LEGAL ASPECTS OF ENGINEERING

OF

ENGINEERING

Fourth Edition

Richard C. Vaughn

Iowa State University

KENDALL/HUNT PUBLISHING COMPANY
2460 Kerper Boulevard   P.O. Box 539   Dubuque, Iowa 52004-0539

Copyright © 1962 by Prentice-Hall, Inc.

Copyright © 1974, 1975 by Richard C. Vaughn

Copyright © 1977, 1983 by Kendall/Hunt Publishing Company

Library of Congress Catalog Card Number: 73–93861

ISBN 0–8403–3038–3

Printed in the United States of America
10 9 8 7 6 5

Contents

Preface

Legal Aspects of Engineering is intended to introduce engineers, architects, and others interested in engineering projects to pertinent legal concepts. It is not intended to replace the services of an attorney. Rather than replace those services, it should make them more useful to the recipient. If the services of a member of the bar are sought by one who is aware of basic legal principles pertaining to his activities, his contacts with the attorney can be expected to be more efficient and satisfactory. In addition, an engineer who has some knowledge of the law as well as his engineering specialty is better prepared to act as an expert witness if the need arises.

Earlier editions of this text evolved from classroom notes for engineering classes I have taught. Some of the changes and additions to this fourth edition stem from this source, but more of them are due to user comments. The material added to this edition consists of a rather large number of carefully selected cases and a chapter on safety. These additions were made in response to requests from users. Dividing the text into six sections was also a response to user request. As changes in the law have occurred since the third edition was printed, it has been necessary to make corresponding changes in the text. The most significant such change is the bankruptcy discussion in Chapter 13.

Law cases are presented at the ends of most chapters. The cases serve to illustrate the principles and concepts in the chapters, but, more importantly, each case also provides an example of legal reasoning. Because legal reasoning is somewhat different from engineering problem-solving logic, the cases have been preserved virtually intact. The only deletions are the case references; while such references are of interest to an attorney, they can tend to break an engineer's trend of thought as he reads a case.

It may be observed that roughly half the population is female and that a substantial proportion of these women have the courage and intellectual capacity to attempt and succeed in the formerly all-male profession of engineering. The trend seems highly desirable; in fact, one may regret the loss of talent this all-male image caused over most of our engineering history. Unfortunately, textbooks of all sorts, law cases, legislative enactments, proclamations and declamations were written with reference to the male gender. "He" and "his" appear where the obvious intent is to include both sexes. Textbooks have been edited and rewritten to remove this gender bias, but the rewrites involved have often destroyed the meanings or severely battered the rules of English grammar. I have chosen not to change this text in this manner. Rather, I ask the forgiveness of my engineering colleagues and colleagues-to-be who are women for my gender indiscretions. Where "he" is used in such a manner that the reference should be all inclusive, please believe that I mean "he or she".

The author is deeply indebted to many persons for their help and comments. Especially helpful have been the comments of students and former students in I.E. 480 classes here at Iowa State University. Also valuable were the comments of John Imhoff of the University of Arkansas. I must also acknowledge the value of conversation and correspondence with others who teach similar courses at other schools.

R. C. Vaughn

Introduction

The first jobs of most engineers after they receive their B.S. degrees are in the employment of others. They become members of management teams. Many of them rise to higher positions of management where they continue to use their engineering backgrounds even though their titles may imply only management responsibilities. Other engineers find the solving of engineering problems so exhilarating that they go on to solve such problems for others as consultants. Still other engineers pursue careers in the military, academia, and in federal, state, or local governments. In any of these endeavors the engineer's relationships with others are prescribed by rules of law and ethics. A knowledge of these rules, then, is valuable to the engineer. We shall study these rules as well as relationships and controversies that spring from them.

The Engineer in Management

The engineer is a problem solver. He possesses unique tools for stating problems in such a manner that they can be solved, and for giving answers. His facility at this results from screening, natural selection, and specialized training in problem-solving techniques. It is this ability to state and solve problems that employers hope to find when they hire an engineer; and it is because of the many uses for this knowledge that there is presently a substantial demand for engineering graduates.

Most of the training offered to an engineer equips him to solve problems of a mathematical nature—problems that may readily be reduced to symbolic form. However, not all problems lend themselves to such an attack. The stress resulting from force application to a particular design of beam is easily stated in mathematical terms. It is a little more difficult, but still quite possible in most cases, to assume probabilities and solve for the number of parts to be run or warehouse space to be required for next year's production. It is exceedingly difficult, though, if not downright impossible, to state laws governing relationships between people in terms of x's and y's with proper coefficients and thereby solve legal and ethical problems. Most such problems involve the interpretation of man-made laws and the use of discretion and judgment in determining rights. Despite their difficulty, the solution of legal problems and problems involving human relations are no less important to a successful engineer than the solution of mathematical problems.

In most engineering jobs the engineer is part of a so-called management team. Before turning to the aspects of law with which the engineer should be familiar, it may well be desirable to consider certain management skills he should strive to acquire.

Engineering Management

For the vast majority of engineering graduates the first job secured is merely a steppingstone to higher things. Most people, including engineers, are ambitious. It is only natural that the engineering neophyte should raise his sights toward positions that offer greater rewards.

Normally the engineer's first job requires a large amount of technical skill. As he moves up, the percentage of time in which he uses his technical skills usually decreases. Regardless of the ladder the engineer has chosen to climb—research, manufacturing engineering, consulting, sales, or any other—progression to higher levels depends upon at least four factors in addition to his engineering ability.

Communication Skills. An idea possessed by an engineer may have very great latent value, but until it is used or communicated in some way, the idea is worthless to him. In addition, the very mental work necessary to put the idea in coherent word-form is in itself of value. Nearly everyone has had the experience of gaining new insight or of discovering added features of an idea when faced with the task of trying to explain it to someone else.

Handling People. A promotion from a strictly technical position to something higher almost always leads to handling people. Being "boss" isn't easy. People can be forced to work under threat of being deprived of their paychecks, but such threats usually stifle initiative. The manager who takes time to explain to his subordinates "why" and to keep them informed is likely to be more successful than one who does not.

Sense of Cost. Most operations are undertaken with a profit motive. Even in those operations that are not expected to make a profit, cost is usually important. If the selling price of a company's product is unchanged, money saved in manufacturing or raw material cost represents added profit; conversely, added cost decreases profit. Many engineers have won promotions, and many consultants earn their livelihoods on their ability to analyze operations and reduce costs.

Knowledge of Law. The engineer is not expected to become an attorney from exposure to one survey course in law, any more than an attorney could become an engineer by taking one survey course in engineering. However, the engineer should be cognizant of the probable effects of carelessness in dealing with others. He should know when he is in trouble and needs the advice of an attorney. The law background is a "preventive" asset; that is, with a basic knowledge of law, the engineer should be equipped to prevent costly lawsuits against his company. Meticulous reading of contracts before signing is an important preventive measure. It is often surprising how little attention is paid to contracts and supporting documents, particularly in view of the fact that these documents outline the rights and responsibilities of the parties.

Executive Qualities

In recent years there has been an increasing trend toward filling top management or executive positions with engineers. There has been recognition of the value of the engineer's analytical approach to executive problems.

While there is a good deal of truth to the often quoted comment that "there is always room at the top," those who get there usually possess special abilities. Engineering training is beneficial to the executive aspirant, but so is a knowledge of many other fields.

What makes an executive? Why does one person achieve this goal while many others strive and fail? At first glance the behavior of one successful executive appears to have little in common with that of another who is equally successful. One is the brusque bull-of-the-woods; another is as smooth as silk. However, upon closer examination certain similar behavior patterns become apparent. Each usually possesses the four above-mentioned qualities of a manager, one or more to a high degree. There are other qualities, too, that are seen to be common to most top executives and which deserve consideration.

Leadership. The quality known as *leadership* is difficult to define. It is clearly evident in one person and strangely lacking in another. Psychologically, leadership indicates an identification of the group with the one who leads—it is necessary that the leader be considered by the group as one of them. It is also required that the leader be somewhat superior to the others in the group in one or more qualities esteemed by them.

It is doubtful that anyone is truly a "born leader." It is more probable that leadership qualities result from training acquired both consciously and unconsciously—study and observation so ingrained that the leader's responses to various situations are almost as natural as breathing. Thus the term "born leader" has come to be used in reference to the leader who seems to do everything right at the right time in a very natural way.

Leadership qualities seem to be enhanced by practice. Opportunities to practice the poise and purposefulness of leadership occur in virtually limitless ways.

One of the main reasons job application blanks nearly always contain space for listing organizational activities is to determine the amount of practice in leadership the candidate has had.

Two outstanding leadership characteristics are the ability to keep the ultimate goal uppermost in mind and the ability to pursue it enthusiastically. Enthusiasm is infectious—it rubs off on others. The relative success of dictators and would-be dictators attests to this. A speech delivered in a monotone makes dull listening; however, the same speech using virtually the same words but delivered enthusiastically can move people to action.

A leader does not need a leaning post—either literally or figuratively. Leadership stems partly from the ability to stand firm on principles. There is a popular misconception that a leader should not admit mistakes. Few people bat 1,000 on all decisions, however. Not only must the leader admit his own mistakes; he must also take responsibility for the mistakes of his subordinates, since their actions result from his direction or lack thereof. Scapegoating is a popular art, but few effective leaders in top management will stoop to it to avoid criticism.

Delegating. A characteristic of most top executives is the facility for delegating authority and responsibility to others. It is virtually impossible for anyone to rise to the top of a modern industrial organization without the ability to delegate. There is just not time to cover effectively and thoroughly all of the requirements of a top management job. The executive who delegates very little is robbing himself of time needed for adequate thought before making decisions. Also, failure to delegate routine tasks to others is a bar to his own promotion; if no one can be found who has performed a portion of the executive's task with the authority necessary for that performance, it is natural to leave the executive where he is.

Specialization is an inherent advantage of effective delegating. No one is a specialist in everything. By assigning some of his tasks to others, the executive can obtain the advantage of specialized treatment.

Delegation, as the term is used industrially, is something more than the mere assignment of tasks to be performed. Delegation includes clothing the delegee with the necessary authority to carry out his assigned function. It is this parting with a portion of his authority that causes the shortsighted executive consciously or unconsciously to oppose delegation to others. It is this very aspect of delegating, however, that is valuable in contributing to the growth of assistants. The able executive realizes this and takes full advantage of it in helping others develop.

Decisions. All of us must make decisions involving choices among alternatives. In this choosing we are not always correct. One attribute that seems characteristic of those people who reach top management is their ability to be right a higher percentage of the time than the average person. Of course, top management decisions are decisions on particularly difficult problems. Decisions run all the way from a single-variable problem such as the checking of a part with go-no go gage to multivariable problems where little, if anything, is fixed or known. Generally, routine decisions are delegated to others; the top manager is the one who makes the decision when major uncertainties are present. The man to make decisions such as these is a venturer—a man who will assume risks in his decisions. Generally, the greater the risk undertaken the greater the possible reward. The conclusion to expand a plant or install new production facilities based on an apparently expanding market is such a decision. No one can predict the future—the further into the future the planning, the more inaccurate it is likely to be.

Top management decisions generally consist of five elements: a gathering of facts; a recognition of limiting conditions; assumption of facts and conditions as they are expected to be and recognition that these are assumptions; analysis of the facts, limits, and assumptions; and decision. Many of the assumptions can be reduced to probabilities. If enough of this can be done, the problem can be programmed for a computer, which will then give the executive some answers. However, the answers are based on assumptions and probabilities, and it is still up to the executive to decide whether to go ahead or not. The risk is still his, not the computer's.

A few top executives possess such vast knowledge and ability at analysis and synthesis that they can make rapid-fire policy decisions that are nearly always right. However, such people are rare. Generally, people in top management do not make hurried policy decisions. There is often grumbling from below because of apparently undue procrastination. Despite the grumbling, such delay is usually the course of wisdom, since the risks are frequently sizeable. A decision based on inadequate facts is hazardous, and delay in waiting for more facts is often inescapable. Even the rare management genius who makes correct decisions rapidly usually has had many years of experience in more methodical decision making which has equipped him for his present role.

Discipline. Discipline is a necessary component of any well-run organization. People must be taught; old habit patterns must be changed. Most top executives are masters of the use of reward and punishment in changing the behavior of subordinates. To be effective, executive orders must imply some form of reproof for disobedience; rewards of some sort must follow outstanding performance if the effort required for the performance is to be continued.

The extent to which reward and punishment are necessary depends to a great degree upon the personal stature of the executive. If he is held in high regard by his subordinates, a word or so of reproof is often the equivalent of the proverbial ten lashes.

In addition to his drives for food, water, and the means of satisfying other basic needs, man has a whole host of derived needs, not the least of which is the need of recognition. Every person needs recognition or respect from others—lack of it causes loss of self-respect and, eventually, diminished effort. Recognition can be either tangible or intangible, and both forms are required. Verbal praise sounds hollow after awhile if it is not accompanied by some material reward. Similarly, material rewards without praise for accomplishments are incomplete.

It has often been stated that rewards should be public; criticism or punishment private. The truth in the statement is inescapable. Most top managers observe this principle in the interest of preserving their organizations.

These are only a few of the principles that guide a top executive in his management of discipline. Most of them he understands and observes without conscious thought when disciplinary occasions rise.

There are many qualities that can make a person successful in top management. Only a few have been mentioned here. Nevertheless, these few are basic and must be mastered by executive aspirants.

The purpose of an industry and its management is to produce something. Converting time and raw material into goods and services requires production facilities. Assembly of the machines and equipment required to produce something is normally undertaken as an engineering project. Not only must the original facilities be planned and built; every design change or functional change of the product requires changing machines and equipment. The job of setting up production facilities becomes, then, not a "one-shot" enterprise, but an almost continuous replanning and rearrangement. The burden of deciding when and how much to change—and what to change to—falls on top management; the job of planning and carrying out the details of rearrangement is assigned to the engineering department.

ENGINEERING PROJECTS

A large proportion of the capital wealth of our country has resulted from engineering projects. Civil engineering projects—roads, bridges, buildings and the like—are most familiar to the public. As a result, whenever the term *engineering project* is used, visions of a dam or cloverleaf are likely to come to mind. The value of civil projects cannot be denied, but contributions by other engineering fields are also significant, even though the public is not as aware of their activities or results.

Since the development and adoption of mass-production methods in the United States, a new combining of engineering talents has taken place. People are needed who can apply knowledge of civil, mechanical, electrical, chemical, industrial, and other engineering fields to manufacturing problems. This combining of engineering talents to solve manufacturing problems has come to be known by many names, but the term *manufacturing engineering* seems more appropriate than most. Typically, manufacturing engineering is concerned with the process required to mass-produce some product. It starts with an analysis of someone's brain child and continues as long as there are engineering problems to be solved.

Manufacturing Engineering

In any engineering project there are three phases or stages of development: (1) the idea, (2) the construction, and (3) making it work. The stages are fairly separable, and a particular engineering group may have responsibilities in one or more of the stages.

Idea. Just about everything we enjoy started as someone's idea or "screwball notion." Neither products nor the processes by which they are manufactured can be developed without someone's original idea. Not all ideas are practical, however. A large number of those that are adopted require alterations before they are acceptable. Many ideas appear attractive in the beginning only to be demonstrated as impractical by objective examination. This objective examination of a possible engineering project is known as a *feasibility study*.

A feasibility study is a preliminary examination of a proposed idea. It is meant to answer such questions as: What will it cost to produce various quantities per year? Can we market enough to make a reasonable return on the required investment? How many can be sold at a given price? What processes will be better in the long run? The answers given determine whether it is desirable to go to the next stage—actually setting up to produce.

Construction. The job of turning someone's idea into a reality can be quite complex in a manufacturing situation. Planning is necessary. The planning requires imagination—a vision of the future; and the planning continues until everything is firmly in place. Even then,

maintenance should be planned. Changes are made easily in the planning stage—it costs little to erase a machine location on a layout and place the machine in another location. Even rearrangements of the entire process are inexpensive at this point. It is here that questions pertaining to equipment sizes, locations, and added features must be answered and the answers justified if the process is to be successful. Layout changes after the process equipment has been placed are very expensive. For this reason, questions that should have been raised in the planning stage but were never brought up reflect on the process engineer's ability. A member of a manufacturing engineering department does not have to be omniscient, but it would help if he could be.

The process engineer designs a layout of the process, complete with machines and equipment, and writes specifications for the machines to function as desired. The specifications are then sent out, proposals received, and contracts let to the successful bidders. The engineer is the owner's agent; as such he must supervise the building of machines or other structures to fit the layout and then supervise their installation. Just as a good cook times everything so that nothing will be cold when it is served, the engineer must control times of completion of the elements of his layout. It is rare that a process is completed and functioning properly within the time it apparently should take. There is nearly always at least one contractor who is late. If the engineer is wise he will allow some time for this in his schedule.

Making It Work. It is probably safe to state that in every manufacturing process ever installed there were special problems to be solved before full-scale production could begin. The presence of "bugs" in a newly installed process is about as normal as any expectancy can be. The bugs must be removed before the process can be considered complete. The engineer who set up the process is the logical person to remove these bugs before the operation is turned over to the production people.

Law and Engineers

In any engineering project the engineer is the representative, or agent, of the owner. It is his function to act in the best interests of the owner—to get the best possible results with a minimum of delay and problems. The engineer must deal with the rights of others. His actions affect others' property rights and personal rights; rights they have due to ownership of property, contractual obligations, torts, or crimes. He is a guardian of the owner's rights and, in a manner of speaking, of the rights of others with whom the owner deals. Since court proceedings are costly in both time and money, he should do all in his power to avoid entanglements which would lead to them. And, since violation of the rights of others is likely to lead to court, the engineer must know the characteristics of these rights if his preventive job is to be well done.

The relationships between the owner and his contractor are set forth in a series of documents drawn up by the engineer. The Instructions for Bidders, Proposal, General Conditions, Specifications, and Drawings comprise parts of the contract. Careless errors in the preparation of these documents can cause legal controversies or place the owner and engineer in indefensible positions when controversies arise. He must formulate the documents in such a way that the owner's position is protected, and do this without imposing undue hardship on the contractor.

In some respects the engineer's position is between the owner and the contractor. When disputes arise he is likely to be called upon to mediate or at least enter into the controversies. To do a reasonable job in this intermediate position the engineer must be acquainted with the legal rights and responsibilities of both parties. He does not have to be an attorney, but some knowledge of the law is essential. He should be able to recognize situations in which it is necessary to consult an attorney. Some knowledge of the law is required even for this; you can't very easily recognize legal troubles unless you have some knowledge of the rights involved.

There is a second reason for the engineer to acquire a knowledge of the law. He is a citizen as well as a representative of his employer or client. The law controls many of his day-to-day dealings with others. When he buys insurance or signs a chattel mortgage for the purchase of a refrigerator, his own rights and responsibilities should be clear to him. At the very least, the idea of reading the document before he signs should occur to him.

An engineer is a member of society as well as a person possessing technical skills. As an educated member of society and a professional person, his knowledge and abilities should extend well beyond his technical skills. One popularly accepted criterion of the cultured person is the ability to analyze and discuss news events with some perception. Much of the news presented to us by radio, television, newspapers, and magazines has legal significance. If the engineer is to be accepted and respected as a learned man in his community, his interests and knowledge must be broad enough to justify this acceptance. An acquaintance with legal matters is a step in this direction.

REVIEW QUESTIONS

1. Why should an engineer have some knowledge of the law?
2. Name at least three more qualifications an engineer should possess for success in management. Name at least three additional qualities of successful executives.
3. What are the stages of an engineering project? What would each stage be composed of in the proposed manufacture of, say, tie clasps?
4. What is manufacturing engineering?

2

Ethics

An engineer is a professional person; the occupation he has chosen is one of the newer professions. Until quite recently the only callings of sufficient dignity and dedication to public service to be termed *professions* were law, medicine, and theology. These three "learned professions" are still looked upon by the public as the pinnacle of professions. Because of the intimate contact between members of these professions and the public, it is doubtful that this thinking will ever change.

Engineering has existed as a separate calling for about a century and a half. Considering the short span of its existence, the progress of engineering toward top professional standing is quite striking. Certainly there was engineering prior to one hundred fifty years ago, as the ancient pyramids, the aqueducts of Rome, and other engineering works mutely testify; but the designing and building of these structures was not known as *engineering*. Most of the early engineering was done by or for the military.

Civil engineering was first to be recognized as a separate calling. Around 1750, John Smeaton, an English engineer, made the first recorded use of the term *civil engineering*. In 1818 the Institution of Civil Engineers was founded in Great Britain; it defined *engineering* as "the art of utilizing the forces of nature for the use and convenience of man." With the development of new fields of technological knowledge since then, many other fields of engineering have been established.

A separate, recognized field of learning and the presence of societies of its members do not make a "profession." A person does not have "professional" status merely because he has graduated from a school and joined a society. Perhaps it is best to consider for a moment the meaning of the term *profession*.

It is not difficult to find definitions of *profession*. Webster's dictionary says it is "the business which one professes to understand and to practice for subsistence; a calling, occupation, or vocation distinguished from a trade or handicraft." *Black's Law Dictionary* calls it "a vocation, calling, occupation, or employment involving labor, skill, education, special knowledge, and compensation or profit, but the labor and skill is predominantly mental or intellectual rather than physical or manual."

While each of the above definitions serves a purpose, each is brief at the expense of completeness. Probably one of the best and most complete definitions was given by the United States Congress in the Labor Management Relations Act as amended in 1947 (the Taft-Hartley Law). In this act Congress defined the term *professional employee*.

Professional Employee

The term "professional employee" means:

a. any employee engaged in work (1) predominantly intellectual and varied in character as opposed to routine mental, manual, mechanical, or physical work; (2) involving consistent exercise of discretion and judgment in its performance; (3) of such a character that the output produced or the result accomplished cannot be standardized in relation to a given period of time; (4) requiring knowledge of an advanced type in a field of science or learning customarily acquired by a prolonged course of specialized intellectual instruction and study in an institution of higher learning or a hospital, as distinguished from a general academic education or from an apprenticeship or from training in the performance of routine mental, manual, or physical processes; or

b. any employee, who (1) has completed the courses of specialized intellectual instruction and study described in clause (4) of paragraph (a), and (2) is performing related work under the supervision of a professional person to qualify himself to become a professional employee as defined in paragraph (a).

The four requirements stated in the Taft-Hartley Law are repeated in some form by most people who attempt to define a profession. In addition, various other criteria are frequently added to the list above: (a) registration requirements for practicing the professions; (b) representation of members and control of activities by a professional society; (c) the public service nature of the occupation; and (d) adherence to a code of ethics.

7

State Registration Laws

The state laws of each of the United States require that an engineer be registered before being allowed to practice professional engineering in the state. Registration in any one state does not give the engineer a right to act as a professional engineer in another state; however, many states have reciprocal agreements whereby registration is much simplified if the engineer is already registered in another state.

The primary purpose of the state engineering registration laws is to protect the public from shoddy engineering practices. To this end, it is necessary that the prospective licensee convince a board of examiners that he is qualified to practice professional engineering. The usual method for this is a scrutiny of the individual's past engineering work and training by the board, and a qualifying examination. This examination commonly lasts two days and is either oral and written or entirely written. It usually covers the basic sciences and specialization in a particular field of engineering. Full registration as a professional engineer allows the licensee to act as a professional engineer within the state and to resort to the courts to collect fees for his services. Penalties in the form of fines and/or confinement are specified for practicing without a license.

According to at least one court decision[1] engineering became a profession upon enactment of the state registration law. Such a landmark is, perhaps, convenient in legal interpretations within a state. However, professions do not magically spring into existence on the day a law is passed. Obtaining acceptance of a field of knowledge as a profession is a never-ending job, and efforts to maintain high standards of service to the public must continue and grow as the profession grows.

Professional Societies

Each of the recognized branches of engineering has formed at least one society of its members. In addition to these there are three organizations that represent and serve all engineers.

A.B.E.T. In 1932 the Engineers Council for Professional Development was formed. For 47 years it was concerned with accrediting engineering curricula and with other nonaccrediting activities such as guidance, ethics, and the development of young engineers. In 1979 E.C.P.D. restructured itself into an accreditation board and joined with the American Association of Engineering Societies for its other functions.

Accredited engineering and technology curricula are examined at least once every six years by an examiner from one of two commissions of the Accreditation Board of Engineering and Technology (A.B.E.T.): the engineering Accreditation Commission examines engineering curricula; the Technology Accreditation Commission examines technology programs. In 1982 there were 1302 accredited engineering programs in 250 institutions, and 670 accredited technology programs in 188 institutions.

A.A.E.S. The American Association of Engineering Societies was founded in 1979, superseding the Engineers Joint Council (founded in 1945). Its objectives are to advance the science and practice of engineering in the public interest; and to act as an advisory, communication, and information exchange agency for member activities. As noted above, A.A.E.S. also acquired some of the functions of the Engineers Council for Professional Development upon its restructuring.

N.S.P.E. The National Society of Professional Engineers, formed in 1934, is concerned with the social, economic, political, and professional interests of all engineers. N.S.P.E. activities were largely responsible for the passage of engineer registration laws in the various states, public recognition of engineering as a profession, and recognition of the value of engineering activities.

Professional Life

A degree in engineering is a foundation; a life's career in the engineering profession can be built on it. An engineer can reasonably expect to be treated as a professional person by his clients and his superiors. However, complete public recognition of engineering as a profession has not yet occurred. The service rendered by a doctor, an attorney, or a member of the clergy is obvious to the public. A person experiencing a strange pain seeks out a doctor for diagnosis and treatment. One who has been accused of a crime requires personal contact with an attorney. A family experiencing domestic difficulties may turn to a member of the clergy for aid. The public has little knowledge, though, of the engineer whose work makes crossing a bridge or riding an airplane safe and convenient. The engineer's work is just as vital and his contributions are as great as those of the other professions—a member of the public can be just as dead from an accident caused by mechanical malfunction as from cancer. The engineer's contribution is unseen; it is for this reason, among others, that the engineer must act as a professional person if he is to establish and maintain the respect accorded professional people.

1. H. C. Downer and Associates, Inc., v. The Westgate Realty Company, No. 4892, Court of Appeals, Ninth Judicial District, Ohio, Nov. 25, 1959.

55

The medical doctor must keep abreast of new developments and the lawyer must peruse recent cases to improve the services they render. Similarly, an engineering education is never finished. The engineer has a duty to his clients and his profession to learn the new developments in his field. Unquestionably, the professional person's day-to-day bread-winning efforts are important to him; but so is the extra time in the evenings and on weekends that is required for reading technical periodicals and attending engineering society meetings. A lathe operator or maintenance man in a shop may work from 7:00 A.M. to 3:30 P.M. and forget his job and everything connected with it at the end of the day. For the dedicated professional, however, the day does not end when the office doors close behind him. There is always more to learn.

CODE OF ETHICS

Definition. According to Webster's dictionary, *ethics* is "the science which treats of the nature and laws of the actions of intelligent beings, these actions being considered in relation to their moral qualities; the science which treats of the nature and grounds of moral obligations; the science of human duty."

Ethics are the ground rules of our moral conduct. They consist of our attitudes toward honesty, integrity, trust and loyalty; they are exhibited in our day-to-day contacts with others. No laws compel an engineer to take an interest in community affairs or to give a completely unbiased report of the results of an investigation. The manner in which the engineer acts depends upon his own moral code, or ethics.

Establishment of Moral Patterns

A person does not acquire a code of ethics or sense of moral duty by reading a passage in a textbook and then deciding to abide by what was stated. Rather, a personal code grows out of the experiences and observations of one's life.

Perhaps we each inherit a predisposition toward a certain type of moral behavior. This, though, is rather doubtful. Certainly we are influenced by what happens after birth—by the environment in which we mature. Examples set by parents, friends, classmates, teachers, and professors all contribute. Punishment for censured acts and praise for achievements are the building blocks for individual codes of ethics. All of these help to make up the engineer's moral structure; to these will be added his experiences and observations on the job.

In 1978 the N.S.P.E. adopted the Code of Ethics presented below. This code is not meant as a body of inflexible laws, to be observed "or else." It is meant as a guidepost, to be worked into and be the basis for changes in the engineer's moral standards. It has been in existence in various stages of development for several decades and has been found to be of value in dealing with others. It provides our professional standards.

CODE OF ETHICS FOR ENGINEERS

Preamble

Engineering is an important and learned profession. The members of the profession recognize that their work has a direct and vital impact on the quality of life for all people. Accordingly, the services provided by engineers require honesty, impartiality, fairness and equity, and must be dedicated to the protection of the public health, safety and welfare. In the practice of their profession, engineers must perform under a standard of professional behavior which requires adherence to the highest principles of ethical conduct on behalf of the public, clients, employers and the profession.

I. Fundamental Canons

Engineers, in the fulfillment of their professional duties, shall:

1. Hold paramount the safety, health and welfare of the public in the performance of their professional duties.
2. Perform services only in areas of their competence.
3. Issue public statements only in an objective and truthful manner.
4. Act in professional matters for each employer or client as faithful agents or trustees.
5. Avoid improper solicitation of professional employment.

II. Rules of Practice

1. Engineers shall hold paramount the safety, health and welfare of the public in the performance of their professional duties.
   a. Engineers shall at all times recognize that their primary obligation is to protect the safety, health, property and welfare of the public. If their professional judgment is overruled under circumstances where the safety, health, property or welfare of the public are endangered, they shall notify their employer or client and such other authority as may be appropriate.
   b. Engineers shall approve only those engineering documents which are safe for public health,

property and welfare in conformity with accepted standards.

c. Engineers shall not reveal facts, data or information obtained in a professional capacity without the prior consent of the client or employer except as authorized or required by law or this Code.

d. Engineers shall not permit the use of their name or firm name nor associate in business ventures with any person or firm which they have reason to believe is engaging in fraudulent or dishonest business or professional practices.

e. Engineers having knowledge of any alleged violation of this Code shall cooperate with the proper authorities in furnishing such information or assistance as may be required.

2. Engineers shall perform services only in the areas of their competence.

a. Engineers shall undertake assignments only when qualified by education or experience in the specific technical fields involved.

b. Engineers shall not affix their signatures to any plans or documents dealing with subject matter in which they lack competence, nor to any plan or document not prepared under their direction and control.

c. Engineers may accept an assignment outside of their fields of competence to the extent that their services are restricted to those phases of the project in which they are qualified, and to the extent that they are satisfied that all other phases of such project will be performed by registered or otherwise qualified associates, consultants, or employees, in which case they may then sign the documents for the total project.

3. Engineers shall issue public statements only in an objective and truthful manner.

a. Engineers shall be objective and truthful in professional reports, statements or testimony. They shall include all relevant and pertinent information in such reports, statements or testimony.

b. Engineers may express publicly a professional opinion on technical subjects only when that opinion is founded upon adequate knowledge of the facts and competence in the subject matter.

c. Engineers shall issue no statements, criticisms or arguments on technical matters which are inspired or paid for by interested parties, unless they have prefaced their comments by explicitly identifying the interested parties on whose behalf they are speaking, and by revealing the existence of any interest the engineers may have in the matters.

4. Engineers shall act in professional matters for each employer or client as faithful agents or trustees.

a. Engineers shall disclose all known or potential conflicts of interest to their employers or clients by promptly informing them of any business association, interest, or other circumstances which could influence or appear to influence their judgment or the quality of their services.

b. Engineers shall not accept compensation, financial or otherwise, from more than one party for services on the same project, or for services pertaining to the same project, unless the circumstances are fully disclosed to, and agreed to, by all interested parties.

c. Engineers shall not solicit or accept financial or other valuable consideration, directly or indirectly, from contractors, their agents, or other parties in connection with work for employers or clients for which they are responsible.

d. Engineers in public service as members, advisors or employees of a governmental body or department shall not participate in decisions with respect to professional services solicited or provided by them or their organizations in private or public engineering practice.

e. Engineers shall not solicit or accept a professional contract from a governmental body on which a principal or officer of their organization serves as a member.

5. Engineers shall avoid improper solicitation of professional employment.

a. Engineers shall not falsify or permit misrepresentation of their, or their associates', academic or professional qualifications. They shall not misrepresent or exaggerate their degree of responsibility in or for the subject matter of prior assignments. Brochures or other presentations incident to the solicitation of employment shall not misrepresent pertinent facts concerning employers, employees, associates, joint venturers or past accomplishments with the intent and purpose of enhancing their qualifications and their work.

b. Engineers shall not offer, give, solicit or receive, either directly or indirectly, any political contribution in an amount intended to influence the award of a contract by public authority, or which may be reasonably construed by the public of having the effect or intent to influence the award of a contract. They shall not offer any gift, or other valuable consideration in order to secure work. They shall not pay a commission, percentage or brokerage fee in order to secure work except to a bona fide employee or bona fide established commercial or marketing agencies retained by them.

III. Professional Obligations

1. Engineers shall be guided in all their professional relations by the highest standards of integrity.
    a. Engineers shall admit and accept their own errors when proven wrong and refrain from distorting or altering the facts in an attempt to justify their decisions.
    b. Engineers shall advise their clients or employers when they believe a project will not be successful.
    c. Engineers shall not accept outside employment to the detriment of their regular work or interest. Before accepting any outside employment they will notify their employers.
    d. Engineers shall not attempt to attract an engineer from another employer by false or misleading pretenses.
    e. Engineers shall not actively participate in strikes, picket lines, or other collective coercive action.
    f. Engineers shall avoid any act tending to promote their own interest at the expense of the dignity and integrity of the profession.
2. Engineers shall at all times strive to serve the public interest.
    a. Engineers shall seek opportunities to be of constructive service in civic affairs and work for the advancement of the safety, health and well-being of their community.
    b. Engineers shall not complete, sign, or seal plans and/or specifications that are not of a design safe to the public health and welfare and in conformity with accepted engineering standards. If the client or employer insists on such unprofessional conduct, they shall notify the proper authorities and withdraw from further service on the project.
    c. Engineers shall endeavor to extend public knowledge and appreciation of engineering and its achievements and to protect the engineering profession from misrepresentation and misunderstanding.
3. Engineers shall avoid all conduct or practice which is likely to discredit the profession or deceive the public.

    a. Engineers shall avoid the use of statements containing a material misrepresentation of fact or omitting a material fact necessary to keep statements from being misleading; statements intended or likely to create an unjustified expectation; statements containing prediction of future success; statements containing an opinion as to the quality of the Engineers' services; or statements intended or likely to attract clients by the use of showmanship, puffery, or self-laudation, including the use of slogans, jingles, or sensational language or format.
    b. Consistent with the foregoing, Engineers may advertise for recruitment of personnel.
    c. Consistent with the foregoing, Engineers may prepare articles for the lay or technical press, but such articles shall not imply credit to the author for work performed by others.
4. Engineers shall not disclose confidential information concerning the business affairs or technical processes of any present or former client or employer without his consent.
    a. Engineers in the employ of others shall not without the consent of all interested parties enter promotional efforts or negotiations for work or make arrangements for other employment as a principal or to practice in connection with a specific project for which the Engineer has gained particular and specialized knowledge.
    b. Engineers shall not, without the consent of all interested parties, participate in or represent an adversary interest in connection with a specific project or proceeding in which the Engineer has gained particular specialized knowledge on behalf of a former client or employer.
5. Engineers shall not be influenced in their professional duties by conflicting interests.
    a. Engineers shall not accept financial or other considerations, including free engineering designs, from material or equipment suppliers for specifying their product.
    b. Engineers shall not accept commissions or allowances, directly or indirectly, from contractors or other parties dealing with clients or employers of the Engineer in connection with work for which the Engineer is responsible.
6. Engineers shall uphold the principle of appropriate and adequate compensation for those engaged in engineering work.
    a. Engineers shall not accept remuneration from either an employee or employment agency for giving employment.

b. Engineers, when employing other engineers, shall offer a salary according to professional qualifications and the recognized standards in the particular geographical area.

7. Engineers shall not compete unfairly with other engineers by attempting to obtain employment or advancement or professional engagements by taking advantage of a salaried position, by criticizing other engineers, or by other improper or questionable methods.

    a. Engineers shall not request, propose, or accept a professional commission on a contingent basis under circumstances in which their professional judgment may be compromised.

    b. Engineers in salaried positions shall accept part-time engineering work only at salaries not less than that recognized as standard in the area.

    c. Engineers shall not use equipment, supplies, laboratory, or office facilities of an employer to carry on outside private practice without consent.

8. Engineers shall not attempt to injure, maliciously or falsely, directly or indirectly, the professional reputation, prospects, practice or employment of other engineers, nor indiscriminately criticize other engineers' work. Engineers who believe others are guilty of unethical or illegal practice shall present such information to the proper authority for action.

    a. Engineers in private practice shall not review the work of another engineer for the same client, except with the knowledge of such engineer, or unless the connection of such engineer with the work has been terminated.

    b. Engineers in governmental, industrial or educational employ are entitled to review and evaluate the work of other engineers when so required by their employment duties.

    c. Engineers in sales or industrial employ are entitled to make engineering comparisons of represented products with products of other suppliers.

9. Engineers shall accept personal responsibility for all professional activities.

    a. Engineers shall conform with state registration laws in the practice of engineering.

    b. Engineers shall not use association with a non-engineer, a corporation, or partnership, as a "cloak" for unethical acts, but must accept personal responsibility for all professional acts.

10. Engineers shall give credit for engineering work to those to whom credit is due, and will recognize the proprietary interests of others.

    a. Engineers shall, whenever possible, name the person or persons who may be individually responsible for designs, inventions, writings, or other accomplishments.

    b. Engineers using designs supplied by a client recognize that the designs remain the property of the client and may not be duplicated by the Engineer for others without express permission.

    c. Engineers, before undertaking work for others in connection with which the Engineer may make improvements, plans, designs, inventions, or other records which may justify copyrights or patents, should enter into a positive agreement regarding ownership.

    d. Engineers' designs, data, records, and notes referring exclusively to an employer's work are the employer's property.

11. Engineers shall cooperate in extending the effectiveness of the profession by interchanging information and experience with other engineers and students, and will endeavor to provide opportunity for the professional development and advancement of engineers under their supervision.

    a. Engineers shall encourage engineering employees' efforts to improve their education.

    b. Engineers shall encourage engineering employees to attend and present papers at professional and technical society meetings.

    c. Engineers shall urge engineering employees to become registered at the earliest possible date.

    d. Engineers shall assign a professional engineer duties of a nature to utilize full training and experience, insofar as possible, and delegate lesser functions to subprofessionals or to technicians.

    e. Engineers shall provide a prospective engineering employee with complete information on working conditions and proposed status of employment, and after employment will keep employees informed of any changes.

"By order of the United States District Court for the District of Columbia, former Section 11(c) of the NSPE Code of Ethics prohibiting competitive bidding, and all policy statements, opinions, rulings or other guidelines interpreting its scope, have been rescinded as unlawfully interfering with the legal right of engineers, protected under the antitrust laws, to provide price information to prospective clients; accordingly, nothing contained in the NSPE Code of Ethics, policy statements, opinions, rulings or other guidelines prohibits the submission of price quotations or competitive bids for engineering services at any time or in any amount."

Statement by NSPE Executive Committee

In order to correct misunderstandings which have been indicated in some instances since the issuance of the Supreme Court decision and the entry of the Final Judgment, it is noted that in its decision of April 25, 1978, the Supreme Court of the United States declared: "The Sherman Act does not require competitive bidding."

It is further noted that as made clear in the Supreme Court decision:

1. Engineers and firms may individually refuse to bid for engineering services.
2. Clients are not required to seek bids for engineering services.
3. Federal, state, and local laws governing procedures to procure engineering services are not affected, and remain in full force and effect.
4. State societies and local chapters are free to actively and aggressively seek legislation for professional selection and negotiation procedures by public agencies.
5. State registration board rules of professional conduct, including rules prohibiting competitive bidding for engineering services, are not affected and remain in full force and effect. State registration boards with authority to adopt rules of professional conduct may adopt rules governing procedures to obtain engineering services.
6. As noted by the Supreme Court, "nothing in the judgment prevents NSPE and its members from attempting to influence governmental action. . . ."

Law and Ethics

There is no penalty at law for a violation of ethics. Neither the examining boards nor the courts have any rights or responsibilities in the ethical practice of engineers. Whatever formal reproof there is for moral misbehavior must come from the engineering societies. In the short history of the engineering profession there has not yet been developed a society equivalent to the American Medical Association or the local and state bar associations for handling ethical infractions. Nearly all the engineering societies are concerned with ethical practices, but few seem deeply concerned. At present,

enforcement efforts vary from apparent tacit condonation of the unethical in some sections of the United States, to very active policing in others. However, the need has been generally recognized and it is likely that systems for detecting, investigating, and holding hearings on unethical practices will soon be developed and vigorously maintained throughout the United States.

Despite the present lack of uniformity in formally policing ethical practices, informal penalties for infractions exist everywhere. The ultimate formal penalty is removal of membership in an engineering society. While loss of membership in a society can be quite harmful to an individual member, the informal penalties are often much more severe. Loss of a job on a weak excuse or social censure within a community is often mute testimony of the presence and effectiveness of informal sanctions.

Codes of professional ethics are not necessarily meant to be of practical value to an individual, yet in most cases they are. The person who is honest and loyal in his adherence to a code of ethics in dealing with others often finds that, as a result, others are honest and loyal in dealing with him. Adherence to ethics tends to inspire confidence and admiration of colleagues, clients, and employers.

Gifts and Favors

Strict interpretation of the Code of Ethics indicates that anything offered to an engineer by a present or prospective contractor should be shunned. This would seem to include all manner of gifts, favors, and evidences of hospitality. If a ball point pen or a cigar is acceptable, why wouldn't also a set of golf clubs or a silver tea service? If there is no stigma attached to a free lunch, then why not also an evening of nightclubbing at the vendor's expense? If an inexpensive favor is to be condoned, where should the line be drawn?

It must be recognized that the "ivory tower" approach is unpopular in many circles. There are numerous companies in which buyers and engineers seldom buy their own lunches, where pen and pencil sets and other gifts are accepted with no qualms. In such places an engineer's refusal of such "advertising"

Reprinted with permission of the National Society of Professional Engineers.

Note:
In regard to the question of application of the Code to corporations vis-a-vis real persons, business form or type should not negate nor influence conformance of individuals to the Code. The Code deals with professional services, which services must be performed by real persons. Real persons in turn establish and implement policies within business structures. The Code is clearly written to apply to the Engineer and it is incumbent on a member of NSPE to endeavor to live up to its provisions. This applies to all pertinent sections of the Code.

would mark him as a bit odd. Perhaps minor gifts and favors should be accepted; maybe even those larger than "minor." However, the engineer should consider well what is at stake when he does accept them.

Whenever the engineer accepts a gift, favor, or hospitality from a contractor or potential contractor, the engineer's freedom of action is inhibited. The obligation to deal with the particular contractor may not be very evident—many times it acts only as a subtle reminder. Nevertheless, at least slight inhibition of completely free action does result. The engineer is a person, a human being capable of being persuaded even against his best engineering judgment. Influence of this nature is against the best interests of the engineer's company. In recognition of this, many large companies have adopted policies restricting or eliminating receipt of gifts from vendors.

It has been said that everyone has a "price." Perhaps this is true. However, we in the engineering profession feel that an engineer's integrity cannot be bought—it has no price tag. If the engineer cannot afford to buy his own lunch or pocket knife he should look to a new employer for economic improvement, not to his present employer's vendors.

Recruiting Practices

In recent years there has been a shortage of engineers. It is occasionally contended that anyone with a reasonable pulse and a diploma certifying him to be a graduate of an engineering curriculum is eligible to be hired as an engineer. This demand for engineers is not likely to decline substantially in the forseeable future.

As might be expected, this unprecedented demand for engineers has led to some peculiar and even reprehensible recruiting practices. Proper use of the talent and problem-solving ability of qualified engineers can make or save money for a company; therefore, pressure is brought to bear on those whose duty it is to acquire such people. The results are not always in keeping with the highest ethical practices. It is, for instance, considered quite unethical for a company to contact an engineer working for another company in an effort to lure him away. If the engineer makes the first move, though, the resulting job change is considered to be above reproach. Often the efforts used to cause the engineer to make this first move are ludicrous (from an objective point of view).

The blame for a company's loss of engineers may sometimes be laid at its own doorstep. A distressingly large number of companies have a tendency to overlook contributions made by their engineers. If a method or design change is made by an engineer and it results in a sizable saving to the company, he may feel that

there should be some recognition for him as a result of the achievement—after all, he could have accepted paychecks and performed only as his boss required. The company, on the other hand, may feel that the engineer is paid both for periods in which his contributions are outstanding, and for many other periods in which seemingly little is accomplished. As a result of these conflicting views, engineers often become dissatisfied and are easy marks for competing offers. Most companies find that some form of tangible recognition (salary increase or bonus) along with words of praise for outstanding jobs will inhibit such dissatisfaction.

The engineer owes a duty of full service to his employer. During the first few months after a new engineer is hired his contributions are not likely to be great, yet his employer has invested time and money in him. If the engineer quits before he has repaid this investment, the company loses money. An engineer who has frequently "job-hopped" may find that even though a demand for engineers exists, he will have a rough time getting another job.

To aid in the development and maintenance of high ethical standards in college recruiting of engineers, the American Society for Engineering Education formulated a code of ethics. This code of ethics, "Recruiting Practices and Procedures—1959," was endorsed by the E.C.P.D. and has been distributed to placement offices on engineering college campuses. It outlines the responsibilities of the employer, the college, and the student applicant in an attempt to secure fair treatment of each by the other two.

The Ethics Tool

The professional engineer is taught to be an ethical person. His code of ethics is as much a tool as his knowledge of the grain structure of steel or the deflection of a beam. Proper use of the tools he possesses will give him a rewarding career; improper use will lead to frustration and disaster.

REVIEW QUESTIONS

1. A process engineer was about to recommend the purchase of equipment for a new manufacturing process for his employer. A vendor calling upon him told him of a new and apparently cheaper means of accomplishing the same end result. The engineer was familiar with the type of work in question, but had never heard of the new process. The vendor invited him to go (at the vendor's expense) to several places in which the new process was used. Should the engineer go to see the new process? At the vendor's expense? What canons have a bearing on the situation?

2. If the engineer took the trip mentioned above and the vendor suggested an evening at a local night club to avoid the boredom of a hotel room (with the vendor picking up the night club tab), should the engineer accept or decline? Why?

3. In going through the files on a process in which his employer finds himself in trouble, an engineer finds several instances of very poor judgment and miscalculation by his predecessor who set up the process. Most of the present problems in the process are caused by the previous engineer's errors. The previous engineer left the company and is now working for another firm. The present engineer's assignment is to improve the process. How should the improvements be justified to the employer? What, if anything, should the engineer say or do about his predecessor's mistakes? What canons apply?

4. About a month ago an engineer made an outstanding improvement in a process. His company produces approximately 300,000 parts per year through the process, and direct labor saving alone amounts to approximately $.10 per part. The foreman of the department in which the process is lo-cated has complimented the engineer on his achievement, but no one else in the plant has done anything more than mention it to him. What, if anything, should the engineer do?

5. Summarize in a few words each of the four requirements for a "professional employee."

6. Just before Christmas an engineer receives a package from a vendor with whom he has dealt in the past. The engineer is now concerned with work entirely outside the field of the vendor's interest. The package contains eight place settings of sterling silver. Should the engineer keep the gift or return it? Why?

7. An engineer is approached by a friend who argues stoutly for joining an engineer's union. It is pointed out that promotions will be based largely on seniority, that wages will be paid according to the class of work undertaken (which is likely to improve the engineer's economic situation), and that overtime will be paid for all work in excess of forty hours per week or eight hours per day. Should the engineer join the union or not? What are the counter arguments?

3

Development of Law

Our activities are regulated by laws. As we live and work we become familiar with many laws, particularly those having to do with the physical world—the laws of nature. We know that if we are near the earth when we drop something it will fall to the earth in obedience to the law of gravity. We can even predict accurately how fast the object will fall and where it will strike the earth if we consider the laws of motion and the retarding forces. Such *natural laws* form a particular kind of universe of laws. They are not man-made laws, only man-discovered. These laws would exist even if we passed a legislative act against them. It is interesting to note that such an act was once attempted; a state legislature tried to set the value of π as 3.000 to make calculations involving the diameter and circumference of circles more convenient.

In this text we are concerned with man-made laws, the laws governing relationships between people. As we will talk about it here, *law* refers to a set of rules and principles set up by society to restrict the conduct and protect the rights of its members.

A person living by himself in such a way that he had no contacts with others would have no need for man-made laws. Add another person and the need for law would become apparent. Each of the two would have rights that might be infringed upon by the other. In fairness, each must control his behavior in such a manner that the other's rights are protected. In such a simple society the relationships would not be complex; simple rules would be sufficient.

Man is gregarious; his social instincts are highly developed. Judging from the steadily increasing percentage of urban residents in our population, our social tendencies appear to be increasing, due either to the strength of the "pull" or to the ease of succumbing to it. As we become a more urban society we require more laws and restrictions of greater complexity to govern our behavior.

Beginnings of Law

Laws began as social customs. It was considered proper to behave in certain manners in particular circumstances. At first the tribal chief and later the priest was charged with the preservation of these customs, including punishment for infractions. In the hands of the priests, the idea that laws were of divine origin was fostered. Thus many of our early laws, as well as the present Islamic system, were said to have resulted from divine manifestations.

Divine Laws. Two codes of divine laws have made a contribution to the laws of Western civilization. The first of these is the Code of Hammurabi (about 2000 B.C.), based on the idea "an eye for an eye, and a tooth for a tooth." Early justice in the United States was sometimes not far removed from this concept, and the sentence of death for first degree murder is similar.

The second set of divine laws that has influenced our law is the Ten Commandments. Present influence of these laws in our legislation and court decisions is easily found. As rules, these Mosaic Laws have an outstanding feature—they are short and simple.

Each person is presumed by the court to know the laws under which he lives. It is necessary that this presumption be made; if it were not, anyone could plead ignorance of the law and thereby avoid it. Yet how valid is this presumption? How many United States citizens know the local ordinances under which they live? Or the state statutes? Or the federal laws? Or even the rights guaranteed or the restrictions imposed by the Constitution and Bill of Rights? A child can be taught the Ten Commandments, on the other hand, and he will be able to recall many of them when he reaches adulthood, even though he may have little contact with them in the intervening years.

Civil Law. Two great systems of law are used in the Western nations. *English common law* is used in most of the English-speaking countries; *Roman civil law* is used in the remainder of Western societies. Civil law (sometimes called the Continental system) originated about 450 B.C. as the Law of the Twelve Tables. This was the law of the Roman Empire as it expanded and contracted during the next ten centuries. During that time statutes were passed and meanings clarified in court decisions. Under Emperor Justinian in the sixth century these laws were all boiled down to their essentials and published as the *Pandects*. This civil law spread to other countries and became the foundation of the legal systems of continental Europe.

In operation, Roman civil law and English common law are quite different, though in practice the results are usually the same. Civil law is based on written codes or statutes, the court's task being to apply the correct statute to the particular set of facts in the case. Common law is built on cases—prior decisions in similar factual situations.

Most of the law brought to the United States by its early settlers was common law. However, in the states settled by French and Spanish settlers, remnants of civil law may be found. Thus, in Louisiana, Texas, and California principles of civil law have had some influence.

The term *civil law* has come to have a dual meaning. It means a code of law based upon the Roman codes, but also it has come to be used today to describe our system of private law, as opposed to criminal law. When the term is used in the remainder of the text it will refer to the system of private law.

Enforcement

A man-made rule to govern the behavior of individuals in a society has little practical value unless there is enforcement of the rule. Enforcement takes one of three forms. *Punishment.* Fines or imprisonment are the usual means of punishing someone who has committed a crime. *Relief.* In actions involving private rights the relief sought is usually money damages for the person who has been harmed at the hand of another, or prevention of future harm. *Social censure.* Frequently the strongest enforcement factor is the fear of social ostracism—the fear of public opinion. Although, strictly speaking, public opinion is not a recognized legal means of enforcement, its existence and strength cannot be denied.

Few of us possess a formal knowledge of the laws that govern our actions. Yet we obey them. Even the worst of criminals obey nearly all the laws almost all the time. We comply unconsciously. The laws have become a part of each of us—they have been a part of our lives since earliest childhood. Thus, even though we may not know the specific laws to which we conform, we do conform, and we are aware when others do not. Often we are not aware of the definite rule violated or the rights infringed. An attempt is made here to bring such an awareness to the reader.

COMMON LAW AND EQUITY

Types of Laws

Our laws are of four basic types: constitutional, statute, common law, and equity. The terms constitutional law and statute law almost define themselves.

Constitutional law sets up the operation of a government, including its powers and limitations. It states fundamental principles in the relationships between citizen and state, including rights which may not be infringed.

A *statute* is a law stating the express declaration of the will of a legislature in the subject of the statute. A state law prohibiting gambling and setting forth a maximum penalty of $500 or six months in jail for nonobservance would be an example of statute law. Similarly, federal laws, such as the Interstate Commerce Act, and municipal laws (or ordinances) regulating traffic are statutes.

COMMON LAW

Our law, as we originally obtained it, was the common law brought over from England by the colonists. It is still our law; it is used when no statute or constitutional law covers the particular legal problem involved. Along with equity it forms a foundation for our legal system.

Origin

The law that existed before the Norman conquest of England was local law. Each town or shire had its own law, and each town's law differed somewhat from those of other towns. The king took an interest in the law only in a very exceptional case.

The Norman conquerors were organizers. Under them a national council, known as the King's Council, was established to make laws and decide cases. Eventually, the council evolved into Parliament and a system of king's courts.

In the first century or so following the Norman Conquest, what we know as common law began. It arose from the practice of judges to write their opinions, giving the general principles and the reasoning they followed in deciding cases. When the facts were similar, judges tended to follow earlier opinions of other judges.

Stare Decisis. Abiding by previous decisions is known in legal terminology as *stare decisis*. The main feature of common law is that the law itself is built on case decisions. When a case is decided, that decision becomes the law for that court and other courts within its jurisdiction[1] in deciding similar future cases. (In the cases in this text you will see many references to previously decided cases. Many other references have been

---

1. A court's jurisdiction, in the manner used above, indicates the area in which the court may operate. For example, the jurisdiction of the Supreme Court of Ohio is the State of Ohio, and a common law decision by the Ohio Supreme Court would be binding on all other courts in Ohio.

omitted to allow easier reading of each case.) A judge uses precedent cases as the foundation for his decision.

About 200 years after the Norman Conquest a justice named Henry Bracton compiled the decisions which had been rendered under the king's court systems. This was the beginning of case reporting. These and later decisions formed the common law of England and, eventually, of nearly all of the United States.

Shortly before the American Revolution, Sir William Blackstone, an English jurist, completed his *Commentaries on the Laws of England*. In this lawbook, the first major contribution since the time of Bracton, Blackstone clarified and made intelligible the English common law. An American jurist, James Kent, made a similar contribution in this country about sixty years later. *Common law* is defined in Kent's Commentaries as "those principles, usages, and rules of action applicable to the government and security of persons and property, which do not rest for their authority upon any express or positive declaration of the will of the legislature." In both books the principles of common law were extracted from decisions on record. These two books provided the basis for further development of common law in both countries.

It is frequently stated that courts do not make the laws, that they merely enforce them. The statement is largely true of constitutional law and statute law, but not for common law or equity. As decisions are made for new types of cases, new interpretations of law are made by the court; and the law is amplified in this way continuously.

Business Custom. In deciding cases the courts make use of business custom. For instance, as will be discussed later, silence on the part of one to whom an offer is made usually cannot constitute acceptance. However, if there has been a history of dealings between persons, or if there is a practice in a particular business such that silence constitutes acceptance, the court will consider this and decide accordingly. Terminology peculiar to a trade is given its trade usage interpretation in court.

Change

Frequently one hears the complaint that the law is behind the times, that it is slow to change in a rapidly changing world. The complaint is fairly well founded; law *is* slow to change. However, it is usually far better to have a law or fixed principle upon which one can depend, than to have a law or principle which may this time decide one way and the next time another way.

The law does change, slowly, to reflect changes in society and changes in technology. By way of illustration we can look back a few years to the changes that

became necessary when the automobile took over personal transportation from the horse and buggy. Similarly, we can look ahead to changes which are likely to be needed when space travel becomes a commercial reality.

Common law changes in two basic ways: by overruled decisions and by passages of statutes.

Overruled Decisions. When a case goes to court, the attorneys for both of the parties in the case have usually done some research on the law involved. It is likely that both will be armed with decisions in previous cases on which the judge in the present case is expected to base his decision. Let us assume that one of the cases used is based on facts quite similar to those in the case at hand. Let us further assume that the decision in the precedent case was handed down by the state supreme court. If the present case is in a lower court and the facts of the case are in all ways the same, the judge should follow the prior decision. However, since there are nearly always differences in the facts of two cases, let us assume that the judge, on the basis of slightly different facts, did not follow the precedent case and that an appeal resulted. The case at hand is finally taken to the state supreme court. If the supreme court justices see the facts in the two cases as being essentially the same, but render a decision different from the decision rendered in the precedent case, the precedent case has been *overruled*. The law has been changed. There is no effect as to the parties in the earlier case; that case was decided by the law of that time. The law was not changed until the state supreme court changed it in the process of overruling. In the interest of retaining stability in the law, courts are quite reluctant to overrule prior decisions, but at the same time they recognize that nothing is as permanent in this world as change itself.

Statutes. One of the many reasons for passage of a statute is dissatisfaction with the law in a particular field. Frequently, when decisions have for some reason become quite muddled in dealing with a problem, an appeal is made to the legislature for a law to clarify the issues involved. Passage of a statute voids the common law covering the same point within the legislature's jurisdiction. The statute must not, of course, conflict with the Constitution of the United States or with the state constitution involved. If, when a case arises, the courts find that a statute conflicts with the constitution, the constitution is protected and the statute eliminated.

Limits of Remedy

In the beginning the common law was administered by *royal writs*. These writs were orders, in written form, to a sheriff or other officer to administer justice in a particular way or to summon a defendant before the royal justices. We still use writs—written and sealed court commands or mandates ordering that some specified thing be done. Following a court judgment, a writ of execution, for instance, may be issued to an officer, telling him to take possession and sell some of the loser's property to satisfy the judgment.

During the first two or three centuries following the inception of the King's Court in England, the law underwent a hardening process. The writs accepted by a common-law court and the remedies offered became standardized and limited. The limitations of common law still exist today. There are three remedies available: money damages, return of real property, and return of personal property. If none of these remedies will suffice, the case is not a common-law case; the common law court has no remedy.

EQUITY

The limited remedies of common law brought about the fourth basic type of law, equity. Consider an example. Black, a contractor, is hired to build a structure for White. During the excavation, Gray, next door, notes an impending separation of his house from its foundation. The walls start to crack and the ceiling begins to bulge. At this point, at common law, Gray has no remedy. At common law he would have to await whatever damage might be forthcoming and sue to get compensation for it. However, in equity he can do something about it *now*. He can obtain a temporary injunction or restraining order to prevent the excavation next door until something more appropriate can be done to prevent his house from sliding into the hole.

Origin

With the limiting of common-law writs (the Provisions of Oxford, 1258, put an end to the making of any new kinds of writs) certain injustices could take place without any relief being offered by the courts.

Common law could not, and still cannot:

1. Prevent a wrong from taking place.
2. Order persons to perform their obligations.
3. Correct mistakes.

It soon became apparent that these gaps in the law had to be filled.

Courts of Chancery. With the King's Court system the king had become established as the "fountain of justice." As such, he could offer redress beyond that available in the common-law courts. In unusual cases the king was petitioned and he settled the cases with

"unusual" remedies. When the load became too heavy for the king the task of hearing the unusual cases was delegated to his chancellor and, eventually, to vice-chancellors. From this the new courts took on the name of *courts of chancery*.

In the United States, courts of equity exist in three ways. In some states there are separate court rooms and judges for equity cases. In other states, the court rooms are the same and the judges are the same ones who deal with other types of law, but the procedure is different. In still other states and in the federal court system, law and equity have been completely combined.

Unusual Remedies. The remedies available in a court of equity are quite different from those offered in common law. They are *in personam* remedies; that is, they are directed to a person, whereas common law acts *in rem*, or upon a thing. Probably the most common and well-known equity remedies are the injunction and specific performance. The list of equity remedies, though, is quite long and includes divorces, mortgage foreclosures, accountings, reformation of contracts, and many others. In fact, an equity court can act in any way necessary to secure a right or remedy a wrong. The very word *equity* implies that justice will be done, and if a remedy must be invented to serve the purpose, that will be done.

The *injunction* exists in two general forms: temporary and permanent. A temporary injunction (a restraining order or injunction *pendente lite*) is readily obtainable for cause. Any attorney, as a member of the bar in the court's jurisdiction is also an officer of the court. As such, he can request a temporary injunction from the court. As soon as the judge signs the temporary injunction, it is an act in contempt of court for anyone who has knowledge of the order to fail to obey it. The object of a temporary injunction is to hold the status quo until a hearing can be held on the merits of the case. The complaint may be dismissed at the hearing, or some other type of remedy may be given, or a permanent injunction may result when the facts are heard. If a permanent injunction is issued, the order is effective as long as the cause of the injunction exists.

Specific performance usually arises in connection with contracts involving land. Land is considered to be unique; no one piece of land is exactly like another. When a contract is made for the sale of a piece of land and the seller refuses to deed the land to the buyer, he may be forced to do so by an order for specific performance from a court of equity. Property other than real estate is treated the same way only when it is recognized as being unique; e.g., an antique or a rare painting.

Equity is reluctant to give a remedy that will require continuous supervision over an extended period. In some cases such remedies have been given, but where another remedy will suffice, such other remedy is preferred.

The remedies afforded in equity courts are not limited to equity remedies. Once a cause of action is legitimately in an equity court, the court will settle all the issues involved, including the remedies afforded at common law and the equity remedy. For instance, an equity decree might include money damages for injuries already suffered as well as an injunction against further injury. Equity, however, will not give a remedy that is directly contrary to common law; neither will equity act when an adequate remedy exists under a statute or under common law.

Features of Equity

Certain features of equity law are different from those of common law.

Requirements. In most actions the plaintiff does not have the right to choose whether the case will be decided by the rules of equity or by common law. There are two basic requirements for equity that determine where the case will be settled, and both of these requirements must be met: (1) it must be shown that the remedy at law would be inadequate, and (2) there must be a property right involved.

The showing that the remedy at law would be inadequate can be made in several ways, but generally one of three things is shown: (a) There is a threat of irreparable injury to the plaintiff. For instance, under a short-term lease the property owner is ordinarily entitled to the return of his property in virtually the same condition as it was when leased. Threatened extensive alterations or removal of trees or shrubs by the leaseholder could be cause for an injunction based on impending irreparable injury. (b) No remedy at law would permanently solve the problem involved; the cause of action would remain for a later suit. A common example of this is the situation in which a survey shows that one person has built a structure that is now found to rest partly on his neighbor's land. (c) Money damages would be incalculable or insufficient as a remedy. A nuisance, such as smoke or noise, making a home untenantable would be basis for getting into equity jurisdiction with this reason.

The showing of a property right being involved is the second requirement. Early equity cases adhered strictly to this requirement, but the more modern interpretation includes also personal rights (such as the right of free speech or freedom of assembly).

Speed. A court of equity generally acts more rapidly than does a court of law. As previously pointed out, a temporary injunction may be obtained with very little delay. In addition, there is usually no jury involved in equity cases, which eliminates the necessity for a time-consuming selection of members and deliberation over the evidence.

Privacy. Since there is no jury involved, a case in equity may be decided more privately. This feature is particularly significant when a case involving a trade secret is tried. If a jury were to hear the facts, there would be twelve more people to hear the secret. The secret would become virtually public information.

Injustices. There are occasions when equity decisions appear to work injustices on defendants. Black owns an industrial plant bordering a stream. The plant discharges waste materials into the stream. White owns property downstream from the plant, which also borders the stream. White's property is far enough downstream so that the water purifies itself before it gets to his property. White has never been injured as a result of the waste discharge into the stream, and does not use the stream except as a location of the boundary of his property. White brings suit to enjoin waste disposal into the stream by Black. A court of equity would be likely to enjoin the waste disposal, even though no one has been injured by it. If the court were to allow the waste disposal to continue, it is possible that, with the growth of the plant, harmful contamination could result. Also, the possibility exists that someone else might later obtain and use property between Black's plant and White's property, and be injured by the pollution of the stream. If the court dismissed the suit and the contamination became harmful, the dismissal could stand in the way of future relief, giving Black an apparent right to continue. Therefore, the court would have to find some solution other than outright dismissal of the case. Any solution other than dismissal is likely to add to Black's cost of operation.

Principles

Many equity principles and maxims form the background for equity decisions. Five prominent equity maxims are the following:

1. For every right a remedy.
2. He who seeks equity must do equity.
3. He who comes to equity must come with clean hands.
4. Equity regards substance rather than form.
5. Equity aids the vigilant, not those who sleep on their rights.

HOLZWORTH v. ROTH

101 N.W. 2d 393 South Dakota (March 2, 1960)

Rentto, Judge

This suit in equity commenced on July 18, 1958, claimed a breach of the covenants of title in a series of standard form warranty deeds by which the title to Lot 37, Harmony Heights Addition in Spearfish, South Dakota, went from the Lampert Lumber Company to the Holzworths, as ultimate grantees. Those named as defendants are the grantors in this series of deeds. They interposed numerous objections to the suit, one of them being that in the circumstances of this case a suit in equity did not lie.

During the time that these named defendants successively owned the property, between June 26, 1956, and April 26, 1957, the construction of a residence thereon was commenced and carried on. Eight of the laborers and materialmen contributing to this improvement were not paid so they filed mechanic's liens.[2] Six of them were filed for improvements commenced during the period when these defendants were the owners, and two for improvements started after the plaintiffs acquired their title. Subsequently on October 22, 1957, two of these lien claimants instituted an action to foreclose their liens naming the other six lien claimants and Martin Holzworth as defendants. This is urged by the plaintiffs as a breach of the covenants of title. None of the grantors in these various deeds were made parties to this foreclosure action nor does it appear that they had notice of it. Whether it was further prosecuted and with what results does not appear in this record. However, plaintiffs still occupy the premises.

In the suit here involved the Holzworths as the ultimate covenantees asked that the defendants be required to remove the mechanic's liens or pay the amount thereof. The defendants by motion for judgment, by their answer, and by a requested conclusion of law directed the trial court's attention to their objection that a suit in equity was not the proper remedy. The trial court overruled this contention and entered judgment requiring the defendants to remove the various liens or pay to the plaintiffs an amount equal to any judgment entered in the lien foreclosure action. From this judgment the defendants appeal.

In this state the distinction between actions at law and suits in equity is abolished by statute. . . . All relief is administered through one proceeding termed a civil action. However, this statutory abolition of distinctions applies only to the form of action, and not to the inherent substantive principles which underlie the two systems of procedure. . . . In other words, the essential and inherent differences between legal and eq-

uitable relief are still recognized and enforced in our system of jurisprudence. . . . One of these principles is that if the primary right which is the foundation of the litigation is legal in nature and there is a remedy at law, the action is one at law. . . . Equity has jurisdiction in such cases only if the legal remedy is not full, adequate, and complete.

When property is conveyed by our standard form warranty deed, SDC 51.1403 writes into it these covenants on the part of the grantor, his heirs, and personal representatives:

> that he is lawfully seized of the premises in fee simple, and has good right to convey the same; that the premises are free from all incumbrances; that he warrants to the grantee, his heirs, and assigns, the quiet and peaceable possession thereof; and that he will defend the title thereto against all persons who may lawfully claim the same.

They spell out the obligation on the part of the grantor, his heirs, and personal representatives arising out of the agreement between the parties. A breach of any of them is in effect a breach of their contract for which an action for damages will lie.

Significantly the chapter of our statutes concerned with damages for breach of contract, . . . prescribes the measure of damages to be allowed on breach of the covenants contained in our standard form warranty deed. . . . It seems to us that an action for breach of these covenants is clearly an action at law. . . . We think it follows that equity has no jurisdiction in this case if the remedy at law is full, adequate, and complete. . . .

Concerning the jurisdiction of equity the question of adequacy of the remedy at law appears in two aspects. Where the suit is properly cognizable in equity the existence of an adequate remedy at law may justify a court of equity in refusing to entertain the matter. . . . On the other hand, where the matter is legal in nature the absence of an adequate remedy at law is necessary to confer equitable jurisdiction. This is the aspect in which it is here involved. Accordingly, the burden of establishing this is on the plaintiffs.

We are unable to find that such inadequacy was urged by them or that it exists. On this feature the record is silent except as it is referred to in the contentions of the defendants. The complaint does not plead the inadequacy of an action at law nor are there any factual allegations from which such conclusion is inferable. In the findings and conclusions proposed by plaintiffs and adopted by the court this matter is not

---

2. Note: A *mechanic's lien* is a claim established against property to secure priority of payment for work done to improve that property; it may be established by almost any unpaid person who had a hand in the improvement.

mentioned. Nor did the plaintiffs in either their brief or argument in this court make a claim of such inadequacy. In the absence of fraud or some other unusual circumstances rendering the remedy at law inadequate equity will not interfere in this type of case. . . . Since it does not appear that plaintiffs' remedy at law was inadequate we must hold that equity is without jurisdiction.

Their remedy at law would have been even more efficient if Holzworth, who was a defendant in the lien foreclosure proceeding, had given these defendants notice of it and requested them to come in and defend the title they had warranted. This is called "voucher to warranty." . . . After such notice and request the judgment in that proceeding would be binding on them if they did not defend it. . . . That he neglected to utilize this privilege is of no help in getting this matter into equity. . . . The trial court should have dismissed this suit.

Reversed.

FRANKLIN v. SING-WILKES, INC.

112 S.E. 2d 618 Georgia (Jan. 8, 1960)

Duckworth, Chief Justice

This case is here on an exception to an order granting a temporary injunction after a hearing on a petition to enjoin certain lawful acts, wherein the purpose of said acts are for the illegal purpose of harassing the defendant by making continued calls and complaints to the police of the City of Thomasville about alleged noises and other breaches of the peace emanating from the petitioner's business in Thomasville. The allegations show that the complaints are not for the purpose of prosecuting the commission of any crime or violation of city ordinances, but for the purpose of harassing the petitioner in its lawful business to cause it to discontinue its night service station operations at this particular station. By cross action the defendants sought an injunction to prevent certain noises and disturbances originating at said service station. The order excepted to enjoined the defendants, until the further order of the court, from interfering with or harassing the petitioner's employees and customers as prayed in the petition. The prayers of the petition sought among other things to prevent the defendants from making telephone calls to the police department and making prosecutions and suing out warrants against the petitioner's employees in the operation of said station and its customers. At the hearing it was stipulated that approximately 8 cases had been made against a person or persons for alleged breaches of the peace at the service

station, involving noise. These cases had been disposed of in the Recorder's Court of Thomasville but are now pending on appeal in the superior court. The evidence and the stipulations showed that the property, which had been residential, has been zoned for business; that the noises around such stations are the usual noises made by the operation of such a business; that since the beginning of the business, the petitioner's officers and employees and the defendants have been in continuous altercation and discussion over the operation of the service station; that one of the defendants had made the statement that, if the petitioner did not close at night he would see if he couldn't get him closed; that the arrests of customers and employees had hurt the petitioner's business; and that the defendants had called the police complaining of noises of tire changing, loud talking, air compressors running, and other varied noises and that cases had been made by the police after being so summoned. *Held:*

1. This court has repeatedly held that where the evidence is conflicting at an interlocutory hearing to determine whether or not the lower court should grant or deny a temporary injunction, it can not be said that the court abused its discretion in either granting or denying the injunction. . . . It follows that the court did not err in granting a temporary injunction against the defendants and in refusing to grant the temporary injunction prayed for in the cross action.

2. The exception to the failure of the court to rule on and sustain the demurrers to the petition, after a hearing thereon in which the court reserved its rulings thereon, is treated as abandoned since counsel for the plaintiff in error has failed to argue it either in the brief or orally before this court. Furthermore, the exception is to no judgment and hence presents nothing for a decision.

Judgment Affirmed.

REVIEW QUESTIONS

1. Why do we need man-made laws? What purpose do they serve?
2. What are the four basic types of laws in our legal system? What does each consist of?
3. What is the meaning and significance of the term *stare decisis*?
4. How do changes in common law take place?
5. What factors led to the establishment of equity as a separate system of law?
6. What types of remedies are offered by common law? By equity?

7. A owns a factory that emits large quantities of foul-smelling smoke. People in a nearby housing development are annoyed by the odors whenever the wind shifts to an unfortunate direction. B, a resident in the housing development, has lodged a complaint against A for public nuisance. In what kind of court would the case be likely to be tried in your state? Why? What would be the probable result of the legal action?

8. What are the two general requirements for equity jurisdiction? How might these requirements be met?

9. In Holzworth v. Roth the decision of the trial court was reversed with the statement that the case should have been dismissed. Does this mean that Holzworth must give up his attempt to recover for the apparent injustice he has suffered? What else can he do?

10. Why was *Franklin* v. *Sing-Wilkes, Inc.,* an equity case? What property or personal rights were involved?

4

Courts, Trial Procedure, and Evidence

The fact that one person accuses another of a wrong does not mean that the accusation is proper. Since the beginning of civilization the problem of determining the truth of an accusation has existed. Court trials with a judge, a jury, and attorneys for both plaintiff and defendant have not always been used. Probably the earliest form of trial was *trial by battle*. Accused and accuser (or their representatives) faced each other in battle, with the outcome determining the justice of the accusation. In many of the early civilizations trial by battle was replaced either by *trial by ordeal* or *trial by jury*. The codes of Hammurabi required trial by ordeal. For certain acts the accused was to be thrown in the divine river. If the river held him (if he couldn't swim), the guilty verdict and punishment were delivered at the same time. Trial by jury, in one form or another, existed in many ancient civilizations. Our present jury trial system developed with the common law. Its continuance in criminal and civil cases is guaranteed in the sixth and seventh amendments of the United States Constitution.

COURTS

In the United States we have a system of courts for each state as well as a system of federal courts. The systems are somewhat similar. In both the federal and state systems there is an ultimate tribunal, a supreme court. At the next lower level are the appellate courts (in the federal system and some state systems) which handle appeals from the lower courts. The lower courts are the district courts in the federal system, and usually county courts in the state systems.

Federal Courts

Supreme Court. The United States Supreme Court is our highest tribunal. It is our final court of appeal. Article 3 of the Constitution gives us our Supreme Court and whatever inferior federal courts Congress may from time to time require. The jurisdiction (as to types of cases) is limited in the Constitution to nine categories. The only cases that may originate in the Supreme Court are those involving ambassadors, public ministers, and consuls, or in which a state is a party. In these the Supreme Court has original jurisdiction; all other cases go to the Supreme Court by appeal.

Cases are appealed to the Supreme Court from either United States Courts of Appeal or from state supreme courts in the normal course of events in an appealed case. However, cases may go directly from any court to the U.S. Supreme Court if the question to be settled involves the U.S. Constitution or is of very great public interest. Appeal is made by a petition to the court for a writ of *certiorari*. If the petition by the appellant is successful, a writ of certiorari will be issued to the lower court demanding that the case be sent up for review. Only a very small portion of such petitions are successful—something like one out of twenty.

The nine justices who sit on the U.S. Supreme Court have the final say as to what our law shall be. They do not, of course, make formal statutes—this is the function of the legislative branch of the government. Their highly significant function is to interpret what is meant by the Constitution or the wording of a statute. The interpretation given by the Supreme Court determines the lawful interpretation to be used in future cases in lower courts.

Courts of Appeal. Eleven United States Courts of Appeal exist. Appeals on federal questions are normally settled by the three justices who preside over each court. These courts were first established by Congress in 1891 because of the burden of appeals upon the United States Supreme Court. They function as appeal courts only and do not conduct trials. Issues between parties are appealed on the basis of a conflict in the law, the facts of the issue having been decided previously in a lower court.

District Courts. The trial courts of the federal court system are the United States District Courts. The districts presided over by the 100 or so U.S. District Courts are formed in such a way that no state is without a Federal District Court. The number of justices in a U.S. District Court is determined by statute and is based on the amount of federal legal controversy arising in the district.

For a case to be tried in a federal court, it must:

1. Arise from the U.S. Constitution, federal laws, or treaties of the United States, or
2. Affect ambassadors, other public ministers and consuls, or
3. Arise in admiralty or maritime jurisdictions, or
4. Involve two or more states as parties, or
5. Involve the United States as a party, or
6. Be between citizens of different states with the amount in controversy greater than $10,000, or
7. Be between citizens of a state who claim land grants in another state, or
8. Be between a state and a foreign country, or
9. Be between a United States citizen and a foreign country or its citizens.

Most of the controversies handled involve federal statutes or the Constitution.

Common examples of cases tried in United States District Courts are bankruptcy, admiralty, patent, copyright and trademark, restraint of trade, tax cases, and cases involving infringement of personal rights. Many other cases arise from decisions of administrative boards (e.g., National Labor Relations Board) which operate as quasi judicial entities and look to the federal courts for enforcement of their orders. Claims against the federal government may be filed either in a U.S. District Court or in a U.S. Court of Claims if the amount in controversy is less than $10,000. If the amount is greater than $10,000 the suit must be filed in a court of claims.

The U.S. Court of Claims is a special court in the federal system. Other special courts include the U.S. Customs Court, the U.S. Tax Court, and the U.S. Court of Customs and Patent Appeals.

State Courts

State court systems are far from uniform throughout the United States. Not only do the systems differ from state to state, but the names of the courts differ as well. A few generalities, though, can be stated.

Each state has a final court of appeal, usually called the supreme court of the state. Nearly always the highest court confines its work to appeals of cases tried in lower courts. Courts of intermediate appellate jurisdiction are interposed between the supreme court and lower courts in many states.

The next lower tier of courts consists of the trial courts of general jurisdiction, known variously as circuit courts, courts of common pleas, county courts, superior courts, or, in New York, the supreme court. Probate courts or surrogate courts handle cases of wills, trusts, and the like. Such courts are limited in geographical jurisdiction to a particular county, district, or other major political subdivision of the state.

At the lower end of the judicial hierarchy are various municipal courts. Police courts, justices of the peace, small claims courts, juvenile courts, and recorders' courts are common examples of these courts of very limited jurisdiction.

Jurisdiction

The jurisdiction of a court means its right or authority, given either by a legislature or constitution, to hear and determine causes of action presented to it. A court's jurisdiction relates to geographical regions (as to location of persons and subject matter), to types of cases, and possibly to the amount of money concerned.

Courts have jurisdiction over property, both real and personal, located within their assigned geographical limits. Even though the owner may not be available, his property may be taken in satisfaction of a judgment. A court has no authority over property lying outside its territorial limits. Let us assume that a Tennessee court has awarded Black $5,000 as a result of a damage action against White. If White does not pay and cannot be made to pay in satisfaction of the judgment, justice for Black is rather hollow. The Tennessee court could take and sell that part of White's property which could be found in Tennessee until the judgment was satisfied. However, it could not touch any of White's property in, say, Georgia.

A court has jurisdiction over all persons found within its geographical limits, whether the persons are residents or not. Jurisdiction over a person is exercised by serving that person with a summons or other legal process—a defendant would be served with a summons; a witness with a subpoena. How service may be made is a matter clarified by each state's statutes. Generally, a sheriff or other officer is directed to serve the process upon the person; however, if the person cannot be found there is usually an alternate means of service. In certain types of cases, such as quieting title to real property, divorce, probate of a will, and others where the thing involved is within the court's jurisdiction, a process may be served even though the person on whom it is to be served is outside the court's jurisdiction. The means by which this is done is known as *constructive service*. This service on an absentee is made by publication of the process in a local paper. In most damage actions, though, absence of both defendant and his property acts as a serious obstacle—action against him would be pointless unless some recovery could be anticipated.

Jurisdiction of courts is also limited as to types of cases which they have authority to handle. A probate court, for instance, ordinarily has no authority to handle criminal cases; criminal courts usually do not handle civil suits.

A monetary limitation is placed upon many of the courts. Justice of the peace courts and small-claims courts are limited to cases involving no more than the statutory limit—usually $150 to $1,000, but up to $5,000 in some states.

TRIAL PROCEDURE

Jury trials involve a great deal of human interest. Newspaper articles, television shows, and movies often deal with courtroom activities. With these sources available it is a rare individual who has no concept of courtroom procedure.

Trial at Law (as opposed to equity)

Although most people have some knowledge of courtroom procedure, the preliminaries and the aftermath are not so well known. Let us assume that you are involved in a controversy in which you have been injured in some way and, apparently, are entitled to damages. How do you go about taking the controversy to court? The most obvious and correct course is to see a competent attorney. But what steps does the attorney take?

Complaint. If, after hearing your story, the attorney decides that you have a reasonable cause of action, his first step will be to draw up and file a complaint in the court where the remedy is sought. Although *complaint* is the common term, it is often called a *petition* or *declaration*. The complaint has a two-fold function:

1. To state the facts constituting the cause of action as clearly and concisely as possible, and
2. To demand the remedy sought by the plaintiff.

Summons. Following receipt of a complaint, the court issues a summons to the defendant. The summons is simply a notice to the defendant that he is about to be sued. A copy of the complaint may or may not accompany the summons, depending upon the jurisdiction. If the complaint does not accompany the summons, it is made available to the defendant by the clerk of the court. If the defendant is served a summons but does not answer it, the result is a judgment against him by default.

Defendant's Answer. The defendant has a statutory time in which to answer the complaint lodged against him and avoid a judgment by default. Three usual answers are made by defendants: demurrer, motion to dismiss, and counterclaim.

A *demurrer* alleges that even if the factual situation is proved to be as stated in the complaint, these facts are insufficient to support the legal action. A demurrer, then, raises a question of law: do the facts alleged give the plaintiff a cause of action at law?

A *motion to dismiss* quarrels with the facts. The defendant may point out specific defects of a factual nature in the plaintiff's complaint.

A *counterclaim* usually admits the facts stated in the complaint, but alleges other facts and, on the basis of these, demands damages from the plaintiff. The plaintiff is then given an opportunity to make a *reply* or *replication* to the counterclaim.

An issue must be framed before a trial can be held. There must be a question of fact or of law, or questions of both, to be settled by the trial. The pleadings are not complete until an issue has been presented. When an issue is clear, the case is ready to go to trial.

The Jury. Parties to a court conflict at law have a choice as to whether or not they will have a jury decide the facts of the case. Both parties may agree to submit all the issues, including issues of fact, to the judge. If there are questions of fact (e.g., "Did the plaintiff act reasonably?"), both parties must be in agreement if they are to dispense with the jury.

A trial jury is known as a *petit jury*. It usually consists of twelve persons, but, by statute in several states, a petit jury may consist of fewer people for civil cases or for crimes less than capital offenses. Selection of the individual members of the jury involves both attorneys and the judge. Grounds for challenging prospective jurors are established by statute. The two opposing attorneys may use these grounds to disqualify prospective jurors being examined. Generally, the established grounds for disqualifications are those that show a financial or blood connection between the prospective juror and one of the litigants. In addition to disqualifying a juror on established grounds, each attorney may usually disqualify a limited number of prospective jurors arbitrarily by exercising the right of *peremptory challenge*. The judge supervises the qualification proceedings. When the jury has been impaneled the case is ready for trial.

Courtroom Procedure. When the pleadings are complete, the case has come up on the court's docket, and the jury has been chosen and sworn in, the trial begins. Following opening statements by the attorneys, witnesses are sworn in and the evidence is examined.

Each attorney sums up his case to the jury, the judge charges the jury, and the jury retires to reach a verdict. In his charge to the jury the judge sums up the case and instructs the jury as to the issues to be decided by it. After reaching a verdict the jury returns to the courtroom and the foreman (usually the first juror chosen) announces the decision. The judge then gives the judgment which is the official decision of the court in the case.

New Trial or Appeal. Within a certain, statutory time after the judgment has been rendered, a new trial or an appeal may be requested. Generally, a new trial is concerned with error in the facts of the case, while an appeal is concerned with a mis-application of the law.

A successful motion for a new trial may be made upon the basis of an almost unlimited number of circumstances. It is argued that if a new trial is not granted, there will be a miscarriage of justice. The following are only common examples of reasons given for requests for new trials.

1. Unfairness or trickery in selection of members of the jury.
2. Prejudice stemming from financial or blood relationship between a jury member and a party to the trial.
3. Misconduct by a jury member, e.g., sleeping during the trial, or gambling on the outcome.
4. Error by the judge in failing to allow evidence which should have been admitted, or in admitting evidence which should have been excluded.
5. False testimony (perjury) of a witness.
6. Unforeseen accident preventing the appearance of a witness.

If the motion to the trial court for a new trial is unsuccessful, appeal may be made to a higher court to order a new trial.

Either party may appeal a decision in a civil case; only the defendant may appeal from an adverse criminal judgment. Appeals are based on questions of law—the trial court has decided issues of fact.

Reasons for appeal are presented to the appeal court in a *bill of exceptions*. Stated here are objections or exceptions taken to the ruling of the trial court. These objections are usually concerned with objections to and rulings on the admissibility of evidence, errors in the conduct of the trial, and instructions by the judge. Evidence presented and testimony taken are usually included along with the judge's instruction to the jury.

The appellant (the appealing party) is usually required to post an *appeal bond* upon taking the case to a higher court. The purpose of the appeal bond is to insure that the appellant will pay court costs and damage to the appellee if the trial court decision is upheld.

In addition to the bill of exceptions and the bond, appellant must present a *brief* of the case to the appellate court. The brief contains a statement of the case from the appellant's position and a list of errors forming the basis of appeal.

Equity Suits

Equity acts when common law or statutes offer no remedy. Equity procedure is different from that of common law. The judge decides both questions of fact and questions of law. There is no jury unless the judge specifically requires a jury recommendation on a question. Even then, the verdict of the jury is only a recommendation and the final conclusion as to fact rests with the judge. If factual questions are long and involved, the judge may appoint a "master" to take testimony and make recommendations.

Equity terminology is somewhat different from that of common law. The first pleading (complaint or declaration or petition in common law) is usually known as either a *bill* or a *complaint* in equity cases. The court's judgment is known as a *decree*.

Equity acts *in personam*. By the decree, a person is directed to do or not to do a certain thing. The decrees are either interlocutory or final. An *interlocutory decree* reserves the right of the court to act again in the case at some later time. A temporary injunction is an example of such a decree.

Cases

In both common law and equity the doctrine of *stare decisis* is followed. Similar prior cases are followed in deciding present issues. Since cases must be known to be followed, it may be desirable to consider for a moment how cases are recorded and reported.

The West Publishing Company, St. Paul, Minnesota, publishes reports of state cases that reach the appeal courts, and all federal cases. The case of *O'Neill* v. *Chicago Transit Authority*, 283 N.E. 2d 99, 5 Ill. App. 3d 69, (1972) appears at the end of this chapter. In this case O'Neill and Chicago Transit Authority were plaintiff and defendant in the trial court. O'Neill won a judgment in the trial court and Chicago Transit Authority appealed that judgment. It is now the function of the appeal court to examine and uphold or overturn the work of the trial court. The numbers and letters following the case name tell how to locate it. The 283 N.E. 2d 99 indicates one place where the case may be found. It begins on page 99 of volume 283 of the second series of North Eastern case reporting books. In like manner, 5 Ill. App. 3d 69 indicates that the case may also be found starting on page 69 of the 5th volume in the third series of Illinois Appeal case reports.

The case reporters used by the West Publishing Company for reporting state cases divide the United States into seven districts. Each district covers several states. In addition to the North Eastern Reporter, there is the Pacific Reporter, the South Western Reporter, the Southern Reporter, the South Eastern Reporter, the North Western Reporter, and the Atlantic Reporter. The cases reported in these reporters are state cases that have been appealed from lower court decisions. The reason for this is that appeal decisions become controlling law for that type of case in that state's courts. A particular decision in an appealed case may even be the basis for decisions on similar cases in other states or in the federal courts.

Another set of reporters covers federal case decisions. The Federal Reporter reports U.S. Circuit Court of Appeals cases; U.S. District Court opinions are found in the Federal Supplement; Supreme Court decisions are reported in the Supreme Court Reporter. Federal special court cases and decisions of administrative boards are found in other series of West volumes.

Cases are reported in the West publications in three sections. A short summary of the facts is followed by a list of the legal points brought out in the case; then the full text of the judge's opinion is given.

EVIDENCE

Evidence is used to prove questions of fact. The facts, as presented by the contestants in a law case, often stray somewhat from the truth. The truth may be shaded a bit in the presentation. Each contestant must be willing to prove that what he said is true. The judge or jury then has the task of determining the true situation. Evidence is the means of establishing proof.

In a criminal case the evidence must prove guilt "beyond any reasonable doubt" for the defendant to be found guilty. A civil case, by contrast, is won or lost on the comparative weight of the proof.

The burden of proof in a criminal case is always assumed by the state. In a civil case the burden usually rests on the plaintiff to prove his charge but, under certain circumstances, may shift to the defendant; one such circumstance occurs when a counterclaim is made.

Real Evidence and Testimony

Evidence may be classified in many ways. It is classed as *real evidence* if it is evidence the judge or jury can see for themselves. For example, a fire extinguisher shown in court to be defective would be real evidence; so would a defective cable or a ladder that broke because of a defective rung. *Testimony* consists of statements by witnesses of things that have come to

their knowledge through their senses. Testimony might be used to prove that a driver was operating his car unsafely, and thus contributed to the cause of an accident.

Judicial Notice

Certain facts are so well known and accepted that the court will accept them without requiring proof. The court takes such *judicial notice* of logarithm tables, provisions of the federal or a state constitution, Newton's laws of motion, and the like. Evidence would not be required to prove that gasoline is combustible, but the presence of gasoline in a particular situation might require proof.

Witnesses

Determination that a witness is competent to testify is part of the court's (judge's) function. Competence is usually questioned on the basis of the witness's mental capacity or mental ability.

The witness is required to testify only as to information having some bearing on the case at hand. If the testimony given under examination or cross examination gets too far afield, either the opposing attorney or the judge may object. Wandering by the witness under examination is likely to result in an objection from the other counsel on the basis that the testimony is "incompetent," "irrelevant," or "immaterial." Each of the three words has a particular meaning in a trial court.

Incompetency refers to the inadmissibility of the testimony. As a matter of law, certain testimony may be excluded. Testimony as to the terms of a written agreement would be incompetent if the terms are apparent from the contract itself.

Irrelevancy refers to the lack of relationship between the issues of the case and testimony requested or given. In a case involving machinery specifications, a question pertaining to an engineer's home life would hardly be relevant.

Immaterial evidence is evidence that is insignificant. The color of tie worn by a salesman when he sold a piece of machinery would be immaterial.

The right of a witness not to testify on certain matters is known as *privilege*. According to the Fifth Amendment to the U.S. Constitution, no person may be compelled to testify against himself. Communications between certain people need not be revealed in court. Examples of such privileged communications are those between husband and wife, doctor and patient, and attorney and client. Neither party may be made to testify unless the privilege is waived by the party affected by the trial.

Conclusive evidence is evidence that is incontestable. It is evidence that can in no way be successfully challenged. The existence of a written contract is conclusive evidence that someone wrote it.

Prima facie evidence is something less than conclusive. It is rebuttable. It is capable of being countered by evidence from the opposing side but, if allowed to stand, is sufficient to establish some fact. A signature on a written document would be evidence of this nature.

Direct and Circumstantial

Direct evidence goes to the heart of the matter in question. It is evidence which, if uncontested, would tend to establish the fact of the issue. A witness to a signature could establish the fact of signing by a particular party.

By contrast with direct evidence, *circumstantial* evidence attempts to prove a question of fact, for instance, as to the authenticity of a claimed oral contract. Circumstantial evidence might be taken to show that the person now denying the contract would not have acted as he did at some past time unless he had entered into the contract. A net of circumstances is often woven to show a high probability that a particular version of an issue is true.

Best or Primary Evidence

The court will require the best evidence possible in a particular case; that is, the highest and most original evidence available. "Secondary" evidence will not be used unless, for some reason, the primary evidence is not obtainable. In a case involving a written document, for instance, the document is the best evidence of its existence and provisions. If the original document were destroyed or lost, a copy of the document or testimony as to its existence and contents would be admissible. The document, itself, would be best or *primary* evidence; the copy or testimony would be *secondary*.

Hearsay

Hearsay evidence is second hand. It is testimony as to something that the witness has heard another person say. Most hearsay evidence is objectionable to the court for three main reasons: first, because the person whose observation is quoted is not present in the court to be seen by the jury; second, the original testimony was not under oath; and third, there is no opportunity for the original testimony to stand the test of cross examination.

There are a few exceptions to the exclusion of hearsay evidence by the court. Statutes vary somewhat in this respect from state to state. Hearsay is sometimes permitted where other evidence is completely lacking. Hearsay testimony as to dying declarations is usually admissible. A prominent exception to the hearsay rule is the *res gestae* statement.

Res Gestae

In common English, the term *res gestae* means "things done." In courtroom procedure *res gestae* refers to allowable hearsay testimony as to spontaneous utterances closely connected with an event. Consider an industrial accident situation in which the victim was killed. If, just before the accident occurred, the victim shouted that the safety device didn't work, testimony to that effect by a fellow worker might be allowed as *res gestae*. The statement explains the cause.

Parol Evidence Rule

A contract or statement that has been reduced to writing is the best evidence of the meanings involved. Testimony *(parol evidence)* that would tend to alter these meanings is objectionable. Only where the terminology is ambiguous or where unfamiliar trade terms are used will testimony be allowed to clarify the meaning, and then an expert witness may be called upon for an interpretation.

The parol evidence rule is confined to interpretations of wording of a document; it does not apply to a question of the validity of the instrument. In a question as to the reason why a person entered into a contract— for instance, a claim of duress—oral evidence would be allowed. Similarly, an attack as to the legality of consideration offered would permit testimony.

Opinion Evidence

During the taking of testimony in a trial, the objection is occasionally heard that the "counsel is asking for a conclusion of the witness." An ordinary person appearing on the witness stand is not allowed to give his opinions or conclusions in evidence. Such is the rule, but, as with many other rules of law, there are exceptions. In some instances the nature of the testimony requires that *opinions* be given—otherwise the evidence will not be clear. In fact, just about any perception of anything is a conclusion based upon sensory responses and experience.

The main thing objected to in opinion evidence is that logical deduction or reasoning is being required of a witness. If such reasoning and conclusions are required in the progress of a trial, an expert from the field of knowledge involved should be called upon to give his opinion as to facts or the meaning of a series of facts. If an opinion is necessary it is desirable to have the best possible opinion. Engineers are qualified by training and experience to act as expert witnesses in certain types of cases. Occasionally it is by giving expert testimony that members of engineering faculties obtain fees which enable them to afford to remain teachers.

THE ENGINEER AS AN EXPERT WITNESS

Most opinion evidence is excluded from a trial; the opinion of an average person acting as a witness is inadmissible. *Opinion* implies conjecture, and the law looks with disfavor upon indeterminate factual situations. Nevertheless, such factual situations do arise and the truth in them must be determined as closely as possible. Such questions as the adequacy of design of a structure or the capabilities of a specially designed machine often must be answered.

Expert

Attorneys and judges are usually quite learned people. Knowledge of the law requires a broad general knowledge of many specialized fields to understand the factual situations presented in cases. Most lawyers, though, would admit that their knowledge of a particular technical field is quite general and that, therefore, they would be incapable of drawing intelligent conclusions on complicated technical questions. For such purpose an expert is needed.

An expert was once facetiously defined as "any person of average knowledge from more than fifty miles away." Such a criterion would hardly stand up in a court of law. An *expert* is a person who, because of technical training and experience, possesses special knowledge or skill in a particular field which would not be possessed by an average person. Qualification before the court as an expert witness is part of the expert testimony. The prospective expert witness can expect to be asked questions as to his background, projects in which he has been involved, his training, whether he is registered, and other questions of a similar nature. The court then determines if he is qualified to give expert testimony.

Expert Assistance

There are three important ways in which an expert may assist an attorney in a case involving a technical matter: (1) advice and consultation regarding technical matters in the preparation of the case; (2) assistance in examining and cross-examining technical witnesses; and (3) expert testimony on the issues involved.

Advice and Consultation. In engineering, as in other technical fields, it is necessary that a person be thoroughly familiar with technical concepts to explain them to laymen. A jury is made up of a cross section of a community (or some near approach to that). Part of the engineer's function as an expert witness is to present to his attorney and to the judge and jury the facts of the case in such a manner that laymen can understand them. The minimum requirements for this are technical proficiency and the ability to effectively communicate the knowledge.

The basis of any effective presentation is investigation. The engineer as an expert witness should be so thoroughly familiar with the facts of the case that nothing the opposition can propose will come as a surprise to him. Drawings and specifications may have to be carefully read, materials tested, and building codes or other laws examined. All should be analyzed for the presence of flaws if the engineer is to do an effective job. Assistance in the preparation of the attorney's brief requires the best of an engineer's investigative powers.

The engineer's obligation to his client and attorney requires an objective approach to the case. Not only should the facts to substantiate his client's claim be present, opposing facts should also be shown. There are two sides to any controversy. In the interest of winning the case, opposing arguments must be considered and rebuttals prepared.

Trial Assistance. In a case involving technical fields, both parties normally obtain experts to aid them and testify in their behalf. In addition to assistance in preparation of a case and testimony in court, the expert may also be valuable in suggesting questions to be asked by the attorney. *Direct examination* questions are prepared in advance, but most *cross-examination* questions and *redirect* and *recross* questions must be planned during the course of the trial. A flaw in the technical argument posed by the opposition might escape an attorney's notice but it should not escape the notice of a technical expert in that field. The questions suggested may be aimed at the opposition by way of cross-examination; or they may be in the form of direct questions to be asked of the expert when he is put on the stand to counter the opposition's evidence.

Testimony. The judge, attorneys, and jurors are laymen as far as the technical expert's field is concerned. The expert, therefore, must present his information in a simplified manner so that it will be readily understood by the layman. Such presentation is quite akin to teaching. A simple foundation must first be laid and then the complexities based on it. The preparation of such a presentation is not always easy. It necessitates comparison of technical principles with everyday occurrences and the use of pictures, slides, models, and drawings to make a meaning clear. Many hours of preparation are required for an hour of effective presentation. Each part of the presentation must be as nearly perfect as possible—incapable of being successfully questioned by opposing counsel.

It is almost essential that the expert witness be present at the entire trial if he is to do an effective job on the witness stand. Prior evidence established by opposing counsel may require alterations in the expert's presentation and changes in the attack on the opposing witnesses.

Honesty in answers is one of the prime requisites of any witness under examination. The opposing attorney will look (with expert assistance) for any point upon which he can attack the expert's testimony. Once found, and properly worked on, a small loophole in the presentation can destroy the effect of laboriously developed testimony. If the engineer does not know the answer to a particular question, the least damaging answer is a simple "I don't know." If the question involves prior testimony, the witness may request the reading of that prior testimony before answering the question. If the question requires calculations or a consultation between the witness and his attorney or other experts, time for such calculation or consultation may be requested from the court.

The demeanor of the expert witness on the stand is important. His appearance and answers to questions posed should inspire confidence in his ability. A professional appearance, professional conduct, and a professional attitude toward the entire proceedings come through clearly to the others in the courtroom. During cross-examination the opposing counsel will usually try to belittle or pick apart testimony damaging to his case; usually the more damaging the testimony, the greater the effort to reduce it to a shambles. Failing this, the attorney may attempt merely to enrage the witness in hopes that an opening in the testimony may occur. Calm and considered answers by the witness are the best defense against the opposing counsel's attack. Courtesy and self-control must be exercised.

Reference use of writings by acknowledged authorities in the technical field is advisable. Often it seems that a quotation excerpted from a textbook has more weight than an oral statement on the witness stand by the author.

Depositions. There are occasions when a witness may be unable to attend a trial to testify. On such occasions his testimony may be taken in some place other than the courtroom prior to the trial. The testimony is taken under oath and recorded for use in the trial. Both opposing attorneys must be present, and the rights to direct examination, cross-examination, redirect, and recross are the same as they would be in the courtroom. At the time of the trial the deposition is read into the court record and becomes part of the proceedings. A deposition is generally considered to be less effective than testimony given in open court where jurors can see and hear the presentation. However, there are times when it is the only means available and is far preferable to the alternative of omission.

To Take the Case or Not. An engineer who is asked to be an expert witness should decide whether or not he really believes in his prospective client's position. The quality of support rendered by the engineer in the case will often depend upon how firmly he believes in the case. On the witness stand the engineer will be required to tell the truth of the case as he sees it. Conviction that his client is right is often apparent in the manner in which the testimony is given.

Fees. The fee to be charged by the engineer for acting as an expert witness in a case should correspond to the fee he would normally charge for other important consulting work. It should be based on the amount of time required and the relative importance of his role in the proceedings. In *no* case should the fee be contingent upon the outcome of the case. "Double or nothing" is closer to gambling than it is to payment for services. Contingency fees are seriously frowned upon by the court as tending to cause inaccurate testimony; opposing counsel will not hesitate to take full advantage of this arrangement if it appears.

In every section of the United States there are minimum fees for professional engineering services. In most states these fees are published by the state society of professional engineers. A typical minimum charge is $400 per day in addition to such expenses as required travel and hotel accommodations. However, the minimum varies considerably in the various geographical sections of the United States.

O'NEILL v. CHICAGO TRANSIT AUTHORITY
283 N.E. 2d 99, 5 Ill. App. 3d 69 (1972)

Goldberg, Presiding Justice:

After a bench trial, William O'Neill (plaintiff), recovered a judgment of $4000 for personal injuries against Chicago Transit Authority and David Wright, a bus driver (defendants). On their appeal, defendants urge that the court erred in granting plaintiff leave to file an amended complaint and that the proof showed that the injuries of plaintiff occurred because of his own condition and not because of negligence of defendants.

Plaintiff alleged in his original complaint that the mishap occurred when he was about to board a bus bound west on 63rd Street. He also alleged that the driver negligently permitted the door of the vehicle to close upon plaintiff and that the bus started before plaintiff had reached a safe place. The complaint also contained other allegations regarding negligence including a charge that the door was inoperative so that it closed on plaintiff.

Plaintiff called no occurrence witness other than himself. He testified that he was attempting to board a southbound Ashland Avenue bus on the northwest corner of Ashland and 63rd Streets. Two people boarded before plaintiff and he had one foot on the second step when the driver put the bus into motion. Plaintiff fell backwards, was rendered unconscious, and awoke in the hospital. On cross-examination, he testified that shortly before he had visited a friend who was a bartender in a tavern. He remained there for three-quarters of an hour and he was positive that he drank two beers and no whiskey.

The only other witness called by plaintiff was his own wife who merely testified to his debilitated condition after his injuries. At the close of plaintiff's case, he requested, and the court granted, leave to amend his complaint upon its face so as to allege that the bus was being operated in a southerly direction upon Ashland Avenue (not in a westerly direction upon 63rd Street); that the bus had stopped on the north side of 63rd Street (rather than on 63rd Street east of Ashland Avenue) and that plaintiff started to enter the bus to go south upon Ashland Avenue (rather than west upon 63rd Street).

The driver testified for the defendants that the bus had stopped on the southwest corner of Ashland and 63rd Streets. The driver entered the bus as relief for a preceding operator. The vehicle was halted at the curb, out of gear, and did not move. Several passengers boarded. Plaintiff then appeared and started to board. Plaintiff was very unsteady, appeared intoxicated, and had no control over his equilibrium. He was holding the door bar; but, as he reached into his pocket for change, he lost his grip and fell backwards through the open door and out of the bus. Plaintiff was some four feet away from the driver and the entire incident took three or four seconds "more or less."

Defendants also called two eyewitnesses who were seated on the bus at the time. It appears from their testimony that the bus was proceeding east on 63rd Street and that it had stopped on the southwest corner of the intersection to change drivers. Both of them were

seated on the long seat immediately behind the driver running parallel to the length of the bus so that both were facing south toward the front door. They saw plaintiff standing in the doorway, staggering or weaving. One witness testified that plaintiff was too far from the driver for the driver to touch him and that the occurrence happened very quickly. An ambulance arrived and the plaintiff was removed to the hospital. Defendants' final witness was a police officer who testified that plaintiff was intoxicated at the time in question.

At the close of all the evidence, over objection by defendants, the court granted plaintiff leave to file instanter a so-called second amended complaint. This new complaint alleged that the bus was going east on 63rd Street near its intersection with Ashland Avenue and that it had stopped on 63rd Street to take on passengers. It alleged that plaintiff was "in an intoxicated, helpless, and irresponsible condition" and that he entered the bus and then fell out of the open door to the ground. It alleged that plaintiff ". . . was in the exercise of ordinary care and caution for his own safety consistent with a person in such intoxicated, helpless and irresponsible condition." It alleged that the defendants knew plaintiff's condition and failed to take precaution to protect him from injury while on the bus.

The right of a litigant to amend his pleading to conform to the proofs is established in the Civil Practice Act, Ill. Rev. Stat. 1969, ch. 110, par. 46(3). Our courts have been liberal in permitting amendments of pleadings. . . . It has often been held that the filing of amendments to pleadings is a matter within the discretion of the court and that this discretion should be liberally exercised. . . . However, the test to be applied in determining whether the discretion of the court was properly exercised is whether the order entered by the court furthered the ends of Justice. . . .

In this case, plaintiff testified that he drank only "a couple of beers" before the accident, and that he was in the act of boarding a bus on the northwest corner of the intersection to go south on Ashland Avenue, that the driver negligently started the bus and that this act of negligence was the cause of his fall. This testimony was a judicial admission by plaintiff. A judicial admission is the highest and best type of evidence. It is sufficient to dispense with the need for proof of the facts admitted. . . . Plaintiff cannot be permitted to contradict the allegations of his own complaint by a solemn judicial admission and then in turn to contradict this admission by completely inconsistent allegations in a newly tendered amendment. . . . Plaintiff cannot abandon his own sworn evidence and then attempt to recover by adopting completely inconsistent evidence produced by other witnesses. . . . The right to amend pleadings is not absolute and unlimited.

A legal proceeding is basically adversary in its nature. However, of paramount importance, it is an attempt to reach justice by ascertainment of truth. It is not a contest in which each party is permitted to take an unfair advantage over the other for his own gain. Under the particular circumstances of this case, in view of plaintiff's own sworn admissions, the court should not have permitted the complaint to be amended in the manner requested. Plaintiff's evidence is overcome and destroyed by the testimony of the driver and two apparently credible and impartial eyewitnesses. Under these circumstances we need not consider the contention of defendants that there is no proof of negligence.

The judgment in favor of plaintiff and against defendants is accordingly reversed.

Judgment reversed.

GLOBE INDEMNITY CO. v. HIGHLAND TANK & MFG. CO.

345 F. Supp. 1290 (1972)

MEMORANDUM AND ORDER

Newcomer, District Judge.

The plaintiff in a previously tried indemnity and/or contribution action seeks to gain a new trial based on many grounds. The Court seeks to direct its consideration on the disqualification of plaintiff's expert witnesses as the only ground which may have any arguable merit in granting a new trial, all other grounds being without merit.

It is well settled law that the trial court must be left to determine the qualifications of an expert witness. . . . The decision upon the fitness of the individual witness is based upon the circumstances of the expert's experience and the factual setting in which the expert's testimony is necessary. Further, the expert's qualifications must be expressly shown. . . .

This Court is well aware that the witnesses which the plaintiff attempted to qualify have distinguished themselves in the academic world and has no difficulty in accepting and recognizing their credentials. However, their credentials alone do not qualify them as experts to testify on the factual setting which was in issue—the design of a molasses storage tank.

An analogy involving expert testimony would be as follows: A properly licensed driver with ten years of driving experience being called upon to testify as an expert witness involving the circumstances of a collision in an auto racing mishap. The witness would be knowledgeable in the general rules of driving, i.e. staying to the right of the road, passing on the left, etc., but

would not be qualified to testify as an expert on the more specific area of driving in an auto race just because he was a licensed driver, without the showing of other specific qualifications. Therefore, the trial court would be acting within its discretion in disqualifying the witness as an expert on auto racing, and still permitting the witness to testify on the general rules of driving. This Court within its discretion felt that the analogy put forth applied to Mr. Maurer, an electrical engineer, and Mr. Bradley, an industrial hygienist.

Mr. Maurer was generally qualified as an engineer. However, Mr. Maurer was asked to testify on the design criteria necessary to insure the safe use of molasses holding tanks in an industrial setting. Such a question is not within the expertise or experience of every qualified engineer. One needs specific training or experience to be able to comment on this question. Some engineers may have this training or experience. Indeed, in the opinion of this Court, it would not even be necessary to be an engineer in order to make expert statements concerning the criteria to be set up for engineers to follow to insure a safe design in a particular industrial situation. There are people in the world who would qualify to give expert testimony on this question. However, there was no evidence that Mr. Maurer had any experience or expertise regarding the proper formulation of safety criteria to be followed in the design of molasses tanks in this particular industrial setting. The defective safety criteria in the design of the tank was a kingpin in the plaintiff's case, and there are experts in the field of holding tank design with an expertise in safety criteria available. Therefore, Mr. Maurer was not allowed to testify.

The Court also ruled that Mr. Bradley was qualified in the areas of industrial toxicology, environmental health, air pollution, but not safety unless qualified within the areas of his expertise, nor safety design. . . . The above analogy also applies to Mr. Bradley and that was the reason for his disqualification as a safety design expert.

In making these decisions as to the qualifications of the plaintiff's experts, the Court was well aware that an expert witness may not have personally and cannot be expected to have personally experienced the factual situation in question about which he is to testify in order to qualify. The plaintiff does not have to get the best possible expert available on the subject, but should have produced an expert more specifically and expressly qualified in the safety aspects of the design of storage tanks. Neither expert here had any prior experience or observational knowledge to testify as to the proper design of a molasses storage tank under the factual setting presented. Therefore, the disqualification of plaintiff's experts in this area was proper and resulted in plaintiff failing to make out a prima facie case. All other grounds for a new trial are without merit, and plaintiff's Motion for a New Trial is denied.

REVIEW QUESTIONS

1. Describe the federal court system. Describe the court system in your state.
2. Assume that you have been the unfortunate victim of someone's negligence. What steps will you or your attorney take in attempting to get compensation for the loss you have suffered?
3. Distinguish between the proof required in a criminal case and the proof required in a civil case.
4. How would you prove the existence and terms of an oral agreement if there were no third parties present to overhear the agreement?
5. Why does a court hold in disfavor:
   a. Oral testimony as to the meaning of a written document?
   b. Hearsay testimony?
   c. Expression of an opinion by a witness?
6. Why is circumstantial evidence so often used in criminal trials?
7. In the case of *O'Neill* v. *Chicago Transit Authority*, which of the pleadings would have placed plaintiff in the best position to win his case?
8. Interpreting from the case of *Globe Indemnity Co.* v. *Highland Tank and Mfg. Co.*, what might be the qualifications for one to be considered an expert in the design of an automobile brake system?

Contracts

The world of the engineer is an environment of serious communications, nearly all of which have contractual implications. A contract to build a bridge or road or building may necessitate numerous subcontracts—contracts with material suppliers, labor contracts, leasing contracts, easements, utility contracts, and many, many others. A contract to manufacture and ship parts to an appliance manufacturer on a continuing basis may similarly precipitate many contracts. The day-to-day engineering management of such contracts as these requires a very large number of activities and communications, almost all of which involve contracts. For one example, the quality of a final product is spelled out or implied in the contract for that product. The product's quality is determined by the production processes used, the manner in which they are used by the production work force, and the materials upon which the processes operate. All of the design and operating decisions involved with such production have quality overtones and for that reason, if for no other, are important contract considerations.

In the next few chapters we will briefly examine the law of contracts. Then, in the following section, we will look at engineering contracts.

5

Introduction to Contracts

Modern civilization is a world of contracts. Each one of us depends upon them. Every purchase is a contract whether it is of a pair of socks or a restaurant meal or a battleship. When you turn on your television set in the evening to watch your favorite program it is done in execution of a contract. The utility company has agreed to furnish electric power and you have agreed to pay for it. You go to work as your part of a contract with your employer. On the job you do what he wants you to do and at the end of a week or a month he pays you for it. It is all part of the same contract. If he pays you by check it is because he has a contract with a bank to safeguard his money and give it out on order. If he pays you in cash, the currency represents a contract between the bearer and a Federal Reserve Bank. When you die and are buried, the security of your last resting place may depend on the terms of the contract under which the land was obtained. You can't avoid contracts, even by dying.

Even a simple thing like leaving your watch at the jeweler's for repair involves you and the jeweler in a complicated legal situation. Everything is resolved painlessly when you pick up the watch and pay him for his work a week later. Meantime the relationship between you and the jeweler involved: (1) personal property—the watch, (2) agency (quite likely a clerk represented the owner), (3) the law of bailment (personal property was left with another for repair), (4) insurance law (had the watch been lost), and (5) a contract (his agreement to repair and your agreement to pay for the service).

All contracts are agreements and, morally at least, all agreements are contracts, but moral duties are not always enforceable at law. Suppose that Black accepted Dr. White's invitation to dinner on Tuesday, then forgot the engagement and did not appear. Black broke a social contract and in doing so committed a serious breach of social ethics. But Black's contract was not an enforceable one and, no matter how much pain and suffering Black caused Dr. White, the doctor could not collect damages.

Now, suppose Dr. White is a practicing dentist and Black is a prospective patient. Black calls and makes an appointment with White for 3:00 P.M. Thursday. In breaching this appointment, Black may be breaching a contract. The commodity in which White trades is his time and ability as a dentist. Many jurisdictions would hold that unless White could otherwise gainfully use the time set aside for Black's appointment, he could collect for that time. In deciding the case the court would examine business practices in the area, and these practices would largely determine the outcome of the case.

If the two parties mentioned above were to enter into an agreement whereby Black agreed to purchase a car from White for $6,000, such agreement would be a contract, and thus enforceable in a court of law. Each party to the contract would have an action at law available to him if the other failed to perform as agreed.

Definition

The only kind of an agreement the law recognizes as a *contract* is defined in *Black's Law Dictionary* as "a promissory agreement between two or more parties that creates, modifies, or destroys a legal obligation."

Stated even more simply, a contract could be defined as "an agreement enforceable at law."

To be enforceable at law a contract must have certain elements.

Elements of a Valid Contract

Analysis of a valid contract shows it to be made up of five elements, each of which must exist according to law. These five elements are:

1. Agreement
   a. Offer
   b. Acceptance
2. Competent parties
3. Consideration
4. Lawful purpose
5. Form

Each element will be given only a brief introduction here, but will be treated in more detail in the next six chapters.

1. The agreement consists of an offer and acceptance. The *offeror*[1] states the terms of the proposed contract. The *offeree*[2] must accept the terms as they are proposed to him to complete a binding contract.
2. For a contract to be thoroughly binding it must be made by at least two parties, none of whom will be able to avoid his duties under the terms of the contract by pleading as a defense that he was incompetent to contract.
3. Consideration in a contract consists of the money, promises, and/or rights given by each party in exchange for the money, promises, and/or rights which he receives.
4. The purpose and consideration in the contract must be lawful if the contract is to be capable of enforcement in a court of law. A contract to perform an unlawful act could not be upheld by a state which imposes a penalty for committing the same act.
5. Difficulties in proving the existence, validity, and terms of contracts have brought about the requirement that certain types of contracts be in written form. Failure to comply with this requirement renders such contracts unenforceable by the court.

Stage of Completion

As soon as the offeree expresses his acceptance of the terms offered to him, a contract comes into existence. Usually the contract at this stage is *executory*, and as long as something remains to be done by either or both of the parties under the terms of the agreement, it remains so. Even when one of the parties has performed his obligations completely and the other party has not yet completed his performance, the contract is *partially executed*, but in a legal sense it is still executory. After all parties to the contract have performed everything according to the agreement, the contract is *executed*. A contract to purchase a refrigerator is executory when the sales agreement is made between the buyer and the seller; it is partially executed (but legally executory) when the refrigerator is delivered to the buyer, and executed when he has finished paying for it.

Parties

The common, "garden variety" of contract involves two parties as *promisor* and *promisee*. However, it is more difficult to determine the liabilities of the individuals where there are several parties and the individual interests of some have been merged. When there are merged interests the relationships of the parties are treated either as *joint* or *several*, or in some cases as *joint and several*.

Individuals who merge their interests into a joint relationship to form a party to a contract may be thought of as partners in the promises made. If the individuals together agree to "bind themselves" or "convenant" to do a certain thing in the terms of an agreement, it is treated as a joint contract. The liability is much the same as it is in a partnership. That is, should they breach the contract, each is liable for complete performance of the contract until the full value has been satisfied. Black and White agree jointly to hire Gray, a contractor, to make alterations in an existing building and to pay him $4000 for the alterations. If, after completion of the alterations, payment is refused by Black and White, Gray must sue them jointly. If Black cannot pay part of the debt, White may have to pay the entire amount. If either White or Black dies, the survivor will be liable for the full amount of the debt.

Restriction of the liability of individuals merging their interests is a feature of the several contract. If, in the above contract, Black and White had agreed to "bind themselves severally," or "covenant severally" to pay $4000 for the alterations which Gray was to make (restricting themselves to, say, $2000 each), the liability of Black and White, each would be limited to the amount stated. In case of default of payment, Gray could take only separate actions against Black and White.

If merging individuals agree to "bind themselves and each of them" or to "covenant for themselves and each of them," the contract is treated as a joint and several contract. If the Black and White contract above were joint and several, and Gray found court action necessary, such action could be taken either jointly or severally, but not both ways.

In a *third-party beneficiary* contract the purpose of the contract is to benefit a third party. If the intent to benefit the third party is clear from the agreement, he has a right to a court action to enforce those benefits. If, however, the consideration under the contract benefits one of the parties to the contract and only incidentally benefits a third party, no right of court action is available to the third party. Probably the most common example of a third-party beneficiary contract is life insurance.

---

1. An offeror is the person who makes an offer to someone else.
2. An offeree is the person to whom an offer is made.

Means of Acceptance

A *unilateral* contract is a promise of a consideration made without receiving a promise of consideration from another party. A common example of the unilateral contract is the reward notice. White publishes a promise of a reward of $500 for the return of his diamond-studded wrist watch. Black, upon finding the watch, claims the reward. To obtain the reward in a legal action, Black must have been aware of the reward promise when he returned the watch.

A *bilateral* (or reciprocal) contract is a mutual exchange of promises, present consideration, or both, by two or more parties.

Formation of Contracts

Express contracts involve overt agreements by the parties, the terms being expressed between them either orally or in writing or both.

Implied contracts are based upon implications of fact. If the parties, from their acts or conduct under the circumstances of the transaction, make it a reasonable or necessary assumption that a contract exists between them, it will be held that such a contract does, in fact, exist.

Quasi contracts are contracts implied in law. They are generally based upon the theory of *unjust enrichment;* that it would, in all justice and fairness, be wrong to allow one person to be enriched by another without having to pay for it. It amounts to a legal fiction created by the courts to permit recovery in cases where, in fact, there would be no recovery otherwise. Black contracts orally to pay $50,000 for White's services for a period of eighteen months. The Statute of Frauds[3] requires such a contract to be in writing if it is to be enforceable. In ignorance of this requirement, White performs the services for Black and now sues for payment. White cannot recover on the original contract, but may recover the reasonable value of his services under a quasi contract on the theory that it would be unjust to allow Black to be enriched by White's services without having to pay for them.

Legal Status

Contracts are classified as to legal standing into valid, unenforceable, voidable, and void.

A *valid* contract is an agreement voluntarily made between competent parties, involving lawful consideration, and in whatever form may be prescribed by law for that particular kind of subject matter. It contains all the essential elements previously described.

An *unenforceable* contract is one which creates a duty of performance which may be recognized in a court of law but which, because of some defect in the contract, may not be enforced by the court. A common example of such a contract is one which is not made in accordance with the statute of frauds. An oral contract, which, because of the subject matter, should have been in writing, is an unenforceable contract.

A *voidable* contract is one in which one or both of the parties may avoid the contract if he so desires. Black, a minor, purchases a bicycle from White, an adult. Black may return the bicycle and demand his money back. White has no similar right of avoidance.

A *void* contract is, strictly speaking, not a contract. A contract to commit a crime is an example of a void contract. The courts ordinarily treat contracts for an unlawful purpose as nullities.

Formality

Contracts may be classified as *formal* and *informal.* Most contracts are informal in nature. Contracts to perform services or surrender ownership of goods to another are usually informal contracts. There are three general types of formal contracts (so called because the contract derives its validity from its form): (1) sealed contracts, (2) recognizances, and (3) negotiable instruments.

Sealed Contracts. Contracts under seal are required by law for certain agreements—for example, transactions involving real property. Under common law and in many jurisdictions if a contract is sealed, the court will not inquire as to the presence or absence of consideration. The promise of a gift, for instance, will be construed by the courts as a contract if the promise is in writing and signed and sealed by the promisor. In most jurisdictions the life of a sealed instrument is extended (frequently to twenty years). In other words, the promisee has a longer time in which to bring suit after breach of the contract by the other party.

Recognizance. A contract which is entered into before a court of record or a magistrate to perform some particular act, such as to appear in court, to keep the peace, or to pay a debt, is a *recognizance.*

Negotiable Instrument. A *negotiable instrument* is a contract for the payment of money. It derives its negotiable characteristics from its form. The requirements for a contract to be a negotiable instrument are

---

3. See Chapter 11, "Statute of Frauds."

set forth in the Uniform Commercial Code which has been adopted by the various states. Briefly, these requirements are as follows:

1. In writing and signed.
2. Unconditional promise or order.
3. To pay, in money, an ascertainable amount.
4. On demand or at a fixed or determinable future time.
5. To order or bearer.
6. If there is a drawee, he must be identified.

1. The instrument must be in writing and signed. It is obviously impossible to have an oral negotiable instrument. The writing may be in long-hand or printed; a negotiable instrument could be written on wrapping paper. The signature may be written or stamped (as is frequently the case with payroll checks), and may appear anywhere on the instrument, although it is commonly placed in the lower right-hand corner.

2. It must be an unconditional promise or order. An acknowledgment of an existing debt is not a promise to pay it unless such a promise is made or implied in the instrument. A mere request or authorization is not considered to be a promise or order to pay. The promise or order must not be conditioned upon any future contingency other than the passage of time.

3. It must call for the payment of a definite amount of money in legal tender. The amount to be paid must be fixed or be capable of being determined from the instrument itself. Payment may actually take the form of goods or services, but the instrument must give the holder the right to call for payment in money.

4. It must provide for payment on demand or at a fixed or determinable future time. If no time of payment is stated, the instrument is assumed to be payable on demand. The instrument is also considered to be payable on demand if it is past due. "Determinable" future time may be tied to some event which is certain to take place, but about the only future event certain enough for the courts is death. Very few people have been known to live forever.

5. It must be payable to order or bearer. Certain *words of negotiability* are required in a negotiable instrument. These words are *order* or *bearer*. The negotiable instrument must contain one or both of these words used in such manner as to indicate that the maker intended the instrument to be capable of being negotiated. Commonly such phrases as *pay to bearer* and *pay to the order of* _____ serve this purpose.

6. It must identify the drawee. If the negotiable instrument calls for payment by a third party (as a check or other bill of exchange), the party who is to make the payment *(drawee)* must be indicated with reasonable clarity.

Promissory Note. Negotiable instruments are of two general types—promissory notes and bills of exchange. A promissory note is a two-party negotiable instrument in the form of a promise by one person to pay money to another. The two parties to the instrument are the *maker*, who undertakes the obligation stated in the instrument, and the *payee*, the person to whom the promise is made. The classification of promissory notes includes conditional sales notes, chattel mortgage notes, real estate mortgage notes, and the coupons on coupon bonds.

Bill of Exchange. The bill of exchange is a three-party negotiable instrument. The *drawer* (corresponding to the maker of a promissory note) orders a third party (the drawee, usually a bank) to pay money to another party, the payee. Common forms of the bill of exchange include checks, bank drafts, trade acceptances, sight drafts, and time drafts.

Negotiation. A negotiable instrument made payable to "bearer" *(bearer paper)* is negotiated by delivery alone. If the instrument is made payable to "order" *(order paper)* it is negotiated by *indorsement* (the signature of the holder of the instrument) on the back of it. Three general types of indorsement exist for negotiation of negotiable instruments: indorsement in blank, special indorsement, and restrictive indorsement. An *indorsement in blank* consists of the signature of the payee on the back of the instrument. Such an act makes the instrument, in effect, bearer paper in that it may be further negotiated by nothing more than delivery (anybody can cash it). A *special indorsement* names the indorsee. "Pay to the order of Jed Black, Sam White" is a special indorsement and must be indorsed by Jed Black if he wants to negotiate it. If the indorsement had read just "Sam White," it would have been an indorsement in blank. A *restrictive indorsement* restricts future negotiation on the instrument. "Pay to the Graytown Bank for deposit only" is an example of a restrictive indorsement.

A *holder in due course*[4] of a negotiable instrument has certain rights superior to those of the original parties. He is entitled to payment on the negotiable instrument in spite of certain personal defenses available to the original parties. If, for instance, the maker was induced by fraud to draw up the note, this is no defense against a subsequent holder in due course, although the maker still has his action available against the person who defrauded him. Certain so-called real defenses may, however, be used successfully against a holder in

---

4. A party other than the original parties to the negotiable instrument, to whom the instrument has been negotiated in good faith and for value and without notice of defect in the instrument.

```
                                                          No. 1001

                                        Sylvania, Ohio    August 11, 19 —

Pay to the order of _____Jed Black_____    $    100.00

One hundred and no/100 ———————————————————— Dollars

For ____P. O. No. 1001____

Bank of Sylvania                                          Sam White
Sylvania, Ohio
```

Bill of Exchange (Check)

```
$100.00                              Gainesville, Florida    August 11, 19 —

Ninety days              after date        I       promise to pay to
the order of                         Jed Black
        One hundred and no/100 ——————————————————————Dollars
at    Graytown Bank, Graytown, Florida

Value received.

No. _____1001_____    Date    Nov. 9, 19 —         Sam White
```

Promissory Note

due course. The most prominent of these is forgery. If your signature has been forged, you should not be held liable.

The law of negotiable instruments is a broad and complicated field. For our purposes it is sufficient that we only touch upon the specialized field briefly.

KUENZI v. RADLOFF
34 N.W. 2d 798, 253 Wis. 575 (1948)

Rosenberry, Chief Justice

The plaintiff is licensed under provisions of sec. 101.31 as a professional engineer. He has 40 years' experience in designing buildings, and was licensed in 1932.

In December 1945 the defendants were considering the erection of a building in the city of Waupun to be occupied by bowling alleys and a tavern. The defen-

dant Radloff consulted the plaintiff and as a result of this consultation the plaintiff wrote the following letter:

Dec. 29, 1945

Mr. Harold Radloff
Waupun, Wisconsin

Dear Sir:

I wish to confirm our conversation of some time ago wherein I named you a fee of 3% of the estimated value of the project for services in making up plans for the construction of a proposed bowling alley to be built at Waupun, Wis. This also includes the services of securing a full approval of the Industrial Commission.

Respectfully submitted
Yours truly,
Arthur Kuenzi

Accepted
O. A. Krebsbach
H. Radloff

Upon receipt of the signed proposal from the defendants the plaintiff proceeded with the design and preparation of the plans for the proposed building. The defendants from time to time during the preparation of the plans consulted with the plaintiff and his associates and changes were made in accordance with the suggestions made by the defendants. The plans were completed early in March 1946, and were presented to the Industrial Commission and duly approved by it and then promptly delivered to the defendant Radloff.

On April 11, 1946, an application for the allocation of construction materials, to which application was attached a copy of the plans, was made on behalf of Radloff and Krebsbach to the Civilian Production Administration. A second application to the Civilian Production Administration, signed by both defendants, was submitted to the Civilian Production Administration on April 25, 1946. In each of these applications the cost of the structure, including fixtures and building service, is stated to be $80,000. The following statement was made in the application.

"A site has been obtained and an architect engaged for the construction of such building and the plan submitted to a contractor who has in turn ordered various materials for the construction thereof. All of said obligations and commitments made previous to March 26, 1946." Both applications were denied on May 1, 1946.

On April 28, 1946, the plaintiff sent to the defendant Radloff an invoice for $1350 based upon the estimated value of the building of $45,000. The plaintiff also demanded payment from the defendant Krebsbach before the commencement of this action. The plaintiff received the following letter from the defendant Radloff:

Monday morning

Dear Sir:

Sorry to keep you waiting but we are still working through Washington to get started building.

We will make payment to you just as quickly as possible. Milan Nickerson one of our partners dropped out, didn't want his money laying idle so he went into the cement block business.

We are picking out another good partner and will get in touch with you or write when we have the partners lined up.

This Nickerson was undecided for some time and that's why we didn't send you any money, until we have the other party lined up.

How is the steel coming? We will have to pay you and have it on hand when it comes and wait for the permit to start to build. You said in your last letter of

quite a while ago that the steel would be here within a couple of weeks.

Yours very truly,
H. Radloff

P.S. Keep this under your hat about a third party and if you should happen to know of someone who has 15 or 20 thousand and wants to put it in a good business of a bowling alley and tavern let us know.

The letter was undated; neither the plaintiff nor the defendant Radloff can fix the date on which it was sent. Evidently it was sent after the receipt of the invoice from the plaintiff because payment is promised.

Upon notice of the denial of their application by the Civilian Production Administration on May 1, 1946, the defendants abandoned the project, and the building for which the plans were prepared has never been erected.

Upon the facts it appears as a matter of law that the plaintiff had a contract with the defendants for the making of plans for the construction of the proposed building; that he proceeded to carry out his part of the contract by preparing the plans, procuring their approval by the Industrial Commission, and delivering them to the defendants; that they were accepted by the defendants and used by them in their efforts to procure a priority order from the Civilian Production Administration.

The defendants seek to defeat the plaintiffs' claim on a number of grounds. We shall first consider the contention of the defendants that there is a defect of parties plaintiff. While there was no allegation in the answer of either defendant to the effect that there was a defect in the parties plaintiff, an attempt was made upon the trial to establish the fact that the plaintiff was a member of a partnership and as such could not maintain an action upon the contract entered into between the plaintiff and the defendants. The contention of the defendants is that the other partners were necessary parties plaintiff. In his testimony the plaintiff made statements to the effect that he had partners and that the arrangement with his associates was a partnership. Other witnesses were called and from the testimony introduced it is clear that whatever arrangement the plaintiff had with other parties who performed some services in connection with the preparation of the plans, they were not partners. Sec. 123.03 (1) defines partnership as follows: "A partnership is an association of two or more persons to carry on as co-owners a business for profit."

It is said in *Montello Granite Co.* v. *Industrial Commission* 227 Wis. 170, 278 N.W. 391, that what parties call themselves is not conclusive on the question of the existence of a partnership. In order to constitute an element of partnership the "profits" in which a partner is to share must be real profits, not wages. . . .

It appears from the evidence that the plaintiff makes contracts for the preparation of plans for buildings. That thereafter he is aided by some members of what might be referred to as a panel. Those who assist him are paid for their services whether the plaintiff collects on his contract or not. In this case the plaintiff had already, before the commencement of this action, made some payments. It does not appear that the associates share in the losses or that their approval is necessary for the plaintiff to enter into a contract, nor are they bound to render service to the plaintiff.

Plaintiff was asked if he had an agreement with his associates. He answered: The agreement is if they want anything I am willing to pay them for it. They generally give me a bill for it.

Q. What is the bill based on?
A. Whatever they may base it on. That is up to them.
Q. Well, you pay them whatever they ask for, is that right?
A. That's right.
Q. And that is what you will do in this case, regardless of whether you collect?
A. That's right.

He further stated: "The men that worked on these plans for me or with me have an interest in recovering this money to the extent that they may bill me for it regardless of whether I collect or not."

It is evident that what the plaintiff referred to as a partnership is some kind of a loose association which does not amount to a partnership.

Robert A. Phillips was the person who rendered the most service in the preparation of the plans. He testified: "I'm an independent operator. I don't work for Mr. Kuenzi. I go and come as I please. When I am through with a job Mr. Kuenzi and I get our heads together and—or he has already arrived at the cost and if that is satisfactory to me I submit my bill to him."

The arrangement between plaintiff and his associates resembles more closely a fee-splitting operation than any other relation. Despite what the plaintiff said, the evidence does not establish a partnership. The necessary elements of a partnership relation are not present in this case. Under the undisputed facts in this case the plaintiff could properly maintain this action against the defendants.

It is also contended that nonlicensed persons can not render service to a licensed professional engineer for which he can collect compensation. Sec. 101.31 (7) provides:

(7) Exempt persons. The following persons shall be exempt from registration under the provisions of this section, to wit: . . . (B) an employee of a person holding a certificate of registration in this state who is engaged in the practice of the profession of architecture or of professional engineering . . . provided, such practice does not include responsible charge of architecture or professional engineering practice as defined in this section.

The plaintiff testifies: "In preparing these plans I did some design work but not the actual drawing. Mr. Phillips did the drawing. Mr. Phillips is not licensed as an architect, but under the law he can work on such plans and specifications under a licensed man as an associate. I would have to assume full responsibility. I put in 42 hours actual time on these plans."

It is considered that plaintiff complied with the provisions of the statutes relating to the practice of professional engineering.

It will be observed that the contract provided that the fee should be 3% of the estimated value of the project for services in making up plans for the construction of the proposed bowling alley. The defendants place a great deal of emphasis on the term "estimated value." The defendants made the claim, and the court sustained it, that this meant the value of the building after its erection. In so holding it is considered that the trial court was in error. The basis upon which plaintiffs' fee was to be computed was the estimated value of the project, not of a building which might never be erected. In its opinion the trial court said: "The court refused to allow this testimony as to cost due to the fact that the letter which comprised the basis for the case said value of the project as the basis rather than cost of construction," and excluded all testimony as to cost except that of plaintiff, and restricted the evidence to what the building would be worth upon the site after it was constructed. Just how the value of a building which has never been constructed can be determined does not appear. "Value" in the sense in which the trial court used the term, means market value, what the property could be sold for after the building was erected. Even if that were the test, evidence of the cost would be relevant and material, but it is not the test in this case.

It is considered that this case is ruled by *Burroughs* v. *Joint School District*, 155 Wis. 426, 144 N.W. 977. It was there held that if when the term "value" is applied to a particular contract, or conditions growing out of it, it leads to results clearly not contemplated by the contract read as a whole, and it is susceptible of another meaning which harmonizes with all the provisions of the contract, such other meaning should be given to it. In that case a building contract provided for payment in each month of a sum equal to 90% of the value of the work done and material furnished during the preceding month, as assessed by the architects. In that case the word "value" was construed to mean not market but contract value. It is considered that in this case the term "estimated value" of the project referred to the estimated cost of the material and services necessary to complete the building according to the plans. There is not a scintilla of evidence in this case that plaintiff was to wait for his compensation until the completion of the building and an appraisal thereof. The idea that the base upon which the fee was to be computed can be established by the sale of a mythical building owned by a mythical owner, and sold to a mythical buyer, is too elusive and indefinite a standard to apply to practical affairs. So in this case we hold that the term "estimated value of the project" means the estimated cost of completing it.

Upon this point the plaintiff testified as follows: "I made an estimate of $45,000 being the value of this building, which is the same amount as the estimated cost. My estimate was the sum of $45,000 as I recall it. I made a charge against the defendants based on $45,000 and charged 3% of that amount or $1,350."

Two witnesses were called on behalf of the defendant who testified that the value of the completed building would be fifteen to twenty thousand dollars, around twenty thousand dollars. This was on the theory that the building when completed would have to be rebuilt if used for any other purpose than a bowling alley. One witness testified: "You would have quite a job getting $20,000 for it because it would have to be torn apart and fixed over for something else." This sort of evidence comes far short of establishing the estimated value of a project.

Considerable evidence was received in regard to the income tax returns of the plaintiff. So far as we are able to ascertain this evidence was immaterial. Whether the proper income tax returns were made or not is a concern of the Department of Taxation, and has no relevancy on the question raised in this case. It was introduced in an effort to establish that the real plaintiff was a co-partnership, a matter which has already been considered.

It is considered that the plaintiff having fully performed the contract between the parties, including the procurement of the endorsement of the Industrial Commission, and defendants having accepted and acted upon the plans as delivered to them, the plaintiff is entitled to compensation on the basis of the lowest estimated cost of the project appearing in evidence, to-wit the sum of $45,000 with interest and costs.

The judgment appealed from is reversed and the cause is remanded with directions to the trial court to enter judgment for the plaintiff as indicated in the opinion.

REVIEW QUESTIONS

1. Name the essential elements of a valid contract. Identify these elements in *Kuenzi* v. *Radloff*.
2. Draw up a valid negotiable instrument with John Doe as payee and Richard Roe as maker or drawer.
3. Distinguish between a joint contract and a several contract. Give an example of each.
4. What is a quasi contract? Who creates it? For what purpose?
5. Distinguish between unenforceable contracts and voidable contracts. Give an example of each.
6. In reference to *Kuenzi* v. *Radloff*, what would be the probable effect if the court had found Kuenzi's organization to be a partnership?
7. Consider the word *value*. How many ways are there to estimate the value of a project that exists only in the planning stage? How many ways are there to estimate the value of something that has been in existence for a period of time—for example a five-year-old hydraulic broach?

6

Parties

There must be at least two parties to a contract. Two minds must have met in agreement. There may be more than two; in fact the only upper limit is the number of parties it is practicable to identify.

No man may make a contract with himself. Consider Black, who is executor of White's estate and otherwise just an ordinary citizen. If Black, as executor of White's estate, agrees with Black, as an individual, to do something, no valid contract will result.

The law protects the innocent. The law also offers its protective shield to those who, due to their immaturity or for some other reason, are held to be incompetent to contract. The law will not usually offer its protective shield unless it is asked to do so, however. A person must plead his incapacity to contract to receive the protection available.

Among those whose ability to contract is in some way limited are infants, married women, insane persons, intoxicated persons, corporations, governments, and professional people. To illustrate the rights and defenses of the parties, infants' contracts will be treated at greater length than the contracts of other incompetent parties.

INFANTS

Age of Infancy

It is probably best to consider first how old a person must become before he is no longer considered an infant or a minor. According to common law, infancy ends at 0:00 hours on the day before a person's twenty-first birthday. This rather peculiar holding appears to result from the fact that the law does not usually recognize parts of days. Reasoning from this, a person will have reached the last day of his twenty-first year, and therefore must be 21, on the day before his twenty-first birthday. The reasoning is faulty, but the practice is well established at common law.

There is no legal *adolescence*. On one day a person is an infant according to law; on the next day he is an adult. The only status that might come close to a legal adolescence is that of *emancipated minor*. Emancipation of a minor takes place when his parents or guardians surrender their rights to his care, custody, and earnings. Such an emancipated minor is usually treated somewhat more sternly by the courts than a nonemancipated minor. Still, according to law, until 20 years and 363 days have passed since a person's birth, he is protected and restricted in his dealings. His ability and knowledge are considered to be less than that of an adult. A day later (at common law) he is vested with the full powers, rights, and responsibilities of an adult.

Statutes in many of the states have altered the age that ends infancy, or have provided for removal of the incapacity under other circumstances. Several states provide that legal majority is reached on a person's eighteenth birthday. Some make it nineteen. Many statutes provide that marriage will remove the infant's incapacity. Statutes of various states provide means by which an infant may remove his incapacity by request to a court of law. This is often done when an infant undertakes a business venture.

Partnership

When an adult becomes a partner he stands to lose some or all of his personal fortune as well as his investment in the business if the partnership becomes bankrupt. However, when a minor becomes a partner in a business venture he can lose in bankruptcy only whatever values he has contributed.

Agency

Generally, an agency contract in which a minor is the principal is *void* (not voidable) at common law. There has been a recent trend, however, to consider such contracts as *voidable*, which appears to be more logical. Infancy is no bar to acting as an agent for another, however, since it is the principal who is bound rather than the agent. An adult, therefore, may enter into a binding contract with a third person through an infant agent.

Disaffirmance

In general it is true that if one party to a contract is not bound, neither is the other. However, the law recognizes certain exceptions to this generality. Infants' contracts form such an exception.

An infant may avoid his obligations under almost any contract. He needs merely to notify the other party of his disaffirmance. The infant's right to *disaffirm* is his personal right; no one else may disaffirm for him.

If a minor elects to disaffirm a contract that is still completely executory, no major problem is involved. Since no consideration has changed hands, none needs to be returned. The problems arise when consideration has been given. If a minor disaffirms a contract with an adult after having given the adult his consideration, return of the consideration to the minor is mandatory. The minor must also return whatever consideration he has received if it is possible for him to do so. It has been stated, though, that a minor's right to avoid his contract is a higher right than the adult's right to get back his consideration. If the consideration received by the minor has been demolished or depleted in value in the minor's hands he may still return it and demand the return of his consideration. Destruction of the subject matter in the minor's hands is only further evidence of his incapacity. Even if the minor cannot return any of the consideration received by him, he may still be successful in getting back what he has given. White, a minor, buys a used car from Black Auto Sales. White pays $1,500 down and agrees to make a series of monthly payments for the car. Two weeks later White loses control of the car while driving it and, upon hitting a tree, the car becomes a total loss. White could return the wreck and get his $1,500 back. If the car were not insured for theft and White lost it to a thief, White could still disaffirm and get his down payment back.

While the above is representative of the rulings in the majority of courts, a substantial minority of courts require that the minor return the consideration received by him or its equivalent in value to disaffirm. The minor still has the right to avoid the contract, but the courts will not allow him to harm the other party when he disaffirms. In one such case a minor had taken his car to a garage for repairs. When the repairs were finished he refused to pay for them and demanded his car.[1] In requiring the minor to pay for the repairs the court compared the legal protection offered to minors to a shield. The judge stated, in effect, that while a defensive shield is afforded by law, it is not intended to be used as an offensive weapon. There was nothing defensive in the acts of the minor in this case. In fact, it represents a bald swindle more than it does a contract. If the repairs had amounted to replacement of rod bearings, main bearings, and piston rings, for instance, the inherent difficulty of returning the consideration to the adult would be quite apparent.

If the infant poses as an adult to get the adult to deal with him, the court may demand that the adult be left unharmed or, at least, that the harm be minimized. It would seem unreasonable to allow an infant to harm another by his deceit and then to protect the infant.

If the subject matter of the infant's contract is something other than real property (real estate) he may disaffirm the contract at any time before he becomes an adult. In addition, the infant has a reasonable period of time after reaching adulthood to disaffirm the contract. He may disaffirm either by an express statement or by implication. If the contract is executory and the infant does nothing about it within a reasonable time, it will be implied that he has disaffirmed it.

If the subject matter is real property the infant must wait until he is an adult to disaffirm the contract. There seems to be good reason in distinguishing between real and personal property in infants' contracts. Land sold by the infant will always be there. This is not necessarily true of personal property with which the infant has parted.

Ratification

It is possible for an infant's contract to be ratified as well as disaffirmed. However, to agree to be bound by the terms of his agreement, the infant must wait until he becomes an adult. This seems reasonable in that if an infant, in the eyes of the law, is incapable of making a binding contract, he could hardly be expected to ratify one he has previously made. Contracts involving both real and personal property must wait until the infant reaches adulthood before they can be ratified. Ratification may be either express or implied. The law merely requires the infant to indicate his intent to be bound if he so elects.

Binding Contracts

Certain contracts made by an infant cannot be avoided by him. Most prominent among such contracts are agreements by which the infant obtains the necessities of life. If a minor is not provided with such things as food, clothing, or lodging by a parent or guardian he may make contracts for them himself. If the minor is already supplied with the necessaries, he cannot be made to pay for an additional supply of them. Where payment is enforced by law, it is payment for the reasonable value of the goods or services, thus putting the liability on a quasi-contractual basis.

The goods and services to be considered necessaries vary according to the infant's station in life. Food, clothing, lodging, medical and dental care, vocational education, and tools of a trade are necessaries for any-

1. Egnaczyk v. Rowland, 267 N.Y.S. 14 (1933).

one. But it is conceivable that such things as a car or a university education could be considered as necessaries for an infant from a very wealthy family.

If the infant has reached the minimum age to enter the armed forces, his enlistment agreement is not avoidable at his option. Marriage, although strictly speaking not a contract, cannot be avoided by a minor who is old enough to marry according to the state law.

Parents' Liability

Ordinarily a parent (or guardian) is not liable for an infant's contract unless the parent has been made a party to it. For this reason, many who deal with infants insist that the adult responsible for the infant's welfare also agree to be bound. Only in cases where the parent (or guardian) has failed in his duty to provide the minor with necessaries will the parent be required to pay reasonable value to third parties for needs supplied.

Minor's Torts

There appears to be a rather popular misconception as to parents' and guardians' responsibility for the *torts*[2] committed by infants in their charge. The usual position taken by the law is that an infant is responsible for his own torts. Unless he is either acting under the parent's direction or should have been restrained by the parent, the parent is free of liability. The law seems reasonable in this. An adult can choose not to contract with a minor and thereby avoid difficulty. However, it is often impossible to avoid tortious harm instigated by a minor (for instance from an object propelled toward one's back). Knowledge that the *tort-feasor*[3] was a minor rather than an adult doesn't help much after the injury occurs. In a situation in which the occurrence of tortious injury is inevitable, knowing the age of the tort-feasor is of little value to the victim. Therefore, the minor must answer for his torts or crimes himself, even though the courts will allow him to avoid his contracts.

MARRIED WOMEN

Under common law a woman lost her right to contract independently when she married. A man and woman were one after marriage and the husband had all the contract and property rights. However, nearly all states have adopted statutes that make a married woman's right to contract and own property at least the equivalent of her husband's. A diminishing number of states, though, have remnants of limitations which have not yet been removed. The wife may not be able to enter into a *binding surety contract*[4] or to make a contract with her husband once he has become her legal spouse.

INSANE PERSONS

Early court decisions involving contracts in which one party was insane declared such contracts to be void. The courts agreed that there could not be a meeting of the minds if one of the minds did not exist legally (*non compos mentis*). Court decisions today usually hold that such contracts are voidable at the option of the insane person when he recovers his sanity.

The law today recognizes that there are various forms and degrees of insanity. An insane person may have sane intervals in which he is capable of contracting. A person may be sane in one or more areas of activity and insane in others. If a contract was made during the person's rational moments, providing he had not been adjudged insane, it is binding despite previous or subsequent irrational behavior. Quite obviously, there can be some difficulty in establishing proof of sane behavior of an insane person or the limits of an area of activity in which he is rational. These are questions of fact, though, and usually are left for a jury to decide on the basis of expert testimony of psychiatrists and psychologists.

Consideration

Although it is generally true that courts will not examine the value of the consideration exchanged in a contract, they appear to make an exception where an insane person's contract is involved. If it appears that the other party to the contract took advantage of the insane person's mental condition, the courts will allow the insane person to avoid the contract. If it can be shown that the other party had no knowledge of the insanity of the party with whom he was dealing and did not take advantage of him, the courts will usually let the contract stand. This is especially true where the parties cannot be returned to their previous status (contract for services performed, for instance, where the work has been completed).

Necessaries

Insane persons are generally held responsible for contracts they make for necessaries. Recovery may usually be obtained for the reasonable value of the goods on the basis of quasi contract.

Guardian Appointed

Adjudication of insanity or other improper behavior and appointment of a guardian changes the picture

2. A tort is an offense against an individual's personal rights or property rights.

3. A tort-feasor is a person who commits a tort.

4. A contract, according to which one person agrees to pay another's debt if the other does not pay it.

somewhat. When the court appoints a guardian for an insane person, habitual drunkard, spendthrift, or aged person, the guardian is expected to act for his charge in all legal matters. Consequently, a contract entered into by anyone who has a legally appointed guardian is treated as void. An exception exists where the contract is one for necessaries the guardian should have provided but did not provide.

Torts

Insane persons are liable for their torts in much the same manner as minors. Mere knowledge of impending tortious injury at the hand of an insane person does not give the intended victim much by way of self-help; one could, however, refuse to contract with another who is known to be insane.

INTOXICATED PERSONS

If a person tries to avoid a contract by pleading intoxication, he must prove he was so inebriated that he could not be expected to understand the consequences of his actions in entering into a contract. A minority of the courts take a very dim view of a suit pleading intoxication. They hold that intoxication is a voluntary state and that the person should have had foresight enough to avoid getting drunk.

In most jurisdictions, however, intoxication of a party when he entered into a contract is sufficient ground to allow him to avoid the contract. If, however, an innocent third person would be harmed by avoidance of the contract, the contract usually will be allowed to stand. Even in jurisdictions where intoxication is frowned upon by the courts as a means of avoidance of a contract, it can be used to show susceptibility to fraud. An intoxicated person is, of course, liable for his torts.

CORPORATIONS

State laws provide means whereby an organization may become incorporated. The purpose and scope of its activities are set forth in the organization's articles of incorporation or charter. The corporation is an artificial person and possesses full power to act within the limits of its charter. If a contract of the corporation goes beyond its charter limits, it is an *ultra vires contract*.

Before the corporation is given the right to do business in a state, it has no recognized capacity to contract. Until a corporation is formed (or registered as a foreign corporation if it was formed in another state), someone must make contracts for it. The corporation may then take over these contracts after it is permitted to operate lawfully. The capacity to contract is also lost if the corporation's charter or its right to operate as a foreign corporation is suspended for some reason.

Ultra Vires Contracts

There appears to be considerable variation in court decisions in cases involving ultra vires contracts. They can, however, be classified in a general way and some general statements can be made about them.

It is probably best to consider ultra vires contracts from the standpoint of their stage of completion. If an ultra vires contract is entirely executory the courts will not enforce it. If it has been completely executed the courts will leave it alone. Where the contract performance has been completed by one of the parties but not by the other (partially executed), the courts will generally give a remedy. Some courts allow recovery on the contract, and others place the remedy on a quasi-contractual basis, holding that the contract itself is void but allowing recovery on the basis of unjust enrichment.

Since a corporation is an artificial person, it cannot personally commit a tort; but its agents can. Through the laws of agency, then, a corporation may be held liable for tortious injury to another by one of its employees. The employee must, of course, be engaged in the corporation's business at the time of the injury. As a general rule, the corporation is still liable even though the injury arose from an ultra vires act.

A corporation, as an artificial person, cannot commit crimes involving intent or violence of a personal nature, but there are many other crimes for which it may be held responsible. It is liable for criminal acts of its agents carrying out the business of the corporation, for antitrust law violation, Bankruptcy Reform Act violation, and numerous other crimes. Anticipated torts or crimes by a corporation may be prevented by an injunction. The penalty for a crime may be a fine or loss of the corporation's right to do business either in a particular state or in the United States.

The corporate device provides limited liability to stockholders and the corporate officers. A stockholder generally risks losing only the amount he has invested. The same is true of corporate officers (president, vice-presidents, secretary, treasurer, and, perhaps, some managers) if the corporation has been fair and honest in its dealings with others. The "corporate veil" protects them. But there is a limit to this protection and a reason to pierce the corporate veil when the people who run the corporation have deceived, defrauded, and injured others. When this occurs these corporate officers (who are charged with the knowledge of the corporation's affairs) may be held personally liable. The title of engineering vice-president may sound sweet, but with that title comes the joint and several responsibility for the acts of the corporation.[5]

GOVERNMENTS

People who do business with federal, state, or municipal governments have a practical need to know the contracting restrictions imposed. For example, where a city charter indicates the manner in which contracts are to be made, the city will not be bound to contracts made in some other fashion. If the Greenville city charter requires that certain contracts must be accepted by a public works board, acceptance by Mayor Brown will not bind the city. Someone performing a contract on the basis of the mayor's acceptance might find himself an unwilling donor to the municipality.

PROFESSIONAL PERSONS

The case of *Kuenzi* v. *Radloff* at the end of Chapter 5 implied that there might be restrictions on an engineer's right to practice. Nearly all recognized professions have such restrictions placed upon them by state statutes. The statutes customarily require professional persons to be registered as such before they are allowed to contract for their professional services. One who performs professional services without being registered may not resort to the courts to collect fees for such services, and he may even be penalized for making such a contract.

White, an engineer working for Black Manufacturing Company, designs a product that is built by Black and later involved in an injury to Brown. Brown brings a negligence action alleging that faulty design of the product caused his injury. If the design is proved to be faulty, against whom does Brown have a right to recover? The general answer is that Black Manufacturing Co. would be likely to bear the loss. The reason for this is the idea known as *respondeat superior*, that the employer is responsible for the acts of his employees during their employment. However, if White made the design while working as a consultant for Black, White would be liable for the design faults. In a similar situation, if White were an employee of Green Consultants in making the design for Black, Green is then liable, again under *respondeat superior*.

SPRECHER v. SPRECHER

110 A. 2d 509 (1955)

Henderson, Judge

This appeal is from a decree of the Circuit Court for Washington County setting aside a deed from the appellee to Martin L. Ingram, Trustee, dated July 28, 1950, and a deed of the same date from Ingram, Trustee, to Myron A. Sprecher[6] and Teresa I. Sprecher, as *joint tenants*,[7] with right of survivorship. The ground of the Chancellor's action was that the deeds were executed while the appellee was still an infant, and were disaffirmed by her within four months after she became of age. The appellant contends that the Chancellor erred in refusing to find that the appellee ratified and confirmed the deeds, or at least failed to seasonably disaffirm them.

The property conveyed, a six-room bungalow and a lot known as 345 S. Cleveland Avenue, in Hagerstown, was purchased as a home by the appellant and her then husband, Frank B. Sprecher, on May 16, 1939. Title was taken in their names as tenants by the entireties.[8] The price was $3,750, and they executed a mortgage to the First Federal Savings and Loan Association of Hagerstown in the amount of $2,700. The appellee, their daughter, had been born on July 14, 1932, and lived with her parents in the home until they separated on July 12, 1948. At that time the mortgage had been fully paid, out of the husband's wages, or perhaps out of their joint earnings since they were both employed, but on July 29, 1948, a new mortgage was obtained in the amount of $1,725. The proceeds were paid to Mrs. Sprecher, who testified that she used the money in part to repay a loan of $1,500 made to her by her mother, who resided in the home with them. On September 10, 1948, the parents and the daughter, who was then sixteen years of age, met with their attorneys, and it was

5. See the case of Mobridge Community Industries v. Toure at the end of this chapter.

6. The wife and mother in this case.

7. Joint tenancy—an estate in fee-simple, fee-tail, for life, for years, or at will, arising by purchase or grant to two or more persons (*Black's Law Dictionary*). In this case, apparently, an estate in fee-simple in which the Sprechers joined as owners.

8. Tenancy by the entirety—It is essentially a "joint tenancy," modified by the common-law theory that husband and wife are one person, and survivorship is the predominant and distinguishing feature of each. (*Black's Law Dictionary*)

agreed that the property be deeded unconditionally to the daughter, subject to the mortgage. On the same day the parents executed a deed of the property to trustees, who were in fact their respective attorneys, which recited that the conveyance was "upon trust to convey the same by deed to Teresa I. Sprecher. On September 13, 1948, Frank B. Sprecher filed a bill for divorce against Mrs. Sprecher, and obtained a decree of absolute divorce on October 8, 1948. On November 13, 1948, the trustees executed a deed to the daughter.

The Chancellor found as a fact that at the time of the meeting to discuss a property settlement the father was unwilling that the mother should retain an interest in the property, but agreed that both should convey to the daughter. While the subsequent decree of divorce did not provide for custody, the daughter continued to live with her mother in the property, and the father contributed to the daughter's support until she was eighteen years of age and obtained employment. The Chancellor rejected the appellant's contention that she did not understand that she was parting with her interest in the property, in view of the plain language of the deed and the circumstances of its execution. The validity of these conveyances is not questioned on this appeal, and it is conceded that the infant was competent to take title to the property. . . .

It appears, however, that on June 4, 1949, the appellant took the appellee to the office of the appellant's attorney and had her sign an agreement whereby Myron A. Sprecher agreed to support Teresa I. Sprecher during the period of her infancy and to maintain a home for her and cause her to attend school and high school. Teresa agreed, "as soon as practical after she shall attain the age of eighteen years," to reconvey the home property to Myron and herself as joint tenants. The appellee was sixteen years old at the time. On July 28, 1950, shortly after her eighteenth birthday, there was another visit to the attorney's office, and the execution of a deed to the attorney, as trustee, and a reconveyance to her mother and herself as joint tenants.

The appellee had graduated from high school in June 1950, secured permanent employment in August 1950, and thereafter paid her mother $10 a week board. She testified that she also paid three or four hundred dollars on the mortgage out of her earnings, but this was denied by the mother. On January 25, 1951, the appellee married Francis A. Pheil and shortly thereafter moved to her husband's apartment. Mrs. Sprecher continued to live in the property in question, and is still there. In 1952 she obtained an improvement loan on the property in the amount of $747 and spent it on improvements. The daughter was not asked to join in the application for this loan, or to execute any papers in connection therewith. On September 23, 1953, Mrs. Sprecher married Leroy S. Hite, who moved into the property with his child. The appellee became twenty-one years of age on July 14, 1953. In August 1953, the appellant asked the appellee to join her in placing another mortgage on the property. The appellee declined to do so and a quarrel ensued. In October she consulted an attorney and on November 10, 1953, she wrote a letter to her mother formally disaffirming the deed she had executed on July 28, 1950. Shortly thereafter she filed the present bill.

At common law the period of infancy extended to the age of twenty-one years in the case of both sexes. . . . By statute in Maryland certain disabilities were removed in the case of females at the age of eighteen. One of the earliest of these statutes was Chapter 101, Acts of 1798, now codified as Code 1951, Art. 93, sec. 206, requiring a guardian to distribute the personal property of a female ward when she became sixteen (later changed to eighteen). . . . But in *Davis* v. *Jacquin & Pomerait*, 5 Har. & J. 100, it was held that although she could receive the property she could not dispose of any of it until she attained the age of twenty-one years. . . . Likewise, in *Greenwood* v. *Greenwood*, 28 Md. 369, 385, it was held that the right of a father to services of a female minor continued until she was twenty-one, despite a statutory limitation to eighteen in the case of apprenticing a female child. Statutes have been passed dealing with the right of females between the ages of eighteen and twenty-one to release dower . . . to make a will . . . to release an executor, administrator, or guardian . . . to release a trustee . . . to execute a release for any money paid, property delivered, or obligation satisfied . . . to make a deed of trust of her property, real, personal, or mixed, provided the same is approved and sanctioned by a court of equity. . . . We do not find any statute altering the rule stated in *Davis* v. *Jacquin*, supra. A conveyance made by an infant under twenty-one years of age is not void, but is voidable, if disaffirmed, within a reasonable time after he or she attains the age of twenty-one years. . . . We think four months is a reasonable time under the circumstances.

The appellant contends that the appellee ratified the deed prior to her disaffirmance. The appellant testified that in August 1953, the appellee and her husband, Mr. Pheil, both said they didn't want to live in the property, that the appellee said: "I don't see why you don't let me sign the property over to you, my share of it, then you won't have to have anyone else to sign a deed, or a mortgage, either one." The appellant also testified that the Pheils wanted $5,000 for their interest; she offered them $3,000, but they would not take it. The appellant's husband, Mr. Hite, her sister, and her brother-in-law testified that Teresa, in the presence of her husband, made statements in August 1953 to the effect that the property belonged to her mother and she did not want it. The appellee and her husband denied that such statements were made. We cannot hold that the Chancellor was clearly wrong in finding these statements, if made, did not amount to ratification under the circumstances. The offer to convey her share for a consideration did not ripen into an agreement. At most, it was no more than a tacit recognition of the fact that she had previously conveyed a half interest to her mother. As pointed out by the Chancellor, the appellee had not then consulted counsel and was unaware of her rights. Indeed, it seems to have been assumed by everyone that the appellee was absolutely bound by her conveyance when she was eighteen years of age. Some of the authorities hold that ratification may be effective although made in ignorance of one's legal rights. . . . But the rule in Maryland seems to be to the contrary. . . . In any event, mere acquiescence or inaction, if not continued, is not enough. All of the authorities seem to recognize that there must be some positive act or declaration of an unequivocal nature in order to establish ratification. . . . We think the general statements testified to in the instant case fall short of this.

The appellant also contends that the appellee is barred or estopped from disaffirming her conveyance by the acceptance of benefits during her infancy which she is unable to restore. If we assume, without deciding, that the right of disaffirmance and recovery of the consideration paid may be barred under some circumstances . . . we think the principle cannot properly be invoked in the instant case. The appellee was under no legal or moral duty to reconvey a one-half interest to her mother. The prior conveyance to her had been made as a result of a property settlement between her father and mother, by which the mother was bound. The conveyance was upon a good consideration and in the nature of an advancement that would negate the implication of a resulting trust. . . . Nor did the mother undertake to perform any services for the appellee that she was not legally obligated to render. As the natural guardians of the infant child, she and the father were jointly and severally charged with its support, care, nurture, welfare, and education. . . . The appellee graduated from high school before she was eighteen, and thereafter until the time of her marriage in 1951, when she left the home, was employed and paid board to her mother. Until she was eighteen her father contributed to her support. These facts distinguish the case of *Wilhelm* v. *Hardman*, 13 Md. 140, where necessaries, in the form of support and education, were supplied by a third party.

The decree appealed from set aside the deeds and declared the property to be the sole and absolute property of Teresa I. Sprecher Pheil, subject to a balance of $408.92 due on the mortgage of $1,725 placed on the property July 29, 1948. The Chancellor held that the appellant was not entitled to reimbursement for mortgage payments made by her during the period from that date to March 1953, when she discontinued making payments. The daughter did not become twenty-one until July 14, 1953. We see no occasion to disagree with the Chancellor's finding. If we assume, without deciding, that reimbursement might be allowed under some circumstances, the appellant here failed to make out a case for equitable relief. . . . The entire proceeds of the mortgage were paid to her and not to the infant, and most of the payments made by the mother were made during the period when the property stood in the name of the daughter alone. The appellee claimed to have made payments of more than $300 in 1951. The daughter is now required to assume payment of the balance due. Moreover, the mother has occupied the premises rent-free during the whole period.

The Chancellor impressed an equitable lien on the property in the amount of $897.28, representing sums expended by the appellant in improvements to the property, and to pay the balance due on her personal loan for that purpose, and required the appellee to pay the costs below. The appellee has not appealed from that part of the decree, so its propriety is not before us. Under all the circumstances, we think the decree appealed from should be affirmed.

Decree affirmed, with costs.

MOBRIDGE COMMUNITY INDUSTRIES v. TOURE
273 N.W.2d 128 (1978)

Dunn, Justice.

This case involves a breach of contract action brought by Mobridge Community Industries, Inc. (MCI), against Toure, Ltd. (Toure), an Illinois corporation, and its board of directors. The trial court ruled that MCI was entitled to recover the sum of $250,000 plus interest, advanced insurance premium, and cost from Toure and directors Cook, Bisbee, Spruck, and Zwald, jointly and severally. Directors Cook and Bisbee appeal. We affirm the judgment.

The breach of contract centers around an agreement dated November 25, 1975, between MCI and Toure. The agreement provided for the sale to Toure of personal property and equipment located in a plastics plant in Mobridge, South Dakota, together with a lease and option to buy the plant building. The agreement required the payment of $250,000 in five equal annual installments, insurance on the property, and rental payments on the building. Toure further agreed that if any personal property or equipment were sold or removed from the plant building it would be replaced with personal property or equipment of equal value to retain the overall value of the plant.

At the time the agreement was executed, MCI was fully incorporated in the State of South Dakota and Toure was duly incorporated in the State of Illinois. Toure, however, had failed to register and qualify to do business as a foreign corporation in South Dakota prior to or subsequent to the execution of the agreement.

Toure failed to make the first annual installment of $50,000 for personal property and equipment in the plant. The entire property was not insured as required by the agreement. Toure also failed to make several rental payments to MCI. Over a period of time, various items of personal property and equipment were removed from the plant building and sold without replacement of items of equal value as agreed.

The fact that the agreement was breached is apparent from the record and is not in serious dispute. The real question is the attachment of liability for the breach. The trial court found Toure and its directors Cook, Bisbee, Spruck, and Zwald to be jointly and severally liable for the breach[9] on three basic theories as follows: (1) statutory liability under SDCL 47-2-59; (2) liability for negligent and wrongful acts resulting in piercing the corporate veil; and (3) the trust fund doctrine.

On our review of the appeal, the successful party is entitled to the benefit of his version of the evidence and of all inferences fairly deducible therefrom which are favorable to the judgment of the trial court. . . . The findings of the trial court upon conflicting evidence are presumed to be correct, and we will not set such findings aside unless they are clearly erroneous. . . . In applying the clearly erroneous standard of review, the question is not whether we would have made the same findings that the trial court did but whether, on the entire evidence, we are left with a definite and firm conviction that a mistake has been committed. . . .

With the proper standard of review in mind, we address the trial court finding of liability under SDCL 47-2-59 which reads as follows:

> All persons who assume to act as a corporation without authority so to do shall be jointly and severally liable for all debts and liabilities incurred or arising as a result thereof.

This statutory provision has been thoroughly analyzed in a well-reasoned opinion written by Federal District Judge Bogue in which he held that SDCL 47-2-59 does not require that the board of directors of a foreign corporation be held personally liable for the obligations of the corporation undertaken while doing business in South Dakota without a certificate of authority to do so. . . . The terms "corporation" and "foreign corporation" are defined separately in SDCL-47-2-1 and context of Title 47 does not require the first term to be read as including the second term.[10] SDCL 47-2-59 refers only to persons who purport to act as a corporation without incorporating and has the effect of negating the possibility of a de facto corporation. . . .

The trial court attempts to distinguish the *Cargill* case on the fact that American Pork Producers, Inc., was a bona fide Iowa corporation and remained a recognized foreign corporation, even though its certificate of authority to do business in South Dakota had been revoked for a period of time, whereas Toure never did exist or function as a bona fide foreign corporation and never sought a certificate of authority to do business in South Dakota. The record contains a letter from the Illinois secretary of state to MCI's counsel stating that Toure was duly incorporated in that state on May 29, 1974, and had designated its registered agent along with his address pursuant to statutory dictates. Since SDCL 47-2-59 applied only to persons acting as a corporation without incorporating and Toure was duly incorporated in Illinois during all times pertinent to the misrepresentations made in this case, the trial court finding that appellants were personally liable under SDCL 47-2-59 is clearly erroneous.

The second theory of liability relied upon by the trial court is that of piercing the veil of the corporate entity. The general rule is that the corporation is looked upon as a separate legal entity until there is sufficient reason to the contrary. Such reason exists when retention of the corporate fiction would "produce injustices and inequitable consequences." . . . In order to promote the ends of justice in appropriate cases, the corporate veil will be pierced and the corporation and its stockholders will be treated identically. . . . In deciding

9. The trial court entered judgment against Toure, Spruck, and Zwald by default and dismissed the case as to defendant Krohn pursuant to stipulation. The trial court found that the record did not support recovery against defendant Raby by virtue of his association with Toure. Raby, however, did leave his position as manager of the Mobridge plant and removed some equipment because Toure had failed to pay his wages. The trial court found that MCI would be entitled to judgment against Raby upon a proper showing of the value of the equipment taken.

10. This is true in part because SDCL 47-2-59 is in the chapter dealing with the formation of domestic corporations, and foreign corporations are treated separately in chapter 47–8.

whether the corporate veil will be pierced, we recognize that "each case is sui generis and must be decided in accordance with its own underlying facts."

Disregarding the corporate entity or piercing the corporate veil may result from the occurrence of numerous factors. The primary factor considered by the trial court was the misrepresentation of Toure's financial condition by the directors during negotiations prior to execution of the agreement. Five basic requirements for the recovery from individual directors on the theory of fraudulent representation of financial condition are listed as follows: (1) a false representation of a material fact made by the directors; (2) the directors making the representation knew the fact was not true or made the statement recklessly with no reasonable grounds for believing it to be true; (3) the misrepresentation was made with the intent to induce MCI to act upon it; (4) MCI took action or refrained from acting in reliance upon the misrepresentation; and (5) MCI incurred damage from such reliance. . . .

The trial court found that various representations were made by the directors as to the financial ability of Toure to improve and operate the Mobridge plant and the investment money that was forthcoming. The Toure financial statement exhibited by the directors to MCI during the negotiations showed a net worth of $90,000, and a second statement showed a net worth of $65,000. This discrepancy was explained as the good will factor of approximately $25,000. At the time the statements were exhibited to MCI, Toure had approximately $62.08 in its corporate account. Thus, the first requirement is satisfied. Regarding the second requirement of knowledge on the part of the directors, the trial court found that the directors were experienced in business affairs, were accompanied by a banker, and, considering outstanding obligations, certainly knew that Toure was "broke." We find that this requirement is further satisfied due to the fact that directors of a corporation are "presumed to have knowledge of the financial affairs of their corporation when making statements concerning its financial condition." . . . The third requirement is satisfied by the very nature of the facts and circumstances surrounding the negotiations between Toure and MCI regarding the Mobridge plant. The financial statements were padded or inflated to induce MCI to close the transaction. The final two requirements are met in that MCI acted in reliance on the inaccurate financial information given by the directors in entering into the agreement for sale and lease and incurred damages as a result of its reliance, as Toure was not in any financial condition to fulfill its side of the agreement. Therefore, the trial court finding that the theory of fraudulent represen-

tation of financial condition rendered the directors liable jointly and severally is supported by the record and is not clearly erroneous.

A further factor justifying a disregard of the corporate entity in this case is inadequate capitalization. An obvious inadequacy of capital, measured by the nature and magnitude of the corporation's undertaking, is an important factor in denying directors and controlling shareholders the corporate defense of limited liability. . . . The rationale is more completely explained in *Briggs Transp. Co.* v. *Starr Sales Co.*, supra, as follows:

> If a corporation is organized and carries on business without substantial capital in such a way that the corporation is likely to have no sufficient assets available to meet its debts, it is inequitable that shareholders should set up such a flimsy organization to escape personal liability. The attempt to do corporate business without providing any sufficient basis of financial responsibility to creditors is an abuse of the separate entity and will be ineffectual to exempt the shareholders from corporate debts. It is coming to be recognized as the policy of the law that shareholders should in good faith put at the risk of the business unencumbered capital reasonably adequate for its prospective liabilities. If capital is illusory or trifling compared with the business to be done and the risks of loss, this is a ground for denying the separate entity privilege. . . .

The record supports the conclusion that Toure was inadequately capitalized in view of the magnitude of its undertaking embodied in the agreement, and therefore the corporate entity must be disregarded.

The directors of Toure made several false representations to MCI in addition to that of financial ability to carry out the agreement. Cook's banker accompanied him during the negotiation process, and Cook's role as treasurer of Toure was emphasized to the point that he would "ride herd" over and be "watchdog" of the funds. There were also misrepresentations regarding marketing networks that were waiting for Toure's products. The fact that appellants were involved in the venture provided considerable credibility to the representations and negotiations. Further misrepresentations came in the form of a Toure management resumé which included several reputable individuals in the business community who were to join Toure management within a month's time. There were other misrepresentations as to start-up time, worldwide patents owned or pending, availability of molds, plant improvements, and an influx of investment money.

Appellants argue that representations as to future events are not actionable and that the false representations must be of past or existing facts. Although this is the general rule, we have stated that an exception comes into existence when the misrepresentation of a future event is in regard to a matter which is peculiarly within the speaker's knowledge. . . . For example, the directors of Toure collectively exhibited a particular expertise in the products involved and represented that some of the products were so new and superior to others on the market that the Mobridge plant was ideal so that production would remain a secret in the industry and the product ideas would not be stolen prior to patenting and marketing. These representations as to the innovative nature of the products were also tied into the anticipation of the market, addition of management personnel, and influx of investment money. We conclude that the exception applies under these circumstances and the representations as to future events are actionable along with the representations of past or existing facts.

Appellants further argue that they acted in good faith and were not aware of what was going on at all times pertinent to this case. This is without merit, because corporate officers and directors are held to a high degree of diligence and due care in the exercise of their fiduciary duty to shareholders. By accepting such duty, each director is charged with monitoring the heartbeat of the business and knowing where the corporation stands in regard to finances, obligations, goals, policies, etc. Where such a duty exists, ignorance due to neglect of that duty "creates the same liability as actual knowledge and a failure to act thereon." . . . Since appellants failed to exercise the duty imposed on corporate directors, they can hardly claim ignorance and lack of awareness "by emulating the three fabled monkeys, hearing, seeing, and speaking no evil." . . .

We conclude that the conduct of the directors constitutes the kind of a dealing which would make it inequitable for the trial court to recognize the corporate entity of Toure and thus permit the individual directors to escape personal liability. While we have held that a corporation existed during the material time when the misrepresentations were made in regard to the assets of this corporation, we are aware of the fact that the Toure board on February 17, 1976, voted to dissolve the corporation by March 15, 1976, and that the corporation was officially dissolved by the State of Illinois on December 1, 1976. It was during this dissolution process that most of the property was removed from the Mobridge plant. This may not meet the requirements of SDCL 47-2-59 for purposes of holding the members of the board jointly and severally liable, but it certainly adds weight to our decision that this is a

proper case to pierce the corporate veil because the legal corporation was of short duration (two and one-half years), was never used for any purpose except the personal immunity of the members of the board in their questionable activities, and was in the process of being dissolved when the assets were actually looted from the Mobridge plant. We are not compelled to say that the trial court finding of sufficient facts to warrant piercing the corporate veil of limited liability is clearly erroneous, and we will not disturb such finding on appeal.

The third theory of liability relied upon by the trial court is the trust fund doctrine that once Toure became insolvent the directors were charged with the fiduciary responsibility of holding the corporate assets in trust for the benefit of creditors. On the basis of our conclusion that the theory of piercing the corporate veil as discussed above warrants a finding of personal liability of the directors of Toure, it is unnecessary to discuss the third theory that the trial court used to charge the directors with personal liability on the breach of contract.

The appellants also allege that MCI has failed to prove damages in the amount of $250,000 by credible evidence. SDCL 21-2-2 provides:

The determinant caused by the breach of an obligation to pay money only is deemed to be the amount due by the terms of the obligation with interest thereon.

The contract breached in this case was an obligation to pay money only ($250,000 in equal installments of $50,000, none of which was ever paid), and the trial court finding that the amount due by the terms of the obligation was the proper measure of damages cannot be held to be clearly erroneous.

The finding of personal liability and the award of damages is supported by the record, and the judgment of the trial court is affirmed.

WOLLMAN, C. J., and ZASTROW and MORGAN, J. J., concur.

PORTER, J., deeming himself disqualified, took no part in this decision.

The case is therefore—*Affirmed*.

REVIEW QUESTIONS

1. Black, a minor, sells a piece of real estate that he inherited. He spends the money he received rather foolishly and, by the time he reaches adulthood, he is deeply in debt. His creditors force him into bankruptcy. The creditors find that the land Black sold as a minor is quite valuable; in fact, the value is sufficient to pay Black's debts and give him a

substantial remainder. Black refuses to disaffirm the sale. May the creditors disaffirm for him? Why or why not?

2. What is an *ultra vires contract?* Give an example of such a contract.

3. How could a married woman's capacity to contract be determined?

4. Gray, a salesman, contracted with Green to sell Green a piece of equipment at a price about ten percent below the usual market price for such equipment. The contract occurred in a local restaurant during an extended lunch hour. Gray had two or three martinis before eating lunch. He now claims he was drunk at the time the contract was made and, on this basis, seeks to avoid the contract. Green has established that all of Gray's other acts (including paying both restaurant tabs) gave no indication that Gray was under alcoholic influence. Is it likely that Gray will be held to his contract? Why or why not?

5. Are contracts for professional services voidable by the recipient of the services if the professional is not licensed?

6. In the case of *Sprecher* v. *Sprecher*, what acts by the daughter would have amounted to ratification under the circumstances?

7. In the case of *Mobridge Community Industries* v. *Toure*, suppose there is another White who could show that his membership on the board of directors of Toure was nominal only and that he was unaware of Toure's fraudulent activities. Would White still be liable? Suppose further that White is the only person on the board with sufficient assets to pay the court's judgment (all the other directors are "broke"). How much would White have to pay?

Agreement

A contract is an agreement, although not all agreements are contracts. According to *Black's Law Dictionary,* an *agreement* is "the coming together in accord of two minds on a given proposition." An agreement consists of an offer and an acceptance of that offer.

Offer

An offer contemplates a future action or restraint of action. It is a proposal to make a contract. In general, an offer states two things: what is desired by the offeror, and what the offeror is willing to do in return.

The offer does not have to be a formal statement to be binding upon the offeror. When the intent to offer is conveyed from the offeror to the offeree, an offer occurs. Under certain circumstances the law will consider a series of acts by the parties to be an offer and acceptance of the offer resulting in a binding contract. A man entering a hardware store where he is well known, grasping a shovel marked $14.95, motioning to the owner who is busy with another customer, and then leaving the store with the shovel, has made an offer to purchase. Though no word was spoken, an offer to buy the shovel at the suggested price of $14.95 was made. By allowing the man to leave with the shovel, the hardware store owner accepted the offer, and a contract resulted.

Intent

The usual test of both offer and acceptance is the *reasonable man* standard. Would a reasonable man consider the statements and acts of the party to constitute a binding element of the agreement necessary in a contract? The circumstances surrounding the passage of ideas between the parties are examined to determine the existence of serious intent to contract. In the formation of a contract, the meeting of the minds is determined by the expressed intentions of the parties, not by their secret intentions. In one contract case[1] a blacksmith shop owner, enraged at the loss of a harness, stated in his irate ravings about the supposed thief that he would pay anyone $100 for information leading to the capture of the thief, and an additional $100 for

a lawyer to prosecute him. The court held that the language used, under the circumstances, would not show an intention to contract to pay a reward. In another case,[2] Justice Holmes stated, "If, without the plaintiff's knowledge, Hodgdon did understand the transaction to be different from that which his words plainly expressed, it is immaterial, as his obligations must be measured by his overt acts."

It is often quite difficult to determine by the language used by the parties whether or not a valid offer and acceptance has occurred. In the haggling, "horse-trading," or bargaining which so often occurs in attempting to reach agreement words are used that, removed from context, sound very much as though the parties had formed a contract. One person may say to another, "I would like to sell my car for $1500," or "Would you give me $1500 for my car?" These are not offers. The courts, in recognition of business practices, view such statements as solicitations to offer and not as binding offers.

Advertisements

When a serious offer is made, the person making it must be ready for acceptance of his offer. Acceptance would complete the contract, and if the offeror could not perform his contractual obligation the offeree would have a legal action for damages available against him. For this reason advertising, prices marked on merchandise in stores, and similar publicity are considered by the courts to be mere invitations or inducements to offer to purchase at a suggested price. Expression by a customer of willingness to buy the merchandise at the price stated does not form a contract. The customer, not the store, has made the offer. The store has the right to accept or reject the offer. It is possible that the store, having sold the last of its merchandise in that line, would find performance impossible. If an offer of the price by a customer were to be construed as acceptance and the store could not perform, it would be liable for breach of contract. To hold that the store has made a

1. Higgins v. Lessig, 49 Ill. App. 459 (1893).
2. Mansfield v. Hodgdon, 147 Mass. 304, 17 N.E. 544 (1888).

contract in all cases in which a customer tenders the price of merchandise of his choice would therefore be unreasonable.

It is, of course, possible to so word an advertisement that it will constitute an offer. Acceptance by anyone will then form a binding contract. A common example of an advertisement that constitutes an offer is an ad offering a reward. To accept, anyone with knowledge of the advertisement may perform the act required in the ad, thus completing the requirements for a valid unilateral contract.

An advertisement for bids on construction work generally does not constitute an offer. Unless the advertisement specifically states that the lowest bid will be accepted, the advertiser has the right to reject any or all bids submitted.

Continuing Offer

A proposal made to be accepted within a given time is referred to as a *continuing offer.* When such an offer is based upon consideration it is an *option,* a contract in itself. In either case the offeror agrees to bind himself to perform or not to perform certain acts upon acceptance by the offeree, providing only that the offer be accepted within the specified time limit.

Termination of Offer

An offer may end in various ways: by acceptance, by revocation or withdrawal, by rejection, by death of a party, or through passage of time. The expiration of an option supported by consideration, however, ends only upon expiration of the time period for which it is open. It cannot be revoked, and rejection of the offer or death of one of the parties usually does not end its life.

The offeror has the right to revoke his offer at any time before acceptance. The withdrawal must be communicated to the offeree before his acceptance. If the offeree has knowledge of the sale to another of goods offered to him on a continuing offer, he has effective notice of withdrawal of the offer.

Rejection by the offeree ends the offer. The rejection of the offer often takes the form of a *qualified acceptance*[3] of the offer or a request for modification of the offer. Either act usually amounts to rejection. Mere inquiry as to whether or not the offeror will change his terms, though, does not constitute rejection of the offer.

Generally, the death of either party before acceptance of an offer terminates the offer. It is necessary that there be a meeting of the minds for a contract to be formed. If one of the minds is no longer among the living, no contract can occur.

If a time limit is specified in a continuing offer, the offer dies with the expiration of the period of time in which the offer was to remain open. If no time was specified in the offer, the offer will be open for acceptance for a reasonable time, the reasonableness of the time depending upon the subject matter of the offer.

Acceptance

Generally, for a contract between two parties to exist there must have been an acceptance of an offer. However, an offer may be accepted and a contract thus formed only during the life of the offer. With the above-mentioned exception of an option contract, once an offer has been rejected, revoked, or its time has run out, it cannot be accepted. Similarly, once an offer has been accepted, it is impossible for the offeror to withdraw the offer. The rules sound simple, but in actual practice it is often difficult to determine whether or not an acceptance has taken place.

An offer may be accepted only by the person to whom it was made. A person other than the offeree, who obtains the offer, cannot make a valid contract by accepting. The best that he can do is to make a similar offer to the original offeror for his acceptance.

An offer must be communicated to the offeree by the offeror or his agent to constitute an acceptable offer. Black tells Gray, a friend of both Black and White, of his intent to offer White his TV set for $500. Gray reveals this to White. White cannot at this point create a valid contract with Black by stating his acceptance. He must either wait for Black to communicate the offer to him or offer Black $500 for the TV set. At this point there is no offer to be accepted. Black could have used Gray as his agent, requesting him to give the offer to White. This, then would have constituted a valid offer.

Acceptance of an offer is held to consist of a state of mind evidenced by certain acts and/or statements. Mere determination to accept is not sufficient; it must be accompanied by some overt act which reveals that the offeree accepts the offer. Without such an overt act it is impossible for the offeror or the court to determine that the offer has been accepted, despite the offeree's secret intent to accept, unless previous dealings have established the offeree's inactivity as acceptance.

Communication of offer and acceptance creates a contract regardless of how it is done. When the offer and acceptance are oral, the contract is formed as soon as the offeree speaks his words of acceptance. Only one

---

3. Such as: "I accept your offer providing you will—in addition." Such a statement may not constitute acceptance, but rather a new offer open now to be accepted. The Uniform Commercial Code is more liberal than the general law of contracts in interpreting acceptance in situations such as this.

sticky problem arises in regard to acceptance communication. Suppose the parties are not in voice contact with each other. Suppose, for example, they are communicating by mail. Then let us suppose the acceptance is made in timely good order but gets lost in transit. Is there a contract or not? This is rather important information for the offeror because he may wish to make the same offer to someone else if the original offer is rejected. After some years of confusion on this point the law is now pretty well settled—there *is* a contract. It sprang into being when the letter of acceptance was posted. About the only way the offeror can protect himself from possible breach of contract action in such a situation is to include a requirement that acceptance be in his office by some fixed time to be effective.

Time of Revocation

An offer may be withdrawn by the offeror up until the time it is accepted. Withdrawal is never effective until it has been communicated to the offeree. When the negotiations are carried on by mail or telegram, a question may arise as to whether or not a contract exists. To point up this difficulty, consider the following example. Black and White have been negotiating by mail as to the sale of White's land. White finally makes an offer that Black finds acceptable, and Black sends a letter at 12:00 noon to White accepting the offer. Previous to this, White has sent a letter to Black revoking the offer, but the withdrawal is not received by Black until some time later than noon on the day he mailed his acceptance. The courts would hold that there is a contract between the parties, and even loss of the letter of acceptance would not change the holding, providing only that Black could prove he had sent such a letter and that the letter constituted acceptance of the contract.

Silence as Acceptance

Unless there is some record of practice or agreement between the parties to the contrary, silence cannot be construed as acceptance. Generally, wording an offer to the effect that "if I do not hear from you, I will consider my offer accepted by you" has no legal effect upon the offeree. Mere silence will not bind him.

Conditions Precedent and Subsequent

If the parties to a contract agree that upon the occurrence of some future event an obligation will come into existence, the event is known as a *condition precedent* to the contract. The parties are not bound by the terms of the contract until the occurrence of the event or condition. A contract to build a garage on a certain piece of property providing that a permit to build the garage can be obtained, is an example of a condition precedent. If no building permit is obtained, neither party is obligated to perform under the contract.

A frequent source of confusion to the engineer learning about contracts is the distinction between a condition precedent and a condition subsequent. A *condition subsequent* is a condition which, when it occurs, ends an existing contract. Assume, for example, that White's house is insured by the Black Insurance Company. The insurance policy states that if the house is ever left untenanted for a period of 30 days or more, the insurance will no longer be in effect; vacancy of the house for 30 days will terminate the insurance. Such a condition is a condition subsequent. In some jurisdictions the law has taken a more liberal view, holding that, in such a case as the example above, only for the period in which the house remained unoccupied in excess of 30 days would the insurance be terminated. According to this view, if White should resume occupancy after 45 days, the insurance would again be in effect. If the building were destroyed on the 40th day of vacancy, though, White could not recover.

MELVIN v. WEST
107 So. 2d 156 (1958)

Sebring, Harold L., Associate Judge.

West, a real estate broker, sued Melvin, a property owner, to recover a real estate commission allegedly earned by West for effecting the sale of certain of Melvin's lands to one Buchanan and his associates. By stipulation, the case was tried before the Circuit Judge without a jury and judgment was for the plaintiff. The defendant has appealed from the judgment, assigning as grounds for reversal that the evidence does not support the judgment and that the evidence shows that a nonlicensed employee of the plaintiff actively participated in procuring the listing of the land and in procuring the purchaser, and hence the plaintiff is barred by law from recovering a commission.

According to the evidence most favorable to the plaintiff, the defendant owned a piece of land which plaintiff understood contained approximately 3,000 acres and was for sale at $1,100 an acre. The defendant orally listed this property for sale with the plaintiff, and several other brokers, with the specific understanding that "the first registered real estate broker who brought in a check and a signed sales contract would be the successful negotiator of the deal."

About a month after West had been given the listing, he informed Melvin that he had a prospect who was interested in buying the 3,000-acre tract at $1,100 an acre. In reply Melvin told West that the price was not $1,100 an acre for 3,000 acres, as understood by West, but was $3,500,000 whatever the acreage. West conveyed this information to his prospect, Buchanan, and thereafter and with full knowledge of the fact that the price of the property had been fixed at $3,500,000, West and Buchanan inspected the property. Shortly after viewing the property, West and Buchanan conferred with Melvin about the purchase of the property by Buchanan and two associates, but came to no definite agreement in regard to a sale. A few days after this conference, Buchanan informed West that he had ascertained that the tract did not contain 3,000 acres, as had been originally represented by West to him, but a lesser acreage, and hence that he and his associates were not interested in buying the property at the quoted price of $3,500,000 but might be willing to pay $2,750,000, and that if the counter offer was not acceptable they "would have no further interest in the matter."

After receiving this counter offer from Buchanan, West phoned Melvin and told him that if he was interested "in helping save the deal" he and West should "get (their) heads together and see if (they) could work out some way to work the situation out . . . (that) Mr. Buchanan was still interested in the property as such . . . and if the price and terms could be worked out to (Buchanan's) satisfaction . . . (he, West) felt the deal could still be made."

The evidence shows that a few hours after this conversation, West, Melvin, and L. V. Hart, one of West's employees, met in West's office at Ft. Lauderdale to discuss what might be done to "save the deal." The meeting ended when Melvin decided, with West's approval, that since he and Buchanan "were the two principals in the situation" he, Melvin, would negotiate directly with Buchanan, if someone would drive him to Miami Beach for the purpose. Thereupon Hart, West's employee, agreed to drive Melvin to Miami Beach where Buchanan was found and a conference was held, which began at approximately 5 o'clock in the afternoon and ended about three hours later, when Melvin finally agreed, after much discussion, to reduce the property from $3,500,000 to $2,900,000, provided $600,000 was paid in cash and the remainder was paid in specifically agreed annual installments, with interest, over a 10-year period; and also agreed that since Buchanan had no authority to commit his associates to the purchase of the property at the new price and terms agreed on at the conference he, Buchanan, might have "until two o'clock the next day (Friday, March 16,

1958) to obtain the permission of (his) associates to continue with the business on the basis of this present agreement and to authorize the contract to be drawn up on this basis"; that in the event permission was obtained "to continue with the business," Buchanan would inform West and would "deposit" with him a check in the sum of $50,000 as a "binder payment"; and that Mr. and Mrs. Melvin would meet with West and Buchanan, at Buchanan's office, on Saturday morning, March 17, 1956, to execute a contract of purchase, to be prepared by West's attorney, which would bind the parties to the sale and purchase of the property.

The evidence is to the effect that on Friday morning, March 16, Buchanan got in touch with his two associates and obtained their permission to purchase the property at the price and terms agreed to by Melvin at the Thursday afternoon conference; that Buchanan called West, at about 11:30 Friday morning, to advise him that he had had "the matter confirmed and . . . had a check available"; and that West immediately phoned the Melvin residence to inform Melvin of what Buchanan had said, but was told by the person answering the phone that Melvin was away from the premises.

West continued calling the Melvin residence at frequent intervals throughout the remainder of the day but was never able to contact Melvin. That night, at a few minutes past midnight, Melvin called West to inform him that on that day he had sold the property to two prospects produced by a real estate salesman, one Harris, who also had an open listing on the property; that a down payment check had been offered and accepted, and that a sales contract had been executed by seller and buyers and hence that he could not sell the property to Buchanan.

The testimony of plaintiff's witness, Harris, the real estate salesman who produced the purchasers to whom the property was sold, was to the effect that on Thursday, March 15, 1956, he had interested two prospects in buying the property at the price of $3,500,000 that was being asked by Melvin; that around 6 o'clock Thursday evening his prospects had offered him a "binder" check which he had refused because "they had not stepped on the property"; that he thereupon attempted to call Melvin between 8:45 and 9 o'clock on Friday morning to inform him that he had the property sold and to request Melvin to meet with the purchasers so that the transaction might be closed without delay; that he met with Melvin one hour and ten minutes later and introduced him to the purchasers; that Melvin then went with Harris and the purchasers to the property, where a purchase contract was executed and a check was delivered between 2:45 and 3 o'clock in the afternoon.

The evidence shows, that after receiving this information late Friday night, West went to Miami Beach early Saturday morning to inform Buchanan that Melvin had sold the property to another prospect. While there West presented a contract of purchase for Buchanan's signature, had Buchanan execute it, and received from Buchanan his personal check in the sum of $50,000 which was dated March 16, 1956, and was made payable to the order of "Wm. H. West, Realtor." According to West, he accepted the check because "Buchanan felt that there might still be a possibility that Mr. Melvin would change his mind and that the other transaction would not go through . . . (and) he wanted to be on record that he had carried out the part of the deal that he had made with Mr. Melvin."

About thirty days later, after it appeared certain that Melvin had no intention of honoring his oral promise to Buchanan, West returned the check to Buchanan and instituted the present suit to recover a commission for selling the property.

The first question on the appeal is whether the foregoing evidence, when viewed in the light most favorable to the plaintiff, is sufficient to support the judgment rendered in his favor.

Two types of brokerage contracts are generally used in the business of selling real estate. Under the first type, the seller employs a real estate broker to procure a purchaser for the property, and the broker becomes entitled to his commission when he produces a purchaser who is ready, able, and willing to purchase the property upon the terms and conditions fixed by the seller, leaving to the seller the actual closing of the sale. Under the second type, the seller employs a broker to effect a sale of the property, and the broker, to become entitled to his commission, must not only produce a purchaser who is ready, able, and willing to purchase the property upon the terms and conditions fixed by the seller but must actually effect the sale, or procure from the purchaser a binding contract of purchase upon the terms and conditions fixed by the seller. . . .

Where a broker employed to effect a sale procures a purchaser who is ready, able, and willing to purchase the involved property upon the terms and conditions fixed by the seller and before he can effect the sale or procure a binding contract of purchase the seller defeats the transaction, not because of any fault of the broker or purchaser but solely because he will not or cannot convey title, the broker will be entitled to his commission even though the sale has not been fully completed, if the buyer remains ready, able, and willing to purchase the property upon the terms and conditions fixed; the strict terms of the contract between the seller and the broker requiring him to actually

complete the sale or procure a binding contract of purchase being deemed, in such case, to have been waived by the seller. . . .

As pointed out in *Hanover Realty Corp.* v. *Codomo,* Fla., 95 So. 2d 420, the rule excusing the broker from complete performance where performance has been made impossible by arbitrary acts of the seller is simply an application to brokerage contracts of the rules relating to contracts generally to the effect that "where a party contracts for another to do a certain thing, he thereby impliedly promises that he will himself do nothing to hinder or obstruct that other in doing the agreed thing," and "one who prevents or makes impossible the performance as happening of a condition precedent upon which his liability by the terms of a contract is made to depend cannot avail himself of its nonperformance."

It is vigorously contended by West that when Melvin went to Miami Beach, with West's acquiescence, and made the oral promise to Buchanan to reduce the price of the property from $3,500,000 to $2,900,000 and to allow Buchanan until 2 o'clock the following day to ascertain from his associates whether or not they would be interested in buying the property at the new price, West thereupon became entitled to his commission, because, in contemplation of law, he became "the first broker to sell, because he fully performed his contract to sell when (Melvin) took over and made the oral agreement with Buchanan." To support his contention, he relies upon what is said in *Knowles* v. *Henderson,* supra, to the effect that where a broker employed to sell property finds a purchaser who is ready, able, and willing to buy at terms fixed by the seller, but before he can effect the sale or procure a binding contract of purchase the seller arbitrarily refuses to go through with the transaction, the broker will be entitled to his commission, if the purchaser remains ready, able, and willing to buy at the terms fixed.

We fail to see how the facts of the case at bar bring the case within the exception stated in *Knowles* v. *Henderson,* supra.

It is perfectly plain that when Melvin went to Miami Beach to confer directly with Buchanan and thereby attempt "to save the deal," West had not become entitled to a commission, because he had not found a purchaser who was ready, able, and willing to purchase the property at the price demanded by Melvin. Since Buchanan and his associates had flatly refused to buy the property at $3,500,000 and Melvin had rejected Buchanan's counter offer of $2,750,000, the most that can be said for West's legal position at the time was that he had three possible prospects, one of whom was willing to confer further about the property but had no power to bind his associates beyond the counter offer that had already been made and rejected.

It is equally plain that since West had utterly failed to perform his nonexclusive oral contract within the terms of his listing, Melvin was not legally obligated to West to negotiate with Buchanan, at the conference, in any particular manner, except to refrain from entering into an arrangement with West's prospects for the purpose of fraudulently preventing West from earning a commission.

So far as can be ascertained from the record, nothing was said or done by Melvin throughout his conference with Buchanan that could be deemed a waiver of the terms of West's original brokerage contract, or that would have, or could have, prevented West from becoming entitled to a commission if a sale had been made to his prospects at the new purchase price, prior to the time some other broker had effected a sale of the property within the terms of his listing. For, as has already been stated, when the conference ended between Melvin and Buchanan no sale had been made of the property. Melvin had orally promised to reduce the purchase price of the property from $3,500,000 to $2,900,000—which Buchanan had been unable to accept because he had no authority from his associates to do so—and had given Buchanan until 2 o'clock the following afternoon to ascertain from his associates whether or not they were interested in purchasing the property at the reduced purchase price.

Even though the oral promise made by Melvin to extend the time for Buchanan to talk with his associates was not enforceable as an option, since no consideration was given for the promise . . . it is impossible to understand how, if West had been negotiating with Buchanan in place of Melvin, he could have accomplished as much as, or more than, was accomplished by Melvin in an effort to effectuate a sale. Manifestly, West could not have lawfully made the concession as to price that was made by Melvin, since he had no authority, in respect to price, except to offer the property for sale at $3,500,000—a figure that had already been presented to Buchanan and rejected by him. And, assuming for the sake of argument, that West had been given authority, prior to the conference, to make concessions in regard to price and terms and thereby bind Melvin, it is plain that Buchanan could not have accepted a single concession on behalf of his associates, since at the time of the conference he had no authority to bind his associates beyond the amount of the counter offer of $2,750,000 that had already been made to, and turned down by, Melvin.

Consequently, when the conference between Melvin and Buchanan ended, West occupied no weaker position, because of anything said or done by Melvin during the conference, than he had occupied prior to that time; indeed, it appears that he was in a stronger position. Before the conference, all that West had were three prospects whom he had been unable to interest in the property at the price and terms fixed by the seller; hence he had failed to fulfill the terms of his nonexclusive contract. After the conference, West not only still had his three prospects but also had, in effect, an oral nonexclusive contract to sell that authorized him to sell the property to Buchanan and his associates for $2,900,000 (while other brokers had to sell, under the terms of their contracts, for $3,500,000) provided, of course, he actually effected a sale of the property or procured a binding contract of purchase, prior to the time some other broker did, and provided the sale was effected prior to the time the gratuitous offer to sell the property at the reduced price terminated or was lawfully withdrawn by the seller.

As we have already stated, Harris, who also had a nonexclusive contract to sell the property on a "first come first served" basis, called Melvin not later than 9 o'clock on Friday morning March 16, 1956, to inform him that he had sold the property at the fixed price of $3,500,000; and at 10:10 on the same morning Harris introduced his purchasers to Melvin. All of this occurred more than an hour before Buchanan advised West that he and his associates were willing to buy the property and hence occurred prior to the time that West could have notified Melvin of the fact, even if the latter had chosen to remain at home throughout the whole of Friday morning. The contract of sale was executed by the seller and the purchasers produced by Harris at 2:45 or 3:00 Friday afternoon. As a matter of law, the execution of this contract terminated all nonexclusive brokerage contracts that were then outstanding. . . .

We find nothing in the oral concessions made by Melvin at the conference that could be construed as an agreement on his part to pay West a commission regardless of whether a sale was made in the meantime by some other broker; nor was there anything said or done by Melvin to indicate that Melvin intended to give West an exclusive agency to sell the property at the new price stated at the conference.

We conclude, therefore, that the trial court erred in giving judgment to the plaintiff; and consequently, that the judgment should be reversed and the cause remanded for further proceedings according to law.

The conclusions we have reached make it unnecessary for us to consider the second point urged for reversal by the appellant.

Reversed.

LORANGER CONST. CORP. v. E. F. HAUSERMAN CO.

384 N.E. 2d 176 (1978)

Braucher, Justice.

The plaintiff, a contractor, was preparing its bid for construction at the Cape Cod Community College. It received an "estimate" of $15,900 for movable steel partitions from the defendant, and used the estimate in preparing the bid it submitted. The construction contract was awarded to the plaintiff, the defendant refused to perform in accordance with its estimate, and the plaintiff engaged another company to supply and install the partitions for $23,000. The Appeals Court upheld an award of damages to the plaintiff, we allowed the defendant's petition for further appellate review, and we affirm the judgment for the plaintiff.

The action was filed in 1970. Demurrers to the declaration and to an amended declaration were sustained, and leave to file a second amended declaration was then denied, the judge "being of opinion there is no cause of action." The Appeals Court held that count 1 of the amended declaration did set out a cause of action and reversed the order, denying leave to amend. . . . Thereafter the plaintiff filed an amended declaration containing four counts, the case was tried to a jury in October 1974, and a verdict was returned for the plaintiff in the amount of $7,100. The Appeals Court held that the plaintiff was "foreclosed from recovery on any traditional contract theory," but could "recover on the theory of promissory estoppel, a basis for recovery not previously explicitly accepted in the courts of this Commonwealth." . . . The defendant argues that "the adoption of this new theory of law is procedurally unfair, unwarranted by the facts in the case, and contrary to the statutory policy of the Commonwealth."

We summarize the evidence most favorable to the plaintiff. On May 20, 1968, the plaintiff was preparing its bid to become general contractor on the construction project. The specifications called for movable metal partitions from the defendant or one of two other suppliers, "or equal." About fifteen days earlier, a sales engineer employed by the defendant had prepared a "quotation" or "estimate" of $15,900 for supplying and installing the partitions. The figure was based on information received from the architect's office, and the engineer knew that the general contractor would submit a bid based on such estimates from subcontractors. The estimate was given to the plaintiff by telephone on May 20, 1968; it was also given to other general contractors. The engineer waited until shortly before bids

were due on the general contract to prevent the general contractor from shopping for a lower price from other subcontractors. The plaintiff received no other quotations on the partitions, and used the defendant's quotation in preparing the bid on the general contract, submitted the same day.

The general contract was awarded to the plaintiff on June 21 or 26, 1968. Sometime in August or September, the plaintiff informed the defendant that it was getting ready to award the partition contract and asked whether it had the defendant's lowest price. Thereafter, on September 12, 1968, the plaintiff sent the defendant an unsigned subcontract form based on the $15,900 figure. The defendant rejected the subcontract, and the plaintiff engaged another company to supply and install the partitions for $23,000. The partition work was not scheduled to begin until the summer of 1969; in fact, work began in the summer of 1970, and the last payment for it was made in 1972.

At the close of the plaintiff's evidence, it waived counts 2, 3, and 4 of the declaration. The defendant rested and moved for a directed verdict. The motion was denied. After verdict, the defendant moved for judgment notwithstanding the verdict, and that motion was denied. The questions argued to us relate to the question whether the evidence made a case for the jury.

1. *The offer or promise.* The defendant argues that the "quotation" or "estimate" made by its sales engineer was not an offer or promise, but merely an invitation to further negotiations, citing *Cannavino & Shea, Inc.* v. *Water Works Supply Corp.* 361 Mass. 363, 366, 280 N.E.2d 147 (1972). But the *Cannavino* case involved the circulation of a price list without specification of quantity. Here there was more; the defendant was to do a portion of the work called for by the plans and specifications. Of course, it was possible for the engineer to invite negotiations or offers. . . . But it was also possible for him to make a commitment. His employer stated in answer to interrogatories that it was "unable to determine whether or not an employee of the defendant spoke with any of the plaintiff's employees on or about May 20, 1968," and the only direct evidence of the estimate was the testimony of the engineer. We think the jury were warranted in resolving ambiguities in his testimony against the defendant, and in finding that the estimate, in the circumstances, was an offer or promise. . . .

2. *Reliance on the promise.* It seems clear enough, as the Appeals Court held, that the evidence made a case for the jury on the basis of the plaintiff's reliance on the defendant's promise. "An offer which the offeror should reasonably expect to induce action or forebearance of a substantial character on the part of the of-

feree before acceptance and which does induce such action or forebearance is binding as an option contract to the extent necessary to avoid injustice." . . . This doctrine is not so novel as the defendant contends. . . . When a promise is enforceable in whole or in part by virtue of reliance, it is a "contract," and it is enforceable pursuant to a "traditional contract theory" antedating the modern doctrine of consideration. . . . We do not use the expression "promissory estoppel," since it tends to confusion rather than clarity.

3. *Procedural unfairness.* The defendant contends that the decision of the Appeals Court, resting on "the new theory of promissory estoppel," departed from the pleadings and from the theory on which the case was tried. So far as the pleadings are concerned, count 1 of the declaration alleged an exchange of promise for promise and also the submission of a bid by the plaintiff in reliance on the agreement between the parties. If either allegation was sustained by proof, the other could be treated as surplusage. The pleadings could have been amended to conform to the evidence, even after judgment; failure so to amend does not affect the result of the trial. . . .

In view of the defendant's claim of procedural unfairness, we requested and received a transcript of the judge's charge to the jury. The defendant does not assert any error with respect to the charge, and did not include the charge in its record appendix. We do not treat the charge as the "law of the case". . . . But we find that the case was presented to the jury on the basis of offer, acceptance, and consideration; there was no reference in the charge to reliance on a promise. We therefore cannot attribute to the jury a finding that the offer or promise of the defendant induced action "of a substantial character" on the part of the plaintiff. We consider the case on the basis on which it was submitted to the jury. . . .

Pursuant to the charge and on the evidence before them, the jury might have found that the defendant's offer was accepted in any one of three ways. First, there might have been an exchange of promises in the plaintiff's telephone conversation with the defendant's engineer, before the plaintiff's bid was submitted. Second, the offer might have been accepted by the doing of an act, using the defendant's estimate in submitting the plaintiff's bid. Acceptance in this way might be complete without notification to the offeror. . . . Finally, the offer might have remained outstanding, unrevoked, until September 1968, or it might have been renewed or extended when the plaintiff asked whether it had the defendant's lowest price; in either case it might have been accepted when the plaintiff sent the defendant a subcontract form on September 12. The evidence warranted the jury in finding that the defendant invited acceptance in any one of the three modes, and in finding that the plaintiff's promise or act furnished consideration to make the defendant's promise binding.

"In the typical bargain, the consideration and the promise bear a reciprocal relation of motive or inducement: the consideration induces the making of the promise and the promise induces the furnishing of the consideration." . . . In the present case, the jury could infer that the defendant's engineer intended to induce the plaintiff's promise or action in the hope that defendant would benefit, and thus that his offer or promise was induced by the hoped-for acceptance. Even more clearly, the jury could find that the plaintiff's promise or action was induced by the defendant's offer or promise. Such findings would warrant the conclusion that there was a "typical bargain," supported by consideration. . . . Indeed, review of the cases suggests that many decisions based on reliance might have been based on bargain. . . . Once consideration and bargain are found, there is no need to apply sec. 90 of the Restatement, dealing with the legal effect of reliance in the absence of consideration.

4. *Statutory policy.* The defendant did not argue any question of statutory policy to the Appeals Court. It argues to us that the decision of the Appeals Court is contrary to the policy of G.L. c. 149, secs. 44A–44L, regulating bidding on contracts for the construction of public works. The argument seems to relate primarily to subcontract bids described in sec. 44C. Such bids must be listed in the general contractor's bid under sec. 44F, and must be filed with the awarding authority under sec. 44H. The defendant was not in any of the trades to which those provisions apply. In any event, the argument relates only to the reliance doctrine on which the Appeals Court based its decision. We decide on a different basis.

5. *Other issues.* Several other matters argued by the defendant to the Appeals Court are discussed in the opinion of that court: unreasonable delay by the plaintiff in notifying the defendant that it was to be the subcontractor, "bid shopping" by the plaintiff, and application of the statute of frauds, G.L. c. 106, sec. 2–201, and c. 259, sec. 1, Fifth. The defendant has not emphasized these matters in its argument to us. The Appeals Court held that they did not bar recovery based on reliance, and they have no more force to bar recovery based on bargain plus reliance. We therefore do not consider them.

Judgment of the Superior Court Department affirmed.

REVIEW QUESTIONS

1. Black is in need of a turret lathe similar to a used one White is trying to sell. White offers Black the lathe for $2,500. Black: "I accept, providing you will deliver the lathe and have it in my shop tomorrow noon." White: "Sorry, but my truck will not be back in town before tomorrow night." Black "Then I will pick it up myself, since I need it immediately." White: "I believe I will wait awhile longer before selling it." Black: "You can't; we made a contract." Was there a contract? Why or why not?

2. On January 3, Gray sends Brown the following offer by first class mail: "I offer you my vertical milling machine in the same condition it was when you last saw it for $4,200. This offer will remain open for your air mail acceptance until Jan. 15." On Jan. 9, at 10:00 a.m., Brown sent the following telegram to Gray: "I accept the offer of your vertical milling machine for $4,200. Am sending truck for it immediately." Is there a contract? Why or why not?

3. In question number 2, assume that Brown received a withdrawal from Gray at 9:00 a.m., January 9, but, since the original letter stated that the offer was open until Jan. 15, Brown sent an air mail acceptance an hour later. Was there a contract? Why or why not?

4. In question number 2, assume that Brown's air mail acceptance on January 9 was lost in the mail and not delivered until January 16. Was there a contract? Why or why not?

5. Green required parts for an appliance he intended to manufacture. He sent out blueprints and specifications to several manufacturers, including the White Manufacturing Company, requesting bids on 100,000 of such parts. White Manufacturing Company submitted what turned out to be the lowest bid. The bid was refused, however. Can White Manufacturing Company demand and get the job on the basis of its bid? Why or why not?

6. Brown lost an expensive watch that had his name engraved on it. He placed an advertisement in a local paper offering a $100 reward for its return. Black found the watch, noticed Brown's name on it, found Brown's address in a telephone book, and returned the watch to him. Later, he read the reward notice and demanded the reward. Is he entitled to the $100? Why or why not?

7. Use examples to distinguish between condition precedent and condition subsequent as they apply to contracts.

8. The price of White's product is $50. Newspaper advertising inadvertently lists the price as $30, precipitating a deluge of orders. White honors the advertised price even though his cost is $35. He has begun an action against the newspaper for $20 for each unit sold. Who will win? Why?

9. In the case of *Melvin* v. *West*, the judge speaks of two kinds of brokerage contracts. How do they differ?

10. In the case of *Loranger Const. Corp.* v. *E. F. Hauserman Co.,* in what ways could you change the facts so defendant must win?

8
Reality of Agreement

In Chapter 7 it was stated that there must be an agreement or meeting of the minds between contracting parties. The meeting of minds must be voluntary and intentional. It is implied that neither of the parties has been prevented from learning the facts of the proposed contract. In short, the assumption is made that each contracting party has entered into the agreement "with his eyes wide open."

If this is not true about a particular agreement, the contract can be avoided. Although the law will uphold a person's right to contract as part of his freedom, and will hold him, as well as the party with whom he bargains, to the agreement they have made, it would be unjust to do so in the absence of free and voluntary action on his part. Where one person knowingly attempts to take advantage of another, it would not seem right to enforce the attempt.

The rules and principles of contracts are very practical and logical as, of course, they should be when they govern practical events. Probably there is no place where this is better demonstrated than in the handling of cases where agreement by one of the parties is not voluntary and intentional.

Contracts in which the *reality of agreement* is questionable fall into five general categories: (1) mistake, (2) fraud, (3) innocent misrepresentation, (4) duress, and (5) undue influence. These will be treated separately.

Mistake

A mistake may be either unilateral or mutual. A *unilateral mistake* is a mistake by one party to a contract as to material circumstances surrounding the transaction. Usually the law will not allow relief for unilateral mistakes. A *mutual* or *bilateral mistake* occurs in circumstances in which both of the parties were mistaken as to some material fact. When both are mistaken the law will not bind either of them.

Unilateral Mistake. Where the mistake involved results from poor judgment of values or negligence by the injured party, the law will hold the party to his bad bargain. Black sells White a used automatic screw machine for $15,000 and White finds later that a similar machine could have been purchased for $10,000. White can not avoid the contract because of the difference in value.

An agreement in writing binds the parties to the agreement according to the wording on the paper. When a person has signed such an agreement he is held to have understood the terms set forth. If he did not understand it, he should not have signed; or else he should have insisted that any questionable parts be rewritten. If one wishes to enter into a written agreement with another, but disagrees with some of the terms, he has the right to eliminate these terms, get the other party to the contract to agree to the change, and obtain his signature to the change before signing. Most written contracts are either typed or hand-printed. If, in reaching an agreement, one of the parties changes the contract in longhand (cursive) with knowledge of the other party, this writing will stand in lieu of the preexisting part with which it is in conflict. Where the terms of a written agreement are capable of two different interpretations, they will be construed most strongly against the person who drew up the contract.

There are certain instances of unilateral mistake in which a party may rescind his contract. If the other party to the contract, in full knowledge of the mistake, took advantage of the situation, the courts will not hold the injured party to his bargain. Such a situation might easily fit into the picture of fraud given below. Certain types of clerical or calculation errors will also allow rescission. If a contractor in preparing a bid on a job, makes a clerical error or a mathematical miscalculation, courts may, in some instances, allow the contract to be avoided. Such judgments have occurred. This is particularly likely if the error is an obvious one and the other party must have known or reasonably suspected an error in the quotation.

Mutual Mistake. If both parties to a contract are mistaken as to a material fact regarding the subject matter involved, the courts generally hold the contract to be void. There are two possible situations: mistakes as to identity and mistakes as to existence. Suppose Black agreed to purchase White's horse for $500, and that the two parties had two different horses in mind. The courts would say that the minds of the two parties had not met, and that therefore, no enforceable contract resulted. In the foregoing example, the two parties may have contracted for the sale of the horse at some location away from the place where the horse was kept. If the horse were found to be dead, the contract would not be enforceable. The subject matter would have ceased to exist (at least in the manner assumed by the parties). The situation would be the same if the parties had agreed to the sale of a house that was discovered to be burned down. The assumed existence of the subject matter would have been a mutual mistake.

Where the value is something different from that assumed by both of the parties, though, a different view is taken by the law. For instance, Black purchases farmland from White at a reasonable value for farmland. Later, a valuable mineral deposit is discovered in the land. If Black had no prior knowledge of such deposits, the sale stands and it is Black's gain. There are, of course, many instances of purchases of valuable paintings and antiques where the parties involved knew nothing of the true value of the subject matter. Such sales are generally quite valid.

Where the mistake concerns legal rights and duties involved, it is not ground for rescission of the contract. Every person is supposed to be familiar with the law and is charged with that knowledge.

Fraud

Six basic elements must be proved to sustain a charge of *fraud*. There must have been:

1. A false representation
2. of a material fact
3. knowingly made
4. with intent to deceive
5. which was relied upon by the injured party
6. to his detriment.

Let us examine what is meant in the law by each of these elements. The first element may be an outright misstatement, but it does not have to be put into words. It may, instead, take the form of an omission of information which should have been passed along to the injured party. Or it may result from an artful concealment such as, for instance, using S.A.E. 90 oil in the crankcase of a car to conceal the need for an overhaul. In certain instances, particularly where a previous relationship of trust has existed between the parties, there may be a duty to speak and reveal all information concerning the subject matter. The courts have been quite general in describing how fraud may arise, preferring not to set up a fixed blockade for the sharp operator to attempt to avoid.

The false representation must be of a material fact which is *not obviously untrue:* For instance, if you are told that a car you are thinking of buying is in perfect condition when, in truth, it has a broken rear window that anyone could see, the statement would not support an action for fraud. It must be a *material* thing that is falsely represented. If the seller represented the car mentioned above as having brand-X spark plugs when the spark plugs were really another brand of equivalent quality, the statement would hardly be considered material. The representation must falsely represent a *fact*. When you stop to think of it, it may be a little difficult to define what is *fact*. Certainly, what you did yesterday, and what you are doing today at the present time may be stated as facts. But, aside from a few accepted certainties, it is impossible to state something about the future as fact. In attempting to get Black to buy land from him, White tells Black, "I intend to start a housing development in a section very near this land." If Black buys in reliance upon the statement and no housing development is begun, there might be some question as to whether or not White ever intended to build. Was the statement a statement of fact? It could very well be, since it is a statement of a present *intention*. If a statement is made in such a way as to express an *opinion* it is not held to be a statement of fact. Sales talk, puffing, statements that a certain thing is the "best," or is "unsurpassed," or a "good buy" are not fraudulent statements. The only exception to this occurs where a person holds himself out as qualified to give an expert opinion on the subject matter. If a party is injured in reasonable reliance on this opinion, he may be able to recover for fraud. Generally, then, the representation of material fact must be a false representation, other than opinion, having to do with something past or present. It is not necessary for the statement to be the sole inducement to action by the injured party. It is only necessary that, if he had known the truth, he would not have taken the action he did take.

Knowledge of the truth or falsity of a statement made does not necessarily determine the existence of fraudulent representation. If the person making the representation knows it to be false, it is fraudulent. If the person does not know whether it is true or not, but makes the representation in reckless disregard of the truth to persuade the other party, he may be charged with having made a false representation.

A misrepresentation for the purpose of fraud is normally made with the intent that the party to whom it is made will act upon it. If the other party does not act upon it there is no fraud. If a third party (for whom the representation was not intended) overhears it and acts upon it to his detriment, it is still not fraud. Action must be taken by the person for whom the false representation was intended.

The injured party must have acted in reliance upon the representations made to him. People are assumed by the courts to be reasonable, and the courts assume that they will take ordinary precautions when dealing with others. One is charged with the knowledge or experience that anyone in his trade or profession would normally possess. For instance, an auto mechanic should be far less gullible than a lingerie salesperson when purchasing a used car. If a person has conducted his own investigation before the agreement, rather than relying upon another's representations, it is far more difficult to sustain a charge of fraud.

The false representations of material fact for the purpose of fraud may be proved; they may have been made with full knowledge of their falsity and with intent to deceive; action may have been taken in reliance upon the misrepresentations, but if no injury resulted there cannot be recovery for fraud. Black is induced by White, as a result of various fraudulent misstatements, to purchase 1000 shares of "Ye Olde Wilde Catte" oil stock at $1.00 per share. Upon discovery that he has been taken, Black sues, but before the case comes up on the court docket the oil company strikes oil and the stock price increases to $2.00 per share. Black quite obviously would not continue the action, but even if he wanted to he couldn't recover damages because he has not been injured.

Several remedies are available to a person who has been defrauded. He may, first of all, wish to continue the contract with full knowledge of the fraud. If the contract has been completed he may wish to retain what he has received and institute a damage action for whatever damage he has suffered. He may rescind the contract, return his consideration, and get back what he has given. If the contract is still executory the defrauded party may merely ignore his obligations under it, relying on his proof of fraud if the other party brings an action against him. In any event, if the defrauded party wishes to bring a court action after he discovers that he has become a victim, he must do so in a reasonable time. If he does not take action within a reasonable length of time, his right to take action will be lost by laches or the statute of limitations.

Misrepresentation

To point up the distinction between fraud and misrepresentation, consider the following example. Black contracts to buy a hunting dog from White for $200. During the negotiations White tells Black that the dog is three years old. A few months later the dog becomes ill and Black takes him to a veterinarian. After treatment the vet tells Black that he has a fine ten-year-old dog. Black has been a victim. He has been defrauded or has been victimized by an *innocent misrepresentation.* The distinction depends upon the presence or absence of the third and fourth elements of fraud (knowledge and intent). If White was present ten years ago when the dog was born, then he can certainly be charged with knowledge of the dog's age. If White knew the dog's age, the statement to Black indicating that the dog's age was three years could have been made only with an intent to deceive Black. If, however, the dog was acquired by White six months ago from Gray, who stated the dog's age to be two and a half years, the statement made by White was an innocent misrepresentation (or *mistake,* in some courts).

Although no fraud results from an innocent misrepresentation, the injured party has the right to rescind his contract, giving up the consideration which he has received. However, in innocent misrepresentation there is no right of tort action for damages as there is in fraud or deceit.

Duress

Duress consists of forcing a person to consent to an agreement through active or threatened violence or injury. The threat must also be accompanied by the apparent means of carrying it out. It places the victim in a state of mind such that he no longer has the ability to exercise his will freely. In the early court decisions, a holding of duress was limited to cases in which the victim's life or freedom was endangered or in which he was threatened with bodily harm. Modern courts take the view that duress is the deprivation of a person's free will; the means of accomplishing this is immaterial as long as unlawful violence is involved. Threat of injury to other persons, even to property, could conceivably be the means employed to gain the desired end. White is an art lover and has a collection of paintings. Black, to obtain White's signature on a promissory note, threatens to cut up one of White's paintings with a pocket knife. This could constitute duress.

Some courage is inferred by the courts. It must be shown not only that threats of unlawful violence occurred, but that they were sufficient to overcome the person's will. When duress has been used the victim has the right to rescind the contract formed.

Undue Influence

Duress and undue influence are quite alike in at least one respect. When either has been successfully exercised, the free will of the victim has been overcome.

The means of accomplishing the objectives are somewhat different. Duress requires violence or a threat of violence. *Undue influence* results from the use of moral or social coercion, usually arising where a relationship of trust or confidence has been established between two people. Common relationships of this nature where undue influence may arise are those between husband and wife, parent and child, guardian and ward, doctor and patient, and attorney and client. It also may be suspected where a person is in dire need, or in some physical or mental distress which would put him at the mercy of the other party.

Three things must be proved in undue influence. First, it must be shown that there was a person who, because of a trust relationship, was in position to be influenced. Second, there must be the fact of improper pressure being exerted by the person in the dominant position. Last, there must be proof that the pressure, being sufficient, did influence the victim; that he acted upon it and was injured as a result.

PUGET SOUND NATIONAL BANK
v. McMAHON

330 P. 2d 559 (1958)

Weaver, Justice

Plaintiff appeals from a judgment dismissing with prejudice her action for rescission of an exchange contract of real properties.

In October 1955, plaintiff conveyed the Liberty Bell Motel, in King County, to the defendants, A. J. and Bernice McMahon, in exchange for the Broadway Cut-off Apartments, in Snohomish County. Plaintiff alleged that defendants misrepresented certain observable physical facts; namely, that there was new plumbing throughout the Broadway Cut-off Apartments, and that the equipment and furniture were new and in good condition. Plaintiff also alleged that defendants represented that the property produced gross annual earnings of twelve to fourteen thousand dollars, from which a net profit of five to seven hundred dollars a month was realized. These allegations were controverted in the answer and the evidence. The court made no finding of fact as to whether or not the misrepresentations were actually made.

The trial court found, however, that plaintiff, eighty-one years of age, had ". . . many, many years' experience in the ownership, management, and control of a considerable number of apartment houses, motels, and other rental units"; and that ". . . plaintiff inspected the Broadway Cut-off Apartments on an undetermined number of occasions in the company of the defendant

Taylor and also of others. She consulted with counsel and was advised against the proposed exchange. If the plaintiff believed that she was to receive from the operation of the Broadway Cut-off a net income of $500.00 per month, that the plaintiff was a woman of such vast business experience that upon her extensively viewing and examining the premises, it was impossible for her to have any reasonable belief that the net income from the property would be $500.00 per month, and that her viewing and inspecting of these premises and her personal experience in handling large properties would not permit her to say that she believed the property would afford her a net income of $500.00 per month. Further, her experience in handling properties for a number of years and her inspection of these premises were such that she could not close her eyes to the condition of the plumbing or of the furniture in the furnished units of the Broadway Cut-off Apartments. In other words, the court finds that she exchanged these properties with full knowledge of the conditions surrounding and after full and complete inspection of an experienced person. That if any representations were made, the plaintiff had no right to rely thereon, due to her multitude of years of experience in owning and managing rental units and operating properties of similar character."

Plaintiff died pending appeal. Although the Puget Sound National Bank, as executor of her estate, has been substituted as appellant, we will refer to plaintiff as appellant.

It appears from her proposed findings of fact that appellant has no particular quarrel with the court's findings that she had no right to believe any misrepresentations that may have been made as to the observable condition of the plumbing, furniture, and equipment in the apartments.

The gravamen of the appeal is appellant's contention that past net profits from operation of the apartments is not an observable physical fact; hence, the finding that she had no right to rely upon defendants' alleged representation of net earnings is a bare conclusion of law, without any supporting finding of fact or evidence upon which it can be based.

From these facts, appellant asks us to assume that a representation as to net earnings was made, that it was false, that she believed it, and had a right to do so. Upon this theory, appellant seeks a reversal of the judgment.

This court said in *Marr* v. *Cook, 1957 . . . :* "It is unnecessary to discuss again all of the elements which a purchaser must prove to be entitled to recover in an action for fraud in connection with a sale. They have been set out in almost identical form in a long line of cases beginning with *Webster* v. *L. Romano Engineering Corp., 1934,* . . . and repeated as recently as *Swanson* v. *Solomon, 1957.* . . ."

In an action for fraud, the burden is upon plaintiff to prove the existence of *all* the essential and necessary elements "that enter into its composition". . . one of which is that the representee had a right to rely upon the representation. All of the ingredients must be found to exist. The absence of any one of them is fatal to recovery. To be remedial, a representation must have been of such a nature and have been made in such circumstances that the injured party had a right to rely on it. It is this element that the trial court found was missing in the instant case.

"The right to rely on representations is inseparably connected with the correlative problem of the duty of a representee to use diligence in respect of representations made to him.". . .

The trier of the fact is justified in finding that the representee did not have the right to rely on a representation, if made, if the representee had expert knowledge of the general subject matter and was peculiarly fitted and qualified, by knowledge and experience, to evaluate that which he sees and appreciate the obvious falsity of the claimed representation. . . . A finding that the representation was actually made is not a necessary condition precedent to a determination that the representee did not have the right to rely upon it; such a determination assumes, for the purpose of argument, that the representation was made.

The past net profits from operation of the Broadway Cut-off Apartments is, as appellant contends, not an observable physical fact; but the evidence supports the trial court's finding that the combination of the condition and extent of the apartments, as disclosed by appellant's investigations, with her vast business experience in the ownership and management of such projects, could lead only to one conclusion: She was not entitled to rely upon representations as to net profits.

The evidence has failed to establish one of the essential and necessary elements that enters into the composition of fraud, and the judgment must be affirmed.

It is so ordered.

Hill, C. J., and Ott and Hunter, J. J., concur.

Mallery, Justice (concurring). The trial court predicated its conclusion that the appellant had no right to rely upon representations, if made, relating to income from the Broadway Cut-off Apartments upon the ground that they were in a bad physical condition, which was open to the inspection. It is the condition of the Broadway Cut-off Apartments that is the crux of the appeal. Appellant aptly points out that there is no

testimony on the question. However, the trial court *knew* their condition from its own inspection of the premises. Its conclusion was therefore not speculation.

COMMUNITY BK., L. OSWEGO, OR. v. BANK OF HALLANDALE & T. CO.

482 F. 2d 1124 (1973)

Roney, Circuit Judge:

The critical question on this appeal is whether the plaintiff bank in Oregon, in making a personal loan, relied on misrepresentations of the trust officer of the defendant bank in Florida regarding the borrower's financial condition. Although the District Court found the representations to be false, it held that the plaintiff's tort claim for damages must fail for want of reliance. We think that the evidence compels a finding of justified reliance and reverse.

On May 31, 1971, Jerome A. Lurie executed a $50,000 promissory note payable to plaintiff, The Community Bank, Lake Oswego, Oregon. The loan had not yet been approved and was to be secured on a two-for-one basis by I.B.M. grade securities in Lurie's trust account with the Bank of Hallandale.

On June 2, 1971, Maldyn C. Evans, Community Bank's president, telephoned Craig G. Kallen, the Bank of Hallandale's sole trust officer, introduced himself, and inquired about Lurie. Evans indicated that the Oregon bank was considering lending Lurie $50,000 and sought information concerning Lurie and his trust account with the Florida bank. Kallen replied that he had discussed this matter with Lurie, who was an extremely good customer of the bank, had a high seven-figure trust with the bank, and had good balances on his accounts. Kallen offered, if Evans would send him a copy of the promissory note, to set aside securities held by Lurie at the defendant bank as collateral for the loan. All of this information was in the hands of the Florida bank, and Kallen neither qualified these statements nor raised any suspicion about his representations.

The facts reported by Kallen were false. As of June 2nd, Lurie had a zero balance at the Bank of Hallandale. At no time, either before or after that date, were the securities referred to by Kallen in the Florida Bank's possession.

On June 3rd, during an audit, it was discovered that certain securities which the Florida bank held as collateral for its own loans to Lurie were in street name, had been stolen, and were subject to stop orders. Consequently, Kallen was relieved of his duties, but remained in his office and received telephone calls as a bank officer until his employment was terminated on June 11th. The Court found, despite denials by Kallen, that in a second telephone conversation with Kallen, on June 10, 1971, Evans asked if collateral had been set aside for the proposed loan and Kallen responded, "I told you already they had." When asked if he would forward a list of securities, Kallen replied, "I told you I would."

After the June 10th call, Evans approved the loan. On his instructions, the cashier and vice-president of Community Bank telephoned Lurie at Kallen's office in the Florida bank. Kallen answered the telephone, indicated that Lurie was in his office, and then turned the telephone over to Lurie who authorized disbursement of the $50,000. The funds were then disbursed.

On June 16, 1971, Evans wrote Kallen a letter which the District Court held evidenced an intent to obtain future documentation before disbursement. Since the Court apparently relied exclusively on this documentary evidence to find no reliance, it is set out in full:

"Dear Mr. Kallen:

In connection with the loan transaction we have with your client, Dr. Jerome A. Lurie, we enclose herewith a certified photocopy of the note executed by Dr. Lurie and payable to us in accordance with the terms therein.

It is our understanding that this copy together with Dr. Lurie's instructions to you will permit you to collateralize his loan at this bank on a two-for-one value ratio. We enclose our form of collateral agreement which we presume will be executed by your Department for us, and that a collateral receipt describing the securities pledged (or the equivalent thereof) will be forthcoming for our files.

When replying, we would appreciate it if you would include either a photocopy of Dr. Lurie's financial statement or sufficient narrative information to indicate his general financial strength and reputation.

Thank you for your assistance.

Very truly yours,
/s/M. C. Evans, President"

We think that this letter cannot serve the Bank of Hallandale as a defense. This action is based not on an agreement or an understanding between the parties, but on the tort claim of misrepresentation. Plaintiff predicated this action upon Kallen's fraudulent telephone misrepresentations and the doctrine of apparent authority in regard to the Bank of Hallandale. . . .

We conclude the evidence compels a finding that, in authorizing the Lurie loan, Community Bank's president did rely on Kallen's factual misrepresentations that Lurie had securities in proper form in his trust account with the Bank of Hallandale and that these could be used as collateral for the loan and had been set aside for this purpose. The June 16th letter could not preclude recognition of Community Bank's reliance on earlier telephone conversations regarding Lurie's financial condition. Although paperwork needed to be completed to conclude the collateralization, it was not the Bank of Hallandale's failure to comply with the collateral agreement, but the fact that the Florida bank never possessed the securities in proper form that was fundamental to the damage to Community Bank.

It is the general law, as well as the controlling law in Florida, that recovery may be had for misrepresentation as to a third party's financial condition where a person, for the purpose of inducing another to lend money to said third person, misrepresents the financial responsibility or solvency of such third person. . . .

The District Court, in its final judgment, listed elements essential to proving misrepresentation: (1) a false statement of fact, (2) known by the defendant to be false at the time it was made, and (3) made for the purpose of inducing the plaintiff in reliance thereon; (4) action by the plaintiff in reliance on the correctness of the representations; and (5) resulting damage to the plaintiff. . . . The court recognized in this fact situation each of these elements except reliance.

For reliance to be proved, (i)t is enough that the representation has had a material influence upon the plaintiff's conduct, and been a substantial factor in bringing about his action. It is not necessary that the representation be the paramount, or the decisive, inducement which tipped the scales, so long as it plays a substantial part in affecting the plaintiff's decision. . . .

It is clear from the record that Evans sought information from Kallen, as the Bank of Hallandale's trust officer, as to facts concerning Lurie's financial position, the existence of the subject securities, and their segregation in his trust account. Thus, Kallen's misrepresentations had a "material influence" on and were a "substantial factor" in Community Bank's loan decision. No stricter standard of reliance is required. A false representation is actionable if it substantially contributed to the formation of plaintiff's determination to act. . . .

To constitute remediable fraud, however, it must appear not only that there was reliance on the misrepresentations, but that the reliance was justified under the circumstances. . . . For the reliance to be justified, the misrepresentation must concern some material thing unknown to the plaintiff either because he did not examine it, because he had no opportunity to become informed, or because his entire confidence was reposed in the defendant. . . .

In the light of Kallen's position as trust officer of the Florida bank, the fact that essential information regarding Lurie's financial condition was in the hands of the Bank of Hallandale and the fact that Kallen obviously intended for Evans to believe the information given, Evans was justified in relying on Kallen's telephone communications.

On remand, the District Court need consider only the question of damages.

Reversed and remanded.

On Petition For Rehearing
Per Curiam:

It is ordered that the petition for rehearing filed on behalf of Bank of Hallandale and Trust Company, Appellee in the above entitled and numbered cause be and the same is hereby denied.

Although the Court's opinion indicated that the District Court need consider on remand only the question of damages, that reference applied only to Community Bank's action against Bank of Hallandale and would not preclude consideration of Bank of Hallandale's third party action against its former trust officer, Craig Kallen, or any other related actions.

REVIEW QUESTIONS

1. Black is a representative of a company making computers. He tells the White Manufacturing Company that installation of a system for cost control and rental of his machines to process them will save the company $6000 per month. As a result, the White Manufacturing Company rents the machines and installs the system. After six months of operation, it is determined that the system is losing money for the company at the rate of $3000 per month. The White Manufacturing Co. sues Black's employer for the $18,000 lost by use of the system to date and the $36,000 that would have been saved if Black's claim had been correct. White Manufacturing Co. charges fraud. How much can White Manufacturing Co. recover? On what basis?

2. List the six elements required for fraud. Which four of these elements are required for misrepresentation?

3. Gray, an engineer for a manufacturer of die cast parts, inadvertently used the weight of the parts rather than the labor cost in calculating the bid price. As a result the price bid per part was about 25% above the cost of the raw die cast material rather than about 80% above the raw material cost (which would have resulted from proper bid calculation). The manufacturer to whom the bid was submitted immediately accepted. Gray's employer claims that he should be allowed to avoid the contract since an error was made in the calculation. Will the court be likely to uphold the contract or dissolve it?

4. Distinguish between *duress* and *undue influence*.

5. Brown, a machine operator in Green's plant, lost his left hand in the course of his employment. Because of the character of the work, the state workers' compensation laws do not apply. Brown threatens to sue Green for $80,000 for damage to his ability to earn a living for the remainder of his working life. Brown claims, with apparent good reason, that the machine should have been guarded at the point where the injury occurred. Green offers to pay $20,000 to Brown if Brown will drop the court action. Brown agrees, and Green pays him $5,000 on account. It soon becomes apparent that this is all Green intends to pay. Brown starts a court action for the remaining $15,000. Green sets up as a defense that the contract resulted from duress. Who would win the court action? Why?

6. In *Puget Sound National Bank* v. *McMahon,* assume the plaintiff to be an electrical engineer whose only other delving into the real estate field involved the purchase of his home. Purchase of the apartments was to be merely a sideline investment venture in real estate. Would this be likely to change the outcome of the case?

7. Considering the case of *Community Bk., L. Oswego, Or.* v. *Bank of Hallandale & T. Co.:*
   a. Why was the Hallandale bank named as defendant rather than Kallen?
   b. What do you suppose Kallen intended to gain by the deception?
   c. What policy should Community Bank adopt in the future to prevent a recurrence of such frauds?

9

Consideration

Consideration is the price (in terms of money, goods, or services) paid for the thing that the promisor wishes to have. It is required in all contracts. It may take the form of a benefit to one of the parties or a detriment to him or a forbearance by him. Whatever form it takes, if the price is freely bargained by the parties, it is construed by the courts as their consideration.

Essentials of Consideration

The consideration given by each party to a contract must meet four general requirements:

1. The consideration *must have value*. With the lone exception of money given in satisfaction of a debt, the amount of which has been acknowledged by both parties, it is not required that the values exchanged by the parties be equal. Usually it is assumed that in the free play of bargaining, the parties have arrived at what each believes to be a reasonable consideration. If the consideration appears grossly insufficient, this insufficiency may be used to establish a case of fraud or other unreality of agreement, but inequality of value usually is not sufficient proof by itself. Black promises his uncle, White, that he will not smoke until he has attained the age of 22. White, in turn, promises to pay his nephew Black, $5,000 for not smoking until he, Black, is 22. Each consideration has value. Black's consideration is a forbearance of a legal right to smoke before age 22. White's consideration is the $5,000. It may seem to an outsider that $5,000 is a high price to pay for the value received. Or it might seem to others that no price would be sufficient to pay for giving up the use of tobacco. However, in this contract, Black and White set the price—the value of the forbearance to *them* was $5,000. A court would not question their determination of values.

2. The consideration *must be legal*. The courts usually will not enforce a contract in which the consideration given by one of the parties to the contract is contrary to an established rule of law. If, in the above example, a statute pronounced the act of smoking before age 22 a crime, Black's forbearance of smoking would not have been valid consideration; legally, he couldn't smoke anyway. To be valid consideration, Black's forbearance would have to be forbearance of something which he was lawfully entitled to do. Similarly, if it is a positive act which is promised as consideration, the act must be lawful. If Black's consideration had been a promise to use narcotics or, for that matter, not to use them, the contract would not be enforced.

3. The consideration *must be possible* at the time the contract is made. If the impossibility of performance was known to either or both of the parties at the time of the offer and acceptance, the courts ordinarily will not grant damages for nonperformance. The situation is a little more difficult, though, if the contract calls for performance which later becomes an impossibility. The subsequent destruction of an item essential to the contract, through no fault of either party, renders performance of the contract impossible and ends the obligations of both parties to the contract. For instance, destruction by fire of a building onto which a builder has contracted to add a room would discharge the contract for the work. It would no longer be possible to add something to the original structure. Impossibility of performance is discussed further in Chapter 13 on discharge of contracts.

4. The consideration *must be either present or future*. A present contract cannot be supported by a past consideration. An exception to this may exist in certain instances resembling gifts. For the past consideration to be sufficient to support a contract it must not have been intended as a gift when it was given to the other party. If the past act or forbearance was not intended as a gift, then an unliquidated (undetermined) obligation was created by it. A present promise to pay for such past act or forbearance is binding upon the promisor. The unliquidated obligation has become liquidated. Past relationships between the parties concerning similar acts or forbearance will often be determinative of their intent either to make a gift or to

create an unliquidated obligation. But valid past considerations form a rather minor exception to the rule.

Contracts generally look to the future. Exchange of valuable, lawful, and possible present or future consideration for similar consideration has virtually unquestioned standing at law. If Green orders 10,000 die castings of a particular design to be delivered by August 31, and agrees to pay for them, both considerations are to take place in the future. Either this or present payment for future delivery sets up an obligation which the other party must carry out or risk action for breach of contract.

Seal as Consideration

In ancient times an impression was made on a piece of clay or (later) a blob of wax attached to a document. The seal took the place of the signature. Later certain documents of exceptional importance or high security were required to be sealed. Under the common law the seal came to have such significance that the courts would not inquire as to whether or not any consideration existed for a contract if the contract bore a seal. The formality of the act of sealing the document made it legal and binding. Today in the United States a great deal depends upon the jurisdiction in which the contract is brought into court. In some states the effect of the seal is similar to that under common law. Generally, in those states where the seal is recognized, the effect is to lengthen the time of obligation for performance under a contract and remove any question of consideration. In many states documents concerning transactions in real property must be sealed by the parties to the transaction. Black promises in a letter to White to make White a gift of $1,000. At this point White has nothing, since the present promise of a future gift either orally or in writing is worthless if it is unsupported by consideration from the other party. However, if the promise of the $1,000 had been sealed, it would be supported as a contract in many states.

In private transactions the seal is no longer an impression made on wax. Now it is comprised of the word *seal* or the letters *L.S. (locus sigilli,* "location of the seal"), or any other notation intended by the parties as a seal, following the signature.

Theories of Consideration

Certain theories of consideration form the basis of court opinions in contract cases. A primary one is the *bargain theory* which, in effect, holds that the parties have bargained in good faith for the consideration to be received. Each of the parties has determined the value of the consideration to him. If the agreement to exchange consideration was voluntary and intentional, the values involved, regardless of how dissimilar they may appear, are not subject to question.

The bargain theory is the basis of court decisions where it appears that the parties negotiated freely. But what happens when one party deals from a position of great strength with a much weaker party? Is it fair when a dominant party may dictate terms on a "take it or leave it" basis to one who is almost forced to take it? Should landlord Brown, for example, be allowed to hold tenant Green to a very one-sided contract which Green was forced to take because he had no alternative? Recent cases have indicated that gross inequities of this nature may not be enforced. Where the contract wording would perhaps require the weaker party to assume responsibility for not only his own but also the dominant party's negligence, such terms may not be given their literal effect. These so-called *adhesion* contracts have gradually come to be less enforceable. The modern trend seems to favor a balancing of the equities rather than following the contract language.

Another theory is the *injurious reliance theory* which is based on the principle of *estoppel.* Where one of two innocent parties must suffer, he whose act occasioned the loss must bear that loss. Gray promises to contribute $10,000 to a charitable organization's building fund. In reliance upon Gray's promise, the charitable organization contracts with others for a structure to be built. Gray's promise to contribute will be enforced in the courts if this is necessary to pay for the building.

A third theory, the *moral consideration theory,* is generally confined to those cases in which a preexisting debt has been discharged by law and the debtor, subsequent to the termination of his obligation to pay the debt, agrees to pay it anyway. The basis of the argument here is that though the *obligation to pay* the original debt has been relieved by law, the debt still exists. The debtor, in reaffirming this obligation to pay his debt, has created for himself a moral obligation to pay. This moral obligation is sufficient consideration to sustain court action to recover on the debt. Cases of this nature often arise from bankruptcy proceedings and creditor's compositions.[1]

Mutuality

Generally, both parties must be bound to a valid bilateral contract or neither is bound. The promises constituting consideration in a contract must be irrevocable. If either party to a contract can escape his

---

1. See Chapter 13, "Discharge," for bankruptcy and creditor's compositions.

duty under it as he so desires, there is no contract between the parties. The contract must fail for lack of consideration and mutuality. In one case,[2] a contract was made to sell and deliver 10,000 barrels of oil. The price per barrel was stipulated in the contract. Delivery, though, was to take place in such quantities per week as the buyer might desire. Payment was to be made upon delivery. No minimum quantity per week was agreed upon; the buyer apparently could, if he so chose, refuse delivery of any oil each week during the life of the contract. The buyer, in other words, really had not agreed to do anything as his part of the agreement. A contract may be sustained, however, if the quantities are ascertainable with reasonable certainty. If, in the above case, the purchases had been tied to the buyer's needs, the contract probably would have been upheld. In a case similar to the one above,[3] the contract was to furnish coal for the steamers of a certain line. Although, in one sense, the quantity was indefinite, it was limited to the requirements of the steamers. Since the quantity was ascertainable at the end of any period of time, the contract was sustained.

LEGAL DETRIMENT

Consideration for a contract may consist of a legal detriment. *Legal detriment* means that the promisor agrees, in return for the consideration given by the other party, either to give up some right which is lawfully his or to do something which he might otherwise lawfully avoid doing. Agreeing, for consideration in the form of a discount in price, to restrict this year's purchases of raw material requirements to a particular source, is an example of legal detriment. A company agreeing to so restrict its purchases would be giving up its legal right to choose to purchase its raw materials from any other source for the years' time.

Forbearance

Forbearance or a promise to forbear or give up a legal right is sufficient consideration to support a contract. One instance of forbearance occurs when one party gives up his right to sue another. A person has a legal right to resort to the courts to have his claim adjusted. For such forbearance to sue to constitute consideration, the claim upon which the suit would be based must be a valid one. The party that forbears must have at least reasonable grounds upon which to bring court action. If the claim is reasonably doubtful, or would be a virtual certainty in favor of the plaintiff, the promise to forbear is sufficient consideration. In a small minority of cases, some courts have extended this reasoning even further allowing as sufficient consideration for-

bearance to sue when only the party who would be plaintiff thinks, in good faith, that he has a valid claim. However, if a person brings court action maliciously (e.g., only as a nuisance to the defendant), he renders himself liable for tort action. Forbearance of court action in such a circumstance does not constitute consideration upon which a contract may be based.

One type of case in which forbearance of court action often occurs is that in which the amount of a debt is in dispute. If, in a compromise, the disputing parties agree upon the amount to be paid, this agreement is binding upon them. Each has given up his right to have the court decide as to the correct amount of the debt. It would be a different situation if the amount of debt were certain and due or past due. When such is the case, the acceptance by the creditor of a lesser sum does not discharge the complete debt. The creditor may bring an action at law later for the remainder of the debt.

Time has value. Prepayment of a lesser sum may, by agreement, discharge a fixed debt. Also, payment by means other than money may discharge a liquidated debt. The court ordinarily will not examine the value of goods or services tendered and accepted in payment of a fixed debt.

Existing Duty

The law allows you to collect only once for what you do. If a person already has a duty to perform in a certain way, he cannot use that same performance as consideration in another contract. For example—the house next door is on fire. The city firemen are attempting to extinguish the blaze. An offer by you to pay a fireman $500 extra to spray water on your roof to keep the fire from spreading to your house would not create a valid contract upon acceptance. The fireman is already paid for doing everything in his power to keep the fire from spreading. He can give nothing that he is not already paid to do in exchange for the $500.

An exception exists to the rule that consideration must not be something which one already is bound to do. Assumptions are usually made before entering into a contract. The actual conditions may not exist in the manner assumed by the parties. Where this is found to be true and the performance of the resulting contract is thereby made more difficult, the added difficulty may be treated as consideration to support an addition to the contract price. If, under these conditions, the parties agree to added compensation, the courts will often enforce the added payment. The additional difficulty, though, to be enforceable, must be something that could

2. American Co. v. Kirk, 68F,791, 15 C.C.A. 540.
3. Wells v. Alexander, 130 N.Y. 642.

not be anticipated by normal foresight. Black, a contractor, agrees to build a structure for White for a fixed price. Test borings have shown the soil to be mainly clay. However, upon excavation for the foundation and basement it is discovered that the test borings somehow missed a substantial rock layer. If White agrees to pay extra because of the necessity of excavating through the rock, he will be held to his agreement. This is true even though the original contract did not require White to make such payment if unusual conditions were met. White might successfully refuse to pay extra, but once he has agreed to pay, he will be bound. If the price increase agreement had been based upon something normally considered forseeable, such as a labor or material cost increase, there would have been no lawful consideration. Such contingencies could be anticipated and covered in the original price agreement; these would not support added consideration.

MEADOWS v. RADIO INDUSTRIES
222 F. 2d 347 (1955)

Lindley, C. J.

Plaintiff sued in the District Court to recover damages occasioned, as he averred, by defendant's wrongful termination of his contract of employment. At the conclusion of his evidence, the court directed the jury to return a verdict for defendant and entered judgment against plaintiff. On appeal plaintiff contends that the court erred in directing a verdict.

On the 30th day of April, 1950, plaintiff was, and for some years prior thereto had been, a mechanical engineer residing in Wisconsin. In response to defendant's advertisement, he contacted defendant's officials and, as averred by plaintiff, the parties entered into a parol contract whereby he was to undertake production of resistors for defendant in its plant in Chicago. The agreement rests entirely upon the parol discussion between the parties, as related by the plaintiff. He testified that the parties made "an agreement and I (the plaintiff) was supposed to go with them," first, to make cold molding resistors, and then, to develop hot molding devices, for which defendant agreed to pay him $10,000 a year, and one-half of 1% of the gross sales; that he was supposed to be plant manager in exclusive charge of operating that part of the enterprise relating to resistors; that he went to work with this understanding without any further contract, was paid $190 per week, and stayed with the company for almost a year, when he was discharged. In the meantime he had twice threatened to quit, but on each occasion had been prevailed upon to stay. He admitted

that nothing was said about whether his employment was to be for a year, two years, or for life. He "supposed" it was permanent. There is nothing in his testimony to indicate that he ever promised to remain in employment for any certain period of time, or that there was any definite term of employment. He expressly denied that he was hired for a year and said that he did not at any time before he began working for defendant, offer to work for one year, two years, three years, or "whatever the time was."

His work during this period was largely the designing and building of machinery for the purpose of making hot mold resistors. At the time of his discharge, defendant told him the company was no longer going to continue the process that he claimed to have designed, and, upon his inquiry as to what that meant with regard to him, he was told "you're through." The evidence discloses that the defendant engaged in the resistor business for a few months after terminating plaintiff's employment and then dropped out of it entirely. On appeal plaintiff insists that his employment was to run until the resistor campaign had been fully launched and as long as it continued in operation.

It is apparent, therefore, that, if there was a contract of any character, it was of nebulous substance only, with absolute uncertainty as to duration and with lack of mutuality of promises upon the parts of the respective parties. In that situation, it seems clear (first) that the contract was void for lack of mutuality, and (second) that if any agreement existed it was one wholly at will, which either party had the right to terminate at any time.

It is well settled in Illinois that whenever a contract is incapable of being enforced against one party, that party is equally incapable of enforcing it against the other. . . . As the Appellate Court has said, in *Farmers' Educational and Cooperative Union* v. *Langlois* . . . . "Mutuality of obligation means that both parties are bound or neither (is) bound. In other words there must be a valid consideration. Without a valid consideration, a contract cannot be enforced in law or in equity." In various Illinois cases contracts have been held void for lack of mutuality. . . .

In the present case, a careful examination of the record discloses that there was not the slightest bit of evidence that plaintiff ever agreed that he would continue in the employment of defendant for any specified time. In other words, he had a right to terminate his employment at any time and did not promise to perform for any definite length of time. Therefore, the contract could not have been enforced against him and was lacking in mutuality. Consequently, he cannot enforce it against defendant.

Plaintiff is in no better position if we consider his alleged agreement from the point of view of its term of existence, for the period of its continuance is indefinite. It is a contract at will, which may be terminated at the option of either party at any time. See *Davis* v. *Fidelity Fire Insurance Co.,* . . . and *Joliet Bottling Co.* v. *Brewing Co.* . . . where the court held that, no time being fixed during which the agreement shall remain in force, it may be terminated at the will of either party. . . .

Nor can it avail plaintiff that his contract was, in his own words, permanent. *Davis* v. *Fidelity Fire Insurance Co.* . . . the court approved of the decision in *W. L. Milnert Co.* v. *Hill,* . . . where the document recited that the employment "(would) be a permanent one." The court held that either party might terminate it at any time, even though the business was permanent rather than temporary. In other words, the Supreme Court of Illinois has expressly held that a contract for "permanent employment" is one at will. This is in accord with the decisions of other jurisdictions that contracts not expressly made for fixed periods may be terminated at the will of either party. . . .

Plaintiff's complaint also charged that two certain notes, aggregating $2,300, given by him to defendant were void and that collection thereof should be enjoined; he also claimed that $380.00 is still due him for unpaid accumulated salary at the time of his discharge. However, it appears undisputed that the balance due on the notes had been reduced to judgment which stands unimpeached. The court could grant him no relief in a collateral action against an unreversed judgment. Inasmuch as the amount of the judgment exceeds the amount he claims due him for unpaid wages, he had no right to recover therefor. Consequently, there was no basis for relief. The judgment is affirmed.

PARIS CONST. CO. v. RESEARCH-COTTRELL, INC.
451 F.Supp.938 (1978)

Weber, Chief Judge.

Paris Construction Company (Paris), plaintiff in the above action was a second-tier subcontractor in a contract with Nick Istock, Inc. (Istock). Istock in turn was a subcontractor to Research-Cottrell which was the prime contractor for construction of a facility for Jones and Laughlin Steel Company in Aliquippa, Pennsylvania.

Paris has not been paid for the work performed on the job and has sued Research-Cottrell for these items.

Research-Cottrell has moved for summary judgment on the claims of Paris and has filed evidentiary matters in support thereof. Paris' response to the motion relies to a very great extent on the same evidentiary materials, largely excerpts from depositions.

Plaintiff's Amended Complaint alleges that its claim against Research is based on the following facts: (1) plaintiff's bid as a subcontractor became part of Istock's bid which was accepted by the general contractor; (2) pursuant to the direction of Research-Cottrell and Istock, plaintiff entered into performance of its work; (3) at the specific request of agents and/or employees of Research-Cottrell, plaintiff agreed to do additional work; and (4) the additional work or "overages" performed by plaintiff were authorized by plaintiff's invoices which were initialed by the on-site supervisor of Research-Cottrell who acted in the capacity of agent of Research-Cottrell.

Defendant's contention, supported by evidentiary materials presented, and not refuted by any evidence produced by plaintiff, is that there was no contractual relationship between Research and Paris; that the subcontract between Research-Cottrell and Istock prohibited any subcontracting by Istock; and, that any relationship between Istock and Paris was an arrangement of their own.

Research-Cottrell's position is further fortified by the testimony that all extra work authorizations for the work claimed by Paris in this suit were on Istock forms (prepared by Paris) rather than on Paris forms, as alleged in the Amended Complaint. The Paris forms were used with respect to matters outside the Istock contract.

Fundamental to this lawsuit is the fact that Paris has filed an identical suit in the Common Pleas Court of Beaver County, Pennsylvania, against Nick Istock, Inc., for the same work and the same damages as those sought from Research-Cottrell. The sworn Complaint in that case alleges that Paris' contract on this job was with Nick Istock, Inc.

We conclude that there is not a genuine issue of material fact and that the plaintiff here, Paris Construction Company, had no express contract with the defendant Research-Cottrell.

Plaintiff also claims that it is entitled to recover from Research-Cottrell on a quantum meruit and/or implied contract theory in that it performed extra work at the request of the supervisor for Research-Cottrell. The primary inquiry in determining this matter is whether or not any circumstances exist which would reasonably have led Paris to believe that Research-Cottrell rather than Istock would pay for Paris' performance.

The evidence produced shows that all extra work performed by Paris on written orders signed by Research-Cottrell's on-site supervisor, Mulholland, were processed through Istock and that Paris billed Istock for such extra work, as well as for regular progress payment and payroll accounts.

There is no countervailing evidence to create an issue of fact here. Research-Cottrell had a contract with Istock which provided for the mechanism of payment for extra work ordered. The fact that Research-Cottrell ordered such work performed and signed authorizations for it is not inconsistent with the conclusion that Research-Cottrell was dealing at all times with the Nick Istock, Inc., contract and Istock personnel. The mere fact that the person to whom the request was made was an employee of Paris does not affect the result. Mulholland was dealing with Istock on the job. Research-Cottrell had no contractual relation at any time with Paris.

Count IV of the Amended Complaint asserts a claim based on detrimental reliance on the representations made to Paris by Research-Cottrell.

The elements of detrimental reliance are: (1) a promise to a promisee (2) which the promisor should reasonably expect to induce action by the promisee (3) which does induce such action by the promisee, and (4) which should be enforced to prevent injustice to the promisee. . . .

Unlike a claim in quasi-contract or implied contract, detrimental reliance does not establish a relationship giving rise to legal liability in absence of express contract. The doctrine of detrimental reliance is "not so much one of contract, with a substitute for consideration, as an application of the general principles of estoppel to certain situations." . . . Before detrimental reliance can be successfully alleged, a promise inducing action or forbearance by the promisee in reasonable reliance thereon must form the basis of the claim.

Again we find no evidence here creating an issue of fact. No promise or arrangement between Research-Cottrell and Paris existed upon which Paris could reasonably rely to induce it to perform. Any promises made with respect to work performed at the Aliquippa project were between Paris and Istock. Therefore, with respect to plaintiff's claim based on detrimental reliance we must grant summary judgment in favor of defendant.

REVIEW QUESTIONS

1. Does a conditional promise, such as a promise to resell a piece of property if you are able to buy it, constitute a legal consideration? Why or why not?
2. Black agreed to pay White, a member of the state house of representatives, $1,000 to do everything "reasonable and lawful" to defeat a bill that was to be presented to the legislature. Can White collect the $1,000 whether the bill passes or not? Why or why not?
3. What is the effect of sealing a contract in your state?
4. Black hires White Automation to build a piece of automatic machinery for him for $150,000. During the construction of the machinery, union pressures result in a wage increase for the electrical suppliers. As a result, electrical equipment costs more than anticipated. White demands $8,000 more for the automation and Black agrees to pay. After installation, Black refuses to pay more than $150,000 for the machine. White sues. What will be the result? Why?
5. Gray owed Brown $600 on an old debt. Gray refused to pay the debt several times, claiming lack of funds each time. Brown finally attempted to collect the debt at a time when he knew Gray had sufficient money. Gray offered to pay $400 and give Brown a wrist watch worth about $30 if Brown would consider the debt paid in full. Brown accepted. Later Brown brought an action for the remainder of the debt. Can he get it? Why or why not?
6. In *Meadows* v. *Radio Industries,* would the outcome of the case have been different if the employment contract had been made for ten months and Meadows was then fired after eight months?
7. In the usual employment contract between an engineer and his employer, how much notice is required for termination of the employment by either party?
8. In the case of *Paris Const. Co.* v. *Research-Cottrell, Inc.,* suppose Paris lost its case against Istock as well as its case against Research-Cottrell, Inc. In this circumstance, would it appear to have a case against Jones and Laughlin Steel Company? Could Paris perhaps establish a mechanic's lien against the property improved?

10

Lawful Subject Matter

Freedom to deal or to refuse to deal with others is one of our guaranteed rights. Just as limitations must be placed upon freedom of speech and the right to bear arms to protect the public, limitations must also be placed upon the right to contract. The necessity that any contract have a lawful purpose is fundamental in the law. Generally, a contract based upon illegal subject matter is considered by the courts as void.

Subject matter considered by the courts to be illegal may be classified in three categories: contrary to statutes (federal, state, local), contrary to common law, or contrary to public policy. More generally, illegal consideration consists of any act or forbearance, or promise to act or forbear, which is contrary to law or morality or public policy. Ignorance by the parties as to what constitutes illegality cannot make valid a contract which is void because of illegality.

Intent

The intent of the parties at the time the contract was made often determines its legality. If both parties intended the contract to be performed illegally it usually will not be enforceable in the courts. This is true even though actual performance was lawful. If only one of the parties intends to perform illegally, the courts will usually uphold the contract.

A very large number of contracts are capable of being performed either legally or illegally. A contract to drive a truck, for instance, may be performed either according to the law or in violation of it. If there is no evidence of intent by both parties to perform the contract illegally, the truck driving contract would be valid. Generally, the contract must be incapable of being performed in a legal manner for the courts to declare it void on the basis of illegality.

Knowledge that the subject matter of a contract is intended for later unlawful use by one of the parties usually will not void the contract. However, where the subsequent unlawful use involves a heinous crime (treason or murder, for instance), an exception is made

to this rule. An action to collect for the sale of a gun where the seller knows the buyer intends to commit murder with the gun would not be successful. If the seller had no knowledge of the intended use of the gun and complied with the law in all other respects in the sale, the contract of sale would be valid.

CONTRARY TO STATUTE OR COMMON LAW

If the subject matter of a contract is contrary to an existing statute, the contract is usually void. The statute concerned may be a federal or state statute or a local ordinance. It is not necessary that the contract be in violation of the wording of the statute; the contract may be legally void if it is in conflict with the implied meaning of the statute or the intent of the legislature when the law was passed.

Law Passage Following Contract Formation

If a continuing contract[1] is formed and later a law is passed making performance unlawful, the entire contract is not voided. Performance of the contract subsequent to the passage of the statute cannot be recovered for in the courts, but the contract is enforceable as to performance prior to passage of the statute. Shortly after the United States' entry into World War II, several regulations were passed by Congress outlawing the sale of various items and restricting the sale of others. In a case resulting from these restrictions where a new car sales agency had leased premises for the sole purpose of display and sale of new cars (so stipulated in the lease), it was held that because of the U.S. Government restriction on the sale of new cars, the lease contract was terminated. If the lease had been so written that the use of the premises had not been restricted to the sale of new cars, the governmental restrictions would have had no effect.

1. A contract, the performance of which will take place over a considerable length of time.

Type of Statute

In considering the legality of subject matter the courts attempt to draw a distinction between laws passed for the protection of the public, and statutes, the primary purpose of which is to raise revenue. If a contract violates a statute passed for the protection of the public, it is treated as void and completely unenforceable in the courts. If the contract violates a revenue statute, though, it is usually enforceable, subject to court penalties for avoidance of the statute. An excellent example of this is to be found in the state licensing laws (e.g., for business establishments and professional people). If the purpose of the law is to protect the public and safeguard the lives, health, property, and welfare of citizens (for instance, licensing of professional engineers), a contract for professional services made by one who is not licensed in the state will not be enforced in the courts. If the primary purpose of the law is to collect revenue only (for instance, state gasoline taxes), the courts will usually enforce the contract and impose a penalty upon the violator.

Harm to Third Person

If a third person would be harmed by a crime or tort in the performance of a contract, the subject matter of the contract is unlawful. It is, of course, quite evident that a court could not punish for the commission of a crime or tort on one hand and support a contract to commit such a crime or tort on the other. Where the contract is an inducement to commit a crime or tort, but the commission of such crime or tort is not a necessity in performance of the contract, the courts will examine the strength of the inducement and the general nature of the contract. Life insurance may be an inducement to murder; fire insurance an inducement to arson. For this reason an insurable interest often must be shown before insurance can be obtained. A contract, in the performance of which a party to the contract must breach an existing contract, is usually unenforceable in the courts.[2]

Contracts That Restrain Trade

Our economy is based on the principles of free enterprise and freedom of competition. Under the Sherman Anti-Trust Act, the Clayton Act, and amendments to them, contracts that tend to create a monopoly or maintain price levels or in other ways restrain trade are unlawful. The penalty for violation of these acts is up to triple the amount of damages shown plus payment of the court costs and reasonable attorney's fees for plaintiff's attorney.

Despite the seeming restraint of trade present in such agreements, the court will protect the purchaser of a business and the "good will" that goes with it. The "good will" portion of the sale of a business is often protected in a radius agreement between buyer and seller. By such an agreement the seller states that he will not compete with the buyer of his business. Typically, the agreement will state that the seller agrees not to enter into the same type of business in the same market area for a given period of time. If the restrictions as to type of business, market area, and time are all reasonable, they will be upheld in court. It is only when these restrictions are unreasonable that a court will hold them to be in violation of the law.

Usury

Most states have passed laws limiting the rate of interest that may be charged for the use of money. Considerable variation exists in the attitudes of the various states when these laws are violated. In some states, when usurious interest is charged, the courts will not aid in collection of principal or interest; in other states, all interest may be forfeited as a result of usury; and in still other states collection of principal and maximum allowable interest results. Borrowing by corporations is listed as an exception in most state laws.

Wagering Contracts

In most states wagering contracts are illegal. It is often difficult for the courts to determine whether a particular contract is a legitimate business transaction or a wager. The test used by the courts in making their determination is centered about the creation of the risk involved. Is a risk created for the purpose of bearing that risk? If so, the contract is deemed a wager. In a dice game, on the first throw, a total of seven or eleven on the two dice pays off for the holder of the dice. The two bettors have created a risk of loss by placing their bets before the dice are thrown, with the score on the dice determining who shall lose his money. In a business contract calling for future delivery of a commodity for the payment of a present price, risk of loss resulting from a change in price of the commodity between the present and the delivery date is assumed by the parties. Has a risk been created for the purpose of assuming it? The courts answer no, providing future delivery is actually intended. Manipulations in the stock and commodity markets are often open to this criticism

2. See Reiner v. North American Newspaper Alliance, 181 N.E. 561 (1930), in which a contract to breach the contract of passage on the Graf Zeppelin was held illegal.

in that the final result in the contract is, and was originally intended by the parties to be a transfer of money rather than commodity.

Others

A contract to withhold evidence in a court case is unlawful; so are contracts that tend to promote litigation. This is one reason why contingency fees for attorneys or others connected with a trial are frowned upon. If a would-be plaintiff stands to lose nothing in a court case, this is an actual incentive for him to undertake the litigation.

A large category of unlawful contracts is included in those which either restrain marriage or promote a divorce action. The courts do everything within their power to promote matrimony and to restrain its dissolution.

Contracts that are immoral in subject matter or tend to promote immorality are declared by the courts to be unlawful and against public policy.

CONTRARY TO PUBLIC POLICY

Contracts must conform to the common law and statutory regulation to be lawful and enforceable. However, these are not the only limitations imposed by the courts on contract subject matter. In addition to the requirement that contracts conform to the written and unwritten laws of the community, the courts require conformity to public policy. *Public policy* is rather difficult to define because it is continuously changing. It must change to conform to changing ideas and changing technology, just as city planning, for example, has had to change to incorporate cloverleafs and jet transportation. Generally, those contracts which would be held contrary to public policy are those which, if allowed, would be injurious to society in some way. It is not necessary that someone, or the public in general, be injured by the performance of the contract. Courts frequently have held that a contract may be unenforceable because of an *evil tendency* found to be present in it. Unenforceability because of the "evil tendency" of a contract is particularly characteristic of contracts in which the judgment or decision of public officials might be (or has been) altered by the contracts. In fact, any contract that tends to cause corruption of a public official may be subject to censure in the courts. This brings up a rather sensitive problem with which the courts often are faced—What acts of lobbying are to be condoned? First, the end sought to be accomplished must be a lawful objective—one which, if accomplished, would improve the public welfare, or at least would do it no harm. Second, the means

used must be above reproach. Generally, a lobbyist must be registered as such; his lobbying practices must not involve threats or bribery or secret deals.

Courts generally treat contingent fees as being against public policy. Assume Green to be hired as consultant for an engineering design job, with payment to depend on his achieving acceptance of the design by political officials. Green, being human, might be tempted to go beyond what is considered right and ethical to obtain his fee. In the court's eyes, contingent fees are an inducement to the use of sinister and corrupt means of gaining the desired objective. Although the court may in certain cases overlook the presence of contingent fees, it nearly always detracts from the case presented by the proposed recipient of the fee.

Fraud or Deception

A contract that has the effect of practicing fraud or deception on a third person is against public policy. Black agrees to pay White $1000 if White (a prominent nuclear engineer) will recommend Black to Gray for a job as a nuclear engineer. White knows nothing of Black's qualifications for the job. Even though White wrote the recommendation and Black succeeded in getting the job, it is likely that White could not get the $1000 by court action. The contract would be void as against public policy. In contrast, payment for a recommendation from an employment agency would be quite enforceable. The employment agency is in the business of recommending people for jobs for a fee. Thus, those who hire employees through an employment agency have knowledge of the usual arrangement; those who hire based upon individual recommendations have a right to assume that such recommendations are given freely and without prejudice.

Breach of Trust or Confidence

Contracts that breach a trust or a confidential relationship are against public policy and will not be supported in a court. Agency is one such fiduciary relationship—the agent acts for his principal in dealing with others. White, as Black's agent, contracts with Green for the purchase of steel. Unknown to Black, White is to receive a five percent kickback from Green for placing the order with him. Even though the steel purchase occurred, the five percent kickback agreement could not be enforced in court.

Contracts having the effect of compounding a crime are against public policy; tax evasion agreements are unlawful. In general, almost any contract that is intended to be hidden from the public for reason other than national security is questionable. The agreements mentioned here represent only a few areas in which public policy sharply restricts the right to contract.

Sources of Public Policy

Public policy is to be found in the federal and state constitutions, in statutes, in judicial decisions, and in the decisions and practices of government agencies. Lacking these, the court must depend upon its own sense of moral duty and justice for its decision.

EFFECT OF ILLEGALITY

The general principle followed by the court in dealing with the subject matter of contract is that no action will be allowed in law or in equity if it is based upon an illegal agreement. That is, court actions based upon agreements that are illegal, immoral, against public policy, have as their purpose the commission of a crime, or are forbidden by statute will not be enforced. In the interest of justice and fairness this principle has been slightly tempered in certain cases.

The reason for the court's dismissing unlawful contracts as void is that the defense of illegality is allowed, not as a protective device for the defendant but as a disability to the plaintiff. The public is better protected against dishonest transactions if the court places this stumbling block in the path of those attempting to avoid the law. Suppose a member of a gang of thieves, upon being cheated out of his share of the loot, went into court to try to force a split. What should the court do as to the division of the spoils? The court would contend that the agreement to split is void, being based on a crime. The public interest is best served if the court does everything in its power to discourage the crime. Thus, as far as the loot-splitting is concerned, the case would be dismissed.

Public interest, then, is the determining factor in such cases. The court's decision is based upon its opinion of what would be the greatest aid to the public. If the public interest would be promoted better by a decision for the plaintiff, the court will so decide. Consider a confidence game in which the victim is placed somewhat afoul of the law by his agreement with the confidence men (as is usually the case). Swallowing pride and guilt alike, the victim asks the court to order the return of his money. The court may decide to do just that as a discouragement to continued practice of such con games on the public.

Disaffirmance of an illegal contract while the illegal portion of the agreement is still executory will allow the person disaffirming to recover lawful consideration given by him. A person paying money to another to have him commit a crime ordinarily may disaffirm the contract so that the crime may be stopped and thus obtain restoration of his money. Here again, the public interest is the determining factor, with the court acting as the representative of the public.

VAN HOSEN v. BANKERS TRUST COMPANY
200 N.W. 2d 504 (1972)

Rawlings, Justice

By action in equity plaintiff Hugh Van Hosen seeks declaratory relief from the forfeiture provision of a private pension plan established by defendant Bankers Trust Company and administered by it as trustee. Trial court adjudged the controverted proviso violative of public policy, therefore void and unenforceable. Defendants appeal. We affirm.

Van Hosen worked for defendant bank almost 33 years prior to his resignation in 1967. Starting as a messenger he ultimately became a vice-president and manager of installment loans. While so employed certain pension and profit-sharing plans were initiated and at times amended by the bank. Among them was the instantly involved "Bankers Trust Company Primary and Supplemental Pension Plan and Trust Agreement." Relevant provisions thereof will be later set forth.

Upon termination of his aforesaid employment, plaintiff sold insurance with a Des Moines agency for about 18 months. He was then offered a position in the commercial loan department of another Des Moines bank, admittedly an institution in competition with defendant bank. Thereupon Van Hosen requested a waiver by defendant of the subject pension forfeiture clause. After some apparently unavoidable delay, during which plaintiff accepted proffered employment with the competing institution, his requested forfeiture waiver was refused. Defendant bank has since withheld retirement benefits payable to plaintiff under the plan here involved. Incidentally no issue regarding trade secrets is instantly presented.

In support of their appeal, defendants contend (1) the forfeiture provision is not a part of the plaintiff's employment compensation, and not in restraint of trade, (2) the court may enforce a forfeiture provision in a pension plan to that extent reasonably necessary to protect the employer's legitimate interest without imposing undue hardship upon the employee so long as public interest is not adversely affected. We shall deal generally with these propositions.

I. Any attempt to rationalize the fractionated postulates heretofore enunciated on the subject at hand would serve to unduly extend this opinion. . . .

II. *Murphy* v. *R. J. Reynolds Tobacco Co.* involved a problem akin to that instantly presented. In the cited case we approvingly quoted this from *Cantor* v. *Berkshire Life Ins. Co.*

" 'The concept of employees' rights and of the place of the so-called fringe benefits in relationship to employees' remuneration has undergone a substantial change in recent years.

. . . .

" 'There has been . . . in recent years a gradual trend away from the gratuity theory of pensions. The courts, recognizing that a consideration flows to an employer as a result of such pension plans, in the form of a more stable and a more contented labor force, have determined that such arrangements will give rise to contractual rights enforceable by the employee who has complied with all the conditions of the plan, even though he has made no actual monetary contribution to the fund.' "

To the same effect as 1A Corbin on Contracts, sec. 153, at 18–20:

"A promise by an employer to pay a bonus or a pension to an employee in case the latter continues to serve for a stated period is not enforceable when made; but the employee can accept the offer by continuing to serve as requested, even though he makes no promise. There is no mutuality of obligation; but there is sufficient consideration in the form of service rendered. Indeed, the employer's offered promise becomes irrevocable by him as soon as the employee has rendered any substantial service in the process of accepting; and this is true in spite of the fact that the employee may be privileged to quit the service at any time."

It is thus evident plaintiff's action stands squarely in contract and this is true whether defendants' pension program be characterized as a contributory or noncontributory plan.

III. These are the relevant portions of the Agreement here involved.

Under Article III "competing institution" is defined as a financial organization doing a correspondent bank business or any financial enterprise in Des Moines, Polk County, Iowa.

Article XI provides, in essence, a participating "member," upon completion of 20 or more years' continuous regular service with defendant bank shall, upon leaving for any reason, have a vested right under the Agreement, subject to the following material part of Article XII: "In the event a Member shall become employed by a competing institution without the consent of the board of directors of the Bank, . . . then in . . . such event all of the rights of such Member, and the rights of any person claiming by, through, or under such Member, to benefits under the terms of this Plan shall be *forfeited and terminated;* and, in the event that any annuity benefits shall have been purchased for such Member, such benefits shall be terminated both as to the rights of such Member thereunder or the rights of any joint annuitant or other beneficiary thereunder and such benefits as may thereafter accrue under the terms of any such annuity shall be paid to the Trustee and applied by the Trustee to the costs of administering the Plan." (Emphasis supplied)

"Forfeited," in the contractual sense, ordinarily means the taking away or loss of rights and interest in property. . . .

Forfeiture is also here unquestionably made positive and interminable by conjunctive use of the word "terminate." This terminology unquestionably denotes an expiration, extinction, and cessation of all affected contractual rights. . . .

From the foregoing flows the unavoidable conclusion that under the terms of Article XII, if it be held enforceable, plaintiff forever lost any and all rights held under the Agreement by merely becoming an employee of a competing institution.

IV. Trial court likened Article XII to restraints on postemployment competition, sometimes contained in employer-employee contracts. In so doing the court leaned heavily on *Baker* v. *Starkey,* and thereupon found Article XII, being in restraint of trade, was violative of public policy, therefore unenforceable. . . .

In that regard, as heretofore disclosed, various courts have recently espoused diametrically opposing views on the subject at hand. Some hold such a pension forfeiture clause as that now before us, unlike those restraints often embodied in employment contracts, does not preclude a benefited retiree from engaging in work for a competitor of the pension-paying former employer, therefore is not in restraint of trade. . . . Other courts have held the threat of economic loss to a pension recipient by affiliation with a competitor of the former employer constitutes, in effect, an impermissible restraint on competition. . . .

For reasons later revealed, however, it is neither essential nor do we here adopt trial court's analogical approach, or the divergent concepts enunciated in *Rochester* and *Food Fair Stores,* supra.

V. It should be inceptionally understood:

"(A) man is permitted to make a contract which will result in a forfeiture, and when it is clear from the terms of the contract that the parties have so agreed, a court of equity, as well as a court of law, will enforce the forfeiture. . . . If one contracts for a forfeiture, while the law will scan it closely and will look upon it with disfavor, yet as a part of the contract it must be enforced. . . . While it is true forfeitures are not favored in the law, they are not outlaws. In *Fairgrave* v. *Illinois Bankers Life Association* we said: 'If the parties have by the terms of their agreement fixed the consequences of a forfeiture on the violation of it, this becomes the law of their contract, and by it they are to be governed.'. . .

On the other hand, since forfeitures are not favored, those claiming them should show the equities are clearly on their side. . . .

In the absence of a statute declaring void any such *in terrorem* provision as that contained in Article XII, and we have none, the enforceability of a contractual divestiture is usually determined by application of the public policy or reasonableness standard. This in turn necessitates a balancing of interests. . . .

It also appears preestimated liquidated damages are, as a rule, similarly evaluated. . . .

So we resort to a weighing of interests in order to determine the enforceability or unenforceability of Article XII. If that proviso be found reasonable then it is enforceable. Conversely, in event such imposes an unconscionable burden on plaintiff it will be deemed unenforceable.

VI. First to be considered is defendant-employer's objective in providing for a divestment of pension rights acquired by a former employee who engaged in post-termination competition.

As indicated by the quote in *Murphy* v. *R. J. Reynolds Tobacco Co.,* . . . an employer's basic purpose in creating an employee pension program is to encourage loyal and productive career service on the part of all possible participants. In fairness it must be conceded that most if not all employers, like employees, are participating

in a constant struggle for survival. To that end they must make every reasonable effort to gain and hold the good will of all possible customers.

It is thus apparent that in the organization and administration of an employee pension program an employer does have legitimate business interests at stake, including good will, as to which he is entitled to reasonable protection.

But there are counterbalancing factors which must also be evaluated.

Under existing economic conditions a person accepting employment will generally evaluate both take-home pay and fringe benefits. In any event, when a career employee retires, either voluntarily or involuntarily, he or she often experiences a traumatic economic change. Furthermore, many pensioners cannot, at the moment, qualify for social security and must resort to other employment for supplementary income. Usually, in such cases, work openings in the employee's accustomed field of endeavor are not readily available. And if such a position is obtained, comparatively inconsequential or no attendant marginal benefits are ordinarily provided, or ultimately acquired.

Also, while engaged in working for a second employer, such pension rights as may have been acquired during service with a prior employer are, to the retiree, relatively insignificant. But when retirement from any subsequent employment occurs, the result can be chaotic, absent restoration of any pension rights acquired through extended service with a prior employer. The harshness of such a situation is self-evident.

Moreover, private pension plans have a humanitarian purpose in that, like employment security, they extend to those benefited some degree of financial independence at a time when earning ability and related income may be impaired or ended. See The Code 1971, Section 96.2. It is in turn evident these programs have become increasingly vital to our socioeconomic community welfare. By the same token society today has a material interest in the orderly development and administration of all pension plans, public or private. Thus public policy comes into play. . . .

It therefore follows, the infinite forfeiture and termination of all pension rights instantly acquired by plaintiff through prior affiliation with defendant bank, merely by accepting employment with a competing institution, imposes an unjust and uncivic penalty on plaintiff at the same time disproportionately benefiting these defendants.

We now hold Article XII of the Agreement, being so unreasonable as to be in violation of public policy, is accordingly unenforceable.

VII. Trial court, in reaching the same result, did so upon a different premise from that here adopted. But such is of no consequence. . . .

Affirmed.

REVIEW QUESTIONS

1. Black, an engineer, agrees to act as an expert witness for White in a court case. In return, Black is to receive $500 plus expenses for his services. Is the contract lawful? Why or why not?

2. In the above example, assume that Black agrees to accept $1200 if White wins, or payment for expenses only if White loses. Is the contract lawful? Why or why not?

3. Gray is a process engineer for Brown. Green has made the low bid on equipment for a manufacturing operation which Gray had begun setting up. The equipment meets the specifications as well as equipment proposed by other bidders. To improve the chance for acceptance of his bid, Green offered to give Gray two percent of the bid price if Green's equipment is used. If the equipment is bought, can Gray get the two percent? After receiving the two percent offer, what if anything, should Gray have done about it?

4. Explain why an insurance contract is not a wagering contract.

5. What is *public policy*?

6. Give two reasons why contingency fees are looked upon with disfavor by courts.

7. In the case of *Van Hosen* v. *Bankers Trust Company* the employee's acts clearly violated a provision of the pension section of his employment contract. Outline the legal reasoning by which the court affirmed the judgment for the employee.

11

Statute of Frauds

An oral contract is generally just as enforceable as a written contract, but a written one has at least one major advantage—its terms are easier to ascertain. The relationships of the parties are set forth for interpretation by the individuals concerned and by a court of law if need for the court should arise. Although it is true that in most circumstances an oral contract is as good as a written one, it is sound common sense to put into writing any contract of more than a trivial nature.

In England during the reign of Charles II, the courts were faced with many cases concerning oral agreements. Instances of perjured testimony were frequent as the contending parties attempted to prove or disprove the existence or terms of contracts. In 1677, the English Statute of Frauds was passed as "An Act for the Prevention of Frauds and Perjuries" to relieve the courts of the necessity of considering certain types of contracts unless their terms were set forth in writing and signed. The statute does not require a formally drawn instrument. The only writing required is the minimum needed to establish the material provisions of the agreement. The writing need not be all on one instrument, but if it is not, a connection between them must be apparent from the documents themselves. The statute does not require a signature from both parties. Only the defendant must have signed. The signature itself may consist of initials, be rubber stamped, in ink or pencil, or apparently anything intended by the party to constitute identification and assent; it may appear anywhere on the document.

The English Statute of Frauds consisted of several sections, but only the sections numbered four and seventeen are of major importance to us today. These two sections have become law in all of the states in the United States with only minor modifications of the original statute. The principles are the same.

Fourth and Seventeenth Sections

According to the fourth section, "no action shall be brought" on certain types of contracts unless the agreement that is the basis for such action is in writing and signed by the defendant or his agent. The following types of contracts are specified in the fourth section:

1. Promises of an executor or an administrator of an estate to pay the debts of the deceased from the executor's or administrator's own estate.
2. Promises to act as surety for the debt of another.
3. Promises based upon marriage as a consideration.
4. Promises involving real property.
5. Promises that cannot be performed within a year.

The seventeenth section states the requirements for an enforceable contract having to do with the sale of goods, wares, or merchandise. It says that unless one of three things is done to secure such a transaction where the consideration is at least ten pounds sterling, the contract will be unenforceable at law. Either:

1. Part of the goods, wares, or merchandise must be accepted by the buyer, or
2. The buyer must pay something in earnest toward the cost of the goods, or
3. Some note or memorandum of the agreement must be made and signed.

The ten pounds sterling minimum has been changed to $500 by each of the states with the adoption of the Uniform Commercial Code.

Promises of Executors or Administrators

In law an executor is a person appointed in a will by the *testator*[1] to execute, or put in force, the terms of the instrument. An administrator serves a somewhat similar function where the deceased died without a will (*intestate*). He is appointed by a court to collect the assets of the estate of the deceased, pay its debts, and distribute the remaining estate to those entitled to it by law.

If the executor or administrator of an estate agrees to pay the debts of the deceased out of his own estate, he is acting as *surety* for the debt of another. In effect,

---

1. Person making the will.

he is saying: "If the estate of the deceased is insufficient to pay you, I will pay the debt." This situation is covered under surety contracts, below.

Promises to Act as Surety

The requirement that a contract to answer for the debt, default, or miscarriage of another person must be in writing covers all types of guaranty and surety contracts. Lending institutions frequently require either collateral or a responsible cosigner as security for a loan. If White wishes to borrow $1000 from Black Loan Company, a cosigner may be required for the loan. If Gray is to act as surety, agreeing to pay if White does not pay, such a contract must be in writing to be enforceable against Gray.

It is appropriate here to distinguish between *primary and secondary promises*. An oral primary promise is enforceable but an oral secondary promise is not. Wording of the promise can be quite important, but the apparent intent of the promisor when the promise is made is even more important. If the wording and other facts make clear an intent such that "If White does not pay, I will" it is a secondary promise. However, if the circumstances show the intent to be that "I will pay White's loan" the promise is a primary one. The primary promise is enforceable against the promisor if it is made either orally or in writing. Similarly, where the defendant had agreed to make good any loss sustained by the plaintiff if the plaintiff would act as surety for a third party, the defendant's promise was held to be primary in nature and enforceable against him even though the promise was oral.[2] This comes closer to an undertaking of indemnity or insurance than surety.

Indemnity (insurance) contracts need not be in writing. Under such contracts no liability is held to exist until obligation arises between the insured and some third party.

Promises in Consideration of Marriage

Marriage is the highest consideration known to law. This provision of the statute of frauds applies particularly to situations in which the agreement to marry is based upon consideration such as a marriage settlement. If Mr. White agreed to pay Black $10,000 in consideration of marriage to White's daughter, the contract would have to be in writing to be enforceable. The statement that contracts in which marriage is to be a consideration must be in writing does not mean that when a man and woman simply agree to get married, with neither giving up anything but his unmarried

status, such an agreement would have to be in writing. Under common law oral mutual promises to marry are quite actionable at law if one of the parties attempts to breach his promise.

Real Property Transactions

Transactions involving "lands, tenements, and hereditaments" (i.e., real property) must be in writing to be enforceable at law.

Real property law is treated more thoroughly in Chapter 19. It is necessary here, however, to make some distinction between real and personal property. *Real property* is anciently defined as consisting of land and those things permanently attached to it, or *immovables*. *Personal property,* then, includes the *movables,* or things not firmly attached to the land. These definitions comprise only a part of the distinction currently applied by the courts.

The courts also distinguish between *fructus naturales* and *fructus industriales*. Fructus naturales is usually held to consist of things present on or in the land that are not the product of human attention or cultivation. Minerals in the soil, trees on the land, and natural grass, for instance, are fructus naturales, and are considered by the courts as real property requiring a writing for their sale. An exception exists, though, in dealing with these natural fruits of the land. When the contract contemplates immediate severance or removal of these things, an oral contract to such effect will be enforceable. Black orally sells White a stand of timber to be cut and sold by White with Black to receive payment as cutting proceeds. If cutting is to begin immediately the oral contract is enforceable; if it is to begin ten months from now, it is unenforceable under current interpretations of the statute. Fructus industriales are those things, such as cultivated crops, which result from human effort. An oral contract in which such things are to be a consideration is enforceable. For instance, a contract to sell the fruit in an orchard as it ripens would be enforceable under the statute of frauds, even though made orally.

Lease contracts involve an interest in land but, for most purposes, are considered as personal property. An oral lease for a year or less is valid, but a lease must be in writing if it is to run longer than a year.

Part performance of an oral contract for the purchase of real property can influence the court to disregard the statute of frauds. It is only in an unusual case, however, that the courts will enforce such an oral contract. It must be a case in which the extent of improvements made by the buyer is so vast and material

---

2. Gilinsky v. Klionsky, 251 N.Y.S. 570.

as to make it unjust to hold the oral agreement unenforceable. In such circumstances an equity court may decree for specific performance by the seller.

Promises Requiring More Than a Year to Perform

The legal interpretation of a *year* is important here. Generally, the time starts to run from the time of making the agreement, not from the time when performance is begun. An oral contract, then, to work for another for a year, starting two days from now, would be unenforceable under the statute of frauds. In most jurisdictions it is held that parts of days do not count in the running of time. If a contract is made today, time will start to run on that contract tomorrow.

The statute refers to contracts "not to be performed within one year of the making thereof." The court interpretation of this statement is that it means contracts which, by their terms, *cannot* be performed within one year. White promises orally to pay Black $80,000 if he (Black) will build a certain house for him. No time limit is set on the construction. The fact that actual construction took place over a two-year period would not bring the contract under the statute of frauds. If the contract could be completed within one year, an oral contract for its performance is binding. By this reasoning, a contract to work for someone "for life" or to support someone "for life" is capable of being performed in one year and need not be in writing to be binding.

If an oral contract, performance of which is to take place in less than a year, is extended from time to time by increments of less than a year, but in such a way that performance continues for more than a year, such a contract is valid. For instance, an oral lease contract for nine months might be continued orally at the end of the period to run to eighteen months.

Sale of Goods

A large majority of the states have adopted the Uniform Commercial Code, which governs the transfer of goods, wares, and merchandise within those states. It incorporates the seventeenth section of the statute of frauds in slightly altered wording.

If the transaction undertaken involves goods of a value great enough to be governed by the statute of frauds in the particular state, an oral agreement will be valid only if (1) part of the goods are accepted by the buyer, or if (2) the buyer pays part of the purchase price in earnest, or (3) signs some note or memorandum as to the terms of the sale. Payment of part of the purchase price may be made in money or in anything of value to the parties.

What actually constitutes goods, wares, and merchandise under the statute has led the courts into some difficulty on occasion. It is apparent that if the goods exist, a contract for their sale will involve merely passage of title to those goods. However, if the contract is for the purchase of goods not now in existence but to be made by the seller, there is a question as to whether this is not a contract for services to be performed. A contract for services would not involve the seventeenth section of the statute of frauds. Generally, the courts have settled upon what is known as the *Massachusetts Rule* for the answer to that question. According to the Massachusetts Rule, if a contract is made for the purchase of goods not in existence at the time, coverage by the seventeenth section will depend upon the nature of those goods. If the goods are the usual product of the seller and are made by him for an established market, the seventeenth section will apply. If the goods are specially made for the particular buyer under an oral contract with him, he will be obligated to take them. Black wishes to purchase a gate to match a very old wrought iron fence around his house. Black contracts orally with White to have such a gate specially made for him. The contract will be enforced. This, of course, is a logical rule since the gate probably would be unsaleable to anyone else.

Effect of the Statute

The words "no action shall be brought" on oral contracts that should have been in writing according to the statute of frauds do not render the contracts either voidable or void. Such a contract may still be valid for some purposes. Where one party has performed his obligations under such an oral contract, he has probably enriched the other party. A court of equity may recognize the obligation created by such a performance and enforce payment by the other party under a quasi-contract. Generally, when the result would be inequitable or grossly unfair, the courts will not allow the statute to stand as a defense.

Where the oral contract that should have been written is either completely executory or completely executed, the courts will not consider it. The parties, generally, are left where they are found.

MAZZOTTA v. GORA
110 A. 2d 295, 19 Conn. Sup. 96 (1954)

Fitzgerald, Judge

In this action the plaintiff is seeking to recover of the defendants, husband and wife, the sum of $684 for the plastering of their home on Barbara Road, Middletown, while under construction by a general contractor. Since the decision turns on technical aspects, the essential facts require a general statement.

On September 24, 1951, the defendants entered into a written contract with one Fred Dean, a building contractor, for the construction of a dwelling house and incidentals connected therewith. The total cost was to be $12,500, payable in specified installments as the work progressed. The plaintiff is also a contractor and specializes in masonry work. On February 26, 1952, he entered into a written subcontract with Dean in which he agreed to build the fireplace in the defendants' house and plaster certain rooms therein. The agreed total price to be paid the plaintiff by Dean was $1,134. This latter contract did not provide for installment payments as the work thereunder progressed.

The plaintiff built the fireplace in the following month over a four-day period. Dean found fault with the plaintiff's work, taking the position that the placement of the fireplace was several inches at variance with its proper location. As a result the plaintiff quit the job without commencing the plastering work. It does not appear that the defendants had any altercation with Dean or the plaintiff regarding the variance in the placement of the fireplace. Neither up to that time nor at any later time did the plaintiff ever receive any money from Dean. Nor did the plaintiff ever file a mechanic's lien against the property to protect his interest.

Sometime in the middle of May 1952 the defendant wife urged the plaintiff to complete the plastering work under his subcontract with Dean. She told the plaintiff that she would shortly be making a $2000 installment payment to Dean through her attorney, and added: "I'll see that you will get your money." She further testified, and the court finds it to be a fact, that she told the plaintiff that she would let him know the day that her check would be turned over to her attorney for transmission to Dean. Such a check, dated June 2, 1952, and cashed by Dean a few days later, was issued by the defendant wife pursuant to the foregoing stipulation. Thereafter Dean defaulted in the balance of his contract with the defendants.

The plaintiff did complete the plastering work after the request of the defendant wife and before the June payment to Dean. In resisting the plaintiff's claim that they are owing money to him for the plastering work, the defendants take the following stand: (1) The plastering work done by the plaintiff is reasonably worth $684 but, contrary to the plaintiff's complaint, there was not in law and in fact an express promise by them to pay for the undertaking; (2) the statement of the defendant wife—"I'll see that you will get your money"—

being oral, is unenforceable under the statute, General Statutes, sec. 8293, as an agreement upon which they can be charged.

It is found that the statement by the defendant wife to the plaintiff—"I'll see that you will get your money"—was never intended by her to signify, or understood by the plaintiff as meaning, that the defendants would become primarily liable for the plastering work to be performed by the plaintiff. Hence the plaintiff must fail in this action. . . .

The short answer to the plaintiff's suggestion that he should be entitled to a recovery in any event under the doctrine of unjust enrichment is that the case as pleaded and tried does not warrant the invoking of that doctrine.

For all that appears, the general contractor in the person of Dean has imposed in a rather vicious manner upon both the plaintiff and the defendants. He has cost the parties hereto money and heartaches. That he has dealt dishonorably with the parties by running out on his contractual obligations with them does not advantage the unfortunate plaintiff in this action against the equally unfortunate defendants.

Judgment is required to be entered for the defendants.

DAVIS v. CROWN CENTRAL PETROLEUM CORPORATION

483 F. 2d 1014 (1973)

Donald Russel, Circuit Judge.

These two cases, combined on hearing because of their similarity of issues, are unfortunate by-products of the current oil shortage. Both plaintiffs and defendant are victims of the shortage in one form or another. They may properly be termed independents in their own particular type of operation. The plaintiffs, both citizens of North Carolina, on the one hand, are small independent oil dealers with their main operations in North Carolina. The defendant, on the other hand, is a refiner, dependent almost entirely on producers for its supply of crude oil. It has for some years been selling its product to the plaintiffs. In anticipation of the oil shortage, which all parties in the industry apparently foresaw, discussions were had among the parties as to future supplies. It is contended by the plaintiffs that the defendant agreed to supply them with certain fixed quantities of gasoline. As the energy crisis deepened, the suppliers of the defendant reduced drastically its supply of crude oil. It accordingly proceeded to allocate on a lower percentage its deliveries to its contract customers and to notify customers such as the plaintiffs, whom it denominated noncontract customers, that it would make no further sales to them. These actions followed that notification. The plaintiff Davis filed his action originally in the Western District of North Carolina, seeking injunctive relief against what he claimed was a breach of contract involving irreparable injury and damages for violation of the Sherman Act. Jurisdiction was based on diversity of citizenship and federal question. The other action was first instituted in the State Court and removed to the District Court for the Middle District of North Carolina. The plaintiff in this action sought similar relief to that demanded in *Davis,* and federal jurisdiction was predicated on similar grounds.[3] Preliminary injunctive relief was sought in both cases by the plaintiffs and were granted in both instances by the District Court having jurisdiction of the actions. It is from these grants of injunctive relief that the defendant has appealed in each case. Since there is similarity both of facts and issues in both cases, we ordered the appeals argued together and we shall dispose of both together. We reverse in both cases.

In granting temporary injunctive relief, the District Court in each instance made specific Findings of Fact. The defendant contends that these Findings show on their face that the temporary injunctive relief was improvidently granted. Specifically, it attacks the Finding made by the District Court in each case that the plaintiffs were likely to prevail eventually on the merits. Such a finding is necessary for the granting of preliminary injunctive relief. . . . This basic contention presents the issue on appeal.

In support of its conclusion that the plaintiffs were likely to prevail, the District Court in each case found that there was an oral agreement between the plaintiff and the defendant whereby the defendant was to supply the plaintiffs with their gasoline requirements. In the *U-Fill 'Er-up* case, the District Court found that, since the plaintiff had expended considerable sums in developing gasoline outlets, termination of supply by the defendant was "not reasonable." It, also, based its conclusion in part at least on considerations of public policy, stating that "as a matter of equity, suppliers should ration their product to historical customers in times of national shortage on a pro rata basis and that this principle has been recognized by the Congress of the United States in passing certain legislation that calls for a pro rata distribution of petroleum products to historical customers based upon the product purchased during a base period defined as the fourth quarter of 1971 and the first three quarters of 1972" and "that the public has a definite interest in preserving a competitive retail gasoline market and the elimination of

the Plaintiff and other independent oil jobbers would be against the public interest." The District Court in that case ordered the defendant to supply the plaintiff U-Fill 'Er-Up with gasoline "on the basis of 2.12% of the total gasoline sold by the Defendant while this Order is in effect."

In the *Davis* case, the District Court found there was an agreement between the plaintiff and the defendant "for the purchase of goods vastly exceeding $500.00," which was "not written nor evidenced by any writing" and which, though obligating defendant to supply the plaintiff as much 1,200,000 gallons per month, did not obligate the plaintiff "to purchase that quantity nor any set quantity of gasoline." Although it recognized that the defendant was suffering hardship too, on account of the oil crisis, the District Court found that "(T)he balance of hardship favors the relief sought by the plaintiff" and "(T)hat the public interest will not be harmed by the issuance of an injunction." It accordingly ordered the defendant to "continue to supply plaintiff with at least 300,000 gallons of gasoline products per month . . . pending further orders of this Court. . . ."

The defendant denied in both cases the existence of any valid agreement. In support of this position, it asserts the alleged agreements are lacking in mutuality and definiteness of duration. Moreover, it argues that if there were any agreement, it was void as violative of the controlling Statute of Frauds. It is conceded by all parties that the North Carolina law is controlling on these several contentions.

We find it necessary to consider only the contention based on the Statute of Frauds. The Findings of Fact in each case make it clear that any agreement between the plaintiffs and the defendant was within the North Carolina Statute of Frauds. That statute, unlike its counterpart in other jurisdictions where its scope is merely remedial, "affects the substance as well as the remedy." . . . On the basis of the present Findings of Fact in each case, the statute would be a complete bar to a ruling that there was a valid contract or agreement between the plaintiffs, on the one hand, and the defendant, on the other. It is true, as the plaintiffs have argued, that in exceptional cases, courts of equity will find an estoppel against the enforcement of the statute, but such an estoppel can arise in North Carolina only "upon grounds of fraud" on the part of him who relies on the statute. . . . The District Court in neither case made a finding of "fraud" on the part of the defendant and, absent such finding, there can be no estoppel. Nor, on the facts in the record before us, would it appear

3. The State Court clearly lacked jurisdiction of the action under the Sherman Act but, whether jurisdiction existed after and as result of removal to Federal Court, *see* Freeman v. Bee Machine Co. . . .

that any such finding would have been in order. In *United Merchants & Mfrs.* v. *South Carolina El. & G. Co.* (1953) . . . it was stated:

" 'A mere failure or refusal to perform an oral contract, within the statute, is not such fraud, within the meaning of this rule, as will take the case out of the operation of the statute, and this is ordinarily true even though the other party has changed his position to his injury."

After all, as the District Court in one of the cases observed, the plight of the defendant was not substantially different from that of the plaintiffs. It was experiencing hardships which forced it to take action it obviously did not relish.

The claim of the plaintiffs is appealing and our sympathies are with them. As the District Courts indicated, it is equitable in periods of scarcity of basic materials for the Government to inaugurate a program of mandatory allocations of the materials. This, however, is a power to be exercised by the legislative branch of Government. The power of the Court extends only to the enforcement of valid contracts and does not comprehend the power to make mandatory allocations of scarce products on the basis of any consideration of the public interest. Public reports indicate that Congress is cognizant of the problem presented by these actions and is giving active consideration to the establishment of a program of mandatory allocations that would apply from the oil producer down to the oil retailer. It is earnestly hoped that Congress will take the necessary steps to establish such controls. For that control, however, the parties must look to the Congress and not to the Courts.

The District Courts were in clear error in finding on the record before them that there was the reasonable likelihood that the plaintiffs would prevail on the merits. For that reason, the granting of injunctive relief during the pendency of the actions was improper in both cases and the injunctions are hereby vacated.

Reversed.

Butzner, Circuit Judge, dissents.

McCOLLUM v. BENNETT

Ill. App., 424 N.E. 2d 90 (1981)

Stouder, Justice:

This is an appeal from a judgment of the circuit court of Peoria County in favor of the defendants, Harvey and Catherine Bennett, and against the plaintiffs, Robert and Mona McCollum. On January 31, 1976, the parties executed an agreement, the pertinent part of

which reads: "We, Harvey M. & Catherine A. Bennett agree to sell said Business known as Harvey's Towing and Used Auto Parts & Property located at 1601 S.W. Adams St." The crux of the issue in the instant case is the meaning of the aforementioned passage. Plaintiffs contend that the passage refers not only to the business and personal property located at the address mentioned, but to the real property there as well. Defendants agree that the passage refers to the business and personal property but contend that it does not refer to real property.

In March 1976 the plaintiffs filed suit for specific performance of the agreement. They then filed an amended complaint requesting instead damages for breach of the agreement. The defendants filed an answer to the amended complaint admitting they operated the towing business, that the parties had executed the agreement, and that the agreement states in part that the defendant agreed to sell the business and property located at 1601 S.W. Adams Street. Defendants also asserted their readiness to perform the terms of the agreement. In response to the plaintiffs' request for admission of facts, defendants admitted that the lot at that address matched the legal address listed in the request for admission.

In May 1980 plaintiffs filed a second amended complaint. The second amended complaint alleged that the agreement was for the sale of real property as well as personal property. Defendants filed a motion to dismiss, raising the issues of the Statute of Frauds and election of remedy. The trial judge granted defendants' motion to dismiss the complaint with prejudice for the reason that the agreement sued on "is in violation of the Statute of Frauds in that the alleged real estate to be sold is not described or mentioned in the contract, and further that the contract does not contain the essential terms and conditions of the alleged agreement upon which the claim for damage is based."

On appeal, plaintiffs raise three issues: (1) whether the agreement violated the Statute of Frauds; (2) whether the plaintiffs waived their right to assert the Statute of Frauds; and (3) whether the doctrine of election of remedy precludes plaintiffs from amending their complaint from specific performance to recovery of damages. We affirm.

We initially deal with whether the agreement violated the Statute of Frauds. We believe the trial court's holding that the Statute of Frauds was violated was correct. There is nothing in the terms of the written agreement that indicates an agreement that the defendants were selling the real property located 1601 S.W. Adams Street. It merely recites that the business and property located at that address are to be sold by the defendants and purchased by the plaintiffs. As the trial court stated, the real property to be sold is not mentioned in the written agreement, nor are any of the terms and conditions mentioned. Therefore, any agreement between the parties to sell the real property was oral and, therefore, unenforceable under the Statute of Frauds, unless this defense was waived by the defendants.

Therefore, we next examine plaintiff's second issue: whether the defendants waived the defense of the Statute of Frauds. We find no such waiver. The plaintiffs correctly state that the Statute of Frauds may be waived by an acknowledgement of the agreement and the subject matter thereof. However, in the instant case, while the defendants admit the existence of an agreement, they have steadfastly denied that the agreement referred to real property. Plaintiffs contend that the defendants' admission that the property 1601 S.W. Adams Street was the same as the legal description contained in plaintiffs' request for admission of facts is evidence of an agreement to sell the real property. We disagree. Simply admitting that the address of real property conforms to its legal description is inadequate to prove the existence of an agreement to sell that real property. In the absence of any evidence showing defendants acknowledged an agreement to sell the real property, we find no waiver of the defense of the Statute of Frauds.

Because we hold that any agreement to sell the real property is unenforceable under the Statute of Frauds, we need not reach plaintiffs' final issue. Accordingly, the judgment of the trial court of Peoria County is affirmed.

Affirmed.

Barry and Heiple, JJ., concur.

REVIEW QUESTIONS

1. Why is a written contract better than an oral one?
2. Name three ways in which the seventeenth section of the English Statute of Frauds differs from the fourth section.
3. What is the difference between *surety* and *insurance* or *indemnity*?
4. Are the following things real property or personal property?
   a. A gas-operated water heater.
   b. A bird bath.
   c. Flowers and shrubs in a flower bed.
   d. A television aerial mounted on a roof.
   e. A window-mounted air conditioner.
5. Black orally contracts with White to build a brick garage for Black for $5000. When the garage is finished Black refuses to pay the price claiming that the garage is an addition to real property and, therefore, should have been in writing to be enforceable. Can White collect? Why or why not?
6. Green orally contracts with the Gray Die Shop to build a punch press die for $2,000. The production for which Green was going to use the die is cancelled and Green refuses to accept and pay for the die. Gray claims that the contract was for a service and, thus, he is entitled to payment. Green points out that dies are the usual product of the shop and, therefore, that the contract had to be in writing to be enforceable. Who is right? Why?
7. In *Mazzotta* v. *Gora* the defendant stated, "I'll see that you will get your money." This sounds like a primary promise. Why did the court hold it to be a secondary promise?
8. In *Davis* v. *Crown Central Petroleum Corporation,* suppose Crown Central had arranged binding contracts with all its outlets to supply them based on their "needs." What recourse would it have if its supply of crude oil were suddenly cut in half?
9. In the case of *McCollum* v. *Bennett,* the statement in question refers to ". . . Business known as Harvey's Towing and Used Auto Parts & Property located at 1601 S.W. Adams St." Would it have been unreasonable for the court to interpret this to mean *all* property at that address, both personal and real?

12

Third Party Rights

A contract is a voluntary, intentional, and personal relationship. The parties involved determine the rights and obligations to be exchanged. Ordinarily, only those who are directly involved have rights stemming from the contract. In law, the relationship between parties to a contract is known as *privity of contract;* generally, only a person who is *in privity* with another may enforce his rights in the contract.

Strict interpretation of the privity of contract principle would prevent some common transactions of considerable value and convenience in our economy. Therefore, the courts recognize two major exceptions:

1. Rights assigned by a party to a contract to a third party are enforceable by the third party.
2. Rights arising from third-party beneficiary contracts are enforceable by the beneficiary.

Assignment

Probably the most common form of assignment occurs when an indebtedness which is not yet due is assigned to another for value. In payment for a machinery installation, the White Company holds a $10,000 note to be paid by Black six months from now. If the White Company finds itself in need of funds, it may be able to sell this right to payment from Black to someone else (possibly a local bank). The bank would pay something less than face value (known as *discounting*) and then take over Black's note with the same rights White had.

Assignment involves at least three parties. The *obligor* (or debtor) is the party to the original contract who now finds that because of the assignment he owes his obligation to someone not in privity of contract with him. The *obligee* (or creditor, or assignor) is the person to whom the obligor originally owed the duty to perform. Now, because of the assignment, the right to that performance has been delegated to another. The *assignee* is the one to whom the obligor now owes the duty of performance.

Most contract rights are assignable if there is no stipulation to the contrary in the contract. Generally, an assignment in violation of a contract provision renders the contract voidable at the option of the obligor.

Assignment Parties

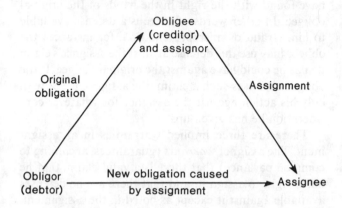

Contract rights to personal services and services based on the skill of an individual are treated exceptionally; and it seems right that they should be. If Black contracts to perform personal services for White, it should not be possible to force him into a choice of either performing those services for a third person or breaching his contract. The same reasoning applies where the rights involved are in the nature of a trust or confidence (services of a lawyer, for example).

Rights and Duties. Rights can be effectively assigned, but not duties. At least, one cannot relieve himself of liability for nonperformance or poor performance by delegating his duties to someone else. The duties may be delegated to another, but the person delegating the duties is still responsible for their performance. He is essentially a *guarantor* of the performance. Black hires White to build a structure. White subcontracts the plumbing to Gray. White's subcontract with Gray does not relieve White of his responsibility for Black's structure, including the plumbing. But White is only responsible as guarantor if he was the one to deal with Gray. His responsibility is relieved if Black makes the plumbing arrangements with Gray.

Assignment differs from *novation*. In a novation both rights and duties are effectively transferred. The distinction depends upon the number of parties involved. If all three parties agree to the substitution of one party for another, the effect is a new agreement by means of a novation. Assignment of rights requires only an agreement between assignor and assignee. The obligor or debtor must, of course, be informed of the assignment if it is to be binding on him. Also, the obligation must be made no greater as a result of the assignment—the obligor may not be forced to do more than he originally agreed to do.

Assignee's Rights. The assignee (the third party) acquires no better right than the assignor had. His right to performance is subject to any fault the obligor could have found with the right in the hands of the original obligee. In other words, if there is a defense available to him (fraud or misrepresentation, for instance) the obligor may use this defense against the assignee's claim just as he could have against the original obligee. If the obligor exercises such a claim, the assignee is left with only his action against the assignor for whatever consideration he has given up.

There are three implied warranties in an assignment. The assignor *warrants* (guarantees, according to common parlance) that there is a valid claim, that he has a right to assign it, and that there are no defenses available against it except as noted in the assignment. If any of these is not as warranted, the assignee has a right of action against the assignor. However, the assignor does not warrant that the obligor will be able to perform. If the obligor becomes bankrupt, for instance, the assignee may have to settle for considerably less than he bargained. He takes the same risk here as he does in any claim where he is obligee.

If the obligor has made part payment to the assignor, or if he has a counterclaim against the assignor, the right obtained by the assignee may be subject to these claims. Black has a $6000 claim against White for installation of a machine. He assigns this claim to Gray in return for operating cash. If the installation proves to be substantially less than a proper performance, requiring White to spend $1000 more to put it in operating condition, this amount might be used as a set-off against the $6000 claim. As a result, Gray would get only $5000 from White and have to look to Black for the other $1000.

A *gratuitous assignment* creates no rights. If an assignment is made gratuitously (the assignor getting nothing back for it), the assignee gets nothing but a promise of a future gift. Such a promise is unenforceable. Until the assignee actually gets something, the gratuitous assignment may be recalled and avoided at will by the assignor.

Notice. A debtor cannot be charged with nonpayment of his debt if he innocently pays a creditor who has assigned the obligation. To make the assignment legally effective, there must be *notification*. When an assignment of rights is made, the assignee obtains, along with his rights, a practical duty to notify the obligor of the assignment. If such notice is not given and the obligor pays his debt to his original creditor, the obligor's debt is discharged. The assignee is then left with his action for recovery against the assignor. If notice has been given to the obligor and he still pays the assignor, such payment does not discharge the obligor's debt.

It is possible, though unlawful, to make subsequent assignments of the same right. The results as to the respective assignees are somewhat controversial. Some court holdings are based on the argument that after the first assignment the assignor had nothing more to assign; consequently, subsequent assignments are null and void. Another view is taken by other courts. According to them, the first assignee to notify the obligor has priority in his claim. The argument here is that only proper notification completes the assignment. The losers, in either instance, have only their actions against the assignor.

Wages. The assignment of future earnings for a present debt is governed by statute in most states. These statutes vary considerably, some making such assignments void. Many set a maximum amount (e.g., 25 percent) that may be assigned from expected wages. In states where wage assignments are upheld, the right to lawfully assign future wages usually depends upon present employment. One must be presently employed to make an effective assignment of expected wages. Generally, if a person is employed he can assign his wages, even though it might be argued that the employment may be terminated at the option of his employer. However, an unemployed person cannot assign expected wages from hoped-for employment, even though his hopes may be well founded.

Third-Party Beneficiary Contracts

If Black and White make a contract that will benefit Gray, what right does Gray have? The nature of the contract, the intent of the parties, and prior indebtedness existing between them all have bearing on Gray's rights. Courts are not in complete agreement in their holdings in such cases. Given the same set of facts a case may be decided quite differently in two different jurisdictions. Only in insurance contracts is the law regarding third-party beneficiaries likely to be applied uniformly.

Insurance. Probably the most common type of third-party beneficiary contract is the life insurance contract. There are two possibilities relating to the beneficiary's right to recover following death of the insured. First, if the insured has purchased insurance from an insurer, he has the right to name anyone as beneficiary. When the insured dies, the beneficiary has a right of action to enforce his claim against the insurer. White contracts with the Black Insurance Co. to insure his own life, agreeing to pay the stipulated annual premiums, and naming Gray as beneficiary. When White dies, Gray can collect.

The second situation differs from the first in that it is the beneficiary who purchases the insurance. Gray contracts with the Black Insurance Company to insure White's life. Gray agrees to pay the annual premiums and is to be beneficiary. For Gray's right as beneficiary to exist, he must be able to show an *insurable interest* in White's life; he must risk a loss which would occur upon White's death. In other words, there must be some anticipated benefit resulting from White's continued existence. Insurable interest is present where the insured is a member of the beneficiary's immediate family. It does not extend to outsiders unless there is an economic tie involved, as between creditor and debtor or partners in an enterprise.

Insurable interest in property extends to those who have an owner or lien interest in the property or merely possession of it with the attendant risk of loss. Both mortgagor and mortgagee, for instance, have an insurable interest in real estate being purchased under a mortgage contract. There is a limit to the insurable interest created by an economic tie, though; usually the courts will not see justification for insurance very much in excess of the amount of economic benefit expected or the risk of loss involved.

The time when insurable interest must exist differs in the two types of insurance. In life insurance it must be shown to have existed at the time when the insurance contract was made. A later change in the relationship does not serve to terminate the insurance. In property insurance the insurable interest must exist when the loss is suffered.

Donee Beneficiary. An unsealed promise of a future gift is worthless as far as enforceability is concerned. That is, it is worthless if the donee tries to enforce it against the donor—as a contract it is unenforceable for lack of consideration. A *donee beneficiary* and an assignee in a gratuitous assignment are in about the same legal position. The difference between the two types of contracts essentially depends upon the time of the intent to benefit the third party. A contract *created* to benefit a third party is a beneficiary type contract; assignment of a right occurs after formation of a contract. Black is creditor and White is debtor to the extent of $500. If Black gratuitously assigns to Gray his right to collect the $500 from White, Black can renege on

his promise at any time before Gray gets the money; Gray has nothing enforceable from Black until he receives payment. However, he does have an enforceable claim against White. In fact, either Black or Gray may undertake enforcement of the claim against White. In the above example Gray would have been third-party beneficiary if the original contract between Black and White had given him the right to collect the $500. However, his rights would be the same in either case. In neither instance would he have a right of action against his benefactor.

Creditor Beneficiary. Assume that Gray is to receive $500 in payment of an obligation Black owes him. If Black and White make a contract whereby Black's consideration is to be paid for by White's paying $500 to Gray, Gray is a *creditor beneficiary*. As such he may enforce his claim against either Black or White. As a creditor beneficiary Gray is in a stronger position than he is as a donee beneficiary. He may collect from either the promisor or the promisee. He can sue the promisee on the previous debt or he can elect to force the promisor to perform.

Incidental Beneficiary. Many contracts are made that indirectly benefit third parties. Failure of the promisor to perform properly does not necessarily give an *incidental beneficiary* the right to take legal action. Generally, if there was no intent by the contracting parties to benefit the third party, the third party has no legally enforceable interest in the contract. Brown hires White (a landscape architect) to landscape his estate. Gray, who lives next door, will incidentally benefit as a result of the landscaping. However, Gray has no legally enforceable interest in the completion of the landscaping. Gray was not a party to the contract, and whatever benefit he might have received was merely incidental to the contract's primary purpose. Brown is a manufacturer and supplier of parts for the automotive industry. He contracts with Green, a builder of automation equipment, for Green to build and install an automatic machine. Gray supplies most of Green's steel. Although Gray would be likely to benefit from the automation contract, the agreement is not for his benefit and he could not enforce it.

Contracts in which the government is a party are sometimes considered to be third-party beneficiary contracts. This is the case when it is reasoned that citizens are to benefit from contracts made by the governing body, and that they have an interest in these contracts since they pay taxes and thereby acquire rights to benefits. If a small segment of a community is to receive benefits, and possibly pay a special assessment toward them, the argument for enforcement by a citizen is even stronger. However, the right of a citizen to take action as a third-party beneficiary to enforce a government-made contract is largely a matter of local statute.

FRAZIER, INC. v. 20TH CENTURY BUILDERS, INC.
198 N.W. 2d 478 (1972)

Spencer, Justice

This appeal is from the sustaining of a motion for summary judgment in a third party action. The principal action was a mechanic's lien foreclosure brought by Frazier, Inc., against Majors, Inc., et al., in which Omaha Poured Concrete Company was subsequently included as a defendant. Majors filed a cross-petition against Frazier and Omaha Poured, alleging damages as the result of the negligence of Frazier in the installation of the plumbing system which resulted in the collapse of a cement floor poured by Omaha Poured. Omaha Poured was given leave to file a third party complaint against Transamerica Insurance Company as a third party defendant, to recover under the terms of an insurance policy providing coverage to Omaha Poured for consequential damages. We affirm.

Frazier, as a subcontractor under Omaha Poured, installed the plumbing in a building being erected for Majors. The plumbing was installed with removable sleeves around the floor drain to permit the installation of a poured concrete floor. After the completion of the building, Majors moved its plastic moulding machines onto the concrete floor and started operations. These machines required the discharge of large quantities of water through the drain. After the first day's operation, the concrete floor pulled away from the wall, buckled, and collapsed. It was then discovered that the sleeves had not been properly installed, and after they were removed the water, instead of running off through the drain, went through an unsealed gap into the ground under the floor, undermining it, causing the floor to sink. Notice was immediately given to Transamerica who investigated the damage. Omaha Poured replaced the floor at its own expense. The present third party action involves the amount paid to settle the consequential damages sustained by Majors because of the collapse of the floor, and does not include any part of the cost of replacing the floor.

Omaha Poured was granted leave to file its third party action against Transamerica January 22, 1969. The petition filed January 30, 1969, alleged that Transamerica is obligated to defend Omaha Poured,

and to pay any sums of money which may be awarded against Omaha Poured as the result of consequential damages sustained by Majors. Omaha Poured alleged it complied with all of the conditions precedent of said policy, but Transamerica refused to provide coverage for said incident which falls within the terms and conditions of the policy, and has refused to defend Omaha Poured. On June 5, 1969, the issues raised by the third party petition were ordered separated for trial purposes from the issues raised by the principal pleadings.

On July 14, 1969, the day the main action was called for trial, Omaha Poured made a settlement with the other defendants, and judgment was entered against it for Majors' consequential damages in the amount of $14,298.22. The agreement included a covenant that the judgment creditor would not execute against the personal assets of Omaha Poured for more than $1,500 of the judgment, and would thereafter look to the Transamerica policy for all remaining sums thereunder.

Immediately previous, and on the day judgment was entered, Majors amended its cross-petition to include a special allegation of negligence against Omaha Poured. No notice was given Transamerica of this amendment, but a copy of the judgment entry was mailed to it the same day the judgment was entered.

The trial court sustained Omaha Poured's motion for summary judgment, specifically finding that there was no substantial controversy as to the following material facts: (1) Transamerica knew of the collapse of the floor shortly after it occurred and knew that the potential loss and claim by Majors, Inc., would include not only damage to the floor itself but the very consequential damages which Majors, Inc., ultimately sought by the instant litigation. (2) Pursuant to investigation by representatives of Transamerica, it unequivocally and unconditionally denied any coverage on the policy of insurance for the incident involved herein. (3) Transamerica refused to accede to the demand of Omaha Poured that it take over and defend the cross-petition filed against Omaha Poured by Majors, Inc. (4) Omaha Poured, without the knowledge or consent of Transamerica, entered into a compromise settlement and agreement with Majors, Inc., resulting in a consent judgment against Omaha Poured for the consequential damage sustained by Majors, Inc., with an agreement that no more than $1,500 of the judgment would be collected from Omaha Poured personally. (5) The amendments to the cross-petition of Majors, Inc., just prior to the entry of the judgment were made without the knowledge or consent of Transamerica. (6) The evidence is sufficient to support a finding of legal liability by Omaha Poured to Majors, Inc., for the consequential damage loss to Majors, Inc., resulting from the collapse of the floor, in the amount of the judgment.

The trial court made the following specific findings of law: First, the policy in question affords coverage to Omaha Poured for the consequential damage claim asserted by Majors, Inc. Exclusions raised by Transamerica in support of its denial of coverage do not apply.

Second, once Transamerica denied coverage to Omaha Poured in the manner in which it did, Transamerica breached its contract with Omaha Poured, relieving Omaha Poured of any obligation under the contract to notify or deal with Transamerica any further regarding the claim.

Third, the allegations contained in the cross-petition of Majors, Inc., prior to the amendments made on July 14, 1969, together with all the pleadings in the case, were sufficient to compel Transamerica to assume the defense of Omaha Poured, and its refusal of Omaha Poured's demand that it do so constituted a breach of its contract with Omaha Poured.

Fourth, Transamerica's breach of its contract with Omaha Poured, by denying coverage and refusing to defend its insured, entitled Omaha Poured to enter into the most favorable settlement and consent judgment possible, which it did.

Fifth, the consent judgment, supported by the evidence, was obtained in good faith and without fraud or collusion. Therefore, having declined to defend the action when called upon to do so, Transamerica may not again litigate the issues that resulted in the judgment.

Transamerica alleges the following assignments of error: (1) sustaining the motion for summary judgment; (2) determining that Transamerica unequivocally and unconditionally denied any coverage on the policy of insurance; (3) determining there was no genuine issue of material fact; (4) determining that the consent judgment was obtained in good faith and without fraud and collusion; (5) determining that Omaha Poured owed no duty to Transamerica to notify it of amendments to the cross-petition; (6) determining that Transamerica had a duty to defend Omaha Poured under the allegations contained in the cross-petition prior to its amendment; (7) admitting into evidence affidavits offered by Omaha Poured; and (8) failing to sustain Transamerica's motion to vacate the judgment.

Only one of the court's findings of fact set out above is questioned in Transamerica's brief, that being No. (2), which is made the subject of assignment of error No. 2. However, even as to this assignment, nowhere in the brief does Transamerica point out in what manner this finding is incorrect or the subject of any factual controversy. Dwight Stephens, Transamerica's claim representative who first investigated the claim, stated

in his affidavit that after completing his investigation he informed Omaha Poured's representative that no coverage was afforded to the insured for the collapse of the floor for the reason that the aforementioned policy did not provide coverage for completed operations and products liability, and that he thereafter reported his findings to his superior, Harold Pace. The affidavit of Harold Pace states that coverage was denied under said policy shortly after May 27, 1967, for the reason that coverage was not afforded thereunder to the insured for completed operations and products liability coverage. There can be no question that Transamerica at all times was insisting that the damage was for completed operations and products liability coverage and it was not covered under the policy.

Transamerica overlooked the fact that its policy did insure Omaha Poured for consequential damages and that the action brought by Majors, Inc., was for consequential damages resulting from the incident. Nowhere in Transamerica's brief does it challenge, by assignment of error or discussion, the finding of the trial court that the Transamerica policy in question affords coverage to Omaha Poured for the consequential damage claim asserted by Majors, Inc. Nor, incidentally, does Transamerica challenge in any manner the trial court's conclusion that as a matter of law the "exclusions raised by third party defendant in support of its denial of coverage" do not apply. There is no merit to Transamerica's first and second assignments of error.

The purpose of a summary judgment proceeding is to pierce allegations of pleadings and to show conclusively that controlling facts are otherwise than alleged and that the moving party is entitled to judgment as a matter of law. *Growers Cattle Credit Corp. of Omaha* v. *Swanson. . . .*

As to Transamerica's third assignment of error, when we pierce the allegations of the pleadings there is no question the material issues are those of law and not of fact.

As to Transamerica's fourth assignment of error, there is not the slightest evidence of fraud or collusion. The settlement was consummated on the morning of the scheduled trial of the main action. Omaha Poured, left to its own resources, at the last moment made a settlement to avoid increased liability. Omaha Poured must have realized, as would any reasonable person in its position, that prudence required it to protect its assets as best it could. There was no question about its liability for consequential damages. There is not the slightest merit to this assignment.

Nor is there merit in Transamerica's fifth assignment of error. Transamerica investigated the incident and denied coverage. It further refused to tender a defense for Omaha Poured. Exhibit 84 to the deposition of Transamerica's claim manager, is a letter from attorneys for Omaha Poured to Transamerica under date of January 10, 1969, reminding it of two previous denials of coverage and of a previous letter dated August 31, 1967, to the effect that Omaha Poured was taking steps to protect itself from the effects of the wrongful denial of coverage. The letter of January 10, 1969, gave Transamerica the trial date of the main action, again tendered the defense of Omaha Poured, and advised that in the event it again declined to provide a defense, a third party petition would be filed. To hold that Omaha Poured had any additional obligation to keep Transamerica informed of the developments would be absurd.

Transamerica's sixth assignment of error misconstrues the decisions of this court on the point in question. In *National Union Fire Ins. Co.* v. *Bruecks,* . . . we said: "It would seem that the obligation to defend a suit for an insured should be determined on the basis of whether the petition filed against him attempts to allege a liability within the terms of the policy." Clearly, the inference from the cross-petition and the prayer before the amendment included Omaha Poured, and sufficiently inferred liability to require action on the part of Transamerica. If there was the slightest question, certainly the proceedings culminating in the filing of this third party action, which occurred six months before the amendment in question, would have removed any doubt.

Transamerica's seventh assignment of error is predicated on its assertion that affidavits offered into evidence, notarized by an attorney of record, are improper and should be excluded. We direct counsels' attention to section 25-1245. R.S. Supp., 1969, which provides: "An affidavit may be made in and out of this state before any person authorized to take depositions, and must

be authenticated in the same way. An attorney at law who is attorney for a party in any proceedings in any court of this state shall not be disqualified as the person before whom the affidavit is made by reason of such representation."

In view of previous comment, Transamerica's eighth assignment of error requires no further discussion. The trial court correctly sustained the motion for summary judgment. The judgment is affirmed.

Affirmed.

REVIEW QUESTIONS

1. What is meant by *privity of contract?*
2. Black is purchasing a house under a real estate mortgage held by the White Mortgage Company. Under the terms of the mortgage Black is obligated to make a payment to White Mortgage Company each month. Part of the payment is for interest, another part reduces the mortgage balance, and a third part is deposited in an escrow account to pay for taxes and insurance. Black sells his house to Gray, with Gray agreeing to take over the mortgage payments. If Gray defaults, can White Mortgage Co. take action to recover from Black?
3. Why must the obligor be notified of an assignment?
4. What is meant by *insurable interest?*
5. Distinguish between *assignment* and a *third-party beneficiary contract.*
6. In the case of *Frazier, Inc.* v. *20th Century Builders, Inc.,* if the insurer reimbursed the owner for the damages caused by collapse of the floor, would the insurer then have a right to take action for reimbursement against the subcontractor, Frazier, Inc., based upon Frazier's alleged negligence?

Discharge

Contracts, as you have observed, are made every day. They are quite ordinary things. Agreements are made and the terms of the agreements are usually carried out in a reasonable manner. This chapter deals with the exceptions, where a party has bargained away more than he intended, or where performance became more difficult than was expected. Public attention is called to exceptions; they are publicized in court cases and newspaper articles. It must be kept in mind, however, that these cases are exceptions, and that the vast majority of contracts are carried out satisfactorily and with benefit to both parties.

In this chapter we shall see how the court interprets contracts. We shall see how well the parties are held to their bargain, what constitutes performance, or a real offer to perform. We shall see when the law will discharge a person's obligations for him. Then, in Chapter 14, we shall examine the remedies available if a contract is breached by one of the parties to it.

Before the court can rule in a contract case it must know what the parties have agreed to do. This is the first job and sometimes actually the only job with which the court is faced. Determining what the parties have obligated themselves to do is known legally as *construction*. Essentially, this means interpretation. The court attempts to interpret from the wording of the contract the legal relationships of the parties. To do this the law has settled upon certain rules and guides, only the more prominent of which will be reviewed here.

RULES ON CONSTRUCTION

Which Law Governs

Contract law varies somewhat from state to state, and parties to contracts are often residents of different states when the contracts are made. For example, after a series of offers and counter-offers, Black, in Detroit, Michigan, makes an offer that appeals to White in Chicago, Illinois, and White accepts. If a question concerning the contract arises, according to which state's law will the question be settled? The courts are not entirely in accord in the answer to this. However, as a general rule, questions involving the validity, reality, and construction of a contract are answered according

to the laws of the state in which the last act necessary for bringing the contract into existence was performed. In the example above, the Illinois law would determine the outcome of a case of fraud or duress in the contract.

As to performance of a contract, generally the law of the state in which performance is to take place governs. If the contract between Black and White were to be performed in Indianapolis, the laws of Indiana would govern the performance.

Intent

The court attempts to interpret the contract according to the apparent intent of the parties when the contract was formed. To do this, the court looks at the circumstances surrounding the formation, and at the parties' conduct since then. Looking at the entire picture, what must have been their intentions? What the parties say about their intentions is not, of course, very good evidence. The intentions may well have changed since the contract was made. Black agrees to build a special machine for White for $120,000. Before he begins work Black is offered an opportunity to completely automate a production line for Gray for $500,000 and at a much greater profit. Black cannot complete both jobs satisfactorily within the time limit set, so he decides to break his contract with White. If taken to court, Black might well attempt to argue that his agreement with White was merely a tentative arrangement rather than a contract. For this reason the court would look into the circumstances surrounding the transaction—such as letters and testimony of disinterested parties—rather than take Black's testimony as controlling the case.

Parol-evidence Rule

One frequently hears of people entering into insurance contracts, chattel mortgages, conditional sales contracts, and other long-term agreements on the basis of what salesmen have told them, without having read the agreements themselves. Mildly speaking, this is foolishness. **Read before you sign!** The written agreement sets forth the obligations of the parties as far as the court is concerned. No testimony about the preliminary negotiations of the parties is allowed to alter the terms of a written contract or add to them. The rule is not absolute or all-inclusive; it is used reasonably. There are circumstances in which testimony concerning a written contract is admissible. Briefly, these exceptions to the parol-evidence rule are:

1. Where there is a question of reality of the agreement (for instance, fraud or duress).
2. Where one of the parties may not have had capacity to contract (for instance, a minor).
3. Where there may have been lack or failure of consideration.
4. Where the language of the writing is not clear to the court, possibly from the use of terms common to a particular trade or profession.
5. Where a new agreement over the same subject matter may have been made.

Black purchases a machine from White for $5,000. In the negotiations White stated that he would repair the machine free of charge until six months after its purchase. When reduced to writing the contract says nothing about this warranty. Black would not be allowed to give oral testimony to establish and enforce the warranty in a court action. If the contract had not been reduced to writing the warranty could have been enforced, once it was established that such a warranty had been given. Even though the warranty could not be enforced, testimony might be allowed as proof that White used the promise to repair fraudulently to persuade Black to enter into the contract.

Wording Used

It is quite apparent that words may be used either to explain or to confuse a meaning. If insurance policies of various companies are examined, examples can easily be found that would confuse almost anyone who might read them. Other policies may be found that say just about the same thing in such clear language that almost anyone who can read could understand them. The court construes a written contract most strongly against the writer. Therefore, it is advisable (at least for those of us who are not lawyers) to write in clear, simple language that allows only one interpretation.

Words are generally given their usual, unspecialized meaning in courts of law. If the words used have a particular meaning in the geographical area involved, or in a certain trade or profession involved in the case, this meaning will be given to the words. If the wording is inconsistent in various parts of the contract, the contract as a whole will be interpreted according to the intentions of the parties, and the wording will be construed to follow those intentions. If two different interpretations are possible, one lawful and the other unlawful, the lawful interpretation will be assumed by the court. If words and figures or words and abbreviations are in conflict, the words will govern.

PERFORMANCE

Theoretically, a party to whom a contractual obligation is owed has a right to precise performance of the obligation. Anything short of the performance to which he is entitled constitutes cause for a damage action against the other party to the agreement. However, performance or nonperformance is not always as self-evident as it might appear. The nature of the obligation undertaken determines the performance. As noted earlier in Chapter 9, on consideration, where a liquidated amount of money is owed, payment of a lesser amount will not satisfy the obligation. Where the contract requires building something, though, exact performance may not always occur and cannot seriously be expected. This is particularly true where research and development is to be part of the performance of the contract. Such is the case in many engineering contracts.

Conditions

Frequently contracts are so written that the apparent intent of the parties is that performance by one party will precede performance by the other. For instance, one might contract to have a machine built and installed in his plant with payment to be made when the installation is complete. A condition such as this would constitute a condition precedent in a contract.

Commonly, the obtaining of an architect's certificate is made a condition precedent. So, also, is the passage of time until the completion date.

Architect's Approval

Where an architect's approval is required by a contract clause, the courts will usually enforce it. It must be recognized, however, that architects are human too, and capable of human failings. The architect may have died or may be insane when his certificate is required, or he may unreasonably or fraudulently refuse to issue his certificate. Under such circumstances the court will ordinarily dispense with the requirement of the architect's certificate. If there is any sound reason for the architect's objections, though, the court will enforce the requirement.

Satisfactory Performance

Where the purchaser of a certain performance must be satisfied, two possibilities exist. The nature of the contract may be such that the only test of satisfaction is the personal taste of the buyer. Black, an artist, agrees to paint White's portrait to White's satisfaction for $5,000. White may *never* be satisfied, even though to a third person the portrait appears to be a perfect likeness. White could conceivably state, after each submission of the portrait for his approval, that "it just isn't me" and require Black to continue. If the court determined the contract to be binding (the consideration of Black's performance might be termed illusory), Black would have to continue to paint or breach his contract.

If the nature of the contract is such that, even though satisfaction of the buyer is specified, it provides for mechanical or operational suitability, it is a different story. In this case, if performance is such that it would satisfy a reasonable person, the court will deem the condition satisfied. Black agrees to install an air-conditioning system for White, to White's satisfaction. After the installation, if White says he is not satisfied, Black may still collect by proving that the air-conditioning system will do all that a reasonable person could expect it to do.

Completion Date

Time limits are frequently stated in contracts. Where performance is to take place by a certain date and it actually extends beyond that date, any of several situations may result. In many contracts there are provisions for liquidated damages (so-called penalty clauses) that state an amount to be paid for each day's delay beyond the date specified in the contract. If the amount specified reasonably covers the damage that would be caused by delay, it will be enforced. If the amount of the liquidated damages is excessive, the court will hold that it is really a penalty clause and will refuse to enforce it. It is the prerogative of the court and not of the private citizen to assess penalties. If there is no liquidated damage clause, and performance runs beyond the time agreed upon, the court may be called upon to estimate damages. Usually, either court-estimated damages or liquidated damages merely serve to reduce the price paid for the work. Ordinarily, nothing but very unreasonable lateness of performance would give the buyer of the performance sufficient grounds to rescind the contract. Where performance is not unreasonable, the buyer must accept the performance, but at a price reduced by the damage he has suffered.

In certain circumstances time of performance is critical in a contract. In this event, a clause to the effect that "time is of the essence of the contract" is usually included. In such instances the courts generally will allow rescission of the contract for late performance.

Substantial Performance

Nearly all building contracts or contracts in which machinery or equipment is to be built and installed are performed in a manner that deviates from what is specified. Some flaw in such a project can be found by looking long enough and thoroughly enough. If variations from specifications were not condoned, few projects would be undertaken and fewer yet would be paid for. Those that were completed would cost so dearly that very few could afford them. As it is, if a building contract calls for a concrete floor of a uniform five-inch thickness, it is not likely that the resulting floor will be precisely five inches thick throughout. However, if the result accomplished approximates closely the result specified, the contractor can still recover his price; his performance has been *substantially* the same as that specified. If gross inaccuracies occur, or if substitutions are found to have been made that do not reasonably satisfy the specifications, it is no longer *substantial performance.* Just where the line is drawn between substantial performance and outright contract breach is a question of fact, and it is properly submitted to a jury. Substantial-performance cases frequently result in the performer receiving the amount for which he has contracted, less damages. The extent of damages is determined by the value of the performance rendered compared with the value of the performance specified, or the cost of additional work to complete the performance properly.

Substantial performance assumes that the performer has pursued his contract in good faith and with the intent that his performance would agree with the standards specified. If this is not the case—if the performer willfully abandons the performance or the work is unreasonably poor—he may not be able to recover anything as a result of his breach of the contract.

Impossibility of Performance

As it deals with impossibility of performance, the law is not entirely clear or settled. In certain cases involving death or illness of the promisor, definite statements can be made. In other cases, particularly where performance has turned out to be much more difficult than was anticipated, general conclusions can be drawn from the majority of decisions, but numerous exceptions may also be cited.

Generally, when a person undertakes a contractual obligation he assumes certain risks. He can hedge against such risks in various ways. He can insert contract clauses which state that if certain things occur he will be excused from performance. He can add enough money to the price to cover "contingencies." He can purchase insurance against the risks he assumes. In fact, almost the only hazard he can't cover in some way when he makes the contract is liability for his performance if the public is injured by it. For example, injuries resulting from the collapse of a public building built by a contractor, which collapse was caused by his negligence, could allow recovery against him by either the injured person or the insurance company.

Death or Illness. Ordinarily death or illness of a party to a contract does not discharge that contract. If a person dies or becomes incapacitated by illness, his estate or those appointed to act for him must take over and complete his obligations. Only where a contract is such that personal services are involved, will death or incapacity due to illness serve as a lawful excuse for nonperformance. For instance, death or illness of a freelance consulting engineer would discharge his remaining obligations to his clients.

Destruction of an Essential to the Contract. By destruction of an essential to a contract is meant destruction of something without which the contract cannot be performed. Black hires the White Construction Company to build an addition to his plant. Before the work is begun the plant is destroyed by fire without fault of either party. White Construction Company's obligation is terminated. If the White Construction Company had begun work and were, say, half finished, White's obligation to complete the structure would be ended, but White could collect for the work his company had completed in addition to any materials that had been accepted by Black. If, as a third possibility, the contract had been for the building of a structure by itself (not an addition to an existing structure), and if the work again were half finished when the building was destroyed, White Construction Company's obligation would not be ended and the contractor would have to rebuild. One cannot make an addition to a structure that no longer exists, but he can build a separate structure even though his first attempt to do so was destroyed.

Unexpected Hardship. As previously indicated, one who contracts to perform in some way runs the risk that conditions may not remain as they are when he enters into the contract, and that conditions may not be as they seem. It is not an uncommon experience to have a materials price increase or a wage increase cut deeply into the profit margin. If the cause of hardship is anything the contractor reasonably could have anticipated, the courts will not relieve him of his duties. It is only where the difficulties that have arisen are of a nature such that no one reasonably could have anticipated them that the court may, in some way, either relieve the burden or lighten the load on the contractor. Under such circumstances a subsequent contract with the owner, whereby the contractor is to receive money for his performance, may be enforceable in court. Or the court may enforce a subsequent contract to give the contractor more time in which to perform. It should be remembered, though, that these rulings are exceptions; if the difficulty was foreseeable the law gives no relief. A subsequent contract based upon a foreseeable difficulty that did arise (e.g., a materials price rise) is void for lack of consideration as to the increase in the contract price.

Commercial Frustration. The doctrine of commercial frustration is often treated in the same manner as the destruction of an essential to a contract. In the United States courts the result is the same. *Commercial frustration* commonly results when a contract is made to take advantage of some future event not controlled by either party. The event is then called off and, as a result, the contract has no purpose. Black leases a concession stand from White for a certain week during which an athletic event is to be held. The athletic event is called off (or moved to a different location). The courts would allow Black to avoid his lease contract. Similarly, if a law were passed preventing such an event, Black would not be held to his contract.

Prevention of Performance

It is implied in every contract that each party will allow the other to perform his obligation. If one of the parties prevents performance by the other, he thereby discharges the other party's obligation, and he subjects himself to the possibility of a severe damage action should the other party be inclined to sue. Black sells White some standing timber, giving White a license to use a private road to the timber. Black prevents White from using the road. White's obligation is terminated and he may sue Black for damages.

Waiver

A *waiver* consists of voluntarily giving up a right to which one is legally entitled. To waive a right a party must first know that he is entitled to it. He must also intend to give up the right. If Black purchases a machine from White according to a description, specification, or sample he can expect to receive the described machine. If the actual machine received varies significantly from the description, Black has a right to refuse to accept it. If, with knowledge of the difference involved, Black keeps the machine and uses it as his own, he has waived his right to return the machine to White and get one more closely resembling the description. Black's failure to do anything about the discrepancy would be an *implied* waiver. If after receipt and examination of the machine Black had told White that he intended to keep it despite its variation from the description, this would amount to an *express* waiver.

Agreement

Renunciation. If two parties have a right to make a contract by an agreement between them, it is only reasonable that they could also agree to disagree. If no rights of a third person are involved, the parties may discharge their contract by mutual agreement without performance in several ways. The parties may agree merely not to be bound by the terms of the original agreement or they may make a new contract agreement involving the same subject matter, thus discharging the old contract. The original agreement itself may specify some event, the occurrence of which will end the contractual relation. Both of the parties may ignore their rights under the contract, each going about his business in such a manner that a waiver of performance may be implied from his actions. When a contract is discharged by these methods, the release of one party constitutes the consideration for the release of the other.

Accord and Satisfaction. Accord and satisfaction occurs when a party agrees to accept a substitute performance for the one to which he was entitled. Ordinarily this occurs when there has been a breach of performance by one party, giving the other party cause to sue. In common terminology, this is the "settlement out of court" one frequently hears about in connection with both contract and tort cases.

To be effective as a discharge, both accord and satisfaction must have occurred. *Accord* refers to a separate agreement substituted for the original one. *Satisfaction* occurs when the conditions of the accord have been met.

Novation. A *novation* replaces one of the parties to a contract. For a novation to be legally effective, all the parties to a contract must agree to it. For a simple illustration, assume that Black owes White $100. White owes Gray $100. If the three parties agree that Gray

will collect his $100 from Black, a novation has occurred that completely relieves White of his obligation to Gray. Black no longer owes White $100, but he has a legally enforceable obligation to pay Gray. Common examples of novation occur when a person buys a house or a car from another, substituting himself as a mortgagor and agreeing to make the loan payments to the lending institution (with consent by the lending institution to the substitution).

Arbitration. A court action for damages is sometimes impractical because of the time required for it, the cost involved, or some other reason. In many states it is possible to substitute a procedure known as *arbitration* for a court action. Arbitration is a procedure in which a dispute is submitted to an impartial umpire or board of umpires whose decision on the matter is final and binding. The legality of the procedure depends upon the statutes of the state in which the controversy arises. At common law, arbitration has no standing; even if a decision were rendered by an arbitrator, the cause might still be taken to court and the arbitration would have no effect. Many of the states have seen in arbitration a means of relieving crowded court dockets and have passed laws setting up the procedure and giving an arbitration decision almost the same force as a court judgment. In these states, almost any controversy in which damages are requested can be submitted to arbitration—not just contract cases, but tort cases and even property settlements following divorces.

Arbitration has several inherent advantages when it is compared to court proceedings. Probably the main advantage is found in specialization—the disputing parties decide among themselves what person is to act as judge and jury. This allows them to select someone who has a specialized knowledge of the field involved—someone who would not have to be educated on the general technical principles before deciding the case. Often this results in a more equitable decision than a judge and jury might render in court.

A second advantage of arbitration is the speed of the procedure. Court dockets are quite crowded; it is not unusual for a year to pass before a particular case comes up, and delays as long as five years occur in some jurisdictions. In the intervening period witnesses may die or move away, and memories dim. Arbitration affords an immediate solution. Today's dispute may be settled yet today or tomorrow if the parties so desire. It is only necessary to select a disinterested person and submit the dispute to him for decision. A minimum of formality is involved.

Cost-saving is a third advantage that may result from arbitration. In addition to the saving of whatever monetary value may be attached to waiting time, the cost of the procedure itself is often less than court costs.

Arbitration is not bound by the evidence rules encountered in a court of law. Whether this is an advantage or a disadvantage is questionable and would depend largely on the case. However, if the arbitrator considers hearsay testimony, for instance, as desirable in determining an issue, such testimony can be taken.

In states where arbitration is used, the proceeding is conducted as an extrajudicial action of a court. Questions of law may be submitted to the court for determination, and the final arbitration award is enforced by the court.

There are three main legal requirements for arbitration. (1) The parties must agree to arbitrate—when the agreement to arbitrate took place is of little matter as long as the parties did agree at some time prior to the arbitration. (2) A formal document known as a *submission* must be prepared by the parties and given to the court. The submission is roughly a combination of the complaint and reply required in a court case; it presents the issue to be decided. (3) The arbitrator(s) must be impartial and disinterested parties. If these requirements are met, the arbitrator's award will bind the parties.

The popularity of arbitration as a means of settling disputes has increased considerably in recent years. Probably the main reason for this is the efficiency of the procedure. It is conceivable that laws *requiring* arbitration in certain types of civil cases may be passed to further relieve the courts of burdensome cases in civil disputes.

Tender of Performance

Tender of performance, if refused, may discharge the obligation of a party to a contract. Three conditions, however, must prevail in a lawful tender of performance:

1. The party offering to perform must be ready, willing, and able to perform the obligation called for.
2. The offer to perform must be made in a reasonable manner at the proper time and place according to the contract.
3. It must be unconditional.

Not only is the obligation discharged if such a tender is refused, but the party who refused has breached the contract and may be sued for damages or specific performance, as the case may dictate.

There is one notable exception to the general rule of tender of performance discharging an obligation. If it is an offer to pay a debt that is due and payable in

money, the debt is not discharged by refusal of the payment. However, there are three rather important effects:

1. The accrual of interest is stopped.
2. Any liens used to secure the debt are discharged.
3. Any surety for the debt is no longer obligated.

If the debt is payable in money, an offer to pay with anything other than legal tender may be refused by the creditor; he is under no duty to accept a check, for instance. If the offer to pay is made before maturity of the debt, the creditor need not accept. In such cases, if the creditor rejects the offer to pay, for the reasons indicated, there has been no tender of performance.

Anticipatory Breach

Breach of contract ordinarily results from someone's failing to perform his obligation as agreed and at the proper time. However, a contract may be breached before the time of performance has arrived. If the party who is to perform notifies the other party that he cannot or will not perform when the time comes for him to do so, an *anticipatory breach* has occurred. Such anticipatory breach gives the would-be recipient of the performance two possibilities if he still desires performance:

1. He may sue the nonperforming party for whatever damage may have been caused by the breach.
2. He may obtain performance from someone else if it is possible to do so.

Black Construction Company agrees, as general contractor, to build a structure for White. Gray is hired as subcontractor to do the electrical work. A month before the electrical work is to be undertaken Gray informs Black that he cannot do it because of other commitments. At this point, if there were no rule as to anticipatory breach, Black would be in quite a dilemma. If he obtained the electrical work from someone else and Gray subsequently had a change of heart, Gray could demand to be allowed to perform and sue if he were denied the opportunity to do so. If Black hired a second subcontractor and then Gray returned and performed the work, the second subcontractor could sue. If he waited until he was certain that the contract was breached, thus causing him to be late with his contract, White could sue him. Anticipatory breach gives him a way out. Black can hire another electrical contractor to do the work without fear that Gray will be able to take successful action against him. Of course,

Gray has the right to change his mind at any time before Black takes such a step, thus resuming his obligation. Generally, information of anticipatory breach must come directly to the innocent party to give him a right to act on it, and the source of the information must be sound enough to justify the action—vague rumors are not enough.

Anticipatory breach cannot occur in regard to payment of a debt. Although a debtor may notify his creditor that he cannot or will not pay his debt when due, the creditor must wait until the duty to pay has actually been breached before he may take action. The creditor, of course, is not likely to be placed in a dilemma similar to that in which Black, in the foregoing example, would find himself in the absence of anticipatory breach.

BY OPERATION OF LAW

Certain laws have been passed and rules developed to provide for contract discharge as a matter of law. In Chapter 10, "Lawful Subject Matter," the result of a change in legislation was discussed, showing the effect of legislation in discharge of contracts. Here we will consider alteration of the contract, the statute of limitations, bankruptcy, and creditor's compositions.

Alteration of the Contract

If a contract is intentionally altered by some of the parties to it, without the remaining parties taking part in or having knowledge of the alteration, the obligations of the remaining parties under the contract are discharged. A party cannot be held to changes in contract terms if he had no hand in making the changes. Black uses White as surety to secure a $500 loan from Gray, dated July 1, and due September 1. During August it appears to Black that he will not be able to meet his obligation on schedule. Black asks Gray for a loan extension to October 1, to which Gray agrees. On October 1, Gray, discovering that Black has moved and left no forwarding address, turns to White as surety. White's surety agreement would not be enforceable against him under these circumstances unless he had been made a party to the extension.

Statute of Limitations

Each of the states has adopted a statute that limits the suable life of a contract. Most of the states specify a certain length of time for oral contracts, a longer time for written contracts, and a still longer time for contracts under seal. The state of Florida, for instance,

specifies three years for oral contracts, five years for written contracts, and twenty years for contracts under seal. A party who has a right of action on a contract must take such action within the time limits stated in the statute or he loses his right to take such action. The time is figured from the date the contract was breached, but with the possibility of renewal whenever the debt is acknowledged in any way, e.g., by part payment. Under most statutes time does not continue to run while the person who has breached is outside the state. Black orally hires White to add a roof to a structure. The contract is made March 1, 1985. White finishes his performance on March 31, 1985, but is never paid. If the statute of limitations states five years for this type of contract, White has until March 31, 1990, to commence his court action for recovery. In most states, if Black made a part payment or in some other way acknowledged the debt on, say, April 15, 1987, the time for White to take action would not expire until April 15, 1992. Similarly, if Black left the state for a year, White would have until March 31, 1991, to begin his suit. If suit is not begun by the dates mentioned, White loses his right to take action for recovery.

Although the legal duty to perform a contract is ended by the statute of limitations, it may be reinstated by the debtor. Any act or promise by the debtor by which he could be said to resume the obligation will revive it and give the contract new life under the statute. If Black made a part payment for the roof in 1993, the statute of limitations would start to run again. Much the same is true of bankruptcy, discussed below. Reacknowledgement by the debtor of a debt discharged in bankruptcy serves to reinstate its legal life despite the discharge.

Bankruptcy

When a person owes more than he can pay, should the law help him or leave him where it finds him? Should one creditor be allowed to receive payment for his entire debt at the expense of other creditors? These and similar questions have been debated by legislatures since the problem of bankruptcy was first recognized.

It is not surprising that the Constitution gives Congress the power to establish "uniform laws on the subject of bankruptcies throughout the United States." Debt was the greatest single cause of imprisonment at the time of the American Revolution. Inability to pay a debt was a prison offense. In fact, forgiving a debtor's obligations and allowing him to begin again with a clean slate is somewhat of an innovation in the law. Bankruptcy proceedings for the purpose of paying off creditors are not new, but it is only recently that the debtor could receive discharge of his obligations in such an action.

Three federal bankruptcy laws were passed and repealed after very short lives before the Bankruptcy Act was passed in 1898. Eighty years later it was replaced by the Bankruptcy Reform Act of 1978. Our present act has two main purposes: (1) to pay off to the greatest reasonable extent the obligations of the debtor to his creditors either by liquidation of assets or by continuing operation of a business or by devoting a portion of wages to the purpose, and (2) to discharge an honest debtor from future liability on the obligations. To accomplish these purposes the Bankruptcy Reform Act provides for:

1. A meeting of the creditors to conduct the business of the debtor's bankruptcy.
2. Possible election of a trustee to take over the debtor's estate.
3. Discharge of the debtor.

The legal machinery enacted to carry out these functions is quite lengthy and complicated. The purpose of this text will be adequately served if we consider only an abbreviated version of the process and some of the concepts.

The Bankruptcy Reform Act is a federal law, Bankruptcy petitions are filed in a Bankruptcy Court (a U.S. District Court); appeal may be taken to a U.S. Circuit Court of Appeals and, finally, to the U.S. Supreme Court.

To Whom the Law Applies. The Bankruptcy Reform Act applies to all entities (individuals, businesses, municipalities, railroads) with one major exception. Financial institutions such as banks, savings and loans, credit unions, and the like generally have separate statutes to govern their insolvency. A special bankruptcy chapter, number 13, is designed primarily to give relief in cases of consumer debt. Two chapters, 7 and 11, are designed primarily to give relief in the form of liquidation and reorganization, respectively. Chapter 9 handles municipalities with debt problems.

The law distinguishes between *voluntary and involuntary bankruptcy*. Almost anyone who has the capacity to make a contract may become bankrupt voluntarily. The prospective voluntary bankrupt is not even required to be insolvent, although as a practical matter bankruptcy would seem pointless otherwise.

Involuntary Bankruptcy. Involuntary bankruptcy is confined to Chapters 7 and 11 of the Act and there are restrictions as to who may be driven into bankruptcy.

Specific exceptions are made for farmers and nonbusiness corporations in addition to the financial institutions indicated above.

Involuntary bankruptcy is begun by three or more creditors, holding a total of $5,000 or more of unsecured obligations, filing a petition in a bankruptcy court. If there are fewer than twelve creditors, only one creditor with at least the $5,000 obligation may file. If the debtor is a partnership, one or more of the partners may file.

Consider the Black Manufacturing Company, a corporation in which Mr. Black holds most of the stock. One of Black's competitors has originated a new product that has captured many of Black's customers, so Black's sales have diminished to a point well below breakeven. With revenues so low, Black has lost the ability to cover current obligations. Payments to several creditors have been postponed. Others have had to be satisfied with minimal partial payments. It has become evident to the creditors that Black Manufacturing is in trouble. Three of Black's creditors decide they have had enough and file a bankruptcy petition in the local U.S. District Court (Bankruptcy Court). The result is a "Chapter 11" bankruptcy.

Chapter 11 Bankruptcy. Generally, under Chapter 11, the debtor is allowed to continue whatever business he may have until there is a court order to the contrary. He may continue to use, acquire, or dispose of property in the same manner as though no petition had been filed. Of course, counter measures are available in case of abuse of the creditors' rights by the debtor. For example, the court may appoint an interim trustee to preserve the estate until the creditors' meeting determines what is to be done with it.

Meeting of Interested Parties (Creditors' Meeting). The idea of bankruptcy is to satisfy the requirements of creditors and others with an interest in the debtor's estate. To accomplish this, one of the first orders of business following the bankruptcy petition in involuntary bankruptcy is the calling of meetings of interested parties. If the debtor is a partnership or corporation, the rights of the various partners or equity interests (e.g., stockholders) are considered.

In the course of the meeting the debtor is examined (under oath) to determine his estate. The debtor is required to reveal all assets, encumbrances on those assets, and the obligations of the estate. It is essentially a fact-finding mission.

A second objective is to allow legitimate claims against the estate. Those creditors with full security for their obligations, of course, are not really involved here—as, for example, one who holds first mortgage on real estate involved. Only if sale of the property might not yield enough to pay off the remaining debt would the mortgage holder have a right to actively participate in the meeting. So then, both secured and unsecured obligations are acknowledged at the meeting.

Along with the acknowledgement of legitimate preexisting debts there is the necessity to approve the costs of the bankruptcy—the administrative expenses. There are court costs, attorneys' fees, accountants' fees, trustee's fees, and the like to be allowed.

In involuntary bankruptcy a trustee is usually appointed at the meeting to take over the estate, collect the assets, and/or run the business according to the creditors' wishes. The bankruptcy court may or may not have appointed an interim trustee following the petition and order for relief. In any case, it is up to the membership of the meeting to appoint someone to continue as bankruptcy trustee.

The final item of business in the creditors' meeting in Chapter 11 involuntary bankruptcy is the formation of a plan. (Chapter 7 contemplates liquidation of a business.) The debtor is generally given 120 days following the "order for relief" to propose a plan that would pay off creditors and continue the business. Confirmation of the debtor's plan could take some time, but if after six months from the start of the action the debtor's plan has not been confirmed, it becomes the committee's business to form a plan.

A Chapter 11 plan must set forth a means of continuing the business (The most likely alternative is to shift to a Chapter 7 bankruptcy, liquidation.) To avoid the shift to liquidation the plan must provide a result for each creditor that is at least as good as he would receive under a Chapter 7 bankruptcy. The plan may provide for retention or sale of property, satisfaction or modification of liens, curing of defaults, changes of security interests, and/or mergers or consolidations. Generally there is a wide latitude in the possible actions to be included in such a plan.

In the *Black Manufacturing Company* case, Black is examined under oath and the extent of his company's obligations and assets is clarified. The creditors are rather worried about their prospects of recovery and must decide to either continue the business or liquidate it. Since Black's management may be partially at fault for the problems, one Gray is appointed by the committee as trustee for the company. The committee's decision as to continuation or liquidation of the company now depends largely on Gray's opinion and Black's plan for the future. Black could, for example, present an appeal plan contemplating a product improvement or an appeal to a new market. Lacking something like this the committee may simply decide to liquidate the company, satisfying committee members' debts with whatever liquidation brings.

The plan must be confirmed. This simply means that the bankruptcy court must hold a confirmation hearing to ascertain whether the plan complies with a) all applicable laws, b) agency rules (e.g., Securities and Exchange Commission), c) provisions of Chapter 11 of the bankruptcy law, and has been accepted by at least one class of claims. The court is not required to confirm a plan unless and until it is convinced of its probable success—that the plan will not lead to eventual liquidation of the debtor.

If Black's plan for the future of his company is unappealing to the committee members, they may well reject it. The logical next step, if that is the case, is Chapter 7 bankruptcy, liquidation.

Chapter 7 Bankruptcy. The objective of an involuntary Chapter 7 bankruptcy is to liquidate the debtor's available assets to pay off the creditors. The case is begun by a creditors' petition followed by the bankruptcy court's response, the *order for relief.*

At the time of the order for relief or before (if the court deems it necessary), an interim trustee is appointed to collect and preserve the assets of the estate, the debtor's property. The interim trustee is later replaced by a trustee (perhaps the same person) whose primary duties are to: a) collect and liquidate the property of the estate in the best interest of all parties concerned, b) investigate the financial affairs of the debtor, c) examine the proofs of claims and object to improper claims, d) perhaps oppose discharge of the debtor, and e) file a final report. If a business is involved, the trustee may be authorized to operate it for a limited period.

The main business of the creditors' committee meeting is electing the trustee, arranging to work with the trustee, and determining the allowances of claims. Secured claims, of course, have superior standing. A mortgagee or other lien holder has first call on the asset on which the lien was established. However, to the extent that the value of the asset is insufficient to cover the debt involved, the lien holder is also an unsecured creditor. On the other side of the coin, excess value of the asset—beyond that required to satisfy the debt—is available to those who hold unsecured claims. Payoff of unsecured claims follows a priority schedule in which administrative expenses have top priority, followed by unsecured claims in which timely notice was given, employees' wages up to a maximum amount, taxes, and other claims.

Now let us assume it is Black rather than the Black Manufacturing Company that is in financial difficulty. Certain personal losses have occurred which convince Black that the prospect of his paying all his bills, including the amounts he is in arrears to his creditors, is dim indeed. If his payments to his creditors were a bit smaller he might be able to make it; and if they could be made a shade smaller yet, he could pay off the arrears and at least be on a current payment status. If his unsecured indebtedness is less than $100,000 and his secured indebtedness is less than $350,000, it may be that Chapter 13 bankruptcy is his way out.

Chapter 13 Bankruptcy. The title of Chapter 13 is "Adjustment of Debts of an Individual with Regular Income." The main problem treated by Chapter 13 is consumer indebtedness. It is available to a debtor on a voluntary bankruptcy basis.

A trustee is appointed by the bankruptcy court to perform most of the same duties as those in Chapter 7 except for the duty of collecting and selling the debtor's assets. It is up to the debtor to devise his own means of paying off his debts. This, of course, may be done by assigning part of his wages to this purpose or by assigning a portion of his earnings from self-employment or his business. Whatever the source of income, the usual court attitude is to allow the debtor almost complete freedom to choose an acceptable plan and operate within it as long as it appears the past due debts to creditors will be paid off. The period of operation of the plan is nominally limited to three years, but it may be extended to five years with the court's permission. Creditors cannot force the debtor into a plan unacceptable to him for the same reasons they can't force him into a Chapter 13 bankruptcy in the first place. (They could, of course, force him into a Chapter 7 bankruptcy.) Only the debtor knows his family requirements, family plans, and other such personal information.

Secured creditors in a Chapter 13 bankruptcy may be paid off in many ways, one of which is for the debtor to return goods on which a lien was placed. Confirmation of the debtor's plan requires only the affirmation of the parties with an economic interest in the action as well as the court's blessing as to the plan's legality. One of the court's confirmation considerations is that the plan contemplate payoff to the unsecured creditors to at least the extent they would realize under Chapter 7.

The Estate. Bankruptcy contemplates rehabilitation of the debtor. Depriving the debtor of all property so that he winds up on public welfare isn't rehabilitation. Because of this, there is certain real and personal property which cannot be taken. Each state has "homestead laws" which specify certain minimums, but the Bankruptcy Reform Act also lists some exemptions. Various forms of income and benefit exceptions are also found in non-bankruptcy parts of the U.S. Code. For example, social security and certain other retirement benefits are exempt, as are veteran's benefits.

The property of the debtor's estate for bankruptcy purposes consists of all the debtor's assets that are not exempted. In addition to obvious property, this includes patent rights, copyrights, trademarks, liens held by the debtor on property owned by a third party, and community property. Generally, the estate rights are limited to those the debtor had at the beginning of the case.

Discharge. Under Chapter 7 and Chapter 13, discharge is limited to individuals. The reason for the Chapter 7 limitation is that even though a corporation or partnership may go through the Chapter 7 liquidation, what is left after bankruptcy is nothing but a hollow shell. The effect of the debtor's discharge is to void existing debts and enjoin the beginning or continuation of any action based on discharged debts.

Certain debts, however, are not discharged by bankruptcy, and some acts by the debtor prevent discharge of obligations. Generally, the following debts are not dischargeable in bankruptcy: a) various tax obligations; b) debts and continuing obligations for alimony, maintenance, and child support; c) liability for fraud or willful or malcious injury; d) certain debts for fines, penalties, or forfeitures for the benefit of a governmental unit; e) debts resulting from fraud, embezzlement, or larceny while acting in a fiduciary capacity; f) debts for educational loans less than five years past due; g) debts remaining after a previous bankruptcy proceeding; and h) debts not listed or listed too late to be included with the bankruptcy.

Discharge of the debtor's remaining obligations is generally forthcoming if the debtor has dealt honestly and fairly with his creditors during the bankruptcy action. Most of the reasons for denying discharge are based on actual or reasonably suspected deceit by the debtor. Discharge is denied for the following reasons (Chapter 7): a) the debtor is not an individual; b) the debtor transferred, destroyed, or concealed some of his property within a year prior to the filing of the bankruptcy petition intending thereby to defraud his creditors; c) the debtor failed to keep or preserve accounts of transactions; d) the debtor made fraudulent statements in bankruptcy examination regarding his estate or financial affairs; e) the debtor failed to explain satisfactorily any losses of assets; f) the debtor refused to obey a lawful court order during the proceedings; g) the debtor was granted a discharge under Chapter 7 or Chapter 11 (or their predecessors) in a case commenced within six years prior to the date the petition was filed; or h) the debtor was granted a discharge under Chapter 13 within the past six years unless the debtor had paid at least 70 percent of the amounts of the unsecured claims in the prior case.

Generally, confirmation of a Chapter 11 plan discharges the debtor. The main exception to this is where the Chapter 11 action essentially amounts to the Chapter 7 liquidation. In such an instance the Chapter 7 limitations, above, would apply.

Under a Chapter 13 bankruptcy the court is required to discharge the debtor after all payments under the plan have been made. However, there is a noticeable reluctance of courts to confirm plans that do not contemplate the payment of at least 70 percent of the amounts of claims by unsecured creditors.

Once the debtor has been through the bankruptcy mill and has received his discharge, his contractual obligations are ended. New property acquired by him, new transactions and business dealings are free from interference by his former creditors. He is given new economic life.

Creditors' Compositions

It is often to the advantage of both the creditors and the debtor to avoid bankruptcy proceedings. There are many costs of bankruptcy and each cost reduces the assets to be divided. It is costly, for instance, to pay the trustee to maintain and then dispose of the property involved. There is a much less expensive procedure available. The *creditors' composition* accomplishes almost the same thing as bankruptcy. It discharges the debtor's obligations. Each participating creditor gets some return on his account receivable. The procedure is informal but binding. It is not necessary that all the creditors join in the composition; two or more are sufficient—if only one creditor is involved it is not a creditor's composition and the remainder of the debtor's obligation is not discharged, as pointed out in Chapter 9, "Consideration."

For example, Black owes White $1,000, Gray $2,000, and Brown $3,000. Black has $3,000 cash available plus various other assets, but finds that he cannot pay all his debts and remain solvent. Black meets with White, Gray, and Brown, telling them of the situation. The creditors are faced with the possibility of bankruptcy proceedings where, after the costs are paid and Black's asset sold for whatever price they may bring, the creditors may get $.25 for each dollar of debt. As an alternative the creditors may choose to divide Black's cash assets in any way they see fit, $.50 for each dollar being one such possibility. The creditors may agree, instead of taking a straight percentage, to divide the assets in some other way that is satisfactory to each. They might agree, for instance, that White will receive $600, Gray $1,000, and Brown $1,400.

There are several explanations of the consideration involved in a creditor's composition. Perhaps the most common one holds that the consideration received by each creditor for giving up his right to sue for the remainder of his debt is found in the forbearance of the same right by the other creditors. Several states have statutes that specify the conditions and procedures for creditors' compositions. Where such statutes exist, examination of the consideration involved is, of course, unnecessary.

COOK ASSOCIATES, INC. v. COLONIAL BROACH & MACH. CO.

304 N.E. 2d 27 (1973)

English, Justice.

Defendant, a Delaware corporation doing business in Michigan, hired an employee, Dean Averbeck, who had been referred to defendant a year earlier by plaintiff, an Illinois employment agency. When plaintiff filed suit in Illinois to recover the fee for its services, defendant filed a special appearance and motion to quash service of summons alleging that the court had no jurisdiction over its person. This motion was denied, and a trial on the merits was conducted. Defendant made a motion for judgment at the close of plaintiff's evidence, and, after the jury rendered a verdict in favor of plaintiff, a post-trial motion for judgment notwithstanding the verdict, but these motions, too, were denied. Defendant now appeals from the judgment entered against it and from the denial of the three motions described. Defendant raises two issues on appeal: (1) the Circuit Court of Cook County did not have in personam jurisdiction over defendant; and (2) Michigan law, which requires that an employment agency contract be in writing, governed the agreement between the parties and, therefore, the contract involved is not enforceable.

There is no dispute over the essential facts. Plaintiff is a private employment agency incorporated in Illinois with its place of business in Chicago. Plaintiff places men only in executive positions paying $15,000 or more. Personnel placement in these higher-paid positions can be very sensitive, and, at times, prospective employers can supply the employment agency with only the qualifications of the needed employee without being able to name the particular job available. With executive placements, it is not unusual for there to be a lag between the time the applicant is referred to an employer and the time he is hired by that employer. In all instances, the fee for plaintiff's referral services is paid by the prospective employer, not the applicant placed. Although plaintiff's policy was that a referral would be applicable to a placement for a two-year period, such policy was not printed on its fee schedule in effect at the time of the referral involved, but was added to the schedule April 1, 1968. Plaintiff's fee schedule is on file with the Illinois Department of Labor. It is not plaintiff's custom to have the applicant sign a contract with the agency.

In December 1967 Dean Averbeck, a resident of Wisconsin, responded to an advertisement placed by plaintiff in *Metal Working News,* a business journal in the field of machine tools. This he did by sending a résumé to Robert Danon, an employment counselor and research man with plaintiff agency, and telling him that he was looking for new employment. A week later Averbeck came to plaintiff's office in Chicago for an interview with Danon. Danon explained to Averbeck that the agency would work with him, and that the agency expected to be advised by Averbeck of all interviews he had with employers to which plaintiff might refer him. Danon made out a résumé which represented Averbeck as a sales manager and which contained Averbeck's personal data and education and employment background. This "flyer" was sent to prospective employers in the machine tool industry, and by way of a large mailing, along with the résumés of 3,000 other applicants, to prospective employers in the metal working industry in general. Both mailings went to companies located throughout the United States.

Defendant is a manufacturing company which, as stated above, is incorporated in Delaware, with its place of business in Michigan. Defendant is not registered as a foreign corporation in Illinois, does not maintain offices in Illinois, is not listed in the Illinois telephone directory, and none of its employees reside in Illinois.

On January 23, 1968, E. H. Jones, Executive Vice-president of defendant Company, telephoned Danon and expressed an interest in the man represented by code number RD390 (Averbeck). He asked for the man's name, the name of his employer, and his earnings at that time. Before giving this information to Jones, Danon advised him that plaintiff was licensed to operate its agency only if the employer were to pay the referral fee upon hiring the job applicant. Jones indicated that such an arrangement would be agreeable to him. According to Danon's testimony, he also told Jones that the referral was good for two years, and that the employer would have to pay the applicant's interview and relocation expenses if the applicant were hired. Jones requested a copy of Averbeck's résumé and asked Danon to have Averbeck call him for an interview the next time he was in the Detroit area. In response to Danon's question as to the type of job which defendant had available, Jones said, "Something in sales."

That same day, Danon called Averbeck at his home in Wisconsin and learned that Averbeck was in Lansing, Michigan, looking for employment in that area. The next morning, Danon called Averbeck in Lansing and told him to call defendant and arrange an interview. Danon then called Jones to say that Averbeck was in the Detroit area and would be telephoning him later that day.

On January 25, 1968, Danon sent Averbeck's résumé to Jones and enclosed a copy of plaintiff's fee schedule. On March 12, 1968, Danon called Averbeck to check various referrals with him and was told that he had not yet had an interview with defendant. On March 18, 1968, Danon called Jones, who stated that he had not yet interviewed Averbeck.

However, Averbeck had, in fact, been interviewed by defendant on January 24, 1968, but was not hired at that time. On January 18, 1969, a year later, defendant contacted Averbeck to return for another interview. Averbeck was hired on January 30, 1969, and began to work for defendant on March 3, 1969. He started in the Sales Department at $17,000 per year with the understanding that he would be made a Sales Manager at a later date. His salary was subsequently increased to $18,000 per year. He left the firm in January 1971.

On December 9, 1969, Averbeck called Danon to inform him that he was considering a change in jobs and incidentally advised him that he had started to work for defendant on March 1, 1969, after defendant had offered him a job as a sales manager at $18,000 per year. He was unhappy with the company, however, and wanted to relocate in either Cleveland or Chicago.

Danon sent Averbeck his old résumé to be updated, and when it was returned, it bore the notation in Averbeck's handwriting, "3/1/69 to present, Colonial Broach & Machine Company, Warren, Michigan, sales manager."

On January 6, 1970, Danon called Jones to say that he was glad Averbeck had been hired and that defendant must have overlooked plaintiff's fee. Jones agreed that Averbeck had been contacted, interviewed, and hired due to plaintiff's services, but that Averbeck, when interviewed, had denied being represented by plaintiff. When Danon stated that plaintiff had, indeed, represented Averbeck at the time of the referral for the original interview in January 1968, Jones replied that he would talk to his people and call back the next day. On January 7, 1970, when Jones did not call back, Danon had an invoice prepared and sent it to defendant. Plaintiff's fee was computed on the basis of 1% per each $1000 of Averbeck's starting annual salary. Since Jones had told Danon, in their telephone conversation of January 6, 1970, that Averbeck's starting annual salary had been $16,000, the fee billed 16% of $16,000 or

$2560. The bill was never paid, and plaintiff brought suit. (It was later confirmed that Averbeck's starting annual salary had been $17,000, and the complaint was amended to state that fact and to increase the amount payed to 17% of $17,000 or $2890 plus interest.)

Defendant first contends that the trial court did not acquire jurisdiction over its person by way of Section 17 of the Illinois Civil Practice Act, known as the Illinois "long-arm" statute . . . and that, therefore, the court first erred in denying its motion to quash service of process and dismiss the suit, and erred again in denying its subsequent motions for judgment in its favor.

The "long-arm" statute provides, in pertinent part, that a non-Illinois resident submits himself to the jurisdiction of the Illinois courts by "the transaction of any business within this State." . . . Defendant asserts that by merely telephoning plaintiff in response to an unrequested solicitation sent to it in Michigan by plaintiff, its conduct did not amount to a "transaction of any business" within the meaning of the statute, and that therefore it cannot be subjected to the jurisdiction of the Illinois courts without a violation of due process.

As noted by the Supreme Court in *Nelson* v. *Miller,* 11 Ill. 2d 378, 143 N.E. 2d 673, Section 17 of the Civil Practice Act, which that court held to be valid, reflected the legislative intent to assert jurisdiction over nonresident defendants to the extent permitted by the due process clause. Due process requires only that before an Illinois court can acquire in personam jurisdiction over a nonresident defendant, that defendant must have had certain minimum contacts with Illinois such that maintenance of the suit in this state does not offend traditional notions of fair play and substantial justice. . . .

Personal jurisdiction over a nonresident does not depend upon the physical presence of the defendant within the state; it is sufficient that the act or transaction itself has a substantial connection with the forum state. . . . It is also sufficient if the nonresident defendant's contact with the state involves only a single business transaction. . . .

Reviewing the facts of this particular case, plaintiff initiated the contact between the parties by sending to defendant a "flyer" regarding available job applicants. However, the mailing of the "flyer" represented only an offer to do business, and defendant was under no obligation to respond. It was defendant, then, who initiated the business transaction in question by telephoning plaintiff and requesting that plaintiff divulge the name of a possible prospective employee whose partial identification had been gleaned from the "flyer." Defendant also asked plaintiff to send defendant a résumé of that applicant, and notify him to contact defendant for an interview. In the same conversation, a contract was created when defendant agreed that, in return for plaintiff's services, it would pay plaintiff's fee if it were subsequently to hire the applicant.

An employment agency's business is to put a prospective employee in touch with a prospective employer, and the agency's services end once the two principals are made aware of each other's identities so that negotiations can be commenced between them. Although defendant's only contact within this state was a telephone call, that call was all that was necessary for defendant to achieve its purpose. Once defendant informed plaintiff that it was interested in a certain person to fill a position and agreed to pay plaintiff's referral fee if it eventually hired that person, defendant knew, or should have known, that it had entered into a contract with an Illinois agency, that the agency would perform its services from its office in Illinois, that the fee, if due, would be paid to plaintiff in Illinois, and if the fee were not paid as promised, defendant might be liable to suit in the Illinois courts.

We find that the necessary jurisdictional minimum contacts for the purposes of in personam jurisdiction over this defendant resulted from that single business transaction between the parties, and we are of the opinion that this conclusion does not violate notions of fair play and substantial justice in requiring defendant to defend this suit in the Illinois courts.

At the time of oral argument in this case, defendant cited an opinion of a federal judge (Northern District of Illinois) in *U.S. Railway Equipment Co.* v. *Port Huron and Detroit Railroad Co.,* 58 F.R.D. 588, holding that the Illinois "long-arm" statute had not served to bring the defendant into court for in personam jurisdiction. We have studied that opinion and believe it is distinguishable on the facts from the case at bar.

Defendant contends, however, that even if Illinois courts had properly acquired in personam jurisdiction over defendant, the court erred in denying its motions for judgment in its favor because the contract, under Michigan Law, was unenforceable because plaintiff was not licensed in Michigan as an employment agency and the contract between the parties was not in writing.[1]

Although plaintiff questions whether a nonresident employment agency must first obtain a license in Michigan before referring a job applicant to a Michigan employer, we need not reach that issue as we find that Illinois law is applicable to construction of the

1. Mich. Stat. 17.393, M.C.L.A. sect. 408.603. No person shall open, operate, or maintain an employment agency in the state of Michigan without first procuring a license from the state superintendent of private employment bureaus. . . .
Mich. Stat. 17.406, M.C.L.A. sect. 408.616. Every employment agent licensed under class 2 (the appropriate class for employment agencies placing executives) shall enter into a written agreement with every employee, employer, or both, for service to be rendered for which a charge is to be made. . . .

contract between the parties and resolution of the instant case.

Under Illinois law, if a contract is made in one state with the intention that it be performed in another, and the states are governed by different laws, the law of the place where the contract is to be performed will control as to the contract's validity and will prevail over the law where the contract was entered into. . . . The contract in question, providing for payment by defendant in exchange for services rendered by plaintiff, was oral, and the parties did not specify in their telephone conversation as to where the services were to be performed. However, as previously mentioned herein, the nature of the contract was such that both parties knew plaintiff's services would be performed from its office in Illinois. The fact that the interviewing and hiring took place in Michigan is of no consequence since the services which were the basis of the contract and for which defendant would be liable for payment to plaintiff had already been performed in Illinois. Therefore, since Illinois is the state where the contract was to be performed, and the contract is valid and enforceable under Illinois law, the trial court did not err in denying defendant's motions for judgment in its favor.

It should also be noted that we are dealing with a contractual situation and, therefore, with obligations voluntarily undertaken. That fact, in itself, creates a presumption in favor of applying the law of the state which would validate the contract. . . . Since the contract, under defendant's analysis, would have been unenforceable under Michigan law, the trial court, as an additional ground for its decision, could properly have presumed that the parties intended to enter into a valid and enforceable agreement, necessarily in this case involving the application of Illinois law.

The judgment of the circuit court is affirmed.

Affirmed.

DIVERSIFIED ENVIRONMENTS v. OLIVETTI, ETC.

461 F. Supp. 286 (1978)

Herman, District Judge.

This is an action for damages brought by a lessee of a computerized accounting system manufactured and sold by the Defendant, Olivetti Corporation of America (Olivetti). Plaintiff, Diversified Environments, Inc., (Diversified) alleges that the Olivetti computer that it leased has never been made operational and that Defendant is liable for damages on theories of breach of express and implied warranties. Olivetti defends on the bases that it has fully performed and alternatively that it was excused from performance because Diversified unreasonably refused to permit it to effectuate its contractual duties. Plaintiff seeks relief for the total payments made under the lease agreement for the computer, the cost of paper products, and other consequential damages. The following are the Court's findings of fact and conclusions of law.

Findings of Fact

1. Plaintiff, Diversified Environments, Inc., is a Pennsylvania corporation engaged in the selling of temperature and energy control systems with its principal place of business at Camp Hill, Pennsylvania.
2. Defendant, Olivetti Corporation of America, is a Delaware corporation engaged in the business of selling computer services with local business offices in Harrisburg, Pennsylvania.
3. Jurisdiction is based upon diversity of citizenship and an amount in controversy in excess of ten thousand dollars.
4. In July of 1974, Tim L. Fleegal, a sales representative of Olivetti contacted Diversified's President, Charles E. Andiorio, Jr., for the purpose of inducing him to buy or lease a computerized accounting system.
5. Mr. Andiorio subsequently met with Mr. Fleegal and explained in detail the nature of Diversified's business and particularly noted that the most tedious part of his duties was the preparation of specifications to be used in submitting bids on jobs.
6. Mr. Fleegal also met with Mr. Warren Beck, who was primarily responsible for the Plaintiff's accounting system, during July and Mr. Fleegal was made aware of all of the accounting procedures of Diversified and that Diversified's accounting records had to be compatible with Barber-Colman Co., for whom Diversified was a manufacturing representative.
7. Neither Mr. Beck nor Mr. Andiorio was familiar with computer systems and they relied upon Mr. Fleegal's expertise.
8. After Mr. Fleegal became thoroughly familiar with the operations of Plaintiff's business he stated that the Olivetti P-603 Computer System would meet all of the Plaintiff's requirements and perform all of the functions that were discussed.
9. Mr. Fleegal was qualified to sell only the P-603 Computer System, which was an accounting computer, and not the Olivetti word-processing machines.

10. At the time of the discussions, Mr. Fleegal stated to both Mr. Beck and Mr. Andiorio that utilization of the P-603 Computer System would save the Plaintiff both time and expense by reducing manpower and record keeping.

11. Mr. Fleegal represented to Mr. Andiorio that he would only need to push a button and he would have the specifications, that Mr. Andiorio would save half of his time, and that the computer would enable Diversified to do without one of its secretaries.

12. On July 26, 1974, Mr. Fleegal submitted a proposal to Mr. Andiorio and advised that the P-603 accounting computer could effectively meet all of the objectives discussed between the parties.

13. The proposal specifically set forth that the P-603 computer could perform the functions of specification writing, estimating, accounts payable, job cost, prime cost analysis, accounts receivable, and check.

14. The proposal stated that the total cost of the system was $9,590.00 which included all programming, forms design, initial operator training, delivery, and installation of equipment.

15. It further provided: "in dealing with Olivetti you do business with a firm which herein guarantees in writing the exact performance of the system both machine and program. Only after these assurances have been met can we ship the machine and bill you as a customer. In addition, you have my personal assurance and that of the Harrisburg Management that all of our resources will be employed toward your complete satisfaction in the system."

16. During July or August of 1974, parts of the proposed computer package were demonstrated to Mr. Beck in the Defendant's office; however, at no time were either the specification writing or estimating demonstrated.

17. On August 7, 1974, Mr. Beck signed in two places, on behalf of Diversified, a "Customer Software Acceptance" form provided by Mr. Fleegal.

18. The Customer Software Acceptance form contains three places for signatures and Mr. Beck signed his name after the following statements on the form:
    1. "I agree that the system explained to me with regard to this application is correct in all respects and that any alterations after this date could result in additional charges according to the current published program rates.
    2. This application as described in section 1 has been demonstrated to me in its final programmed form and I accept it as being a complete and workable solution."

19. Mr. Beck did not sign after the third line which stated:
    "The program described in section 2 above has now been installed and the relevant personnel have been fully advised of its capabilities. I have received complete program documentation."

20. Mr. Fleegal advised Mr. Beck that Diversified would owe absolutely no financial obligation until the third line of the form was signed, and it was this promise that actually prompted Mr. Beck to sign the first two lines of the form.

21. This "Customer Software Acceptance" form was considered by the defendant as an agreement or contract between the parties.

22. After the signing of the form, the computer and various programs were ordered by Mr. Fleegal.

23. Around this same period of time, in July or August of 1974, Mr. Fleegal also assured Mr. Andiorio that Diversified would not be bound to accept the computer unless and until a third signature was placed on the acceptance form as acceptance and approval of the complete system.

24. Mr. Fleegal promised to personally oversee the installation and implementation of the complete computer system and also promised that Plaintiff's operators would be fully trained and if the training proved unsuccessful that Olivetti girls would be available to run the computer.

25. Mr. Fleegal also promised both Mr. Beck and Mr. Andiorio that either he or other Olivetti staff would transfer all the necessary information onto the computer cards and the Plaintiff's only obligation was to show the Olivetti staff where the information that was needed as a data base was stored.

26. Along with the other representations, Mr. Fleegal told Mr. Andiorio that Plaintiff would not owe one cent until the computer was fully in operation and they were completely satisfied.

27. On these conditions, the computer was placed at Plaintiff's business during September of 1974; however, it was not operational at that time.

28. Mr. Fleegal then contacted an equipment leasing company, Equipment Funding, Inc., (Equipment Funding) and made the arrangements for Equipment Funding's purchase of the computer and software, and the subsequent leasing of it to the Plaintiff.

29. Mr. Fleegal received a lease agreement from Equipment Funding and took it to Mr. Beck for his signature on October 3, 1975.

30. Mr. Beck signed the lease agreement on October 3, 1975, after Mr. Fleegal assured him that it was just a mere formality, an application for a lease,

and that Plaintiff would not be obligated to keep the system or to make any payments until it was completely satisfied.

31. Subsequently, Mr. Beck received a payment or coupon book from Equipment Funding and on approaching Mr. Fleegal, he was told to disregard it as no payments were due until the computer was operative and until they signed the third line of the Software Acceptance form as their acceptance.

32. The lease was not to be effective until an "Acceptance Certificate" was signed by the Plaintiff.

33. In mid-November, Mr. O'Brien, from Equipment Funding, and Mr. Fleegal went to Plaintiff's place of business for the purpose of obtaining execution of the "Acceptance Certificate" and Mr. Beck initially refused to sign the certificate.

34. Mr. Fleegal then induced Mr. Beck to sign the acceptance on the promises that the computer would be running by the first of the year and on the guarantee that the computer system would be acceptable to the Plaintiff.

35. Subsequently, Mr. Fleegal and another Olivetti employee, Barbara Slagle, made several visits to Diversified for the purpose of installation.

36. Mrs. Slagle, a customer software representative, met with Plaintiff's employee on December 18, 1974, and together they set up the payroll data base and the employee was taught how to update the data.

37. The payroll function was the only function Mrs. Slagle was supposed to teach, as Mr. Fleegal was to teach all of the other functions listed in the proposal.

38. Mrs. Slagle incurred no problems in either teaching Plaintiff's employee or in getting the base data for the payroll function.

39. Mr. Fleegal made several visits during the month of December 1974 for the purpose of training Plaintiff's employee on the numerous other functions; however, he neither transferred the data as previously promised nor was he successful in training the designated employee on any of the other functions.

40. Mr. Fleegal spent a substantial amount of his time during these visits in discussing his religious beliefs with Plaintiff's employees.

41. After receiving complaints from his employees, Mr. Andiorio refused to allow Mr. Fleegal to return to the premises.

42. During Mr. Fleegal's visits at Plaintiff's business in December of 1975, he never requested any information from Mr. Andiorio with respect to the specification writing or estimating, even though the specification writing was to be the primary use of the computer.

43. By January 7, 1975, the only data that had been transferred was the payroll base data, and the computer was only capable of being utilized for this minor function at that time.

44. Plaintiff, pursuant to prior representations, in early January, stopped further training and requested the Defendant to remove the computer from their premises, as the computer was at that time nearly worthless because data had not been transferred, employees had not been trained, and Plaintiff was completely unsatisfied with the computer.

45. Defendant refused to remove the machine and by letter of January 20, 1975, District Manager, T. F. Meade, Jr., replied, "The relevant personnel have been trained," and "(o)ur only remaining obligation is to continue to assist you in the fullest implementation of this sytem which you requested and for which you contracted."

46. Plaintiff continued making the lease payments after consulting with counsel, as it did not want to place its credit rating in jeopardy, and was advised to institute suit against Olivetti instead.

47. A meeting was subsequently held in February 1975 with Mr. Meade, Mr. O'Brien, Mr. Andiorio, and others in attendance, and Defendant took the position that it had fully performed.

48. No further training was conducted in 1975 and Defendant was not requested by Plaintiff to conduct training during this period.

49. This suit was filed on April 13, 1976.

50. Subsequent to the institution of this action, Mrs. Slagle returned in December of 1976 to train another employee and to attempt to prepare the computer for Plaintiff's utilization.

51. After one day or a day and one-half this installation attempt was rejected by the Plaintiff on the advice of his employee who was trained in computer systems for the reasons that the P-603 was not compatible with the Barber-Colman bookkeeping system and because use of the accounting computer for specification writing was cost prohibitive.

52. Use of the P-603 computer for specification writing required that the information be placed on cards at the rate of one paragraph per card, which for Plaintiff's needs would have required likely over a thousand cards at two dollars each, and which would have required someone to manually pick the necessary cards out of a file and insert them into the P-603 computer.

53. The P-603 computer was not designed to perform word processing as that required for specifications writing, which was the Plaintiff's primary concern.
54. Expenses incurred by Plaintiff with respect to this transaction include $15,126.00 for payments due under the lease, $145.54 for paper products, and an accountant's bill of $387.50.

Discussion

While a number of the theories raised by the Plaintiff are indeed relevant and applicable to the facts of this case, it is unnecessary to discuss the theories of warranty and misrepresentation, as Defendant's breach of its contractual duties is sufficient to impose liability. The parol evidence rule is clearly inapplicable here, as there was no integrated written agreement between the parties that fully and completely stated the entire agreement. The only writings involved are the written proposal and the Customer Software Acceptance form, neither of which completely embody the agreement between the parties. We find that the oral agreement to provide certain services formed part of the contractual relationship and that the oral agreement obligated Defendant to perform the transfer of data, the training of employees, and generally to make the computer functional. These obligations were breached as the base data has only been transferred for the relatively minor payroll function and the only training that has been completed is to this payroll function. Plaintiff's employees have not been trained on the remaining functions, the ones most important to the Plaintiff, and the base data has never been transferred onto the computer cards.

Defendant asserts that it should be excused from performance because the Plaintiff prevented it from performing its obligation. While not totally devoid of merit, this argument fails to relieve the Defendant from liability. As noted in the findings, the computer was installed at Plaintiff's place of business in September of 1974 and the Plaintiff was fully receptive to having the computer made operational until sometime in early January of 1975. Plaintiff assigned an employee for the computer training and Mrs. Slagle encountered no problems in either the training or the transfer of data for the payroll function. The problems arose from Mr. Fleegal's failure to succeed in training the employees on the other numerous functions and failure to transfer the base data as was initially promised and which formed a part of the understanding between the parties. This could have been due to the fact that this was Mr. Fleegal's first sale and his first attempt at training individuals in the use of the computer. Regardless of this, it is clear that no one was trained to perform the other functions and that Mr. Fleegal interfered with

Plaintiff's employees to some extent with his religious discussions.

It was only after Defendant's attempts at performance were proving unsuccessful that Plaintiff demanded the computer be removed and training halted. This was reasonable under the circumstances as Defendant had advised Plaintiff numerous times that it had no financial or contractual obligation until they signed the third line of the Customer Software Acceptance form as an indication that they were completely satisfied and that the computer was fully operational. As noted above, the Defendant took the position that it had performed and that the employee of Plaintiff had been trained, which was simply not true. The Plaintiff remained receptive to having its employees trained, even after suit was filed, until it determined that the computer was neither economically feasible nor compatible with other bookkeeping requirements. In short, Plaintiff's refusal to permit training at the two times noted was reasonable under the circumstances and was not a material interference with Defendant's obligation. The argument that it was excused because base data was not supplied is similarly unpersuasive as Mrs. Slagle encountered no such problem, Mr. Fleegal never advised Mr. Andiorio of any uncooperative conduct of his employees, and because the letter of Mr. Meade of January 1975 never raised the problem of obtaining base data. Therefore, no excuse exists for Defendant's non-performance. . . .

Defendant also argues that Plaintiff has failed to join an indispensable party, Equipment Funding, because complete relief cannot be accorded among those already parties. This argument is not valid for at least two reasons. First, complete relief can be accorded between the present parties. Defendant breached its contractual obligation, and defendant has made no showing that Equipment Funding is an indispensable party. Second, the Defendant should be stopped from even raising the issue, as it was only due to Defendant's misrepresentation that the lease was initially entered and the acceptance certificate signed.

The final argument of the Defendant is that Plaintiff failed to mitigate its damages. While Plaintiff was under an obligation to mitigate damages, it was Defendant's burden to prove that Plaintiff failed in this obligation. . . . Defendant did not present any facts at trial that established a means of mitigation for the Plaintiff. Instead, the evidence showed that Plaintiff tried to return the computer and that after this was rejected by the Defendant, Plaintiff gave Defendant other opportunities to perform its contractual duties. The breach was material and the measure of damages is that which was caused by the breach. . . . Under the circumstances of this case, the damages are the cost of the computer and paper products, the interest that Plaintiff was obligated to pay under the lease, and the expense incurred for an accountant on the request of Defendant's agent, totaling $15,659.04.

Conclusions of Law

1. A contractual relationship exists between Diversified and Olivetti, part of which is the oral agreement by Olivetti to perform the transfer of all base data and to train Plaintiff's employees.
2. The contractual duty owed to the Plaintiff was breached by the defendant as Defendant substantially failed to carry out its obligations of transferring the base data, of training Plaintiff's employees, and of making the computer system operational.
3. The injury suffered by the Plaintiff due to Defendant's breach is $15,659.04, and judgment will be entered for the Plaintiff in this amount.

An appropriate order will be entered.

MARKSILL SPECIALTIES, INC. v. BARGER

428 N.E. 2d 65 (1981)

Hoffman, Presiding Judge.

Marksill Specialties, Inc., appeals the judgment of the trial court awarding damages to Theodore Barger for Marksill's breach of a written contract to pay R.B.I. Sales commissions. Issues raised by Marksill include:

(1) whether the trial court erred in failing to grant Marksill's motion to dismiss the cause because Barger was not the real party in interest;

(2) whether the trial court erred in excluding evidence that Marksill's president lacked authority to enter into the contested contract when the issue was included in Marksill's contentions in the pretrial order;

(3) whether a proper foundation was laid for the introduction of a form contract into evidence;

(4) whether the contract was terminable at will due to the lack of a specific termination date;

(5) whether the contract is void for lack of certainty and mutuality;

(6) whether the court erred in its construction of the contract;

(7) whether the contract was void for lack of or failure of consideration; and

(8) whether the evidence is sufficient to sustain the judgment.

On February 15, 1973, Marksill entered into an employment agreement with Theodore Barger. Barger was employed to perform certain engineering and design duties. Prior to the time of the employment agreement, Marksill entered into a representative agreement with R.B.I. Sales, a partnership formed by Barger and Noel Ryan.

The representative agreement provided that in return for R.B.I. Sales' efforts in securing new accounts, Marksill would pay R.B.I. Sales a 5% commission based on the amount of sales to Dexter Axle Company. The employment agreement provided: "In the event Theodore Barger should no longer be employed, commission checks for the Dexter Account will continue to be paid as per prior Representative Agreement." The representative agreement provided: "This agreement is valid and payment shall continue as long as ——— sells any product to any company listed."

Marksill contends initially that the trial court erred in denying its Ind. Rules of Procedure, Trial Rule 12(B)(6) motion to dismiss. The motion was based on the requirement of Trial Rule 17(A) that "(e)very action shall be prosecuted in the name of the real party in interest." Marksill argues that it entered into the representative agreement with R.B.I. Sales, not Barger, and therefore R.B.I. Sales is the real party in interest.

The motion to dismiss was made at the close of Barger's case. The trial court denied the motion as being untimely filed. Marksill is correct in its contention that such a ruling is in error. In *Childs* v. *Rayburn, Adm.* . . . . this Court held that a motion to dismiss premised on TR. 17(A) is timely even though it is made at the midpoint of a trial. The trial court's error in this regard is, however, harmless.

Marksill argues that if Barger is permitted to maintain the action, it would still be possible for Ryan, the other partner of R.B.I. Sales, to also bring an action on the contract. Marksill could thus be liable for two judgments based on the same contract. The record shows that R.B.I. Sales was a partnership composed of only Barger and Ryan. Ryan abandoned the partnership sometime after the representative agreement was entered into.

IC 1971, 23-4-1-29 (Burns Code Ed.) provides:

"The dissolution of a partnership is the change in the relation of the partners caused by any partner ceasing to be associated in the carrying on as distinguished from the winding up of the business."

Ryan's abandonment of the partnership clearly effected a dissolution. IC 1971, 23-4-1-37 (Burns Code Ed.) provides:

> "Unless otherwise agreed the partners who have not wrongfully dissolved the partnership or the legal representative of the last surviving partner, not bankrupt, has the right to wind up the partnership afffairs: Provided, however, That any partner, his legal representative, or his assignee, upon cause shown, may obtain winding up by the court."

Included within the winding up of the partnership's affairs is the performance of existing contracts, the collection of debts or claims due the partnership, and the payment of partnership debts. . . . Pursuant to IC 1971, 23-4-1-37, Barger, as the sole remaining partner, is entitled to wind up the partnership's affairs. Barger is therefore the real party in interest to maintain this action. Ryan, as the abandoning partner, may be entitled to a share of the proceeds, but his cause of action would be against Barger, not Marksill.

Marksill next contends that the trial court erred in excluding evidence that Marksill's president lacked authority to enter into a lifetime or perpetual agreement. Although the issue was included within Marksill's contentions in the pretrial order, the trial court did not err in excluding the evidence. The representative agreement provided that the commission would be paid so long as Marksill continued to sell certain products to Dexter Axle. The contract is therefore neither a lifetime, nor a perpetual contract, but rather, a contract terminable upon the happening of a certain condition. Whether Marksill's president had authority to enter into a lifetime or perpetual contract is irrelevant to the issues involved in this case.

The next issue raised by Marksill is whether there was a sufficient evidentiary foundation for the admission of a form contract into evidence. Marksill argues that Barger did not make a showing that a diligent search had been made in order to locate the original contract. Admission of secondary evidence absent such a showing of diligence violates the best evidence rule.

Generally, it is within the discretion of the trial court to make the preliminary factual determination of whether an adequate showing of diligence has been made. . . . Accordingly, the trial court's determination will be disturbed only upon a showing of an abuse of discretion.

In the present case, Barger testified that his former partner, Ryan, informed him that the original contract had been destroyed and that no copies had been retained. It is within the province of the trial court to judge the credibility of the witnesses. Marksill has failed to establish that the trial court abused its discretion in accepting Barger's testimony and determining that an adequate showing of diligence had been made.

Marksill also contends, citing 12 I.L.E. *Evidence* sec. 83 (1959), that Indiana law requires that:

> "(t)he loss of the writing must be proved by the person who had it at the time of the loss or into whose custody it is traced, if he still is alive."

Recent Indiana decisions have not construed the exceptions to the best evidence rule as narrowly as does the Indiana Law Encyclopedia. The proponent of secondary evidence need only satisfactorily demonstrate to the trial court that the original writing is lost. . . . The determination of whether an adequate showing of unavailability is made is within the discretion of the trial court. Barger's testimony that the contract was destroyed in 1972, before this litigation was contemplated, obviously persuaded the trial court that the original representative agreement was unavailable through no fault of Barger. Marksill has again failed to establish as an abuse of discretion.

Marksill next contends that the representative agreement was terminable at will, by either party, because it contains no specific termination date. It is true, as Marksill asserts, that a contract providing for continuing performance and which has no termination date, or which provides that it will last indefinitely, is terminable at will by either party. . . .

The representative agreement in the present case does not fall within the category of contracts which have no termination date or which provide that they will last indefinitely. Although a date is not specified, the representative agreement does contain a provision that sets out a condition which would terminate Marksill's obligations. As noted previously, that condition is the discontinuance of the sale of certain products to Dexter Axle Company. The representative agreement, containing a provision for termination, is terminable in accordance with its terms and not at the will of either party.

Marksill next argues that the representative agreement is unenforceable because of a lack of mutuality. Marksill also contends that the representative agreement lacks sufficient certainty to be enforceable.

The existence of a valid contract depends upon mutuality of obligation; i.e., there can be no contract unless both parties are bound. . . . Where, however, one party to the agreement acts upon the promise of the other party and performs his part of the agreement, the contract is not unenforceable for lack of mutuality. . . . In the present case, Marksill promised to compensate R.B.I. Sales for its efforts in securing new accounts. R.B.I. Sales made efforts to secure new accounts. Marksill is therefore obligated to perform its part of the bargain. The contract does not lack mutuality.

Likewise, the contract does not lack certainty. Although the form contract which was introduced into evidence contained blank spaces, there was sufficient testimony from which the trial court could ascertain the terms of the original agreement. This testimony is therefore sufficient to establish the requisite certainty.

The next issue raised by Marksill is whether the trial court erred in not construing the agreement so as to give effect to the reasonable expectations of the parties. Marksill contends that the contract is ambiguous and that the ambiguities should be resolved against R.B.I. Sales, the drafter of the agreement.

A contract is ambiguous only where reasonable people could find its terms susceptible to more than one interpretation. . . . Ambiguity is not established by the mere fact that a controversy exists. . . . Where no defect in the formation of a contract is alleged, the terms of the contract, if unambiguous, are conclusive upon the question of the parties' intentions. . . . Whether an ambiguity exists must be determined by application of the following principles:

1) Words used in a contract must be given their common meaning unless, from the entire contract and the subject matter thereof, it is clear that some other meaning was intended; and
2) Words, phrases, sentences, and paragraphs of a contract are not to be read alone; the intention of the parties must be gathered from the entire contract. . . .

The representative agreement is not ambiguous. By the express terms of the contract, in exchange for the efforts of R.B.I. Sales in securing new accounts, Marksill agreed to pay R.B.I. Sales a 5% commission so long as it continued to sell products to Dexter Axle Company. The representative agreement was correctly construed in accordance with its express terms by the trial court.

Marksill contends next that the representative agreement was void for lack of, or failure of, consideration. According to Marksill, if the consideration recited in the agreement is the efforts of R.B.I. Sales in securing new accounts, there is failure of consideration, because the evidence shows that no new accounts were in fact secured. On the other hand, Marksill argues that if the trial court was correct in finding that the agreement did not require R.B.I. Sales to service the accounts, there is a total lack of consideration.

Initially it must be noted that specific findings of fact were neither requested, nor required. Indiana Rules of Procedure, Trial Rule 52(A). The fact that, in its opinion, the trial court found that the agreement did not require R.B.I. Sales to service the accounts, does not represent an exclusive finding with regard to consideration. On the contrary, the trial court made no specific findings regarding consideration.

The contract provides for the efforts of R.B.I. Sales in securing new accounts. This is adequate consideration for Marksill's promise to pay a commission. Additionally, Marksill's assertion that no new accounts were secured is not supported by the record. Although Marksill had been doing business with Dexter Axle prior to the execution of the representative agreement, the evidence shows that R.B.I. Sales negotiated with Dexter Axle for the introduction of a new line of products manufactured by Marksill. This new line of products may rightfully be viewed as a new account. The contract is therefore supported by adequate consideration.

Finally, Marksill challenges the sufficiency of the evidence. The only new issue Marksill raises in its sufficiency argument is whether the evidence is sufficient to establish that the form contract entered into evidence contained the same provisions as the representative agreement which R.B.I. Sales and Marksill entered into.

Barger testified that the form contract contained the same provisions as the representative agreement Marksill entered into with R.B.I. Sales. Mark Norman Sill, president of Marksill, testified that he could not state that the form contract did not contain the same provisions. This Court will neither weigh the evidence nor judge the credibility of the witnesses. These functions are within the province of the trial court. Based on the testimony, the evidence is sufficient to sustain the trial court's judgment.

Having found no reversible error, the judgment of the trial court is affirmed.

Garrard and Staton, J. J., concur.

REVIEW QUESTIONS

1. Black Tool and Die Company agreed to make a punch press die for White for $10,000. A one-month delivery time was agreed upon. Black was ready to begin work on the die when White called and told Black to hold up until further notice. White then shopped around in an attempt to improve upon the price. White could not find a better price and called Black about two weeks later to tell him to go ahead on the die, but Black refused, saying that his work schedule was now such that he

could not complete the die within six months. White claims breach of contract and threatens to sue. What is the likely outcome of the case? Why?

2. Why is it necessary for courts to recognize anticipatory breach on contracts in which a structure is to be built and installed?

3. Does your state have an arbitration statute? If so, what are the provisions and limitations in the statute?

4. Black, under a contract with White, built an automatic assembly machine to assemble drive mechanisms for automobile window regulators. The contract calls for a machine capable of producing 1,500 assemblies per hour. The resulting machine ran at a speed that would easily produce 1,500 assemblies per hour. However, its longest run since installation a month ago has only been about two minutes before it jammed. Frequently it will run only one or two pieces before stopping. The cause of jamming is slight variations in the dimensions of the component parts of the window regulator assemblies. The parts are manufactured by White in the same manner they have been produced for many years. Black had access to unlimited quantities of the parts while the machine was being built. According to the contract, Black's performance was finished when the installation of the machine was completed. White has paid $162,000 of the $180,000 agreed price of the machine. Black demands payment of the remainder. White claims a right to retain part or all of the $18,000 to compensate him for efforts spent in making the machine work. Has Black substantially performed? Can he get the $18,000? Why or why not?

5. Green leased a building near two metal working plants for a period of five years. The lease specified no restrictions as to use of the building. Green set up a tool and die shop that operated profitably for about a year when the first plant left and relocated in another city. Shortly thereafter the second plant was dissolved in bankruptcy. Green wants to avoid his lease, claiming commercial frustration in that the remaining tool and die work is insufficient to be profitable. Is he stuck with the lease or can he get out? Why?

6. In *Cook Associates, Inc.* v. *Colonial Broach & Mach. Co.*, how did the Illinois employment agency obtain jurisdiction with regard to a Michigan firm? What could the Illinois court do if Colonial refused to pay the judgment against them?

7. In *Diversified Investments* v. *Olivetti*, etc., how could Diversified have prevented its computer disaster while still accomplishing its desired objectives?

8. In *Marksill Specialties, Inc.* v. *Barger*, outline the agreement between Marksill and Barger in regards to satisfying all of the elements of a valid contract and discharge according to the judge's logic.

14

Remedies

We have considered the requirements for the formation of a lawful contract. In Chapter 13 we considered the discharge of obligations imposed on the parties by such contracts. We have observed that not all contractual obligations are discharged as the parties originally intended. When the actual performance is materially less than that which was intended, a breach of contract has occurred. Each party to a contract has a right to obtain proper performance for the rights or performance he gives up. If this right is not satisfied, the law affords a *remedy*. The extent and type of remedy afforded is determined by the nature and extent of the breach.

We have defined a *contract* as an agreement enforceable at law. The enforceable-at-law part of the definition sets the contract agreement apart from other agreements. Saying that contract rights are enforceable at law implies that there must be remedies available for their breach. "For every right, a remedy;" so runs an equity maxim, and this pertains to contract rights as well as to other rights the law protects.

In law, remedies exist to enforce a right, or to prevent the violation of a right, or to compensate for an injury. Probably the most common remedy sought and obtained is money *damages*. However, there are numerous instances in which damages will not afford an adequate or complete remedy. For this reason other remedies have been developed. Such remedies as *restitution, specific performance,* the *injunction, rescission,* and *reformation* are examples of those available under particular circumstances. In addition, a court of equity, with its origin based on unusual remedies, can combine and select remedies or, if necessary, invent new ones to fit new circumstances. Here we will consider only the common remedies of damages, restitution, specific performance, and the injunction. One or a combination of these remedies will be appropriate in nearly any case in which an engineer is likely to be involved.

It has become almost standard practice to provide some form of remedy such as liquidated damages[1] in the wording of engineering contracts. Such provisions are enforceable in court if they are made in good faith by the parties and are reasonable in the extent of the remedy provided.

Damages

Damages are compensation in money, recoverable in court by one who has suffered a loss, detriment, or injury. Any breach of contract situation allows a damage action of some sort unless it is very unusual. Even when the breach is not of a nature such that compensation is really justified, the injured party may still win his case and be awarded *nominal damages* (e.g., six cents or one dollar). An award of nominal damages merely means the court has recognized that there was an invasion of a technical right of the plaintiff. Of course, as with any other award, the loser will probably be assessed the court costs. The loser pays the court costs but, win or lose, each party usually must pay his own lawyer.

Compensatory Damages. The usual reason for undertaking a damage action is to obtain *compensation* for an injury to one's person, property, or rights. To obtain compensatory damages it is not only necessary to prove that a right existed and was invaded; in addition, the amount of damage must be established with reasonable certainty. If the amount of damage cannot be reasonably established, the result is likely to be an award of nominal damages. The amount of compensation to which the plaintiff may be entitled is a jury question. The judge must accept the jury verdict unless he feels the jury has incorrectly weighed the evidence.

There are two basic theories of damage measurement:

1. The contract measure of damages
2. The tort measure of damages

The *contract measure of damages* attempts to return any out-of-pocket costs to the plaintiff. In addition, it tries to compensate for such things as profits missed as a result of the contract breach. The objective of this method is to place the plaintiff in the position he would have enjoyed if the contract had not been breached.

Of course, the damages claimed must be directly connected to the contract breached if the plaintiff is to be compensated. Black has a contract to build auto-

1. Liquidated damages are *liquidated* in the sense that they are known, predetermined damages, such as a $100 forfeit by the contractor for each day he is late in completing his contract.

mation equipment for White. Gray states that if the automation works properly for White he will be interested in a similar installation. Black may even have submitted preliminary plans and drawings to Gray. White then breached his contract. Black could collect compensation for his costs so far on White's contract plus the profit he could reasonably expect from White. However, Black could get nothing from White to cover anticipated profit from Gray. The claim here would be termed too speculative.

The *tort theory of damage measurement* attempts to return the plaintiff to the position in which he would be if nothing had happened. According to the tort theory, the plaintiff's out-of-pocket costs are covered in addition to compensation for any mental anguish he may have suffered. The results, in terms of money damages, can be quite different depending upon which theory is followed in a particular case. It might be noted that a tort case can look very much like a contract case, and a breach of contract can appear to be a tort. The dividing line is delicate and, at times, not too well defined.

Exemplary Damages. In certain cases the court will allow more damages than the reasonable compensation for the injury or wrong suffered. Where the right was violated under circumstances such as fraud, malice, oppression, or other despicable conduct by the defendant, *exemplary damages* may be awarded. Double or triple the bare compensation may result. Such damages have a primary purpose of punishing the defendant for his conduct and setting him forth as an example. Secondarily, exemplary damages are added compensation for the shame, degradation, or mental anguish suffered by the plaintiff.

Exemplary damages are much more likely to be allowed in tort cases than in contract cases, according to the state laws on damages. The idea behind this is that contract breaches are not likely to cause as much resentment or physical or mental anguish as are torts or crimes.

Duty to Mitigate Damages. If there were no recourse to law when a person's rights have been invaded, he would certainly make every effort to keep the damage as small as possible. All the law asks in requiring the plaintiff to *mitigate* (abate or minimize) the damage suffered is that he follow just such a reasonable course of action. If one is injured he must make every reasonable effort to keep the injury to a minimum. For instance, if an employment contract (to run for a certain period of time) is breached by the employer, the employee must actively seek work elsewhere. If he is successful, he will be allowed the difference between the two salaries (assuming his original job paid him

more); if he is unsuccessful after a reasonable effort to find subsequent employment, he may sue for his total lost pay. If he does not make a reasonable effort to find subsequent employment, or if he refuses suitable work, he may find himself with considerably diminished damages. He would not, of course, be required to take work for which he was not suited (for instance, an experienced engineer would be unlikely to be criticized for refusing employment as a farmhand); neither would he be required to move a great distance from his community.

Black is a manufacturer of appliance parts, particularly chrome-plated ones. He has a contract with White whereby White is to supply Black with nickel, at a stated price, for use in the copper-nickel-chromium plating process. During the life of the agreement, White raises the price of the nickel supplied, thus breaching the contract. Black could try to find an alternate source of nickel or he could pay White's increased price. He might even use the increased price as an excuse to cease manufacturing appliance parts for his customers, relying on White's breach to cover any losses he might sustain. Either of the first two alternatives might be considered reasonable as an attempt to mitigate the damage. Black would not, however, be allowed to renege on his contracts with the appliance manufacturers and pass along to White damages assessed against him. Neither could he maintain an action for lost profits if he ceased manufacturing parts on this basis. Black's damage suit will get him only the difference between the contract price and the price he actually had to pay for the nickel.

It might appear in the situation above that the equity remedy of specific performance would be available to Black. Such is not the case unless a statute exists to make it available—and some states do have such statutes. Without statutory provision, however, specific performance would be denied on the basis that money damages would be a sufficient remedy. Black could, conceivably, obtain the same quality and quantity of nickel from other suppliers, with the difference in price being the only loss to him.

Restitution

Restitution, as currently applied, is not greatly different from damages. Awards are usually made in money. They are based on the plaintiff's having parted in good faith with his consideration and the defendant's having breached his duty. The difference between restitution and damages is in the purpose and amount of the award. *Restitution* only restores what is lost or the value of the thing given. There is no attempt, as in a damage action, to compensate the plaintiff for lost profits. Only the out-of-pocket cost is covered. In effect, the plaintiff is required to return whatever consideration he has received from the defendant. The courts, however, do not adhere strictly to this rule. They will not apply it where, by so doing, they offer a shield to the defendant for his wrongdoing. The injured party is required to return what he has received where it is reasonably possible for him to do so, but it is not made an unwavering prerequisite to recovery by him.

Equity Remedies

Specific performance and the injunction are the principal equity remedies. Neither remedy may be used where an adequate remedy at law (e.g., damages, restitution, or a statute) is available. However, either remedy may be used in conjunction with damages where damages alone would be an insufficient remedy. Where either remedy would require extensive supervision of the court for enforcement, an attempt will be made to find a different remedy. Where, for instance, specific performance of a contract to maintain something is requested, it is likely that the court would deny the remedy. Such a remedy requires supervision; the court would look for a more appropriate remedy and only turn to one of the two standard remedies as a last resort.

Specific Performance. The most common, though not exclusive, use of the remedy of specific performance occurs when a unique piece of property is involved. A piece of land, such as a city lot or a farm, is unique. So is an original painting by an old master, or a tailor-made piece of automation equipment. Courts, since ancient times, have considered land as unique (extension of the concept to other property items is of more recent origin). If a contract to sell a particular piece of land is breached by the seller, sufficient money damages might be awarded to allow neighboring property to be purchased. However, no two pieces of land have the same location, and it is likely that there would be other tangible and intangible differences; the purchaser's spouse, for instance, might claim that the view from the location gives a sense of security or that the trees are appealing.

Injunction. Originally injunctions were only *prohibitive* in nature ("thou shalt not"). Now, in most jurisdictions, an injunction may be either prohibitive or *mandatory* ("thou shalt"). Even where injunctions must be prohibitive, it is possible to write what is, in effect, a mandatory injunction. In one case a tenant, enraged at his landlord, piled garbage on the front lawn of the tenant house before leaving. Though a mandatory injunction could not be issued in that state, a prohibitive

injunction did the job just as well. The tenant was prohibited from allowing the garbage to remain on the lawn at his former residence.

The injunction is often used where irreparable injury to real property is imminent—not just "possible," but imminent, very probable. The probable damage must also be damage that could not be satisfactorily repaired.

A court will not require specific performance of personal service contracts; such a holding would violate long-established legal policies. Rather, a person who has contracted his service to another might be enjoined from performing the same service for anyone else.

The speed and convenience of the injunction as a means of enforcing a law has appealed to legislators. If a particular law can be made to call for an injunction or a "cease and desist" order to be issued when the law is violated, the time and expense of a jury trial is often avoided. It is only necessary that the order be issued and probable violators informed. Any further violation is contempt of court resulting in a jail sentence or a fine. The speed and simplicity of the injunction is appealing. However, it should be carefully used in the statutes; wholesale use could deprive us of our jury trial right.

Enforcement of Remedies

A remedy without enforcement would be meaningless. The law must "have teeth" if it is to be effective. There are three common means of enforcing court awards against the loser in a suit at law; execution, garnishment, and attachment. Equity enforcement usually takes the form of contempt of court.

After a judgment is rendered in court the loser is expected to comply with that judgment. Where security has been posted, the loss may be deducted from it. Where no security has been pledged and the loser does not comply with the court's order, the other party may return to court for an order to confiscate property in satisfaction of the judgment. Such an order is a *writ of execution.* It is addressed to the sheriff or other enforcement officer, giving him the right to seize as much of the loser's property (both real and personal) as may be necessary to satisfy the judgment. The property so obtained is sold at an execution sale, the proceeds being used to satisfy the award of damages, with any remainder going back to the loser.

Garnishment is the means used to obtain the loser's property which is held by a third party. Notice is given to the third party to turn over the judgment debtor's property in satisfaction of the obligation.

Attachment is a process used when the defendant himself is not within the jurisdiction of the court, but some of his property is available. Because the attachment process usually takes place before the court proceedings, the plaintiff is required to post a bond to protect the defendant. Such attachment prevents the defendant from removing his property from the court's jurisdiction prior to the court's judgment. If the defendant wishes to remove the attachment, he may do so by posting a counter bond in sufficient amount to cover the plaintiff's claim.

Execution, garnishment, and attachment are all limited by statutes in the various states. The homestead laws which limited creditor's rights also protect the loser in a damage action. Also, many state laws severely restrict garnishment, particularly when the wages of the head of a household are concerned.

Another device that should be considered as security or enforcement is the *mechanic's lien.* It is a lien against not only the structure built, improved, or worked upon, but also generally against the land upon which the structure rests. It may be established by any unpaid laborers, contractors, subcontractors, material men, or others having a hand in the work involved. The mechanic's lien did not exist under common law or equity and is, therefore, entirely a creation of state statutes. The statutes tend to be quite similar and tend to emphasize benefits to laborers, materialmen, and subcontractors rather than those to contractors and engineers or architects. The reason for this is that the latter group is much more likely to be in position to pursue a remedy for nonpayment by means of breach of contract.

Contempt of court is the principal means of enforcing equity remedies. The extent of the enforcement is pretty much within the court's discretion. Statutes frequently limit the length of contempt-of-court jail sentences and the amount of fines. However, repeated offenses lead to repeated sentencing. Each day in which the court order is avoided represents a separate offense, so the confinement could run for years.

KROEGER v. FRANCHISE EQUITIES, INCORPORATED

212 N.W. 2d 348 (1973)

Boslaugh, Justice.

This was an action for damages for breach of contract. The defendant appeals from a judgment for the plaintiff in the amount of $4,000.

On November 9, 1970, the plaintiff entered into a subcontract with the defendant whereby the plaintiff agreed to furnish labor, materials, and equipment and perform all carpentry work required to construct a service station and restaurant in Omaha, Nebraska. The contract provided the plaintiff would begin and terminate his work according to a "Critical Path Schedule" which was a detailed construction schedule set out in the contract. It provided the carpentry work would be performed between December 3, 1970, and January 28, 1971.

The plaintiff commenced work on November 20, 1970. In December the plaintiff received a telephone call from the defendant's job superintendent, Burt Smith, who said he "was shutting the job down." The plaintiff heard nothing further from the defendant until April 1971. The plaintiff then did 8 hours' additional work on the job but refused to complete the contract because carpenters' wages were about to increase and the job had been figured originally on the basis of being winter work.

The entire evidence at the trial consisted of the written contract and the plaintiff's testimony. The defendant's answer alleged the plaintiff had agreed to the closing down of the job because of the weather. The evidence was to the contrary. The plaintiff testified he did not agree to closing down the job; that there was temporary shielding and a portable heating unit on the job; and the weather did not prevent construction from proceeding.

The defendant also claimed it had a right to reschedule the work under the contract. The contract provided that if the critical path schedule was revised, the plaintiff would receive 3 days' notice when the job was to be ready for him and claims for damage for delays were to be made promptly. We believe that a delay in all construction from December to April was not a "revision" of the critical path schedule within the meaning of the contract and the contemplation of the parties.

The petition alleged the plaintiff had performed work and services in the amount of $800 and was further damaged in the amount of $3,500. The plaintiff testified he and his employees had spent 139½ hours on the job; the job had been estimated on the basis of 1,000 hours' work at $8 per hour plus 15 percent profit; and he had been paid $241 by the defendant.

The plaintiff was entitled to recover the value of the work performed plus the profit he would have received if he had been allowed to complete the job within the time provided in the contract. . . . The plaintiff was required to furnish appropriate data to enable the trier of fact to find the damages with reasonable certainty. . . . Damages for breach of contract that are susceptible of definite proof are recoverable only to the extent the evidence affords a basis of ascertaining their amount in money with reasonable certainty. . . .

There was no satisfactory evidence of the reasonable value of the work performed and no evidence as to the profit the plaintiff would have realized if he had been permitted to finish the job as the contract originally provided. The contract required the plaintiff to furnish both labor and materials for "carpentry per plans and specifications" but there was no evidence concerning the plans and specifications and no evidence concerning the labor cost to plaintiff and his overhead expenses.

The evidence was not sufficient to sustain the finding that the plaintiff was damaged in the amount of $4,000. The judgment is reversed and the cause remanded for a new trial on the issue of damages only. Reversed and remanded.

WIEBE CONST. CO v. SCHOOL DIST. OF MILLARD

255 N.W. 2d 413

Clinton, Justice.

This is an action by Wiebe Construction Company against the School District of Millard, arising out of a contract entered into by the parties on July 22, 1969, under the terms of which Wiebe agreed to construct for the district a project identified as the Millard High School stadium at a cost price of $556,365. In accordance with provisions for changes in the contract contained therein, the contract was modified by the parties by change orders Nos. 1, 2, 3, and 4, calling for additional work and payments in the amount of $2,172.18, $2,067, and $8,553. The original contract required completion of the work within "350 consecutive calendar days" after " 'Notice to Proceed.' " The contract also provided that the contractor pay liquidated damages in the sum of $100 per day for each day of delay in performance.

Wiebe's petition contained three causes of action as follows: (1) $56,915.72 for balance unpaid on the contract price; (2) $42,042 for increased costs by reason of delay caused when problems not anticipated by the parties arose and the district and its engineers delayed in making decisions as to necessary specification changes; and (3) $1,361.21 for extra work performed in reconstruction of a sidewalk.

The district filed an answer and counterclaim. In its answer the district alleged that Wiebe failed to complete the work properly. It denied that unanticipated conditions were encountered and alleged that in any event they should have been anticipated by the contractor. In its counterclaim the district made factual allegations, and prayed for liquidated damages at $100 per day for 224 days' delay in completion of the project and for damages for certain defects in performance, including, among others, the claim that planks for certain stadium seats were not in accordance with contract specifications. Its total prayer for damages was in the sum of $62,112.65. In its reply Wiebe alleged, among other things, that the delay in construction was caused by indecision of the district's engineers and agent as to whether specification changes were required and what these changes would be.

The trial of the case began before a jury and after 5 days before the jury the parties waived a jury trial, presenting the remainder of the evidence and submitting the case to the trial judge.

The trial court entered a judgment in part as follows: ". . . the court finds generally in favor of the plaintiff and that there is due to the plaintiff from the defendant on the causes of action set forth in plaintiff's petition the sum of $44,880.68." The court also allowed interest at 6 percent from October 1, 1971, until April 30, 1976, the date of judgment, in the amount of $12,342.18. The court dismissed with prejudice the counterclaim of the district.

We will first discuss the claim of the district that it was entitled to liquidated damages for delay in performance. The entire project consisted of a football field, stadium, appurtenances, and a running track. The delay in performance arose only in connection with the running track portion of the contract. The evidence would permit the trial court to find the following. After construction was commenced a part of the site was found to be underlain with ground water and to be in a very spongy condition. When this matter was called to the attention of the engineers in November of 1969, it appeared that the condition would require a change in contract specifications and not merely more difficult work on the part of the contractor. As a consequence of this situation the engineers, in a letter from Wiebe, stated: "It would seem to us that a more reasonable approach to resolving this matter would be to wait until spring of 1970 to determine the change in the work." In a letter dated June 1, 1970, the engineers wrote to Wiebe: "We will provide you with additional details on the extra work to be performed for stabilization of the running track subgrade in the very near future." A letter from the engineers to Wiebe dated June 15, 1970, contained the following item: "6. The track stabilization detail will be made available, for construction purposes, upon the completion of all items listed above and no work should be performed on the track curb, subgrade base, etc., until these items have been corrected." As one consequence of the water condition, change order No. 4, dated September 1, 1970, and executed by the parties a few days later, was entered into. It called for an extra in the form of a drainage system which was in fact constructed. The system was not, however, completely effective. After that there were extended discussions between the parties as to what, if any, further specification changes were required. The engineers hired a soil expert who made recommendations. Under date of September 3, 1970, a fifth change order, which was a revision of several previously proposed change orders, was offered by the district's engineers. This change order made some additional specification changes in the preparation of the subgrade of the track and also provided for a 120-day additional time extension on the contract period in addition to a 28-day extension which had been granted by one of the earlier change orders. The proposed changes in change order No. 5 were not agreed to by Wiebe because of, among other things, a claim that it could not, on the basis of the proposed specification changes, make any reasonable estimate of quantities of certain materials involved.

It is now necessary to note portions of the four change orders which were in fact adopted as these portions pertain to the "contract period." In change order No. 1 the contract period was designated as August 18, 1969, to August 3, 1970 (350 days). The second change order provided for the same contract period. The third change order stated the contract period as 378 days and contained no substantive contract changes otherwise. Change order No. 4, dated September 1, 1970, in addition to the drainage system change, provided: "Contract period to be determined." Following change order No. 4 there were no further determinations as to what would be the contract period, but on September 15 or 16, 1970, Wiebe was instructed to proceed under the original track specifications. On October 28, 1970, the engineers performed a test of soil conditions and it was found the ground was too wet to proceed at that time. Wiebe, however, indicated that he would proceed nonetheless if the district would accept the risk of frost damage to the track. No agreement was reached at that point. The track was completed on October 25, 1971.

The foregoing evidence would be sufficient to support a finding that the district had waived the provision for time of performance, or that the parties had modified the time for performance of the contract. A contractual provision providing for an award of liquidated damages for delay in performance may be waived. . . . Thus dismissal of the part of the counterclaim concerning liquidated damages for delay in performance was supported by the evidence and cannot be said to be clearly wrong.

The evidence as to whether some of the work done was not in accordance with contractual specifications is to some limited extent in conflict. It presented simply a factual issue for the trial judge to determine. The court's dismissal of the counterclaim for defective work is therefore also supported by the evidence.

We now turn to the issue of the propriety of the award of prejudgment interest. The district argues that a reasonable controversy existed as to Wiebe's right to recover the contract balance and the amount was a matter of dispute, therefore the claim was unliquidated and under the previous holdings of this court no prejudgment interest could be allowed. It cites *Frank McGill, Inc.* v. *Nucor Corp.,* . . . and other opinions of this court. In the cited case, although the contract price was a fixed amount, we upheld the trial court's denial of prejudgment interest because the contract was ambiguous as to the amount of work to be done for the stated contract price and there was a factual question as to whether all the required work had been done. This, we said, made the plaintiff's right to recovery, as well as the amount, a subject of dispute, therefore the claim was unliquidated even though the jury awarded the plaintiff the exact amount of his claim.

In none of the Nebraska cases cited by the district do we have the situation which confronts us here. Wiebe, in its first cause of action, sought a sum certain fixed by the terms of the contract. The district sought to offset the amount owed by a claim for liquidated damages for delay in performance as well as by amounts for claimed defects in the performance of the work. Wiebe relies upon the proposition that where the plaintiff's claim is liquidated, the existence of an unliquidated setoff does not prevent the recovery of prejudgment interest. It cites the following authorities, among others, *Raymond International, Inc.* v. *Bookcliff Constr., Inc.* . . . . It seeks to distinguish *Wilson Concrete Co.* v. *A. S. Battiato Constr. Co.* . . . which latter case did not involve an offsetting counterclaim.

It is apparent that Wiebe's claim on its first cause of action for the balance owed on the contract is, by itself, a liquidated claim. It is the amount owed, computed in accordance with the terms of the contract. The amount was disputed only because of the claims the district made in its counterclaim. Because of the limited assignment of error, the only part of the counterclaim before us on this appeal is the claim for the contractually stipulated daily damages for delay in performance. The trial judge found against the district on that part, as well as on those for defective performance.

The situation in *Wilson Concrete Co.* v. *A. S. Battiato Constr. Co.,* supra, was similar to that before us here, that is, there was a claim by the plaintiff for a contract balance and the defendant asserted an offset by reason of defective performance. However, in that case the jury had found that certain of the materials furnished in the performance of the contract did not meet the specifications and allowed an offset. The trial court then allowed prejudgment interest on the contract balance, less the amount of the offset. A division of this court reversed that portion of the judgment, placing reliance upon *Hays* v. *County of Douglas,* supra. In the case here before us, the trier of fact found against the district on its counterclaim. The *Hays* case, on which the Wilson opinion rested, did not involve a plaintiff's liquidated claim and an offsetting counterclaim, but an ambiguous contract, and contested factual details relating to claimed nonperformance which clearly rendered the amount of recovery uncertain. In our judgment, the opinion in the *Wilson* case is not controlling here because (1) in the case before us the trier of fact found against the defendant on the counterclaim, and (2) it may be that the *Wilson* opinion's reliance upon *Hays* is misplaced, but we need not decide that at this time.

We hold that in an action for a liquidated sum which represents a balance owing on a contract, the amount claimed does not become an unliquidated claim merely because of the assertion of an offset, and that if the trier of fact finds against the defendant on the offset, prejudgment interest should be awarded on the plaintiff's claim. In accord is *Raymond International, Inc.* v. *Bookcliff Constr., Inc.,* supra, a diversity case in which the trier of fact was the judge, a jury being waived, and where the court was required to apply Nebraska law. There the trier of fact found against the party asserting the offset and, after pointing out that where the contract if clear and unambiguous and the defense untenable, the Nebraska Supreme Court held that prejudgment interest is to be awarded. The federal court then went on to say: "The existence of an unliquidated set-off or counterclaim does not in this case bar interest prior to the entry of judgment. . . . In *Hansen* v. *Covell,* supra, cited by Wiebe, the California court has gone a bit further. It treats the offset, if allowed, as a payment and awards interest on the contract balance after deducting the offset. Whether we wish to go that far can be decided when a pertinent case reaches us. The trial court did not err in awarding prejudgment interest.

We now turn to Wiebe's cross-appeal in which it asserts that it should be awarded the full balance of the contract price in the amount of $56,915.72 instead of the $44,880.68 awarded by the court, a difference of $12,035.04. The only basis for reducing the contract balance would have been by allowing some portion of the counterclaim. This the trier of fact expressly disallowed. The general finding for the plaintiff and the disallowance and dismissal of the counterclaim cannot be reconciled with the award to the plaintiff of an amount less than the contract balance. "In a contract action, if the plaintiff has fully performed his contract he is entitled to the contract price." . . . Wiebe has not assigned as error disallowance of the counterclaim except that part on liquidated damages. This we have already treated.

The judgment is reversed and the cause remanded for further proceedings consonant with this opinion.

Reversed and Remanded.

REVIEW QUESTIONS

1. Black hired White Automation to build a special machine to be used by Black in the manufacture of automobile door handles. The door handles were to be sold to Gray Motor Company. The price of the special machine was to be $100,000. Shortly before work was to begin on the special machine, Gray cancelled his order for door handles and Black immediately cancelled the contract for the special machine. Does White have a right to resort to legal action? If so, against whom and for how much?

2. What is the purpose of: (a) nominal damages, (b) compensatory damages, (c) exemplary damages?

3. Distinguish between damages for tort and damages for breach of contract.

4. Green bought a new car from Brown Motor Sales for $10,000. A few days after he bought the car he attempted to pass another vehicle, and the steering linkage locked when he turned his wheels to the left. The resulting crash destroyed the car and sent Green to the hospital. Green's hospital bill amounted to $4800; the first month away from his job he received full pay from his employer ($3000 per month), but the next two months he did not. When he returned to work with a 20% disability he was asked to take a job paying $2000 per month because of his inability to perform his former job. He is 45 years old. Examination of the wrecked automobile showed that one joint in the steering linkage appeared too tight and that there was no grease fitting at the joint and, apparently, there

never had been one even though a hole had been drilled and tapped for the fitting. Does Green have a right of action against anyone? If so, for how much? Based on what theory?

5. Why should penalty damages be awarded to a plaintiff in a tort action but denied when the action is based on a breach of contract?

6. In *Kroeger* v. *Franchise Equities, Incorporated,* what added evidence will be required to establish the extent of damages?

7. In the case of *Wiebe Const. Co.* v. *School Dist. of Millard,* calculate the total award of damages Wiebe may expect based on Justice Clinton's opinion.

15

Sales and Warranties

The building of any kind of structure, be it a productive machine, a process or a building to house it, a road, or a bridge, requires the purchase of a good many things. In a large organization a purchasing department buys what the engineer specifies; in a small concern the engineer may find that he must do some of the buying. In either case the engineer is concerned with the purchasing activity. The engineer's job includes at least effective recommendation of items to be purchased. A manufacturing engineer or process engineer may not be charged with the responsibility of actually purchasing; nevertheless, he is very much concerned with the items to be bought, since they are to be components of his final structure. A target date for completion must be met, and delay in receipt and installation of components may be quite costly. From this standpoint he must be concerned with transportation of the things purchased and even with the financial arrangements involved.

The engineer is vitally concerned with the adequacy of the components of his structure. If a vendor said his product would render the service intended, but the product simply does not perform, for example, is there any recourse? Are we stuck with the purchase or do we have rights based on warranty? Such problems do arise, and the engineer is involved with them.

The term *sale* can refer to transfer of either real or personal property, but as it is used in this chapter it refers to transfer of the ownership of personal property only, for a price usually stated in money. The sales law which was developed to govern such transfers is set forth in most states by the Uniform Commercial Code.

OWNERSHIP

It is often desirable to know who owns goods at a particular time. One who does not own goods cannot lose them. When goods are stolen or destroyed by fire, flood, or other catastrophe, the one who loses (at least, initially) is the owner. Consequently, the time when title passes from seller to buyer and the shifting of ownership risks is important.

Specific and Identified. For title to pass, the goods must be specific and identified. They must exist and be in a deliverable state such that no material thing remains to be done to them by the seller. If any of these requirements is not met, the sales contract is interpreted not as a *sale,* but as a *contract to sell.* Title does not pass in a contract to sell until the seller unconditionally appropriates the goods in the buyer's behalf. Black, in need of 20 cooling fans for his shop, visits White's warehouse where White has about 100 such fans stored. After examining sample fans, Black agrees to take 20 of them at an agreed price per fan. At this point there is no sale; White still owns the entire 100 fans, and should anything happen to them, the entire loss is White's. Now let as assume that the two men separate out 20 fans. If no other material thing remains to be done, Black has title to the 20 fans so separated. If the parties agreed to have White deliver the fans to Black, and if it appeared to be their intent to have title pass on delivery, title would not pass until delivery had occurred. Of course, if the fans were not yet in existence and were purchased merely by a description or a sample, title could not pass until the fans were made and appropriated to Black's contract.

F.O.B., F.A.S., C.I.F., and C.&F. Several abbreviations are commonly used in shipping goods from seller to buyer. Among other considerations they specify the point at which the risks of ownership pass from seller to buyer. For instance, *F.O.B. San Francisco* indicates that when the seller has delivered goods into the carrier's possession in San Francisco, to be delivered to the buyer, the ownership risks pass to the buyer. Until the goods reach this point it is the seller who suffers the loss if some tragic event terminates the existence of the goods or damages them. *F.A.S.* means the same thing with respect to delivery by ship. *C.I.F.* and *C.&F.* are similar to F.O.B. and F.A.S., but require more performance by the seller than just handing over the goods to the common carrier. In a C.&F. (cost and freight) sale the seller is required to obtain a negotiable bill of lading for the goods, load the goods, and send all the documents plus an invoice to the buyer. C.I.F. (cost, insurance, and freight) requires him not only to do the things required in a C.&F. sale, but to insure the goods as well. The buyer is required to pay the price of the goods (which, of course, includes shipping costs and any other extras) when the documents arrive. He has no right to wait for the goods or inspect them prior to making payment. If the goods are lost or damaged in transit the buyer has no action available against the seller; but, of course, he does have an action available against the carrier.

Despite the meanings above, the buyer and seller are not necessarily tied to these interpretations even though they have used these abbreviations in their contract. That is, if the wording of their agreement makes it clear that another meaning is intended (for instance, giving the buyer the right to approve of the goods before paying for them), such will be the interpretation. Where these terms are used and not modified by other language in the contract, the Uniform Commercial Code dictates their meaning.

Security Interest

In our economy, credit buying accounts for a large number of sales. People (and industries) buy goods and services and agree to pay later. But the simple promise to pay later leaves something to be desired. When "later" comes the buyer may have many debts and very few assets. Without some added security the seller may be reduced to the status of creditor in bankruptcy and receive only a few cents for each dollar of the debt. So arrangements have been devised to improve the seller's position. Under the Uniform Commerical Code the arrangement is known as *security interest* (replacing various predecessors, the most common of which were known as conditional sale and chattel mortgage). Under the security interest (which might still be termed a conditional sale or a chattel mortgage in a given state) the seller retains certain rights to the goods sold until the buyer has paid for them.

The previous security arrangements located title to the goods in either the seller or the buyer. Under some of the arrangements, then, recovery of the goods from a defaulting debtor would be simply an exercise of a right of ownership. Under the present law of security interest the location of the title is immaterial. The security of the secured party's interest in the personal property is simply a right based on the debtor's default.

Consider Black, who is in need of a refrigerator and lacks funds sufficient to pay the entire cash price. Having located the refrigerator of his choice, he arranges to purchase the refrigerator by paying $90 immediately and agreeing to make a series of ten monthly payments of $90 each to the Brown Appliance Company.

In other words, the parties have made a *security agreement*. To complete (or perfect) the security agreement, assuming that Black will possess the refrigerator while the payments are being made, the two parties must properly file a *financial statement* regarding the transaction. This financial statement must contain at least Black's and Brown's names and addresses, a description of the refrigerator, and the parties' signatures. The place of filing may differ from state to state, but it is a place designated by each state's Secretary of State. If Brown were to keep the refrigerator pending full payment, the filing of the financial statement would not be required.

The refrigerator purchase example above tacitly assumed a retailer-consumer agreement involving consumer's goods. Security interest transactions involving something other than tangible consumer goods sometimes require special rules. For example, if the goods purchased are to become fixtures or additions to real property, the place to file the security interest must be where interests in real estate are filed rather than the customary filing place for consumer's goods interests. As a second example, if the goods purchased are inventory items intended to be involved in the production of some final product, identification of the goods may be lost. Steel might be formed into a cabinet or into piston rings; oil might be used to obtain heat for processing or it might be altered to form a plastic. Special rules give the secured party rights in the final product in such instances. Other special rules have had to be devised to handle security interest in intangibles such as patents and copyrights, the jurisdiction of products intended to be moved from state to state (e.g., semi-truck trailers), and other situations.

Default. Considering again Black's refrigerator purchase, suppose that he makes eight of the ten required payments and then becomes incapable of making the last two payments. In other words, he *defaults*. The possibility of this happening was, of course, Brown's reason for obtaining the security interest in the first place. So now what can Brown do about it?

Debtor default allows the secured party to regain possession of the goods. Brown can *repossess* Black's refrigerator. However, Brown has certain obligations and Black has rights even after default and repossession. If the secured party elects to repossess (he may elect other methods of enforcing the security interest), he must proceed in a commercially reasonable manner. If he resells the goods he must use the proceeds to pay the debtor's obligation and the reasonable costs of repossession, and then turn any remainder back to the debtor. The resale itself must be above reproach. It can be either a public or private sale and the secured party can buy the goods himself at the sale, but if he does buy the goods he must pay at least the going market price for such things. Brown cannot legally repossess Black's refrigerator, sell it to himself for, say, $1.00, and then collect from Black for the remainder.

If the secured party repossesses the collateral, the debtor still may get his goods back. To do that he must pay the balance remaining due on the goods as well as the secured party's costs of repossession, etc. He can only exercise this right up to the time when the secured party resells the goods to another, however. If Black could borrow enough money from a friend to pay off the balance he owed on the refrigerator plus repossession costs, he could get the refrigerator back from Brown by paying this amount before Brown resells it.

Repossession and resale upon debtor default is only one of numerous possible remedies available to the secured party. The remedy the secured party will elect to use depends to a considerable extent, of course, on the nature of the goods involved. One alternative is simply to obtain a court judgment against the debtor in default, using the security agreement as proof of the debt. The debtor, then, would retain possession of the goods. Another alternative is to repossess the goods and lease them, using the rental payments to satisfy the balance due and costs. The secured party may even repossess the goods and keep them as his own in satisfaction of the debt, but this move requires the debtor's agreement—the debtor must be notified that the secured party intends to do this. Then the debtor has 30 days in which to object to this solution. If he doesn't object within that 30 days, the secured party gets title to the goods. There is one exception to this retaking of the title to the goods in satisfaction of the debt. If the debtor has paid 60 percent of the cash price of those goods, the secured party is required to sell or dispose of the goods in a commercial transaction, balancing the equities with the proceeds.

The Uniform Commercial Code rather nicely balances the rights of both parties. Brown, as secured party, has a variety of remedies if Black defaults on his refrigerator payments. On the other hand, Black has a right to expect equitable treatment from Brown if, for some reason, it becomes impossible for him to make the payments.

Sale on Approval and Sale or Return

A device frequently used to sell goods is to place them in the prospective buyer's hands for a period of time. The buying motive of possession is strong in most members of our society, and when we have goods on a trial basis it is often difficult to surrender possession of them at the end of the trial period. It is also a persuasive sales argument to be able to assure a merchant that he can take goods to sell and then return them if they do not sell. The law concerned here determines title passage and risks in two distinct types of such sales activity.

In a *sale on approval* the buyer is given possession of the goods for a period of time to become his if he approves of them. While the goods are in the prospective buyer's hands the title to them rests with the seller. Thus, any loss of the goods is the seller's loss, with, of course, the right to recover if the prospective buyer caused the loss. *Approval* may be either express or implied. Expression by the buyer of willingness to take title to the goods is approval. If a time limit is stated and the goods are held beyond the time limit, approval is implied. If there is no time limit and the goods are held beyond a reasonable period, approval is also implied. The third implication of approval occurs when goods are used as the buyer's own, in such a way that a reasonable trial of them is exceeded in their use. Until he has registered his approval, though, the prospective buyer in a sale on approval arrangement is merely *bailee*[1] of the seller's goods.

A *sale or return* is generally treated as a sale to a merchant—with the privilege of returning the goods. The risks of ownership of the property pass to the dealer. A sale in which the seller gives the dealer the right to return the goods at his option is a sale or return transaction. Frequently such sales take the form of sales to a merchant "on consignment" or "on memorandum." Return of the goods revests the ownership risks in the seller. If a time limit is stated and the goods are not returned in that time, the sale is final. If no time limit is stated the merchant has a reasonable time in which to return the goods.

AUCTION

A sale by auction is complete when the auctioneer's hammer falls. Such is both custom and law. But certain questions sometimes arise during auctions. For example, can the owner withdraw his goods from the auction after there have been bids, but before the hammer falls? And can the owner or someone acting for him enter the bidding competition to bid the price up? What if a bid is made while the hammer is falling (or during whatever act is used to signify completion of the sale)? Can a bidder withdraw his bid before the hammer falls?

Consider Gray who has goods to be sold at auction. The terms of the sale may be specified in an advertisement, but if there is no such specification Gray will be held to the following: He may withdraw his goods (or

---

1. A bailee is one who possesses property belonging to another (the *bailor*) with that person's acquiescence.

any item or lot) at any time prior to completion of the sale of the item or lot. In other words, the fall of the hammer changes ownership of the goods and terminates Gray's right to withdraw whatever was being sold.

Gray might try to bid the price up or get someone else to do it for him, but if the auctioneer knowingly receives such a bid, a "good faith" bidder may object. If the "good faith" bidder finds this to be the case, he has a right to rescind the sale. Or, if he so chooses, he may go back to the last "good faith" bid and take the goods at that price. Of course, if such a bidder discovers bidding in the owner's behalf (so-called shill bidding) he has the right to withdraw any of his bids. But then, he has this right anyway. That is, anyone has the right to withdraw a bid he has made at any time before the hammer falls if he so desires.

If a bid comes in at virtually the same time as the completion of the sale (while the hammer is falling someone bids at an increased price), the auctioneer has two options. He can simply declare the goods sold at the price bid while the hammer was falling or reopen the bidding competition.

It is the seller's right to make alterations in the auction rules to suit his purpose. Of course, the prospective bidders must know what the rules are. That is, if the seller advertises the auction "without reserve" he must sell the goods at whatever is the highest price bid. And, if he so states, he may reserve the right to bid on his own goods. in short, he may very well make his own "ground rules" for the auction "game."

SALES CHANGES TO THE LAW OF CONTRACTS

The law of contracts sets forth certain rules for the formation, interpretation, and discharge of contracts. Over the years it has become apparent that certain modifications of these rules might be desirable as they pertain to the sale of goods, wares, and merchandise. All of these rules, of course, presume that nothing in the contract agreed to by the parties specifies something to the contrary.

In the ordinary law of contracts an *option* is a contract. That is, Green (prospective buyer) may wish to have a week to consider White's (seller) offer of a piece of real estate at a stated price. If White agrees to give Green that week to consider the offer and Green pays something for the right to accept the offer within a week, the result is an option. Consideration is given by each party. But, now, if Green does not give some consideration (e.g., $20), no contract results. White can then sell the property to Black within the week even though he has given Green the week to think about it.

In sales, the law is different. If a similar situation involving goods occurred, White would be held to his promise to Green even though an option was not formed. If White sold the goods to another within the week, he would be liable to Green for whatever damage Green suffered as a result.

According to the law of contracts the offeror makes the terms of acceptance (even, perhaps to the means of acceptance). Any alteration of the offer by the offeree in his intended acceptance constitutes a counter offer. Under sales law response by the offeree may make minor changes in the offer and still remain, effectively, an acceptance, creating a contract. Of course, if the attempted acceptance constitutes a significant or "material" change, no contract results. And acceptance may occur by any reasonable means, including an act (such as shipping conforming goods) which would not be likely to occur unless a contract had been made.

Many contracts which would be called "unenforceable for uncertainty" under contract law are preserved under the law of sales. For example, the quantity of product may remain to be determined later by the parties. Or the price may depend on a future market quotation or a later arrangement by the parties. At best, these would be nothing more than "gentlemen's agreements" under the law of contracts. But under sales law they have the legal status of full-fledged contracts.

The main thrust of the Uniform Commercial Code modification of contract law is to more truly reflect the intent of the parties. If it is apparent that the parties truly intended to make a contract, the law attempts to enforce the essence of the agreement even if some components are missing or indefinite.

WARRANTY

A *warranty* (or guarantee) is added assurance to a buyer. It is necessarily connected to a sale. In fact, it cannot exist unless it is based on a sale. If the warranty is made at the time of the sale, the consideration for the warranty is part of the sale price. If the warranty is made later, however, it must, as any other contractual promise, be supported by separate consideration to be legally binding.

Warranty Benefits. Mention was made earlier of privity of contract. One who is not a party to the formation of a contract (or a member of his household) does not have the legally enforceable right to reap the benefits of it. This is also true of warranty promises. The original promisee is the only one who has a right to warranty benefits. When goods are resold the warranty is not passed along to the new buyer unless some provision for this is made in the warranty. The rule is a general one and there are some exceptions to it. Where the goods in question consist of food or drugs, for example, public policy and many statutes dictate the protection in the law.

Good Title. In a sale or contract to sell there is a warranty that the buyer will receive *good title*. This warranty is that there are no rights or liens on the property other than those of which the buyer is aware. It means that no other person has valid claim to the merchandise in question. Specific exceptions to the warranty of good title exist in the form of sheriff's sales, certain auctions, mortgagee's sales, and the like. Such sales are often authorized by law, but there is no assurance that a prior owner or lien holder does not exist to disturb quiet enjoyment of title to the goods. The title obtained is, in some respects, similar to the quit-claim deed in real estate where the seller, in effect, says, "I give you my claim to title however good it may be."

Express Warranties

A statement of warranty is a promissory statement. It is here that the main distinction can be made between statements that may be fraudulent and warranty statements. You recall that *fraud* involves a false representation of a fact—something past or present. *Warranty* has to do with either the present or the future. When Black sells White an automatic screw machine and tells White that it has just been overhauled, when in truth it has not been, such a statement is fraudulent. If Black, on the other hand, promises to repair the machine if it should break down in the first year White uses it, this statement constitutes a warranty. Statements having to do with the present, though, are a little harder to distinguish. A statement by Black that all the collets and pushers have been replaced and are new would be factual; if untrue, it could be the basis of fraud. In contrast, a statement that the machine is in such a condition that it will be useful in the manufacture of White's product would constitute warranty. Another distinction between warranty and fraudulent representations is that a warranty becomes part of a contract, whereas the representations are inducements to contract. Clarity of this distinction, though, may be questionable in many situations. In certain cases where a false representation has been made, the buyer may elect either his remedy for fraud or that for breach of warranty.

Opinions. A warranty is a statement other than opinion or judgment. With very rare exceptions a statement made as the seller's opinion cannot constitute warranty. A statement by the vendor that the merchandise is "first rate" or "the best" or "superior quality" is usually construed as sales talk or "puffing" the goods. The courts have long adhered to the idea of *caveat emptor* ("the buyer beware"). According to this logic the buyer is free to inspect goods before he buys them and free not to buy if he is not allowed to inspect, or if he finds something wrong.

The recent tendency in the law is to place more responsibility upon the seller. It might even be called *caveat venditor*. The trend is based upon the notion that many statements made by a vendor actually have the effect of relieving the buyer of the duty to ascertain the value of the goods for himself. An affirmation of value having this effect has often been held to be a warranty in recent decisions.

In making a warranty of his merchandise, the vendor makes a contract somewhat similar to insurance. He agrees to assume a risk that would normally be borne by the buyer. In the example above, if Black warranted the automatic screw machine for a year as to breakdown, he would be promising to take over White's risk of repairing the machine for a year.

Description or Sample. Contracts for sale often involve samples of the goods the buyer is to receive or descriptions of them. The use of such descriptions or samples constitutes an *express warranty* of what the buyer is to get. Since the buyer normally does not have an opportunity to examine the merchandise he is buying when a description or sample is used, the seller would have a chance to short change him. The warranty is meant to prevent this. Goods must conform in all respects to the kind, quality, and condition described or as shown by the sample.

Implied Warranties

In addition to express warranties which may be made by the seller at the time of sale, there are two *implied warranties*. These implied warranties exist in all sales contracts unless they are expressly omitted by the parties.

Fitness for Described Purpose. The seller is assumed to be more familiar with his goods than is the purchaser. For this reason, if the purchase is made on the basis of a buyer's description of what the goods are to do, with the seller supplying the goods for that purpose, the goods supplied must be adequate to do the job. This warranty is defeated if the buyer orders goods according to a trade name or trade specification. Where this is done it makes no difference if the seller knows of the intended purpose and believes the goods will not fit the purpose. For example, Black requires a punch press for a blanking operation on a production line he is setting up. His calculations (in error) show a requirement of a 40-ton press. White, with full knowledge of the purpose intended, is called upon to supply the press and does so. On the first day of operation the punch press crank breaks and Black brings an action on the implied warranty of suitability for purpose. Since Black specified the press, he would not be allowed to recover. If, on the other hand, Black had asked White to supply a press for the blanking operation, allowing White to determine the required press size, suitability would have been warranted.

Merchantability. The implied warranty of merchantability is somewhat akin to suitability for a described purpose. The distinction is in degree and in the manner in which the warranties arise. All goods sold by a merchant are subject to the warranty of merchantability. To be *merchantable,* goods must be of the usual quality sold in the market; they must be sound and undamaged, free from hidden defects; they must be fit for the general purpose for which such goods are sold. In the above example if it could be shown that the punch press crankshaft had not been properly heat treated and, therefore, would not withstand a 40-ton force, Black might recover under merchantability.

Express Non Warranty. Parties to a sales contract are free to contract in any lawful manner they choose. Frequently, sales contracts contain *disclaimer clauses*—clauses which, in effect, state that the buyer takes the goods at his own risk. As long as public policy is not seriously involved, such clauses are usually lawful and binding. The provision that the buyer takes the goods "as is" or "with all faults" will be held to relieve the seller of many of his usual warranties. Of course, even in an "as is" sale the merchandise sold must be what it is purported to be. That is, sale of a vertical milling machine indicates that what is bought will constitute a vertical milling machine even though the term *as is* is used in the sale. The "as is" pertains only to the condition of the subject matter, not to its existence.

To be effective the statement excluding the implied warranties must be conspicuous. It must stand out from the rest of the writing and attract the attention of the reader. And, if it is to effectively exclude the warranty of merchantability, it must use the term, *merchantability*. In other words, if one wishes to exclude implied warranties he cannot hide his wishes from the buyer at the time of the sale.

BREACH

If the goods received by the buyer are not as warranted by the seller, the buyer has an election of remedies. The buyer may, at his option, do one of three things: (1) He may keep the goods sent and pay for them at the contract price. He might then take an action for *breach of warranty* to try to recover the cost to him of the non-conformance of the goods. (2) He may reject the entire shipment of goods. If he rejects the goods, however, he must inform the seller and state the reason for rejection. The seller may then instruct the buyer as to disposition of the goods. If no instruction as to disposition of the goods is forthcoming, the buyer is simply required to act reasonably according to the nature of goods and the circumstances. (3) The buyer may reject part of the goods and accept part (any commercial unit). The units accepted would be paid for at the contract price, but the buyer could recover the cost of non-conformance.

Suppose Green ships the Brown Company 10,000 zubit components known as ZIP-2s. Brown Company's receiving inspection shows the lot of ZIP-2s to consist of about 20% defective units and, therefore, to be classed as unacceptable. Brown Company rejects the 10,000 ZIP-2s and so notifies Green. Green may require the entire lot of 10,000 to be returned, or he may ask Brown Company to sort all 10,000. If the non-conformance would shut down a production line, mitigation (minimization) of damages would require some such disposition as sorting and using the good ones. In any event, Green is liable for any added costs caused by non-conformance. If the ZIP-2s are non-conforming Green is even liable for the receiving inspection cost. On the other hand, he would not be liable for the receiving inspection cost if the goods entirely conformed to specification.

BUYER'S RIGHTS

If the seller breaches the sale contract the buyer has a right to take legal action to recover damages. The damages, of course, may be anticipated by the parties in a "liquidated damage" clause in the contract. If the liquidated damage amount truly represents a reasonable approximation of the anticipated damage it will be honored and enforced. If it is obviously too large to be realistic it may be unenforceable as a penalty clause. On the other hand, if it is too small it may simply be ignored as not representing true agreement between the parties.

Failure to Deliver. If the seller breaches his contract by failing to deliver the goods or repudiating the contract, the buyer has an election of three courses of action and the right to whatever compensatory damages he can prove: (1) The buyer may *cover;* that is, he may procure substitute goods from another source. Damages, of course, would reflect costs resulting from the delay involved, or the cost of obtaining the goods from another source. (2) The buyer may *replevin* the goods. He may prove the transaction, post whatever bond the state law requires, and obtain a *writ of replevin* with which to obtain possession of the goods. Such action anticipates a court determination of true ownership of the property in question. (3) If the buyer can make a case for the goods being unique (even the source of the goods offering some special service might be sufficient to call them unique), he can resort to the equity remedy of specific performance.

If the buyer has made part payment or has encountered other material costs by the time the seller breaches the contract, he has a security interest in the goods to the value of the part payment or costs. At that point, then, his rights are those of the secured party in a security interest transaction. This is a particularly useful device if the seller should become insolvent prior to delivery. The buyer's security interest would then prevent the seller's creditors from legally disposing of the goods.

Damages for breach of contract including, of course, breach of warranty may take the form of a set-off or deduction from the price to be paid for the goods. If the payment is to leave the buyer in something other than a state of default, though, it must include an explanation of the reason for the payment of an amount less than the agreed price.

The buyer's right to take legal action based on the seller's breach eventually ends if the buyer does nothing about it. The statute of limitations on sales contracts limits this length of time to no longer than four years. The parties can shorten this time limit in their agreement as long as the agreed length of time is not less than one year. So, effectively, the time limit for legal action to be begun might be any time between one and four years after the breach.

SELLER'S RIGHTS

If the seller delivers goods to the buyer and those goods conform to the buyer's specification, the seller may reasonably expect to be paid for them. But, of course, the buyer might refuse to accept the goods or he might repudiate the contract or he might not pay the price. So the seller has a set of rights to be exercised in such cases. One rather obvious right he has is to take a legal action for damages. Of course, he is also within his rights to simply cancel the contract if the buyer breaches. The seller has other alternatives, too, and they are discussed here.

Withholding Delivery. If the buyer breaches the contract, the seller has a right to retain any of the goods still in his possession. If the goods are in the hands of

a common carrier or other bailee to be turned over to the buyer, breach by the buyer allows the seller to reclaim the goods from the bailee.

One problem arises when the goods are being manufactured for the buyer and breach occurs. If the goods are to be shipped in a series of shipments and the manufacture occurs in a manner such that the goods may be in various stages of completion, the seller is simply charged with using his best judgment as to whether to finish any work in process. Depending on the nature of the goods they might conceivably be finished and sold to another. If the buyer is the only customer for them, however, further work on the inventory would seem pointless.

Seller's Resale. If the buyer breaches the sale contract, the seller has a right to resell the goods to another. He may do this either by public or private sale, and the conditions of the sale are very nearly the same as they are for a sale by a secured party in a security interest transaction. The terms, method, manner, time, and place of resale are subject to the test of being commercially reasonable. If the sale is public the seller may purchase the goods himself. Any buyer at the resale takes the goods free of any claim by the original buyer.

If the resale yields a lower price than the original buyer was to pay, the seller, of course, has a right to the difference plus costs from him. However, if resale yields a profit for the seller, the original buyer has no claim on that profit.

When the buyer breaches a sale contract, the seller has a right to claim compensatory damages. He may expect to be reimbursed for all losses suffered at the hand of the buyer, including lost profit. In other words, the seller is to be placed in the position he would have been in had no breach occurred.

GROSS v. POWELL

181 N.W. 2d 113 (Minn., 1970)

Chester G. Rosengren, Justice.

These are consolidated appeals by Robert H. Powell defendant and third-party plaintiff, from judgment entered against him and from an order denying his motion for a new trial.

Without attempting to detail all of the facts to which the parties have stipulated, the pertinent ones appear to be as follows:

On April 10, at about 3:30 p.m. defendant Leo A. Hendrickson arranged to purchase a 1962 four-door Oldsmobile from Proctor Motor, Inc., a Minnesota corporation in St. Louis County (hereinafter referred to as Proctor). At the time of the purchase the bill of sale in the form printed on the reverse side of the 1968 Minnesota motor vehicle registration card covering the Oldsmobile was executed by Hendrickson as buyer and Proctor as seller and acknowledged before a notary public. At the same time (according to the stipulation) Hendrickson delivered to Proctor the agreed purchase price of said automobile in the form of a check for $600 dated April 10, 1968, drawn on the First State Bank of Floodwood, and signed by Veronica Hendrickson, the wife of defendant Hendrickson, as maker. The seller accepted said check in full payment of the purchase price of the automobile. Hendrickson paid Proctor the sales tax in cash in the sum of $18. On the same date, Proctor delivered the keys to the car and the car to Hendrickson with the unrestricted right to use it as his own. Hendrickson thereupon drove the car from the premises of Proctor.

After taking possession of the car, Hendrickson encountered appellant, Robert H. Powell, and arranged to have him drive the 1962 Oldsmobile back to Floodwood, while Hendrickson drove his 1957 Oldsmobile. Powell thereafter drove the 1962 Oldsmobile as driver and sole occupant and while en route to Floodwood was involved in an automobile collision resulting in the death of Michael James Culbert, Jr.

Hendrickson had arranged with the First State Bank of Floodwood to bring the 1962 Oldsmobile to the bank on April 11, 1968, with the expectation of using said car as security for a loan to cover the $600 check issued to Proctor, but because of the demolition of the 1962 Oldsmobile in the collision, Hendrickson was not able to proceed with obtaining the loan. The delivered check was subsequently dishonored for insufficient funds, and thereafter Proctor commenced an action against Hendrickson and his wife to recover the purchase price of said automobile.

Plaintiff, Donald J. Gross, as trustee for the heirs of Michael Culbert, commenced an action for death by wrongful act against Hendrickson and Powell, as owner and driver, respectively, of the automobile involved in the accident. Appellant Powell instituted a third-party action against The Travelers Indemnity Company, alleging that title to the automobile had never passed to Hendrickson from Proctor and, therefore, Travelers, as Proctor's insurer, was obligated to defend Powell and would have the primary obligation to pay any judgment claims against him resulting from the accident.

The only issue presented in the case is: Who had ownership of the automobile involved in the accident for purposes of the Minnesota Safety Responsibility Act, Minn. St. 170.54? This statute provides:

"Whenever any motor vehicle shall be operated within this state, by any person other than the owner, with the consent of the owner, express

or implied, the operator thereof shall in case of accident, be deemed the agent of the owner of such motor vehicle in the operation thereof."

The parties agree as to the results which follow from our determination of the ownership issue.

The trial court found that Hendrickson had purchased the car involved and had title thereto at the time of the accident and that Powell is not entitled to any benefits under Proctor's insurance coverage provided by Travelers. The court based its decision on the ground that title to the automobile had passed, under Minn. St. 336.2-401, at the time of delivery of the vehicle to the buyer, Hendrickson, as the buyer and seller had contemplated.

On this appeal, appellant contends that in a "cash sale," as between the parties only, no title passes to a buyer who pays the purchase price with a check which is subsequently dishonored. He bases his argument on two Minnesota cases, *Gustafson* v. *Equitable Loan Ass'n*, . . . and *Guckeen Farmers Elev. Co.* v. *Cargill, Inc.* . . . , the reasoning of which, though not the result, is claimed to have been continued under the Uniform Commercial Code, specifically Minn. St. 336.2-511(3), which provides in part:

". . . (P)ayment by check is conditional and is defeated as between the parties by dishonor of the check on due presentment."

Respondent, Travelers, argues that here there was an agreement that title was to pass on delivery sufficiently explicit to pass title under Minn. St. 336.2-401(1), which provides:

"Each provision of this article with regard to the rights, obligations and remedies of the seller, the buyer, purchasers, or other third parties applies irrespective of title to the goods except where the provision refers to such title. Insofar as situations are not covered by the other provisions of this article and matters concerning title become material the following rules apply:

"(1). . . Subject to these provisions and to the provisions of the article on secured transactions (article 9), title to goods passes from the seller to the buyer in any manner and on any conditions explicitly agreed on by the parties."

In the alternative, Travelers contends that title passed on delivery of the car to the buyer in the absence of explicit agreement, citing Minn. St. 336.2-401(2), which provides:

"(2) Unless otherwise explicitly agreed title passes to the buyer at the time and place at which the seller completes his performance with reference to the physical delivery of the goods, despite any reservation of a security interest and even though a document of title is to be delivered at a different time or place. . . ."

As a third contention, Travelers asserts that title passed to the buyer on delivery because the seller elected to affirm the sale after dishonor of the buyer's check through an election to sue the buyer for payment due pursuant to Minn. St. 336.2-511(3).

This court cannot accept appellant's contention that in a cash sale, where a check given in payment of the purchase price is subsequently dishonored, no title passes as between the parties. The opinions cited by appellant in support of his contention are distinguishable from this case. In those actions each of the sellers respectively sought to rescind the transactions of sale through an action against a third party, in *Gustafson* for replevin and in *Guckeen* for conversion. The sellers' actions in those instances were obviously inconsistent with any claim that title had passed to the buyer. The rule as laid down in *Gustafson* and quoted with approval in *Guckeen* states. . . :

" '. . . Where goods are sold for cash on delivery, and payment is made by the purchaser by check on his banker, such payment is only conditional, and the delivery of the goods also only conditional; and if the check on due presentation is dishonored, the vendor may retake the goods.' (Citations omitted)"

This rule was elaborated upon in *Guckeen* as follows. . . :

"In this state it is well settled that, where a cash sale of goods is intended and a check in payment thereof is accepted, there is an implied representation that the check will be paid upon presentation at the bank upon which it is drawn; and that if not so paid title to the goods will remain in the seller who may recover the goods or their value from a third party who has purchased them from the seller's vendee."

The rule was correctly stated upon the facts presented in both *Gustafson* and *Guckeen;* but it was not intended, and did not purport, to cover the situation in which, as here, the seller has chosen to affirm the sale through a subsequent action to recover the purchase price from his vendee. Had this situation arisen prior to the passage of the Uniform Commerical Code, this court undoubtedly would have followed the lead of cases such as *Redmond* v. *Lilly*, . . . which repeated the "rule" saying. . . .

". . . (I)f the owner of a chattel contracted to sell it to a buyer for cash and delivered it to him in exchange for a check, believed by the seller to be good at the time it was accepted, the seller could, upon the dishonor of the check, recover the chattel from the buyer on the ground that the legal title had not passed from the seller to the buyer."

Continuing, the court then stated what we believe would have been the precode law in Minnesota. . . :

". . . If, however, such seller elected to treat the transaction as a sale and to recover judgment from the buyer for the agreed purchase price, he could do so. . . .

". . . As between the plaintiff (seller) and the individual defendants (vendees), his filing suit against them for the contract price vests title to the goods in them as of the time it would have vested in them had no fraud been perpetrated."

This statement summarizes the law as it would have been found prior to the enactment of the code, had the issue of title ever arisen before this court under facts similar to those before us. Thus, it would appear that the rule which appellant would have this court find preserved under Minn. St. 336.2-511(3) was, in fact, never the law in this state.

We are reluctant to accept the so-called third contention made by Travelers, which in effect would require this court to find that title as of the time of this accident depended on subsequent conduct of the seller. Despite what would have been the law in precode days had the matter arisen then, the code prompts the opinion of this court that rights and obligations, including those flowing from title, should vest as of the occurrence of the transaction under scrutiny (here, the sale) and should not depend on the subsequent conduct of the parties—in this case the election by the seller to recover on the check rather than to rescind the transaction.

The drafters of the code felt it important to deemphasize the amorphous concept of title as the source of all rights and obligations concerning goods in order to achieve greater certainty in commercial dealings. As is succinctly stated in appellant's brief:

"The (Uniform Commercial) Code adopts a step by step approach, which by reference to its various provisions, determines the rights and duties of the various parties to a transaction at each juncture of the transaction regardless of where title lies. . . ."

Accordingly, the code subordinates the title concept to a residuary position, leaving it to determine case results only where no other specific section of the code is applicable. Sect. 336.2-401.

We agree with the trial court that no other section of the code applies here and that sect. 336.2-401 therefore governs this case. On the view we take of the case, and because there is some slight doubt in our minds as to whether Proctor and Hendrickson "explicitly agreed" on the passage of title as contemplated in sect. 336.2-401(1), by which the code allows parties to set the conditions on which title will pass, we do not address ourselves to Travelers' first contention but assume arguendo that here there was no explicit agreement which would bring this case within sect. 336.2-401(1).

We find that title passed to the buyer here no later than at the time when unrestricted possession was delivered to the buyer under sect. 336.2-401(2), which provides in part:

> "Unless otherwise explicitly agreed title passes to the buyer at the time and place at which the seller completes his performance with reference to the physical delivery of the goods. . . ."

Thus, at the time of the accident, title to the automobile rested in Hendrickson, who is deemed the owner of the automobile for purposes of Minn. St. 170.54 pursuant to sect. 170.21, subd. 9, which provides:

> " 'Owner' means a person who holds the legal title of a motor vehicle, or in the event a motor vehicle is the subject of an agreement for the conditional sale or lease thereof with the right of purchase upon performance of the conditions stated in the agreement and with an immediate right of possession vested in the conditional vendee or lessee, or in the event a mortgagor of a vehicle is entitled to possession, then such conditional vendee or lessee or mortgagor shall be deemed the owner for the purposes of this chapter."

This result is clearly correct in "imposing liability on those who have ownership and the power and right to prevent use of the vehicle.". . . .

Under the statutory definition, it appears this court must reach the same result even were it to accept appellant's contention. In essence, appellant's claim would seem to be that the sale was conditional because title passage depended on honor or dishonor of the check accepted as payment in a cash sale. As a conditional sale, other provisions of sect. 170.21, subd. 9, would control and we would reach the same result as under the first portion of the definition—the buyer is deemed "owner" for purposes of sect. 170.54. This corroborates our first expressed conclusion. We do not believe

that this conclusion is contrary to the language contained in . . . which we have carefully reconsidered.

The respective policies of insurance were presumably written on vehicles garaged and licensed in Minnesota and included by implication pertinent statutes related to ownership, title, and operation of the insured vehicles. Thus, it seems impossible to ignore the inclusion and impact of the cited sections of the Safety Responsibility Act.

In light of the foregoing, the decision of the lower court must be and is affirmed.

Affirmed.

CITY OF MARSHALL, TEX. v. BRYANT AIR CONDITIONING
650 F. 2d 724 (1981)

Goldberg, Circuit Judge

One short year after the now legendary heat wave of 1980 burned its way through the South, we are forced to consider the paradoxically chilling thought of a Texas summer without air conditioning. Plaintiff-appellees claim that they were forced to simmer through several summers due to defendant-appellant's deceptive trade practices and breach of warranty with regard to the sale and maintenance of air-conditioning equipment. While we can certainly sympathize with appellees' frustration and perspiration, we are required by Texas law to reverse the judgment in their favor and remand the case to the trial court.

I. "Summer in the City"

In 1973 defendant-appellant Carrier Corporation ("Carrier"), through its Bryant Air Conditioning Company division, manufactured six air conditioner units which were sold for use in the City of Marshall, Texas ("Marshall") public library. In 1974 Carrier, again through its Bryant division, manufactured ten air conditioner units which were sold for use in the Wiley College men's dormitory. Each of these units was sold by Carrier pursuant to an express warranty which provided that (1) Carrier warranted the components and parts of the air-conditioning equipment to be free from defects in material or workmanship for a period of one year after installation, (2) Carrier agreed to "repair or replace, at its option" certain components or parts which were found to be defective during the one-year period, and (3) for an additional four-year period, Carrier agreed to "repair and replace, at its option, certain parts or components in the 'Refrigeration System' found to be defective." Record at 49.

According to plaintiff-appellees, the equipment never worked properly and required considerable maintenance and repair by Entex Corporation ("Entex"), a gas utility company. Plaintiff-appellees claim that the problems were due to the unavailability of replacement parts and hence the failure of the Carrier warranty. In 1977 the sweltering situation allegedly reached near-crisis proportions, and in October of that year Carrier sent the late Ralph Kemp ("Kemp") to look into the matter. During his visits to Marshall and Wiley College, Kemp apparently stated that the air-conditioning equipment could be repaired and adjusted to give satisfactory performance, that Carrier would supply necessary replacement parts, and that Carrier would provide factory-trained personnel to work on the units. However, shortly after Kemp examined the allegedly defective air-conditioning equipment, Wiley College and Marshall entered into an agreement with Entex which provided that Entex would replace the Carrier air conditioners with new equipment at its own cost in return for Marshall's and Wiley College's legal rights against Carrier. Pursuant to this agreement, new air-conditioning equipment was installed at the Marshall library and Wiley College dormitory.

Both Marshall and Wiley College brought state court suits against Carrier seeking damages for breach of warranty and violations of the Texas Deceptive Trade Practices-Consumer Protection Act ("Deceptive Trade Practices Act"). Carrier removed the actions to federal court based on diversity of citizenship, and the federal district court granted Entex's motions to intervene as assignee of Marshall's and Wiley College's claims. The actions were then consolidated and tried before a jury. After a four-day trial, the jury returned a verdict in favor of plaintiffs on both the breach of warranty and deceptive trade practices issues. Because the two claims represented alternative grounds of recovery, the trial court entered judgment pursuant only to the greater of the two verdict amounts, awarding treble damages and attorney's fees under the Texas Deceptive Trade Practices Act. Carrier appeals from the trial court's judgment.

II. "We CAN Work it Out": The Deceptive Trade Practices Act Claim

It is undisputed that the basis of plaintiff-appellees' Deceptive Trade Practices Act claim in this case centers around statements made by Carrier's representative Ralph Kemp during his visits to Wiley College and the Marshall public library in the autumn of 1977. As noted above, after examining the allegedly defective air-conditioning equipment, the late Mr. Kemp apparently stated that the units could be repaired and adjusted to give satisfactory performance, that Carrier would provide factory-trained personnel to work on the units, and that Carrier would supply necessary replacement parts.

Plaintiff-appellees argued at trial that had these representations been fulfilled, there would have been no need to replace the allegedly defective air-conditioning equipment. Plaintiff-appellees then reasoned that they were entitled to the cost of replacing the Carrier air conditioners with new units. The jury apparently agreed, and the trial court entered judgment trebling the $77,000 replacement cost verdict for plaintiffs.

On appeal, Carrier raises a number of issues which it claims preclude a Deceptive Trade Practices Act judgment in the case at bar. However, we need go no further than a consideration of one of the basic elements of a Texas Deceptive Trade Practices Act claim: the requirement that a plaintiff recover only for damages actually caused by the allegedly deceptive trade practice. Because there is no proof in the record of this case of any damages caused by an allegedly deceptive trade practice, the trial court should have directed a verdict in favor of defendant on the Deceptive Trade Practices Act claim.[1] We therefore must reverse the trial court's judgment and order dismissal of the Deceptive Trade Practices Act claim in this case.

It is clear that under the Texas Deceptive Trade Practices Act, the allegedly deceptive trade practices must cause the plaintiff to be actually damaged before he can recover. . . . In the case at bar, plaintiff-appellees' damages, if any, were caused solely by the failure of the air-conditioning equipment and alleged breach of warranty. There is no evidence that Kemp's allegedly deceptive trade practices caused any actual damages whatsoever. While it is true that if Kemp's alleged representations were fulfilled by Carrier, plaintiff-appellees would not have incurred the replacement cost of new air-conditioning equipment, the statements themselves in no way caused this cost or additional costs. The allegedly defective equipment had been purchased years before Kemp's statements were made, and so this is not a case in which an allegedly deceptive trade practice caused a plaintiff to buy defective equipment. Moreover, shortly after Kemp's visit, plaintiff-appellees purchased new air-conditioning equipment, and so this is not a case in which an allegedly deceptive trade practice caused a plaintiff to enter into a detrimental transaction, or to refrain from entering into a beneficial transaction. Rather, it is a case in which the allegedly deceptive trade practice did not cause plaintiffs to alter their plans or behavior, and did not cause them any harm whatsoever. The only damage in the case at

1. "A directed verdict should be granted if, considering all the evidence in the light most favorable to the party against whom the verdict is directed, reasonable men could not reach a contrary verdict." . . . In the case at bar, the defendant moved for a directed verdict but the trial court refused to grant the motion. . . .

bar—if any—was the result of an equipment failure beginning some time before the allegedly deceptive statements were made. Plaintiff-appellees may have suffered through several summers because of the air-conditioning equipment failure and alleged breach of warranty, but they did not suffer any more due to Kemp's statements made in the autumn of 1977.[2]

Because "reasonable men could not reach a contrary verdict," . . . the trial court should have directed a verdict in defendant's favor. We therefore reverse the judgement of the trial court and order dismissal of plaintiff-appellees' Deceptive Trade Practices Act claim.[3]

III. "Promises, Promises": The Breach of Warranty Issues

As an alternative ground of recovery, the jury awarded plaintiffs breach of warranty damages in the amount of $49,000. Appellants argue that this verdict cannot be sustained due to a number of errors below. We agree with appellants that the jury was not properly instructed on the issue of reasonable notice under Texas warranty law, and we therefore reverse the jury verdict and remand for a new trial on this issue.[4]

Texas law "requires notification by the buyer to the seller that a breach of warranty has occurred," so that the seller has an opportunity to cure the breach. . . . In the case at bar—despite timely objection by defendant-appellant—the jury was not instructed that such notice was required.[5] Rather, the jury was told that the essential elements of a breach of warranty claim in the case at the bar were simply that the air-conditioning equipment was defective in material and workmanship, and that defendant failed to repair or replace defective components or parts in accordance with the warranty. . . . Because the issue of reasonable notice was improperly omitted from the trial court's jury charge, we must remand for a new trial on the breach of warranty issue. . . .

Plaintiff-appellees note that the jury was asked—via special interrogatory—whether Carrier was given a reasonable opportunity to cure the equipment defects or malfunctions. Since the jury answered that Carrier was given such an opportunity, plaintiff-appellees reason that the notice issue has been resolved in their favor. . . . While this argument looks persuasive at first glance, upon closer scrutiny it is seen to lack merit. The special interrogatory made it clear that the jury was to consider the notice issue only if the *Deceptive Trade Practices Act claim* was resolved in favor of plaintiffs. Hence, the jury was asked to resolve the notice issue only with regard to claims arising from statements made by Carrier representative Kemp in the autumn of 1977. Since the allegedly defective equipment was installed in 1973 and 1974, since plaintiff-appellees complained that the equipment never worked properly, and since the primary warranty was for only one year, adequate notice with regard to claims arising from allegedly deceptive trade practices in 1977 is irrelevant with regard to claims arising from an alleged breach of warranty.[6] Moreover, as noted above, the court's instruction on the essential elements of a breach of warranty claim clearly omitted the notice issue. The jury was not asked to consider whether Carrier was given a reasonable opportunity to cure equipment defects with regard to the alleged breach of warranty, and the instruction below was therefore erroneous.[7]

2. Shortly after Kemp's autumn visit to Wiley College and the Marshall public library, and before the start of the next sweltering summer, Entrex—the company handling virtually all air-conditioning matters for Wiley College and the Marshall public library—replaced the allegedly defective equipment with new air conditioners. However, the decision to replace the Carrier air conditioners with new equipment appears to have been made before Kemp's visit. . . . Hence, Kemp's visit was viewed by plaintiff-appellees as nothing more than as an opportunity to bargain for a cash settlement with Carrier. . . . and the alleged representations made by Kemp could not have caused plaintiff-appellees to do anything differently or to suffer any harm.

3. Because we reverse the Deceptive Trade Practices Act judgment on this ground, we do not reach the remaining Deceptive Trade Practices Act issues raised by appellant.

4. We reject appellant's contentions that, as a matter of law, Carrier fulfilled its warranty, and that, again as a matter of law, plaintiff-appellees failed to give Carrier adequate notice of the breach. There was ample evidence both of the breach and of notice to Carrier to submit these issues to the jury. . . . Likewise, we reject appellees' contention that adequate notice was proven as a matter of law. . . . Considering the record as a whole, the issue of reasonable notice was clearly a jury question and the court's erroneous instruction on this issue therefore requires reversal.

Because we reverse and remand with regard to the breach of warranty claim based on the trial court's erroneous instruction regarding notice, we do not reach appellant's other breach of warranty claims which—if correct—would require the same result.

5. Contrary to plaintiff-appellees' contention, the issue "whether Carrier was given a reasonable opportunity to cure the alleged defects or malfunctions" was presented in the pre-trial order by defendant-appellant and hence the issue of notice was adequately raised. . . . Moreover, defendant-appellant raised a timely objection to the court's jury charge on breach of warranty, arguing that the trial court erroneously failed to instruct the jury that notice is a necessary element of a breach of warranty claim. . . .

6. For example, the jury's answer to this special interrogatory may simply mean that the jury found that plaintiffs gave Carrier reasonable notice of Carrier's failure to fulfill the alleged representations made by Kemp. This notice is a far cry from the reasonable notice required with regard to an alleged breach of warranty for equipment installed several years earlier.

7. Appellant also suggests that the plaintiffs' claim is time barred by the applicable statute of limitations. Because the record below is not sufficiently developed concerning when plaintiffs' cause of action accrued for statute of limitations purposes, we do not reach this issue. Nothing in this opinion should be read as in any way precluding defendant-appellant from raising the statute of limitations issue on remand.

IV. Conclusion: "The Second Time Around" . . .

Because there is no evidence that plaintiff-appellees were actually damaged by the allegedly deceptive trade practices in the case at bar, we reverse the judgment of the trial court and order that the Deceptive Trade Practices Act claim be dismissed. Because the jury was improperly instructed on breach of warranty, we remand for a new trial on this issue.

REVERSED and REMANDED.

REVIEW QUESTIONS

1. Brown, in Seattle, Washington, ordered a machine from the White Company in Detroit, Michigan. The contract stated that the machine was to be shipped F.O.B. Detroit. At the bottom of the sheet the note "we will deliver the machine to you in Seattle at our cost" was written in longhand and signed by White. En route between Detroit and Seattle the machine was destroyed in a cyclone. Whose machine was lost? Why?

2. Black bought an automatic machine from White to replace a machine that had previously required two men to operate. In selling the machine to Black, White pointed out the saving in the cost of two men's time. He also stated that "productive capacity will be doubled" with the new machine. Hourly production increased even more than double—1,100 pieces per hour against 500 pieces per hour previously. However, there was a problem involved. The machine seldom ran an hour without breaking down. Whenever it broke down, either one or two machine repairmen would be called upon to fix it. After a month or so one machine repairman was ordered to stand by for breakdown whenever the machine was scheduled to run. Weekly production on the automatic machine is only slightly greater than previous weekly production on the hand-operated machine. Black has charged White with fraud. Can he recover on this basis? Why or why not? Is he stuck with the machine? What defense does White have?

3. Distinguish between *express* and *implied* warranties.

4. How does the existence of a security interest protect a creditor from debtor default?

5. What rights does the debtor have in a security interest arrangement?

6. Distinguish between *sale on approval* and *sale or return.*

7. What is required of the seller to sell something *as is?*

8. What election of rights does a seller have if the buyer refuses to pay for goods he has received?

9. Location of title to goods at a particular point in time can be important. In the case of *Gross* v. *Powell* how could the facts be changed so that Proctor Motor, Inc. would be responsible for the injuries arising from the accident?

10. What must plaintiff in *City of Marshall, Texas* v. *Bryant Air Conditioning* prove to recover under the Carrier Corporation warranty when the case comes up for retrial?

Engineering Contracts

The general public is well aware of construction contracts that determine how buildings are to be erected, bridges built, and highways created. The media often report the stories of such construction projects and refer to the contracts. Such construction projects, and their inherent contracts, are also well known because the finished products are very evident. Legal problems and entanglements occur frequently enough in the use of contracts in the civil engineering, architectural engineering, and construction engineering fields that special courses in contract writing are commonly included in those curricula. The need for such education in mechanical, industrial, electrical, chemical, and other engineering curricula may be less apparent. However, *all* engineers seem to be involved in writing specifications and interpreting contract documents at some time during their careers. Some, especially those who rise in management, spend their entire working lives dealing with contracts. Thus there is a need for all engineers to be aware of laws regarding ownership, independent contracting, and agency, and of contract documents that spell out work to be done and the responsibilities of the parties to contracts.

16

Contracting Procedure

Before discussing contracting procedure several terms and relationships between the parties involved need to be discussed.

Owner. The *owner* is the party for whom the work is to be done. He is the one to whom the others look for payment for services. He is the final authority in questions as to what is to be included or left out of a project being undertaken for his benefit. He may be a private individual, president of a corporation, chairman of a board of directors, or a public official charged with the responsibility for the project.

Engineer or Architect. As the terms will be used here, *engineer* and *architect* are virtually interchangeable. There is, at present, considerable controversy (including court cases) over the meanings of the terms and the work to be considered the proper field of each. No attempt will be made to add to that controversy here. It will be assumed that the person is properly employed whether he be architect or engineer. The function of such a person is that of *agent* of the owner. He furnishes the technical and professional skill necessary in the planning and administration of the project to accomplish the owner's purpose. He is the designer, supervisor, investigator, and adviser of the owner. Most state laws require him to be registered as a professional in his field. He may be a consultant or an employee of the owner. He is the one with whom the contractor deals directly.

Contractor. The contractor is the one who undertakes the actual construction of the project. He furnishes the labor, materials, and equipment with which to complete the job. The term *contractor* is frequently further broken down into *general contractor* and *subcontractor*. The general contractor agrees to accept the responsibility for the complete project, frequently undertaking the major portion of it himself. Subcontractors are hired for particular specialties by the general contractor and, in effect, work for him while completing the portions of the project for which they have been hired. The general contractor is responsible for the entire project, even when the wiring, the plumbing, and the roofing are done by various subcontractors.

Types of Construction

Much of the capital wealth of our country is constructed by independent contractors. Most of the buildings, machines, bridges, utilities, production facilities, and other items of wealth that are primarily responsible for our standard of living were built under contract. There are two major types of such construction—public and private. There are significant differences in the motives and relationships involved with each.

Private Works. Private projects are those that are undertaken for an individual or a company. The restrictions imposed upon the parties are those of contracts in general. The agreement may be achieved by advertising and then choosing the best bid, or by direct negotiation without advertising. The acceptance may be oral or in writing; in fact, the entire contract could be oral if the parties so chose.

The profit motive is the usual reason for construction of private works. The owner believes the project will give him a desirable return on his investment. However, this need not necessarily be the reason for the project. In private work, the reason could be nothing more than a personal whim of the owner. The desirability of the project is not open to question by the public as long as no one is harmed by it.

Public Works. In public projects much of this is different. The motive for construction of public works is public demand or need. Financial return sufficient to justify the investment is frequently of less than primary importance.

Money for private works comes either from direct payments from available funds or from loans (e.g., bonds). Payment for public works comes from tax receipts or from loans (bonds or other obligations) to be retired from future tax receipts.

Voluminous statutes govern the letting of public-works contracts. These laws make certain restrictions. Generally, formal advertising and bidding is required to insure competition among the bidders. The "lowest responsible bidder" gets the job. Usually the means of advertising and the length of time the advertisement is to run are specified. Changes in plans or specifications usually cannot be made after the award of the contract even though such changes might be beneficial. Acceptance of a bid may not be effective until it has been ratified by a legislature or a legislative committee.

Once a contractor's bid on a public project has been accepted, the amount he will get is fixed. The official in charge of the project cannot agree to pay more, regardless of the apparent justice of the contractor's claim.

The purpose of the restrictions in letting public projects is, of course, to prevent dishonesty, collusion, and fraud among bidders and between bidders and public officials. Sometimes the restrictions seem unfair; and sometimes the results are less than might have been accomplished without them. At times well-meaning contractors fail to survive their ignorance of the law. The results in general, though, seem beneficial to the public.

Construction and Manufacturing

A construction project and the manufacture of goods for a market are basically similar. Each is concerned with the use of labor and equipment to turn raw materials into a finished product of some sort. Each must deal with economic considerations in acquiring raw material and labor. Each aims for efficient management in an effort to show a profit. Both are concerned with production schedules that must be met if penalties of one nature or another are to be avoided. Quality must be maintained, and costs must be minimized.

The main distinction between *construction* and *manufacturing* stems from the location of the product. In most construction, whether it is a building or a piece of productive equipment, the place where the product is built is the place where it will stay. A construction product is usually custom-made, built to specific requirements and not to be reproduced. Such a product does not lend itself to the economies of standardization of method as do the products of most manufacturing companies.

DIRECT EMPLOYMENT OR CONTRACT

After the decision has been made by the owner to undertake a construction project, the question frequently arises as to whether the work should be done by the available staff, by contract, or by a combination of both. The decision involves many factors; two very important ones being the relative size of the job and the skill of the staff. Many jobs are too large for the present staff or too small to be submitted to an outside

contractor, hence there is no problem. But there are also many projects of intermediate size which could be completed either way. It is with these jobs that the present discussion is concerned. There are a number of benefits and disadvantages the owner (or engineer) should consider in choosing the best procedure.

Cost. Certain savings in cost are apparent when direct employment is used: (1) The owner does not have to pay the contractor's *profit* margin if he does the work himself. (2) The amount added in by the contractor for *contingencies* is saved if no contingencies arise. The expected cost saving here is really anticipation of winnings from a gamble and if the owner's staff is inexperienced, the odds are against him. An experienced contractor can often see and avert incidents that would otherwise be contingencies. (3) The cost of making *multiple estimates* is avoided if the owner's staff undertakes the job.

Flexibility. A project undertaken by direct employment is more flexible if it becomes necessary to make changes while the job is under way; the owner has only to order the changes made. When a contractor is hired to build according to plans and specifications and work is under way, change proposals will usually meet with resistance. The contractor is interested in completing the project as soon as possible so that he can receive his money and go on to the next job. He will be tempted to charge heavily for the delay caused by a change.

Subsequent Maintenance. There is something to be said for subsequent maintenance as an inducement for the owner to use as many of his own people as possible. A machine or other structure is more readily repaired by the original builder than by maintenance men who have had no experience with it.

Grievances. Labor (union) problems are usually somewhat reduced by using present crews. There is the possibility of jurisdictional disputes, but the likelihood of these and other issues arising is minimized. The individuals forming the nucleus of the crew, at least, have learned to live with each other and with others employed by the owner in different jobs.

Specialization. The great and sometimes decisive advantage of hiring a contractor for a project is that the contractor is a specialist. His specialty is in labor, supervision, and procurement of materials—the so-called know-how of that particular kind of contracting. It is probably this factor, more than any other, that gives the contractor an advantage.

Public Relations. The public relations programs of many large concerns tip the scales in favor of hiring contractors to undertake jobs for them. This is especially true when a company sets up an operation in a new community. To establish itself in favorable light in the community, the company may hire local people to set up its facilities, even though it has a staff capable of doing the job.

PAYMENT ARRANGEMENTS

There are four basic ways in which an owner may pay for work undertaken by a contractor. In addition to the basic payment arrangements, there is an infinite number of variations and combinations of them, each adjusted to a given project. The features of each basic arrangement will be considered primarily from the owner's standpoint.

Lump-Sum Contract

If a manufacturer or an individual purchases a product manufactured by a company, he usually knows the price before he makes the agreement to purchase. The price of an automobile is arranged between the dealer and the buyer, for instance, before the sale is actually made. The *lump-sum* contract arrangement gives the owner the same assurances as to the price he will have to pay for the job. This aspect of the lump-sum contract appeals to people, and it is the main advantage of the arrangement from the owner's standpoint.

There are several inherent disadvantages in the fixed price or lump-sum contract. Probably the main one is the antagonistic interests of the owner and the contractor. Once the contract is signed, the contractor's main interest is in making a profit on the job and in doing it as quickly as possible. There is an incentive for him to do no more than the minimum requirements set forth in the plans and specifications. With an unscrupulous contractor the results may be shoddy workmanship and a poor structure. Even a responsible contractor may be tempted to cut corners if contingencies start eating into his profit margin or if he is already losing on the job. The owner's interest on the other hand, is to obtain the best possible structure he can get for the money he has agreed to pay.

Changes, under a lump-sum contract, can be quite costly. The change represents an impediment to the contractor's speedy completion of the job. He is in the position to dictate the cost of changes if he so desires. The owner has hired him to do the job; he is on the premises with his equipment to render the service called for in the contract. The owner's alternative to paying the contractor's price for a change is to wait for completion of the job and then hire someone else to make the change. This is often very costly.

A lump-sum contract requires that considerable time and money be spent by the contractor in examining the site, estimating, and drawing up and submitting a bid before the job can start. The delays may run to months or even years and the cost of delay can be considerable. If the job is to be started as quickly as possible, the lump-sum contract is not indicated.

If the work required is at all indefinite or uncertain, the lump-sum conract should not be used. The contractor will have to add in a sufficient amount to cover the uncertainty if he is to show a profit. The greater the degree of uncertainty, the greater the probable spread in bidders' proposals. Prices on a 500-ton press, for instance, might vary as much as six or seven percent between high and low bids among five or six press manufacturers. If the equipment were a piece of automation with only the raw material and the end product known, the highest bid might be four or five times that of the lowest. Each contractor would try to cover himself as best he could against a large number of unknowns and gamble that the amount submitted would result in a successful bid for him.

Lump-sum contracts are used commonly and successfully, but their successful use is pretty well restricted to situations in which unknowns are at a minimum. They are not appropriate: (1) where uncertainties exist; (2) where a speedy start is necessary—emergency work, for instance; (3) where ongoing plant operations will interfere with the contractor's work.

To overcome these objections one of the two basic "cost-plus" types of contract can be used.

Cost-Plus-Percent-of-Cost Contract

The most rapid means of starting a project is through the use of the *cost-plus-percent* pricing arrangement. In an emergency an owner may be faced with the necessity of starting work immediately, while the plans for the completed structure are still being drawn up. Using a cost-plus-percent arrangement, today's phone call can result in action today. It is this feature that prompted the widespread use of such contracts by the federal government during World War II. Valuable time would have been lost in estimating and bidding if they had not been used.

According to the cost-plus-percent arrangement, the owner usually pays all the contractor's costs plus an added percentage (often 15%) of these costs as the contractor's profit. *Cost* refers to the cost of materials and services directly connected with the owner's structure. Such items as the contractor's overhead, staff salaries, and the like are usually excluded unless direct connection to the project can be shown.

A major advantage of the cost-plus-percent contract is its flexibility. Changes may be made readily when the owner desires them. Since the cost to the owner for making changes includes profit to the contractor, the contractor has little reason to object to them.

The risks involved in construction are assumed by the owner in the cost-plus-percent contract. He does not know with any certainty what the project will cost until it is completed. On the other hand, if no adverse conditions (contingencies) arise, the benefit is his rather than the contractor's.

The cost-plus-percent contract is not an unmixed blessing to the owner, though. Since the contractor's profit is tied to costs, the costs may be quite high. Gold-plated doorknobs may show up. The contractor has what amounts to an incentive to dishonesty—a financial reward for running up costs. The most honest of contractors (or people in any profession, for that matter) would be tempted to be inefficient under the circumstances. The need for the owner to police the project is apparent. It is because of this one disadvantage that the federal government now looks with disfavor on the cost-plus-percent contract. Renegotiation of contracts and the recapture of excess profits on government contracts following World War II left the government with a rather bitter attitude toward the arrangement.

Even if the contractor pursues the completion of the project in the best interests of the owner, efficiency is not assured. Supervisors and workers alike are not likely to put forth outstanding effort for their employer if nothing will be gained for them as a result.

Cost-Plus-Fixed-Fee Contract

The remedy for the main undesirable feature of the cost-plus-percent contract is found in the *cost-plus-fixed-fee* arrangement. Here the contractor is paid a fixed fee as his profit, and the owner picks up the tab for all the contractor's costs of undertaking the project. The amount of the fixed fee is subject to negotiation between owner and contractor or bid by the contractor based upon estimates of the cost of the completed project. The advance settlement of the amount of the fixed fee precludes an immediate start on the project, but the time required is not nearly as great as that necessary for a lump-sum contract.

The cost-plus-fixed-fee contract is probably the best basic arrangement from the standpoint of all parties concerned. The contractor has no incentive to run up costs or work inefficiently. In fact, with a view toward maximizing his profit in a given period of time, he has an incentive to hasten the completion of the project to obtain his fee.

There can be less flexibility with this arrangement due to the contractor's desire to complete the job rapidly. A proposal by the owner for a major, time-consuming change in the project is likely to be met with objections and an "outstretched hand." If the contractor is required to spend a longer time in pursuit of his fee, it is only fair that his fee be increased.

As in the cost-plus-percent contract, the owner runs the risk of contingencies, but he is in a somewhat better position. Under the cost-plus-percent arrangement, the occurrence of contingencies tends to increase the contractor's ultimate profit. There is incentive to bring about contingencies or, at least, not to actively avoid them. In the cost-plus-fixed-fee arrangement, the desire for early completion is an incentive for the contractor to avoid contingencies if possible. Thus, the owner's interests are better protected.

Unit-Price Contract

Certain kinds of structures may be conveniently built under the *unit-price* type of arrangement. This scheme applies best where there is a large amount of the same kind of work to be done. In the building of a road, for instance, the main elements are excavating, filling, and pouring of concrete. A unit-price contract could be conveniently used. The contract would specify so much per cubic yard of excavation (plus an extra amount if rock formation is encountered), so much per cubic yard of fill, and so much per cubic yard of concrete. The price per unit includes the contractor's cost per unit plus an amount for contingencies, overhead, and profit. The engineer or architect usually estimates the quantities required ahead of time for the benefit of both owner and contractor. The actual quantities may be considerably different from the estimate, but the contractor is paid according to the actual quantities required.

Usually the unit-price arrangement is used in conjunction with a lump-sum contract. In nearly every job there are some elements (such as clearing, grading, and cleaning up the site) that do not lend themselves to unit pricing. The combination is usually quite beneficial, largely because it is flexible.

With a unit-price contract much of the contractor's uncertainty is relieved, and this is reflected in his lower estimate for contingencies. The risks not assumed by the contractor, though, must be borne by the owner. The owner has no precise knowledge of the cost of the job until its termination.

Just as is true with a lump-sum contract, the job cannot begin immediately under a unit-price arrangement. The contractor requires time to examine the premises and prepare an estimate for the owner. Normal bidding procedure is usually used in the award of such contracts.

Variations

The types of contracts described above are the four basic forms. In addition to these there are many variations, or hybrids, many of them tailored to particular needs of projects. Probably the most common variation is the addition of an incentive system of some sort. Profit-sharing and percentage of cost saving are examples. One variation is the addition of a kind of reverse liquidated-damage clause. That is, the contractor is offered a fixed amount per day additionally if he finishes ahead of schedule.

Another form of contract is the *management contract*. In such a contract, the owner hires a contractor, not necessarily to undertake the work with his own organization, but to oversee the job, often hiring others to do the work. Frequently this includes managing work to be done with the owner's labor force. Work undertaken by the owner's people is said to be work under a *force account*. The contractor under a management contract still holds independent contractor status. He agrees to produce a result. His actions do not bind the owner under a management contract as an agent would bind his principal. The management contract is, therefore, distinct from the agency relationship, which exists between an owner and his engineer or architect. Usually the services of an engineer or architect are not used.

STAGES OF A PROJECT

A project starts as an idea or a dream for the future. If it is soundly conceived, planned, and developed, the dream may be realized. Failure in any of these things may turn it into a nightmare. For discussing the development of a project let us consider the lump-sum or the unit-price type of contract arrangement, since each requires extensive preliminary work.

Feasibility Studies

Regardless of how beneficial a project may seem to its originator, it is nearly always advisable to conduct a preliminary investigation. It is recognized that wars and other emergencies may preclude such an investigation, but in most organizations a state of emergency is somewhat unusual. The purpose of the *feasibility study* is to obtain preliminary information on several things:

1. What is the cost of undertaking the project? This cost is determined usually on the basis of either annual cost or present worth (or capitalized cost if perpetual service is contemplated).
2. Can the objective be attained better (or cheaper) in some other way? The comparison is made on the basis of annual cost or present worth.
3. What benefits will result from the use of the various alternatives? In most private projects and some public projects the ratio of economic benefit to cost must be sufficient to justify the project. In many public works, a crying need may push consideration of economic benefit into the background.

The preliminary investigations and reports are usually not intensive. Some schemes are shown to be obviously impractical after only a minimum of data is obtained. Where the scheme appears to be profitable, though, the expenditure of considerable time and money on the feasibility study may be justified. Surveys and investigations of such elements as markets, sources of raw material and labor, cost of transportation, and applicable laws and ordinances may become necessary. Even when a tentative decision has been made to go ahead with the project, based upon reports that show it will pay off, it is usually worthwhile to spend some time and money investigating whether there is a cheaper way of achieving the same goal. Most such studies can be undertaken at a reasonable cost. However, the more closely balanced the evidence, the more detailed must be the study. Wise use of investigations can save money in the long run, but wisdom also dictates the point at which a study should be terminated. When a course of action (or inaction, as the case may be) is clear, the feasibility study has usually served its purpose.

Design

If the feasibility study indicates the project is desirable and the decision is made to go ahead, the next step is the design of the structure. Normally, all designs are complete in some detail before work is started. A complete feasibility study usually includes sketches of layouts considered. The design completes consideration of functional requirements, layouts, and the dimensions involved. Preparation of the drawings is a part of the engineer's or architect's task. When the drawings and specifications are completed, they combine to give the basic information on the project.

Legal Arrangements

If such arrangements have not already been made, land must be obtained by purchase, or by exercise of eminent domain if it is to be a public project. Railroad sidings, highway connections, and utility services must all be considered.

In the design drawings the owner and engineer have a picture to use in talking to others about the project. If a building is being constructed, zoning is likely to be a consideration, and building codes must be satisfied. A copy of the design drawings of the proposed construction ordinarily must be filed with the proper authorities to obtain a building permit.

Another legal matter is the engineer's or architect's right to practice in the state. State licensing laws generally require that a registered professional engineer sign construction plans or have them issued under his seal. It is not required that all members of the engineering staff be registered. If a member of the staff who is registered takes the responsibility for the plans, the law is satisfied.

If the project is to be undertaken for the public, strict adherence to laws governing such projects is necessary. It is necessary that the order and appropriation for the project be passed before the work is undertaken. In many types of public construction there are minimum standards to be met.

Preparation of Contract Documents

During the preliminary stages of a project it is necessary to prepare contract documents that will guide the remainder of the project. One of the main purposes of these documents is to set forth the relationships between the parties. If this purpose is to be accomplished adequately, the documents must be prepared with great care and skill. The engineer's task of preparing these documents often seems dull and routine—as an obstacle to be overcome to get to something more interesting. Dull and routine it usually is, but it is also important. Careful attention to this task prevents many future controversies, and it may make controversies that do arise easier to settle.

The pieces that fit together to make up a construction contract are (1) the advertisement, (2) the instructions to bidders, (3) the proposal, (4) the agreement, (5) the bonds, (6) the general conditions, and (7) the specifications and drawings.

Each component of the array of documents comprising a construction contract has a name or heading. The parts are not called by the same names in all contracts, and the material covered under the headings is not always the same. That is, what is covered in "general provisions" in a federal government contract might be covered in "general conditions" where a state or a private party is owner, or the coverage might be found under "information for bidders." There seems to have been only one major attempt at a general standardization—The American Institute of Architects has drawn up and copyrighted contract documents for use in building construction contracts. Although these do not entirely fit the picture here, our discussion will center around them since they are national standards in closely analogous construction. The federal government and most of the state governments have standardized contract components; the same is true of most large companies. Only a short indoctrination is necessary to familiarize a new engineer with his employer's particular terms and usages.

Certain instances of overlap may be noted. Ideally, a subject should be thoroughly treated in only one place and reference made to this treatment whenever the occasion arises again in the documents. In larger projects, though, duplication of coverage is fairly common.

Advertisement. The advertisement is usually the last contract document to be prepared, but is the first one seen by the contractor.

The primary purpose of the *advertisement* is to obtain competitive bidding on the project. In public contracts a minimum of three bidders on any project is normally required and a special authorization is needed if an award is to be made otherwise. In private work there is, of course, no legal requirement to advertise. Contract awards are often made to contractors with whom the owner has successfully dealt on previous occasions. Many companies consider competitive bidding to be desirable, however, and formal procedures have been established by them to require it.

A second purpose to be accomplished by the advertisement is to attract only prospective bidders who would be interested in the type of work involved. The advertisement should not attract those who have insufficient capacity or who are not interested in the type or location of the work. To accomplish this end the wording of the advertisement should give a clear, general picture of what is to be done.

The title of the advertisement has two functions. It must attract attention and it should also state very generally what is to be built. The phrase "Notice to Contractors" or "Call for Bids" together with a phrase generally describing the type of structure, such as "Elementary School," serves these functions well. A glance attracts the qualified contractor and prompts him to read further.

The information to be included in the advertisement varies with the type of project contemplated, but the following details are often found desirable:

1. The kind of job.
2. Location of the project—construction equipment is rather costly to move.

3. The owner and the engineer—previous contracts with owner or engineer may influence a contractor.
4. Approximate size of the project.
5. The date and place for receipt of bids, and the date and place of opening and reading bids.
6. If an award is to be made, e.g., "to lowest responsible bidder," or if the owner reserves the right to reject any and all bids; and when the contract is to be signed.
7. Deposits to be required, bid bonds, performance bonds.
8. Procedure for withdrawing bids if withdrawal is to be allowed.
9. The place where copies of the contract documents may be obtained.
10. Any special conditions.

To accomplish the purposes of advertising for bids, the advertising medium should be carefully selected. Public contracts must be advertised in local newspapers. For private contracts, local newspapers and trade journals make good advertising media.

Instructions for Bidders. The purposes of advertisement are best served by brevity. Contractors who remain interested in the project after reading the advertisement are offered the opportunity to obtain more information, usually from the engineer. It is customary to require a deposit (usually from $50.00 to $500.00) from the contractor when he obtains a set of the contract documents.

The contract document known as "Instructions for Bidders" or "Information for Bidders" may be a separate document. Probably just as frequently it is the beginning portion of the specifications. Much of the information contained in Instruction for Bidders is the same as that given in the advertisement, but it is in expanded form—the "what," "where," "when," "how," and "for whom" are given in more detail.

Additional inclusions in the Instructions for Bidders vary considerably from one project to another. Items included in Instructions for Bidders in one project may be found in the general conditions document or in the general provisions section of the specifications in other projects. Additional items usually included in the Instructions for Bidders section are listed below:

1. A requirement that the bidders follow the proposal form.
2. A statement as to whether or not alternative proposals will be considered.
3. The proper signing of bids; e.g., the use of a power of attorney.

4. Qualification or prequalification of bidders. This is a requirement to satisfy the owner that the contractor has the necessary skill, financial means, staff, and equipment to do the job.
5. Discrepancies. Provision is usually made for review with the engineer of any discrepancies appearing in the contract documents.
6. Examination of the site. An invitation is normally extended to bidders to examine the site with a warning that no additional compensation will be allowed as a result of conditions of which the bidder could have informed himself.
7. Provision for return of required bid deposits to unsuccessful bidders.

The Proposal. The *proposal* is a formal offer by the contractor to do the required work of the project. Acceptance of the proposal makes it a binding contract, so considerable care must be exercised by the engineer in drawing it up.

Proposal forms are usually standardized for all bidders on a job. If the proposal is broken down into components (as in a unit-price contract), it is necessary for comparison purposes that the breakdown be the same for all bidders. Where just one lump-sum bid is requested, it is still necessary for the proposal form to be the same for all, since bids should be on an equivalent basis. The following elements may be contained in a proposal form:

1. The price or prices for which the contractor agrees to perform the work involved.
2. The time when work is to start and when it is to be finished.
3. A statement that no fraud or collusion exists. Of particular concern is the possibility of fraud or collusion among bidders or between any bidder and a representative or employee of the owner.
4. A statement that the bidder accepts responsibility for having examined the site.
5. Proffer of any required bid bond or guarantee and agreement to furnish whatever other bonds may be required as well as an agreement to forfeit these bonds or portions of them under conditions stipulated.
6. Acknowledgement that the various other documents are to become parts of the contract.
7. A listing of subcontractors if required.
8. Signature and signatures of witnesses.

Agreement. To a lawyer, the agreement probably would be the most important of the contract documents. It is the focal point of the entire relationship between owner and contractor and the other contract documents are drawn to support it.

The term *agreement* is used advisedly for this document, because the term *contract* is preferred when referring to the complete array of contract documents.

Usually the agreement is quite short—one page or possibly two—and it describes the work to be done largely by reference to the other contract documents. The owner's consideration (the price to be paid for the work) must be stated, as well as the means and time of payment.

Although they are included in the other contract documents incorporated by reference, there are a few items which are usually repeated in the agreement. If time of completion is an essential element of the project, that time and liquidated damages for failure to complete on time are mentioned. If there is to be a warranty of the work by the contractor for, say, a year after completion, that is usually included. Any amounts to be held back from payments to the contractor are set forth.

Bonds. A bond gives the owner financial protection in case of default by the contractor. There are three types of bonds in common use in contracting—the *bid bond,* the *performance bond,* and the *labor and material payment bond.* Each protects the owner by assuming a risk he would normally run in hiring a contractor to undertake work for him.

The function of a *bid bond* is to assure the owner that the bidder will sign the agreement to do the work if his bid is the one accepted. In theory the amount of the bid bond is supposed to cover the owner's loss if the lowest responsible bidder fails to sign the agreement and the owner must then turn to the next higher bidder. Usually the owner does not require a bid bond as such. He requires a deposit which may be satisfied by a bid bond or a certified check or some other security by the contractor that the owner will be reimbursed in case of failure to sign. The bid security is forfeited only if the chosen bidder fails to agree to the project. It is returned to the bidder after the agreement is made. The bid securities of unsuccessful bidders are, of course, returned to them.

Through the *performance bond* the owner's risk that the contractor may fail to complete the project is passed on to a surety company. The risk involved may be very slight—most contractors are in business to stay. However, a contractor deals in the future, and predictions of what will happen sometimes go awry. Risks are involved. The contractor may meet with insurmountable obstacles. Such things as unforeseen price rises, strikes, fires, floods, storms, or unsuspected subsoil conditions can financially ruin even the best-backed contractors. If the contractor is faced with such disaster, insolvency may result, and the owner, if he has not provided for a performance bond, may be left trying to obtain blood from a stone. However, if a performance bond has been required, completion of his structure is guaranteed. Many surety companies maintain their own facilities to be pressed into service on such occasions; more frequently the surety company hires another contractor to complete the job.

The cost of a performance bond will, of course, be passed on to the owner in the price he pays for the work. This price normally runs somewhat less than one percent of the bid price for the contract. For this price the owner not only gets risk protection, but a preselection of contractors. Surety companies are quite choosy about the contractors they agree to back. The irresponsible and the "fly-by-nights" are poor risks, and a reputable surety company will not back them. The requirement of a performance bond, then, allows the owner to select from the best.

The *labor and material payment bond* offers protection against labor and material men's liens, known generally as *mechanics' liens.* The lien laws of the various states differ considerably. In any state, though, if a contractor fails to pay for his labor or material, a lien may be obtained against the property it was used to improve. In addition to the labor and material supplier's liens, the contractor, subcontractor, engineer, or architect may secure payment by recording a lien. Based upon the assumption of the owner's honesty and integrity in dealing with his contractor and engineer or architect, discussion here will be confined to labor liens and material suppliers' liens.

Mechanics' liens secure payment for anything connected with the improvement of real estate. The security is an encumbrance upon the property which then makes it more difficult to sell or mortgage. Technical procedures and delays are necessary in following the lien laws to remove encumbrances. There are two ways in which the owner may protect himself:

1. By withholding sufficient funds from payments to the contractor to pay for labor and materials if the contractor fails to do so, or
2. By requiring the contractor to obtain a labor and material payment bond.

Withholding part payment requires that the owner know the amount he may have to pay. This, in turn, usually requires a sworn statement from the contractor as to his outstanding bills before payment is made to him. Some state lien laws require such a sworn statement if a payment bond has not been provided in the contract. The procedure can become somewhat cumbersome.

Requirement of a labor and material payment bond from the contractor is much simpler for the owner. According to the bond, the surety company assumes liability for the contractor's unpaid bills.

When the federal government is owner in a project, a performance bond and a labor and material payment bond are automatically required. The Miller Act (passed in 1935) requires such bonds for federal contracts exceeding $25,000.

General Conditions. In a set of contract documents the document that states the general relationships among the parties is usually known as the *General Conditions.* This document deals with rights reserved and assigned among the parties, authority, and responsibility. Topics covered in the General Conditions vary from contract to contract, but some are almost invariably present.

There is nearly always a statement near the beginning of the General Conditions as to the *unity* of the contract documents—that a requirement in one document is just as binding as if it appeared in all of them. Such unity is necessary since the specifications for even a small project would reach tremendous size if each specification item had to be followed by all conditions pertaining to it.

The right of inspection by the owner or his representative at any time is usually reserved. It is common also to allow inspection by public officials as a general condition.

Conditions for termination of the contract by the owner and by the contractor are set forth in the General Conditions. Bankruptcy of the contractor and failure by the owner to make scheduled payments to the contractor when due are conditions for termination.

The insurance program for the project is usually outlined in the General Conditions. Provision is made that workers' compensation will cover medical costs and partial wage payments in case of injury to a worker as a result of his employment by the contractor. The owner's protective liability insurance protects the owner from contingent liability if the contractor's operations should injure anyone. Fire insurance and vehicle liability are among many other types of insurance commonly required by the General Conditions.

The engineer or architect is to make decisions on the work involved in the project. He has the right to stop the work when it appears necessary to do so. The extent or limits of his authority should be spelled out clearly. Provision is often made for arbitration as a final step in an altercation between the owner and the contractor.

Finally, the General Conditions usually include a requirement that the contractor keep the site clean as work progresses and that he clean up the site thoroughly when he finishes.

The Final Steps

Time. Almost invariably there is considerable pressure by the owner to get things started soon after the decision has been made to undertake a project. Advertising and bidding procedures require time, however, and to shorten the time allowed for the initial stages is nearly always an act of folly. The prospective bidders need time to investigate the work site and to plan their work. If there is not enough time for the investigation and planning stages, many unknowns will remain. Generally, the more that is *not* known by a bidder, the higher will be his bid price. There are few fears greater than fear of the unknown, and fear of a proposed project drives the price up.

Collusion. Most owners, engineers, and contractors are honest people. There are some of each, though, who will eagerly forget ethics and the law to seize an unfair advantage. Unfair advantages take many forms, and there are many "shades of gray" between fair, honest practices and illegal ones. One is giving preference to one contractor over another, either by giving him added vital information privately or by writing the specifications so as to give him an advantage. Another form of collusion occurs occasionally when there is a limited number of responsible bidders on a project. The bidders get together and decide who will take the job and for what price; the other bidders then submit prices higher than that submitted by the "successful" bidder. The result of these and other forms of collusion is higher cost to the owner. The existence of such practices is the main reason for governmental restrictions in letting public contracts. Collusion is, of course, against public policy and the Sherman Anti-Trust Act. It is punishable by both fines and imprisonment. In addition, up to triple damages can be recovered in a civil action by those injured.

The time for receiving proposals should be fixed and inflexible. It is unfair to give one contractor a longer time to prepare his proposal. Similarly, the opening of the proposals should take place at the time specified.

Lowest Responsible Bidder. A contract award normally goes to the "lowest responsible bidder." Many factors enter into the determination of the contractor who is to be awarded the contract. If *prequalification* has been required, the decision is based upon price alone. The nonmonetary factors used to determine the lowest responsible bidder are those that indicate a reasonable likelihood of completing the contract. The chief factors to be considered are:

1. The contractor's *reputation*. Such things as shoddy work, constant bickering for extra payments, and an uncooperative or lackadaisical attitude are cause for caution. Rejection of a bidder on the basis of reputation often leads to arguments, but each person builds his own reputation and should have to live by it.
2. The contractor's *finances*. Inadequate finances or credit can be a source of trouble in a project. Even though a bond is required of the contractor, finding a substitute would cause delay, and the project may suffer.
3. The contractor's *experience*. If the project is a new field for the contractor, he may have to experiment, whereas an experienced contractor would automatically know what to do. There is, of course, the possibility that the work of an inexperienced contractor might be better because of a new approach or new ideas. The best guide is the contractor's past performance. The size of the project is also an important consideration. A contractor's success on a $40,000 job does not insure success on a million-dollar project.
4. The contractor's *equipment*. Most contracting work requires expensive, often specialized equipment. Without access to the proper equipment, the contractor may be doomed to failure despite good intentions. A trip by the engineer to examine the contractor's machinery and equipment may be recommended.
5. The contractor's *staff*. The skill of each of the contractor's staff members in his respective area of specialization can mean the success or failure of an enterprise. Purchasing of materials and supplies, for instance, can add to profit or be an excessive addition to cost. There are many instances of the same or similar items being sold for widely divergent prices by different suppliers.

Disqualification of a bidder is a rather serious step, and the engineer should be sure of his reasons before taking this action. The prospect of charges of favoritism or debates over qualifications compels the engineer to overlook any personal feelings he may have toward a particular bidder. With all bids, the right to reject any and all proposals should be reserved for use if needed.

CONTRACTOR'S COSTS

What is the major reason why contractors lose money on jobs? Probably the best answer is that they bid too low. And why would a contractor bid too low? Because he has overlooked one or more of the elements of a proposal. Five basic components are necessary to a contractor's proposal if he is to "make out" on the job. These are (1) direct labor, (2) materials, (3) overhead, (4) contingencies, and (5) profit.

Direct Labor

In putting together the necessary elements for any kind of structure, be it a special machine or a building, direct labor is an important item. The cost-per-hour for toolmakers, carpenters, brick layers, and other specialists is a significant amount. This direct payment cost can be anticipated and is usually estimated with reasonable accuracy. There are other costs, though, which are tied to direct labor and which are often overlooked.

Fringes. The costs involved in direct labor which are often overlooked are those that are usually termed *fringe benefits*. Fringe benefits are payments (other than direct wages) by an employer caused by the presence of the worker on the payroll and imposed on the employer by a governmental requirement or by collective bargaining. Many payments are fringes according to this definition.

Workers' compensation is one such payment. To conform with a state's workers' compensation law, the employer usually pays an insurance company or a state agency a set amount per $100 of payroll. The amount paid by the employer is determined either from a rate manual or according to the employer's injury experience. These costs run from a few cents per $100 on office employees to nearly $20 per $100 of payroll on certain types of construction work.

Social security is another government-required fringe benefit. Employer's payments to social security are equal to those deducted from the worker's wage; e.g., at 16 percent total deduction, the employer would pay 8 percent and the employee 8 percent of the employee's wages. When the Social Security Act was passed, these payments were little more than a trivial annoyance; now they constitute a significant cost to the employer.

Holiday pay and vacation pay are common fringe costs to the employer. A recent collective bargaining goal has been the addition of each employee's birthday as a holiday for him. Although these payments are made for time when no work is performed, they are still costs of direct labor.

It is the policy of many employers to share the cost of medical insurance and life insurance with their employees. Overtime premiums and shift premiums add to the cost of direct labor. Maintenance of a retirement fund for employees, payments from which will supplement social security benefits, is common.

Two of the means used to increase employee interest in the company are stock-buying plans and profit-sharing plans. In a stock-buying plan, the employer usually helps the employee become a part-owner in his or other companies. Frequently, this takes the form of making deductions from the employee's wages and then adding to the employee's investment a few years later. Turnover is reduced if the employee must wait for the employer's addition to the investment. Profit-sharing plans work in many ways, one way being the division of company profits after the first, say, $100,000 of profit in a particular year. The increased incentive and company loyalty that result from such plans cannot be denied—but neither can the added cost.

Availability and Transportation. With increased automation, it has become more and more possible—and even desirable—to locate plants without reference to labor supply. Structures are being built in the frozen regions near the Arctic Circle and the Antarctic and in desert regions, for example. The contractor who undertakes such installations has the problem of getting people to go with him and work on the projects. Often this requires that relocation expenses and housing be furnished. In less spectacular instances the cost is often overlooked. There are many locations where, though there may be an abundance of people, there is a shortage of particular specialists. Getting these specialists may entail payment by the contractor for daily time in transit or for moving them to the location.

Materials

One of the largest costs of a project is the cost of the materials that go into it. Purchasing can make or break a contractor. There is, in effect, an added profit for the contractor who, because of his knowledge of sources of materials and supplies, is able to make fortunate procurements throughout his project. A characteristic that often marks an efficient contractor is his prompt payment of invoices. It is common practice among suppliers to offer discounts for prompt payment, such as two percent off for payment within 10 days, net in 30 days. Although two percent on any one bill may not amount to much, the accumulation is significant.

Availability and Transportation. Local availability of materials and supplies is an important consideration. *Apparent* local availability may not be sufficient. The legality of local "tying agreements" is quite questionable, but the practical results are apparent. One story runs something like this: It seems that the Black Construction Company, of a neighboring state, was successful bidder on a contract, bidding in competition with local contractors. The bid was made on the basis of cement, mortar sand, and gravel being locally available (suppliers in the area were quite plentiful). Black set up to begin operations on the site, and when he tried to buy concrete ingredients he found they were "earmarked" for his former bidding competitors. As a result, Black had to transport cement, mortar sand, and gravel several hundred miles, resulting in a loss to him on the contract. Other contractors have run into very high local prices. Usually, it pays a contractor to investigate and make sure of local supplies before bidding on work in unfamiliar settings.

Storage. The owner often allows use of his storage facilities if such facilities are available. In many contracts, though, such facilities are not available or are inadequate. The successful bidder should include storage in his planning.

Overhead

A discussion of all the items that normally constitute *overhead* would be beyond the scope and purpose of this book. These are the costs that many small contractors or those new in the field may tend to overlook; as a result, they seem to "make out" on their contracts but lose money in the long run.

The contractor's overhead consists of many things: maintenance of his office, equipment maintenance, taxes, supervision, depreciation on equipment, utilities, and others.

Cost of Estimating. Of particular interest is the cost of investigation, planning, and estimating. This cost usually runs somewhere around two percent of the bid price on a project. Two percent isn't bad, but very few contractors get every job on which they bid. It is likely that the average would be about one successful bid out of every six or so submitted. If these figures are accepted, then the cost of making a successful bid is about twelve percent of the bid price. If the bidding is realistic, the cost is passed on to the owner. It is worth noting that this cost constitutes one of the wastes of competitive bidding practices. There have been instances in which owners solicited bids with no real intention of going through with their projects. Such practices should be discouraged.

Contingencies

Very few projects run smoothly from start to finish. It is rare that every day is a weather-working day or that delays do not occur for one reason or another. To cover the unexpected events the contractor usually adds an item known as *contingencies* into his bid. The cost of the item runs anywhere from 5 percent to 15 percent of the total, depending upon the likelihood that hazards will occur. If liquidated damages are in prospect, contingencies may be quite high. If all work to be done is clearly and completely shown, and the probability of hazards is small, the amount for contingencies will be reduced.

Profit

People who work for others as independent contractors do so in an endeavor to make a profit. Much of the growth of our economy can be attributed to the intent to make such a profit. The contractor is entitled as is anyone else to be paid a reasonable return on the projects he undertakes. The percentage of profit varies with such things as the size of the job, competition, and other factors, but profit there must be if the contractor is to survive.

HAYNES v. COLUMBIA PRODUCERS, INC.
334 P. 2d 1032 (1959)

Finley, Judge.

E.R. Haynes, a general contractor, brought this action to recover money allegedly due him from the defendant, Columbia Producers, Inc., under four contracts entered into between the parties.

At the trial the work done pursuant to each of the four contracts was referred to by a separate job number. For convenience, we will refer to the contracts in the same manner. The first contract (Job 5-14) was the only one of the four in writing. It provided for the construction of a grain elevator and was a "fixed-price" contract. The second contract (Job 5-16) was also for a fixed amount. It was for the construction of a foundation and concrete slabs for a steel warehouse to be erected adjacent to the elevator. The third and fourth agreements were both "cost-plus" contracts. One of them (Job 5-19) provided for the labor and material for the construction of an under-tunnel and foundation, and a slab, for a storage warehouse. The fourth contract (Job 5-26) was for the installation of machinery to be used in the storage warehouse building.

One of the principal causes of the difficulties between plaintiff and defendant was that all four contracts were being performed simultaneously, and the work was being done at the same location. During the trial, the corporation contended, *inter alia,* that the contractor had billed many items to the cost-plus contracts, whereas, in fact, these items should have been charged to the "fixed-price" contracts.

Plaintiff Haynes performed all work required under the contracts. The sole dispute at the trial concerned the amount, if any, which defendant corporation owed the plaintiff. The trial court entered judgment for the plaintiff in the sum of $28,052.99, plus interest. Both parties have appealed, the plaintiff claiming a greater amount than was awarded to him, and the defendant claiming that the amount of the judgment was too large. For convenience, we shall hereinafter refer to the appellant as Columbia Producers and to the respondent–cross-appellant as Haynes.

Under the machinery installation contract (Job 5-26), Haynes agreed to install certain machinery in Columbia Producers' elevator. Columbia Producers purchased this machinery from a third party, the Carter-Miller Company, thereby receiving a discount of $1,948. Columbia Producers directed Carter-Miller to credit the $1,948 discount to Haynes, who had an account with Carter-Miller for other purchases completely independent from the work he was then doing for Columbia Producers. The obvious effect was, of course, that Haynes owed Carter-Miller $1,948 less than he had owed before the discount was credited to his account.

Columbia Producers contended that the "plus" amount agreed to as the contractor's fee on Job 5-26 was the discount that the corporation caused to be credited to Haynes' account with Carter-Miller. The trial court found that the parties had agreed that the "plus" amount would be ten percent of cost, and made no finding relative to the Carter-Miller discount.

The appellant, Columbia Producers, does not assign error to the finding of the trial court that the parties agreed to a contractor's fee of ten percent. Its assignment of error is directed to the failure of the trial court to make any finding relative to the discount. It is urged by Columbia Producers that the effect of the trial court's decision on this point is to give a double allowance to Haynes. With this we agree.

Columbia Producers directed Carter-Miller to credit Haynes with this discount, under the mistaken impression that this was what the parties had agreed to as the contractor's fee on Job 5-26. The fact that Columbia Producers was mistaken on this point does not entitle Haynes to a ten percent fee and the discount. Haynes' contention that Columbia Producers gave him this discount merely as a gratuity is not supported by the record, and is not consistent with the business relationship existing between these parties. In short, Columbia Producers' first assignment of error is well taken, and it should be allowed $1,948 as an offset against the judgment awarded Haynes.

As part of Haynes' costs on the machinery installation contract (Job 5-26), the trial court allowed him $1,061.30 for labor used to install certain bin dividers. Columbia Producers contend that the obligation to install these dividers existed under Job 5-14, and that, consequently, it was error to allow these costs as a part of Job 5-26. This is not merely a dispute without substance, as it will be remembered that Job 5-14 is a "fixed-price" contract, whereas Job 5-26 is a "cost-plus" contract.

The contract entered into between these parties for the construction of the elevator (Job 5-14) obligated Haynes to furnish labor and all other costs necessary to complete a reinforced concrete elevator as shown on certain plans. These plans were introduced into evidence, and it is readily apparent that they provided for the construction of bin dividers.

The oral contract made for the installation of machinery (Job 5-26) was subdivided as follows: (a) hopper bin bottoms; (b) spoutings; (c) belt conveyors; and (d) general machinery installation. It will be noticed that there was no obligation under this contract for installation of any bin dividers. Rather, this obligation clearly existed under the contract entered into for the construction of the elevator. Accordingly, the judgment awarded Haynes should be reduced in the further amount of $1,061.30 (independent of any interest calculation).

Columbia Producers next contends that the trial court erred in refusing to credit it with $2,467.18, representing the amount charged by Haynes for certain sheet steel, and the transportation thereof, for use in the construction of bin bottoms and hoppers on Job 5-26. The total bill for this item was $4,164.18, representing 38,352 pounds of steel, plus transportation. Columbia Producers claims that only 20,000 pounds were actually used on Job 5-26. The trial court, faced with conflicting testimony, found for Haynes on this issue. We have carefully examined the record and conclude that it supports this finding.

Finally, Columbia Producers urges that the trial court erred in allowing Haynes interest on the amount found due him. In this connection it asserts that a trial of this case was necessary in order to determine how much was owing from it to Haynes, and that, consequently, this amount was not liquidated in the sense that it could have been determined prior to trial. Columbia Producers bases this assertion on the fact that Haynes allegedly failed to furnish adequate or proper billings, in that many items were being charged to the cost-plus contracts which should have been charged to the fixed-price contracts. Columbia Producers asserts that, in addition, many other items on the bill were overcharges. Even assuming these facts to be substantially true, we conclude that the trial court was correct in the allowance of interest.

In *Mall Tool Company* v. *Far West Equipment Company*, . . . this court quoted with approval from *McCormick* on Damages 213, para. 54, that

'A claim is liquidated if the evidence furnishes data which, if believed, makes it possible to compute the amount with exactness, *without reliance upon opinion or discretion*. Examples are claims upon promises to pay a fixed sum, claims for money had and received, claims for money paid out, and claims for *goods or services to be paid for at an agreed rate*.' (emphasis supplied.)

and that

'If the claim is one of the kinds mentioned above, it is still "liquidated," by what seems the preferable view, even though it is disputed in whole or in part.'

In further explanation of the above, McCormick continues by stating:

'Doubtless all courts would agree that a specific sum of money named in and convenanted to be paid by an express contract, where the liability to pay the principal sum is undisputed, is a "liquidated" sum. Such admitted claims rarely give rise to any controversy interest. Is the claim for such a sum still a "liquidated" demand, where the defendant denies all liability under the contract, *or disputes liability for certain items and admits others*? It would seem that the existence of a dispute over the whole or part of the claim should not change the character of the claim from one for a liquidated, to one for an unliquidated, sum. And this conclusion finds support in the cases. . . .

. . . In short, *it is the character of the claim* and not of the defense that is determinative of the question whether an amount of money sued for is a "liquidated sum.' " (Emphasis supplied.)

We are convinced that the *character of the claim* in the case at bar is liquidated. Two of these contracts were for fixed amounts. The other two were costs, plus ten percent of costs, as the contractor's fee. All were subject to mathematical computation to arrive at the amount owed. It was not necessary to rely on opinion evidence. In short, the amounts owed were determinable within the meaning of the *Mall Tool* case, supra. The trial court did not err in allowing interest.

We turn now to a discussion of the assignments of error raised by Haynes on his cross-appeal, only one of which we need to discuss in detail.

The written contract entered into for the construction of the elevator (Job 5-14) provided that Haynes should be allowed extra compensation if it became necessary for him to excavate any "rock." The trial court found that Haynes had expended $1,814.11 for extra excavation within the terms of the contract. However, the trial court also found that, under the original plans, Haynes was obligated to construct a basement, size 40' by 40'. It is admitted that the basement as it was finally constructed was only 20' by 40'. The trial court determined that there was a saving to Haynes of $1,690 in the construction of the smaller basement; consequently, the $1,814.11 allowed for the rock excavation was reduced by the amount of $1,690.

Haynes contends that there is no substantial evidence in the record to support the trial court's finding that, under the contract, he was originally obligated to construct a basement, 40' by 40'. Haynes argues that the agreement between the parties was originally for a basement 20' by 40'. We believe there is merit to this contention.

The written contract did not specify what the dimensions of the basement were to be. The contract merely required Haynes to construct the basement in accordance with certain plans. From the plans it is difficult to ascertain the actual size the basement was to be. For example, one of Columbia Producers' witnesses, an engineer, testified that the plans called for the basement to be 40' by 40'; on cross-examination, however, he admitted that the plans showed only a one-sided view of the basement. The only probative evidence concerning the agreement between the parties which we have found in the record is the testimony of Haynes. He testified, that, originally, it was agreed the basement would be 40' by 20'. As there appears to be no evidence to contradict this testimony, it follows that the trial court erred in finding that the original plans specified the basement should be 40' by 40', and in awarding the amount of $1,690 as a credit to Columbia Producers.

The remaining four assignments of error raised by Haynes are all directed to the trial court's findings of fact. By his pleadings, as modified by a pretrial order, Haynes claimed (1) that he was entitled to $3,874 for extra work done on Job 5-16 for the reason that he was required to level certain ground before commencing construction of the warehouse required by that job; (2) that he was entitled to $980.27 for cement delivered, and (3) to $982.25 for excavation done on Job 5-19 over and above the amount allowed by the trial court; (4) that he had filed a claim of lien against Columbia

Producers within ninety days after the termination of work as required by statute. The trial court found adversely to Haynes on each of these claims. Our examination of the record discloses that the evidence amply supports these findings.

The net effect of our decision is to allow Haynes $1,319.30 (independent of any recalculation of interest) less than was allowed him by the trial court. Under the circumstances, neither party shall recover costs on this appeal.

The cause is remanded with directions to the trial court to enter judgment in accordance with the views expressed herein.

HOUGH v. ZEHRNER
302 N.E.2d 881 (1973)

Staton, Judge.

I.
STATEMENT ON THE APPEAL

Hough delivered 1,944.6 tons of crushed stone to Zehrner's junk and salvage yard where a new commercial garage for trucks was being constructed. The crushed stone was used for the driveway and parking area around the commercial garage where the muddy condition of the ground would not support commercial truck travel. When Hough was unable to obtain payment for the delivered crushed stone, he filed a mechanic's lien under I.C. 1971, 32-8-3-1. . . . His foreclosure suit resulted in a judgment against him. The trial court concluded that Hough's lien was not within the scope of the statute. Hough filed his motion to correct errors which presents this question on appeal:

> Does the scope of the mechanic's lien statute encompass a materialman who delivers crushed stone for a driveway and parking area which is to be used in conjunction with a commercial garage being constructed?

Our opinion construes the above statute and concludes that such a materialman is entitled to a mechanic's lien. We reverse the trial court's judgement.

II.
STATEMENT OF THE FACTS

Hough entered into an oral contract with Caprio and Phebus in October 1968 to supply crushed stone which would be used in the construction of a driveway and parking facility at Zehrner's junk and salvage yard where a new commercial garage was being built. The first delivery of stone to Zerhner was on October 16, 1968, and the last load of crushed stone arrived on November 1, 1968. The total deliveries amounted to 1,944.6 tons of crushed stone for an agreed price of $2,916.90. Caprio and Phebus had a commitment to Zehrner for the delivery of the crushed stone. All parties knew of the agreement with Hough and the intended use of the crushed stone. When Hough was unable to receive payment from Caprio and Phebus, he filed his notice of claim for a mechanic's lien on December 30, 1968. The foreclosure action which commenced on June 17, 1968, resulted in a judgment against Hough. The trial court entered the following judgment:

> "The Court having had this matter under advisement and being duly advised in the premises, now finds:

> "That the crushed stone delivered by plaintiff to premises of defendant, John Zehrner, a/k/a John Zehner, was used in the filling of holes on the land and in covering certain lands to make a parking and driving area for trucks. Said crushed stone was not used in the erection of any building or structure.

> "The Indiana Supreme Court has often said that the mechanic's lien statutes are in derogation of the common law and must be strictly construed. This Court can find no authority in statute giving rise to a mechanic's lien in this cause.

> It is THEREFORE, ORDERED, ADJUDGED, AND DECREED by the Court that the plaintiff take nothing by way of his complaint from the defendant, John Zehrner, a/k/a John Zehner, and that said named defendants recover their costs herein."

Hough timely filed his motion to correct errors which raises the question set forth below for our consideration on appeal.

III.
STATEMENT OF THE ISSUE

The issue is one of statutory construction. I.C. 1971, 32-8-3-1. . . . We will examine the statute to determine:

> Does the scope of the mechanic's lien statute encompass a materialman who delivers crushed stone for a driveway and parking area which is to be used in conjunction with a commercial garage being constructed?

We conclude in our "Statement on the Law" below that the scope of the statute does encompass such a materialman.

IV.
STATEMENT ON THE LAW

The statute here under consideration, contains the following language:

> "That contractors, subcontractors, mechanics, journeymen, laborers, and all persons performing labor or furnishing materials or machinery for the erection, altering, repairing, or removing any house, mill, manufactory, or other building, bridge, reservoir, systems of waterworks, or other structures, or for construction, altering, repairing, or removing any walk or sidewalk, whether such walk or sidewalk be on the land or bordering thereon, stile, well, drain, drainage ditch, sewer, or cistern may have a lien separately or jointly upon the house, mill, manufactory, or other building, bridge, reservoir, system of waterworks, or other structure, sidewalk, walk, stile, well, drain, drainage ditch, sewer, or cistern which they may have erected, altered, repaired, or removed or for which they may have furnished materials or machinery of any description, and, on the interest of the owner of the lot or parcel of land on which it stands or with which it is connected to extent of the value of any labor done, material furnished or either; . . ."

This statute is in derogation of the common law and should be strictly construed as to its scope. . . . Any lien claimant under this statute has the burden of proof to establish that his claim is within the scope of the statute. Once this has been successfully accomplished, a liberal construction will be given the statute so that its purpose can be accomplished. . . . The purpose of the statute was expressed by our Supreme Court in *Moore-Mansfield Construction Co.* v. *Indianapolis, New Castle, & Toledo Railway Co.* . . .

> "The mechanics' lien laws of America, in general, reveal the underlying motive of justice and equity in dedicating, primarily, buildings and the land on which they are erected to the payment of the labor and materials incorporated, and which have given to them an increased value. The purpose is to promote justice and honesty, and to prevent the inequity of an owner enjoying the fruits of the labor and materials furnished by others, without recompense." . . .

Looking to the language in the statute which would be indicative of its scope, we extract the following:

". . . persons . . . furnishing materials . . . for . . . other structures, or for construction (of) . . . any walk or sidewalk, whether such walk or sidewalk be on the land or bordering thereon, . . . or for which they may have furnished materials . . . of any description, and, on the interest of the owner of the lot or parcel of land on which it stands or with which it is connected to the extent of the value of any . . . material furnished. . . ."

It would be absurd to limit the scope of the statute to those items specifically and expressly mentioned. . . . Descriptive materials are blatantly absent; therefore, materials are inescapably bound with the nature of ". . . other structures." These words should be given their ordinary and literal significance first. . . .

Webster's Third New International Dictionary (1970) defines "other" as ". . . that which is remaining or additional; being the ones distinct from the one or those first mentioned or understood." "Structure" is defined as the ". . . action of building; construction," giving the following example from T. W. Arnold: "demolish any building, highway, road, railroad, excavation or other structure." The *Random House Dictionary of the English Language* (unabridged ed., 1969) defines "other" as ". . . additional or further; different or distinct from the one or ones mentioned or implied; . . ." The word "structure" is defined as ". . . mode of building, construction, or organization; arrangement of parts, elements, or constituents; a pyramidal structure. . . ." It further defines "structure" as ". . . anything composed of parts arranged together in some way; . . ." In *McCormack* v. *Bertschinger* . . . where it was contended ". . . that the labor and material which were furnished in the construction of the garage, driveway, walks, and retaining wall, and not in the construction of the house itself, were not lienable, . . ." since they were not structures, the Oregon Supreme Court held that a driveway was a structure even though it had not been specifically or expressly set forth in the statute. The Oregon Supreme Court applied the maxim of *noscitur a sociis*.

Zehrner urges that the doctrine of *ejusdem generis* would exclude the inclusion of a driveway as a structure under the statute. *Ejusdem generis* is only an illustration of the broader maxim of *noscitur a sociis* that general and specific words being associated together take color from each other.[1] But, when it is clear, as it is in the present case, that the less general words were inserted for a distinct object to carry out the purpose of the statute, then the general word ought to govern.

It would be a mistake to permit *ejusdem generis* to pervert the construction of the statute and defeat the intention of the legislature. . . . The cardinal rule of statutory construction mandates that this Court give effect to the intent of the legislature. . . .

The drilling of a water well was held to be a structure. . . . Architectural services are within the scope of a mechanic's lien statute. . . . In other jurisdictions where the statutory language is similar, grading was held to be reasonably necessary for the proper construction of a house and a part of its "erection." Even landscaping in Illinois has been included as part of the "erection" of a structure thereby bringing it within the lien statute. . . .

The rationale of our Supreme Court in *Wells* v. *Christian* . . . might well be applied to the present case. In *Wells* v. *Christian, supra,* our Supreme Court stated:

"The mains and pipes laid down . . . are clearly a part of the apparatus necessary to accomplish the objects for which such heat plant was erected. They constitute a part of the machinery by means of which the business of supplying heat to others must be carried on. The laying of these connecting pipes, essential to the exercise of the franchise held by the appellees, was a part of the erection of the manufacturing plant. . . . The hauling of materials to be used in the performance of the work, and hauling away the surplus earth excavated, were incidental matters inseparably connected with the principal undertaking, and constituted items of labor for which a lien may be acquired. . . .

"The work which appellant performed being directly and necessarily connected with the erection of the appellees' heating system. . . . The claim sued upon and found to be due and unpaid is within the protection of the statute, and appellant, having taken the steps necessary to perfect a lien upon the real estate described, was entitled to a decree of foreclosure."

Without the crushed stone, heavy trucks attempting to use the commercial garage would become mired down in the soft, moist earth. Moving heavy trucks about the parking area would be cumbersome and difficult. Crushed stone for the driveway and parking area was

---

1. The rule of statutory construction known as *noscitur a sociis,* which means that the meaning of a doubtful word may be ascertained by reference to the meaning of words associated with it, is the underlying authority for the application of the *ejusdem generis* rule. . . . The rule of *ejusdem generis* is that general words following an enumeration of particular cases apply only to cases of the same kind as expressly mentioned. . . .

a necessary and essential part of the commercial garage structure and its subsequent functional use. Hough's claim of lien is well within the scope of the statute. We do not deem it necessary to draw obvious analogies with walks or sidewalks or the obvious value imparted to Zehrner's commercial garage by having a usable driveway.

V.
DECISION OF THE COURT

Crushed stone delivered for a driveway and parking area to be used in conjunction with a commercial garage is a structure within the scope of the mechanic's lien statute. I.C. 1971, 32-8-3-1. . . . The judgment of the trial court should be and the same hereby is reversed.

YALE DEVELOPMENT CO. v. AURORA PIZZA HUT, Inc.
III. App., 420 N.E. 2d 823 (1981)

Reinhard, Justice:

This case involves an appeal and cross-appeal from a judgment against defendant, Aurora Pizza Hut, Inc., finding it breached a written contract but limiting plaintiff's recovery to $1,000 under the terms of a liquidated damages clause. The sole contention of plaintiff, Yale Development Co., on appeal is that the liquidated damages clause should not be enforced and that it should be able to recover compensatory damages in excess of the amount stipulated. Defendant, in its cross-appeal, argues that its termination of the contract did not constitute an anticipatory breach and, in the alternative, that if such action did amount to a breach, the plaintiff is not entitled to recover because of its subsequent inability to perform under the terms of the contract.

The parties executed a contract on September 19, 1975, in which defendant agreed to pay $90,000 in exchange for property located at Route 53 and Butterfield Road in unincorporated Du Page County. The sale was specifically made contingent upon plaintiff being able to obtain a zoning change and liquor license which would allow the construction and operation of a Pizza Hut restaurant. Although time was made of the essence, no specific time was mentioned in the contract.

Plaintiff filed an application for rezoning with the Du Page County Zoning Board of Appeals on December 14, 1975. After a public hearing, the Zoning Board of Appeals recommended denial of plaintiff's petition, and on February 23, 1976, the County Board of Du

Page County concurred in the denial. Plaintiff then filed a complaint in the circuit court seeking a declaratory judgment that the existing zoning was void and that the intended use of the premises be permitted. A bench trial was conducted on October 7, 1976, and the case was taken under advisement on January 5, 1977, after trial briefs were submitted. On February 24, 1977, before the court issued a decision, defendant sent plaintiff a letter purporting to terminate the contract "inasmuch as the city (sic) has denied our right to rezone the property." Subsequently, the court denied rezoning of the property of which the court below took judicial notice in its written reasons for decision. Plaintiff then filed the present action alleging that defendant was in breach for repudiating the contract prior to the time performance was due. The trial court held for the plaintiff but entered an order limiting plaintiff's recovery to $1,000 under the terms of the liquidated damages clause. This appeal and cross-appeal followed, and we reverse on the basis of the defendant's cross-appeal. We find the second issue raised by defendant's cross-appeal to be dispositive of the case at bar but turn first to the question of breach.

Defendant's first contention on cross-appeal is that its good faith termination of the contract did not constitute an anticipatory breach under these facts and circumstances since plaintiff was unable to obtain the rezoning of the subject property within a reasonable period of time. We disagree. Defendant's notice of termination came at a time when the plaintiff had an action for declaratory relief to rezone the property pending before the circuit court. Defendant reasons that the rezoning had not been accomplished in the 17-month period between the time of execution and the notice of termination and that there was no reason to believe the pending action would be successful when proceedings before the Zoning Board of Appeals and the County Board were not.

Although the contract did not specify the time for performance, the law will imply a reasonable time. . . . The intention of the parties controls what time is reasonable, and the court must look to the surrounding circumstances to discover the intention of the parties. . . . A reasonable time for performance is such time as is necessary to do conveniently what the contract requires. . . . Under the facts and circumstances of the present case we do not view a 17-month period as being unreasonable when the necessity of rezoning was contemplated by both parties. The record also indicates that the parties had had previous similar dealings which required rezoning actions and that two of such dealings required periods in excess of two years to be resolved. In light of these previous contracts and the period of time typically involved in obtaining a rezoning, we cannot say that a 17-month period was manifestly unreasonable and not within the intention of the parties. The trial court, therefore, correctly viewed the February 24 letter as an anticipatory breach.

Under the law of anticipatory repudiation, when one party to a contract repudiates his obligations before the time performance is due, the other party may elect to treat the repudiation as a breach and sue immediately for damages. . . . This leads us to defendant's second contention and the one we find dispositive of the case at bar. Defendant contends that, assuming the letter of February 24 is regarded as an anticipatory breach, the plaintiff cannot maintain an action on the contract due to his subsequent inability to fulfill the condition precedent of obtaining the rezoning. We agree. Although it was not necessary for plaintiff to actually tender performance since an anticipatory breach excuses the non-repudiating party from further performance, . . . we hold that a plaintiff suing on an anticipatory breach must still show a willingness and ability to perform had not the breach occurred. While it appears that no Illinois court has yet had the opportunity to consider this precise question, Illinois courts have consistently held that where both parties to a contract are in default, there can be no recovery by either against the other. . . . It has also been held that where one party has put it beyond his power to perform, although no demand or tender is necessary to allow the other to recover for breach, the plaintiff must show that he was ready and willing to perform the contract on his part. Similarly, in *Nation Oil Co.* v. *R.C. Davoust Co., Inc.,* . . . the court held that a party seeking to recover for breach of contract must show that he has performed or offered to perform his own obligation under the contract or that such performance was excused. Although none of these cases involve anticipatory breach, we consider their basic principles to be applicable to the case at bar.

As these cases demonstrate, if plaintiff had elected to wait until the time for defendant's performance to sue, instead of bringing suit immediately on the anticipatory breach, it would have been required to show a tender or offer of performance on its part, or that its performance was excused. Due to plaintiff's inability to procure a rezoning, it could not have tendered its performance and thus could not have maintained an action for breach at the time when defendant's performance was due. It would be anomalous to allow plaintiff to put itself in a better position by suing immediately on an anticipatory breach and thus avoid the necessity of proving its tender of performance. We therefore hold that where a plaintiff sues on an anticipatory breach prior to the time when defendant's performance is due,

he must show an ability and willingness to perform his part of the contract within the time specified in the contract.

Indeed, this seems to be the law in those jurisdictions which have considered the question. For example, in *Ufitec, S.A.* v. *Trade Bank and Trust Co.,* . . . the question before the court was whether a holder of a draft drawn against a letter of credit issued by the defendant bank could sue the bank for an anticipatory repudiation due to the bank's act of revoking the letter of credit before it had expired. The court concluded that since the holder never complied with the letter of credit, nor had it shown that it could ever comply during the term of the letter of credit, it could not maintain an action for anticipatory breach. The court stated, "(a)n anticipatory breach, in a proper case, may excuse one from performing a useless act, but it does not excuse one from the obligation of proving readiness, willingness, and the ability to have performed the conditions precedent."

The problem is also discussed in the third edition of *Williston's Treatise on Contracts:*

"The difficulty is not peculiar to cases of supervening illegality, but is involved in every other case where, after an anticipatory breach, supervening impossibility occurs which would in any event prevent and excuse performance of the contract.

The situation differs, also, in only a slight particular, hereafter referred to, from one where it appears after the anticipatory breach that, although there was no legal excuse, the return performance could not or would not have been rendered to the repudiator.

In each of these cases, if all the facts could have been known or foreseen at the time of the repudiation, no cause of action on the contract would have arisen.

It is a practical disadvantage of the doctrine of anticipatory breach that an action may be brought and perhaps judgment obtained before the facts occur which prove that there should have been no recovery. Fortunately, in most cases, this evidence, though not available at the time of the repudiation, becomes available before judgment can be obtained.

It seems clear that if the evidence thus becomes available the plaintiff can recover no substantial damages, and in the case of supervening illegality which is not due to the defendant's fault, there seems no reason to allow even nominal damages.

The loss should rest where chance has placed it; and the same should be true in case of any supervening excusable impossibility. Still more clearly, there should be this result if the facts show that the plaintiff could not or would not have performed for reasons which would not be a legal excuse.

The fact that a right of action has already arisen should not preclude the defense. Failure of consideration after a cause of action has arisen bars recovery. . . .

Similarly, *comment a* of section 277 of the *Restatement of Contracts* makes the following rule applicable to anticipatory breach:

"Where in promises for an agreed exchange a promisor commits a breach, and a right of action for the breach arises, the right of action is extinguished if it appears after the breach that there would have been a total failure to perform the return promise, even if the promisor had not justified the failure by his own breach or otherwise." . . .

Since the plaintiff has failed to obtain rezoning of the subject parcel it cannot demonstrate an ability to perform and, hence, is not entitled to recovery under the contract. The judgment of the trial court is accordingly reversed.

Reversed.

Seidenfeld, P. J., and Nash, J., concur.

REVIEW QUESTIONS

1. Describe the relationships between the parties to a construction contract.
2. How do public projects and private projects differ?
3. In what ways are contracting and manufacturing similar? How do they differ?
4. If you planned to build a two-car garage on your lot, what factors would you consider in deciding whether to attempt to build the garage yourself or hire a contractor to do it? How does this differ from an industrial situation in which a company is trying to decide whether to build a special machine or hire someone else to build it?
5. Summarize briefly the advantages and disadvantages of: (1) a lump-sum contract; (2) a cost-plus-percent-of-cost contract; (3) a cost-plus-fixed-fee contract; and (4) a combination unit-price–lump-sum contract.
6. In *Haynes* v. *Columbia Producers, Inc.,* what caused the court action? How could it have been prevented in the original arrangement?
7. What purposes are served by a feasibility study? When should it end?
8. Why do governments strictly regulate competitive bidding practices? What formal procedures are required in your state?
9. Locate in a local newspaper an "advertisement" or "call for bids" for a construction project. What details does the advertisement give its reader?
10. What are mechanic's lien laws? How do your state statutes call for such liens to be established and removed?
11. What are the purposes of each of the three types of bonds commonly required of contractors?
12. What nonmonetary factors determine the qualifications of a bidder?
13. Your employer is about to bid on the building and installation of a shuttle mechanism to automatically move 2" diameter hollow cylinders 1" high from a lathe to a punch press, to locate them in the press die and actuate the press to extrude the cylinders. What cost elements are likely to be encountered in the work and which, therefore, should be included in the price bid?
14. Review the statement of Indiana law in *Hough* v. *Zehrner.* What, if any, work or materials used on a piece of property would not be sufficient basis for a mechanic's lien?
15. In *Yale* v. *Pizza Hut* the defendant was held to have breached the contract. Why, then, did the court refuse damages to the plaintiff?

17

Specifications

As the term is used here, *specification* refers to the description of work to be done or things to be purchased. Specifications are most frequently heard of in building construction, but they exist in every area of engineering. The definition above is broad enough to include many things we encounter daily in our dealings with others. If you hire a painter to paint your house and tell him the house is to be white with gray trim, you have made a specification. If you take your car to an auto mechanic to be repaired, telling the mechanic to do whatever is necessary to remove the "grind" from the transmission, you have made a specification. A person ordering four 1/4-inch stove bolts, 3" long, from a hardware store clerk is using a specification. The specifications mentioned so far have been oral, but they are just as truly specifications as are the voluminous written ones for such a construction project as the Hoover Dam.

There are two main reasons for putting specifications into writing rather than giving them orally in certain situations:

1. To obtain a permanent record for resolving disputes.
2. To assure planning.

If the purchase involved is of sufficient monetary value so that a breach of the specified conditions could cause the purchaser substantial injury, the specifications should be written. The written record of what is specified defines the duties of the parties. The specification is part of the contract. It is likely to be interpreted in court or by an arbitration board if a dispute arises between the parties. Lawsuits on some construction projects have been undertaken years after completion of the projects. Without a permanent record of the rights and obligations of the parties, the result can be utter confusion. Written specifications frequently *prevent* costly lawsuits because they act as a ready reference in controversies between the parties. Building construction is seldom undertaken without specifications; and process engineers, project engineers, accountants, and purchasing agents toil over specifications for machinery and equipment. Very few government

purchases are made without reference to written specifications. In fact, the only occasions when the federal government makes purchases without such specifications are isolated instances of purchases of services.

The second reason for putting specifications into writing is that writing a specification almost necessarily requires planning. It is easy to specify something orally without giving it much thought. When it becomes necessary to reduce the specification to written form, however, the very knowledge that a permanent record is being made induces caution. When one writes, he tends to examine his reasons for whatever he puts on paper. The result, in specification writing, is usually a more efficient purchase. The likelihood that the thing specified will do the job required at a lower overall cost is improved greatly by the writing. In specifying 30 strokes per minute for a punch press he is about to purchase, a process engineer may well be led to question his decision as he writes the specification. Under certain conditions a variable-speed press (say 20 to 40 strokes per minute) might be more appropriate, and the writing of the specification calls his attention to the question again.

SPECIFICATION WRITING

The specification has a communications job to do. It must communicate to the reader what is required by the writer. It is essentially quite a simple job. As such, it can be done best by the use of simple language. Complex sentence structure and complicated wording may often be interpreted more than one way. With simple structure and simple wording this is much less likely to happen. It is best to avoid jargon, abbreviations, and symbols unless they are of a recognized standard, and fully understood in the trade.

Specifications, together with the drawings, show the contractor what is to be done. Each supplements the other. In addition, the specifications indicate the relation between the parties in greater detail than does the agreement. The working drawings show the work to be accomplished, but, frequently, not the quality standards required. The quality standards are usually more conveniently stated in the specifications.

Style

Specifications should be written with the greatest clarity of which the author is capable. The more clear and concise the writing, the better it will be comprehended. A specification is not the place for flowery language or complicated legal terms. Although it is difficult to overemphasize brevity and terse presentation in writing specifications, the specifications still must be complete. Completeness should be considered the limit to which brevity can be taken. In other words, the writer should strive to be brief up to the point where further brevity may be accomplished only by sacrificing some of the meaning in the specification.

Novels and other literature written to be read for entertainment frequently refer to the subject in terms of "he," "his," and other such pronouns. The use of such words adds considerably to the ease and enjoyment of reading such material. The vast majority of the readers will understand the meaning intended by the author. Those who do not will usually pass over the sentence without hesitation to maintain interest in the story. The writer of anything that is likely to be interpreted in a court of law cannot afford to be so entertaining. Where it is at all likely that there may be a misinterpretation, the subject should be repeated. Consider the sentence: "In case of controversy between the contractor and the inspector, he shall immediately refer the question to the engineer." Who is to refer the question? The contractor could say, "I thought the inspector was to contact the engineer," and vice versa. Replacement of the word "he" with "the contractor" or "the inspector" clears up any doubt.

Precise Wording

Our language consists of many words with similar meanings. There are general words and specific words. The word *property,* for instance, has a very broad meaning, including all items of personal possessions as well as real estate. Many other terms have broad meanings and should be used very carefully in the wording of specifications. The words used should indicate what is to be accomplished so precisely that no doubt can exist. Commonly used words frequently are not exact enough in meaning. For instance, it is quite common to hear someone say that something should have an addition on *either* side of it, as "light on either side of the gateway," when what is intended is that the addition must be present on *each* side, as "a light on each side of the gateway." Many other words are commonly used interchangeably, such as *any* and *all, amount* and *quantity, malleable* and *ductile,* and *hardness* and *rigidity,* for example. The inexactness of meaning in oral conversation usually causes no problems; but in specification writing the result can be trouble, measured in dollars. There are few instances in the English language where one word means exactly the same thing as another. Care in wording is definitely called for where the writing may have to be reviewed in court.

Reference Specifications

With the wealth of old specifications, texts on specification writing, and standards published by various organizations, it is a rare specification today that is entirely original. As a practical matter this is desirable. Previous specifications have been tested, errors removed, and the language improved. If the rewriting for the new specification is carefully done, other potential problems may be discovered and eliminated. In addition, there is less likelihood of overlooking something in the present specifications if a pattern can be followed. However, a word of caution is necessary. Wholesale clipping of paragraphs and requirements from previous specifications can result in problems. While frequently there is considerable similarity between specifications, it is unlikely that any two will be exactly alike. If caution is not exercised in adapting paragraphs and clauses from old to new, the requirements for certain features of the new job are likely to be different from what was intended. There may be features of the new job which are found to be completely omitted from the new specification.

Many organizations have written standards for various items of equipment or elemental components, making it unnecessary for the specification writer to do more than incorporate these standards by reference. The United States government has published a vast array of standard specifications. For instance, when the government buys women's slacks for use in the armed forces, the specifications consist mainly of references to military standards and other standardized specifications. The buttons are specified by Federal specification number V-B-781, the fasteners by V-F-106, the shipping boxes by NN-B-631, and so on for the cloth, the stitches, the labels, and all other elements of the purchase. The writing of a specification where such standards exist consists largely of determining the appropriate elements and listing the standards in logical order. The advantage of such standardization is quite obvious. A specialist in one element of the entire assembly has specified the appropriate quality to be used. It is impossible for one person to be a specialist in everything. The specification resulting from the combined efforts of several specialists is quite likely to be better than it would be if the total specification were to be written by any one of them.

ARRANGEMENT

The specification usually consists of at least two parts, one general and the other specific and detailed. The first part is known by different names (such as general conditions, general provisions, or special conditions) in various specifications, and the information included is not well standardized. In most contracts there is a separate document, previously discussed, known as the "General Conditions," that deals with the basic rights and responsibilities of the parties. To avoid conflict with the more basic document, we will use *general provisions* as the name for the general portion of the specifications.

General Provisions

In the relationships between the parties to a construction contract there is a vast middle ground between the provisions in the agreement and general conditions and the detailed specifications. The general conditions are sufficiently general to apply to any contract work the owner may want and to any contractor he may hire. The general provisions part of the specification pertains to a particular contract or type of contract. It sets the owner's policy as to control of the work, the scope and quality of the work, and any special requirements or precautions. It is here that answers are found to many of the day-to-day questions that arise between the parties. To cover these questions the general provisions must consider many topics. A few of the topics appear frequently enough to justify consideration here, these being representative of the contents of a general provisions section.

Sequence of Work. A topic that is almost certain to be covered (usually by a requirement for consultation) is the sequence of work. It is poor policy, from a legal and from a cost standpoint, to rigidly control the details of the work to be accomplished. However, there are occasions when some control must be exercised by the owner in the public interest (as in highway construction) or to dovetail the project with the work undertaken by other contractors. Usually a work schedule is called for in the specifications to help the engineer and contractor plan the work to the best advantage of the owner. Such a work schedule is made by showing graphically the starting and completion dates for the component parts of the project. The work schedule resembles the Gantt Charts so commonly used in production scheduling in industry. The figure that follows shows a simple work schedule chart for multi-station, strip-feed punch-press installation. A schedule such as this provides the engineer with the means of obtaining a weekly (or daily or monthly) check against actual

performance. It may be noted that the schedule also contains percentages assigned to each component of the job. These percentages represent estimated portions of the total job for each component and are usually agreed upon by the engineer and the contractor prior to starting work.

Such schedules are frequently used in a progressive payment scheme (so much per week or month according to accomplishments during the period). The schedule allows a realistic estimate of progress to be made. For instance, assume that the contractor installing the presses shown in the figure is on schedule on February 4 (the end of the week beginning January 30). At this point he would be entitled to payments totaling 50 percent of the total contract price less whatever amount may be withheld until final completion and acceptance. The amount to be so held back is another thing occasionally specified in the general provisions. Frequently this is set at 10 percent. In the foregoing case, assuming a 10 percent hold-back, the contractor should receive 45 percent of the total contract price.

Changes and Extra Work. Very few large contracts are completed without changes being made during the course of the work. Questions of payment for such changes can cause severe disagreement if nothing is provided in anticipation of them. A provision for changes and extra work is usually made in either the general conditions or the general provisions portion of the specification. Just as there are four basic means of paying for a contract, there are also four means of paying for extra work:

1. Lump sum
2. Cost plus percentage
3. Cost plus fixed fee
4. Unit price

The cost-plus-percentage and unit-price types of contract present little or no problem as to compensation for changes or added work. The extra work is compensated at the fixed rate in the unit-price contract; in the cost-plus-percent contract changes are easily made. In the lump-sum and cost-plus-fixed-fee contracts, though, the need to prearrange a way to compensate for extra work is apparent. The contractor is already on the job; it is usually inconvenient and costly to get someone else to replace him for the added work. If the contractor is unscrupulous and the engineer has not provided adequately for changes, the contractor can make these changes costly.

To illustrate this point there is a tale (of rather doubtful veracity). It seems that a rather prominent builder of homes made his living a few years ago by capitalizing on the very human desire to change the

Work Schedule for Press Installation

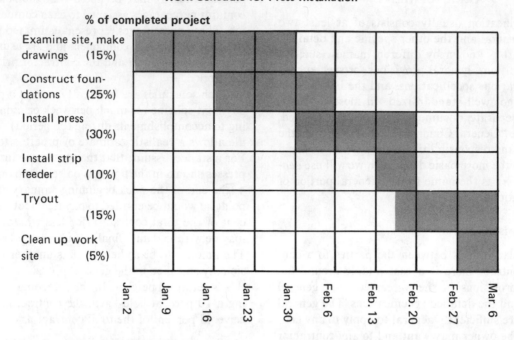

structure while it is being constructed. He had a large selection of standard homes which he offered to build for any married person at cost. The customer would agree to a structure, and work would progress to the point where the rooms were laid out and partitioning begun. At this point almost invariably the customer or the spouse would require one or a series of changes to be made. The cost for the changes was, of course, quite high, for this was where the contractor made his profit. A few of the more cost-conscious customers managed to resist the temptation to change and were rewarded by getting an adequate house at a very low cost, but these were the exception. The engineer's attention to the provision for payment for changes and extra work in the contract documents may well be worth his time.

Other Suppliers. Work or materials to be supplied by others (either by the owner or other contractors) should be shown in the specification. Frequently this takes the form of one or more "right of supply" clauses in which the owner reserves the right to supply motors or other components (often salvaged from worn-out machines). When more than one contractor is to work on a project, the dividing lines must be drawn clearly in the specification. This is necessary for avoiding conflict and assuring that someone will be responsible for the details of each item; in other words, it will avoid overlap or gaps in the contracted work.

Drawings. The drawings are an integral part of a construction contract. The following statement is commonly included in the general provisions of the specification: "The Contract Documents are complementary,

and what is called for by any one shall be binding as if called for by all." The drawings and specifications, particularly, supplement each other as everyday working documents. Occasionally a conflict between a drawing and the specifications becomes apparent. To resolve such conflicts, the general provisions frequently state that "in case of difference between drawings and specifications, the specifications shall govern." Some provision is usually made for submission of working drawings and sketches for the engineer's approval during the course of the construction. Such details as the number of copies of drawings, even size and type of paper to be used, are sometimes specified.

Information Given. Usually, considerable information pertinent to the proposed project is passed along to the bidders and thus, eventually, to the contractor. Some of the information may be of such a nature that the owner and the engineer will not want to warrant its completeness or the indications given by it. This is commonly true of test borings, for instance, where a defect in the subsoil might not show up in the samples that are taken. To protect the owner in such circumstances, the general provisions usually state that neither the owner nor the engineer will warrant that the information given shows the entire true picture. Generally, the contractor is held responsible for having made his own examination of the site.

Services Furnished. When an addition to an existing structure is made, or when machinery or equipment is installed, certain of the services necessary are commonly supplied by the owner. Such services as water, compressed air, electricity, and crane service to unload equipment are frequently furnished by him. It is in the owner's interest to mention the availability of such services in the specification to give the contractor a truer picture of the costs he will not have to bear.

Receipt and Storage of Materials. By similar reasoning, if the contractor is to be allowed to use the owner's receiving and storage facilities, this should be made clear to him in the specification. Such facilities constitute a considerable addition to the cost if the contractor is to supply them himself. The cost will be passed along to the owner if he does not supply such facilities.

Wage Rates. Particularly in government contracts, the wages paid by the contractor are important. There are several federal statutes (and usually similar state statutes) that regulate wages, hours, and even sources of materials on public contracts. By way of example, many federal contracts cite the Davis-Bacon Act (wages), the Buy American Act (purchases of materials), and the Eight-Hour Laws (wages and hours) in their specifications.

The wages paid to workmen are of importance, even when the owner is a private party. Wages and working conditions poorer than those to which the area is accustomed can cause strikes and other labor problems. Projects are sometimes delayed and even partly destroyed as a result of labor strife. It is unpleasant to find oneself an innocent victim in such circumstances. To avoid trouble of this nature, many specifications for private contracts provide that wage rates and working conditions must be equal to or better than those prevailing in the trade or locality.

Safety. A requirement such as the following, as to safety and accident prevention is also a usual inclusion in the specifications. "The contractor shall, at all times, exercise reasonable precautions for the safety of employees in the performance of this contract, and shall comply with all applicable provisions of federal, state, and municipal safety laws and building construction codes."

Detail Specifications

The second major division of the specifications gives the details of the work to be undertaken. These detail specifications, together with the engineer's drawings, state how the job is to be done and what is to be accomplished. In writing the general provisions portion the engineer has access to guideposts and instructions. When he writes the detail specifications, though, he has fewer guideposts and must rely on his knowledge of what is to be accomplished and his ability to express himself.

Detail specifications are concerned with the materials and workmanship in the finished project.

Materials. When something is purchased, it is with the intention of obtaining some *service* that the thing purchased is capable of rendering. All a possession can do for one is give him service of some kind. When he buys a lathe or a punch press, the purchaser is really purchasing the ability to turn, bend, blank, or perform some other operation on materials. Much the same is true in the purchase of materials for a construction project. The materials purchased must render a service. It is up to the engineer to obtain the best service available for the owner at the most favorable cost. There are, then, two factors that normally oppose each other in the selection of material: cost and service. There are many instances in which the same or similar service can be rendered by two quite different materials (or pieces of equipment or machines). Part of an engineer's "stock in trade" is his knowledge of various means of obtaining services for his employer.

Materials are commonly called for in specifications according to established standards. SAE 1090 steel, for instance, indicates a steel with 90 points of carbon, that hardens with proper heat treatment and has some unique physical properties. The various physical properties of materials, such as strength, elasticity, conductivity, and appearance, are important in determining the service they will render in a specific application. Transportation, storage, and inspection costs join other costs to be weighed against the service offered by a particular material.

Very often, specifications are written with "or equal" clauses; for example, "Electrical controls to be XYZ or equal." The *or equal* means "not literally exact equality." Probably a more proper way of stating the meaning would be *or equivalent*. With this, as with other contract language, the courts interpret wording according to trade usage.

Workmanship. When one takes an automobile to a mechanic for a valve job, he usually isn't interested in the order of removal and replacement of the screws, nuts, and bolts. Similarly, it is rare for the owner to be greatly interested in how a particular result is accomplished, providing the result is satisfactory. It is usually far better to specify results to be accomplished rather than the process by which the results are to be accomplished. For instance, it is much better to specify the compressive strength of concrete a week after pouring than to specify the quantities of cement, sand, and broken stone or gravel and the method of mixing.

There are exceptions, of course, to the principle of specifying only results. A particular method may interfere with the rights of others (e.g., blasting, in place of air hammers). It may also be necessary to specify a method or process if interference with other contractors is likely to occur.

Usually it is sufficient in specifications to require that the workmanship be equal to the best available without going into the details of the method. For example, "All sheet-metal work shall be performed and completed in accordance with the best modern sheet-metal practice, and no detail necessary therefore shall be omitted, although specific mention thereof may not be made either in these specifications or on the drawings."

Arbitrary Specifications

Generally, there are two possible relationships between the owner and the contractor. The relationship of owner–independent contractor indicates that the contractor has been hired to produce a particular result. The employer–employee, or master–servant, relationship prevails where the owner (employer) or his agent, the engineer, supervises too closely the work of the contractor. There are two main advantages to the owner in retaining the owner–independent contractor relationship. Probably the primary one is that the contractor retains liability for his acts. There are many cases on record where, because the supervision was too close or the specifications made the contractor a mere employee of the owner, the owner was held directly liable for the acts of the contractor. Statements such as "The contractor shall begin and continue work on whatever parts of the project the engineer shall direct, at whatever time the engineer shall direct," sound like the contractor is to be an employee of the engineer (and, hence, an employee of the owner). Such statements leave the door wide open for a court finding against the owner in a case of public liability.

There is another advantage in specifying the results to be obtained rather than the means of attaining them. If a contractor follows a particular specified procedure, he cannot be held responsible if the result proves faulty. On the other hand, if he agrees to produce a specified result, with the means of accomplishment left up to him, he must produce the result. Failure by the contractor to produce the result according to the specifications may give rise to a damage action against him or assure repair by him.

The following specification was written and used in the purchase of the described automation. The process engineer who wrote these specifications had helped to plan the impact bar manufacturing process. Later he supervised the installation of the automation and worked out production problems concerned with it.

X COMPANY SPECIFICATIONS INSTRUCTIONS

Information

Contractor shall consult the Manufacturing Engineering Department of the X Company, Y Plant in regards to working procedure, production line operations, reference drawings, plant layout drawings, and these specifications.

Responsibility

Contractor shall be responsible for all field dimensions including interference with adjoining machines, building structure clearances, and installation location. Dimensions, speeds, machine sizes, and locations described in these specifications are only approximate. Reliable data must be ascertained by contractors and be verified by the person or persons concerned before proceeding with questioned phase of automation and machine construction.

Testing

Contractors shall completely design, fabricate, machine, deliver, and install special machines and automation described in these specifications. This equipment shall be tested for performance after installation and shall simulate actual production rates, as set forth in these specifications. The contractor shall be responsible for the proper functioning of all contracted equipment. The validity of such functioning shall be borne out in the prescribed test phases herein explained. Test phases shall be conducted under the supervision of suitable representatives of the X Company, and the approval of all equipment will be forthcoming from these representatives.

Drawings

After contract is awarded, five (5) sets of preliminary prints representing proposal drawings of the equipment contracted shall be submitted to the Manufacturing Engineering Department for consideration, subject to approval. One set of submitted proposals will be approved by the X Company and returned to the contractor together with proper contract authorization. The remaining prints shall become the property of the X Company. Errors, omissions, and/or changes affecting these drawings that are discoverd or made as the equipment is manufactured shall be corrected by the contractor and submitted to the Manufacturing Engineering Department for approval before altering contracted construction.

X COMPANY

MANUFACTURING ENGINEERING

DEPARTMENT SPECIFICATION NO. _____

P. N. NO. _____

Subject _____ AUTOMATIC SHEET LOADER FOR IMPACT BARS. _____

PLANT ___ Y PLANT ___ PROJECT _____ ITEM NO. _____

INCLUDED DRAWINGS _____

APPROVALS _____ /s/ _____ /s/ _____

_____ /s/ _____ /s/ _____

_____ /s/ _____

_____ /s/ _____

_____ /s/ _____

_____ /s/ _____

_____ /s/ _____

—— REVISIONS ——

DWG. NO.	SHT. NO.	LOCATION	DATE	REMARKS

ISSUED BY _____ /s/ _____

Y PLANT

SHEET NO. _____ OF ____ 7 ____ SHEETS

The Manufacturing Engineering Department will issue the necessary drawing numbers and titles as required for the various components making up the complete unit. All working drawings shall be supplied by the contractor and shall be made on tracing cloth. Such drawings shall be made on sheets conforming to X Company Standard sizes. They shall be intelligibly drawn and cross-indexed for reference purposes.

Tracings, or tracing reproductions, comprising all drawings of the complete project shall be delivered to and become the property of the X Company on or before filing completion notice. These shall include piping diagrams, electrical diagrams, and detail and assembly drawings of all mechanical and structural components of the contracted equipment.

All drawings must conform to the X Company Standards and to A.I.S.C. and J.I.C. Electrical, Pneumatic, and Hydraulic Standards.

Rights of Supply

X Company reserves the right to supply any items on the proposed automation and equipment or motors which may be available from their source. Therefore, an itemized list of all standard commercially manufactured equipment shall be submitted to the X Company for approval before purchases are made by contractor.

Consultation

Immediately after the contract is awarded, the successful bidder shall confer with the Manufacturing Engineering Department, X Company, Y Plant, and discuss details of time scheduling and working procedure.

Contractor shall then prepare a progress schedule of his work, complete with starting and completion dates for each phase of the machine set-up and equipment he expects to manufacture, and submit it to the Manufacturing Engineering Department, Y Plant, for approval.

Procedure for Delivery

All equipment and machines, either assembled or knocked down, shall be plainly marked with the vendor's name, a description of the article, and X Company Purchase and Item Number. Miscellaneous or loose items shall be crated and marked in a similar manner with a list of contents enclosed in each package. All items or packages shall be listed on the Bill of Lading.

The X Company will receive items and furnish crane service, if available, to unload. Contractor shall move equipment to job site. X Company assumes no responsibility for any loss or damage in transit.

X Company "general conditions" shall become part of the contract.

GENERAL

Purpose

The purpose of these two (2) sheet loaders is to load sheets singly onto a press feed shuttle from a conveyor on which 14" high stacks of 125 sheets each are placed.

Work

All work shall be performed in accordance with X Company Standards and all workmanship shall be equal to or better than the best modern practices. Job site must be completely cleared of all debris caused by the contractor before completion notice can be accepted. Installation and field work shall be done under the direction of the Y Plant Engineering Department.

Power

Contractor shall furnish all wiring from the X Company Distribution panel to the machine control panels. Contractor shall be responsible for all wiring and control devices within his contracted equipment, including mounting, labeling, and operation of all switches, relays, and solenoids. All electrical, pneumatic, and hydraulic installation shall conform to X-J.I.C. Standards. A minimum number of air and water supply lines to any and all equipment shall be furnished by X Company when necessary. 440/220 V., 3 Ph., 60 Cy., A.C. power.

Materials

Machines and allied equipment shall be constructed mainly of casting, rolled structural shapes, gears, chain, and fixtures of good quality, free of rust.

Fabrication shall be accomplished by bolting or welding. All holes must be drilled or punched. Burning of holes will not be permitted. All supports shall be properly spaced for uniform transfer of load to floor. Means of securement shall be fixed anchor bolts set in lead or sulphur. All parts shall be designed and detailed with due regard to allowable stresses in materials used.

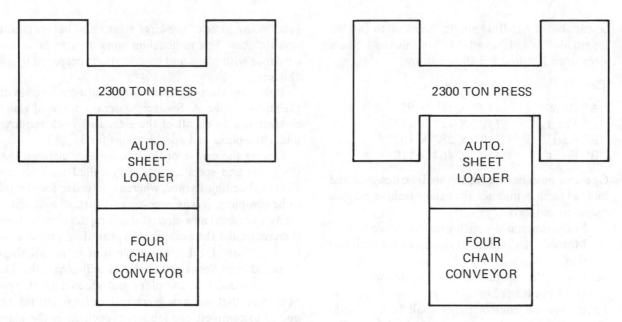

Sketch showing relative location of Automatic Sheet loaders

Contractor shall shop paint all materials with one (1) coat of M-426 Red Lead and field paint with one (1) coat of M-340 Grey. Inside of all removable drive guards shall be painted with one (1) coat of M-314 Alert Orange.

Machines and automatic equipment shall be suitably equipped with alemite or equal hydraulic lubrication fittings wherever necessary. Manifold lubrication lines shall be provided on all equipment wherever feasible, employing alemite or equal lubrication manifolds.

All air or hydraulic cylinders, valves, motors, speed reducers, relays, starters, and other commercial items shall be of approved X Company selection.

All exposed drives, couplings, belts, sprockets, chains, and/or other moving parts shall be completely guarded with enclosed type easily removable metal guards. All guards to be designed and fabricated in accordance with X Company Sheet Metal Standards. All guards to have the approval of the X Company Local Safety Engineer.

AUTOMATION DESCRIPTION

A. Machines and automation equipment shall be fully automatic wherever possible and interlocked electrically or mechanically.

B. Automation equipment shall be designed in such a manner that conveyed parts can be removed from it at any phase of its operation without difficulty. Exception to this rule must have individual approval.

C. Machines and automation equipment shall be provided with guards wherever necessary to prevent loose parts from falling or bouncing from proper locations.

D. All wipers, diverters, and other moving equipment shall be designed and built in a manner which will prevent jamming or damaging of machine parts.

E. All metering devices and automatic equipment must be designed and constructed in a manner which will cause an even and regular distribution and flow of parts.

F. All air cylinders supplied by contractor shall be cushioned at both ends and be provided with suitable speed valves wherever necessary.

DETAILED DESCRIPTION

1. Two (2) magnetic (pneumatic) sheet loaders will be required. They shall be located relative to the 2,300-ton presses and four-chain stack conveyors as shown in the attached sketch. Contractor shall furnish department 240, Manufacturing Engineering, with the approximate overall dimensions of these machines and their allied equipment as soon as possible for Plant Layout purposes.

2. The machines shall be designed to load the 2,300-ton press dies with single sheets removed from stacks of 125 sheets previously placed on a four-chain conveyor. The machines shall be interlocked mechanically or electrically with the 2,300-ton presses and the four-chain conveyors to provide a continuous flow of production. The machines shall

be capable of handling single sheets up to 144" in length, 48" in width, and .125" in thickness. Sheet sizes to be handled are shown below:

Part	Sheet Size
"A" Rear	.110" X 36" X 95"
"A" Front	.110" X 42" X 118"
"B" Rear	.110" X 28" X 103"
"B" Front	.110" X 46" X 110"

3. Operator push button station shall be designed and built in such a manner that the machine may be operated as follows:
   a. Fully automatic—with machine loaded.
   b. Manual—individual push button for each station.
   c. One-cycle operation—automatic with machine not loaded.
4. Each machine control panel shall contain sufficient excess room to accommodate the installations of six (6) additional relays.
5. Outside contractor to furnish:
   a. Necessary labor and materials to design, fabricate, and install two (2) complete sheet loading mechanisms with control panels and operator control stations as described above.
   b. All necessary safety equipment.
   c. All starters, Square "D" type or equal.
   d. Do all field painting.
6. X Company to furnish:
   a. Crane service, if available, to unload.
   b. Plant layout location of all items.
   c. Electric, air, and other plant services to within 40' of contracted equipment.
7. Assigned "Z" number is 121-ZP-124. Drawing title is "Automatic Sheet Loader for Impact Bars."

SWITZER v. BOZEMAN
106 So. 2d 762 (1958)

Fruge, Judge ad hoc.

Defendant-appellant appeals from a judgment costing him in the sum of $269.22 in connection with his contract with subcontractor A. Switzer, plaintiff-appellee, herein.

This is a suit in which the only issue is the interpretation of the provision of the plans and specifications. And that is whether certain electrical work was called for in the plans and specifications.

Louisiana State University, as owner, entered into a contract with defendant-appellant, Robert L. Bozeman, a contractor, to remodel the third floor of Nicholson Hall, which remodeling work consisted only in subdividing some of the large rooms and hallways into small offices. The remodeling work was to be in accordance with plans and specifications prepared by architects.

Bozeman then entered into a sub-contract with plaintiff-appellee, A. Switzer, under the terms of which Switzer was to do all of the electrical work required under the plans and specifications for $1,183.

During the course of the job, Switzer claimed that the plans and specifications only called for one new electrical ceiling fixture, whereas, in order for the job to be complete, it was necessary to furnish and install many additional new electrical ceiling fixtures. Switzer then requested the architects to grant him an extra allowance from L.S.U., to enable him to install these "claimed" additional new electrical ceiling fixtures. The architect ruled that the plans and specifications were clear and that all new electrical ceiling fixtures required to complete the job were specified in the plans and specifications.

Switzer, despite repeated demands from Bozeman, refused to complete the job, so Bozeman hired another electrical company to finish Switzer's contract. This latter company completed the job at a cost to Bozeman of $687.59. Bozeman then deducted this amount from the electrical subcontract price and paid the difference to Switzer. This suit followed, in which Switzer claimed this $687.59, which was the amount deducted from his contract price.

The district court held that Switzer was wrong and that the new electrical ceiling fixtures required to complete the job were all specified in the plans and specifications, and therefore, covered by Switzer's sub-contract; this item included $102.16 paid the new electrical contractor to install the fixtures, and $238.87 paid for the fixtures themselves. The district court also found that Switzer had not "grounded" the outlets to which the fixtures were attached, and recognized the amount paid by Bozeman to this new electrical contractor of $80.32 to have such work done.

However, the district court held that the $269.22 which Bozeman paid this new electrical contractor to install the electrical work for the telephones were not specified in the plans and specifications, and, therefore, not included in the electrical sub-contract that Switzer had with Bozeman. Accordingly, the lower court granted judgement to Switzer against Bozeman for $269.22.

We are not favored with written reasons by the trial court.

The only issue involves the interpretation of a contract. Since the plans and specifications by the architects are made part of the contract, we must determine whether they require that the telephone outlets be connected by conduit with the existing telephone panel in the building.

The plans have a legend thereon where various symbols are listed, with the meaning of each symbol shown opposite thereto. For example, there was a small circle with radiating lines, spoken of during the trial as "rising sun," and opposite which were the words "Elect. Clng. Fixture," meaning electrical ceiling fixture. And there were symbols for bookcase, new partition, electrical base outlet, etc. Additionally, there was a symbol of an inverted triangle, opposite which was the word "Telephone." This inverted triangle, meaning telephone, was shown in six places on the plans, indicating that there were to be six telephone outlets installed.

The question involved is whether, by showing such symbol of an inverted triangle that only the outlet itself was called for, or whether that outlet was also to be connected with the telephone panel already in use in the building. Now, if only the outlets were called for and it was not required to connect such outlets up with the panel so that service could be had, it is obvious that another contract would have to be let to connect the outlets up with the panel in order to use the telephones. It would appear to be an absurd consequence to say that the contract called for the outlets, but did not require that they be connected with the panel, in view of the specifications.

The specifications made it clear that this was to be a completed job "including tying utilities all into existing service," and was to be "ready for immediate use." The plans and specifications called for "work evidently necessary within the general intent (thereof) . . . for the . . . thorough completion of the work." We quote these provisions of the specifications, viz.:

Scope of work and general items: "Extent of work: It is the intent of these specifications to cover all required labor and materials for the remodeling interior of Nicholson Hall, Third Floor, LSU, Baton Rouge, La.; The contractor shall perform all work required for the completion of this work in accordance with these specifications and accompanying drawings ready for occupancy; including tying utilities all into existing services.

Scope: These specifications, together with the drawings, are intended to cover all labor, materials, and appliances of every kind required to provide all necessary electrical work and electrical fixtures for the remodeling job. All the work shall be ready for immediate use before the same will be accepted.

Extra work: No additional compensation will be allowed for work evidently necessary within the general intent of these specifications and accompanying plans

for the proper construction and thorough completion of the work.

Arthur G. McLavy, the electrical contractor who completed the electrical work for Bozeman, testified about this conduit to connect the telephone outlets with the existing telephone panel in the building, viz.:

Q. Now what is your other item?

A. That was to furnish the necessary labor and materials to put in a conduit telephone system as required by the telephone company.

Q. To put in what?

A. A telephone system for existing telephone panels to outlets as shown on the plans according to directions by the telephone company and the University.

Q. Was that work the type of work customarily the telephone company did?

A. No, sir.

Q. Was that work called for in these plans and specifications?

A. You are asking for an opinion now.

Q. Well, you read the plans and specifications, didn't you?

A. Yes, sir.

Q. Was that work called for? Can you point out on the plans and specifications where it is called for?

A. It is not called for on the plans and specifications in so many words, but it's the general practice in any commercial building or any building used as an office building to have a continuous conduit system for the telephone company to install their wires.

Q. What requirement is shown on the plans with reference to telephones?

A. Just the outlets are indicated.

Q. Just the outlets are indicated?

A. Yes.

Q. And from that you draw the conclusion that you are supposed to connect those up with the telephone wires from outside of the building?

A. No.

Q. What is that?

A. You would draw the conclusion from that that you would have to extend from the nearest, I would say, panel or junction box in the building in each and every outlet, a continuous run of conduit.

Q. Is that customary and standard practice in the electrical business in this section in a building such as this?

A. Yes.

Q. Any question about this, any room for debate on that?

A. Of course, there would be room for debate on it.

Q. Well, what is the room for debate?

A. Well, I mean in my mind there is.

Q. Say what is in your mind, Mr. McLavy.

A. Nothing.

Q. The plans indicate here on page A-1 the three-cornered white symbol and marked opposite it is shown telephone, and how many of those do they have on this plan? Will you count them?

A. Six.

Q. When you went on the job what work on the telephone installation had been performed before you got there?

A. The outlet box had been installed. The outlet box had been installed in the partition and the conduit run out at ceiling level.

Q. Then what did you do?

A. I requested a meeting with representatives from Louisiana State University and the telephone company to meet out there and we laid out how they wanted it done.

Q. What was it that you did?

A. There is an existing panel,—I forget which end of the hall it is on, east end, yes. We ran a one-inch conduit from there out into the corridor and down. We could describe it and down close to the west end and from there branched out to the smaller conduits of the existing outlets or close to them as directed by the telephone company.

Q. I ask you again, in a building such as this, is that work customarily done by the electrical contractor and not by the telephone people?

A. The telephone company does not run any conduit themselves.

The electrical work in connecting the telephone outlets to the telephone panel by conduit was obviously necessary in accordance with the plans and specifications.

It is our opinion that this work was clearly called for in the plans and specifications. It necessarily follows that it was included in Switzer's bid which is as follows:

Confirming phoned price this date . . . Nicholson Hall Elec. per plans and specs., $1183.00.

It is significant that the record reveals no effort by Switzer with respect to any claim with Bozeman or anyone else that the electrical work necessary to connect the telephone outlets to the existing telephone panels in the building was called for in the plans and specifications. Switzer testified that he ran a ½-inch conduit from the telephone boxes as shown on the plans by the symbols to points at, in most cases, ceiling height where he could be instructed to bring them to other places. He further testified that he had met Mr. Wilson on the job once or twice to discuss fixtures and other arrangements. He stated that he had written a letter,

but upon a close perusal of the record no letter in evidence disclosed any reference to telephone connections; we therefore conclude that there was no controversy whatsoever with respect to the telephone connections prior to the date of trial. The record disclosed that Mr. Switzer took the position all along by the letters he wrote and by his testimony in the record that he should have been permitted to charge extra for new light fixtures to be installed on the job which request was denied by the architect. To clarify this point, we take the liberty of quoting from the correspondence in the record.

Bozeman's letter of August 29, 1956, to Switzer, in part reads:

". . . we take the position however, that the job must be complete in accordance with the plans, specifications, and job requirements as interpreted by the architect.

We will complete our portion of this job by August 31st, 1956, and unless notified to the contrary, in writing, we shall expect the electrical work to be complete also."

Switzer's answer to Bozeman, dated August 30, 1956, in part says:

"Your letter of the 29th received this date. We appreciate your position in this matter . . . but feel also that the fixtures in question . . . are not specified . . . as part of our work.

It is not possible for us to complete this work . . . other than the installation per plans and specifications . . . which is installed as of this date."

Bozeman's letter to Switzer dated September 4, 1956, by registered mail, in part, reads:

"In your letter of August 30, 1956, you have refused to complete the above mentioned job unless you receive from the architect a change order covering five different items. Since the University officials and the Architects have advised us that this building must be ready for occupancy by Monday, September 10, 1956, and in view of the position that you have taken in this matter, it appears to us that we are forced to act as follows:

We hereby notify you that all of your work must be completed by Saturday, September 8, 1956. Further, if you have not shown sufficient effort by 8 AM Thursday, September 6, 1956, to complete this job within the time set forth, we will take over and complete that portion of the electrical work as is now incomplete, and deduct from your contract the cost to us. . . ."

It is in evidence that Switzer did not examine the site so that he could be in a position to say where the telephone panel was to which the telephone outlets were to be connected. Nor could he know the conditions that were present so that the type and size of conduit could be determined. It is important to quote from the specifications at this point:

> "Examination of Site: . . . each bidder will be held to have examined the site and satisfied himself as to the existing conditions . . . that will in any manner affect the work under this contract."

The specifications did include tying utilities all into existing services and require the remodeled part to be ready for immediate use after acceptance by L.S.U. and called for all work evidently necessary to complete the job. Thus, it appears to us that if Switzer had looked he would have seen the telephone panel on the third floor, and it is obvious that the outlets were to be connected with this panel, and by so doing he would have known the type and size of the panel. Aside from that, he could have called in the architect, the telephone company, and the electrical representative of the University to assist him.

Accordingly, for these reasons, the trial court judgment in favor of plaintiff-appellee is hereby reversed and his suit dismissed at his cost.

Reversed.

REVIEW QUESTIONS

1. Why should specifications be written rather than oral?
2. Distinguish between:
   a. malleable and ductile.
   b. strength and rigidity.
   c. force and pressure.
   d. structure and building.
   e. project and operation.
   f. tool and die.
   g. machine and automation.
   h. precise and accurate.
3. What are the inherent advantages of standardized specifications?
4. What danger is there in requiring a contractor to follow a particular method in his performance?
5. What is the owner's interest in the wages the contractor pays to his employees?
6. What different machines could be used to obtain a 2" X 4" rectangular piece from a sheet of 1/16"-thick aluminum? In what ways could you fasten two pieces of metal together?
7. Write a simple specification for the purchase and installation of a 1/3-h.p. pedestal grinder.
8. What are the inherent advantages and disadvantages in copying portions of old specifications into a new one?
9. Interpreting from *Switzer* v. *Bozeman*, to what extent do trade or area practices have a bearing on meanings or omissions in specifications?

18

Agency

There is a limit to the amount one person can do; he cannot be in more than one place at a time. When a person's duties and desired objectives become too numerous for him to handle, he usually delegates them to others. This delegation of duties may take one of three forms: (1) employer–employee (sometimes called master–servant) relationship, (2) owner–independent contractor relationship, or (3) an agency.

In satisfying the normal requirements of his job, the engineer (whether he is a consultant or an employee) must act as *agent* for his employer at least part of the time. While he is thus engaged, his rights and liabilities are dictated by the law of *agency*.

The agent replaces his employer in dealing with other persons. Herein lies the distinction between the agency relationship and the employer–employee relationship. The agent is still an employee for many purposes, but special rights and duties are involved in agency. A lathe operator in a plant is an employee. Since he does not deal with other persons as a representative of his employer, he is not an agent.

An independent contractor agrees to produce a result. The intent of the parties and the degree of control exercised by the owner determine whether the relationship is that of owner–independent contractor or employer–employee. The degree of liability of the employer (or owner) is determined by the relationship he has created. He is liable for tortious injuries caused by his employees and for harm to them as such injuries may arise from their employment. On the other hand, his liability for injury to, or injury caused by, an independent contractor is extremely limited. The degree of control exercised by the employer is probably the main criterion in determining the relationship. There are many instances, particularly in workers' compensation cases, where a supposed owner–independent contractor relationship was held to be an employer–employee relationship because of the degree of control exercised by the employer (owner).

Black, a manufacturer, hires White as time-study man in Black's plant. In setting production standards and making methods changes, White is Black's employee. White is soon promoted to process engineer, in which capacity he is in charge of the installation of an automatic machine being purchased from Gray Automation. When White deals with Gray Automation and other outsiders, he becomes Black's agent. He fills a dual role, for while he is agent in dealing with others, he is still Black's employee in some of his duties as process engineer. In installing the machine, Gray Automation is an independent contractor unless an excessive degree of control is exercised by either Black or White.

Agency involves three people. The *principal* is the person who is represented by the agent, and is the source of the agent's authority. The *agent* is the person who represents his principal, acting in his place. *Third parties* are persons with whom the agent deals in the name of his principal.

Creation of Agency

The agency relationship may be created in any of four ways: by agreement, by ratification, by estoppel, or by necessity. The responsibility and authority of the agent is a little different under each circumstance.

Agreement. In *agency by agreement,* both parties must intend to create a relationship that amounts to agency. The parties may not consider the relationship to be agency when they enter into it—but if the result amounts to an agency, it will be so construed.

The means used by the parties to express their intentions to form an agency ordinarily is unimportant as long as the ideas are exchanged. An agency contract is much the same as any other contract in this respect. The intent may be either expressed or implied.

The agency agreement is not necessarily a contract, but it usually is. A contract requires consideration, but a simple agreement may create a valid gratuitous agency. Black owns a truck. White does not. Black, without promise of compensation, agrees to transport a machine for White from a freight depot to a machine shop across town. In doing this he must deal with others. Even though Black is to be paid nothing for his efforts, his actions are controlled by White when Black picks up, transports, and unloads the machine. An agency was formed.

An agreement to act as agent for another ordinarily may be either oral or written. However, for certain purposes a written or a sealed instrument may be required. Where the instrument to which the principal is to be bound requires a seal, the agent's authority must be in writing and sealed also. Probably the most frequently used form of this is the *power of attorney,* which establishes the agent as attorney-in-fact for his principal. Where the nature of a transaction is such as to require a public recording of it, any powers of attorney involved are also recorded.

Another form of written agency is the corporate *proxy.* By the use of a proxy, a stockholder appoints some particular person to act for him in voting his shares of stock in a particular way.

Ratification. *Agency by ratification* cures the defect of lack of authority. If a person contracts with another as an agent when he really has no authority to do so, the person for whom he purports to act is not bound to the contract. Much the same is true if an actual agent exceeds the authority given him by his principal. In either of these circumstances the principal may, if he wishes, agree to be bound by the terms of the contract. Such ratification is *retroactive*—the time of entering into the contract goes back to the time when it was made. The effect of ratification is the same as if the principal had previously retained an agent to act in that particular manner for him. Black hires White as a salesman to sell the company's products. In his travels White finds a buyer, Gray, for a used milling machine that Black has wanted to sell for some time. White, without delay, contracts in Black's name to sell the machine to Gray. If Black no longer wishes to part with the machine or, possibly, has contracted to sell it to another, he will not be bound to the agreement with Gray. If Black does not ratify, White will be personally liable for any harm to Gray resulting from the contract. If he does ratify, Black will be held to the contract just as though White had been given specific orders to sell the machine. The fact that White did not have authority to sell the machine does not allow Black to ratify a portion of the contract. Black must ratify all or nothing. Gray is not bound to the agreement until Black ratifies. If he finds that White acted without authority, he may withdraw before Black's ratification.

There are four requirements for a valid ratification: (1) There must be a principal in existence when the supposed agent acts. A corporation, for instance, cannot make a binding ratification of contracts made in the corporation's name before it was formed. New contracts will be required if the corporation is to be bound. (2) The person acting without authority must act as an agent. If he acts for himself, subsequent ratification by another will not create enforceable obligations between the third party and an outsider. If an agent of an undisclosed principal exceeds his authority, later ratification by his principal will not cure the defect. (3) The principal must be aware of the facts when he ratifies. A principal's actions that would imply ratification have little effect unless the principal knows what he is doing. Of course, if the principal does not investigate the details when he has a duty to do so, his negligence may be interpreted so as to give him implied knowledge. (4) The principal must intend to ratify. Intent and ratification may be interpreted from the principal's actions after he obtains knowledge of the transaction. If he does nothing after being informed of the transaction, ratification could be implied from his inaction.

Estoppel. *Agency by estoppel* arises where one person appears to have authority to act for another and, despite lack of real authority, does act in the name of the other. *Apparent* authority is the key to the concept. If the principal acts in such a way that another person appears to be his agent (thus, in effect, deceiving the third party), he is then estopped from denying that the other person is his agent. The third party must, of course, have dealt with the supposed agent because of the principal's actions if he is to prove agency by estoppel.

Necessity. *Agency by necessity* occurs as a result of an emergency. It is a rather rare happening. If, to save his employer from some disaster, an employee must deal with others without an opportunity to obtain authorization, an agency by necessity is created.

Where a wife binds her husband to pay for necessaries (or where a dependent binds his guardian), agency is sometimes said to exist. The most common holding, though, is that the husband (or guardian) had a *duty* to support, and binding him to such contracts is a result of this duty rather than agency.

Competency of Parties

Since, in agency, the principal is the party to be bound to a third party, he must be *competent* to contract. The agent may be a gray-haired man of sixty, but if his principal is a minor, the contract is voidable at the minor's option. From this there arises a practical desirability of investigating the principal before contracting with him. Not only could an incompetent principal avoid a contract made by his agent for him; he might also avoid his contract with his agent.

Though competency of the principal is of major concern to those dealing with him, competency of the agent is not. Almost anyone may be an agent; it is the principal who is bound. A minor agent contracting with a third party would bind his adult principal to the contract.

Agent's Authority

The agent's authority comes from his principal. It consists of *express* orders or directions given to him by his principal in addition to authority that may reasonably be implied. *Implied authority* is based on previous dealings between the parties, or local or trade customs. If none of these control the situation, the extent of implied authority is that which is necessary to accomplish the purpose of the agency.

If the agent contracts beyond his authority, his principal is not bound. From this there is an obvious burden upon the third party to determine whether the agent has authority to contract. The third party is safe in dealing with the agent if he can obtain evidence of the agent's mission. Implied authority necessary to the accomplishment of the purpose is included despite the principal's instructions to his agent to the contrary. Black is a buyer for the White Manufacturing Company. His present assignment is to buy a six-station automatic indexing table, drive, and base, to be used in machining small die castings. He has been specifically told not to buy any tooling with the machine. Nevertheless, he contracts with Gray for a machine with tooling that, he is told, may be reworked for the die castings. The contract for the machine and the tooling will be binding. Black's specific orders to buy the machine might well be taken to imply that he also had a right to purchase tooling for it. If Gray knew of Black's assignment, he would not have a duty to go further and determine any unusual restrictions which might have been imposed on Black.

A third type of agent's authority is *apparent authority*. The reasoning of apparent authority runs so close to that of agency by estoppel as to make the two nearly indistinguishable. Apparent authority exists when, by some act or negligence on the part of the principal, an agent is either clothed with more authority than he really has been given, or one who is *not* an agent is made to appear as though he were.

An agent is chosen for his particular capabilities and fidelity. He is the one in whom the principal places his trust. The agent cannot, therefore, by his act alone delegate his authority to another. If the agent hires a sub-agent, the principal has no liability to the sub-agent for wages or other benefits and is not liable for the sub-agent's acts. The rule is not without exception; if part of the agent's express or implied task is hiring others for his principal, those so hired work for the principal.

Agent's Duties

Agency is a *fiduciary* relationship—the principal's trust and the agent's loyalty are implied. The law enforces these qualities in the relationship; breach of them is a cause for action. The agent is personally liable for the results of his disloyalty.

Obedience. An agent owes his principal a duty of strict obedience in all ordinary circumstances. Disobedience is a breach of the agency agreement. It is not the agent's function to question or judge the wisdom of his principal's orders; it is his function to do everything in his power to obey them. Of course, when the principal outlines to his agent a general purpose to be accomplished, the agent may be required to use judgment and discretion in working out the details. Still, the purpose to be accomplished is not open to question. Direction by the principal is implicit, even in a gratuitous agency, once the agent has begun his performance.

Strict obedience is limited to lawful and reasonable possibility. The agent need not, of course, follow instructions of an unlawful nature. Neither would he be expected to accomplish an impossibility. In an emergency situation an agent may have the right to fail to obey instructions strictly. The reasoning here is the same as that in authority of necessity; if the agent's failure to follow instructions will save his principal from disaster, his right to disobey is apparent.

Care and Skill. The agency relationship normally implies that the agent will use ordinary care and skill in carrying out his duties. The test of whether or not he has done so is the test of *the reasonably prudent man*. Has the agent acted as a reasonably prudent person would be expected to act in like circumstances? Negligence in following the principal's orders may make the agent liable for payments to him; in addition, he may have to pay for losses suffered by the principal that could be reasonably anticipated from failure to follow instructions properly.

If the agent professes to be a specialist (e.g., a consultant in some professional field), the standard of skill expected of him is that which is normally attributed to such a person. The standard is the same whether the person really is such a specialist or not; failure to perform as a specialist would be expected to perform makes the agent liable. Black, a manufacturer, hires White—an engineering consultant on conveyors—to design, recommend, and oversee the installation of a monorail conveyor system in his plant. If, because of very poor planning and design, the conveyor must be removed shortly after its installation, Black may have an action available against White. If Black's action is to be successful, he must prove (usually by expert testimony) that anyone possessing the knowledge and skill normally possessed by an engineering consultant specializing in conveyors would have made a more effective design. Damages could run as high as the total of the consultant's fee plus the cost of the improper installation and the cost of its removal.

To Act for One Principal. An agent has a duty to act for and accept compensation from only one principal. He could not, for instance, reasonably represent both buyer and seller in a sales contract. The buyer's interest and the seller's interest are at opposite poles; each desires to get the best possible deal for himself. If the agent represents more than one party to a contract, the transaction is voidable at the option of either principal.

The agent is relieved of his responsibility to act for only one party if the parties are told of the multiple relationships and acquiesce. An agent's interest that is adverse to his principal's interests is allowable if the principal knows of the interest and continues the relationship in spite of it.

Kickbacks or secret commissions from third parties are against public policy. The agent's compensation should come from his principal.

If the agent acquires in his own name property that should go to his principal, the agent will be deemed to be holding the property as bailee. Similarly, the agent cannot contract with himself as the third party without his principal's consent. To do so gives the principal the right to avoid the transaction at his option.

Accounting. The agent has a duty to account for all money or property involved in agency transactions. Further, the principal's property must be kept separate from the agent's property. If commingled money or property belonging to both principal and agent, is lost, the agent must make good the principal's loss. If the property were kept separate and the loss occurred through no fault of the agent, only the principal would lose.

The agent has no right to use the principal's property as his own without consent to do so. Using property of another without his consent is the same in agency as elsewhere—it is *conversion* (theft).

Closely akin to the agent's duty to account to his principal for money or property is the agent's duty to report information to his principal. Generally, notification to an agent has the same effect as notice to his principal. In either case the principal is charged with possession of the knowledge.

Loyalty. The essence of agency is the identity of the agent with his principal's purpose. The agent is often in position to gain personally from information acquired by him. To use the information so as to add to the agent's personal fortune is an act of disloyalty. Recovery by the principal for such misuse of information is possible.

Principal's Duties

Most agency agreements are contractual in nature, and each party has a duty to live up to the agreement. The principal does not, however, have to pay for disloyal service. Neither will he have to pay if payment is made contingent upon the agent's success (as commissions for sales) and the agent's efforts do not meet with success.

Payment. In the usual agency contract the means and amount of payment are stipulated. If such a stipulation is not made, though, the agent is entitled to reasonable payment for his services. If principal and agent are not close friends or relatives and there is no other reason to assume that the agent acted for nothing, an unliquidated obligation of payment by the principal to the agent exists. A gratuitous agency is, of course, an exception to this.

Payment of an agent on a *commission* basis presents some special problems. When has the agent earned his commission? Does the principal have to pay if he deals directly with the third party? What happens if the principal accepts an order through his agent to sell to a third party and then principal and third party agree to disagree? Such problems arise not only in agencies to sell a company's products; they are also common in real estate and other agencies.

Generally, barring agreement to the contrary, the agent has performed and is entitled to his commission when he has found a buyer and has contracted with him for the principal. A real estate agent (or broker) ordinarily does not have the power to contract for his principal. Therefore, it is only necessary that the real estate agent find a buyer ready, willing, and able to buy the property to be sold at the owner's price. With these conditions satisfied, the principal has an obligation to pay the agent his agreed commission.

If, after the agent has performed his obligation, the principal and the third party do not complete the transaction, the principal is still bound to pay his agent. It matters not that the principal will no longer profit by the transaction.

The agency agreement will often state whether a commission is to be paid to the agent if principal and third party deal directly. An *exclusive agency* for the sale of real estate, for instance, requires that the real estate agent be paid his commission regardless of who sells the realty. Without the exclusive agency feature, the owner's sale of the realty to another would create no obligation to pay the agent. The same is generally true of an agent who sells a product. If the sale is made without his services, he has done nothing to earn a commission and is not entitled to it.

Expenses. The principal is legally bound to pay his agent's expenses. To constitute an obligation of the principal, the expenses must, of course, be connected to the purpose of the agency. Thus, cost of travel, meals, and overnight hotel or motel accommodations connected with an agent's trip to sell his principal's products should be paid by the principal. Similar costs incurred by the agent on a pleasure trip with his family ordinarily would not be covered by the principal.

Indemnity. While the agent has a duty to follow his principal's orders, the principal also has a duty to *indemnify* the agent if the result injures someone and the agent has to pay for the injury. Of course, the agent is not required to perform unlawful acts; he is prohibited in the same manner as anyone else from committing a crime. If, though, a tort or crime is committed by the agent innocently following his principal's instructions, the principal is liable for the result. Both principal and agent are liable to the third party for acts committed out of and in the course of the agent's employment; but if the agent has to pay, he can recover from his principal. The agent alone is responsible for acts not connected with his employment.

Black is an agent of the White Machinery Company. His function is to answer customers' complaints and thus make the sales of the machines permanent. He is a trouble-shooter. As such, he is entitled to compensation according to his agreement with the White Machinery Company. He is also entitled to payment for legitimate expenses in connection with his job. If, while instructing someone in the proper use of a machine, an injury should occur, White Machinery Company would be liable.

Third-Party Rights and Duties

So far we have considered the rights and liabilities of two of the agency parties—the principal and the agent. But there is another party from whose standpoint agency should be considered. The third party also has a stake in the relationship. Normally, an agent's transactions bind his principal and a third party—but are there instances when one or neither party would be bound? Must the third party rely on all that the agent tells him? These and other questions concern the third party.

Duty to Question Agent's Authority. We have noted that the agent has the authority given him by his principal. He also has authority common to other agencies

of a similar nature. The third party is safe in relying upon the agent's authority to this extent once he has established that he is dealing with an agent of an existing principal. If the third party knows nothing of either principal or agent from previous contacts, he is well advised to determine by some objective means if the principal and the agency relationship actually exist. Obviously, if the principal is nonexistent or the principal exists but there is no agency, the third party may part with something of value in good faith and get nothing for it; a person cannot be bound by someone's merely claiming to be his agent. Under such circumstances the third party would be left with an action against the agent only, and it is likely that *he* would be hard to find.

Agent's Right to Collect. Does the agent have the right to collect from a third party? Usually he does not, barring specific authority, or trade or local practice to the contrary. Ordinarily, the third party must give his consideration directly to the principal. Black represents the White Manufacturing Company. He obtains an order from Gray for a quantity of his principal's product and receives part payment for the goods. Black is not seen again locally. The one who is to stand the loss of the part payment depends upon whether Black had express or implied authority to receive payment. If no such authority can be found, Gray is the loser to the extent of the payment. The situation would be different if Black had brought the goods along with him; under this circumstance the right to collect can be implied.

Somewhat akin to the agent's authority to receive payment is his authority to sign a negotiable instrument in his principal's name. Authority to do this must be expressly given to have binding effect.

Transactions Binding Agent. In the normal course of affairs the third party has no action available against the agent in a transaction. If the agent has acted within the scope of his express and implied authority, it is the principal and the third party who are bound. It is possible, though, for an agent to act as surety for his principal; or he may contract with the third party in such a way that it is he, rather than his principal, who is to be bound. Ordinarily an agent will agree in a transaction in such a manner that he indicates his principal and the fact that he is agent for the principal. If the agent however, merely agrees in his own name or signs as "Black, agent," indicating no principal, he may be held personally liable.

Tort. If, while in the course of his principal's business, the agent commits a tort against the third party, the third party may charge either the agent or the principal with the act. Successful action against the agent then gives the agent a right to recover from his principal. An exception to this appears to exist where the principal is a minor and the agent an adult—here the agent must stand the loss.

If the third party, without cause, brings about the discharge of the agent, he has committed a tort. In fact, the rule is more general than this—anyone who maliciously causes another to lose an employment relationship has committed a tort and an action will lie against him.

Undisclosed Principal

Normally the third party is aware that he is dealing with an agent of a known principal. Such is not always the case, though. The agent may not reveal that he is working for any principal, thus allowing the third party to assume that he is dealing directly with the party to be bound. Or the agent may reveal that he represents another without naming his principal (partially disclosed principal).

In either case, where the principal has not been disclosed to the third party, the third party may elect to hold either principal or agent to the contract. If the third party elects to hold the agent, and the agent has acted within the scope of his authority, the agent has a right to be indemnified by his principal. Either the principal or the agent may hold the third party to the transaction, but the principal's right to do so is superior to the agent's.

The enforceability of undisclosed principal transactions appears to be counter to the concept that a contract must be entered into voluntarily and intentionally by the parties. However, the legality and enforceability of such contracts is well established. It is, in effect, an exception to the general rule of contracts.

An undisclosed principal contract will not be enforced where the third party, either expressly or by implication, makes clear his intent to deal exclusively with the agent. White Manufacturing Company wishes to expand its operation into another section of the country. It retains Black to purchase land for the expansion without revealing the company's name. (Such purchases are sometimes undertaken to keep local land prices from soaring.) Black contracts with Gray to buy 200 acres of suitable land. Gray can elect to hold Black to the contract or, when the principal is revealed, hold the White Manufacturing Company. Gray is bound to the contract unless he has either expressed or implied his intent to deal exclusively with Black. If Black, under questioning by Gray, were to deny the existence of a principal, it would be grounds for fraud, making the contract voidable at Gray's election.

Termination

The rules for winding up an agency agreement are about the same as those for winding up any employment agreement, except that a third party must be considered. The usual contract of employment of a so-called white-collar employee is oral and terminable at the option of either employer or employee. If an engineer or a sales agent or an accountant engaged in such employment decides to leave, it is only necessary to so inform the employer, settle the accounts, and leave. The employer's right to terminate such an agreement is similar. Not all agency contracts are of this simple form, though, and they are not always terminated in this fashion.

By Law. Death, insanity, or bankruptcy of either principal or agent automatically terminates an agency relationship. Death or insanity of the principal is effective even if the agent is not aware of the event. That is, if an agent deals with another after his principal dies or becomes insane, but before the agent is informed of it, the transaction is not binding.

If the agency has been created for a specific purpose, destruction of an essential to the accomplishment of the purpose ends the agency. Similarly, passage of a law that makes the purpose of the agency unlawful, terminates the agency.

By Acts of the Parties. An agency created to accomplish a specific purpose or to last for a stated time is generally not terminable at the option of the parties without possible repercussions. If an agency is created to accomplish a particular purpose, it ends when the purpose is accomplished. If a time limit for the agency is set, it ends when the time runs out.

Where an agency has been created for a purpose or to last a certain time, neither the principal nor the agent may unilaterally terminate the agency without giving the other a right of legal action. Both parties may, of course, agree to disagree before the contract is finished. Revocation of the agency by the principal terminates the agency; but if it is done without just cause or agreement, the principal is likely to be held liable for payment to his former agent for the remainder of the term for which the agency was to run. Similarly, renunciation of the principal by the agent ends the agency, but the principal may be allowed recovery. As indicated earlier, disloyalty by the agent would be just cause for early termination by the principal. In any case, termination by a unilateral act of either principal or agent does not become effective until the other party is informed of it.

Agency with an Interest. If the agent has an interest in the subject matter of the agency, the relationship cannot be terminated by an act of the principal. More is referred to by the term *interest* than just the agreed compensation for the agent's services. Essentially, this implies part ownership or an equity in the subject matter. This is more of a partnership venture in most instances; one partner could not very well fire another.

Notice. When an agency is terminated, third parties should be notified. If the agency is terminated by law, notification is considered to have taken place, since death, insanity, or bankruptcy would be a matter of public record. When termination takes place by acts of the parties, though, there is a particular necessity to inform those who have dealt with the agent. If, in ignorance of the dissolution of the agency, a third party deals with an agent as he had dealt with him before, the principal will be bound. The reason for this is the agent's apparent authority to act for the principal. Notification to those who have previously dealt with the agent prevents this, but notification is not effective until the third parties receive it. Thus, a notice in a newspaper or trade journal would not be effective notification to third parties of previous dealings.

Partnerships

Each partner in an enterprise is an agent for it. Generally, the rules of agency apply to partnerships. As long as the transaction involved is in the normal course of business of the partnership, agreement by one partner binds all partners to the contract. Transactions beyond the normal scope of the partnership require approval of all the partners. Just as notice given to an agent is the virtual equivalent of notice given to the principal, notice given to any partner is also notice to the partnership.

VAUX v. HAMILTON
103 N.W. 2d 291 (1960)

Strutz, Judge.

The two actions involved in this litigation arose out of a collision of an automobile driven by plaintiff Vaux, in which the plaintiff Nixon was a passenger, and a Cadillac automobile driven by the defendant Dorothy Hamilton which carried the dealer's license of the defendant Day's Auto Brokers, Inc. The accident occurred just west of Jamestown, North Dakota, on U.S. Highway No. 10.

Both actions are against the same defendants and involve the same facts. The cases were consolidated for trial in the district court of Stutsman County, and both cases were argued together on appeal. Both appeals will be considered in one opinion.

The defendant Day's Auto Brokers, Inc., is a foreign corporation engaged in the business of selling used cars in the city of Seattle, Washington. Through its agent, DeLain Belch, the defendant purchased the Cadillac automobile involved in this litigation in the Detroit area. The employee purchasing the car left it with the Midwest Auto Delivery for delivery to the defendant's place of business in Seattle. The delivery service advertised for a driver to deliver the automobile to Seattle, and the advertisement was answered by the defendant Ruby Cuthbert. The agreement under which she was to drive the car to the defendant's place of business in Seattle provided that all gas and oil and other expenses be paid by the driver. While the car was being driven to Seattle, it was involved in a collision just west of Jamestown resulting in the litigation now before the court.

The plaintiffs alleged in their respective complaints that the defendant Cuthbert was the agent of the defendant Day's Auto Brokers, Inc., in delivering the car. This was denied by the defendant Day's Auto Brokers, Inc. Verdicts were returned by the jury in favor of both of the plaintiffs and against the defendant Day's Auto Brokers, Inc., and the defendant Dorothy Hamilton, who was driving the car at the time of the collision. The defendant Day's Auto Brokers, Inc., has appealed from the judgments and from orders denying its motion for judgment notwithstanding the verdict or, in the alternative, for a new trial.

The burden of establishing agency rests on the party alleging it, as respects the master's liability for negligence of the alleged servant. . . .

Thus, where existence of agency is denied, the burden of proving agency is on the party asserting its existence.

The evidence as to the existence of agency in this case, relied on by the plaintiffs, consists of the deposition of Henry Freymueller, the president of defendant Day's Auto Brokers, Inc. He testified, on cross-examination by the plaintiffs, that the defendant company obtained the automobile in question by having its employee, DeLain Belch, purchase it and then deliver it to the driveaway firm for shipment after attaching defendant's "intransit" dealer's license; that the defendant was to pay to Midwest Auto Delivery a flat fee to deliver the said automobile. Freymueller further testified:

> "Well, we pay them to get the car out here. The discretion of how they deliver it is up to them."

There was the further evidence of the defendant Ruby Cuthbert, the girl who answered an ad of Midwest Auto Delivery, advertising for a driver to deliver a car to Seattle. She stated that she had seen the advertisement of Midwest Auto Delivery in her local paper; that she answered the advertisement and agreed to drive the car in question to Seattle; that she did not know who owned the automobile but that it had a Washington dealer's license on it. She then said:

> "It is quite the thing, they advertise in newspapers in Ontario anyone who wants to go to the West Coast, it is not employment, it is a case if you go to the West Coast it is a cheap way to go, and they—. . . ."

She further stated that she and her two companions, the defendants Dorothy Hamilton and Margaret Jack, were to pay the oil and gas and their own expenses incurred while taking the automobile to Seattle.

On this evidence the jury found the defendant Hamilton to be the agent of defendant Day's Auto Brokers, Inc.

In reviewing the sufficiency of the evidence on appeal from the judgment and from an order denying motion for judgment notwithstanding the verdict or for a new trial, this court will view the evidence in the light most favorable to the verdict. . . .

The record is silent as to whether this was the first occasion on which the defendant Day's Auto Brokers, Inc., had had the Midwest Auto Delivery deliver an automobile for it. While there is evidence that the defendant Day's Auto Broker's, Inc., was in fact the owner of the automobile involved in the collision, ownership of the automobile alone does not establish or prove agency. Neither is ownership alone sufficient to impose liability upon the owner of a car because of the negligence of another who is permitted to use it. . . .

It is true that defendant Cuthbert was performing an act in the interest of defendant Day's Auto Brokers, Inc., but acts of the alleged agent cannot establish agency without evidence showing that the alleged master had knowledge thereof or assented thereto. . . .

In this case, the testimony was undisputed that the defendant Day's Auto Brokers, Inc., did not even know of the existence of the three girls who were delivering the automobile until after the accident had occurred.

The limited evidence presented to the jury on this question is more indicative of a relationship of independent contractor than of master and servant. Here, Midwest Auto Delivery was hired for one purpose, namely, to deliver the car to Seattle, and was responsible only for that result; it could accomplish that result in its own way. The record fails to disclose any right of control by defendant Day's Auto Brokers, Inc., over details as to how that result was to be accomplished. Such evidence may be available, however, on a new trial. While, under the present state of the record, on appeal from the judgment and from the order denying the motion for judgment notwithstanding the verdict or for a new trial, there is a failure to sustain the allegations of the complaints as to agency, this court need not order judgment for the defendant but will order a new trial when it appears that the defects may be remedied upon a new trial. . . .

Other specifications of error alleged by the defendant relate largely to instructions given by the court, or instructions refused by the court, relating to matters of agency, independent contractors, and liability of the owner of a vehicle for negligence of one permitted to use it for the user's own purposes. Since a new trial in these cases must be granted and, in view of what we have said above, it is unlikely that these questions will arise upon a new trial, we do not now consider them.

However, one specification of error deals with a matter which may well arise on the retrial of these actions. The trial court overruled an objection by the defendant to the following question put by the plaintiffs to a medical expert, testifying on behalf of the plaintiffs, as to the future pain and suffering of one of the plaintiffs:

> "Doctor, can you state with a reasonable degree of medical certainty that there is a distinct possibility that this might happen?"

An objection that the question was leading, suggestive, speculative, and conjectural was overruled.

The question in the form in which it was asked was clearly objectionable. While there are exceptions to the general rule that an opinion of a witness may not be received in evidence and although, under certain circumstances, the opinion of an expert is admissible, testimony which consists of no more than a mere guess of the witness is not admissible. Such testimony must be as to a definite probability and must not involve, to an excessive degree, the element of speculation or conjecture. The question directed to the medical expert in this case was calling for a mere guess on the part of the doctor "that there is a distinct possibility that this might happen."

Webster defines *possibility* as "the character, state, or fact of being possible, or that which may be conceivable." Thus, even if an event might occur only once in ten thousand times, it still is within the realm of possibility, though very improbable.

A medical expert is qualified to express an opinion to a medical certainty, or based on medical probabilities only, but not an opinion based on mere possibilities. . . .

For the reasons stated, the orders denying motion for new trial in the above actions are reversed, and new trials are granted.

MOUNDSVIEW IND. S.D. NO. 621 v. BUETOW & ASSOC.

253 N.W. 2d 836 (Minn., 1977)

Todd, Justice.

Buetow & Associates, Inc., (Buetow) entered into an agreement with Moundsview Independent School District No. 621 (Moundsview) to perform architectural services. Buetow agreed to prepare plans and specifications for an addition to a school as well as to provide general supervision of the construction operation. After the completion of construction, a windstorm ripped a portion of the roof off the school, allegedly due to the failure of a contractor to adequately fasten the roof to the building. The trial court granted Buetow's motion for summary judgment based on Buetow's contract with Moundsview, which provided that Buetow was not responsible for the failure of a contractor to follow the plans and specifications. We affirm.

In August 1968, Moundsview retained Buetow to prepare plans and specifications for an addition to an elementary school. At the time of the execution of the agreement, Moundsview had the option of requiring Buetow to provide (1) no supervision, (2) general supervision, or (3) continuous on-site inspection of the construction project by a full-time project representative referred to as a "clerk of the works." Moundsview elected to have Buetow provide only a general supervisory function, the specific language of the contract enumerating the requirements as follows:

> *"The Architect shall make periodic visits to the site to familiarize himself generally with the progress and quality of the Work and to determine in general if the Work is proceeding in accordance with the Contract Documents.* On the basis of his on-site observations as an Architect, *he shall endeavor to guard the Owner against defects and deficiencies in the Work of the Contractor. The Architect shall not be required to make exhaustive or continuous on-site inspections to check the quality or quantity of the Work.* The Architect shall not be responsible for construction means, methods, techniques, sequences, or procedures, or for safety precautions and programs in connection with the Work, *and he shall not be responsible for the Contractor's failure to carry out the Work in accordance with the Contract Documents."*

(Italics supplied.)

The contract further provides:

> "The Architect shall not be responsible for the acts or omissions of the Contractor, or any Subcontractors, or any of the Contractor's or Subcontractor's agents or employees, or any other person performing any of the Work."

Buetow prepared plans and specifications requiring the placement of wooden plates upon the concrete walls of the building. The plates were to be fastened to the walls by attaching washers and nuts to one-half inch studs secured in cement. During the 79-week construction period, the president of Buetow made 90 visits to the construction site in performance of Buetow's general supervisory obligation.

On May 19, 1975, a severe windstorm blew a portion of the roof off the building causing damage to the addition and to other portions of the school. It was discovered that the roof had not been secured by washers and nuts to the south wall of the school as required by the plans and specifications.

Moundsview brought an action for damages caused by the roof mishap against Buetow, the general contractor, and the roofing subcontractor. In response to an interrogatory from Buetow requesting Moundsview to state all facts upon which it relied to support its allegations against Buetow, Moundsview replied:

> Defendant Buetow failed to properly supervise the roof construction, failed to supervise and discover the missing nuts and studs and take proper corrective action."

Thereafter, Buetow made a motion for summary judgment, basing its motion upon the affidavit of one of its officers which stated that Buetow did not observe during any of its construction site visits that the washers and nuts had not been fastened to the studs on the south wall. The motion was also accompanied by the architect's contract which the parties entered into and Buetow's interrogatories and Moundsview's answers thereto. Moundsview did not file a responsive affidavit to oppose the motion.

The trial court granted Buetow summary judgment, accompanying its decision by memorandum which states:

> "Since the contract of the architect did not require detailed supervision by the architect of the construction project, and since the architect was not contractually liable, as a matter of law, for the acts and omissions of the general contractor or any subcontractor, the architect is entitled to summary judgment under the principle enunciated in *J & J Electric, Inc.* v. *Moen Company.* . . ."

Moundsview appeals from the judgment entered pursuant to the order for summary judgment.

The issue presented for consideration is whether there exists a genuine issue of fact in this case that will preclude the entry of summary judgment dismissing the complaint against Buetow.

1. Initially, we note that the rule in Minnesota is that a party cannot rely upon general statements of fact to oppose a motion for summary judgment. Instead, the nonmoving party must demonstrate at the time the motion is made that specific facts are in existence which create a genuine issue for trial. . . .

The general statements included within Moundsview's complaint and the equally general answers to Buetow's interrogatories are insufficient to create a genuine issue of fact to successfully oppose a motion for summary judgment. Thus, since Moundsview failed to present any specific averments of fact in opposition to the motion for summary judgment, our review of the case is limited to a consideration of the contract between the parties.

2. Moundsview argues that Buetow breached its duty of architectural supervision by failing to discover that a contractor had failed to fasten one side of the roof to the building with washers and nuts as required by the plans and specifications. It is the general rule that the employment of an architect is a matter of contract, and consequently, he is responsible for all the duties enumerated within the contract of employment. . . . An architect, as a professional, is required to perform his services with reasonable care and competence and will be liable in damages for any failure to do so. . . .

Thus, consideration of whether Buetow breached a duty of supervision requires an initial examination of the contract between the parties to determine the parameters of its supervisory obligation. The argument that Buetow breached its duty to supervise would be more persuasive had Moundsview contracted for full-time project representation rather than mere general supervision. An architect's duty to inspect and supervise the construction site pursuant to a contract requiring only general supervision is not as broad as its duty when a "clerk of the works" is required. The mere fact that Buetow received additional compensation for performing the general supervisory service does not serve to expand its responsibilities to an extent equivalent to the duties of a full-time project representative. Moundsview cannot be allowed to gain the benefit of the more detailed "clerk-of-the-works" inspection service while in fact contracting and paying for only a general supervisory service.

Thus, the question of whether Buetow breached its duty to supervise the construction project is to be determined with reference to the general supervisory obligation enumerated in the contract. The contract provided that the architect ". . . shall not be responsible for the Contractor's failure to carry out the Work in accordance with the Contract Documents." When this section is read in conjunction with the section which provides that "(t)he Architect shall not be responsible for the acts or omissions of the Contractor, or any Subcontractors, or any of the Contractor's or Subcontractors' agents or employees or any other persons performing any of the Work," it is apparent that by the plain language of the contract an architect is exculpated from any liability occasioned by the acts or omissions of a contract. The language of the contract is unambiguous. The failure of a contractor to follow the plans and specifications caused the roof mishap. By virtue of the aforementioned contractual provisions, Buetow is absolved from any liability, as a matter of law, for a contractor's failure to fasten the roof to the building with washers and nuts.

Thus, based upon the language of the architect's contract, Buetow was entitled to summary judgment. . . .

Affirmed.

McCURNIN v. KOHLMEYER & COMPANY
477 F. 2d 113 (1973)

Per Curiam:

Federal jurisdiction over this case initially was grounded upon a joinder of claims arising under the Commodities Exchange Act, the Securities Act of 1933, and the Securities Exchange Act of 1924 with a diversity claim arising under the Louisiana law of agency. The trial court below determined that none of the customer's (Appellee) federal claims had merit,[1] but, it asserted pendent jurisdiction over the state claim[2] and proceeded to find that the customer was entitled to recovery from the broker (Appellant) under prevailing Louisiana law. We affirm.

---

1. As a discussion of the basis alleged for these federal claims and the reasons for the trial court's rejection of them would add nothing to the disposition of this appeal, we abstain analysis.

2. In deciding to assume pendent jurisdiction of the state claim, the trial court correctly made the following determinations: (i) that the federal question raised was not "unsubstantial and frivolous"; (ii) that the state claims arose from identical facts on which the federal remedies were sought; and (iii) that since the case had been fully tried, it was in the interest of justice as well as judicial economy that the issue be decided on what was already a complete record.

The dispute between the parties arose out of trading in the commodity market by McCurnin, the customer. The broker, Kohlmeyer and Company, through its employee Drake, also a co-Appellant, purchased cotton futures for customer at a price in excess of that authorized. He suffered a net loss in the transaction of $26,725.[3]

Upon learning of the unauthorized purchase, MrCurnin did not immediately and affirmatively repudiate the transaction, at least not by clear and unambiguous conduct. A period of three days elapsed before his market position was liquidated and thus before the full extent of the loss was realized. The broker contends that the customer's delay and his accompanying conduct subsequent to learning of the unauthorized purchase clearly manifested his intention to ratify the purchase and, furthermore, this delay was violative of his duty to mitigate damages.

The trial court, in a thorough and well-reasoned opinion . . . rejected these arguments. The Judge found that the broker's conduct was violative of two codal Articles of the Louisiana Law of Mandate, La. Civil Code Articles 3010 and 3003.[4]

In response to the contention that the customer ratified, the trial Judge wrote:

"The conclusion that McCurnin failed to repudiate is mistaken. McCurnin had manifested his displeasure to Drake. He had been informed—misinformed—by Drake that there was nothing he could do but complete the transaction. It is true that Drake's optimism about the market had made both McCurnin and Drake sanguine that all might turn out well, but his false hope was never transmuted by McCurnin into approval of Drake's actions."

The Court held that the burden of proving ratification was on the broker and an intention to ratify an unauthorized act cannot be inferred when the conduct can be otherwise explained. For ratification to be implied, it must be shown that the principal actually had knowledge of the material and pertinent facts. Here the judge was entitled to conclude that the customer's error, whether error of law or fact, was clearly induced by the broker. The court held that the customer's effort to repudiate the unauthorized transaction was defeated by the broker.

Though the trial court agreed that the customer owed a duty to minimize his damages, it found that he had acted with reasonable promptness under the circumstances. Immediately upon learning that the broker required that he liquidate his position before they would consider making any adjustment, McCurnin ordered the cotton futures sold.

These were essentially all factual questions. The Judge found the facts. There it ends.
Affirmed.

REVIEW QUESTIONS

1. Identify the following persons as agents, employees, or independent contractors according to the usual duties involved in their work.
   a. Research chemist working for chemical company.
   b. Free-lance consulting engineer in the labor relations field.
   c. T.V. repairman for local department store—on house call.
   d. Trouble-shooter for steel company (keeps steel sold to customers by recommending proper treatment of a particular heat of steel).
   e. Engineering vice-president for local company.
   f. Dentist.
2. How may the agency relationship be created?
3. Brown is a process engineer for White Manufacturing Company and is about to recommend the purchase of certain machinery and equipment. The Green Equipment Company is one prospective supplier. On a recent trip to the Green Company, Green offered Brown a new station wagon if Green was chosen as the equipment supplier. Brown has always considered himself to be quite ethical, but he is also human and the station wagon sounds tempting. Neglecting the ethical aspects of the situation, Brown is still faced with certain legal problems. What are Brown's rights if, after recommending Green as supplier, Green fails to produce the station wagon? What can happen to Brown if White Manufacturing Co. finds out about the deal?
4. Gray, engineer for Black, White, and Company, was sent to observe an automation installation at a plant some 50 miles away. On the return trip he approached an intersection and applied his brakes. His car hit a patch of ice. As a result, he hit another car, injuring its occupants, both cars, and

3. The suit below was for $15,286.45. This was the amount of his credit balance at the time of the loss. The broker counterclaimed for $11,438.55, the amount remaining due if the customer had to bear the loss.
4. Article 3010 of the Louisiana Civil Code provides:

"Art. 3010. The attorney cannot go beyond the limits of his procuration; whatever he does exceeding his power is null and void with regard to the principal, unless ratified by the latter, and the attorney is alone bound by it in his individual capacity."

Article 3003 of the Louisiana Civil Code provides in part:

"Art. 3003. The attorney is responsible, not only for unfaithfulness in his management, but also for his fault or neglect."

himself. Who is liable for injuries to the other car and its occupants? Who is liable for injury to Gray and Gray's car?

5. In *Vaux* v. *Hamilton,* what is the relationship between Hamilton and Midwest Auto Delivery? What is the relationship between Midwest Auto Delivery and Day's Auto Brokers, Inc.? Could Midwest Auto Delivery be held liable for the injuries? Give your reasoning.

6. In *Moundsview Ind. S.D. No.621* v. *Buetow & Assoc.,* a) does the summary judgment in favor of Buetow mean that Moundsview cannot recover for the windstorm damage to its school roof? b) rewrite the contract requirements in such a manner that Buetow is responsible for such disasters in the factual situation described in the case.

7. In *McCurnin* v. *Kohlmeyer & Company,* what minimum additional acts or statements by McCurnin would amount to ratification? Does McCurnin have any right of action against Drake?

Section IV

Property

Most engineers work for other people—either for a private enterprise or for the public (a local, state, or federal government). An engineer uses other people's property in his work; hence, he must observe their rights. In numerous instances his work will require him to deal simultaneously with his employer's property and that of others, possibly including his own. Effectively handling property and property rights in these circumstances requires some knowledge of property law.

Property is either physical or intellectual. Because of the obvious differences between, say, an automobile and the patent on a new plastic, the rights and responsibilities of each must be treated differently. The same general thread of ownership rights pertains to both, but the legalities pertaining to those rights are very different.

19

Physical Property

All of us have things which we consider to be ours: our clothing, books, writing instruments, a watch, perhaps a home in the suburbs. The word *property* is used in two senses. It denotes *things* owned by a person; this is the usual concept. It also refers to the *rights* involved in ownership. These rights, known as *property rights,* signify dominion over things owned. That is, the right to use and to exclude others from using the things we own; the right of control over and enjoyment of them, and the right to dispose of them.

Physical property may be classed as real, personal, or mixed. In the discussion of the Statute of Frauds, Chapter 11, it was necessary to distinguish between real and personal property. Generally, *real property* has been defined as land and anything firmly attached to it. *Personal property* is all property other than real, such as goods, chattels, choses in action, money, and accounts receivable, or other evidences of debt. Combinations of real and personal property are *mixed property*.

Property is either corporeal or incorporeal. *Corporeal property* exists in a material state—land, money, an automobile. *Incorporeal property,* on the other hand, does not have material existence. It may be a right-of-way across property, or the good will of an enterprise.

PERSONAL PROPERTY

The term *chattels* is often used synonymously with personal property. *Chattels personal in possession* are the tangible items; e.g., a watch, a truck, or a machine in a factory. *Chattels personal in action,* commonly known as *choses in action,* are intangible rights arising from tort or contract—the right to goods contracted for or the right to recovery for injuries suffered in an automobile collision, for example. A *chattel real* is an interest in land less than fee simple ownership or a life estate—for example, a ten-year lease.

Acquisition

A person may lawfully obtain ownership of personal property by (1) original acquisition, (2) a procedure of law, or (3) acts of other persons.

Original Acquisition. Unowned things in their natural state become the property of the first person to obtain possession of them. Most things are owned by someone today, but, for example, the possibility of reducing wild animals to personal property still exists. Obtaining ownership in this way is known as acquiring title by *occupancy.*

Property which one *creates* by his mental or physical efforts belongs to him unless he has agreed, for compensation, to transfer it to another. Books, inventions, trade names, and other such creations are of this nature.

Property may be acquired by *accession*—adding to other property. A new windshield of a car or a gear in the transmission becomes the property of the owner of the automobile. This is particularly true where the addition becomes an integral, built-in part of the whole in such a way that it is not readily detachable. Even where the innocent purchaser of stolen property adds value to it, he is merely adding value to property belonging to another. White buys a car from Gray who, unknown to White, has stolen the car from Black. White adds a new motor, transmission, and paint job to the car. Later, Black locates his car. Black is entitled to regain possession of his car in its improved state. Probably there is no other place where the law adheres so strictly to the principle of *caveat emptor* (the buyer beware) than in the purchase of stolen property.

Accession also applies to a natural increase of purchased property. Black sells White a mare. Shortly after the sale a foal is born. White is the owner of both the mare and the foal.

Procedure of Law. Property may be distributed according to certain legal procedures. Four of these arise from intestate death, mortgage foreclosure, judicial sale, and bankruptcy.

When a person dies and has not left a will, his death is termed *intestate.* The various states have, by statute, declared how property shall be distributed in case of such intestate death—the laws of *descent.* There is a great variation in these statutes as to who will inherit the estate. If no relatives of the deceased can be found, the property will go to the state—it *escheats* to the state.

Even when a person leaves a will, he is limited somewhat in the way he may leave his estate to his heirs. He may not, according to most state laws, leave his wife or minor children destitute by willing his entire estate to strangers.

Statutes provide for mortgage foreclosure in case of default by the mortgagor. Although it is common in chattel mortgages to provide for the mortgagee to take and sell the mortgaged property in case of default, a court procedure is usually possible if such provision has not been made.

Sales of property may be undertaken to satisfy a judgment of a court. Certain property of the loser is taken from him (within limits stated in the laws of each state) and is sold to satisfy the judgment.

When abandoned property is found by the police or sheriff's department in a community, it is kept for a statutory period of time and then sold at public auction. Such sales usually must be advertised and public, with the property going to the highest bidder.

Under bankruptcy procedures a trustee may be appointed by the court with the duty to convert the assets of the bankrupt into money. The trustee[1] may take over the property with the right and duty to sell it.

Generally the buyer of such property does not get any better title than the seller had. In judicial sales, sales of abandoned property, and bankruptcy sales, title is usually not warranted by the seller. The seller sells by virtue of a legal right or duty to do so; the buyer assumes the risk that title may not be good. Black steals White's car and abandons it in a neighboring town. It is held by the local police department for the required period of time and then sold to Gray at a public auction. Later White finds his car in Gray's possession. White can claim and get his car.

Acts of Other Persons. Title to personal property may be lawfully acquired from others by will, gift, contract, confusion, or abandonment. A person may also acquire possession of property if it is lost or mislaid by another.

The subject of wills is discussed under real property. It is sufficient to note here that, if the testator complies with the law, he may leave his property to whomsoever he wishes.

If property is acquired by gift, title to the property follows possession. Black promises White a gift of $500. At this point White has nothing. The promise of a future gift, either oral or in writing, is unenforceable, since it is unsupported by consideration. Of course, if the written promise of a gift were signed and sealed, a consideration would be imputed under common law and the promise would be enforceable. As soon as Black actually gives the $500 to White, though, it becomes his property and Black loses any claim to it. Under a few exceptional circumstances the gift may be recoverable, particularly when a third party has rights in the gift.[2]

The subject of acquisition of personal property by contract is covered in Chapter 15, "Sales and Warranties." Good title to personal property is warranted in any sale unless there is a stipulation to the contrary in the contract.

Property may be acquired by what is known as *confusion,* primarily when fungible goods are involved. *Fungible goods* are goods any unit of which is replaceable by any other unit—eg., grain of a particular type, crude oil, or screws in a bin. Such goods are usually sold by weight or measure.

If fungible property of two or more owners is mixed together so that the identity of each owner's property is lost, each owner owns an undivided share of the confused mass. After harvest, Black stores 500 bushels of wheat with 700 bushels of wheat belonging to White in a common granary. Each owns an undivided share of the 1200 bushels of wheat. Destruction of a part of the mass will be shared by each party on the basis of his contribution to the total.

If confusion of goods results from the tortious act of one of the parties, the innocent party will, by law be kept unharmed by the act of the other. If ownership by the tort feasor cannot be determined, the innocent party becomes owner of the total.

Abandoned property is unowned. It becomes the property of the first person to take possession of it. Taking possession of abandoned property is about the same as taking possession of something that has never been owned.

Lost and mislaid properties give rise to some legal problems. In each case the owner has unintentionally parted with possession of his property. In each case he still owns the property even though it is no longer in his possession. The finder of *lost* property has a right to the property as his own against all persons except the true owner. By contrast, the holder of *mislaid* property has possession of it as a bailee—in other words, he is holding it to give to the owner.

The distinction between lost and mislaid property is derived largely from the circumstances in which it is found. If the property is found in such a location that it is apparent that the owner intentionally placed it there and then inadvertently left it, it is mislaid. A purse left on a store counter would be mislaid; if it were found on the floor, it would have been lost.

1. See Trusts, p. 207.
2. As where the property was stolen from another, or where the donor anticipated impending bankruptcy, or where the donor was dying and diminished the property which would go to his heirs.

In many states the problems involved in lost and mislaid property have been cleared up by statute. The requirements of the statutes usually are met by advertising the property in a local newspaper. If no one claims the property within a certain time after the publication of the advertisement, the finder obtains title to the property.

Bailment

A relationship that closely resembles property ownership is that of *bailment*. The bailment relationship occurs when personal property is left by the bailor (the owner of the property) with a second person, the bailee.

Requirements. Distinguishing bailment from similar relationships requires careful definition. A bailment is made up of three elements:

1. Title to the property must remain with the bailor.
2. Possession of the property must be completely surrendered by the bailor to the bailee.
3. The parties must intend to return the bailor's property to him at the end of the bailment.

Notice the similarity between a bailment and a sale or a trade with a slight delay in it. Black stores a spare conveyor at White's warehouse for an agreed period and a fee. Black still has title to the conveyor. White has possession, and the same conveyor is to be returned to Black. Therefore, it is an instance of bailment. With certain other types of property, though, an inherent difficulty exists. If, instead of a conveyor, Black were to store grain in a common granary, he might not expect to get back the identical grain that he stored. The same might be true of animals in a herd and a few other instances where the owner does not expect that the identical property will be returned to him. Courts are not uniform in all jurisdictions in their holdings under such circumstances. Generally, though, it is held that where the owner is not to receive back the identical thing given, it is not bailment. It is held that title passed with possession and that title to other similar goods will be passed back later. It is, in other words, a *sale*.

It becomes necessary to find out who owns what when one party or the other goes bankrupt or a writ is issued pursuant to a judgment against someone's property. Property being held for a bailor by a bailee cannot be successfully taken for the bailee's debt. It is possible, though, if a judgment were to be issued against the bailor, to obtain his bailed property from the bailee.

Duty of Care. The person entrusted with the property of another has a duty to care for it. Under a particular set of circumstances the degree of care may be great, ordinary, or slight. There are two primary considerations that determine the necessary degree of care: (a) the nature of the property involved and (b) the purpose of the bailment. As to the nature of the property, it is obvious that a person should take greater care of a new automatic screw machine than of a used anvil.

The bailment relationship benefits someone—the bailor, the bailee, or both. If the bailment is to benefit the bailor only, the bailee need exercise only slight care in protecting the bailed property. He is liable only if he has been grossly negligent. Such a bailment might occur as a result of the owner requesting a friend to care for his property gratuitously.

If property is borrowed for the benefit of the bailee (as one would borrow his neighbor's lawn mower), great care is required of the bailee. The property must be returned in the form in which it was borrowed. About the only damage for which the bailee would not be responsible would be that resulting from an act of God—such as destruction by a cyclone.

Probably the most common form of bailment occurs as a benefit to both bailor and bailee. Whenever the bailor pays the bailee to take his goods and alter them in some way or just to store them for him and then return them, both parties benefit. Thus, mutual benefit bailments would occur in such situations as: leaving a car at a garage with orders to fix the transmission; transferring a machine from Cleveland, Ohio, to Fort Worth, Texas; and storing an unused machine at a warehouse during a slack period. When the bailment is to benefit both parties the bailee is required to use at least ordinary care. By ordinary care is meant the care that a person would be likely to use in preserving his own property. The bailee is liable for damage resulting from his negligence if negligence can be proved against him.

If the bailee has used the requisite amount of care in preserving the bailor's property, he will not be held liable for damages. Loss of the property or damage to it, then, will follow title and be borne by the bailor.

Bailee's Right and Duties. The bailee's right to possession of the bailed property is second only to the bailor's right. The bailee may sue a third party to recover the property if necessary.

The bailee is liable if he gives the bailed property to someone other than the owner or his agent and it is thereby lost. However, if the bailee returns the property to the person who gave it to him originally, assuming that he is still the owner, the bailee is not liable.

The bailor has a duty to disclose any known defects in the bailed property which might harm the bailee or his employees. If harm results from a failure to disclose such defects, the bailor may be held liable for tort.

Negligence Liability. Most bailments are contracts. It is possible, therefore, for the bailee, by contract clauses, to remove any or all liability for his negligence, but only if he is a private bailee. For a public or quasi-public bailee—a hotel or express company, for instance—to make such a contract stipulation would be unlawful. Such a bailee will be liable for negligence when serving the public regardless of contract clauses to the contrary. If a private bailee insists on eliminating his liability, there are only two choices open—to do business with him on his terms or look elsewhere.

Fixtures

A *fixture* is personal property attached to real property. By the attachment the personal property becomes a part of the real property. The concrete and other building materials that are worked into a plant become real property. Similarly, a heating unit or a television aerial becomes a fixture when it is attached to a house.

Generally, ownership of a fixture goes to the owner of the real estate to which it is attached. There are so many exceptions to this generality, though, that it might be restated: *unless something appears to the contrary,* the owner of the real property also owns the fixture. The main condition to the contrary is the intention of the parties when the fixture was attached. If it appears that both parties intended that ownership of the fixture should not go to the owner of the real property, the original owner will have a right to remove it. Black Construction Company undertakes the building of a structure for the White Company. A small building, complete with plumbing and lighting, is erected on the premises as a superintendent's office. Although the superintendent's office is firmly fixed to the ground, it may be removed at the end of the project.

The relationship of landlord and tenant often involves the determination of ownership of fixtures. When real property is leased or rented the tenant normally may install his personal property (e.g., machines or conveyors) and then take them with him when he leaves. If the tenant fails to remove one of his fixtures and take it with him, ownership goes to the owner of the land. Black rented a house from White. Requiring hot water, which White's house did not have, Black bought a suitable water heater from Gray Appliance Store, paying 10 percent down. Black hooked up the water heater to the plumbing and used it for a month, then moved to another state. Gray Appliance tried to get the water heater back, but could not do so since it was now part of White's real property. Gray's only available action is against Black, and he may be hard to reach by court action.

REAL PROPERTY

Real property has been defined as land and anything firmly affixed thereto. When an engineer becomes a party to building a road or renovating a manufacturing plant, he is concerned with real property. As a citizen in a community he will either own real property or lease it. Speculation in real estate is nearly as popular a sport as speculation in the stock market. We will consider here the transfer (or conveyance) of real property and some of the rights and duties created.

We may buy real property, use it pretty much as we please, and transfer it to others with very few restrictions involved. The right to "own one's own home" is almost a part of our heritage. It is only when title is threatened or, perhaps, when prescriptive rights are exercised against real property that we become aware that there are limitations.

It has not always been this way. In England, where our ideas about real property originated, no one other than the king could be said to own much of anything a few centuries ago. Under the *feudal system* there, the land belonged to the crown. The right to hold realty depended upon military service and fealty to the king, and was theoretically terminable at his option. Land was parcelled out to the gentry who, in turn, divided it up among their servants. Originally, when a landholder died another person was appointed to take his place. Very early this was replaced by provisions that tended to insure that the property would remain in the family of the grantee or tenant provided the heir was able to meet the military obligations entailed.

Little remains today in the United States of feudal rights in land. About the only remnants are the state's rights of *eminent domain,* the right of a federal, state, or local government to use private property for public benefit, and *escheatment,* the return of property to the state upon intestate death of the owner when no eligible relatives can be found.

Kinds of Estates

Estates in real property are classed as freehold, less than freehold, and future estates.

Freehold. A *freehold estate* is an estate of undetermined duration in real property. It may be an estate in fee simple or it may be an estate for life. An *estate in fee simple* is the highest real property estate known to law. The holder of an estate in fee simple has the right to complete use and enjoyment as long as this does not harm another, as well as the right to transfer the estate to anyone he chooses. Upon his death his estate will go to his heirs according to his will or according to law if he dies intestate.

A *life estate* is an estate of undetermined duration and, therefore, a freehold estate. The life upon which the term of the estate depends is usually that of the holder of the estate, but it could be that of anyone else. An estate that is terminable upon some contingency other than death but is, in some way, dependent upon the duration of a person's life is treated the same as a life estate. Black gives an estate to a young widow, terminable when she remarries. She might die without remarrying, and this would also terminate the estate. It is therefore treated in law the same as a life estate, but with marriage as an added contingency.

The rights in a life estate are not so complete as they are in fee-simple estate. The holder of a life estate may not sell it to another. Though he is allowed to use and enjoy the real property, he may not destroy its value. For instance, he may not sell the topsoil or remove ornamental trees, although he could cut and sell ripe timber.

Less than Freehold. An estate in real property that is to run for a fixed or determinable time is *less than freehold*. In law it is considered as personal property. Thus, a ten-year lease or a grant of property to run "as long as the property is used for educational purposes" would be less than a freehold estate. By contrast, a lease for "99 years, renewable forever" would be a freehold estate, since the duration is undetermined.

Future Estate. A *future estate* is an estate that someone will have when a future event occurs. According to Gray's will, Black is to get an estate left to White when White dies. Black has a future estate in the property involved.

Transfer of Real Property

Real property and real property rights are transferred in four major ways: (1) by will or inheritance, (2) by sale, (3) by gift, and (4) by legal action. We will consider the documents required in these transfers.

Will

Originally, the word *will* indicated a disposal of real property only—a *testament* disposed of the testator's personal property. Thus the use of the phrase *last will and testament* came to be popular when the testator wished to combine the two functions in one document. By common and legally accepted usage, the term *will* today indicates disposition of both real and personal property.

Age. Under common law anyone of sound mind and 21 years of age could make a valid will in the United States. Most of the states have passed laws that reduce the age requirement.

Sanity. An idiot, an imbecile, or an insane person cannot make a valid will. The law does not require a towering intellect as a testator, however. The law requires only that the testator have: (a) sufficient mental capacity to comprehend his property; (b) capacity to consider all persons to whom he might desire to leave his property; and (c) understanding that he is making a will. In these requirements there is nothing that prohibits an eccentric person from making a will. A person physically or mentally ill may make a will. Even an insane person could, in his rational moments, make a valid will.

Who May Inherit. Inheritance is not limited to relatives of the deceased under a valid will. Almost anyone may inherit. Municipalities, universities, and charitable organizations often have benefited from the terms of wills. The law does prevent inheritance by the murderer of the testator. Also, joint stock companies cannot inherit; neither can a corporation, unless the charter granted by the state allows inheritance.

Similarly, the testator has a right to disinherit as he chooses within the limits of the state statutes. Complete disinheritance of the testator's husband or wife cannot be done successfully in most states, and provision for any minor children may be required. Aside from these statutes, though, the testator may disinherit as he pleases.

Types of Wills. In addition to the ordinary written will with witnesses, two other types of wills are recognized in some states. The *holographic will* is one that is written entirely in longhand by the testator. Usually no witnesses are required. Where the holographic will is recognized—in about half of the states—it has the same standing as any other will.

A *nuncupative will* is an oral will. Such a will must be made to a certain number of witnesses and they, in turn, must reduce it to writing shortly thereafter, according to most state statutes. The testator cannot will real property to another orally. In fact, in the states where nuncupative wills have legal standing, a limit is usually placed on the amount of personal property that may be willed orally.

Witnesses. A witness to a will must be a disinterested party capable of being a witness in any judicial proceeding. It would be possible for a minor to be a witness. A person who stands to gain or lose by the will, though, would be incompetent as a witness.

Essentials of a Valid Will. There are four essentials or requirements for a valid will:

1. To pass the testator's real and personal property along to others, the will must be in *writing*. The law does not require any special kind of writing such as typing or longhand, so long as the will is written. Neither is there a requirement as to the material on which the writing appears. A will chiseled in stone or etched on glass could be as legally binding as one drawn up on a form prepared by an attorney.

2. A valid will must be *signed* by the testator and *sealed* (in those states requiring a seal). The signature normally appears at the end of a will and its validity may be open to question if it appears elsewhere.

3. Wills (except holographic) must be witnessed. State laws require either two or three persons to attest the signing of a will. The will must be signed in the presence and sight of the witnesses and the witnesses must sign in the presence and sight of each other and of the testator.

4. A will must be published. In wills, the word *publication* means something different from its ordinary sense. By publication of a will it is meant that the testator must declare that it is his last will and testament. The witnesses must know that it is a will being signed; not necessarily the terms of it, only that it is a will.

Codicils. A *codicil* is a change in a will. It is used to explain, modify, add to, or revoke a part of an existing will. If there is any question as to the date of the making of the will, the time when the last codicil was drawn is the effective date of the will. The making of a codicil to a will requires the same formality as is required in making a will.

Probate. After the death of the testator the will is presented for probate to a probate (or surrogate) court. State statutes determine the next steps, but the laws follow a general pattern. Opportunity is given to question the validity of a will. It may be held invalid for fraud, undue influence, improper execution, forgery, mistake, or incapacity of the testator. If the validity is unchallenged or any challenges attempted are unsuccessful, it is *admitted to probate*—i.e., received by the court as a valid statement of the testator's intent. If the will is successfully challenged, a previous will may be reinstated or, if no previous will exists, the result is the same as intestate death.

In drawing up a will it is customary to name someone as executor or executrix. Upon the death of the testator and probate of the will, the executor is called upon to carry out the terms of the will. This must be done *under bond* unless the testator has specifically exempted the executor from bond. If no will was left or if no executor was named in the will, the court will appoint an administrator or administratrix. The functions of an administrator are similar to those of an executor. However, if the decedent left no will, the administrator must follow state laws for distributing property following intestate death.

Deed

Conveying real property by sale or gift requires a formal transfer. Each state has jurisdiction over the real property within its boundaries. Each has set forth the formalities required to convey ownership from one person to another. Although the statutes vary from state to state, there is a general uniformity in the requirements.

Kinds of Deeds. There are two kinds of deeds in common use in the United States today: *warranty* and *quit-claim*. There are occasions when each may be used, but the better title is obtained in a warranty deed.

A *warranty deed* warrants that the title obtained by the grantee is good. In any deed the grantee gets only the title that the grantor has to give; but if grantee's title under a warranty deed is ever successfully attacked, the grantee may recover any damage suffered from the grantor. Specifically, the grantor warrants three things: (1) that he has good title and the right to convey it; (2) that there are no encumbrances other than those mentioned in the deed; and (3) that grantee and his heirs or assigns will have quiet, peaceful enjoyment of the property conveyed.

A *quit-claim deed* transfers title but does not warrant it. In effect, it is the conveyance by the grantor of whatever title he may have to the property. Such a deed might be used where inheritance of the property by several members of a family sometime in the past has left a clouded title.

Essentials of a Deed. For a deed to be valid it must be composed of several essential elements. The deed must name grantor and grantee and the consideration involved; the property must be described or otherwise identified; some words of conveyance must be used; it must be signed, sealed (in many states), witnessed, delivered, and then be accepted by the grantee.

Description of property within a city is likely to be by lot number and plat. Rural property may be described according to metes and bounds, or by the Torrens System of sections and fractions. In interpreting a deed the court will endeavor to carry out intents of the parties even when there is an error in the description. Corner markers or monuments and natural landmarks show this intent better than descriptions, since these can be seen by the parties. Thus the presence of such a marker may cause the court to disregard the technical description. If descriptions conflict in a deed, the court will interpret the wording in the grantee's favor.

Recording. Any instrument involving real property must be recorded. The recording of a deed does not pass title to the property; the making of the deed took care of that. It is still essential to record it, though, because if the grantor were to make a second deed to another fraudulently, the first grantee to record his deed would have valid claim to the property; the other grantee would be left with only his action against the grantor.

Title Search and Title Insurance. The law requires any proceeding that affects real estate to be recorded as a notice to the public. Thus, to have full force or standing at law, a deed, mortgage, lien, attachment, or other encumbrance must be filed at the local recorder's office or registry of deeds.

A *title search* involves following the changes in title to a piece of property from the initial grant from the state to the present. The result of the search should show an unbroken chain; a break is cause for suspicion and further search. A will leaving the property to more than one person may be questiond. Any encumbrance on the property is questioned to determine whether or not it has been cleared up. Of course, there is a point in time beyond which it is usually felt it is not necessary to go. If, because of destruction of records or for some other reason, ancient title cannot be cleared it will usually be certified despite the void.

In most communities *title insurance* may be purchased to warrant title to real property. The title insurance company will search the title and issue insurance for a one-shot fee based on the outcome of the search.

Mortgages. A large proportion of the buyers of real property today do not have sufficient assets to pay cash for their real estate. Money to buy the property must be borrowed from someone. The money might be borrowed on a personal loan or a note, but the problem of securing the loan exists. Black borrows $100,000 from White on a note, the money to be used to buy a house and lot. If Black, at some future time cannot pay an installment on the note, White may obtain a judgment in court for the remainder of the note. However, under most state statutes execution or attachment could not be levied upon Black's homestead and much of his personal property. Thus, White would have little real security. A mortgage offers the lender substantially greater security.

A real estate *mortgage* is a contract between the mortgagor (the borrower) and the mortgagee (the lender). The mortgagor borrows funds from the mortgagee, perhaps for the purchase of real estate, promising to return the money with interest, and offering the real estate as security.

Mortgage Theories. Mortgages began under common law as defeasible conveyances. The mortgage took the form of a deed from mortgagor to mortgagee. The mortgagor could *defeat* the deed (get it back) by paying the loan on which the mortgage was based in the time specified. If the mortgagor missed a payment, though, he had nothing. Any default gave the mortgagee absolute right of ownership. The results seemed rather harsh and the treatment has become more lenient.

In equity jurisdiction, where mortgage foreclosures are normally handled, certain mortgagor's rights have come to be recognized. Where common law considered the mortgagee as owner, allowing him to collect rents and profits from the property, mortgagor now has the rights of ownership. A missed payment no longer terminates forever the mortgagor's right; he has a certain time in which to redeem the property under a right known as *equity of redemption.*

In equity the view is taken that the whole idea of the mortgage is security for a loan—that it is nothing more than a lien. This *lien theory* is now the accepted reasoning on mortgages in the majority of the states. Some states, though, still hold to the older common law ideas in modified form, under the *title theory* of mortgages.

Formality. Since a real estate mortgage is an interest in real property, it must be in writing. The form of a mortgage, even in *lien theory* states, is similar to that of a deed, and the same formal requirements usually pertain to both. The mortgage must be signed, sealed (where the seal is recognized), witnessed, and recorded. When the mortgage is satisfied, this too must be recorded. Recording of the mortgage and its discharge serves as notice to the public of this type of property encumbrance.

Mortgagor's Duties. Security is the reason for a mortgage. While the mortgagor is owner of the mortgaged property, his right of ownership necessarily must be somewhat restricted. He cannot tear down all buildings, sell off the trees and topsoil, and then allow the mortgagee to take over the worthless remainder. To do so would diminish the mortgagee's security and constitute the tort of *waste*. With his security so threatened, the mortgagee has reason to institute foreclosure proceedings.

As the loan balance declines, the mortgagor's right to unlimited use and disposal of the property increases, since less security is required to protect the mortgagee's interest.

The mortgagor usually must pay all taxes, assessments, and insurance on the mortgaged property. Unpaid taxes and assessments become liens and endanger the mortgagee's security. Insurance on the property protects mortgagee and mortgagor alike. In case of near total destruction, the mortgage balance is paid and any remainder paid to the mortgagor.

The mortgagor must, of course, make his mortgage payments when they are due. Nonpayment constitutes default and gives the mortgagee the right to institute foreclosure. Generally, early tender of payment of the balance due need not be accepted by the mortgagee; he has a right to the interest which he has contracted for. The standard FHA and Veteran's Administration mortgages have provisions for early payment, but many other mortgages do not.

Mortgagee's Rights. The mortgagee may assign the mortgage note together with the mortgage to a third person who, then has the same rights as the mortgagee or "stands in the mortgagee's shoes." Mortgagor must, of course, be notified of the assignment if he is to be required to pay the assignee. If the mortgagor, lacking knowledge of the assignment pays the original mortgagee, he will diminish the amount of the note by the amount of the payment.

In case of default in payment or a diminishing of the security, mortgagee may foreclose. Generally, foreclosure begins as a bill in equity. The bill outlines the mortgagee's rights and the mortgagor's breach of the agreement. If foreclosure is allowed, the court will appoint a master of chancery to sell the mortgaged property. The purchaser gets a deed to the property; court costs are paid first from the proceeds, then the mortgage balance; and, finally, if anything remains it is returned to the mortgagor.

If the foreclosure sale of the property does not return enough to pay off court costs and the mortgage, the court may issue a *deficiency decree*. Such decree holds the mortgagor personally liable for the unpaid balance of the obligation. Enforcement by execution or attachment will be likely to follow. The courts lately have exhibited some reluctance to issue deficiency decrees. This is especially true where the loan was for the purchase of the real property security. It is felt that the mortgagee lent the money on the security of the realty and not on the mortgagor's personal credit. In

other words, the mortgagee must have evaluated the risks involved and the mortgagor's security when the loan was made. Recovery, then should be limited to the price this property will bring—part of value of the interest charged is payment for risk.

Mortgagor's Rights. The presence of a mortgage on real property does not, of course, prevent reasonable use of the property by the mortgagor or disposal of it subject to the mortgagee's rights. The mortgagor may use and enjoy the mortgaged property in whatever way he wishes as long as he does not harm another thereby, including the mortgagee.

The mortgaged property may be willed to another or sold or given away. The transferee takes the place of the mortgagor except as to personal liability on the debt. If the grantee takes the property merely *subject* to the mortgage he will not be held to have assumed personal liability. In other words, in case of default a deficiency judgment might still be obtained against the original mortgagor. On the other hand, if the grantee *assumes* the mortgage, he is held to replace the mortgagor in all respects.

Land Contracts. An arrangement commonly used in the purchase of real property is the *land contract*. It resembles quite closely a mortgage under the title theory. According to a land contract the purchaser, in addition to his down payment (if any), agrees to make a series of payments. When the balance is reduced to some agreed amount, frequently half the purchase price, the seller will deed the property to the buyer and take a first mortgage.

Land contracts typically include the right of the seller to declare all payments due immediately if a payment is missed or late. This, of course, has the effect of forcing forfeiture by the buyer since, if he has missed one payment, it is hardly likely that he could pay the entire balance. If the buyer gives back the land upon default, the seller takes it back with no problem of foreclosure proceedings and public resale. The seller is still owner and he merely takes over his property.

This removal of the buyer and repossession of property by the seller with no balancing of the equities involved is known as *strict foreclosure*. Strict foreclosure is allowed in connection with both mortgages and land contracts where the prospective buyer has acted very improperly or is insolvent. State laws govern the handling of land contracts as well as mortgages. Where the buyer has acted in good faith under a land contract and has made only a slight default, the equities will usually be balanced in some manner—but the buyer must ask for his relief. If the buyer merely returns the land to the seller he gives up any chance he may have to recoup a part of his loss; his equity is cut off.

Eminent Domain

The right to possession and use of property is a lesser right than the right to take such property for public necessity. The right to take private property for public use is known as *eminent domain* (or condemnation). The right of *eminent domain* may be exercised by the state or municipality or other public entity but it is not limited to these. Quasi-public enterprises or private businesses whose functions serve the public at large (e.g., railroad or power companies) also may petition for and be granted this right.

Only such private rights as are necessary to the public will be taken by eminent domain. If the taking of these rights will disturb the private owner in his use and enjoyment of the property, he will be compensated for his loss. Compensation is made according to an assessment of the market value of the right lost. Either party may appeal the assessment if he is dissatisfied.

Dedication. When land is required for public use such as a road or school playground many owners will donate land for the purpose. Such donations are known as *dedications*. Although dedications are usually made expressly by the owner to the public officials involved, they may also be implied. If public use of private property is made continuously for a period of twenty years or longer, dedication may be conclusively presumed.

No formality is required in the offer to dedicate a piece of property to public use. Similarly no formality is required for acceptance. To complete a dedication, though, there must be some kind of acceptance. When the offer is expressly made, it is usually answered by expressed acceptance. Acceptance may be implied, though, from public activities, such as maintaining the dedicated property. Public maintenance of a privately owned, but publicly used road, for instance would indicate acceptance of the road.

It may seem unnecessary to determine whether or not a particular piece of property has been dedicated to the public use. The question of tort liability, though, makes title determination important. If someone is injured because of a large hole in the road the question arises as to who owned the road and who, therefore, had the duty to maintain it.

Adverse Possession. Title to real property may be acquired by *adverse possession*. The legal requirements make it quite difficult to acquire title to land in this manner; however, if the requirements are met, a new title to the land is issued to its possessor. That is, adverse possession results not in a transfer of present title, but in an entirely new title being issued.

The right to take title by adverse possession results from the theory in law that doubt and uncertainty as to title to anything should be removed. Reasoning from this, owners should be compelled to be reasonably diligent in defending their rights. The compulsion afforded is adverse possession.

There are four general requirements for adverse possession: (1) Possession must be open and notorious actual occupation. The possessor must occupy the realty in the same manner as one might expect of the true owner. (2) The possession and occupation must be adverse to the interests of the owner. Thus, a tenant or lease-holder could not obtain title to the realty by adverse possession. (3) The adverse possession must be continuous over the statutory period required. If the state statute requires twenty years (as a large number do), two ten-year periods separated by a period when the property was occupied only by the true owner would not suffice. (4) There must be either a *claim of right* or *color of title* by the possessor. *Claim of right* is interpreted from acts of the possessor such as improving the land or fencing it. *Color of title* is some symbol of claim of ownership which is in some way defective. Payment of taxes on the property possessed is required by some statutes.

Prescription. Prescriptive rights are just about the same as title from adverse possession. About the only major difference in most states is that prescriptive rights do not give a person ownership of real property. Instead, prescription deals in rights involved with real property, particularly easements. As with adverse possession, the use of the property must be open and notoriously adverse to the owner. Black, for many years (a sufficient number according to the state statute), has crossed White's land to get to his own. Black has established an easement by *prescription*. He does not own the path across White's property, but he has a right to continue to cross it in the same manner in which he is accustomed to crossing it.

Trusts

Titles to both real and personal property may be involved in a trust relationship. Trusts involve at least two people—the trustee, who either holds or sells property, and the beneficiary, who is to benefit from the trust. In courts of equity two titles to trust property have developed. The trustee is held to have *legal title,* with the right to sell or otherwise use the property involved. The beneficiary has *equitable title* to the property. Equitable title is regarded by equity as the real ownership, even though legal title is vested in someone else.

Rights in Common

Ownership of property by several persons arises under five situations: partnership, joint tenancy, tenancy in common, tenancy by the entireties, and community property. In each situation the rights of more than one person are involved in any property dealings.

Partnership. A *partnership* is an association of two or more persons to carry on a business as co-owners for profit. People often join their assets to more effectively carry on an enterprise. Each of the partners has rights in the joined property and in other property acquired by the partnership, and each has attendant liabilities. Every partner has a right to act as agent in the business of the firm, thus adding to or disposing of assets in the particular types of transactions for which the partnership exists. Transactions outside the normal course of business, though, require agreement of all the partners.

Partners in an enterprise have what is known as *unlimited liability* for the debts of the partnership; each stands to lose some or nearly all of his personal fortune if the enterprise folds. However, for many purposes the property of individual partners is separate from that of the partnership. When a solvent partnership is dissolved—possibly because of the death of a partner or agreement to dissolve—each partner has a claim to a share of the partnership assets, but no claim upon the property individually owned by other partners. If a partnership becomes bankrupt, the firm's creditors have first claim upon the partnership assets; the creditors of the bankrupt partner have first claim against his individual property.

Joint Tenancy. A *joint tenancy* is created by a will or deed or other instrument naming two or more parties as joint tenants. Under joint tenancy each tenant has the right to use the property and may not exclude the other joint tenants from it. The right of survivorship is a main feature of joint tenancies. It is for this reason and certain abuses of it that some states take a dim view of joint tenancies.

A joint tenant may sell his share in the property to another, but the buyer then becomes a tenant in common with the remaining joint tenants. The buyer is tenant in common, but the remaining joint tenants are still joint tenants. Since survivorship acts before a will does, a joint tenant cannot successfully leave his interest in the property to his heirs.

Tenancy in Common. A *tenancy in common* is about the same thing as a joint tenancy except for the complications of survivorship. A tenant in common may leave his interest in the property to heirs or sell it to someone. The result is merely a substitution of one or more tenants in common.

Each tenant in common has an undivided part interest in the whole property. Each is entitled to a proportionate share in possession, use of, and profits from the property. If one tenant pays property costs, say taxes, he has the right to contribution from the others.

Tenancy by the Entireties. *Tenancy by the entireties* might be thought of as a special case of joint tenancy. The relation is created by conveying to husband and wife by the entireties. Neither husband nor wife can destroy the relationship without consent of the other. Real property held in this manner cannot be taken to satisfy the debts of either party under an individual judgment. It may be taken, though, to satisfy a judgment against both of them.

Community Property. Some nine of our states[3] have a somewhat exceptional treatment of property owned by husband and wife. Property acquired by a couple after their marriage is known as *community property*. Each has an equal share in it. Upon the death of either party the other is entitled to at least half the community property or to the entire amount if there is no will to the contrary. If they agree to disagree by way of the divorce court, each is entitled to half of the community property (with a few exceptions in some of the states).

Community property is property acquired after marriage. It is possible, though, for either husband or wife to have and acquire separate property either before or after marriage. The property that each has when he leaves the unmarried status is his. Also, if property is acquired by one of the two after marriage by gift, will, bequest, or descent, it is his separate property. Property obtained by trading separate property for it remains separate from community property.

Real Property Leases

Creation and Characteristics. A *lease* is a contract by which a tenant acquires something less than complete rights in real property owned by another, the landlord. The lease, itself is a *chattel real,* that is, personal property. Although a lease is a contract, it involves an interest in land so it is treated somewhat exceptionally. The original Statute of Frauds considered leases as real property transactions and required them to be in writing. The Statute of Frauds has been changed in the various states, however, so that an oral lease contract to run for a year or less (three years or less in some states) is binding.

A lease creates the relationship of *leasor* and *lessee* or, more commonly, *landlord* and *tenant*. The relationship created is not the same as that between a

---

3. Arizona, California, Idaho, Louisiana, Nevada, New Mexico, Texas, Washington, and, to a lesser degree, Oklahoma.

roomer and proprietor of a rooming house or innkeeper and guest. It involves more than these. The tenant is placed in possession of the property to use as he pleases, and as long as he abides by law and the lease, his rights to use and enjoyment are about the same as that of ownership.

The provisions of the lease contract bind the parties. This, of course, is fundamental—but it should be noted that if the lease is written, any oral provisions not reduced to writing are valueless. They are unenforceable. Black leases a building from White for the manufacture of boat trailers. White orally promises to rewire the building, but the written lease is silent about the wiring. If White does not rewire the building, Black is likely to be in the market for some extension cords. Black might be able to use the oral promises to show fraud in the creation of the contract, but this would be about the only value of the oral promise.

Those covenants expressed in the lease agreement will be adhered to strictly in a court interpretation. If the Black and White lease above contained a statement that Black "agreed to return the building in as good condition as when received, save for normal wear and tear and natural decay," such clause would hardly sound ominous. However, if the building burned down, Black might find himself replacing it or paying for it under this clause in the lease.

A lease runs for a definite period of time or is terminable at will by either party. It is this feature that makes it something less than a freehold estate. There are four general types of leases: (1) lease for a definite period of time; whether for one week or for 99 years, it is still a lease; (2) lease from year to year, month to month, week to week; (3) tenancy at will; and (4) tenancy at sufferance.

A lease for a definite period of time, say two years, needs little explanation. The tenant's rights end with the passage of time.

A *lease from month to month,* might arise from the expiration of a lease that was taken for a definite period of time. If the tenant continues to hold the property with the consent of the landlord after expiration of the original lease, he has a lease of this nature. The rent periods in the original lease dictate how long the tenant's new lease right will last; e.g., if the expired lease was to run a year at a fixed amount per month, the new lease runs from month to month.

When the tenant is given possession in such a way that a lease would be presumed and yet no term is called out, he is said to have a *tenancy at will.* It may be terminated at any time by either party.

A *tenancy at sufferance* occurs when the tenant remains in possession of the property without the landlord's consent after expiration of the lease. The landlord may terminate a tenancy at sufferance at any time.

Unless law or lease prohibits it, rights under a lease contract may be assigned to another. The result is known either as *assignment* or *sublease,* depending upon how much of the lease contract was assigned. If the entire remainder of the lease is assigned to another, it constitutes an assignment; if the lessee fails to assign all rights under the lease—he assigns only part of them—it is a sublease. In a sublease the original lessee still has property rights in the lease. Consider the Black–White lease again. Black, finding the manufacture of boat trailers quite seasonal and rather unprofitable, assigns the remaining term of the lease to Gray. If Black has reserved nothing to himself and has assigned the full remainder of the term, Gray is now bound by the terms of the original lease. If Black had assigned to Gray only a part of the building, or had assigned to him only two of the remaining, say, four years under it, this would constitute a sublease. In such a situation Gray would not be bound by the terms of the original lease, but by the terms of the new one between himself and Black.

Landlord's Rights. The landlord is, of course, entitled to the agreed compensation for the use of the premises. He has the right to come peaceably upon the premises for purposes of collecting the rent when it is due. In certain states he has the statutory right to exercise a lien against the tenant's personal property if other efforts to collect the rent fail. As a last resort, the landlord may obtain an eviction order against the tenant, thus removing him, if the rent is not paid when due. If the lease only designates a patch of ground, as many do, the destruction of a building there will not reduce the amount of rent, even though the leased property may become untenantable as a result.

At the end of the term the leased premises must be returned to the landlord in substantially the same condition as when leased. Though the landlord is not allowed to interfere with the tenant's enjoyment of the property, he may, after notice, inspect the premises for waste. Also he has a right to come upon the premises for purposes of repairing damage.

The landlord has available an action for waste against his tenant if waste can be shown. But the landlord's available action does not end with his tenant. The land is still owned by the landlord—he is *remainderman;* he is said to have a reversionary interest in the property. He, therefore, has a right to prevent third persons from injuring the property or obtaining easements upon it. The law will support an action by him for recovery or preventive relief as the case may be.

Tenant's Rights. The tenant has a right to the property he has leased free from interference by the landlord. He has a right to the appurtenances on the property, such as buildings, if such was the intent of the lease. Whether the leasehold will serve the tenant's purposes or not is beside the point unless fraud or concealment can be proved. Here the rule of *caveat emptor* applies—if the property would not serve the tenant's purposes, he should not have leased it. The tenant, of course, is at liberty to use the property for any purpose he wishes as long as the use does not violate the law or a provision of the lease.

The tenant often must improve the premises to suit them to his purpose. When the term of the lease expires, who owns the improvements? The answer depends upon the intent of the parties when the improvements were made. How much improvement could be made? The extent of improvements depends upon two factors: the purpose of the lease and the length of its term. Generally, the landlord is entitled to the return of his property in substantially the same form it was when he leased it. A lease to run 100 years would allow a great deal more alteration than a one-year lease. If the stated use of the premises or restrictions in the lease make changes obviously necessary, agreement to those changes will be implied.

Taxes and assessments are normally paid by the landlord. If the tenant finds he must pay real estate taxes or assessments to retain the leased property, he has a choice of two remedies; he may either pay the agreed rent and maintain a damage action against the landlord, or set off the payments against the rent he has contracted to pay. Of course, the landlord could shift responsibility for taxes and assessments to his tenant as part of the lease agreement if he so desired.

Liability. The tenant is liable for injuries to his employees, guests, or invitees to nearly the same extent as an owner of the property. He has a duty to keep the premises in a safe condition, a duty owed to third persons.

Unless a covenant in the lease requires it, the landlord is under no duty to repair the premises. It follows, then, that he is not liable to outsiders for injuries sustained by them. It is only rarely that the landlord may be held liable for injury to his tenant; only where a defective condition of the premises was known to the landlord and he did not reveal it to the tenant is he liable.

Easement

An *easement* is an interest in land. It gives a person a right to do something with the real property of another or a right to have another avoid doing something with his property.

It is heritable, assignable, and irrevocable. These features distinguish an easement from a license. A *license* is revocable and unassignable permission or authority to use the property of another. A valid license may be given orally. Black and White own adjoining property. Black has secured written permission to cross White's land. The writing states that the right to cross White's land pertains to "Black, his heirs or assigns." Such a grant would be held an easement since it is capable of being assigned to another. If Black sells his land to Gray the easement may be transferred to Gray in the sale. A license, on the other hand, could not be transferred.

There are several types of *natural easements*. An owner of a building owns a right (in the form of an easement) to prevent his neighbor from excavating in such a way as to cause his building to tend to fall into the hole. This is known as the right of *lateral support*. If Black sells White a piece of property that is completely surrounded by Black's property (there is no other means of access except by air travel), there is an implied natural easement across Black's property. This is known as a *way of necessity*. Although the idea did not become popular in the United States, a natural easement to light and air developed in English law; no structure could be built that interfered greatly with the natural light available to a neighbor.

Easements, other than natural, are created by grant or prescription. The grant may be in the form of a deed of the easement right itself, or of a covenant in the deed that transfers the real property. All manner of easement rights are created by grant or prescription—roads, power lines, gas lines, or sewers may cross land under such easements. Even raising the water level and inundating part of someone's land by damming a stream may involve an easement.

A person cannot have an easement in his own land. There must be a *dominant estate* (the owned property) and a *servient estate* (the easement). This, of course, would not be possible if an owner of a piece of property could possess an easement in the property in addition to complete ownership of it.

WATER RIGHTS

When a person owns a piece of real property, his ownership ordinarily extends to things on it and under it. From this, the conclusion might logically be drawn that water on and beneath the land belongs to the owner of that land. Actually, the rights may or may not extend to ownership of the water depending upon the jurisdiction. There are several different ways in which water rights are handled, ranging from individual ownership to state ownership. The question of water ownership has lately become more and more pressing, as our population has increased considerably, bringing with it an increased demand by each individual for water. As public demand for water increases still further we are likely to see continued legislation in this field. Although there is a lack of uniformity in laws and court cases on water rights, some generalities may be stated. When a problem involving water arises, it is advisable to check local legislation and court decisions.

Boundaries

The extent of real property is often limited by a watercourse or a body of water. Under common law the defining of property limits in such a manner has several meanings, depending upon the nature of the body of water.

If a nonnavigable stream separates the property of two *riparian owners,*[4] each owns to the center of the stream channel, or to the "thread of the stream" as it is known. Shifting of the stream to a new channel does not change the rights of the two owners. The property line remains as before if the channel change comes about suddenly or in such a way that the old channel may continue to be identified.

Riparian owners are entitled to additions to their property that come about gradually as a stream adds to one shore or another. If, as a result of these natural accretions, the channel gradually changes, the dividing line of the properties will also change; the property of one riparian owner will be extended at the expense of his neighbor across the stream.

The owner of property bordering on water affected by the tides owns only to the high-water mark. The foreshore (the land between the high-water mark and low-water mark) is public property, belonging to the state.

Land bordering upon navigable lakes or streams is owned to the low-water mark. In addition, the owner has the right to build a pier extending to the line of navigability. The difficulty of establishing a fixed property line by the concepts of high-water or low-water marks has led some of the states to establish riparian property lines by other means. Lines so established are not so apt to fluctuate with droughts or floods.

When a stream divides two states, state ownership does not follow any general pattern. One state may own all of the stream or none of it; or the center of the stream or the channel may be the dividing line.

Riparian Rights and Duties. A riparian owner generally has the right to *reasonable use* of water bordering his property. *Reasonable use* is a little difficult to define, however, and each controversy over the right to use water must be decided on its own merits. Generally, it means that the owner may use the water as long as he returns it in approximately the same quantity and quality as it was when it came to him. He has a duty not to pollute the water on which his property borders. For instance, he cannot dump garbage or sewage into a stream bordering his property. Such would be an unreasonable use since it would infringe upon the right of downstream riparian owners to have the water in its natural state. Domestic use of water (for drinking or bathing) is held to be more important than either agricultural or industrial uses.

Underground Water. Water and the rights to its use are not limited to the rivers and lakes on the surface of land. Who owns water in the soil (percolating water) or underground rivers? Generally, the right to use and the duty not to pollute extend to underground streams as well as surface streams.

A large quantity of water is present beneath the soil—water with no appreciable direction of flow, which is known as *percolating water.* The results of tapping this source of water are often quite unpredictable. The owner of land generally has the right to drill a well and capture a quantity of this water for his own use. However, if in so doing he lowers the level of the water table so that his neighbor cannot get water, an injury is apparent and the neighbor's cause is actionable. Where a watershed supply is quite limited the court will have a tough time assigning the rights to the water.

Irrigation has been the salvation of many areas of our country. If water must be pumped from a watershed, though, the lowered level of the water table may harm neighboring communities. Not all of the water returns to the soil; much is lost by evaporation from the ground surface and through the leaves of the plants fed.

A property owner cannot lower a water table, and thus harm his neighbor; neither may he raise the level of groundwater and do harm. The damming of a stream could result in flooded basements nearby.

Prior Appropriation. Our western states have far more serious water problems than the eastern states. The common law rights mentioned above seem satisfactory where water is plentiful, but other rules have developed in the West.

The rights of *prior appropriation* (roughly—first come, first served) and prescription predominate in the West. The first of two or more persons to appropriate water for his own use has the superior right to continued use. Continued use of water for an extended period of time, even by a nonriparian owner, gives one the

---

4. Riparian owners are owners of property bordering upon a stream or other body of water.

right to further use. Currently, the states that adhere to the doctrine of prior appropriation are: Alaska, Arizona, California, Colorado, Idaho, Kansas, Montana, Nebraska, Nevada, New Mexico, North Dakota, Oklahoma, Oregon, South Dakota, Texas, Utah, Washington, and Wyoming. If a person wishes to appropriate a large amount of water for his own uses, he must first obtain a permit to do so. In this way, use of the water is controlled for the benefit of the public.

BRIDGES v. THOMAS
118 So. 2d 549 (1960)

Allen, Chief Judge.

The appellant, as plaintiff in the lower court, filed an action to have a deed and purchase money mortgage between her and the appellee-defendants reformed so as to reduce the quantity of land that plaintiff intended to convey to defendants. The complaint also stated that "should said defendants be dissatisfied with said transaction" that the same be cancelled. The defendants answered admitting the transaction with plaintiff but averred that it was an arm's length transaction and that the plaintiff instead of setting up any mistake had only manifested a change of mind in regard to the width of the land sold to defendants. After a hearing on the merits and examining the documents involved, the lower court entered final judgment in favor of defendants.

The plaintiff was the owner of two parcels of land contiguous to each other extending from the Florida East Coast Railway across U.S. Highway No. 1 to the Indian River. The parcels are designated as No. 1 and No. 2. The creek, at its confluence with the Indian River, was believed by plaintiff to divide Parcel No. 1 from Parcel No. 2.

In the latter part of 1956, plaintiff negotiated with the defendants for the sale of part of parcel No. 1. Plaintiff did not have a survey of her land nor did she have an abstract of title, but based on the assumption that the creek was supposed to be the boundary between the two parcels, the plaintiff had defendant draw, in the presence of plaintiffs, a map of the land to be sold. This map showed the north-south limits of the land along the river to be 150 feet, the northern boundary meandering westerly along the creek to a point where the creek is 60 feet north of the southern boundary line and then along this 60 foot line west to the railroad. A price of $3,500 was set with $300 to be paid down as a binder. On October 20, 1956, the binder was paid and a receipt given. The deed conveying this land to defendants was dated and acknowledged on November 14, 1956.

Sometime in May 1957 a survey was made for defendants and plaintiff by one Heath. This survey showed the center of the creek to be 193.55 feet (instead of 148 feet as listed in the deed) north of the south boundary of parcel No. 1, with a meandering river frontage of 220 feet. Upon discovery that the creek was actually in parcel No. 2, retained by plaintiff, the defendants were requested to adjust their north boundary to 148 feet north of the south boundary. The defendants refused and this suit was filed.

To better understand this transactoin, a copy of the survey sketch is attached. The defendants contend the transaction was to cover from the center of the creek to the south boundary. Plaintiff contends it was to cover from the south boundary north 148 feet, but in no event was the conveyance to cover any land north of the creek. Plaintiff also contends that she relied on a mistaken assumption that the creek divided the two parcels of land. It appears from the record, however, that the plaintiff told the defendants, ". . . I want you folks to have what is south of the creek, but I don't want you to come across the creek . . . that is the reason I am puting this 148 feet to keep you south of the creek." It also appears that plaintiff furnished a map to an out-of-state mortgagee prior to this transaction showing the creek to be the dividing line and subsequently a similar sketch was furnished to an abstract company by plaintiff. It should be noted that this abstract was not available when the conveyance in question was negotiated and consummated thus could not be the basis of the mistake.

The deed from plaintiff to defendants provides:

Begin in center Creek at confluence with Indian River at a point approximately 148 ft. North of South line of land owned by Mae D. Bridges; thence Westerly along center of said Creek to a point which is 60 ft. North of South line of said land owned by Mae D. Bridges; thence Westerly parallel to South line of said property aforesaid and 60 ft. distance therefrom to Florida East Coast Railway right-of-way; thence Southerly along East boundary of Florida East Coast Railway right-of-way to South line of said property of Mae D. Bridges; thence East along South line of Mae D. Bridges property to the Indian River; thence Northerly meandering the West Bank of Indian River to point of beginning. Together with riparian and littoral rights thereunto belonging, excepting right-of-way of U. S. Highway No. 1 as now located. Said land being part of Government Lot 2, Section 21, Township 29 South, Range 38 East, Brevard County, Florida.

For the purpose of determining whether equitable relief should be granted in this type situation the courts have divided the cases into two general classes: (1) where the sale is of a specific quantity which is usually denominated a sale by the acre, and (2) where the sale

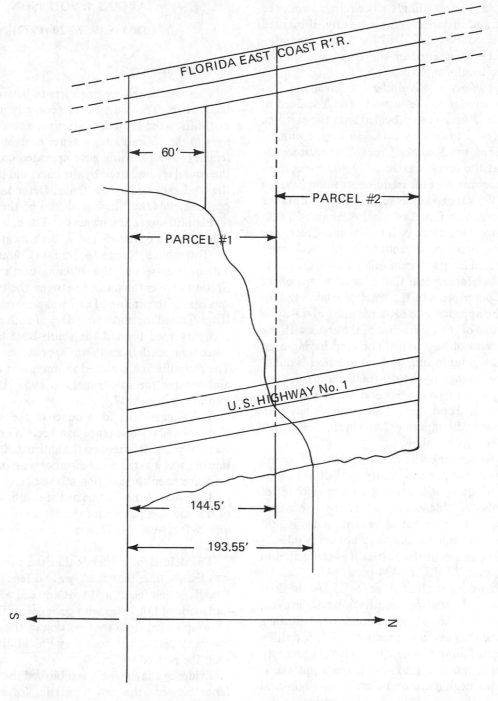

is of a specific tract by name or description, which is usually called a sale in gross. Inasmuch as the present transaction was clearly a sale by description with no mention of price per foot or acre, our discussion will be limited to sales in gross and the principles applicable thereto.

The question whether a sale is one in gross or by the acre is to be determined from the terms of the contract or deed and the surrounding circumstances. It is noted that the deed in question provides a point of beginning at the center of the creek at the confluence with Indian

River but then further describes this point of beginning as being ". . . a point approximately 148 ft. North of South line. . . ." It has long been held that monuments and natural landmarks as a general rule prevail over courses and distances for the purpose of determining the location of a boundary even though this means either the shortening or lengthening of distance. . . . The basis for the rule is that mistakes are deemed more likely to occur with respect to course and distances than in regard to objects which are visible and permanent and are accordingly more reliable evidence than courses and distances. Consequently, if marked trees or water courses be called for in the deed, distances must be lengthened or shortened and courses varied so as to conform to those objects.

The case of *Pierce* v. *Alexander* . . . involved a factual question similar to the instant case. The deed in question in the *Pierce* case provided that the east line of the parcel was to be 385 varas[5] in length with its southern terminus at Wallace Creek. The evidence established that the creek was actually 405 varas from the northern terminus of the east line, or some 20 varas south of the 385 varas point as set forth by the distance call in the deed. The Court of Civil Appeals of Texas held that since the call was for Wallace Creek, the boundary line must be extended to the creek even though the stated length thereof falls short of the creek.

It would therefore appear that in order to give effect to the entire description of the tract of land in the instant case, the approximate distance must give way to the superior call of the confluence of the creek with the river as the point of beginning. The land having been sold in bulk for a lump sum with no mention of quantity being the essence of the contract, the parties are deemed to have assumed the risk of deficiency or excess in the absence of fraud. . . . This principle has been stated by the Florida Supreme Court in *Citizen's State Bank* v. *Jones* . . . as follows:

The rule denying relief in case of a deficit or an excess is frequently applied in equity as well as at law, but a court of equity will not interfere on account of either a surplus or a deficiency where it is clear that the parties intend a contract of hazard, and it is said that although this general rule may not carry into effect the real intention of the parties it is calculated to prevent litigation, 27 R.C.L. 434 para. 147. . . .

The parties having dealt at arm's length and the deed being silent as to the specific quantity of land conveyed, any excess over and above the approximated distance must be deemed to have been precipitated by plaintiff's own conduct in failing to know the extent of property she offered and undertook to sell. If one's mistake is due to his own negligence and lack of foresight and caution, in the absence of fraud or imposition, equity will not grant relief. . . .

Finding no error by the chancellor and for the reasons assigned herein, the judgment of the lower court is affirmed.

Affirmed.

ABOOD v. JOHNSON
200 N.W. 2d 20 (1972)

McCown, Justice.

This is a boundary line dispute between adjoining landowners. The court found generally in favor of the plaintiffs, fixed the boundary line, and awarded damages to the plaintiffs for a fence destroyed by the defendant. The plaintiffs have appealed contending that the boundary line fixed by the court did not include all the land enclosed by the fence. Defendant's cross-appeal contends that the line should be the lot line.

Plaintiffs were the owners of Lot 6, and the defendant was the owner of Lot 7, both located in Section 12, Township 8, Range 16, Buffalo County, Nebraska. The quarter-section line running north and south in Section 12 was the lot line between the two lots. Lot 6 was east of the line and Lot 7 was west of it. The Platte River formed the north boundary of both properties and a county road formed the south boundary. The distance from north to south was approximately 1,500 feet. The plaintiffs first acquired an interest in Lot 6 in 1926, and became the sole owners in 1953. Defendant acquired Lot 7 in 1947.

The allegations and evidence of the plaintiffs were that a boundary line fence had been in existence for at least 50 years. It extended the entire distance of the lot line but was located some distance west of it. Plaintiffs' evidence fixed the location of the boundary line fence 61 feet west of the lot line at the south, 49.2 feet west of the line at a point near the center of the properties, and 28 feet west of the line at the north end of the properties.

The defendant contends that the correct boundary was the lot line; that there was no fence which was a boundary line fence; and that any use which plaintiffs had made of Lot 7 was with permission. Defendant has cross-appealed from that portion of the decree which fixes any part of the boundary line at any point other than the platted lot line.

Evidence convincingly established the existence of a fence between the two properties for more than 50 years. The fence was located at a point west of the quarter-section lot line but the exact distance west of the line at particular locations in prior years was not surveyed or measured. The evidence was undisputed that the plaintiffs had dug and established an irrigation

5. A *vara* is a Spanish-American measure about 33 inches long.

well approximately 40 feet west of the lot line on the south end of the properties and had used it continuously since 1957. The evidence was also undisputed that the plaintiffs had planted and cultivated crops on much of the south half of the disputed area. The evidence was convincing that plaintiffs had built and maintained a silo or ensilage bed at a point some 700 feet north of the south line of the properties. The west edge of the ensilage bed was 49.2 feet west of the lot line. The evidence is undisputed that in 1967, the plaintiffs and defendant jointly removed approximately 400 feet of fence at the north end of the property to permit gravel operations to continue moving easterly along the south side of the Platte River and from defendant's to plaintiffs' property. In April of 1971, the defendant used a bulldozer and destroyed the fence on the remainder of the property. At the trial, the evidence established that there were some broken fence posts at the south edge of the property 61 feet west of the lot line. There was a fence post on the west side of the ensilage bed approximately 700 feet north of the south line and 49.2 feet west of the lot line. There was a broken concrete fence post some 400 feet further north. A line connecting these three specific locations and extended north for the remaining distance of approximately 400 feet ends 28 feet west of the lot line at the north border. Plaintiffs' evidence was that the fence had been located on that line. There is no evidence that a fence was ever located on the lot line at any point.

The court found generally in favor of the plaintiffs, fixed the boundary line, and directed the preparation of a survey accordingly. The boundary fixed by the court commenced 43.7 feet west of the platted lot line on the south, rather than 61 feet as shown by the plaintiffs' evidence; the next point was some 740 feet north, and at that point the line fixed by the court and the line established by plaintiffs' evidence were identical, both being 49.2 feet west of the lot line. From that point, the boundary fixed by the court ran generally north but toward the east where it joined the lot line at a point some 400 feet further north. The boundary then continued to the north end of the properties on the quarter-section lot line. The court also awarded damages to the plaintiffs for the fence destroyed by the defendant.

A thorough review of the record confirms the court's general findings in favor of the plaintiffs. The boundary line fixed by the court, however, does not fully conform to the evidence. The trial court did not indicate the basis upon which the boundary was fixed, nor make specific explanatory findings. The court determined that the dividing line on the north 400 feet of the property should be the quarter-section lot line rather than any

fence line. Comments in the record indicate that determination was made because the plaintiffs and defendant had jointly removed the fence in that area for the sole purpose of removing gravel from both properties in 1967.

We believe this case is controlled by *McCain* v. *Cook*. . . . It is the established law of this state that, when a fence is constructed as a boundary line between two properties, and parties claim ownership of land up to the fence for the full statutory period and are not interrupted in their possession or control during that time, they will, by adverse possession, gain title to such land as may have been improperly enclosed with their own. See also *Ohme* v. *Thomas*. . . .

"After the running of the statute, the adverse possessor has an indefeasible title which can only be divested by his conveyance of the land to another, or by a subsequent disseisin for the statutory limitation period. It cannot be lost by a mere abandonment, or by a cessation of occupancy, or by an expression of willingness to vacate the land, or by the acknowledgement or recognition of title in another, or by subsequent legislation, or by survey." *McCain* v. *Cook,* supra.

Under the evidence here, the plaintiffs had acquired title to the property long before 1967, either by boundary line acquiescence or adverse possession, or both. Plaintiffs' title could be divested by nothing short of a validly executed deed, by adverse possession, or by other legal means not pertinent here.

The county surveyor who testified on behalf of both parties also prepared exhibit 57, describing the boundary fixed by the court. The surveyor also prepared a survey reflecting the fence line as established by plaintiffs' evidence. The survey was exhibit 50, but it was not admitted into evidence because a copy of it had not been furnished to the defendant within the time specified in the pretrial order. The surveyor did testify as to the location of the various points used as the basis of that survey and that he had observed the fence posts at the points shown. Exhibit 50 designates the line on which the dividing line fence was located in reference to the north-south quarter-section line. Exhibit 50 may not be complete insofar as a legal survey description of the property line is concerned, but subject to any such technical completion, it designates the boundary line established by the plaintiffs' evidence.

The decree of the district court was generally correct, but it should be modified by subsituting the division line shown in exhibit 50 for the line shown in exhibit 57 and described in paragraph 2 of the journal entry. As so modified, the decree is affirmed.

Affirmed as modified.

REVIEW QUESTIONS

1. Distinguish between:
   1) personal property and real property.
   2) sale and bailment.
   3) warranty deed and quit-claim deed.
2. In what ways may personal property be lawfully acquired?
3. What are the requirements for a valid will?
4. Why must real estate transactions be recorded?
5. In what ways are a mortgagee's interests in real property similar to those of a landlord?
6. How are water rights controlled in your state?
7. List the points made by the court leading to its decision in *Bridges* v. *Thomas*.
8. The deed in *Bridges* v. *Thomas* mentioned littoral rights. What are littoral rights?
9. Return to the requirements for adverse possession and compare these requirements with the court finding for the plaintiff in *Abood* v. *Johnson*.

20

Intellectual Property

PATENTS

Everything in our civilization that distinguishes us from other forms of life results from man's creative efforts. Some of the most commonplace objects were marvels of invention only a few years back, and inventions keep coming at an ever increasing pace.

Engineers often find themselves in fortunate positions to invent things or to improve upon others' inventions. They are particularly favored by training in science, natural selection, general temperament, and by the nature of engineering jobs for this endeavor. Inventions generally involve the application of scientific principles to practical problems with a practical solution as the objective. The relationship between invention and the training offered by engineering curricula seems quite obvious. Because of the engineer's training and talents he should be alert to the possibilities of making inventions, of patenting them, and of exploiting them.

Suppose that Mr. Black, an engineer, has just invented an entirely new type of internal combustion engine after many months of effort. The engine will run on a most readily available resource and promises to have a longer life than even the best competitors. What should Black do to secure for himself the fruits of his creative efforts? Probably the best course would be for him to contact an expert on patents—a patent attorney or a patent agent. But even though the task of obtaining a patent is delegated to another, there is still considerable information Black should have. What, for instance, may be patented? What is the nature of a patent? Who is entitled to one? What protection does it afford? What could prevent an inventor from getting a patent? How long will it take, and what delays can be anticipated? This chapter represents an effort to answer these and a host of other questions that are likely to arise.

The Patent Right

One meaning of the word *patent* is "open or disclosed, obvious or manifest." In a sense these terms could be applied to the right issued to an inventor by the Patent Office. To obtain the protection afforded by a patent, the inventor must make a full and complete disclosure of his invention. No material feature or component may be withheld. The revelations must be such that a person skilled in the field could, by use of the patent, duplicate the thing patented.

The patent right is often regarded as a contract between the government and the inventor. In consideration for complete revelation of the invention, the government gives the inventor the right to *exclude others* from making, using, or selling his invention. The right extends for seventeen years from the date of issue, after which the content of the patent becomes public property. It is worth noting that the patent right is the right to exclude others from making, using, or selling the invention—it is *not* the right to make, use, or sell it. The reason for this is to avoid conflict with state or other federal laws that might prohibit making, using, or selling such things as those covered in the patent; or a statute might prohibit, making, using, or selling things in a particular *manner* proposed by the inventor. Also, the inventor should not be able to impose upon the prior rights of another or of the public in general merely because he has obtained a patent for his invention. For instance, if use of the invention injures another, the presence of the patent should not allow the injury to continue.

The patent right is usually considered to be a unique kind of personal property. It may be bought or sold, mortgaged, licensed, or given or willed to another nearly as easily as any other personal property.

History of Patents

Concerted efforts by a government to recognize and reward an inventor by giving him a protected monopoly in his invention began during the fifteenth century in the Republic of Venice. In England the practice began as a grant of monopoly from the sovereign. Not only were grants of monopolies made to inventors; there were also grants of trade monopolies of various types. Abuses of these grants led to the passage in 1624 of the Statute of Monopolies which terminated the right of the sovereign to create monopolies. However, the granting of a monopoly to an invention's inventor was preserved in the sixth section of the act, which provided for letters patent to be issued. Letters patent were provided for in the Statute of Monopolies, but no formal procedure for granting patents was set up in England until 1850.

The United States colonists brought the idea of patenting inventions to the new world. Prior to the adoption of the U.S. Constitution, patents were issued by the individual colonies, but there was at least one glaring defect in this system. A patent issued by a colony secured the rights in only that colony. If someone in another colony could obtain the essence of the patent, he was free to make any use of it that he might desire. It is for this reason, among others, that the U.S. Constitution provides that Congress shall have the power "to promote the progress of science and useful arts, by securing for limited times to authors and inventors the exclusive right to their respective writings and discoveries."

The first United States patent law was enacted in 1790. Since then there have been numerous changes of the law and of the governmental department in which it is to operate. The Patent Office[1] is now headed by a commissioner of patents and is part of the Department of Commerce. A 1952 Act of Congress (effective January 1, 1953) revised the law and brought it up to date.

THE RIGHT TO PATENT

The right to patent was neatly summarized in section 31 of the old U.S. Patent Act (35 USCA). It stated that: "Any *person* who has *invented* or *discovered* any *new* and *useful art, machine, manufacture,* or *composition of matter,* or any new and useful *improvements* thereof, or who has invented or discovered and asexually reproduced any distinct and new variety of *plant,* other than a tuber-propagated *plant,* not known or used by others in this country, before his invention or discovery thereof, and not patented or described in any printed publication in this or any foreign country, before his invention or discovery thereof, or more than one year prior to his application, and not in public use or on sale in this country for more than one year prior to his application, unless the same is proved to have been abandoned, may, upon payment of the fees required by law, and other due proceeding had, obtain a patent therefor." The present Act broke this summary into separate elements intended to be more convenient for court use. However, the meaning expressed is virtually unchanged. The only major change concerns foreign patents as a bar to patentability; foreign patents now act as bars to patentability only if they were granted before filing of an application for a similar patent in the United States.

Certain rules of practice have had to be developed in the Patent Office to aid in interpreting the patent law. Congress has declared in the legislation the right of the Patent Office to set up and maintain such rules; there are now some 350 of them.

Any person (other than a Patent Office employee) may be granted a patent if he meets the patent law requirements. A corporation is a legal person, but it cannot effectively apply for a United States patent. The corporation could acquire patent rights from another and exploit those rights, but the patent must first be applied for by a *natural person.* Natural persons include those of foreign nationality as well as United States citizens.

A patent may be applied for by someone other than the inventor under two circumstances. If the inventor is deceased, the executor or administrator of his estate may apply for a patent in his place. If the inventor is insane, his guardian may apply for him.

A patent may be issued to two or more persons as joint inventors. However, under this circumstance it must be shown that all the joint owners had a hand in creating the invention. Mere partnership in an enterprise or financial assistance does not make one a joint inventor.

Assignment. Since a United States patent has the attributes of personal property, it may be assigned to another person. Assignment of the rights may take place either before or after the inventor obtains his patent, but it requires a sworn, written notification to the Patent Office to be effective. Notification of the Patent Office completes the assignment of an existing patent. If the office is not informed within three months and the patent is subsequently assigned to another, the first assignee to record the transaction will be the new owner of the right.

A patent may be issued directly to the assignee. When this is done it is the patent application that is assigned by the inventor. The inventor must still swear to the specification, but any patent resulting from the application will be granted to the assignee.

It is, of course, possible to assign a portion of the rights acquired in a patent. But the interest assigned must be specified in the assignment. That is, assignment of a half interest in the royalties resulting from a patent could be determined and upheld in court. However, if the assignment is of, say, ten percent of *the patent* to another, the assignee would be likely to be held to have a share in the patent equal to that of the

---

1. The correct name is the United States Patent and Trademark Office of the Department of Commerce, but is is most commonly called the *Patent Office,* or abbreviated *PTO,* in patent and trademark cases.

inventor. It is improbable that the court would endeavor to determine what portion of the entire patent would constitute ten percent of its value.

Shop Rights and Contracts to Assign. As a general rule the patent rights to an invention belong to the inventor. If the inventor used his employer's time and equipment in his creative activities, however, it seems only right that the employer *should* have some benefit from the result. The employer's right to benefit under these circumstances is well established in the law. Some difficult questions arise in this connection, though, in regard to contracts made in anticipation of invention, and inventions created wholly or partly on the employee's own time.

A *shop right* is a nonexclusive, nonassignable license to use an employee's invention. It is limited to the particular employer involved and does not imply that compensation or royalties will be paid to the inventor. It arises from implications of the employment rather than from an express agreement to assign patent rights. Both the inventor and the employer have rights arising from the patent grant, and neither can exclude the other.

An employer's shop right to inventions created by his employees on company time and with the employer's facilities is an implied right; or, in some cases, the right may be based on estoppel. However, the duty to assign patent rights may be made the subject matter of a contract. The employee agrees that as consideration for his continued employment he will assign any patents obtained by him to his employer. The duration of the agreement may even be made to run for a period beyond termination of the employee's services; and the scope of the agreement may be made to go well beyond things the employee might invent that would immediately benefit his employer. There is a limit, though, to the all-encompassing extent to which such agreements may be taken. It is considered against public policy for the length of time to be excessive, thus practically forcing a scientist or engineer to be tied to one employer or else change his profession. It is common for such agreements to run for a year beyond termination of the employee's services. In essence, though, the question of an employer's rights to a patent obtained by a former employee is determined by when the creative work was done. If the work on which the patent was based was done for the former employer and if he had a right to the assignment of patents obtained by the employee, he may maintain an action for assignment of the patent.

It has become almost standard practice to require new engineers and scientists to agree to assign patent rights. Some companies even include an agreement to assign patent rights in their employment application forms. In many instances this is merely an added precaution taken by the company. If an employee has been specially hired and retained to do research aimed toward obtaining patents, the patents so obtained must be assigned to the employer, even without an agreement to assign. On the other hand, the right of an employer to patents obtained by someone not hired to invent is a matter of shop rights, unless there exists a contract to assign. Since companies frequently move their technical personnel into and out of research as occasions demand, the precaution of an agreement as to patents seems well founded.

Consider Mr. Black and his engine. Assume him to be an engineer for the White Manufacturing Company. If Black developed an engine as a result of research and development endeavors for which the White Company paid him a monthly salary, Black's patent would have to be assigned to the company. If he was hired as a manufacturing engineer, but spent part of his time developing the engine with company facilities, the company would be entitled to at least shop rights in the engine. With shop rights the White Company could still make, use, and sell the engine even though the patent was granted to Black.

Mr. Black may have used his own facilities in developing the engine at home in the evenings. Would the White Company then have a right to his invention? Yes, they would if he was hired to invent or if he had agreed to assign patents to the White Company as a condition of his employment. Incidentally, an oral contract to assign future patent rights is quite enforceable if the contract terms can be proved.

Invention or Discovery. One of the fundamental requirements of the subject matter of a patent is that it constitute an invention or discovery. These two terms, *invention* and *discovery,* are often used synonymously, despite differences in meanings. Discovery refers to the recognition of something in existence that has never before been recognized; whereas invention refers to the production of something that did not exist before.

To be *patentable,* an invention or discovery must not only be new or previously unrecognized, it must also be something extraordinary. An obvious or normally predictable result is not patentable. That which an ordinary skilled person in the field involved could reasonably be expected to do may not be patented.

There is no fixed yardstick of patentability in law. Each case is judged on its own merits in the light of similar cases and the present state of the art in the field of the subject matter of the proposed patent. The standard is more strict now than it was fifty years ago, and it was tighter then than it was in the early 1800s. This only reflects progress in the various fields of learning. That which might have been patentable at the turn of the century is now commonplace to journeymen in the field involved. In the final analysis, it is the judgment of the court that determines whether true invention or discovery is present. Since the judgment is a human opinion, it is open to the criticism that it could be fallible and must, in some instances, be arbitrary. True though this may be, no adequate substitute for human judgment on the question has yet been found.

New and Useful. A patentable invention cannot be something that is already known and used by others in the art involved. The rule is tempered with reason, though, as are most rules of law. For instance, an invention that duplicates something discovered and used by an ancient Egyptian civilization and then lost by intervening posterity might be patentable even though it was known at one time.

Description of the invention or discovery in a printed publication can be a bar to obtaining a patent. Certainly, if the subject of the invention was published by another prior to the "inventor's" conceiving it, it cannot be said to be new. Publication by the inventor more than a year prior to his application will also prevent him from getting his patent rights. In this connection the courts have found it necessary to determine what is meant by the term *publication*. Publication is held to consist of making information available to the general public. It is not held to occur if the information is given to a restricted group of persons with the express or implied condition that the information is not to become public knowledge. Probably one of the best examples of a publication is a patent; copies of patents issued in the United States are available to anyone at a price of $.50 each ($.20 for design patent copies).

For a publication to bar patenting of an invention it must contain more than mere reference to a new idea. Sufficient details must be present to enable the reader to make practical use of the idea. Black, for instance, might safely refer in a published article to a new internal combustion engine in very general terms. As long as he does not reveal the essence of his secret, he does not start the year's limitation "clock."

Public use or sale of the invention more than a year prior to filing the patent application also defeats patentability. If Black started manufacturing his engines for public sale, time would start to run against the year from the date of his first sale. Of course, there are many shades of gray between black and white. For instance, manufacture of a limited number of the machines for experimental use by certain persons would be unlikely to be held *public use*. This is especially true where the inventor has told the users of the need for secrecy regarding the invention. Court cases have held that use can be experimental even though the inventor may have made some profit in the transactions. *Experimental use*

is essentially determined by the intent of the inventor and the nature of the invention. Some things must be tried publicly. Experimental use of a new road-surfacing material, for example, would almost necessarily require public use in a street or highway if truly typical conditions are to be encountered.

The invention must be useful as well as new. In court the word *useful* is given a rather broad interpretation; essentially, it is required that no harmful effect on society would result from the invention. The primary purpose of the entire patent system is to benefit the public. It follows, then, that the inventor of something that offers the public no benefit or something that is harmful or immoral should not be entitled to a patent.

An invention must be operable or capable of being used if it is to satisfy the test of useful purpose. If there is any question of the ability of the invention to perform as claimed, the Patent Office may require a model to be built for demonstration purposes. Thus, if the examiner had difficulty understanding Mr. Black's use of internal combustion, he might demand a model from Black. However, the requirement of a model is exceedingly rare. It is much more likely that the examiner would require an affidavit from someone who had actually seen the engine in operation.

Patentable inventions extend to ornamental designs and curiosities. But there is one type of invention the patent office refuses to accept as patentable—any "perpetual motion" machine. It is held that such machines are obviously inoperable and will continue to be until the law regarding conservation of energy is repealed.

The Atomic Energy Act of 1954 rather severely restricts the right to obtain a patent on any invention to be used in the production or utilization of fissionable materials. Under this act no patent for an invention or discovery of this nature may be issued without approval of the Atomic Energy Commission.

What Is Patentable. An idea is not patentable, but the machine, process, or thing into which it has been incorporated may be. That is, a physical law or principle, no matter how beneficial it is likely to be to mankind, is not patentable as long as it remains an idea. Its physical embodiment might be patented, though, if the other tests of patentability are met.

There are seven categories of inventions or discoveries which may be patented:

1. An *art* or a *process* or *method* of doing something—for instance, a new type of heat treatment of steel alloys to obtain certain physical properties.
2. A *machine*. By this term is meant an inanimate mechanism for transforming or applying energy, such as Black's newly conceived internal combustion engine.

3. A *manufacture*—anything (other than a machine) made from raw material by hand, machine, and/or art. Many manufactured products would serve as examples—a golf club, ash tray, paper clip, and paper pulp.

4. A *composition of matter*, such as a new dental filling material to be used in place of dental amalgam or gold, or a new drug or an insecticide.

5. A new and useful *improvement* of any of the above. Original patents in a field are often followed by numerous improvement patents. For instance, Morse's original telegraph patent was followed by over 5,000 improvements. Similarly, the basic patent on radio receivers, the automobile, and plastics each began a long parade of patented improvements.

6. A new variety of *plant*—roses, camellias, hybrid corn, etc.

7. A *design*. A particular pattern, form, or contour of a product may be patented. Cloth, door chimes, soft drink bottles, and packages for goods have been subjects of design patents. Design patents run for shorter periods of time than other patents. The prospective patentee may apply for a design patent to run 3½, 7, or 14 years at his option. There is only a slight additional cost for applying for the long-term design patents.

PATENT PROCEDURE

The patent procedure is set up in such a manner that an inventor can obtain a patent on his invention without outside help. Why, then, should a prospective patentee spend money to obtain the services of a patent attorney or a patent agent? There are two main reasons for the expenditure: First, although the procedure as outlined here may appear fairly simple, technicalities and complications may arise requiring knowledge that only a person who has studied patent procedure could possess. Second, unless the patent is properly drawn up and presented, the patentee is likely to find the wording he used (which was so clear to him) to be worthless.

Usually the reason for getting a patent on something is a practical one. The patentee hopes to make money on his patent by selling or licensing it to another, or by using the product, or by manufacturing and selling it himself. An application for a patent, then, is usually based on economic motives. If an invention is worth patenting at all, the inventor should try to get the greatest possible coverage of the rights he wishes to protect. The extent of coverage is largely determined by the wording of the claims. An experienced patent attorney or agent can word claims in such a manner that the broadest possible coverage is obtained.

There is another prominent motive for obtaining patents—one in which the profit resulting from the patent is not so apparent. It stems from the fact that realistic limitations must be imposed upon the claims in any patent—that is, the coverage in the claims can extend only as far as they can be justified by the nature of the invention and its novelty. To prevent others from entering the field of the patent by patenting things similar to what is already covered, the holder of a patent may attempt to "fence in" his invention. This is done by obtaining patents that are not necessarily profitable by themselves, but which serve as protection for a profitable patent. This practice, known as "blocking," is commonly used by many large enterprises. Since the practice causes frustration to outsiders, many criticisms have been leveled against it. It is lawful, however, unless the result would tend to give the patent holder a monopoly over an entire industry.

Preliminary Search. It is often said that "there is nothing new under the sun." Certainly it is improper to assume that because something is not being manufactured and sold commercially it is not covered by a patent claim. Somewhere in the more than four million United States patents, or in the multitude of foreign patents, there is quite likely to be something similar to the subject matter under consideration. The purpose of a patent search is to ferret out any similar patents to find out if a patent can be obtained on the new "invention," and, if a patent can be obtained, the limits of the claims to be made. The preliminary search is not a legal requirement; it is, rather, a practical expedient. It is quite possible to apply for a patent without a preliminary search, but it is not advisable unless the applicant or his attorney is completely familiar with the state of the particular art.

Application

A patent application has three main components: (1) the petition, (2) the specification (including claims and possible drawings or a model), and (3) the oath. In addition to these requirements, the proper fee must accompany the application. The fee for all patents other than design patents is $65.00 plus $10.00 for the second through the tenth added claim and $2.00 for each added claim after that. The cost for issuing a patent is $100 plus $10 for each page of specification plus $2 for each sheet of drawing. The fee for design patents depends upon the length of time for which the patent is expected to be issued. There is a $20 fee for each design application plus a fee for the patent issue. A 3½-year design patent requires a $10.00 filing fee; a 7-year patent, $20.00, and a 14-year patent, $30.00.

Petition. The *petition* is addressed to the Commissioner of Patents and is essentially a request for a *grant of letters patent* to be issued to the applicant. It may also include an assignment of the power of attorney to the applicant's attorney or agent, although the power of attorney may be attached on a separate sheet.

Specification. The purpose of a patent specification is to clearly describe the invention. The clarity of description must be such that any skilled person in the field to which it pertains could, by using the specification, reproduce the invention and use it. One or more drawings or, possibly, a model may be required to make the invention clear. Models, however, are not permitted as substitutes for drawings unless they are specifically requested by the Patent Office.

Drawings are required in all cases in which they are meaningful. This includes almost every type of invention except compositions of matter and processes. There are special rules pertaining to patent drawings and, for this reason, most applicants hire specialists to make them. However, almost any engineer with the required drawing courses and a little experience could make an acceptable patent drawing by following the Patent Office rules. In addition to being technically acceptable, the drawings must meet the following requirements: (1) They must be made with India ink on heavy, high quality paper which is calendared and smooth. (2) The sheets must measure 10 inches wide by 15 inches high, with a marginal line 1 inch inside each edge. (3) A 1¼-inch space must be left under the top margin as a title block. (4) For shading, the light must come from the upper left-hand corner at a 45° angle. Shading lines cannot be less than one-twentieth of an inch apart. (5) Clear and careful lettering is required with a minimum height of one-eighth inch. (6) Each sheet should be signed by the applicant or his attorney in the lower right-hand corner, either just above or just below the lower marginal line. Actually, signature of the drawings is not a legal requirement if reference to the drawings is made in other signed papers; but the practice is to sign the drawings as well.

A substantial portion of the body of a specification is usually devoted to describing the various views shown in the drawing and the functions of the components. Prior to the explanation of the drawing details, though, there should be a brief summary of the substance and nature of the invention and, possibly, its purpose. The claims usually follow the detailed description of the invention.

The *claims* are the operative part of a patent. They are essentially statements of what is considered to have been invented and, therefore, preserved to the patent holder. From the applicant's point of view, the broader the coverage in the claims, the greater the rights he will have in his patent. Others may legally encroach upon his invention only to the point where they enter the area set aside in the claims. It would be to Black's advantage, for instance, to claim "an internal combustion engine." Of course, such a claim would not be allowed; but if it were, he could force manufacturers of any kind of internal combustion engines to cease manufacturing or pay him royalties. The natural end result would be payment to Black to use the right he reserved in his claim. The principles of internal combustion engines are well within the public domain, however, so Black's claim would have to be restricted to a particular kind of engine. His claim might read "an internal combustion engine comprising . . ." with the remainder restricting the claim to what is new in his invention.

Patents are available to the public. If a particular patent appears highly profitable economically, it is likely to attract many people who will try to approach the invention as closely as possible without infringement. It is here that patent claims are really tested. Prospective producers of patented things may go to great lengths to avoid the payment of royalties; and, if they can find a way around the claims in a patent, there is no reason why they should not use it.

Since it is difficult to tell in advance just what portion of an invention will come to be most important in the next seventeen years, a considerable amount of imagination must be used in making the claims. Sometimes an apparently insignificant component of a device becomes more lucrative than the invention itself.

The original claims in a patent application should be as broad as the preliminary investigation will allow them to be. If they are too broad, the patent examiner who investigates the application will require them to be narrowed down. If they are too narrow in the beginning, however, they cannot be broadened without giving up the original patent application date—and there may be good reason for retaining that date. The time lost in making a new start is by itself reason enough.

Oath. The third essential component of every patent application is an *oath* taken by the applicant that he believes himself to be the originator of the thing for which he requests a patent. The oath may be taken before any person authorized by law to administer oaths, either in the United States or in the appropriate foreign country (if the applicant is not a citizen of the United States). A statement of citizenship (e.g., "citizen of Great Britain") is required in the oath.

Examination

When the patent application has been prepared it is submitted to the Patent Office for examination and the hoped-for approval. There, the application will be sent to one of the examining divisions (specializing in particular types of subject matter) and will be assigned to a patent examiner. Actual examination takes place according to filing dates on the applications. An application may wait for six months or even a year before the examiner gets to it.

The application is examined to determine whether it complies with the law and whether it is truly something new. If the form and content of the application comply with the law, the examiner turns next to the question of novelty. The search undertaken by the patent examiner is likely to be considerably more extensive than the applicant's preliminary search. This is particularly true if the patent is allowed.

To determine if the proposed invention is really something new, the patent examiner does not confine his examination merely to old patents. His search is likely to take him far afield. Not only will he compare what is proposed with what has been patented; he is likely to examine trade publications, newspaper articles, even mail order catalog descriptions and goods for sale in local stores.

The result of the examiner's work is communicated to the applicant or his attorney in a letter known as an *Office Action*. If the examiner has found reason to quarrel with the novelty of the proposed invention, the entire application will be rejected.

The Office Action may show that some or all of the claims have been allowed. If all claims are allowed, the patent will be issued promptly. If some claims are allowed and others rejected, the applicant may obtain a patent including the approved claims. Or he may reword or further restrict the rejected claims to resolve the conflict between them and the claims on a previous patent (as cited in the Office Action). Or he may, as some do, just quit in disgust.

Amendment. Amendment of an application that has been wholly or partly rejected as a result of its first examination is nearly always complex and legally technical. Sometimes a visit to the examiner by the applicant's attorney can clear up misunderstandings or indicate rewording of certain claims to make them satisfactory. Much of the attorney's time will be spent in studying the claims in the application and comparing them with other patents and publications with which the examiner has noted a conflict. Amendments to the application are then made. It may be noted that making changes in a patent application requires considerable care as well as knowledge of Patent Office rules.

Generally, nothing may be deleted or replaced by the applicant or his attorney. Rather, a separate paper must be drawn, answering all the examiner's objections and recommending deletions or substitutions to cure the defects. The examiner will then make the corrections upon resubmission of the application. The original numbering of the claims is retained, although some of the claims may have been deleted. That is, if there were twelve claims in the original application and Number 11 were to be eliminated, the last claim would still be numbered "12."

Response. Response to an Office Action (submission of the amended application) must take place within six months. If no response is made within the time limit, the application is considered to be abandoned.

Reexamination of the altered application may require another waiting period of from six months to a year, and these rounds of Office Action followed by response may continue indefinitely. If a year per round may be assumed, considerable time may elapse between the original application and the final outcome. If the applicant persists in his pursuit of a patent, the rounds of Office Action and response will end with either attorney and examiner finally agreeing on the claims and issuing a patent, or with the applicant's receipt of a *final rejection*.

Appeal

A Patent Office final rejection is not always *final*. There is still the possibility of appeal of the examiner's decision to a higher tribunal. Relatively few applications are finally rejected by the examiner and then appealed by the applicant. Generally, the attorney and the examiner can find common ground before appeal is necessary. Nevertheless, an appeal procedure exists as a final recourse in patent law.

There exists within the Patent Office itself a Board of Appeals to which a finally rejected application may be taken. Although the Board of Appeals is a part of the Patent Office, there is no apparent tendency in it to support the examiner's position. Frequently the Board will overrule the examiner and allow claims that were previously rejected.

If the Board of Appeals maintains the examiner's position, a further appeal is still possible. The applicant may take his case to the United States Court of Customs and Patent Appeals, or he may file a civil action against the Commissioner of Patents in a United States District Court. If either action is successful the court will order the patent to be issued. However, just as with court actions involving administrative boards, the Patent Office must be shown to be clearly wrong for the court to overrule its decision.

Interferences

Less than one percent of the patent applications filed in the United States Patent Office become involved in interference proceedings. Nevertheless, the possibility does exist, and the cost involved is sufficient to make consideration of it worthwhile.

An *interference* arises when two patent applications claim the same thing. It may also arise as a conflict between an application and a patent that has been issued for less than a year. As the result of either conflict, one adversary wins and holds the disputed claim or claims, and the other has nothing but experience as a reward for his trouble.

In an interference, just as in any other court case, the winner is determined by the evidence he can present to the court. Records of the conception and pursuit of the invention must have been made and kept if a contestant is to have a chance of winning. This is one reason why nearly all companies require research staff members to keep notebooks of activities (with pages serially numbered and entries dated), and why periodic witnessing of the contents is necessary. Anyone capable of understanding the contents, by the way, may act as witness to research notes.

Interference actions are taken first to the Patent Office Board of Patent Interferences. Appeal may be taken to the Court of Customs and Patent Appeals or to a United States District Court.

The purpose of an interference proceeding is to discover which of two adversaries actually was the first inventor. Two dates become important: the date of conception of the invention, and the date of reduction to practice. If one party to an interference action can prove that he was first to conceive of the invention and first to reduce it to practice, he is apparently entitled to the patent protection.

Proof by one party of his first conception is not enough. He may also be called upon to prove that he pursued the idea with reasonable diligence. If the other party was not first to conceive of the invention but was first to reduce it to practice, he may obtain the desired patent by proving that his adversary temporarily abandoned the idea.

Inventions are often developed in secrecy, but too much secrecy can be fatal to the patent. Proof of reduction to practice requires testimony of someone who actually saw the invention in operation.

Assume that Mr. Black's claims in his application for his engine are met with an interference. That is, one Mr. White has made application to patent a similar engine and has posed claims that conflict with Black's. The case is tried before the Board of Interferences. White proves by records that he has the earlier date of conception of the invention. If White can now prove an earlier date of reduction to practice, the patent will issue to him. It may be noted that his patent application will serve as constructive reduction to practice. If White's application preceded Black's, White is known as the *senior party* in the interference action. However, Black built and ran his engine before witnesses while White was still at the drawing board. At this point White may still get the patent if he pursued his invention with reasonable diligence, since he first conceived of it. Black's hope for the patent rests on his ability to prove that White temporarily abandoned his endeavor for a substantial period—even four or five weeks might be enough. Here, White's records (if he has made and kept them) will protect his rights; without records he could lose what is rightfully his.

Allowance and Issue

Few patent applications become involved in appeals; fewer yet in interference. Most patent issues between applicant and examiner are settled satisfactorily in the early stages, and either a patent results or the application is abandoned.

If the patent is allowed, the applicant is sent a notice of *allowance.* Usually the patent will be issued on the fifth Tuesday following the date of allowance.

INFRINGEMENT AND REMEDIES

The grantee of a patent has a lawful monopoly. His right would be virtually worthless, though, if he could not resort to court action to enforce it. It must be, and is possible to prevent others from encroaching upon the area of activity reserved to the patentee. He should be compensated if another enters the field reserved to him and benefits because the patent exists, and such compensation is available to him.

Action for patent infringement may be brought in any Federal District Court. The nature of the action and procedural rules are those of equity jurisdiction; as you recall from Chapter 3, actions at law and in equity are merged in the federal courts. Thus the action may be taken for damages alone or for an injunction with or without damages.

In a patent infringement action the defendant is charged with having made, used, or sold the subject matter in violation of the protected monopoly created by the patent. The essence of such actions is the test of extent of coverage in the claims compared with the alleged violation. It is here that unnecessary restrictions in claims are likely to prove costly, for the court will interpret the claims literally. What the patentee has given up in the Patent Office he cannot get back in court; he has only the claims allowed. For instance, the claims in one patent referred to "wide, thin members" in a structure. When a competitor used cylindrical members to accomplish the same purpose he was sued for infringement. The court held that this was not infringement. Where another patent claim referred to a semicircular connector, use of a different connector or none at all did not infringe.

Defense

The defendant in an infringement action has essentially two defenses available to him. He may seek to prove either that the patent or the claims in it are invalid or that his action did not amount to infringement.

To support an infringement action the claim must be restricted to the disclosure in the patent. That is, if the patentee has gone ahead and made so many changes in his invention that the claims no longer cover it, he is no longer protected. The reasoning seems obvious, but cases on this point indicate that the discovery of their lack of protection comes as a shock to some patent holders.

All patents are presumed in court to be valid. It may be possible, though, for the defendant to attack the validity of the patent by quarreling with some fact of the application, e.g., the statement in the oath that the applicant believes himself to be the first inventor of the subject matter. Successful attack voids the patent, and the defendant is free to continue his acts.

The defendant may claim noninfringement. He may admit the acts complained of and then show that the claims are not sufficiently broad to cover these acts.

Remedies

Patent infringement usually gives the patent holder a right to a damage action; and from this arises the cause for injunction in such cases. If the defendant were not to be prohibited from continuing to infringe, the right to damage action could be repeated throughout the life of a patent.

The present patent law provides for either an injunction, or damages, or both in patent infringement cases. In addition, the law allows the court to go beyond mere compensatory damages and assess up to triple damages against the defendant if the case appears to warrant it. In exceptional cases the court may even assess a reasonable amount for plaintiff's attorney's fees.

The measure of compensatory damages in an infringement case is the cost to the plaintiff. However, the statute requires that he be compensated at least in the amount that he lost or would have lost in royalties because of the infringement. A question may arise as to the amount of royalties to be assessed if the plaintiff has not made previous royalty arrangements with others. If such is the case, the question is settled either by a jury or by the court with or without the aid of an expert witness.

There is a time limitation on infringement damages. Assessment of damages may not cover more than six years of past infringement.

Patent Markings

If the plaintiff in an infringement case is to get any damages for the injury to him, he must have informed the defendant of his patent. Marking patented goods with the patent number serves this purpose. If he has not so marked the goods, the plaintiff must prove that he informed the defendant of the existence of the patent and that the infringement continued.

Goods sold are often marked *Patent Pending* or *Patent Applied For*. These terms have no legal force as far as infringement is concerned. However, if they are used when, in fact, no application has been filed, it may be assumed that the purpose of their use was to defraud the public. The current statute provides for a $500 maximum fine for each such unlawful use of the term. Half the fine assessed goes to the member of the public who brings the charge.

COMMENTS AND CRITICISMS

Our patent law is not perfect; very few man-made laws are. But despite its imperfections, the present law seems to accomplish the objectives stated by the framers of our Constitution reasonably well.

One common criticism is directed toward the time and money required to obtain a patent. At first, the criticism seems well founded. As to time, few patents are issued in much less than a year after the application is begun; some have required twenty years or more. This sounds like a long time to wait for patent protection but, as a practical matter, the delay is seldom a hardship, and it may be beneficial to the applicant. The greater the delay in securing a patent, the greater is the period of practical patent protection. Theoretically, the applicant is not protected while his application is being processed. However, should he be threatened with an infringement, the patent office will usually expedite issuance of the patent to permit legal action upon the infringement. Thus, practically, the applicant has a large measure of protection during the application processing period. The monetary outlay required is extremely variable, depending upon the complications that may arise. It is possible for the patent to cost only very nominal fees. However, it is more likely to cost somewhere from $500 to several thousand dollars. A patent is somewhat like other business ventures; its probable cost in time and money should be weighed against the expected results. If economic analysis shows that the venture is likely to be profitable, it should be undertaken. If the likelihood of profit is remote, perhaps it is better kept and used as a trade secret. Many large corporations require that a patent be able to pay for all the expenditures required in a certain length of time, or recover a given profit on the investment, to justify the cost of securing it and setting up to produce the patented item. A pay-off period of two or three years is not uncommon; neither is a 20% or a 25% profit margin.

Occasionally the objection is heard that the small inventor has no fair chance to compete with the research staffs of big business. It is true that research staffs are brought together to form a talented team and that in many things teamwork pays off. But even in a research team the best ideas often flow from one individual or a small nucleus of people. Once the idea occurs it is often pursued more rapidly by teamwork, but if a free-lance inventor has the first date of conception and has pursued it diligently, speed by a corporate research team is to no avail.

Members of industrial research staffs sometimes complain that they are not adequately compensated for patents they obtain and assign to their employers. Perhaps the criticism is valid, for many receive only a dollar or five dollars for the assignment. However, the opposite argument is that the staff member is paid not only for the time during which he has produced something worthwhile, but also for other time when was not so productive. It is also argued that the research job, considering only the activities involved, is more enjoyable to many people than the alternatives. The employer also has an investment in research facilities which must return a profit if he is to survive.

Corporations are often criticized because, with large funds available, they can indulge in long legal battles to win infringement or interference suits from less fortunate competitors. Sometimes the mere threat of a long legal battle is sufficient to intimidate a small inventor. While this criticism has merit, there is still an end of the road for all legal battles. If the small inventor is legally right and has chosen his attorney well, the mere preponderance of legal counsel on the other side is not sufficient to win. There is another aspect to this particular problem. Because of the large costs involved and the unpredictability of the outcome of such cases, large businesses frequently pay out of court rather than undertake a court defense. That is, if an inventor claims

that a manufactured product infringes his patent and demands a small royalty, the manufacturer may purchase the patent or pay the royalty rather than go to court, even though the particular patent might be only remotely related to his product. The legal cost to the patent holder could be quite small, since he can usually find an attorney willing to work on a contingency basis.

One criticism which seems to have greater validity than most is concerned with the public welfare. Suppose someone invents something of great public benefit—perhaps a cure for cancer. Under present law it would be possible for him to obtain a patent monopoly on his invention, make very limited amounts of the cure, and sell it at enormous prices. All but wealthy people would be deprived of the cure—a rather appalling prospect.

Other criticisms are directed at the extension of the scope of patent monopolies by pooling arrangements, tying clauses, marketing agreements, and the like. Some of these arrangements are lawful; others are not. Most of the criticisms have some merit.

Despite shortcomings in the patent law, protection is afforded to the inventor, and the rate of technological advance of our economy is testimony to its success. Imperfect though it is, it is successful.

TRADEMARKS

Property consists of intangibles as well as tangibles. The good will attached to a trademark or a trade name is an example of intangible property. Trademarks are like other forms of property in that they can be bought, sold, and used by the owner as he chooses as long as he does not thereby injure someone.

In the United States the law regarding trademarks is primarily the common law plus the Lanham Trademark Act of 1946. Under this Act *trademark* is defined: "The term 'trademark' includes any word, name, symbol, or device or any combination thereof adopted and used by a manufacturer or merchant to identify his goods and distinguish them from those manufactured or sold by others."

Trademarks are products of the Industrial Revolution. When goods were manufactured primarily for local sale, there was little need to identify the manufacturer. With specialization in manufacture and expanded marketing, successful advertising came to require that the manufacturer's products be identified in some way. The trademark resulted.

A trademark differs from other property in that part of its value is in its unique design. It identifies the products of a particular manufacturer. The intent of the trademark is to distinguish the goods of one manufacturer from similar goods of all other manufacturers.

Many distinctive marks and names are successfully used to identify products, but the more common the mark or expression used, the more difficult it is to make a trademark out of it. It would, for instance, be difficult to obtain a trademark right for *pencil* or *automobile* because of the commonness of these words. The words *Eagle Chemisealed* and *Ford,* though, distinguish particular products of specific manufacturers.

Just as the descriptive terms *pencil* and *automobile* would be difficult to establish as trademarks, geographical names and family names present problems. The test of these three categories when used as a trademark is whether the name has been used for sufficient time so that it identifies a specific product. A "Cincinnati" shaper is a product of one manufacturer; similarly a "Ford" car is the product of another. A company manufacturing, say, dental materials could use either "Ford" or "Cincinnati" to identify its products. A new company manufacturing automobiles, though, could not use the Ford name to identify its products, even though the owner might be named Ford. New competitors in a field have a right to identify themselves and the location of their business, but not in such a way that trademarks or trade names are infringed. If a new company in Cincinnati were to manufacture shapers, they could not imprint the name *Cincinnati* on the side of the shapers in such a way that prospective purchasers would be confused as to the manufacturer.

It is quite proper and common to use words ordinarily not connected with a description of the product in establishing a trademark or trade name. The use of "Bluebird" for a television set, for instance, would be lawful as long as it did not conflict with a similar name and product of another T.V. manufacturer. Many companies have made up their own words as trademarks or trade names. This is one of the safest means of identification.

Any trademark or trade name may be lost if the word, after use, becomes established as a term descriptive of many products. "Aspirin" was once a trade name of only one product; so was "Cellophane."

The right to use a particular name for one's products is established by the first user of the name. A person who subsequently uses such established name in the sale of competing products may be enjoined from continuing the use of the name. If the use of the mark or name was made intentionally in violation of another's right, damages may be recovered—even to triple damages.

The market in which a second user of a trademark advertises and sells is important in establishing the right to use a particular mark. As long as the second user does not harm the originator's market he is free to use a similar mark. That is, the simultaneous use of similar marks for goods to be sold in strictly local markets several thousand miles apart probably would not be cause for an injunction until the markets actually overlapped.

Common law and equity have established rights in the use of trademarks as well as penalty for abuse. Federal and state legislation (where statutes have been passed) have modified the established rules only slightly. The federal act (Lanham Act), covering goods in interstate commerce, provides that the user of an identifying mark may register the mark. If the mark is used for five years after registration without protest, the one using such a mark is presumed to be the first user and the mark is his. Registration of the mark continues for twenty years; if the mark is still in use after the twenty-year period, it is renewable upon application by the party using it. Nonuse of a trademark for a two-year period is *prima facie* evidence of abandonment.

Licensing and Franchising

As commonly used, the terms *license* and *franchise* appear to be essentially interchangeable. The meaning as far as trademarks are concerned simply implies that someone (licensor or franchisor) allows someone else (licensee or franchisee) to use his established trademark. The complexities of such arragements range from a simple allowance to use a trademark to a complex system in which the licensee receives the right to use the trademark, confidential know-how in production of a good or service, and the benefit of widespread promotion and, in turn, must submit to strict control of his management and the quality of his product. Licenses and franchises are generally deemed beneficial to the public in that they tend to promote competition and assure a certain standard of quality. They provide an efficient means of combining centralized planning, direction, and standard-setting with local control and initiative.

The licensing and franchising coin has another side, of course. If the use is such as to defraud the public, the trademark will not be protected. Consider the Brown Construction Company, a company so eminently successful in construction contracting in a particular city that it expands to new markets. Since its trade name and logo have become symbolic of high quality in construction, it expands by a licensing arrangement in which it reserves the right to dictate the company management and quality, requiring a monetary return for the use of its well-promoted name. (Similar arrangements are common in the fast food, automotive repair, and numerous other industries.) Suppose the Brown Construction franchises come to be far different from what the original reputation and the promotion imply. The construction practices turn out to be very poor at many of the outlying locations, and this leads to public deception. Under such a circumstance, Brown risks not only legal actions for the poor performances, but also loss of protection of the trademark. Thus, Brown has a legal as well as a practical duty of caution in releasing his trademark to licensees and in monitoring their quality.

COPYRIGHTS

The law of copyrights is primarily the law of the Copyright Act of 1976 (effective 1 January 1978). The copyright is a form of legal protection for "original works of authorship"—literary, dramatic, musical, artistic, and certain other intellectual endeavors. It gives an exclusive right to copy, publicly perform, or display (appropriate as to type of work copyrighted) to the holder of the copyright. It is a property right that may be sold or leased to another by contract. The cost of a copyright is maintained at a fairly nominal level. For example, the cost to copyright a published book is $10 plus two copies of the book, sent to the United States Copyright Office, Library of Congress, Washington, D.C. 20559.

A copyright of a literary work does not preserve the ideas presented in the published material. What is protected is the language used. Anyone is free to use and publish the ideas as long as the wording used is not identical with that in the previous publication.

Notice and Duration

The copyright notice for a literary work is simply the symbol © or *copr.* or *copyright,* followed by the year of first publication and the name of the copyright owner; for example,
© 1983 James Black
Without the notice some of the copyright protection may be lost, and if the notice is omitted from the published work for five years, the copyright itself may be lost.

The life of a copyright of something created after 1978 is the creator's life plus 50 years beyond his death. Works made for hire (e.g., an instruction booklet for a company's product) have a copyright duration of 75 years from publication or 100 years from creation, whichever is less.

Fair Use

Copyrighted works are generally meant to be used, and in our current state of technology a complete prohibition against copying would be unrealistic. There-fore, the idea of *fair use* has become a substantial part of the law. Generally, the use the copyright protects against is use that deprives the copyright owner of the income to be realized from exploitation of his copyright. For example, it is fair use of a textbook to make copies of short excerpts from it for classroom use as long as the amount copied and used in not a substantial part of the text. Permission from the copyright owner, of course, cures a would-be infringement.

DANN v. JOHNSTON
96 S.Ct. 1393 (1976)

Mr. Justice Marshall delivered the opinion of the Court.

Respondent has applied for a patent on what is described in his patent application as a "machine system for automatic record keeping of bank checks and deposits." The system permits a bank to furnish a customer with subtotals of various categories of transactions completed in connection with the customer's single account, thus saving the customer the time and/or expense of conducting this bookkeeping himself. As respondent has noted, the "invention is being sold as a computer program to banks and to other data processing companies so that they can perform these data processing services for depositors." . . .

Petitioner and respondent, as well as various amici, have presented lengthy arguments addressed to the question of the general patentability of computer programs. . . . We find no need to treat that question in this case, however, because we conclude that in any event respondent's system is unpatentable on grounds of obviousness. . . . Since the United States Court of Customs and Patent Appeals (CCPA) found respondent's system to be patentable, *Application of Johnston,* supra, the decision of that court is accordingly reversed.

I

While respondent's patent application pertains to the highly esoteric field of computer technology, the basic functioning of his invention is not difficult to comprehend. Under respondent's system a bank customer labels each check that he writes with a numerical category code corresponding to the purpose for which the funds are being expended. For instance, "food expenditures" might be a category coded "123," "fuel expenditures" a category coded "124," and "rent" still another category coded "125." Similarly, on each deposit slip, the customer again, through a category code, indicates the source of the funds that he is depositing. When the checks and deposit slips are processed by the bank, the category codes are entered upon them in magnetic ink characters, just as, under existing procedures, the amount of the check or deposit is entered in such characters. Entries in magnetic ink allow the information associated with them to be "read" by special document-reading devices and then processed by data processors. On being read by such a device, the coded records of the customer's transactions are electronically stored in what respondent terms a "transaction file." Respondent's application describes the steps from this point as follows:

> "To process the transaction file, the . . . system employs a data processor, such as a programmable electronic digital computer, having certain data storage files and a control system. In addition to the transaction file, a master record-keeping file is used to store all of the records required for each customer in accordance with the customer's own chart of accounts. The latter is individually designed to the customer's needs and also constructed to cooperate with the control system in the processing of the customer's transactions. The control system directs the generation of periodic output reports for the customer which present the customer's transaction records in accordance with his own chart of accounts and desired accounting procedures." . . .

Thus, when the time comes for the bank customer's regular periodic statement to be rendered, the programmed computer sorts out the entries in the various categories and produces a statement which groups the entries according to category and which gives subtotals for each category. The customer can then quickly see how much he spent or received in any given category during the period in question. Moreover, according to respondent, the system can "(adapt) to whatever variations in ledger format a user may specify." Brief for Respondent, at 66.

In further description of the control system that is used in the invention, respondent's application recites that it is made up of a general control and a master control. The general control directs the processing operations common to most customers and is in the form of a software computer program, i.e., a program that is meant to be used in a general-purpose digital computer. The master control, directing the operations that vary on an individual basis with each customer, is in the form of a separate sequence of records for each customer containing suitable machine instruction mechanisms along with the customer's financial data.

Respondent's application sets out a flow chart of a program compatible with an IBM 1400 computer which would effectuate his system.

Under respondent's invention, then, a general-purpose computer is programmed to provide bank customers with an individualized and categorized breakdown of their transactions during the period in question.

II

After reviewing respondent's patent application, the patent examiner rejected all the claims therein. He found that respondent's claims were invalid as being anticipated by the prior art. 35 U.S.C. sec. 102, and as not "particularly pointing out and distinctly claiming" what respondent was urging to be his invention. . . .

Respondent appealed to the Patent and Trademark Office Board of Appeals. The Board rejected respondent's application on several grounds. It found first that, under 35 U.S.C. sec. 112, the application was indefinite and did not distinctly enough claim what respondent was claiming to be his invention. It also concluded that respondent's claims were invalid under 35 U.S.C. sec. 101 because they claimed non-statutory subject matter. According to the Board, computer-related inventions which extend "beyond the field of technology . . . are nonstatutory," . . . and respondent's claims were viewed to be "non-technological." Finally, respondent's claims were rejected on grounds of obviousness. 35 U.S.C. sec. 103. The Board found that respondent's claims were obvious variations of established uses of digital computers in banking and obvious variations of an invention, developed for use in business organizations that had already been patented. . . .

The CCPA, in a 3–2 ruling, reversed the decision of the Board and held respondent's invention to be patentable. The Court began by distinguishing its view of respondent's invention as a "record-keeping *machine* system for financial accounts" from the Board's rather negative view of the claims as going solely to the "relationship of a bank and its customers." 502 F.2d, at 770 (emphasis in CCPA opinion). As such, the CCPA held, respondent's system was "clearly within the 'technological arts,' " id. at 771, and was therefore statutory subject matter under 35 U.S.C. sec. 101. Moreover, the Court held that respondent's claims were narrowly enough drawn and sufficiently detailed to pass muster under the definiteness requirements of 35 U.S.C. sec. 112. Dealing with the final area of the Board's rejection, the CCPA found that neither established banking practice nor the Kirks patent rendered respondent's system "obvious to one of ordinary skill in the art who did not have (respondent's) specification before him." . . .

In order to hold respondent's invention to be patentable, the CCPA also found it necessary to distinguish this Court's decision in *Gottschalk* v. *Benson,* supra, handed down some 13 months subsequent to the Board's ruling in the instant case. In *Benson,* the respondent sought to patent as a "new and useful process," 35 U.S.C. sec. 101, "a method of programming a general-purpose digital computer to convert signals from binary-coded decimal form into pure binary form." . . . As we observed, "(t)he claims were not limited to any particular art or technology, to any particular apparatus or machinery, or to any particular end use." . . . . Our limited holding, id. at 71, 93 S.Ct., at 257, 34 L.Ed.2d, at 279, was the respondent's method was not a patentable "process" as that term is defined in 35 U.S.C. sec. 100 (b).[1]

The Solicitor of the Patent Office argued before the CCPA that *Benson's* holding of nonpatentability as to the computer program in that case was controlling here. However, the CCPA concluded that while *Benson* involved a claim as to the patentability of an "apparatus" or "machine" which did not involve discoveries so abstract as to be unpatentable:

> " 'The issue considered by the Supreme Court in *Benson* was a narrow one, namely, is a formula for converting binary-coded decimal numerals into pure binary numerals by a series of mathematical calculations a patentable *process?*' (emphasis added). . . .
>
> "(T)he instant claims in *apparatus* form, do not claim or encompass a law of nature, a mathematical formula, or an algorithm." 502 F.2d, at 771 (emphasis in CCPA opinion).

Having disposed of the Board's rejections and having distinguished *Benson* to its satisfaction, the Court held respondent's invention to be patentable. The Commissioner of Patents sought review in this Court, and we granted certiorari. . . . We hold that respondent's invention was obvious under 35 U.S.C. sec. 103 and therefore reverse.

III

As a judicial test, "invention"—i.e. "an exercise of the inventive faculty," . . . has long been regarded as an absolute prerequisite to patentability. . . . However, it was only in 1952 that Congress, in the interest of "uniformity and definiteness," articulated the requirement in a statute, framing it as a requirement of "nonobviousness."[2] Section 103 of the Patent Act of 1952, 35 U.S.C. sec. 103 provides in full:

> "A patent may not be obtained although the invention is not identically disclosed or described

or set forth in section 102 of this title, if the differences between the subject matter as a whole would have been obvious at the time the invention was made to a person having ordinary skill in the art to which said subject matter pertains. Patentability shall not be negatived by the manner in which the invention was made."

This Court treated the scope of sec. 103 in detail in *Graham* v. *John Deere Co.,* 383 U.S. 1, 86 S.Ct. 684, 15 L.Ed.2d 545 (1966). There, we held that sec. 103 "was not intended by Congress to change the general level of patentable invention," but was meant "merely as a codification of judicial precedents . . . with congressional directions that inquiries into the obviousness of the subject matter sought to be patented are a prerequisite to patentability." . . . While recognizing the inevitability of difficulty in making the determination in some cases, we also set out in *Graham,* supra, the central factors relevant to any inquiry into obviousness: "the scope and content of the prior art," the "differences between the prior art and the claims at issue," and "the level of ordinary skill in the pertinent art." Ibid. Guided by these factors, we proceed to an inquiry into the obviousness of respondent's system.

As noted, supra, at 1395–1396, the Patent and Trademark Office Board of Appeals relied on two elements in the prior art in reaching its conclusion that respondent's system was obvious. We find both to be highly significant. The first was the nature of the current use of data processing equipment and computer programs in the banking industry. As respondent's application itself observes, that use is extensive:

> "Automatic data processing equipments employing digital computers have been developed for the handling of much of the record-keeping operations involved in a banking system. The checks and deposit slips are automatically processed by forming those items as machine-readable records. . . . With such machine systems, most of the extensive data handling required in a bank can be performed automatically."

It is through the use of such data processing equipment that periodic statements are ordinarily given to a bank customer on each of the several accounts that he may have at a given bank. Under respondent's system, what might previously have been separate accounts are treated as a single account, and the customer can see on a single statement the status and progress of each

---

1. "The term 'process' means process, art, or method, and includes a new use of a known process, machine, manufacture, composition of matter, or material. 35 U.S.C. sec. 100(b).

2. S. Rep. No. 1979, 82d Cong., 2d Sess., 6(1952); H.R. Rep. No. 1923, 82d Cong., 2d Sess., 7(1952).

of his "sub-accounts." Respondent's "category code" scheme, see supra, at pp. 1394–1395, is, we think, closely analogous to a bank's offering its customers multiple accounts from which to choose for making a deposit or writing a check. Indeed, as noted by the Board, the addition of a category number, varying with the nature of the transaction, to the end of a bank customer's regular account number, creates "in effect, a series of different and distinct account numbers. . . ." Petition for Certiorari, at 34a. Moreover, we note that banks have long segregated debits attributable to service charges within any given separate account and have rendered their customers subtotals for those charges.

The utilization of automatic data processing equipment in the traditional separate account system, is, of course, somewhat different from the system encompassed by respondent's invention. As the CCPA noted, respondent's invention does something other than "provide a customer with . . . a summary sheet consisting of net totals of plural separate accounts which a customer may have at a bank." . . . However, it must be remembered that the "obviousness" test of sec. 103 is not one which turns on whether an invention is equivalent to some element in the prior art but rather whether the difference between the prior art and the subject matter in question "is a difference sufficient to render the claimed subject matter unobvious to one skilled in the applicable art. . . ."

There is no need to make the obviousness determination in this case turn solely on the nature of the current use of data processing and computer programming in the banking industry. For, as noted, the Board pointed to a second factor—a patent issued to Gerhard Dirks—which also supports a conclusion of obviousness. The Dirks patent discloses a complex automatic data processing system using a programmed digital computer for use in a large business organization. Under the system transaction and balance files can be kept updated for each department of the organization. The Dirks system allows a breakdown within each department of various areas, e.g., of different types of expenses. Moreover, the system is sufficiently flexible to provide additional breakdowns of "sub-areas" within the areas and can record and store specially designated information regarding each of any department's transactions. Thus, for instance, under the Dirks system the disbursing office of a corporation can continually be kept apprised of the precise level and nature of the corporation's disbursements within various areas or, as the Dirks patent terms them, "Item Groups."

Again, as was the case with the prior art within the banking industry, the Dirks invention is not equivalent to respondent's system. However, the departments of

organization and the areas or "Item Groups" under the Dirks system are closely analogous to the bank customers and category number designations respectively under respondent's system. And each shares a similar capacity to provide breakdowns within its "Item Groups" or category numbers. While the Dirks invention is not designed specifically for application to the banking industry many of its characteristics and capabilities are similar to those of respondent's system. . . .

In making the determination of "obviousness," it is important to remember that the criterion is measured not in terms of what would be obvious to a layman, but rather what would be obvious to "one reasonably skilled in (the applicable) art." . . . In the context of the subject matter of the instant case, it can be assumed that such a hypothetical person would have been aware both of the nature of the extensive use of data processing systems in the banking industry and of the system encompassed in the Dirks patent. While computer technology is an exploding one, "(i)t is but an evenhanded application to require that those persons granted the benefit of a patent monopoly be charged with an awareness" of that technology. . . .

Assuming such an awareness, respondent's system would, we think, have been obvious to one "reasonably skilled in (the applicable) art." There may be differences between respondent's invention and the state of the prior art. Respondent makes much of his system's ability to allow "a large number of small users to get the benefit of large-scale electronic computer equipment and still continue to use their individual ledger format and bookkeeping methods." Brief for Respondent, at 65. It may be that ability is not possessed to the same extent either by existing machine systems in the banking industry or by the Dirks system.[3] But the mere existence of differences between the prior art and an invention does not establish the invention's nonobviousness. The gap between the prior art and respondent's system is simply not so great as to render the system nonobvious to one reasonably skilled in the art.[4]

3. The Dirks patent does allow "the departments or other organizational users (i.e., the analogues to bank customers under respondent's invention) to retain their authority over operative file systems" and indicates that "(p)rogramming is very easy and different programs are very easily coordinated."

4. While "commercial success without invention will not make patentability," *Great Atlantic & Pacific Tea Co.* v. *Supermarket Equipment Corp.,* . . . we did indicate . . . that "secondary considerations (such) as commercial success, long felt but unsolved needs, (and) failure of others" may be relevant in a determination of obviousness. . . . Respondent does not contend nor can we conclude that any of these secondary considerations offer any substantial support for his claims of nonobviousness.

Accordingly, we reverse the Court of Customs and Patent Appeals and remand this case to that court for further proceedings consistent with this opinion.

So ordered.

Reversed and remanded.

Mr. Justice BLACKMUN and Mr. Justice STEVENS took no part in the consideration or decision of this case.

DUNLOP HOLDINGS LIMITED
v. RAM GOLF CORP.
524 F.2d 33 (1975)

Stevens, Circuit Judge.

Plaintiff sued Ram for infringement of its patent covering an unusually durable golf ball.[1] Ram convinced the district court that the patent was invalid because the invention had been made by a third party named "Butch" Wagner. Ram proved that Wagner had publicly used the new golf ball before February 10, 1965, the earliest date that plaintiff can claim invention;[2] however, Wagner had not disclosed his formula to the public. The questions on appeal are (1) whether the district court's findings on the prior invention issue are supported by the record, and (2) whether the nondisclosure of the method of making an article which is in public use is the kind of concealment or suppression that avoids the bar to patentability in Section 102(g).[3]

The patent covers the discovery that certain synthetic materials,[4] when fabricated by themselves (or with minor amounts of compatible materials), produces a golf ball cover with exceptional cutting resistance. An example of the material described in the patent is a DuPont product named "Surlyn." Golf balls made of Surlyn, with or without minor additives, infringe the claims in plaintiff's patent.

As noted, the date of invention claimed by plaintiff is February 10, 1965. In April of 1964, DuPont was trying to find a commercial use for its Surlyn, a recently developed product. Shortly thereafter, Butch Wagner, who was in the business of selling re-covered golf balls, began to experiment with Surlyn as a golf ball cover. He first made some sample balls by hand and then, using a one-iron, determined that the material was almost impossible to cut. He obtained more Surlyn and made several dozen experimental balls, trying different combinations of additives to achieve the proper weight, color, and a texture that could easily be released from an injection molding machine. By November 5, 1964, he had developed a formula which he considered suitable for commercial production and had

decided to sell Surlyn-covered balls in large quantities. The date is established by a memorandum recording his formula, which Wagner wrote in his own hand and gave to his daughter for safekeeping on the occasion of her son's birthday.[5]

During the fall of 1964, Wagner provided friends and potential customers with Surlyn-covered golf balls. By the end of the year he had purchased enough Surlyn to produce more than 20,000 balls, and by February of 1965 he had received orders for over 1,000 dozen Surlyn-covered balls. By the end of 1965, he had ordered enough Surlyn to produce more than 900,000 such balls. Without commenting further on the evidence, we note our conclusion that there is ample support in the record for the district court's findings that Wagner had discovered the use of Surlyn as a golf ball cover before November 5, 1964, had reduced the discovery to practice before February of 1965, and did not abandon the invention before his death in October of 1965.

We recognize that Wagner continued to experiment with different formulae after his decision to go into commercial production and that he encountered some problems with cracked covers. These facts do not undermine any of the district court's findings on the prior

1. U.S. Patent No. 3,454,280 covering "Golf Balls Having Covers of Ethylese-Unsaturated Monocarboxylic Acid Copolymer Compositions," issued to Dunlop Rubber Company Limited, a British company, as the assignee of the two individual inventors, pursuant to a U.S. Patent Application filed Feb. 2, 1966, and a British application filed on Feb. 10, 1965.

2. 35 U.S.C. Sec. 104 provides in part that ". . . an applicant for a patent, or a patentee, may not establish a date of invention by reference to knowledge or use thereof, or other activity with respect thereto, in a foreign country, except as provided in section 119 of this title." 35 U.S.C. Sec. 119 allows priority from the date of filing in certain foreign countries including Great Britain. Plaintiff is thus barred from establishing a date of invention by reference to its activities in Britain prior to Feb. 10, 1965, the date of its British application.

3. 35 U.S.C. Sec. 102 provides: "A person shall be entitled to a patent unless. . . .

* * * * * *

(g) before the applicant's invention thereof the invention was made in this country by another who had not abandoned, suppressed, or concealed it. . . ."

4. The parties use the term "copolymers" which we understand to refer to a kind of synthetic rubber or plastic material. The description in the patent is of

"A golf ball comprising a core and a cover, said cover being formed of a composition comprising a copolymer of ethylese and at least one unsaturated monocarboxylic acid containing from three to eight carbon atoms, said copolymer containing up to thirty percent by weight of said acid." Patent No. 3,454,280 column 6, lines 45–50.

5. In the district court's original findings this handwritten memorandum was erroneously described as a page in Wagner's formula book, whereas it was actually a separate sheet of paper. We attach no significance to this error, which the district judge subsequently corrected, since the testimony unequivocally established the genuineness of the document. We also find no substance in appellant's objection to the district court's making this minor correction in its findings after the notice of appeal was filed. . . .

invention issue. The patent claims are broad enough to encompass any golf ball cover made principally of Surlyn and there is no doubt that Wagner had made a large number of such golf balls and successfully placed them in public use.[6] The only novel feature of this case arises from the fact that Wagner was careful not to disclose to the public the ingredient that made his golf ball so tough.[7] For that reason plaintiff argues that he "suppressed or concealed" the invention within the meaning of Sec. 102(g).

Since 1850 it has been settled that a patentee may be entitled to credit for making a new discovery or invention even though someone else actually made the discovery before he did. . . . That case established the proposition that an abandonded invention will not defeat the patentability of the rediscovery of "lost art."[8] The case has also been cited for the proposition that an inventor who had merely made a secret use of his discovery should not be regarded as the first inventor. . . .

Gillman involved a patent on a machine which had previously been developed by a man named Haas; Haas had used the machine in his own factory under tight security. The output from the machine had been sold, but the public had not been given access to the machine itself. In holding that Haas was not the first inventor, Judge Hand drew a distinction between a secret use and a noninforming public use.[9] There had been only a secret use of the Haas machine and therefore he was not regarded as the first inventor.

This case certainly involves neither abandonment nor a mere secret use, for the evidence clearly demonstrates that Wagner endeavored to market his golf balls as promptly and effectively as possible. The balls themselves were in wide public use. Therefore, at best, the evidence establishes a noninforming public use of the subject matter of the invention.

If Wagner had applied for a patent more than a year after commencing the public distribution of Surlyn-covered golf balls, his application would have been barred notwithstanding the noninforming character of the public use or sale. . . . For an inventor must exercise reasonable diligence if he is to be rewarded with patent protection.[11]

The question of diligence is especially significant in cases arising out of a dispute between two applicants for a patent on the same discovery. For in such a case, when the issue is which of the two applicants is entitled to the monopoly reward, it is often appropriate to weigh the later inventor's diligence in enabling the public to obtain the benefit of the concept more heavily than the earlier date of unexploited conception. . . . But in this case, although Wagner may have failed to act diligently to establish his own right to a patent, there was no lack of diligence in his attempt to make the benefits of his discovery available to the public. In view of his public use of the invention, albeit noninforming, we do not believe he concealed or suppressed the discovery within the meaning of Sec. 102(g).

We recognize, as appellant argues, that portions of Judge Rich's opinion in *Palmer* v. *Dudzik* . . . suggest that a public use which does not disclose the inventive concept may amount to concealment within Sec. 102(g). But that case, like *Gillman,* involved a patent on a machine; the benefits of using the machine were not made available to anyone except the inventor. Moreover, the case arose out of an interference proceeding in which the dispute was between two applicants for a patent, the earlier of the two having been less diligent than the later. In this case, Wagner was not only the first inventor, but also "the first to confer on the public the benefit of the invention". . . .

6. The evidence identifies at least three golfers who used Surlyn-covered balls during the fall of 1964 for rounds of golf played at Riveria Country Club in Los Angeles. . . . By February 1965, two of these golfers, both of whom were favorably impressed with the play of the new ball, had placed orders with Wagner for more than 1,000 dozen Surlyn-covered balls; they began to distribute them commercially although they both lacked knowledge of the Surlyn content in the cover construction. . . .

7. In support of its contention that Wagner concealed his invention, plaintiff relies on (1) the deposition of an acknowledged expert on golf ball construction who failed to discover the Surlyn content of the cover in an analysis of Wagner's ball; and (2) the secretive manner in which Wagner gave the Surlyn formula to his daughter on her son's birthday "to keep in case something ever happened to him." . . .

8. "So, too, as to the lost arts. It is well known that centuries ago discoveries were made in certain arts the fruits of which have come down to us, but the means by which the work was accomplished are at this day unknown. The knowledge has been lost for ages. Yet it would hardly be doubted, if anyone now discovered an art thus lost, and it was a useful improvement, that upon a fair construction of the act of Congress, he would be entitled to a patent. Yet he would not literally be the first and original inventor, but would be the first to confer on the public the benefit of the invention. He would discover what is unknown, and communicate knowledge which the public had not the means of obtaining without his invention." . . .

9. "We are to distinguish between a public user which does not inform the art . . . and a secret user. . . ."

10. Omitted.

11. The second sentence of Sec. 102(g) reads as follows: "In determining priority of invention there shall be considered not only the respective dates of conception and reduction to practice of the invention, but also the reasonable diligence of one who was first to conceive and last to reduce to practice, from a time prior to conception by the other."

A conclusion that Wagner had concealed or suppressed his invention would have to be supported by a stronger showing than a mere lack of diligence. For it is less serious to hold that the first inventor has forfeited his right to a patent monopoly than it is to hold that he has forfeited any right to use his own invention without the permission of a subsequent inventor.

"But we must bear in mind that it was not alone to reward the inventor that the patent monopoly was granted. The public was to get its reward and have the advantage of the inventor's discovery as early as was reasonably possible." . . .

There are three reasons why it is appropriate to conclude that a public use of an invention forecloses a finding of suppression or concealment even though the use does not disclose the discovery. First, even such a use gives the public the benefit of the invention. If the new idea is permitted to have its impact in the marketplace, and thus to "promote the Progress of Science and useful Arts,"[12] it surely has not been suppressed in an economic sense. Second, even though there may be no explicit disclosure of the inventive concept, when the article itself is freely accessible to the public at large, it is fair to presume that its secret will be uncovered by potential competitors long before the time when a patent would have expired if the inventor had made a timely application and disclosure to the Patent Office.[13] Third, the inventor is under no duty to apply for a patent; he is free to contribute his idea to the public, either voluntarily by an express disclosure, or involuntarily by a noninforming public use. In either case, although he may forfeit his entitlement to monopoly protection, it would be unjust to hold that such an election should impair his right to continue diligent efforts to market the product of his own invention.

We hold that the public use of Wagner's golf balls forecloses a finding of suppression or concealment; that holding is consistent with both the decided cases and the underlying purposes of the statute.

Affirmed.

GUNTER v. STREAM
573 F. 2d 77 (1978)

Baldwin, Judge

This is an appeal from a decision of the Patent and Trademark Office Board of Patent Interferences (board) which awarded priority as to two counts of an interference to junior party, Stream. We affirm.

On August 11, 1975, an interference was declared between Gunter's application entitled "Heat Pipes for Fin Coolers," serial No. 507,314, filed on September 19, 1974, and Stream's application entitled "Method and Apparatus for Controlling the Viscosity of Glass Streams," serial No. 511,541, filed on October 3, 1974. The two counts of the interference correspond to claims 6 and 8 of Gunter's application and claims 28 and 29 of Stream's application.

The subject matter of the interference is a method and apparatus for employing heat pipe fins for cooling glass fibers as they are drawn through orifices of a glass fiber forming machine. Counts 1 and 2 define the subject matter:

1. A fiber glass bushing unit comprising in combination a container for the reception of molten glass, a plurality of orifices on the bottom of said container arranged in parallel rows, a plurality of plate-like fin members positioned between the rows of orifices by but below and out of contact with said container, said plate-like fins being mounted at one end in a header member, means to pass the fluid coolant through said header member, each of said plate members having a wick material affixed to the interior surfaces of said plate member and having a central cavity located therein, a vaporizable liquid on said wick capable of being vaporized from the surface of said wick and recondensed on said wick during operation.

2. A method of cooling glass fibers being drawn from a molten glass source from a plurality of glass orifices located on the bottom of said glass source, removing heat from said fibers by positioning a plurality of plate-like heat exchange members between said fibers to thereby absorb the radiant heat from said fibers on the surface of said plate-like members continuously, maintaining the surface of the plate-like members receptive to heat absorption by vaporizing a volatile fluid on the interior surface of said plate-like members continuously from the surface of a wick contained therein and removing heat continuously from said plate-like members by indirect heat exchange with the mounting means for said plate-like members to thereby condense said volatile fluid in said plate-like members and thereby return it to the wick for further vaporization.

Gunter took no testimony and is restricted to his filing date of September 19, 1974, as the date of conception and constructive reduction to practice. Stream, an employee of Owens-Corning Fiberglass Corporation (OCF), assignee of his application, submitted testimony and documentary evidence to support a date of conception and reduction to practice prior to Gunter's filing date. Stream himself testified that, in August of 1970, he read an article on heat pipe technology published in the August 6, 1970, edition of *Machine Design,* which was admitted into evidence as Stream Exhibit 2. According to the testimony, Stream had a conversation, on or before August 27, 1970, with his

---

12. U.S. Const., art. I, Sect. 8, clause 8.

13. In this case, for example, it is not unreasonable to assume that competing manufacturers of golf balls in search of a tough new material to be used as a cover, might make inquiries of Wagner's Surlyn supplier that would soon reveal his secret ingredient. After all, DuPont certainly had a motive to expand the market for Surlyn.

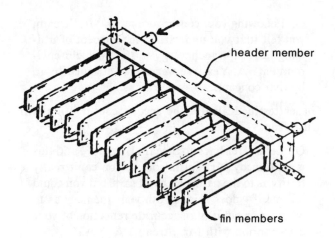

header member

fin members

supervisor, Mr. Hellmut I. Glaser,[1] in which he told Glaser of his idea to apply heat pipe technology to glass fiber making. Glaser corroborated Stream's testimony about their conversation and also testified that he reported on Stream's idea to Mr. Steven R. Gustafson, then patent attorney for OCF. Subsequent to this conversation with Glaser, Gustafson reduced Glaser's report to writing on September 2, 1970. Glaser testified that the contents of the Gustafson memo, which was admitted into evidence as Stream Exhibit 3, was an accurate summary of his report.

To support his reduction to practice of the invention, Stream produced employees of OCF who testified about contracting with Hughes Aircraft Company for construction of prototype fin shields which were eventually completed and shipped to OCF on November 11, 1973. Tests were performed on the prototypes by OCF at its Huntingdon Plant on April 17 and 18, 1974.

In its opinion, the board defined conception as a disclosure of an invention which enables one skilled in the art to reduce the invention to a practical form without "exercise of the inventive faculty." The board was persuaded by the evidence presented by Stream on the question of conception. It found that appellee conceived the invention on August 27, 1970, when he understood it to the extent that he was able to disclose it to another who in turn understood the invention.

Opinion

On the question of reduction to practice, the board found that the Hughes prototype, successfully tested by OCF, embodied every essential element of the counts. The tests conducted on April 17 and 19, 1974, were proof of an actual reduction to practice, which is attributable to Stream. We agree with the board's finding on this issue, and we are not persuaded by appellant's argument that the reduction to practice does not inure to the benefit of Stream, since he took no part in this phase. Stream can prevail if he proves an earlier date of conception by a proponderance of the evidence. . . . The issue before the court, then, is whether

Stream proved, as junior party, by a preponderance of evidence that he had conception on or about August 27, 1970.

Gunter argues that Stream never had conception but only expressed an invitation to experiment with heat pipes in glass fiber forming machines. Stream is required, Gunter argues, to have conceived not only the invention, but the means to accomplish the invention. The conception was not completed by Stream because extensive research by Hughes Aircraft was necessary to achieve satisfactory performance of the invention. Gunter further argues that while Hughes Aircraft was working on the prototype, it suggested to OCF the use of cooling blocks in the construction of the prototypes. This, he argues, militates against Stream being in possession of a conception which included use of a "header member" which is recited in the counts. It is contended also that Stream had no connection with the invention from August of 1970 until September 27, 1974, when he reviewed and signed the application disclosing his invention and that there is no evidence on record to indicate that Stream was ever informed of the progress of Hughes Aircraft or of the tests of OCF.

The board correctly cited the definition for conception initially stated in *Mergenthaler* v. *Scudder.* . . .

> The conception of the invention consists in the complete performance of the mental part of the inventive act. All that remains to be accomplished, in order to perfect the act or instrument, belongs to the department of construction, not invention. It is therefore the formation, in the mind of the inventor, *of a definite and permanent idea of the complete and operative invention, as it is thereafter to be applied in practice,* that constitutes an available conception, within the meaning of the patent law.

We adopted this definition in *Townsend* v. *Smith,* supra. Reviewing the evidence supporting conception, we conclude that the conception of using heat pipe technology in glass fiber forming, as described in the counts, occurred on or about August 27, 1970. We hold, therefore, that Stream established by a preponderance of the evidence that he conceived the invention on or about that date. Having already shown that there was reduction to practice by the assignee, Stream's conception completes the showing necessary to award priority.

The facts show that on or about August 6, 1970, Stream read and understood the article on heat pipe technology. With his working knowledge of glass fiber forming and his understanding of basic heat pipe technology described in the article, Stream conceived the

---

1. Glaser is an engineer who had been with OCF since 1956 as a specialist in glass fiber formation. In 1970, he became a manager of the Process Technology Department.

invention, applying heat pipe technology to glass fiber forming. The Gustafson memo is the only documentary evidence which corroborates the conception.[2] It states, in pertinent part:

> On August 27, 1970, Mr. Hellmut Glaser disclosed to Michael Mitcham and the writer that commercially available "heat pipes" might be advantageous substitutes for our present fin shields.
>
> The heat pipes cool the surrounding area through the vaporization of fluid contained inside the pipe. One such heat pipe is made by Electron Dynamics[3] and is very similar in size and shape to a single fin shield. In operation, one end of the heat pipe is soldered or welded to a cooling manifold.
>
> According to Mr. Glaser the original suggestion for this incorporation of heat pipes was made by Ralph Stream.

The memo was the culmination of two conversations both involving Glaser, who corroborated Stream's testimony about the first conversation.

Q. What do you recall about the conversation?

A. Well, Ralph Stream came to my office with an article out of a trade journal, trade magazine on heat pipes, and disclosed to me that this might be application (sic) to be used on finishields; certainly might be something we could use there, that application.

Q. If I hand you a copy of Stream Exhibit 2, do you recall if that's the article you just mentioned, that Ralph Stream came to you with? A. Yes.

*   *   *   *   *   *   *   *

Q. Okay. Do you recall any of the details of the conversation between you and Ralph Stream which you just referred to? A. I think it's difficult to recall details about that. He brought the article into my office.

Q. Sure. A. He brought the article into my office and I recall that we shortly discussed the concept of heat pipes, and that because of the advantages such a device offers, we should seek to utilize it in the cooling of forming cones, possibly as a substitute for finshields.

Q. Based on your conversation, or at the time of the conversation with Mr. Stream, did you understand in general what a heat pipe is? A. I think the article pretty much describes it, yes.

Q. Following your conversation with Mr. Stream, you felt that you understood the concept of utilizing heat pipe technology in the finshield environment? A. Yes. We were very intrigued by it, by that concept.

Glaser testified also to the second conversation with Gustafson:

Q. Let's refer back to Stream Exhibit 3, and this is written by Mr. Gustafson, so you can't really testify as to the truth of what it says, but you could tell me if—does this refresh your memory as to whether or not it is an accurate reflection of your conversation with Mr. Stream? A. Yes.

Q. Okay. And do you have any reason to believe that your conversation with Mr. Gustafson was after August 27, 1970? A. All I—it's difficult to remember dates, exact dates. We discussed, we, with Steve Gustafson, Ralph Stream's ideas, within a couple of days after Ralph Stream brought it in to me, because Steve came at that time almost weekly or bi-weekly to—

Q. Okay. And Mr. Gustafson in Stream Exhibit 3 says in the third paragraph, "According to Mr. Glaser, the original suggestion for this incorporation of heat pipes was made by Ralph Stream."

A. Right.

Q. Do you agree with that statement? A. Yes.

With this evidence to support conception of the invention on or about August 27, 1970, the inquiry is directed to the substance of the conception. Did Stream conceive, at that point in time, all the essential elements of the counts? To answer this inquiry we compare the counts to the description in the Gustafson memo. The counts reproduced in their entirety, above, include an apparatus count and a method count. The apparatus count describes the fiber glass bushing unit as primarily a plate-like fin member, which has a central cavity for vaporization of a fluid coolant which travels through a wick, in combination with a header member, which possesses a means to pass the fluid coolant. The method count describes the cooling process as vaporization of fluid coolant and indirect heat exchange with a header member (cooling block).

The Gustafson memo describes the invention as a heat pipe, which replaces a standard finshield, connected to a "cooling manifold." This combination corresponds to the description of the apparatus in count

2. Both Gustafson and Glaser testified about the memo. Gustafson identified the document, while Glaser, on direct examination, testified that he understood the memo to be an accurate reflection of his conversation with Gustafson on August 27, 1970.

3. Electron Dynamics is a division of Hughes Aircraft Company.

1. The plate-like fin member corresponds to the heat pipe, both cool through the "vaporization of fluid inside the pipe." The header member corresponds to the "cooling manifold," as both secure one or a plurality of heat pipes or fin members, and both provide a means for indirect heat exchange. Thus, the Gustafson memo describes the process of cooling as set forth in method count 2.

Gunter's argument that, in July of 1972, Hughes Aircraft suggested the cooling block and that, therefore, Stream was not in possession of a complete conception in August of 1970, is fully met by the suggestion of a "cooling manifold" in the Gustafson memo. The comparison of the counts with the description of the Stream invention in the Gustafson memo, we conclude, shows clearly that Stream conceived the invention with all essential elements of the counts at least by August 27, 1970.

Motion to Tax Costs

Appellant request the court to tax appellee for the cost of seventy-one pages of a ninety-three-page addition to the printed transcript. The ninety-three-page addition supplemented testimony of six of appellant's witnesses. Appellee, in opposition to the motion, argues that this testimony is relevant to the issues of conception and reduction to practice raised by appellant in his notice of appeal.

For purposes of allocating printing costs, appellant is required to bear the costs for that material necessary for the court to decide the issues he raised on appeal. . . .

We conclude, after examining the testimony in question, that the material was necessary for consideration of the issues on appeal. Appellant's motion is accordingly denied.

Having reached the above conclusion with regard to conception and reduction to practice, we *affirm* the decision below which awards priority to junior party, Stream.

Affirmed.

REVIEW QUESTIONS

1. Why is the patent right the right to exclude others from making, using, or selling the invention rather than the right to make, use, or sell it?
2. White, an electrical engineer, goes to work for the ABC Company to design automation circuity. No patent agreement is required of him. Using company time and facilities (in part), he develops a new product and makes application for a patent on it. If he obtains a patent, what rights, if any, will the ABC Company have in the product?
3. In question 2, assume that White had signed an agreement to assign patent rights to the ABC Company, but had developed the product at home, using only his own time and facilities. What rights, if any, will the ABC Company have in the patent?
4. Outline the steps of the patenting procedure.
5. Why are records of invention development necessary?
6. Consider trademarks and copyrights. Can you conceive of something that might be the subject of either a trademark registration or a copyright?
7. In the case of *Dann* v. *Johnston,* the court refers to "the general patentability of computer programs." What arguments can you present for and against computer programs being patentable?
8. In *Dunlop Holdings Limited* v. *Ram Golf Corp.,* a) why was Ram the defendant? b) what is the practical result of this case?
9. In the case of *Gunter* v. *Stream,* what would Gunter be required to show to maintain his priority in the patent?

Section V

Torts

Nearly all engineers are concerned with contracts and property; therefore, our time is well spent considering the rights and liabilities comprising the law in these areas. Just as important (perhaps even more important to some engineers) is the law concerning personal rights. We all work with other people, so it follows that what we do may infringe upon their rights, and what they do may infringe upon ours. Where the rights so infringed are recognized and protected in law, there are special defenses and remedies available. As is true for other professionals, an engineer's activities encounter tort risks. What the engineer designs—a product, a process, or a system of some sort—may cause injury to someone's rights. A design is based upon a mental image of the future. Without such plans, progress would cease. But designing a thing or a combination that has never before existed can be hazardous; it is often impossible to conceive of all ramifications of a new concept. Because of this, the price of progress in engineering is sometimes injury to someone—a tort.

21

Torts and Crimes

Numerous man-made laws and rules regulate the behavior of people. The field of law may be broken down into many categories and the categories may be further subdivided. One major breakdown is that shown below:

    I. Criminal Law
   II. Civil Law
       A. Torts
       B. Breaches of Contract

An individual unlawful act is either a public wrong or a private wrong; possibly both. An unlawful act that injures the public is a *crime;* one that injures one individual or a group of individuals less than the general public is a *civil wrong*. Civil law, or the law of private rights, is divided into torts and breaches of contract. We have discussed the law of contracts. The intent here is to cover a few broad, general concepts in criminal law and torts.

In the United States we have many rights and freedoms. We can do just about as we please up to the point where the things we do infringe upon the rights or freedoms of others. A crime is an antisocial act, but, of course, not all antisocial acts are crimes. Relief of internal pressure by means of a loud belch is *generally* considered to be an antisocial act, but it is not yet a crime. Society is injured when a crime is committed. The main purpose of trying a person accused of a crime and punishing him if he is guilty is to prevent recurrences of the criminal act.

One main distinction between a criminal action and a civil action is that the state undertakes prosecution for a crime. When a civil wrong has been committed, the plaintiff must bring his own action. A criminal action is undertaken to punish the wrongdoer; a civil action is pursued to get compensation for a loss suffered or to prevent a loss from being suffered.

The same act may constitute at once a tort and a crime—as such it gives rise to both a civil and a criminal action against the person who committed the act. In fact, it takes some thought to conceive of a tort that may not be a crime and a crime that would in no way be a tort.

CRIMINAL LAW

A crime is an act prohibited by either common law or a statute. In states where a criminal code has been adopted, all crimes are statutory. As time passes and society becomes more and more complex, we tend to increase the number of laws defining certain acts as *crimes*. When a criminal statute is made, it is generally necessary to answer at least three questions in the statute: (1) What is the act (or omission) that is to be prohibited? (2) Who can commit the crime (or, conversely, who cannot)? and (3) What is the punishment for commission of the act? Under common law there is both a physical and a mental component of a crime. The mental element is known as *criminal intent*. In a common law case it is frequently necessary to prove intent as an element in the criminal act. Many state statutes remove the necessity for this proof on the basis that the act speaks for itself and that a person will intend the natural results of his acts.

Under common law a child under seven years of age is incapable of entertaining criminal intent. Between ages seven and fourteen the child is presumed incapable, but the presumption may be rebutted under certain circumstances. Insane persons and idiots are not criminally responsible for their acts. A corporation cannot be guilty of crimes involving malice or intent. Drunkenness might seem to be similar to insanity, but it is rarely a valid excuse. The law usually holds drunkenness to be a voluntary state preventable by proper foresight.

Punishment for a criminal offense ordinarily takes one of the following forms: (1) death; (2) imprisonment; (3) fine; (4) removal from office; (5) disqualification to hold and enjoy any office of honor, trust, or profit under the constitution or laws of the state.[1]

Degrees of Crime

Treason. The highest crime is *treason*. It is defined in the Constitution as: "Treason against the United States shall consist only in levying war against them,

1. California Penal Code.

or in adhering to their enemies, giving them aid and comfort. No person shall be convicted of treason unless on the testimony of two witnesses to the same overt act, or on confession in open court."

Felony. *Felonies* comprise the second level of crime. Early common law punished felonies with a sentence to death. Now a felony is generally defined as an act that is punishable by death or imprisonment in a penitentiary. Every citizen has a duty to do everything in his power to prevent the commission of a felony and to prevent the escape of a felon after the crime has been committed. One who fails to act in a reasonable manner to prevent the crime or the escape of the criminal is, himself, guilty of a misdemeanor. The law does not require a person to walk into a blaze of gunfire—he must only do everything he reasonably could be expected to do under the circumstances.

Misdemeanor. The lowest level of crime is known as *misdemeanor*. It consists of all prohibited acts less than felonies. Traffic violations are misdemeanors, as are zoning law violations and breaches of the peace. Punishment for a misdemeanor usually consists of a fine or jail sentence or, generally, anything less than death or imprisonment in a penitentiary.

Terms Often Misunderstood. *Compounding a crime* refers to an agreement between a person who has committed a crime and another who has knowledge of the crime to the effect that the latter will not report the act. For example, one who has been robbed might agree with the person who robbed him that he will not report the robbery if his property is returned. Compounding a crime is a criminal offense in itself. Society has been offended by the commission of the crime, and no citizen has the right to deprive society of the opportunity to punish the criminal.

Double jeopardy is another misunderstood term in criminal law. The fifth amendment to the Constitution provides (in part): ". . . nor shall any person be subject for the same offense to be twice put in jeopardy of life or limb. . . ." A person is put in *jeopardy* when a valid indictment has been lodged against him, he has been tried, and jury verdict has been given. It is not double jeopardy however when, by a single act, a person violates two laws and is subsequently tried for violation of both of them. Many state laws prohibit acts that are also prohibited by federal laws. Both governments may have laws forbidding the sale of narcotics, for instance. If a person is acquitted in Federal Court on a charge of violating the Federal Narcotics Law, he may still be tried in a state court for violation of the state law.

TORTS

A *tort* is an offense against an individual in the form of injury to his personal rights or his property rights. Prosecution is generally undertaken by the plaintiff to obtain compensation for the injury suffered, or a decree may be sought to prevent harm to personal or property rights.

Just as the law undertakes to prevent acts against society by prosecution of one who has committed a crime, the law also provides procedures to redress wrongs to an individual. Such wrongs fall into two general categories—torts and breaches of contract. *Breach of contract* cases arise when there has been an agreement of some sort between the parties involved. These are treated in Chapters 13 and 14. Tort actions arise from duties and natural rights existing between parties. The driver of a car, for instance, has a duty to avoid hitting others while he is driving. If he is negligent in his duty and as a result injures another, a tort action is available to the victim to make the driver pay for the damage.

In criminal law it is frequently necessary to prove the existence of intent to commit a crime. In tort cases, particularly where negligence is involved, proof of intent is not likely to be as important. It is only necessssray to prove three things in a tort action: (1) that the defendant owed the plaintiff a duty; (2) that this duty was breached by the defendant; and (3) that the damage resulted from the breach of this duty. Whether or not the *tort-feasor* (the one who committed the tort) intended his act to result in injury is beside the point.

Res Ipsa Loquitur. In most tort cases the plaintiff can point to specific negligent acts by the defendant to make out his case. In some instances, however, it is difficult or impossible to show defendant's specific acts or omissions. When this is true the plaintiff may still make out his case based on the doctrine known as *res ipsa liquitur*. Essentially this means "the thing speaks for itself." To use this doctrine, plaintiff may show that the injury would not occur unless someone were negligent; that defendant had control of the instrumentality causing the injury; and that plaintiff in no way contributed to the injury. The result is not proof, but circumstantial evidence which presents to the jury a logical inference to be accepted if they find it reasonable. Defendant, of course, has an opportunity for rebuttal, which may take one of several forms but usually consists of showing that he actually exercised the care he should have exercised.

Occurrence

In general there are three ways in which a tort may arise; through malfeasance, misfeasance, or nonfeasance on the part of the tort-feasor.

A tort is said to arise from *malfeasance* when the tortious act is one the tort-feasor should not ordinarily be allowed to commit. Deliberate destruction of a company's reputation and good will by publication of falsehoods is an example of such torts.

Misfeasance results from an act one would ordinarily be allowed to do, but which is done at such a time or place that it injures another. Assume you are driving down a highway and your left front tire blows out, forcing you into the opposite lane in the path of an oncoming car. Ordinarily you do not violate any rights if your tire blows out—you can have a blowout whenever you wish. However, if the blowout is the direct cause of injury to another, the resulting injury is your responsibility. It was not the other car that caused the injury, but yours.

Nonfeasance takes place when one neglects to do that which he should have done to protect others from injury. When a construction crew leaves an excavation for an evening or weekend, barriers are usually placed around the excavation. If the placing of barriers is neglected and, as a result, someone falls into the excavation, thereby injuring himself, this injury is the contractor's responsibility.

COMMON TORTS

Some of the more common torts will be treated under four general headings: (1) torts against a person, (2) torts against one's reputation, (3) torts against property rights, and (4) business torts.

Torts Against a Person

Assault and battery are two common personal torts. The first of these terms, *assault,* is quite frequently used improperly. Its legal meaning is "threat of violence." It consists of one or more acts intended by the tort-feasor to create apprehension of bodily harm in the victim. There must be an apparent present means of inflicting the bodily harm; for instance, a knife or a pistol (it would make no difference that the pistol was not loaded if the victim had reason to believe that it was). The tort of assault requires that the threat be concerned with immediate injury—not next week or "if I ever see you again." Harm from the tort of assault frequently occurs when the victim has a weak heart or when a pregnant woman receives the threats.

Assault ends and battery begins when the threat is carried out. *Battery* is the intentional and unlawful touching of another in an offensive manner. Battery is often incorrectly reported as assault; the two torts do often go together but there is a distinction between them.

False imprisonment occurs when one is intentionally confined within limits set by the tort-feasor. The victim must be aware that he is being confined and he must not have given his consent to the confinement. The means of imprisonment is incidental as long as the victim's personal liberty is restricted. For example, confinement of a person in a car that is traveling too rapidly for exit to be made safely would be imprisonment. A particular means of confinement might be imprisonment to one, but not to another; that is, an athletic young man might escape through a window, whereas a wheelchair cripple could not.

The right to have a court determine guilt or innocence in a criminal case or who should win a civil suit is sometimes abused. One party may bring suit against another merely as an annoyance to him. The tort involved in such an action is *malicious prosecution* (or *vexatious proceeding* if based on a civil case). The tort hinges principally on the presence or absence of "probable cause." If there were reasonable grounds to believe that the facts warranted the action complained of, this is a perfect defense against a suit for malicious prosecution. Usually, if a reputable attorney recommends an action at law after he has learned the true facts, it can be assumed that there is "probable cause."

Torts Against Reputation

A person has a right to whatever reputation he earns in his day-to-day dealings with others. If false and malicious statements are published (orally or in writing) such statements may constitute *defamation*. Defamation occurs when false and malicious statements made about a person tend to expose him to public ridicule, contempt, or hatred. Even statements about a dead person can constitute a tort if they are false and maliciously tend to blacken the memory of him. Defamation occurs when a statement wrongly attributes a criminal act to a person. It also occurs in statements that tend to injure one in his job or profession.

Defamation takes two forms. Oral defamation is known as *slander*. Printed or written defamation or defamation by pictures or signs is known as *libel*. It is slander to falsely state that White is embezzling company funds; it is libel if the statement is written. In such an instance, slander would not occur if the statement were made only to White with no one else present.

Someone other than White would have to hear the statement for slander to occur.

Libel results from printed matter. Even a radio or television broadcast of a speaker who reads a defamatory statement from a written article may constitute libel rather than slander. The damages recoverable for libel are usually greater than for slander because of the lasting impression created.

According to present day law, *truth* and *privilege* constitute complete defenses to defamation suits. Regardless of the malicious manner in which the statements are made, if they are true there is no defamation.

Privilege refers to the right of one person to defame another. A judge has this right and so does a sworn witness on the stand. Privilege is found when the otherwise defamatory statements are made in carrying out a judicial, political, or social duty. It arises from the necessity of making a full and unrestricted communication.

Torts Against Property

When one owns property, what he really owns is a set of rights. He has the right to possess the property, to use it (as long as he does not infringe upon the rights of others), and to dispose of it. One can normally exclude others from using his property or from taking possession of it. Tort action frequently results from the invasion of these rights.

Trespass. The tort of *trespass to land* occurs whenever a person without license enters upon the land of another. Even simply walking across a person's lawn is a tort. The law, however, does not concern itself with trifles, and a single instance of trespass such as the invasion of one's lawn probably would not be actionable. Even if it were, the result would be likely to be only nominal damages. An action for trespass is more likely when the trespass has been repeated numerous times or when material damage can be shown. Such damage to real property can be shown, for instance, where the foundation of a structure encroaches upon the property of another. Black builds a structure near the edge of his property line (according to a survey). White, the owner of the adjacent property, later has another survey made. The later survey shows part of Black's foundation to be on White's property. The court established White's survey as correct. An equity court (where such a case would be likely to wind up) has the right to order the removal of the foundation. It probably would not do so, however, realizing that it would only be placing a weapon in White's hand to force Black to pay an ex-

orbitant price for a piece of White's land. It is more probable that the judgment would require White to sell Black the piece of land at the reasonable market value.

If trespass to land takes the form of numerous members of the public using the property as they desire, an *easement* may result. If Black, for instance, owns lakeside property and the public crosses his property to reach the lake, he may eventually be prevented from excluding the public. The period of time for such a *public easement* to occur runs from 15 to 20 years in the various states. To create the right of easement public use must be continuous. It is for this reason that one occasionally sees a road blocked off for one day per year.

The right to trespass upon another's land can be given by the person in possession. Such permission is known as a *license* or an *easement*. In addition, certain others may have a license to trespass. A caller at home has the right to go as far as the door by a direct route. If a person must enter another's property to recover his own property, he has a right to do so.

It is the person who is in possession of the land who has the right to exclude others from trespassing. In other words, those who rent or lease property have the right to exclude others from it (even the owner) as long as the property is leased by them.

Personal rights take precedence over property rights. One does not ordinarily have the right to shoot trespassers. The force used must be no more than sufficient to remove the person from the property.

Attractive Nuisance. Ordinarily, one who trespasses upon another's property assumes whatever risk may be inherent in the trespass. If the trespasser is injured by some hidden danger, he has little chance of recovery against the owner. But, just as is true with many other general rules of law, this one has its exceptions. Probably the most prominent exception is known as *attractive nuisance,* pertaining to children of tender age. It is of recent origin as legal doctrines go, and has been rejected by some courts, but the number and size of recoveries in the past decade or so prompts its consideration.

The doctrine of attractive nuisance began in the United States with a case involving injury to a child playing around a railway turntable. In the century or so since then, a multitude of property conditions and instrumentalities (including recently, swimming pools) have come to be considered attractive nuisances for children.

In jurisdictions where the attractive nuisance doctrine is supported, a property owner or occupant may be held liable for injuries sustained by children on his premises under the following conditions: if he knew or should have known the attractiveness of the dangerous instrumentality or property condition to children and failed to reasonably guard against injury to them; or if he had reason to expect children to play there (e.g., having seen them play in the vicinity), and did not warn them or take other suitable precautions.

The owner's (or occupant's) risk of attractive nuisance liability is removed by taking reasonable precautions. He is not expected to foresee very unlikely events—only those that might befall a normal, inquisitive child; and he would not be expected to guard something of danger obvious even to a child. The doctrine is aimed at conditions which would be inherently dangerous to a child, but which the child could not be expected to foresee. Thus, an unguarded piece of machinery could easily be an attractive nuisance, whereas an open pit in a field would be less likely to be one. Generally, the attraction must be something unusual, uncommon, or artificial as against a natural hazard.

Attractive nuisance cases could involve children of any age, but children of an age between five and ten years seem particularly susceptible. The court also considers such things as the child's intelligence, his state of mental health, and other conditions as significant in such cases. The largest factor, though, is the presence or absence of proper precautions by the owner or occupant of the premises. And this question is rightly submitted to a jury.

Conversion. The tort counterpart to the crime of theft is *conversion.* Conversion, though, includes more than just depriving the owner of his right to possession of his property. It also includes wrongful alteration of property and wrongful use of property by persons other than the owner. It may arise in instances of bailment, where something left with another is used or sold by the bailee. Black leaves a television set with White (as bailee) to be repaired. White sells the television set to Gray. White's tortious act is conversion for which Black may maintain a conversion action in court. A successful suit in conversion normally nets the true owner of the property the market value of the converted property and vests title in the converter when the judgment amount has been paid. The owner, though, has an election of two remedies available to him. He may sue on the tort of conversion or maintain an action in replevin to obtain the return of his property. If the owner desires return of his property prior to the replevin action, he may usually obtain it by posting a bond to be forfeited in case the property is found to belong to the other party.

Nuisance. Each person has the right to use his property as he chooses as long as he does not, in some way, injure the person or property of another. If one's person or property is injured by another and the tort fits no other category, nuisance will usually cover it. Nuisance can be just about anything that interferes with the enjoyment of life and property. It may take the form of smoke or sulphur fumes, or it may be pollution of a stream or excessive noise, to mention only a few types.

Nuisances are either public or private. A public nuisance is one which annoys or disturbs a substantial number of the persons in a communtity. A private nuisance produces special injuries to private rights of one or a very few people. Any citizen may successfully lodge a complaint about a public nuisance, but only the person injured can maintain a successful action on a private nuisance.

Black owns a factory in which semi-trailers are manufactured. Since the manufacture requires the use of rivets, the process is quite noisy. When Black first built the factory, several years ago, the building site was a cornfield and the nearest neighbor was some two miles distant. With the passage of time Black's trailer business expanded. Adjoining land was sold to a land development company and houses have been built and sold. Recent orders for trailers have forced Black to put on a third shift at the factory, from 11 P.M. to 7 A.M. Some of the new house owners complained to Black about the noise; one (White) has instituted a nuisance suit. In answer, Black contends that he was there first, that an injunction would force him to close down his plant and deprive workers of jobs, and that the noise just isn't great enough to injure anyone anyway. There are a variety of judgments that would be possible in such a situation. As to Black's being there first and thus acquiring a right (known as a *prescriptive right*) to maintain the nuisance, it is doubtful that this defense would succeed. Such a defense might succeed only if White had full knowledge of the noise problem (as to degree and time of day) and bought his house in spite of the noise. Proof by White that the noise had increased in time and intensity would be likely to defeat the defense. As to the hardship that would be imposed by an injunction, the judgment would be different in various states. Certain of the state legislatures have adopted policies tending to encourage business migration into their states. In such places the courts are very loath to take an action that would result in hardship to an industry or company. The *balance of hardship* doctrine would probably also be considered here—is it a greater hardship to continue operation under the circumstances or to enjoin its continuance? Hardship in terms of job loss and loss of income to the community would be weighed against the noise annoyance. The likely result of such a case as the example presented is a decree requiring Black to do all in his power to abate the noise problem. Many measures can be taken to attenuate such industrial noises.

Torts Against Business Rights

In the United States the right to compete with others in a business venture is protected by the government and the courts. Despite the likelihood that entrance into a particular field by an efficient newcomer may injure or even eliminate an established concern, such competition is favored. Usually the result is healthy. The general tendency is to encourage efficiency, since the public benefits from it in lower consumer costs.

Competition, though, can lead to its own destruction. If all less efficient concerns are driven from the field, a monopoly results. Since unregulated monopoly is usually associated with excessive prices, inefficient operation, and other undesirable effects, laws exist to preserve competition.

Since the field of law treating competitive practices is very large, no attempt will be made to cover the entire field here. Rather, a few of the more prominent and well-defined business torts will be mentioned.

Inducing Breach of Contract. Although breach of contract is treated under the law of contracts, inducing another to breach a contract is a tort. According to the ancient common law, inducing breach of contract was not actionable unless it was accompanied by violence or fraud. This concept was changed by the case of *Lumley* v. *Gye*[2] in which an opera singer was induced to breach her contract and work for another. Though no fraud or violence occurred, the court stated that a right of action for inducing breach of contract existed. Since that time the courts have become quite firm in their opposition to inducing a contract breach. It should be noted that merely advising a prospective buyer of the merits or properties of a product is not inducing breach of contract. The end result may be breach of contract, but the seller must have actively persuaded his customer to breach if he is to be justly accused of having a hand in it. Black has a contract to buy parts from the White Screw Machine Products Company. Gray offers to sell Black better parts at a lower cost. Black breaches his contract, but Gray cannot be said to have induced the breach of contract unless he actively advocated Black's breach.

False Descriptions. The presence of false or misleading advertising is often made apparent in our daily lives. Under common law the only remedy afforded a person injured by such advertising was an action for fraud or deceit. Federal and state statutes have modified the common law, and the courts have become more liberal in this respect. The Federal Trade Commission Act seeks to prevent deceptive advertising as do many state acts. The Pure Food and Drug Acts, both state and federal, emphasize public protection in the area of food and drugs. Enforcement, though, is a major problem.

When false advertising is used to deprive a competitor of customers, his remedy in court is an injunction and an accounting for profits. To obtain this remedy he must show two things: (1) that his customers were lost to another; and (2) that it was by an unlawful means. Both are often difficult to prove.

Closely akin to false advertising is the *disparagement* of another's product. The tort resembles libel and is often called *trade libel*. Essentially, the law prevents a person from making false and misleading statements about a competitor's products. In addition to the preventive relief of injunction, damages for lost profits may be obtained if special damages can be shown. For any relief for disparagement to be forthcoming, the plaintiff must prove that:

1. The statements made by defendant were untrue.
2. The false statements were made as fact (rather than opinion).
3. The statements concerned the plaintiff's goods in particular—that is, defendant's statement that his goods were better than those of all competitors would not be disparagement.

If the plaintiff has a case that will get him into equity jurisdiction and his evidence proves the three requirements above, he can usually get an injunction. To go beyond this and collect damages, the plaintiff must show *special damage*. He must show not only that his business in general has suffered, but that he has lost specific sales as a result of the disparagement.

Disparagement is a little more difficult than libel to establish. The burdens of proof fall upon the *plaintiff;* in libel, the defendant must bear part of the proof burden. Here plaintiff must prove that the statements made were *untrue,* whereas in libel the defendant would have the burden of proving statements true.

Just as in libel and slander, certain persons have the privilege of *disparagement.* If, in the interest of preserving life and health, a doctor warns against the use of certain foods or drugs, he does so with privilege. The same is true if a family member warns another member of the same family against using certain things. In each case there is a personal interest to benefit others. Usually consumer's research organizations are extended the privilege of disparagement because of the public benefit from such services.

Trade Secrets. In the United States a person may obtain a patent[3] to protect certain of his ideas providing they are reduced to pictorial or written form. Many

---

2. Ellis & Blackburn 216, 118 Eng. Rep. 749 (1853).
3. See Chapter 20, "Intellectual Property."

other original and profitable ideas may not be patentable, or the inventors may not desire to patent them for some reason. Obtaining a patent gives its owner exclusive right to use of the idea for a certain number of years. The law protects the owner's use of the patented idea against infringement.

An idea does not have to be patented to be protected by the courts; it may be protected as a *trade secret*. The protection of trade secrets is not based on the same reasoning as that of patents. Patent protection is based on the government-induced incentive to create, the reward amounting to a protected monopoly. The owner of a patent may use his idea publicly without fear of lawful use of the idea by a competitor. The owner of a trade secret is not protected if a competitor obtains the secret by a lawful means through study, research, or general observation. The protection afforded the holder of a trade secret is based upon breach of a trust or confidence.

Many things are classed as secrets. Customer lists, sources of raw material, ingredients, blue prints, and processes are only a few examples. An engineer for a company is in a position where he is particularly likely to obtain trade secrets. The law does not attempt to prevent persons from benefitting from experience they gain while they work for an employer. Rather, the law tries to prevent the employee from passing on to others things he knew *as secrets* of his employer. The employee must, of course, know that information passed along to him is a trade secret of the company for which he works if use of this knowledge is to be restricted.

A secret is, of course, something other than public knowledge. One who has an idea to sell must first obtain the promise of the prospective buyer to pay for it if he uses it. If the seller neglects to obtain such a promise, revealing his idea before getting a promise of compensation, he has no case if the prospective buyer uses the secret without paying for it. Black, conducting research on metals, finds a heat treatment that vastly improves the tone of bells. Black approaches White, a manufacturer of bells, to sell the idea to him. If White obtains the secret by lawful means without promising payment to Black, Black has no action available against White.

Negligence

Most tort cases are based on negligence—someone did something negligently, or neglected to do something he should have done. *Black's Law Dictionary* defines *negligence* as "the omission to do something which a reasonable man, guided by those ordinary considerations which ordinarily regulate human affairs, would do." Negligence is present if harm could have been foreseen and prevented.

Standard of Care. Negligence is the failure to behave in the manner in which a reasonable person would behave under the circumstances. In a tort action the plaintiff usually must show that the defendant owed him a duty of *care*. There is a general standard as to this duty of care; the standard has developed over centuries of growth of the law. In addition, there are many circumstances that tend to modify the standard of care.

The general standard of care, as it has developed, is the care that would be exercised by a *reasonably prudent man* in like circumstances. The average or reasonably prudent man is one possessing normal intelligence, memory, capacity, and skill. He is a man who possesses no handicaps, either physical or mental, which would serve to set him aside as exceptional. It is, of course, easy to talk about an average person, but much harder to find one. Most people have something other than average intelligence or average physical structure. Reaction time (for a visual stimulus), for instance, averages somewhere around 0.19 sec., but most people are either slower or faster. Nevertheless, there must be a standard established and then allowance made for the exceptions.

Modifications of the general standard of care are made to treat the exception. The standard of care required of a surgeon in removing an appendix would be considerably more strict than the standard required of a person whose only claim to a knowledge of medicine came from a course in anatomy, but who, because of an emergency, had to attempt surgery. An engineer works under an exceptional standard of care when he designs or supervises the construction of a machine or structure. On the other end of the scale, people who are deficient mentally or impaired by a physical handicap cannot be held to the same standard as the average or reasonably prudent man.

Gross Negligence. Doing something that should not be done or neglecting to do something that should be done, thereby causing injury to another is negligence. When the act is done or neglected intentionally or with reckless disregard for the consequences, it ceases to be the common variety of negligence and becomes *gross negligence*. The likelihood of recovery by the victim is improved considerably if gross negligence can be shown. Contributory negligence by the victim is not a valid defense for the tort-feasor if gross negligence is proved.

Assumption of Risk. People do not always do what is best for them. Occasionally they assume risks for the experience or thrill of the very danger involved. If one is injured or dies as a result of the risk assumed (e.g., death of heart attack during a roller coaster ride), there can be no recovery.

The picture is a little more complicated where a person accepts employment in a risky occupation. For many years the holding of assumption of risk by the employee prevented recovery. Under the Workers' Compensation laws,[4] though, the employer is deprived of this defense.

Assumed risks are only the risks normally and naturally involved with the undertaking. Going back to the roller coaster ride; if the roller coaster suddenly became unsupported, with the resulting crash killing and injuring people, recovery would be quite possible.

A person often assumes a risk (of sorts) when he becomes a "good Samaritan" volunteer. If aid given to another who is in distress results in further injury to the distressed person, the volunteer is liable for such injury.

Contributory Negligence. Assumption of risks ordinarily arises from a contractual situation of some sort, but *contributory negligence* comes from an improvident act of the injured party. It is essentially the lack of the ordinary care that should be exercised by the victim under the circumstances. If negligence on the part of both plaintiff and defendant is involved in the case, the question becomes one of *comparative negligence*. Ordinarily, contributory negligence bars recovery by the plaintiff. However, under comparative negligence, if both parties were negligent and injury to plaintiff would have occurred anyway, recovery may be allowed but diminished by an amount by which plaintiff's neglect contributed to the total damage.

Proximate Cause

The main cause of most tort injuries is usually quite apparent when the facts are established. There are occasions, though, when more than one act or omission may be a cause of the injury. A motorist driving along a highway at night at a lawful speed may be so blinded by oncoming headlights that he will not see an object he is approaching. If he strikes another car in the rear, is *he* liable or would the person who failed to dim his headlights be liable? The question is one of *proximate* or *substantial cause*. The failure of the oncoming driver to dim his lights would probably be posed as a defense but with a probable lack of success. The driver, upon his failure to see properly, should have slowed down.

A proximate cause of a tort must be of such a nature that it was a substantial factor in the cause of injury. In other words, without the existence of the proximate cause, no tort would have resulted. There must be a direct connection between the cause and effect; it must be part of a natural and continuous sequence. Black and White are engaged in the electrical repair of an overhead crane. Before starting the work Black turned off the electricity at the switch box. White is working as the ground man of the pair. Gray, requiring electricity for a job he is doing, throws the wrong switch at the box. Black, receiving a shock from the conductor, drops a wrench on White, thereby injuring him. The immediate cause of White's injury was the force of the blow from the wrench dropped by Black. The proximate cause was Gray's action in throwing the wrong switch. If the case went to court, the probable result would be a finding for White against Gray.

Justification

Under certain circumstances tortious conduct may be justified. A person is justified in trespassing upon another's land if he must do so to regain possession of some of his personal property. A person is justified in striking another if he must do so in self-defense. License (permission) may be given to commit an act which is tortious in nature—such as a license to trespass upon the land of another in making a survey. Legal authority may be given to allow the commission of tortious acts—as the authority a police officer may exercise.

While a tort may be justified in some way, the person committing the tort still must restrain himself from going beyond the limits justified. A person defending himself against the attack of another is justified in his defense up to the point where he becomes the aggressor. If he goes beyond the point of justification, he becomes answerable for the injury caused by his acts.

A tort may be justified by proving that the injury was caused by an inevitable accident. It must be shown that defendant did everything reasonable under the circumstances to prevent injury. Accidents resulting from natural causes such as lightning, storms, and earthquakes are inevitable accidents.

Discharge of Torts

Discharge of the obligation to pay for damage by a tortious act may occur in several ways. It is apparent that not all causes of action find their way into court. Many are discharged by a simple agreement between the parties concerned that the injured party will not sue. The out-of-court settlement (accord and satisfaction) is a common means of discharge. Rather than take the case to court the tort-feasor agrees to pay the injured party for the damage done, thus avoiding court costs (in both time and money) and, often, lawyers fees.

If the case goes to a jury, a judgment results. The amount of the judgment in a tort case is generally made up of two elements: (1) the out-of-pocket cost to the

4. See Chapter 25, "Workers' Compensation."

plaintiff—such as medical cost, loss of wages, and the like, and (2) compensation for pain and suffering if such be involved.

Under common law only the injured party was allowed to bring a tort action. If the injured party died, the cause of action ended. This has been changed by the almost complete adoption of survival statutes, which allow others to sue in the name of the deceased.

Bankruptcy of the tort-feasor may act as a discharge of sorts for tort obligations. If tort action has been instituted or a judgment rendered or the obligation reduced to a contract before the bankruptcy proceedings are begun, the injured party shares in the bankrupt's estate as any other creditor. If no suit has been brought or contract made on the tort obligation, though, the tort-feasor's assets go to meet his obligations to his creditors. The injured party's cause of action remains after bankruptcy, and he may elect to sue the tort-feasor for whatever remains.

If prompt action is not taken by the injured party, his cause of action may be lost to time. Most states have a statute of limitations for tort actions—the action must be instituted within so many years after the tortious act or the cause of action dies a legal death. Tort actions undertaken in a court having equity jurisdiction also run the risk of losing out to time. The equity term *laches* indicates a cause in which the plaintiff has "slept on his rights" too long. Stale causes are not popular, the feeling being that if the plaintiff wishes to pursue his cause of action he should do so without undue hesitation.

STATE v. H. SAMUELS COMPANY, INC.
211 N.W. 2d 417 (1973)

Hallows, Chief Justice.

Several issues are raised in the briefs, but the only one which is dispositive of the case is whether the repeated violation of a city ordinance constitutes a public nuisance which ought to be enjoined.

H. Samuels Company, Inc., has operated a salvage business in block 137 in the city of Portage since the early 1900s. In 1948 the junk business was expanded to include the salvaging of metals from automobiles and other machinery. Cranes were used after 1949, a guillotine shears after 1966, and a hammer mill after about 1971. At one time Samuels operated around the clock, but at the time of trial the operation at night had been reduced. In the processing of scrap metal, Samuels utilized railroad cars, trucks, heavy-duty cranes, guillotine shears, oscillators, conveyor belts, air tools, hammer mill, and metal-sorting equipment. Prior to 1966, block

137 was zoned commercial and light industry, but in 1966 the zoning was changed to heavy industrial. Block 137 is the only block so zoned in the developed portion of Portage. The areas immediately adjacent to block 137 are zoned either residential, single-family homes or commercial and light industry.

The defendant has a license to operate a junk yard. In its operation, the defendant unloads scrap metal from railroad cars with a magnetized crane and drops the metal into a steel guillotine shears which snaps the metal and drops it onto an oscillating conveyor belt, which in turn drops it on a pile or to a sorting house. Other operations involve a two-ton magnet lifting a car engine to the height of four feet and dropping it onto a large piece of steel wedged into the ground. Air tools are used to dismantle the engines, and the hammer mill is used to hammer metal into pieces in a large drum and to drop them on a conveyor belt where they are washed and sorted. The alleged nuisance consists of the air noise and ground vibrations created by the operation.

The city of Portage has an ordinance prescribing maximum permissible noise and vibration levels. The state contended the Samuels company has repeatedly violated this ordinance and will continue to do so to the injury of the public. At the trial the state of Wisconsin attempted to prove the alleged nuisance by the testimony of two expert witnesses who monitored the noise and by the testimony of neighborhood homeowners of the disruption of their life patterns. The homeowners testified to their loss of sleep, domestic discord, added expense in remodeling their homes, suspension of home remodeling, moving from the neighborhood, rattling of windows, loss of hobbies such as working out of doors, loss of use of porches and yards for relaxation, shaking of pictures and furniture, shaking of beds, and rattling of dishes. The two experts testified their tests showed that at various times the sounds caused by the operation exceeded the maximum permissible decibel levels and sound frequencies established by the city ordinance of Portage. They also testified that the vibrations emanating from the salvage yard exceeded permissible displacement values prescribed by the ordinance for areas zoned heavy industrial.

The defendant's testimony consisted of the testimony of the chief of police who related that of the 32 complaints received in 1970, 24 were by one person and the rest by four persons; in 1971, of the 47 complaints, 38 were from one party and the balance from seven other persons. No action on behalf of the city of Portage has been taken to enforce the city ordinance against Samuels. The president of Samuels testified he had equipped his cranes with silencers, that he had reduced his operation, and intends to reduce the handling of automobiles in the future. In the area where defendant's plant is located, there are other industrial plants.

In its decision the trial court stressed that an injunction to enjoin a public nuisance was a drastic remedy, that the city of Portage had never brought an action for the violation of the ordinance against the defendant and "the defendant had taken considerable steps to improve the situation" and was operating a legitimate business where it had been carried on for many years. The court acknowledged the operation of the defendant's plant "is obviously an annoyance to the immediate neighbors." However, the court was impressed by the reasoning in the concurring opinion in State ex. rel. *Abbott* v. *House of Vision* . . . to the effect that before an injunction will issue when a statute has been violated an effort must be made to prosecute for the violation of the statute, as this remedy is presumably adequate. The court also considered some economic factors although it is stated they were not directly involved, and commented that if an injunction to enjoin the nuisance required the defendant to stop operation, that would be taking of defendant's property without adequate compensation and therefore unconstitutional. The court concluded the case did not constitute such a case as called for the use of an injunction.

We think the trial court was in error. A public nuisance may be proved by a few witnesses. It is the extent and the nature of the acts and the resulting damage which are important, not the number of witnesses. The court questioned the accuracy of the tests performed by the state's experts by presuming noise from sources other than the Samuels plant contributed to the result of the tests. The presumptions are contrary to the testimony and the evidence. The fact the defendant has made some efforts to cut down the amount of noise does not go to the question of the existence of a nuisance. Neither the legitimacy of the business nor the length of time it has been in existence is controlling in determining whether a public nuisance exists. These factors are relevant to the question of whether the court should exercise its discretion to enjoin the nuisance. The reliance on the concurring opinion in State ex. rel. *Abbott* v. *House of Vision,* supra, is misplaced. The concurring opinion is really a dissent on the issue of whether a nuisance existed and whether a crime was enjoined because it is a crime. This dissent relied on State ex. rel. *Fairchild* v. *Wis. Auto Trades Association.* . . . But the language in *Fairchild* must be read in the context of its facts and the express statement, "There is no claim the acts of the respondent constitute a nuisance, public or private."

True, a court of equity will not enjoin a crime because it is a crime, i.e., to enforce the criminal law, but the fact the acts complained of cause damage and also constitute a crime does not bar injunctional relief. The criminality of the act neither gives nor ousts the jurisdiction of equity. . . . In such cases, equity grants relief, not because the acts are in violation of the statute, but because they constitute in fact a nuisance. . . .

This view must be distinguished from the doctrine that the repeated violation of a criminal statute constitutes *per se* a public nuisance. This doctrine justifies the issuance of an injunction not to enforce the criminal statute but to enjoin illegal conduct which, because of its repetition, constitutes a nuisance. Under this doctrine, a violation or a threatened violation of the statute does not constitute a nuisance. The violations of the statute must take place and be repeated to the extent their repetition effects such public rights as will constitute a nuisance.

In the majority opinion of State ex. rel. *Abbott* v. *House of Vision,* supra . . . this court said. . . :

"But the *Thekan* and *Cowie cases* received much study when they were before us and have been re-examined now and we conclude that the language of their opinions, broad as it is, expresses our view of the law and is applicable to acts repeatedly performed and with the avowed purpose of continuing, which do violate a statute whether or not they might be lawful under other and different circumstances. Consequently, we hold that if the statutes are violated as charged in the complaint a public nuisance is committed and the equitable remedy of injunction may be invoked."

The modern concept of injunctional relief is to use it when it is a superior or more effective remedy. This concept is illustrated by the many statutory provisions using an injunction to enforce sanctions and regulations in the commercial world. While the *Thekan* and the *Cowie* cases might be distinguished, their broad language supported this court's view in *State* v. *J. C. Penney Company* . . . upon which this court enjoined repeated violations of a usury statute on the ground that the open, notorious, and flagrant violation of valid laws enacted for the benefit of the people of this state constituted a public nuisance. The court took judicial notice of the widespread use of the revolving charge accounts and the large number of Wisconsin citizens affected by these practices, and thus concluded the violations were a public nuisance which ought to be enjoined.

It would seem this court is now committed to the proposition that the repeated violation of criminal statutes constitutes *per se* a public nuisance. But whether such nuisance should be enjoined depends upon the amount of damages caused thereby and upon the application of the doctrine of the balancing of equities or comparative injury in which the relative harm which would be alleviated by the granting of the injunction is considered in balance with the harm to the defendant if the injunction is granted. If the public is injured in its civil or property rights or privileges or in respect to public health to any degree, that is sufficient to constitute a public nuisance; the degree of harm goes to whether or not the nuisance should be enjoined. The abatement of a nuisance by an *in rem* action is to be distinguished, as those cases generally involve a statutory declaration of what conduct constitutes a public nuisance and a statutory authorization for abatement against the property. . . .

In *Jost* v. *Dairyland Power Cooperative* . . . this court reviewed the theory of public nuisance in the context of a suit for damages. The court relied on *Pennoyer* v. *Allen* . . . in which it was stated it was no defense to show that the business was conducted in a reasonable and proper manner and that the injury might have been done with more aggravation. The court emphasized that the destruction of the enjoyment of the plaintiffs of the comfort of their homes furnished the ground for action. It was pointed out that the lawfulness of the business did not justify the invasion of private rights. In *Dolan* v. *Berthelet Fuel & Supply Co.* . . . the court relied on *Pennoyer* v. *Allen,* supra, and concluded that even though a coal yard was operated properly and was a social and economic business, as was found by the trial court in this case, nevertheless the operation of the coal yard would be enjoined if it caused substantial damage to the adjoining plaintiff.

We need not decide whether defendant's operations in this case amount to a criminal-law nuisance because we think the repeated violations of the city ordinance constituted as a matter of law a public nuisance. We see no valid distinction between a city ordinance regulating business conduct and a criminal state statute. The cases involving city ordinances may be even stronger because ordinances in this state in their nature are not criminal. An ordinance is regulatory and prohibits undesirable conduct, but the consequence for its violation is a forfeiture rather than a fine or imprisonment. . . . A *fortiori* if repeated violations of a public statute as in *Penney* constitute a public nuisance, then the repeated violations of an ordinance constitute a public nuisance. . . .

It does not follow necessarily that the public nuisance resulting from the repeated violation of a statute or ordinance will be enjoined; this depends upon the degree of harm. In the instant case it may well be the amount of harm caused by the repeated violations during the normal work hours of the day is insufficient to call forth an injunction, but the same degree of violation impairing the public's right to the enjoyment of their homes after normal working hours causes a greater injury and ought to be enjoined. If we were to consider the facts in this case in relation to establishing a criminal-law nuisance, it might well be an operation less than that allowed by the ordinance would constitute a public nuisance which should be enjoined. However, the briefs ask for an injunction to limit the operation to what is permitted by the ordinance between 5:00 p.m. and 7:00 a.m. On the theory of our reversal, the injunction can only enjoin operations which constitute violations of the ordinance.

Judgment is reversed, with directions to enter a judgment enjoining the operation of the defendant from violating the city ordinance as to noise and ground vibration during the hours of 5:00 p.m. and 7:00 a.m. each day of the week.

MONARCH INDUS., ETC. v. MODEL COVERALL SERVICE
381 N.E. 2d 1098 (1978)

Hoffman, Judge.

Plaintiff-appellant Monarch Industrial Towel and Uniform Rental, Inc., (Monarch) filed a complaint of tortious interference with a contractual relationship against Model Coverall Service, Inc. (Model). Monarch alleged that Model committed said tort by inducing Emmert Trailer Company (Emmert) to breach its uniform rental service contract with Monarch. (Emmert executed a similar contract with Model after terminating the contract with Monarch).

Following Monarch's presentation of evidence at trial, the trial court granted Model's motion for judgment on the evidence, pursuant to Ind. Rules of Procedure, Trial Rule 50. Monarch perfected this appeal arguing that the court erred in granting Model's motion for judgment on the evidence and in refusing to allow Monarch to reopen its case.

Indiana recognizes the tort of interference with contract relationships by inducing a breach of contract and has defined the essential elements which must be proved for recovery under such an action in *Daly* v. *Nau* . . . , as follows:

"(1) existence of a valid and enforceable contract;
(2) defendant's knowledge of the existence of the contract;

(3) defendant's intentional inducement of breach of the contract;

(4) the absence of justification; and

(5) damages resulting from defendant's wrongful inducement of the breach."

Model's T.R. 50 motion was grounded upon the lack of proper evidence as to damages. But it is well established that the judgment of the trial court will be affirmed on appeal if sustainable on any basis. . . . The evidence presented by Monarch failed to prove that Model intentionally induced Emmert to breach the contract with Monarch. Rather, the evidence shows that Emmert was dissatisfied with the service that Monarch was providing and had been looking at other rental services. The evidence is that Model approached Emmert to inquire as to whether Emmert was being supplied with a uniform rental service and that the Model sales representative was told that Emmert was not happy with the present supplier and intended to cancel the contract. And there was no evidence that Model offered any inducements to Emmert in the form of a better price or better services. Rather, the evidence is that there was no discussion of prices until Emmert had already given Monarch notice of termination of the contract and that the price Emmert was paying under its contract with Model was higher than it had paid under the contract with Monarch.

To sustain a judgment for defendant on the evidence, the evidence must be without conflict and susceptible of but one inference in favor of the moving party. If there is any evidence or legitimate inference therefrom tending to support at least one of plaintiff's allegations, a directed verdict should not be entered. . . . The evidence presented at trial clearly showed that Emmert elected to terminate the contract with Monarch and made the decision independent of Model's approach and subsequent contract with Emmert. There was no evidence from which an inference of intentional inducement to breach on the part of Model could be drawn. . . .

Inasmuch as Monarch failed to prove inducement to breach, this Court need not discuss the sufficiency of the evidence as to the damages incurred by Monarch due to the breach of contract by Emmert or Monarch's argument that granting the T.R. 50 motion denied Monarch its rights to have the jury consider punitive damages.

Finally, whether the court erred in refusing to allow Monarch to reopen its case to present additional evidence as to the net profit it would have earned had the contract been completed is a question this Court does not decide. Error, if any, was harmless since that evidence could not have prevented the failure of the plaintiff's case on the essential element of intentional inducement to breach the contract. . . .

The judgment is affirmed.

Affirmed:

STATON, J., and CHIPMAN, P. J., participating by designation, concur,

BEIDLER v. W. R. GRACE, Inc.

461 F.Supp. 1013 (1978)

MEMORANDUM AND ORDER

Troutman, District Judge.

Plaintiff brings this action against defendant, his former employer, alleging that his discharge was a violation of an implied contract between himself and defendant, and that certain actions of defendant, in terminating plaintiff's employment, constituted wrongful harassment amounting to tortious infliction of mental and emotional distress.

Defendant moves to dismiss, contending that an employment contract is terminable at will and that there was no breach of contract in the termination of plaintiff's employment. Defendant also contends that there can be no tortious infliction of mental distress if there is neither fear of and danger of physical impact nor actual impact, and if the acts complained of are not extreme and outrageous and beyond the bounds of human decency.

Since 1891 the established law in Pennsylvania has been that in the absence of a specific restriction, either statutory or contractual, a contract of employment may be terminated at any time, for any reason or for no reason. . . . This law has recently been reiterated, . . . and has been adopted by the courts of this Circuit. . . .

The law of Pennsylvania regarding contractual provisions of employment, and how they affect terminability, is set forth in *Cummings* v. *Kelling Nut Co.* . . .

"The general rule is that when a contract provides that one party shall render services to another, or shall act as an agent, or shall have exclusive sales rights within certain territory, but does not specify a definite time or prescribe conditions which shall determine the duration of the relation, the contract may be terminated by either party at will * * * (Citations omitted). The burden is on the plaintiff in such cases to overcome the presumption by showing facts and circumstances establishing some tenure of employment * * * (Citations omitted). The intention of the parties governs. One relying on the contract as providing for a reasonable length of time must establish something in the nature and circumstances of the undertaking which would create the inference that a definite or reasonable period of employment was actually contemplated by the parties. . . .

There is no natural or vested right to seniority; seniority arises only as a result of a contract express or clearly implied. . . . In the absence of an agreement for a fixed period of time, a hiring is a hiring at will and gives no right of seniority. Under such a contract of hiring, either party may terminate the contract at will at any time. . . . Stating that an employee's compensation is for a stated amount for a stated period does not make the contract one for a definite period, or even raise a presumption that the hiring was for such period. . . .

In the case before us, there is no indication that there were any provisions for seniority, or if there were, that they applied to plaintiff. Exhibit A to the complaint indicates that there was a procedure to be utilized upon termination of employment. For instance, an "exit interview" was to have taken place outlining the reasons for termination; evaluations were to be made of employee performance and the employee was to be advised as to the basis for the evaluations, the method in arriving at decisions, and the strong points and shortcomings of an employee; penalties of suspension or dismissal, as well as reprimand, could be imposed for a series of offenses; immediate dismissal would be imposed for another series of graver offenses. See Complaint Exhibit A. Despite plaintiff's contentions that these regulations constitute the basis of an implied contract, there is nothing therein to indicate that they are seniority provisions. Absent a seniority provision, the law of Pennsylvania clearly and firmly holds that an employment contract may be terminated at any time for any reason by either party.

We note that *Geary* v. *United States Steel Corporation,* supra, indicated that the absolute right of an employer to discharge an employee at will may be modified, but refused to so modify the law based on the facts before the Court. This potential modification was acknowledged by the Circuit Court of Appeals for this Circuit in *Davis* v. *U.S. Steel Supply,* supra. However, as the Court in *Keddie* v. *Pennsylvania State University,* . . . explained, such modification would occur upon the violation of a clear mandate of public policy, such as dismissal for exercising a statutorily conferred right, such as filing for workmen's compensation benefits. There is nothing in the law of Pennsylvania suggesting that failure to adhere to certain stated guidelines constitutes such violation of public policy. Other courts have held that failure to adhere to certain stated guidelines or policies by an employer in discharging an employee does not constitute a breach of an implied contract. . . . Therefore, we conclude that failure to adhere to company personnel policy does not create a cause of action for breach of an employment contract.

Plaintiff also seeks damages for tortious infliction of mental distress. Such tortious infliction can result from either intentional or negligent conduct. For intentional infliction to occur, there must be intentional, outrageous or wanton conduct, peculiarly calculated to cause serious mental or emotional distress. . . . Plaintiff avers that he was harassed in the following ways:

"(a) being excluded from certain meetings that were necessary to the performance of his job and then being expected to be familiar with the subject matter of said meetings;

(b) finding that the materials and papers located on his desk were constantly being arranged so as to annoy and bother him;

(c) being told on February 22nd that he was being given a new 'assistant'; however, plaintiff had never been conferred with or notified prior to this date of this action nor was the plaintiff informed as to what plans were being made for this new 'assistant';

(d) never received any communication concerning his job performance from his superior, Jan Hansen, but received numerous communications from other employees and rumors that his job was in jeopardy;

(e) plaintiff requested a meeting with his superior, Jan Hansen, for the purpose of ascertaining his employment status; however, Mr. Hansen continually evaded the issue but made several intimations that the new 'assistant' would be replacing the plaintiff."

This conduct is not the type of extreme, outrageous conduct that gives rise to a cause of action. Thus plaintiff has not stated a cause of action for intentional infliction of mental and emotional distress. Nor has plaintiff stated a claim for negligent infliction of mental or emotional distress. For such a cause of action to lie, there must be, if not contemporaneous physical impact, at least personal danger of physical impact from the negligent force and fear of physical impact. . . . Obviously, whatever concerns plaintiff had as regards his employment, he never feared physical impact and, if he did, there is no indication whatsoever that he was in danger of such impact. Thus, he has not stated a claim for infliction of mental or emotional distress.

Accordingly, defendant's motion to dismiss will be granted.

REVIEW QUESTIONS

1. Name a crime that could not be a tort. Name a tort that could not be a crime.
2. Describe and give an example of each of the three degrees of crimes under United States law.
3. What generally must be proved in a tort action?
4. Black, an engineer, is injured while visiting the White Manufacturing Company. The injury resulted from Black being splattered in the face with hot metal from a die casting machine he was observing at the time. What complaint and reasoning might be used by Black? What reply would be likely to be used by White?
5. Gray, an engineer, learned a manufacturing process as a trade secret from White, his employer. Later, Gray quit and went to work for Black. Upon hearing that White had sold his plant to Brown, Gray quit Black's employ and went into business for himself, using the trade secret. Brown is suing for an injunction to prevent Gray from using the trade secret, claiming that the secret process was bought with the rest of the business. Gray claims that he has respected the secret he learned from White in not using it until the business was sold by White. Would the court be likely to issue the injunction? Why or why not?
6. The Green Paper Company has responded to an invitation to set up a plant in a particular community. Several millons of dollars have been spent for buildings and equipment. However, in the first few months of operation numerous complaints have been lodged and injunctions requested. It is claimed that the odors peculiar to the industry have lowered local property values; that the discharge of "black liquor" and dyes in the local stream has eliminated fishing. The plant employs approximately 1,000 people. How would the court be likely to treat the problem?
7. What practical effect does the court's decision have on the defendant in *State* v. *H. Samuels Company, Inc.?*
8. In *Monarch Industries, etc.* v. *Model Coverall Service*, what added evidence did Monarch need to win its case and recover from Model?
9. Based on the court's decision in *Beidler* v. *W. R. Grace, Inc.*, indicate a scenario in which the court would have found for the plaintiff.

22

Product Liability

Tort law consists of a body of rules, statutes, legal theories, and principles designed to assure recovery for private injury. The plaintiff makes his case by showing that defendant neglected a duty he owed to the plaintiff and that this was the proximate cause of plaintiff's injury. But now suppose the defendant is the producer of a product that injured the plaintiff. To what extent may the plaintiff recover? What defense could the producer use? Can the plaintiff obtain evidence held exclusively by the defendant? Must negligence be proved? The answers to these and many related questions comprise the relatively new and currently expanding field of product liability.

History of Product Liability

The idea of recovering from the producer for a product-related injury is of quite recent origin. A century or so ago such a case would have been virtually inconceivable. Even a few decades ago product liability cases and recoveries were quite rare. But in the 1960s revolutionary changes in the field occurred; to understand how and why these changes came about we must review the common law we inherited from England in this regard.

Early English social and legal philosophy reflected the manufacturing nature of the economy. Producers of goods and services were held in high esteem. Their success meant success of the nation. The legal climate fostered their growth. Both logic and social philosophy supported the legal defense available if someone complained about a product—*caveat emptor* (the buyer beware). The logic was simple: one should examine what he is to receive before he buys it. If he is so negligent that he does not examine before he buys, then he should live with his bad bargain. Legal support of an action to recover for a bad product would be, in effect, support of buyer negligence and the law usually will not aid those who are negligent. But then, of course, the products produced in those days were somewhat more easily examined than what we buy today. One can easily see defects in a shovel or wheelbarrow, but automobiles, television sets, automatic washers, and the like have created a rather different product climate. It is a rare consumer who would understand the internal

components and functions of his new car even if he were to dismantle it before he bought it. So is he being negligent when he buys in reliance upon those who produced the vehicle?

Another defense in the producer's armament was *privity of contract*—the idea that one who is not a party to a contract should have no rights arising from it. In other words, if one was injured by a product but he did not buy it directly from the manufacturer, he could not act against that manufacturer to recover for his injury. The producer or manufacturer only needed to interpose a middleman—a wholesaler or retailer—as an insulator. Then, if the injured person could prove he was the buyer of the product, he might sue the middleman, but he could not reach the "deep pocket." Although there is something to be said for the legal generality, the result does not seem quite right. After all, it was the producer and not the middleman who produced the faulty product. Nevertheless, such was the law of a century or so back.

Beginning around the turn of the century the law of product liability began to change. Injured plaintiffs occasionally recovered from producers of faulty products. One decision stands out as being especially predictive of future events. This is the decision as written by Judge Cardozo in *McPherson* v. *Buick Motor Co.*[1] It seems that a wheel on a new Buick collapsed and plaintiff was injured in the resulting accident. In finding for the plaintiff in spite of the defenses mentioned above, Cardozo's reasoning is virtually a statement of product liability law as it became fifty years later. During that half century the law was not entirely predictable or "settled." Courts here and there followed the *McPherson* v. *Buick* decision. Out of all this overturning of previously solid defenses emerged two legal philosophies that came to be used successfully in product liability cases: negligence and warranty.

Negligence. The idea in negligence here is the same as it is anywhere else in tort law. The plaintiff makes his case against the product's producer by showing that the producer owed the plaintiff a duty of careful design and production of the product, that this duty was neglected, and that this neglected duty was the proximate

1. 217 N.Y. 382 (1916).

Plaintiff's case

1. Defective product and defendant's responsibility for it.
2. Defective product was proximate cause of plaintiff's injury.

} Defendant Liability? {

Defendant's case

1. Product alteration.
2. Obviousness (contributory negligence).
3. Abusive use of product.
4. Functional necessity and state of the art.
5. Compliance with standards.
6. Not proximate cause.

Plaintiff's proof (to maximize recovery)

1. "Out of pocket" costs.
2. Lasting effects of injury.
3. Producer neglect of safety considerations.

} Extent of damages (presuming defendant loses) {

Defendant's proof (to minimize recovery)

1. Product abuse.
2. Comparative (or contributory) negligence.
3. Image of care.

cause of plaintiff's injury. Plaintiff problems often arose in attempting to prove producer negligence in design or manufacture, and the producer had a formidable defense if he could prove contributory negligence by the plaintiff. Even so, negligence did win cases for plaintiffs.

Warranty. Other cases were won by plaintiffs based on *warranty*. Specifically, the warranty is the implication that the thing bought will do the job for which it is intended. Not only is it implied that it will do its job, it is also implied that it will not injure the product's purchaser while that job is being done. If injury occurs during the intended use of the warranted product, the injury gives the plaintiff cause to act against the seller of the product; the implied warranty is breached which, in turn, amounts to a breach of contract. But there is a problem in taking a product liability action under warranty. Under the Uniform Sales Act the only person protected by this warranty was the purchaser. Later, under the Uniform Commercial Code, this was changed to include members of the purchaser's household. But note also that the action was based on contract. The purchaser might act against the merchant from whom the product was bought, but there was still no contract basis to act against the product's producer.

Negligence was often difficult to prove, and warranty restricted the parties who might be plaintiff and defendant. Legal statesmen believed that those injured by defective products deserved better treatment. A 1963 case[2] preceded a 1965 change of law[3] which, combined, improved the plaintiff's chances for recovery.

STRICT LIABILITY

In most of the states the law of product liability is set forth as it appears in section 402A of the Restatement (Second) of Torts, as modified by other decisions within the court's jurisdiction. It is therefore important

for us to observe the wording of section 402A: "(1) One who sells any product in a defective condition unreasonably dangerous to the user or consumer or to his property is subject to liability for physical harm thereby caused to the ultimate user or consumer, or to his property, if (a) the seller is engaged in the business of selling such a product, and (b) it is expected to and does reach the user or consumer in the condition in which it is sold. (2) The rule stated in subsection (1) applies although (a) the seller has exercised all possible care in the preparation and sale of his product, and (b) the user or consumer has not bought the product from or entered into any contractual relation with the seller."

Although the statement of *strict liability,* as section 402A is often called, seems clear and unequivocal, we shall observe that many wording interpretations and extensions of meaning have been required. This is currently the product liability arena. This is the setting where opposing attorneys (and expert witnesses) prove the defendant liable or not for a product. It is also the arena where "how much" is determined. Essentially the battles could be pictured in this manner:

Plaintiff's Case

To make a case for recovery against the producer/defendant the plaintiff must prove the product was defective when it left the producer's control. Evidence must then prove a causal connection between the product defect and the injury to the plaintiff. Usually the legal arena includes a jury to which the evidence is presented.

Defective Product. Upon sober reflection one is led to conclude that proof that a product was defective when it left the producer's control may be difficult. At

2. Greenman v. Yuba Power Products, 59 Cal 2d 57, 27 Cal Rptr 679, 377 P2d 897, 13 ALR 1049.

3. Section 402A of the Restatement (Second) of Torts, now adopted by nearly every state.

times it is very simple and so obviously true that the only evidence required is a statement of *res ipsa loquitur* (the thing speaks for itself). At other times it may or may not be true, with expert witnesses contending both ways and with the plaintiff hoping the jury will believe his expert rather than the defendant's expert.

Hidden Defects. The product defect must be a hidden one. Numerous court cases indicate that we have not completely abandoned the idea of *caveat emptor*. Use of an obviously defective product sets up a defense of contributory negligence. In one case the plaintiff was injured while using a fork lift truck in a high stack area.[4] The court held it to be obviously dangerous to operate a fork lift in such a manner without a protective overhead guard and, therefore, the manufacturer of the lift truck should not be responsible for the injury to the operator. On the other hand, the presence of a hidden defect which causes an injury appears to give the plaintiff a right of recovery. In one such case[5] the carbon content of steel upon which the plaintiff was working was high enough to cause the steel to be brittle. In normal use it shattered, causing injury to the plaintiff.

It may not even be necessary to point to the specific hidden defect in the product for plaintiff to recover. During use of a hammer a piece of the head splintered off and struck the plaintiff in the eye. The hammer had been in use eleven months prior to the injury. The hammer head hardness met military standards. No specific fault of the manufacture or design of the hammer was found. There was no proof that a defect existed when the hammer left the defendant's control. Yet the plaintiff recovered from the manufacturer of the hammer.[6]

Several cases have followed a line of reasoning similar to that of the *Dunham* case. In one case[7] the plaintiff could prove only that she was using her five-month-old car in a very reasonable manner in very reasonable circumstances, that she was an experienced driver, was not intoxicated, and did not use drugs, that the car malfunctioned, causing it to crash. She alleged, but apparently did not prove, that the driveshaft became disconnected and dropped to the roadway. Despite an inability to prove a specific defect, she recovered damages.

Discovery. Very often some of the evidence needed by the plaintiff is in the defendant's hands. That is, quality control records, customer complaints, designs and design changes, research and product engineering records, all may have a bearing on the case. In fact, they may be vital to the plaintiff's case. In recognition of this, certain "discovery" procedures have become popular. Usually plaintiff's attorney need only show the court the relevance of the requested information to the plaintiff's case to obtain a court order for it. Defendant's failure to produce that evidence is then contempt of court.

Labels. Sometimes the function of the product and the state of the art of its production and use are such that it is inherently dangerous to use. In this circumstance there is a duty to adequately warn prospective users of the nature of the product. In one case of this nature[8] a man was spreading mastic prior to laying a parquet floor. He had read the label and was aware of the message contained therein which cautioned that the mastic was inflammable. The nature of the substance was actually more than merely flammable—it was explosive and should have been so labeled. The plaintiff was injured in the explosion and recovered because of the inadequacy of the label.

Instructions and Warnings. Most products of more than a trivial nature are accompanied by user instructions of some sort. These may be installation instructions, maintenance procedures, repair details, or, perhaps, something more of the marketing nature. Obviously, following the instructions should not cause the product to injure someone, but suppose the instruction is meant to cure a known problem of the product. Suppose further that one who follows the instruction is, nevertheless, injured by the product.[9] The result can be devastating to defendant, for inadequacy of the product has already been admitted. If the instruction or warning is inadequate to remedy the product defect, its effect on a product liability action is totally negative.

What must the producer do if the hazard is not discovered until a very large number of the products have been distributed? Very simply, the producer must do everything that can reasonably be done to remedy the situation. Automotive product recalls are examples of the extent to which these remedies may be taken. Mailed warnings to all known users could be adequate if sufficient effort were made to identify the likely victims. The producer's position is far from secure in such a circumstance, but the degree and sincerity of effort to warn people likely to be injured at least provides a reasonable defense.

Damages. Plaintiff's action is usually intended to obtain money from the defendant to compensate for plaintiff's loss. Occasionally, because of extremely hazardous or careless behavior by a defendant, a court may go further and award an additional amount to the

4. Posey v. Clark Equipment Company, 400 F. 2d 560 (1969).
5. Moomey v. Massey Ferguson, Inc., 429 F. 2d 1184 (1970).
6. Dunham v. Vaughan & Bushnell Mfg. Co., 247 N.E. 2d 401 (repeated at end of chapter).
7. Hall v. General Motors Corp., 647 F. 2d 175 (1980).
8. Murray v. Wilson Oak Flooring Co., Inc., 475 F. 2d 129 (1973).
9. See Byrd v. Hunt Tool Shipyards, Inc. 650 F. 2d 44 (1981).

plaintiff as a punishment or penalty against the defendant. Damages are discussed in greater detail in Chapter 14.

User or Consumer. The language of section 402A sounds as though there is a definite limitation as to who may be party plaintiff in a product liability case. What about injury to an innocent bystander? This question has been effectively answered in a California case[10] which has been referred to by numerous other states where the question has arisen. The answer is, very simply, that the innocent bystander has the same right as the user or consumer to act against the producer of the injurious product. Logically, the bystander should have even a higher right, since the user or consumer has at least a chance to look at the product before deciding to use it or not. The innocent bystander has no such opportunity.

Defendant's Case

Sometimes the plaintiff's case is so overpowering that defendant has little alternative to settling the matter out of court. This is one area in which the defendant's expert witness may be extremely helpful. If faulty design or manufacture is readily evident to a professional engineer expert in the field, it may be presumed that the fault would also be evident to plaintiff's expert. The best advice the expert can give his client, then, is to settle out of court.

The main reason for defense taking its case to court is that by doing so, defense stands a good chance of winning or reducing the amount of damages to be paid. The decision as to defense course of action depends on what can be proved—what the evidence shows. The nature of the evidence may range from a cause for outright dismissal of the case to virtually nothing that cannot be successfully countered by the plaintiff.

Product Alteration. The producer of a product should be held responsible only for those products he has produced. Close examination of a component part may indicate that it was repaired after manufacture—perhaps replacement brake linings or a rebuilt wheel cylinder failed. If this was the cause of the injury, it may no longer be the automobile producer's responsibility. The question is simply: who produced the product that failed?

Suppose it was the original brake linings (or other component) that failed and caused plaintiff's injury. Suppose further that these linings or other components had been supplied to the automobile producer by another manufacturer. Shouldn't the component supplier be held responsible for the injury rather than the producer who assembled these components into a finished

product? The simple answer is no—it is the producer of the final product as sold to the consumer who is responsible for its safe performance. Whether the producer made the parts himself or bought them is irrelevant as far as his responsibility to the injured plaintiff is concerned. The producer may be able to pass part or all of the loss along to the supplier, but the producer of the final product has primary responsibility.

Proximate Cause. If there is no causal connection between the plaintiff's injury and the producer's product, the plaintiff has no case. One might be able to show a faulty design location of the fuel tank in a car, but if this is in no way connected to plaintiff's injury, the faulty fuel tank location has no bearing on the case. Just as product alteration was a complete defense, so is a successful quarrel with the contention of proximate cause.

Obviousness. As noted above, it is difficult for a plaintiff to maintain a successful action if the product fault causing his injury is an obvious one. The same is true where prominent labels attached to the product have been ignored. Of course, what is obvious to a person experienced with the kind of product in question might not be obvious to a novice, and a label written in English might not be much of a warning to one whose only language is Arabic. Such problems as these and many of those below become questions of fact for a jury to answer.

Abuse. A producer must expect his product to be subjected to all sorts of abuses as well as the use for which it was intended; consider the uses to which you have put screwdrivers. Even T.V. and newspaper advertisements show product abuse as persuasive proof of the rugged nature of products. Still, there is a logical limit to which anticipated abuse may be taken. It is doubtful that a plaintiff's injury resulting from the use of a typewriter as a hammer would be a tolerated abuse. But this sort of question is also often left for a jury to decide.

Functional Necessity and State of the Art. In our present state of technological development it is impossible to accomplish certain functions without some risk being involved. A *completely* safe car would not move; a *completely* safe rotary lawn mower would not mow grass; a *completely* safe knife would not cut. But these functions—movement by car, cutting grass, and other capabilities—are needed by society. So we cannot hold a manufacturer of such things to a standard of complete safety. There is some danger inherent in the operation of most products; perhaps the best we can expect

10. Elmore v. American Motors, 451 P2d 88, 75 Cal Rptr 652, 70 AC 615, 37 LW 2538 (1969).

is a condition we might consider "reasonably dangerous." The standard must run something like this: The manufacturer may be required to produce his product as safely as the state of the art will permit. In other words, a review of the state of the art at the time the product was produced is called for. Returning to that production time, if a survey of the literature and comparison with similar products shows no safer way of accomplishing the function, it seems unreasonable to expect more from the defendant.

Proof of compliance with the state of the art may not necessarily be a complete defense for a producer. The decision could favor the plaintiff for the simple reason that the court believes the state of the art should have advanced more rapidly. Consider Grey Harvester, a producer of agricultural machinery. White, a farmer, was injured while operating a hay baler. Even though Grey successfully shows that he complied with the state of the art and industry standards, he could lose his case. White may be able to show sluggish response by producers of farm machinery to injuries such as these. If the court feels the response should have been more rapid, White may win.

Standards. Hazard reduction and safety have become important considerations. Various federal agencies have become concerned with safety as have the military and industrial organizations. Almost invariably the direction taken by each of these organizations is the formulation and publication of minimum standards to be met by whatever products are being considered. Now suppose that Black Manufacturing Company has complied with all available standards in the manufacture of its product—say, a riding-type rotary lawn mower. Green, in attempting to operate the lawn mower in very heavy grass (or brush, perhaps), manages to injure himself. Green then takes a product liability action against Black Manufacturing. Is Black Manufacturing protected because it complied with the standards? The direct answer is no. The question of liability would probably still be answered according to the section 402A criteria. In fact, if the hazard were so improbable that those who wrote the standards completely missed it, this might be good evidence that what caused the injury was truly a hidden design defect.

On the other hand, noncompliance with published standards resulting in injury to a plaintiff is certainly strong evidence to be used against the producer. It might well be used as a basis for penalty damages beyond mere compensation of the plaintiff for injuries suffered. In addition to this, avoidance of standards published by federal agencies usually occasions fines and/or other sanctions against the offending manufacturer.

Plaintiff's Negligence. Various treatments of contributory negligence by the plaintiff under strict liability appear to exist. Apparently, if the plaintiff has proved a sound case against the product's manufacturer, the defendant's proof of contributory negligence will not relieve the producer of liability. That is, if Green proves a hidden defect in Black Manufacturing's lawn mower and a causal connection between the hidden defect and the injury, Black probably cannot win the case by proving that Green was careless. But that doesn't mean he shouldn't try the defense. Even if contributory negligence fails to win dismissal of the case, it is a valuable point to be made in minimizing damages.

Defense Image. There is nothing in strict liability to indicate that the character of the defendant has anything to do with plaintiff's case. In fact, section 402A would hold the manufacturer liable even though he has done a careful job in preparation and sale of his product. So the defendant may well lose the case. But the amount of loss must be assessed either by a jury or by a judge or by both. If the plaintiff can produce evidence of careless production, sloppy methods, fast and none too careful product engineering changes, insignificant research and overly zealous marketing, this may make an impressive case for penalty damages. On the other hand, if defendant can show great care in design, manufacture, quality control and attention to customer complaints, damages may well be held to a minimal amount. The producer may have to pay for the result of the faulty product, but the risk of penalty damages is minimized.

Design Defects. Products may be defective by reason of faulty design, faulty manufacture according to the design, or faulty labels and warnings. Of the three types of defect, the most serious from the producer's point of view and the most difficult to define is the design defect. A design found to be defective usually involves not just one unit but rather an entire run or lot or, perhaps, many years' production. A defective design decision against one unit of product sets a precedent for recovery in subsequent cases. There is reason, then, for care in determining when a design is defective.

The *Barker* case[11] is particularly thorough in its reasoning as to design defect and presents a logical approach to the definition. The standard announced requires that for the design to be *defective,* (1) plaintiff must establish that the product failed to perform as safely as an ordinary consumer would expect when used in an intended or reasonably foreseeable manner, or (2) plaintiff must show that the product's design proximately caused his injury; and following this, the defendant must fail to establish that the benefits of the

11. Barker v. Lull Engineering Company, Inc., 573 P2d 443 (1978).

challenged design outweigh the risk of danger inherent in such design. Although the risk-benefit, or cost approach has often been a tacit component of product liability cases, *Barker* appears to be the first case in which it is advocated as a formal criterion. Accordingly, a producer should be able to avoid liability for omission of safety devices that would make products virtually inoperable and for failing to include production processes that would double or triple the product cost for miniscule safety improvements. Adoption of the *Barker* case reasoning in other states might provide a foundation for more uniform decisions in product design cases.

State Acts

No one should suffer because of faulty products. Defective products should not have been produced or should have been removed by the producer before they could injure someone. A product liability problem does exist, of course, but some would contend that it suffers from "over-kill." Cases arise where products were not really faulty, were abused, or perhaps were produced many decades ago. The cost of recoveries and out-of-court settlements for such cases is added to production costs, and the public pays in higher prices. In recognition of such apparent abuses many of the states (starting with Utah in 1977) have enacted product liabilty laws.

State product liability acts vary considerably in their content and their degrees of restrictions. The common inclusions are, generally: a) a statute of repose indicating that after a certain period of time (e.g., ten years) the producer's responsibility for the product ends, b) that the "state of the art" is to be usable as a defense, c) that compliance with recognized standards (e.g., military standards) is a reasonable defense, d) that alteration and/or abuse by the plaintiff is a defense, and e) that failure to warn is not a component of strict product liability. Such restrictions as these may become more common in the future of product liability.

DUNHAM v. VAUGHAN & BUSHNELL MFG. CO.

247 N.E. 2d 401 (1969)

Schaefer, Justice.

A jury in the circuit court of Macoupin County returned a verdict in the sum of $50,000 in favor of the plaintiff, Benjamin E. Dunham, and against the defendants Vaughan & Bushnell Mfg. Co. and Belknap Hardware and Mfg. Co. Judgment was entered on the

verdict and the Appellate Court for the Fourth Judicial District affirmed. . . . We allowed the defendants' petition for leave to appeal.

The injury that gave rise to this action occurred while the plaintiff was fitting a pin into a clevis to connect his tractor to a manure spreader. He had made the connection on one side, using a hammer to insert the pin. To insert the second pin he lay on his right side underneath the tractor and used the hammer extended about two and one-half feet above his head. The hammer moved through an arc which he described as about 8 inches. He testified that as he undertook to "tap" the pin into the clevis a chip from the beveled edge of the hammer, known as the chamfer, broke off and struck him in the right eye. He lost the sight of that eye.

The hammer in question is a claw hammer of the best grade manufactured by the defendant Vaughan & Bushnell Mfg. Co. It bore the "Blue-Grass" trademark of its distributor, the other defendant, Belknap Hardware and Manufacturing Co. The plaintiff had received the hammer from a retailer, Hayen Implement Company, located near his home. He received it as a replacement for another "Blue-Grass" hammer, the handle of which had been broken. Before the accident occurred the plaintiff had used the hammer for approximately 11 months in connection with his farming and custom machine work. He had used it in repairing a corn crib and had also used it in working upon his farming implements and machinery.

Each party offered the testimony of an expert metallurgist. Neither expert found any flaws due to the forging of the hammer, or any metallurgical defects due to the process of manufacture. The experts agreed that the hammer was made of steel with a carbon content of "1080." The plaintiff's expert testified that such a hammer was more likely to chip or shear than one made of steel with a lower carbon content of "1040," which would not be so hard. The defendant's expert disagreed; it was his opinion that a hammer made of harder steel, with the higher carbon content, would be less likely to chip or shear than one made of steel with a lower carbon content. Both experts testified that use of a hammer produced a condition described as "work hardening" or "metal failure," which made a hammer more likely to chip or shear.

The defendants apparently suggest that the plaintiff should not have used a claw hammer to tap the pin into the clevis because the mushroom head of the pin was made of steel of "Rockwell" test hardness of C57, which was harder than the head of the hammer, which tested Rockwell C52. But as the appellate court pointed out, the specifications of the General Service Administration used by all Federal agencies, call for a Rockwell

"C" hardness of 50–60 in carpenter's claw hammers and a Rockwell "C" hardness of 50–57 for machinists' ball peen hammers. Those specifications also require that sample carpenter's claw hammers and sample ball peen hammers be subjected to identical tests by striking them against another hammer and against a steel bar, to determine their tendency to "chip, crack, or spall." The specifications thus negate the defendant's suggestion that the plaintiff should have used a ball peen hammer, rather than the hammer in question, in tapping the pin into the clevis.

The basic theory of the defendants in this court is that the requirements of strict liability, as announced in *Suvada* v. *White Motor Co.,* . . . were not established, because the testimony of the experts showed that the hammer contained no defect. *Suvada* required a plaintiff to prove that his injury resulted from a condition of the product which was unreasonably dangerous, and which existed at the time the product left the manufacturer's control. But the requirement that the defect must have existed when the product left the manufacturer's control does not mean that the defect must manifest itself at once. The defective "aluminum brake linkage bracket," with which the court was concerned in ruling upon the legal sufficiency of the complaint in *Suvada,* was alleged to have been installed in the tractor not later than March of 1957; it did not break until June of 1960.

Although the definitions of the term "defect" in the context of products liability law use varying language, all of them rest upon the common premise that those products are defective which are dangerous because they fail to perform in the manner reasonably to be expected in light of their nature and intended function. So, Chief Justice Traynor has suggested that a product is defective if it fails to match the average quality of like products. . . . The Restatement emphasizes the viewpoint of the consumer and concludes that a defect is a condition not contemplated by the ultimate consumer which would be unreasonably dangerous to him. [Restatement, Torts (Second) section 402A, comment g.] Dean Prosser has said that "the product is to be regarded as defective if it is not safe for such a use that can be expected to be made of it, and no warning is given." (Prosser, The Fall of the Citadel, 50 Minn. L. Rev. 791, 826). Dean Wade has suggested that apart from the existence of a defect "the test for imposing strict liability is whether the product is unreasonably dangerous, to use the words of the Restatement. Somewhat preferable is the expression 'not reasonably safe.' " . . .

The evidence in this case, including both the General Services Administration specifications and tests and the testimony of the experts as to "work harden-

ing" or "metal failure," shows that hammers have a propensity to chip which increases with continued use. From that evidence it would appear that a new hammer would not be expected to chip, while at some point in its life the possibility of chipping might become a reasonable expectation, and a part of the hammer's likely performance. The problems arise in the middle range, as Chief Justice Traynor has illustrated: "If an automobile part normally lasts five years, but the one in question proves defective after six months of normal use, there would be enough deviation to serve as a basis for holding the manufacturer liable for any resulting harm. What if the part lasts four of the normal five years, however, and then proves defective: For how long should a manufacturer be responsible for his product?" . . .

The answers to these questions are properly supplied by a jury, and on the record that is before us this case presents only the narrow question whether there is sufficient evidence to justify the jury's conclusion that the hammer was defective. The record shows that it was represented as one of "best quality" and was not put to a use which was regarded as extraordinary in the experience of the community. The jury could properly have concluded that, considering the length and type of its use, the hammer failed to perform in the manner that would reasonably have been expected, and that this failure caused the plaintiff's injury.

Strict liability, applied to the manufacturer of the hammer, Vaughn & Bushnell, extends as well to the wholesaler, Belknap Hardware and Mfg. Co., despite the fact that the box in which this hammer was packaged passed unopened through Belknap's warehouse. The strict liability of a retailer arises from his integral role in the overall producing and marketing enterprise and affords an additional incentive to safety. . . . That these considerations apply with equal compulsion to all elements in the distribution system is affirmed by our decision in *Suvada* v. *White Motor Co.* . . .

The defendant's objections to the instructions to the jury were adequately disposed of in the opinion of the appellate court. The judgment of the appellate court is affirmed.

Judgment affirmed.

GIERACH v. SNAP-ON TOOLS CORP.

255 N.W. 2d 465 (1977)

Heffernan, Justice.

This action for negligence is brought by a user of a ratchet wrench against the manufacturer, Snap-on Tools Corporation. Peter Gierach, the Plaintiff, was an employee of the Riebe Oldsmobile Garage in Grafton, Wisconsin. On May 1, 1973, Gierach was working on an Oldsmobile automobile when the ratchet wrench slipped. Gierach sustained injuries to his face, mouth, and teeth when the ratchet wrench struck him. The evidence showed that Gierach was using the wrench properly at the time the accident happened. After the accident, the wrench was placed in the tool box of Karrels, the service manager at Riebe, to whom the wrench belonged. About a week later, Dick Augers, a salesman for Snap-on Tools, made one of his regular sales calls to the garage and was told about the accident. He took the wrench into the back room and disassembled the gear housing. It was apparent to those present that a gear tooth was sheared. The plaintiff testified that Augers said, "Well, this is what the problem is, that the gear is sheared and this would cause it to slip." Karrels, the service manager, also testified that the sheared gear was discovered when the Snap-on salesman disassembled the housing. Karrels also testified to the salesman's statement.

The action was brought by the plaintiff on the theory that the accident was caused by the manufacturer's improper design or manufacture of the ratchet wrench.

At the trial, Karrels, who was a master mechanic with extensive experience, gave as his opinion that the gear teeth were not properly hardened, and, as a consequence, the gear tooth sheared off. On the other hand, there was testimony by Godlewski, Snap-on's quality assurance inspector, that the gears were properly hardened, that they were built and designed to withstand 5,000 pounds of pressure, and that there was nothing wrong with the manufacture or design of the tool. Snap-on's witness acknowledged, however, that the maximum pressure that could be exerted on the wrench by a worker would be less than 1,000 pounds.

It was Godlewski's testimony that the wrench had not been cleaned and maintained properly, that grease and debris had built up within the gear housing, and the gear pawl could not seat properly to fully engage the gear teeth. He said that it was as a consequence of this improper maintenance that the wrench slipped.

The parties, prior to trial, stipulated that the damages for personal injuries were $4,500.[12] The jury, accordingly, was required only to return a verdict in respect to negligence. Ninety percent of the negligence was attributed to Snap-on Tools Corporation and ten percent to the injured plaintiff, Gierach. Judgment for the plaintiff was entered for the total sum of $4,249.69, including costs and disbursements. The appeal was taken from that judgment.

The trial judge instructed on the elements of negligence, and, in addition, instructed in respect to the duty of a manufacturer to exercise ordinary care in the design and manufacture of its product so as to render that product safe for its intended use. He also instructed that the manufacturer had the duty to exercise ordinary care to give adequate warning of the dangers attendant upon the proper use of the product. A *res ipsa loquitur* instruction was given in the following form:

> "You are further instructed that if you find that the plaintiff was properly using the ratchet wrench in question at the time of the accident and that nothing occurred to cause the ratchet wrench to become defective after it left the defendant's control, and if you further find that the accident in this case ordinarily would not have occurred if the ratchet wrench had not been defective in its design, you may then infer from the accident itself and the surrounding circumstances that there was negligence on the part of the defendant in the design or manufacture of the ratchet wrench."

The court instructed the jury that Gierach had a duty to use ordinary care for his own safety.

The defendants, insofar as the record shows, submitted no proposed instructions to the court and failed to object to any of the instructions that were given. Yet, on this appeal, defendant argues for the first time that, because this is an action for negligence and not for strict liability under sec. 402(A) of the Restatement of Torts, a *res ipsa loquitur* instruction was inappropriate. This objection comes too late, because the defendant fully acquiesced in this instruction. In addition, a *res ipsa* inference is permissible in respect to any tort which occasions unintentional personal injuries if the elements necessary for instructing on that inference are placed in evidence. The evidentiary preconditions for the doctrine were summarized in *Utica Mut. Ins. Co.* v. *Ripon Cooperative*. . . .

> "(1) The event in question must be of the kind which does not ordinarily occur in the absence of negligence; (2) the agency or instrumentality causing the harm must have been within the exclusive control of the defendant."

12. The record is confusing, for the judgment recites that the parties had, prior to trial, stipulated to a $4,500 damage ceiling. Our review of the record indicated, however, that, both in plaintiff's motion after verdict for entry of judgment and in verbal representations by both parties immediately prior to trial, the damage ceiling was stipulated to be $5,000. However, for purpose of this appeal, we accept the statement in judgment that the stipulated ceiling was $4,500.

The instruction given in the instant case was in substantial conformance with these standards and was not objected to. The evidentiary preconditions for the *res ipsa* inference were satisfied in this case. There is no dispute that the slipping of the gears would not have occurred in the absence of negligence. Exclusivity of control does not mean that the instrumentality be in the physical possession of the defendant at the time of the occurrence. . . . As we noted in *Ryan* v. *Zweck-Wollenberg Co.,* . . . quoting from Prosser, Torts, sec. 43, p. 298:

> " 'All that is necessary is that the defendant have exclusive control of the factors which apparently have caused the accident; and one who supplies a chattel to another may have had sufficient control of its condition although it has passed out of his possession.' ". . .

Defendant also asserts that *res ipsa* is inapplicable in a products liability case where negligence is alleged. That assertion is completely without foundation in the law; and we conclude that, under the circumstances, it was within the sound discretion of the trial judge to give that instruction. . . . In the circumstances here, moreover, the *res ipsa* instruction was given without objection.

The defendant, on this appeal for the first time, impliedly objects to the instruction in respect to the manufacturer's duty to warn in respect to the use and care of the ratchet wrench. There was no objection to that instruction when it was offered by the court. However, the point which the defendant now seeks to assert was arguably made when the defendant objected to the special verdict question which inquired:

"Was the defendant negligent with respect to:

". . . (b) Failing to warn of dangers with respect to the ratchet wrench?"

The objection to the question was based, however, not on the lack of an evidentiary basis at the trial, but rather on an answer given by the plaintiff to a question asked by defendant's counsel.

Defendant's counsel asked, "(C)an you think of any further instruction or warning that could have been given to you. . . ." The plaintiff responded that he could not think of any. From this, defense counsel concludes that it was conceded that no warnings were necessary. This position, however, is contrary to the entire tenor of the defendant's case.

It was the position of the defendant throughout the trial that the plaintiff and his fellow employees had failed to clean and maintain the wrench properly and that the consequent buildup of grease and dirt within the gear housing of the wrench caused the slippage. The response appropriately made by plaintiff's counsel to this assertion is simply that, if such hazard existed, the purchasers and ultimate users of the wrench should have been warned by the manufacturer of the necessity of periodically opening the gear box and cleaning it. No warning was ever given by the manufacturer. The record shows that it was the defendant's theory of the case and its evidence that made it reasonable for the trial judge to instruct on the manufacturer's duty to warn of the necessity for the periodic cleaning of the wrench.

It was Godlewski, the defendant's expert witness, who testified that grease and dirt could build up within the gear housing and cause it to slip. It is apparent from the defendant's own testimony that it was aware of the slippage danger and yet it failed to give any warnings or instructions with respect to the maintenance or cleaning of the wrench.

Snap-on Tools, knowing that someone could be injured if the tool were not properly maintained, had a duty to warn and it failed to discharge that duty.

In view of the fact that the defendant failed to object to any of the instructions, and because the instructions given were not legally erroneous, no objection to the instructions can be raised on this appeal.

The defendant on this appeal argues that a verdict question should have been submitted to the jury in respect to whether the service manager, Karrels, was negligent in the supervision of Gierach in respect to the use and care of the ratchet wrench. The trial judge refused that requested question because there was no evidence that Karrels was negligent. The trial judge, therefore, properly excluded a question about Karrel's negligence. Although, as we held in *Connar* v. *West Shore Equipment of Milwaukee, Inc.,* . . . a special verdict question in respect to the negligence of an individual who is not a party may be included in the verdict, it is necessary that there be "evidence of conduct which, if believed by the jury, would constitute negligence on the part of the person or other legal entity inquired about." . . . The trial judge properly concluded that there was no evidence upon which a jury could have found Karrels negligent for the failure to warn or supervise Gierach.

The evidence was sufficient to support the verdict, whether the verdict be viewed in the light of the plaintiff's initial theory that the wrench was negligently designed and manufactured or whether it be viewed in light of the defendant's theory that the accident occurred because of the buildup of grease and dirt within the wrench housing.

There were sufficient facts to support the jury's verdict in respect to negligent manufacture and design, because the evidence showed that the manufacturer represented that the gears were designed to withstand pressures up to 5,000 pounds. Yet, the testimony presented by the defendant's expert indicated that at most a maximum force of 1,000 pounds could have been exerted by Gierach.

Applying the inferences that are appropriate under the *res ipsa* instructions, the jury could reasonably conclude that the instrumentality was within the control of the manufacturer and that the breaking of the gear would not have occurred were it not for some negligence in the manufacture or design.

Looking at the jury verdict in connection with the defendant's theory that the buildup of grime and dirt occasioned the slippage, it is apparent that the evidence showed that the manufacturer was aware of this hazard and yet failed to give any warning or instruction whatsoever in respect to the cleaning or maintenance of the sealed gear housing.

The most difficult question in respect to negligence is one not posed on this appeal at all. Our examination reveals no evidence of negligence on the part of the plaintiff Gierach. Apparently, however, plaintiff's counsel, as a matter of strategy, concluded not to cross-appeal in light of the relatively small amount of reduction of damages occasioned by the jury's attribution of ten percent of the negligence to Gierach.

The question of the sufficiency of the evidence was posed on motions after verdict; and the trial judge, upon re-examination of the record, concluded that there was ample evidence to sustain the findings of the jury.

While there was evidence submitted by the defendant which, if believed by the jury, would tend to eliminate or minimize any negligence on the part of the defendant, the trial judge correctly pointed out that the jury was not obliged to believe such testimony. It did not.

Our review of the record reveals no error of law, and the evidence was sufficient to support the verdict.

Judgment affirmed.

BARBER v. GENERAL ELEC. CO.

648 F.2d 1272 (1981)

William E. Doyle, Circuit Judge.

The question which is here presented is whether the trial court erred in granting defendant's motion for summary judgment in a personal injury case which grew out of a high-voltage transformer explosion in the course of its being installed.

The occurrence took place on May 27, 1976. The transformer was being installed by the plaintiff Barber and other employees of Western Farmers Electric Co-

operative at a Western Farmers substation. General Electric had manufactured the transformer at Rome, Georgia, and had shipped it to Anadarko, Oklahoma, by rail in 1974. Western had stored it for two years. It had been moved to the installation site in May of 1976. During installation there was a malfunction. This caused pressure to build up inside the transformer. A further result was the expulsion of insulating oil through a pop-off valve. There was a protective system which would have caused fuses to blow and turn the circuit off, but it failed to function. Just prior to the explosion Barber had been standing under the pop-off valve, and (he) was covered with the expelling oil. He claims that he was blinded by the oil and while he ran from the vicinity of the expelling oil, he fell and seriously injured himself. Barber's cause of action was based on two theories of strict liability in tort, namely manufacturer's product liability and breach of implied warranty of merchantable quality—fitness for its intended use.

General Electric sued Western Farmers Electric Cooperative as a third-party defendant. Employers Casualty Corporation, the Workmen's Compensation carrier, intervened. It alleged a subrogation interest as against General Electric. It also realleged plaintiff Barber's theories of recovery.

The trial court entered summary judgment in favor of General Electric and against plaintiff Barber. . . .

II. Propriety of the Granting of Summary Judgment

Plaintiff contends that Western Farmers justifiably relied on General Electric's ability to warrant the integrity of the system which was contained in that part of the transformer which was designed, manufactured, and sealed in their Rome, Georgia, plant. His additional allegation is that Western Farmers relied on a statement in General Electric's Transformer Instruction Manual which stated that "transformers are normally shipped completely assembled, liquid filled, and ready to install." Also contended is that the transformer was not "ready to install" or "completely assembled," and that the fire was caused by a defective terminal board, loose or unconnected wires into the terminal board, or a combination of both.

The position of General Electric is that the terminal board was not faulty and that any loose connections into the terminal board occurred after the transformer arrived at Anadarko, Oklahoma. General Electric points to the fact that the transformer was under Western Farmers' control for two years prior to the accident; that the transformer was inspected by Western Farmers at the time it was delivered to Anadarko and nothing was found wrong at that time; that employees of Western Farmers inspected it again prior to its being moved to the installation site; that Western Farmers employees admit that they did not inspect the terminal board connectors on the main tank compartment side of the transformer (where the explosion occurred), although this inspection was recommended by General Electric in its Installation and Maintenance Instruction Manual.

Another point which is advanced by General Electric is that the main tank compartment of the transformer had not been "sealed" by General Electric, since the manual specifically recommended inspection, and the term "sealed" is defined (in *Black's Law Dictionary*) as "fastened . . . so as to be closed against inspection." Barber responds to this by saying that after General Electric filled the compartment with insulating oil, the top of the compartment was "sealed" by means of a plate that was bolted down and was "air tight" according to General Electric publications.

General Electric emphasizes that plaintiff has not come forward with any evidence which shows that any defect was present in the transformer when it left General Electric's hands in 1974. There are simple answers to this assertion. One is that circumstantial evidence is present in the substantial discovery. The other answer is that the summary judgment motion was presented in the midst of the discovery stage of the case.

The legal standards applicable to this products liability case are to be found in *Kirkland* v. *General Motors Corp.,* . . . as follows:

1. It must be shown that the product was the cause of the injury;

2. It must be shown that the defect existed in the product at the time it left the manufacturer.

3. It must be shown that the defect rendered the product unreasonably dangerous to an extent beyond that which would be contemplated by the ordinary consumer who purchased it, with ordinary knowledge common to the community as to its characteristics.

General Electric maintains that Barber has failed to present any evidence which has established all of the above listed elements. It argues that there is no evidence that the defect existed at the time that it left General Electric. General Electric also argues that an ordinary utility customer would not disregard proper installation instructions by the manufacturer, and that a high-voltage transformer could not be dangerous beyond that which would be contemplated by an "ordinary utility customer."

Barber lists some fifteen factual disputes which prevent the grant of a summary judgment. Barber also argues that General Electric viewed and repaired the burned transformer, and after doing so it destroyed the burned parts; that these are the parts which are important evidence. Barber admits that no evidence exists that General Electric intentionally destroyed the internal parts of the transformer in order to cover up evidence. Barber does not accuse General Electric of any wrongdoing. He does maintain that even though the act of General Electric was innocent it would be unfair to prevent him from presenting his case because he is unable to produce any pieces of the transformer which had been destroyed.[13]

Some fourteen depositions were taken in the case. Most of these were on behalf of General Electric. The General Electric depositions focused on the fact that Western Farmers did not follow the inspection procedure which had been recommended in its manual. Also emphasized is that since the accident, Western Farmers has instructed their employees to follow the manual. The facts adduced in depositions show that at the time of the accident Western Farmers employees did not open the sealed compartment in the main tank, drain the compartment of several hundred gallons of oil, and check the terminal board connectors for loose connections. The employees have followed that procedure since the accident. The same employees testified in the depositions that prior to the accident they did not believe that such procedure was necessary. One deponent, Frank Mingus, Station and Equipment Superintendent for Western Farmers, testified that Western Farmers thought, prior to the accident, that such a policy was likely to do more harm than good.

13. The ultimate issue is the sufficiency or lack thereof of evidentiary proof of the factors enumerated in *Kirkland,* supra, which Barber must present in order to avoid summary judgment in favor of General Electric. This court has held that for summary judgment to lie, " '(t)he movant must demonstrate entitlement (to a summary judgment) beyond a reasonable doubt and if an inference can be deduced from the facts whereby the non-movant might recover, summary judgment is inappropriate.' " . . . The court must construe the evidence, and all reasonable inferences therefrom, in the light most favorable to the party opposing the motion for summary judgment. . . . Summary judgment is not to be granted unless the evidence is clear to the point that there is no genuine factual issue upon which reasonable minds might differ. *Williams* v. *Borden,* supra. This standard differs from the standard for a directed verdict. To avoid a directed verdict in a products liability case in Oklahoma, a plaintiff must present enough evidence to permit the inference that more probably than not the product was defective when sold. . . . To avoid summary judgment in a product liability case, however, the party opposing it need only show that the evidence regarding whether the product was deficient when sold is subject to conflicting interpretations of such nature that reasonable men might differ as to its significance. *Id.* The courts recognize that summary judgment is a drastic remedy which is to be granted with caution so as to insure that litigants will have a trial on bona fide factual disputes. . . . The foregoing are the governing standards in the summary judgment evaluation.

General Electric contends that if this procedure had been followed the accident would not have happened. However, the evidence in question does not necessarily bar the plaintiff Barber because it does not establish his assumption of risk or contributory negligence. Nor does it establish this as to Western Farmers. In any event, assumption of risk is relevant only if it shows that there has been a voluntary assumption of a known risk. . . . If General Electric is, in fact, arguing that Western Farmers was aware of a known defect, such a question would be for the jury.

The testimony does raise an important issue, however. That is whether the transformer was defective when delivered to Western Farmers solely because Western Farmers was not warned that an inspection in accord with the suggested procedures was vital, and that in its absence there would be a fire or explosion. If the risk was of this magnitude it seems strange that General Electric did not attach a warning sign to the transformer in a conspicuous place.

From the present record it is plain that summary judgment is not the remedy in this case because there is no lack of a factual dispute as to whether the product was defective when it left General Electric. It is noteworthy that the General Electric emphasis is on its own inquiry which pursues the proposition that Western Farmers failed to heed General Electric's instructions. This in itself involves a question whether the equipment was defective when it departed from General Electric.

Oklahoma follows the well-accepted principle that failure to warn may be, in itself, a defect within the product. . . . There the Colorado Supreme Court noted that the adequacy of warning, or the requirement of a warning, is to be determined only after the consideration of the likelihood of accident and the seriousness of the consequences of failure to warn. Such questions are factual and are to be decided by the jury.

Plaintiff did not specifically raise the issue of the failure to warn in the proceedings below. However, it is a much present issue in the case. The contents of the depositions taken by General Electric make this clear. It is not clear as a matter of law that a suggested means for inspecting a transformer found in an instruction manual is an adequate means for communicating a warning where, as here, the risk of non-inspection is great.

We do not agree that the fact that plaintiff is unable to show a defect in the circuit board, which board was destroyed by General Electric after the fire, should preclude the plaintiff proving his cause of action by circumstantial evidence. The Oklahoma Supreme Court in *Kirkland,* supra, recognized that in a products liability case proof can be through circumstances and inferences rather than direct evidence, since actual or direct proof of the defect in a sophisticated product may be within the sole knowledge or possession of the defendant. . . .

We are not advancing an opinion on the ability of plaintiff to succeed on the merits. We do say that the evidence in the record is sufficient to show the existence of several fact questions in connection with the standards which are set forth in *Kirkland,* supra. There are undoubtedly other fact questions. One of particular importance which comes to mind is the question of whether the fire-explosion occurred as a result of General Electric's failure to warn Western Farmers that its transformer could explode and burn if the suggestions in its installation manual were not followed, thereby rendering the transformer defective under Oklahoma law at the time it left General Electric's hands. This latter issue is relevant to both Points 2 and 3 in *Kirkland,* supra. They must be proved in order to successfully maintain an action for products liability. Depositions of the medical doctors involved also indicate the existence of a factual issue regarding whether the allegedly defective transformer and resulting accident were the factual cause of Barber's injuries. This issue is relevant to the first standard which is set forth in *Kirkland,* supra, and which plaintiff must fulfill in order to succeed in his case.

It is not the duty of the trial court to weigh the evidence between the plaintiff and the defendant on a motion for summary judgment. Nor is it the purpose of the summary judgment remedy to serve as a substitute for a trial by the judge or for a trial by jury. In this case there are factual disputes in connection with each of the three areas or standards which are set forth in *Kirkland,* supra. Therefore, summary judgment is not applicable.

The judgment of the district court is reversed and the cause is remanded for a trial in accordance with the views expressed herein.

REVIEW QUESTIONS

1. Why was *caveat emptor* an appropriate defense 200 years ago but is not appropriate today?
2. What is the meaning of *privity of contract?* Under what circumstances does it make reasonable law? Why isn't it an appropriate defense in a product liability case?
3. Contrast strict liability as stated in the Restatement (Second) of Torts, section 402A, with negligence and warranty as they would be applied to product liability.

4. The White Company produces a combination tool for home use which may be converted to a lathe, drill press, grinder, and many other power tools. Gray bought one of these tools and was injured while using it as a lathe. The injury occurred because the lathe chuck loosened and the piece on which Gray was working flew out of the chuck, striking him in the head. Gray was out of work for several weeks and has lost partial sight of his right eye. What would you as plaintiff's expert witness look for to make a case for Gray to recover? What would you do as defendant's expert witness in the case?

5. Can you make the cost-benefit ideas of *Barker* v. *Lull Engineering* agree with the sec. 402A definition of strict liability? Does it agree better with negligence or warranty?

6. In the case of *Dunham* v. *Vaughan & Bushnell Mfg. Co.* the manufacturer was found responsible even though no negligence in design or manufacture was proved. If such is the trend under strict liability, what could a manufacturer do to protect himself against such losses?

7. In the case of *Dunham* v. *Vaughan & Bushnell Mfg. Co.* is there any indication that the tractor manufacturer or the manure spreader manufacturer could have been made party defendant rather than the producer of the hammer?

8. The *Gierach* case and the *Barber* case involve the presence and absence of written instructions. How should the producer of a product with known hazards warn a distant and unknown user of those hazards? Suppose the hazard is discovered after many products have been sold and distributed—now what measures should be taken?

Section VI

Governmental Regulation

Political considerations dictate engineering activity to a very considerable degree. This is obviously true in projects run by the federal government (e.g., engineering for NASA and the military) and by state and local governments (e.g., roads, bridges, and water supply). Politically inspired intervention is an expected component of such projects. A major problem in exercising such political control of engineering activities is the lack of effective communication between politicians and engineers. Common observation leads one to conclude that many politicians tend to be scientifically naive. On the other hand, many if not most engineers find political involvement and motivations difficult to understand and reconcile with engineering requirements. The results are frequently less than desirable.

Much of the control on engineering activity in private as well as public enterprise is exercised by administrative agencies according to administrative rules and laws. The basic idea is that an administrator with some knowledge of the engineering and business involved will act as the control mechanism according to established rules. Of course, the regulatory statute was politically inspired (and the rules are made according to that inspiration), and the personnel employed to regulate often have backgrounds that leave something to be desired. Under these circumstances it is not surprising that engineers often complain about the controls imposed on them.

Here we will look at the law and activities of administrative agencies in general. Then we will discuss how administrative agency controls are commonly applied to three industrial functions: labor, workers' compensation, and safety.

23

Administrative Law

We have always had administrative agencies or bureaus or commissions. For the first century and a half or so after our government was formed there weren't many of these entities, but since then there has been an ever increasing tide of them. The federal government has the ICC, the FRB, the SEC, the NLRB, the IRS, and the FTC to name only a few. At the state level of government there is usually some sort of industrial commission, a governing board for the universities, a tax commission, numerous licensing boards, and many other agencies. Local agencies include zoning boards, school boards, welfare agencies, and others. All of these boards have powers to investigate, make rules and individual rulings, and supervise activities in some limited geographical area and some sphere of activity. All have delegated powers—powers delegated to them by a legislative body or a chief executive (e.g., President, governor, mayor). We are in almost daily contact with them, and they have an ever-increasing influence on what we may do and how we may go about doing what we do. It seems only reasonable, then, that we should consider what or who controls these agencies, why they exist, and how one learns to live with them.

Why Agencies?

Administrative agencies act like courts of law in some of the things they do—they may rule for or against an individual or a business. Brown may be granted or denied a license to operate a business, or his license may be taken from him because he failed to follow an agency rule. Gray's tax return may be investigated by the Internal Revenue Service and deductions allowed or denied. Black may not be allowed credits for the courses he took at another university when he tries to enter Old Siwash U. White Company may be required to cease and desist air or stream pollution. Green Trucking Company may require agency approval of its rates before it can offer its service to customers. Whenever an agency does something like this it is acting in a fashion that resembles what a court does. Unlike courts, however, agencies do not have to wait until an injury has occurred before they act.

Agencies are also legislative in nature. They have the power to investigate situations that come to their attention and then make rules based on what they find.

The Internal Revenue Service may find it desirable to require people like Green to keep another kind of record. After following appropriate rule-making procedure, the rule requiring Green to keep such a record would appear in an issue of the Federal Register. The Federal Power Commission may wish to make a rule regarding the sharing of power in different sections of the United States. Again, after following a required procedure, the rule would appear in the Federal Register. Publication in the Federal Register is assumed to be adequate notice to anyone affected by the rule.

In many ways agency activities are like those of an executive or supervisor. They generally have the right not only to investigate, but to act to prevent occurrences which they anticipate as harmful to someone. The practicalities are such that the threat of active supervision may be sufficient to obtain the objective sought by the agency.

Agency activities, in other words, do not reflect the separation of powers so carefully assigned in our Constitution. Rather, they blend the powers so separated to govern a segment of the population or business world in the name of the public.

The suggestion is sometimes made that courts could do better what agencies are supposed to do. But one need only consider the traditional nature of courts to see the magnitude of changes that would be required for courts to replace agencies. The main function of courts is to hold trials. Traditional court procedure is designed to obtain all pertinent information regarding some past event. Then, armed with this information, the court makes a judgment. This is the court procedure expertise. Only rarely, and then in the nature of an equity action, will courts concern themselves with things that have not yet occurred. In numerous cases motions to dismiss are granted because the action is *moot,* meaning there is no real and present issue to be decided. Or a court's judgment may refrain from going beyond the minimum reasoning required to answer a present question. To go beyond this point would be *dicta,* or dictating what courts in the future might do in other situations. This rule-making or legislating is usually carefully reserved for a legislature.

Another point may be made in favor of administrative agencies rather than courts for supervision in an area of activity. The point is simply this: judges are experts in law, and usually not expert in the technicalities of a given kind of activity. Judge Brown, for example, probably was an attorney for a period of years before being elected or appointed to his present position. He may have specialized within the law, but even so, he might be classed as expert or semiexpert in almost any area of civil law or criminal law. At least, by brushing up on recent cases in a given area he could make intelligent judgments on questions arising therein. But now, suppose we place him in a position where a knowledge of atomic energy is essential (e.g., the AEC), or where electrical power distribution questions arise (e.g., the FPC). Suppose further that we ask him to supervise activities by companies involved with these questions. By so doing we are probably asking too much of the judge. A better choice might be Black (a nonlawyer), who has been involved with the field for a substantial period. By choosing Black we presumably reduce the chances of horrible and costly errors and increase the probability of sound decisions.

Administrative Abuses.

As one examines the results of our government by agencies, he cannot escape the conclusion that despite all the arguments for them the results can turn sour. Newspaper reports, investigators' comments, law cases, and comments from friends who were victims reveal problems.

Consider Black, above, who was just appointed to a six-year term as a member of the seven-person committee heading XYZ Commission. He was appointed because he is expert in the XYZ field. Of course, he is also likely to be a member of the appointment-maker's political party or at least sympathetic toward it. Now, Mr. Black may be a very ethical sort of a person. But even if he is, there are opportunities and pressures in administrative agencies that can bring about changes in this facet of his personality.

As a government employee Mr. Black's travel costs are covered by an expense voucher at the end of a trip. If his need to travel is caused by a supervised company, however, there is reason to ask the company to pick up the tab. If Mr. Black works it "properly," he may be able to get expense money from both sources. If he can work in visits to other supervised companies at the same time, he may, perhaps, obtain multiple travel payments. If one of the companies supervised is engaged in the business of transporting people, Mr. Black may obtain free trips to "examine" first hand the nature of transportation it offers. And if a company deals in vacations, the nature of vacation must, of course, be investigated in person. Mr. Black may very soon learn

that because of the supervisory power he wields, almost any company he supervises may be called upon successfully for favors.

Mr. Black's appointment to the commission lasts only six years. If Mr. Black intends to live longer than six years, it is desirable for him to be eligible for another job at the end of that period. His most likely future employer is one of the companies he supervises. There is, therefore, a significant practical pressure to induce him to treat at least one large company favorably in tacit agreement as to future employment.

Of course, not all commissioners and administrative agency officials have erodible ethics. But then, neither are they all paragons of virtue. They tend only to be human with human strengths and weaknesses.

ADMINISTRATIVE AGENCY ACTIVITIES

The activities of administrative agencies are primarily those of (a) holding hearings, (b) rule making, and (c) supervision. In carrying out these functions the agencies are often given broad discretionary powers. If an agency steps beyond the boundaries of these powers as outlined by the act creating the agency, it may be called upon to engage in a fourth activity, that of defending itself in court where one of the entities supervised is plaintiff.

Hearings.

The agency counterpart to a court trial is a hearing. The main differences from a trial are that a hearing examiner rather than a judge presides and that there is usually much less formality involved. The result of the hearing is a *finding* which is submitted to the agency for appropriate action. Most hearings are *adjudicative*—that is, there is a plaintiff (often the agency, itself) and a defendant. Some, though, are *legislative*—simply a device for collecting evidence prior to making a general rule of some sort. The legislative hearing is appropriately a part of the rule-making procedure.

Adjudicative hearings are conducted to determine what happened in some instance or set of instances in question. The Gray Company has been accused by the National Labor Association (union) of an unfair labor practice. Specifically, the NLA says that just prior to the recent representation election one or more members of management made statements amounting to threats if the NLA became the elected representative of the employees. (Obviously, the NLA lost the election or there would not be the hearing.) The unfair labor practice complaint was made to the National Labor Relations Board which reacted to the complaint by appointing a hearing officer to investigate. A time and place for the hearing was set, the date came, and a trial-type hearing attempted to elicit the facts of the case. Witnesses were called, sworn in, examined, and cross-examined. Hearsay may have been allowed, and sometimes something less than the best evidence may have been used.

The results were sent on to the NLRB by the hearing officer as his findings, along with his recommendations for action (or inaction). The NLRB is not bound by the hearing officer's recommendation—it may order a new election or not regardless of the recommendation it receives. If an election is ordered the Gray Company or the union that won the election may wish to appeal the order. If the NLRB order is that the situation is to remain as is, the NLA may wish to appeal. Depending upon the nature of the question and other circumstances, appeal may be taken to a U.S. District Court or a U.S. Court of Appeals.

The hearing procedure described above is similar to that required by nearly all federal administrative agencies and some state agencies. The major differences to be noted in lower government levels are the likelihood that the hearing will take place before the entire agency rather than a hearing officer, and that the appeal procedure will go through the state or a local court system.

Rules and Rule-Making.

Rule-making is a legislative procedure. Administrative agencies make rules to regulate the activities of the entities controlled presumably in the public interest. One problem of the procedure is that sometimes the public interest seems to get lost in the process. In some ways this is not surprising, for in the day-in-day-out operations of administrative agencies they are in close contact with the businesses they supervise. Thus, it is often the businesses themselves who propose the rules to be made. In such a set of circumstances one should not expect the resulting regulations to bring excessive hardships to the businesses. A rule so made may very well benefit the business community supervised at a cost to the public.

Rules are usually made pursuant to directives in the statute creating the agency powers. If the rule is one the statute called for the agency to make, it is known as a *legislative rule*. Such legislative rules have much the same force as laws. The other general category of rules made is that of *interpretive rules*—rules that interpret something. An interpretive rule may interpret a law, a policy, another rule, a rate schedule, or something else. Such interpretations are often open to question and court review.

Procedural Fairness. Rules could be made in such a way as to be arbitrary and completely unfair to one or more of those supervised or to the public in general. There is a federal law (and some states also have such laws) known as the *Administrative Procedure Act* designed to prevent such unfairness. This law in conjunction with the act creating the agency sets forth general procedures to be followed by agencies in making rules. The primary means by which fairness is assured is the requirement for agency actions to be open to public scrutiny.

In keeping with procedural fairness, agencies usually do not make rules without first giving notice that such rules are being considered. Thus, an opportunity is given for those who would be adversely affected to attempt to counter the rule. Often legislative hearings are scheduled and those who would be affected are invited to attend. A favorite gimmick is to publish the proposed rule and make its effective date an extended period of time from publication. Such publication acts as a notice. If no one objects, the rule becomes effective on the date set.

Rule making may have both beneficial and adverse effects. Consider Brown, who is licensed by the FCC to operate a television station reaching a given audience. Brown is a very conscientious individual in his occupation. He has taken numerous surveys of his audience and they all show a strong preference for old movies and game shows. Suppose that the FCC, in an effort to "clean up" television, passes a rule banning the types of programs Brown televises. Or suppose the FCC rule simply requires all network stations to televise only network programs during the prime viewing times. Such rules might aid the T.V. networks to sell greater amounts of advertising since they would reach larger audiences. But Brown and his audience might well suffer because of the rule. Brown's audience would be depleted and his ability to sell local advertising would be injured because of his smaller audience.

Ex post facto. Our federal Constitution prohibits Congress making an action or event unlawful and setting the effective date before the law was passed. Accordingly, the "unlawful" act must have violated a law in existence at the time the act occurred. The meaning of this *ex post facto* provision has been interpreted as applying only to criminal acts and criminal laws. Also by judicial interpretation, administrative rules are declared to be civil in nature. So Gray, with his income tax problem may feel that his troubles are over when he pays what the IRS requires. But suppose the Internal Revenue Service passes a new regulation two years from now that would require Gray to pay an amount additional to the tax he has already paid. Gray may have to pay that additional amount or suffer whatever sanctions are specified in the law. "Final" statements by administrative agencies are not always final.

Supervision and Coercion.

Administrative agencies generally have the right to supervise those with whom they are concerned. In other words, they may find fault with those entities and then discipline them for whatever fault was found. Or they may simply require those supervised to "cease and desist" a practice found faulty. The means used by agencies to accomplish their supervision vary from one agency to another, but all of them include "investigation" as one device.

Investigation. Investigating a person or a company may sound like a perfectly innocent and necessary activity, but in capable hands the investigation can turn into coercion. This is very much akin to arresting and trying someone for a crime. The person arrested may be innocent of any wrongdoing, but to many who hear of his plight, the very fact that he was arrested and accused, implies guilt. Similarly, the fact of investigation of a company or a person can cause customers to drop away, lenders to balk, and stockholders to flee in alarm. So publicized investigations become means of coercion, and the threat to "straighten up or we'll investigate you" has teeth.

Of course, he who is so coerced may resort to the court system. He may even be successful in getting the agency "monkey" off his back—but the likelihood of his success is extremely low. Regardless of the guilt or innocence of the victim, the agency's investigation is likely to be supported if it can show a lawful purpose in its nosiness. It may even be supported if no reasonable purpose can be shown. After all, agencies exist to supervise activities; and how can one effectively supervise unless he is aware of the facts in a situation? And to find these facts he must investigate. The agency may even have cause to investigate just to make sure everything is operating as it should. So investigation is a potentially coercive device with an aura of legitimacy but also with potential for abuse by an agency.

Publicity of an investigation can be harmful, but so can some of the tactics used in the investigation. Consider modern discovery procedures—if one has ample reason to do so he may prepare an "interrogatory" which, when signed by an appropriate judge, requires the recipient to reveal any information in his possession bearing on some issue. Obedience to a properly phrased interrogatory can be a rather significant amount of work. Disobedience is contempt of court. If one must answer many interrogatories phrased in rather broad

fashion, he may find it necessary to hire a staff simply for this purpose and, of course, the responsibility for paying the staff salaries is all his. Another problem arises from the fact that very few of the supervised entities are completely without sin of some sort as far as agency regulations are concerned. As a parallel, there are few of us who have never broken any law—it may be observed that few persons come to dead stops at stop signs, for example. Discovery procedures by an agency may turn up unexpected gold mines of trivial violations which could be further investigated. The victim's attention could then be diverted to defenses of accusations rather than the production of whatever goods or services it deals in. It may be that the imposition of such a burden by an agency is necessary and desirable—but it could also be abusive coercion.

Supervisory Variations. The threat of harrassment by investigation is one means used by agencies to control those supervised. The use of direct cease and desist orders is another. But sometimes neither of these devices is as effective as some very practical coercion techniques. Consider, for example, agencies empowered to levy fines against offenders, (e.g., the FCC and the CAB). Suppose the law gives the agency a right to assess a fine of, say, $10,000 for a given violation. Suppose further that fines of this nature are freqently levied, but are nearly always reduced to a much lower figure—perhaps in the neighborhood of $1,000—when payment is made. We now have a handy device not only for supervision, but also to keep those supervised from complaining. If someone refuses to pay his assessed fine, a court action is the natural result and the amount to be paid if one loses is $10,000, not $1,000.

Another practical means of supervising and avoiding court conflicts is known as the *consent decree*. Upon discovery of a violation an agency may threaten to take court action against the alleged violator and give him an alternative—a means to avoid the action. All he need do is to essentially admit that he was guilty and agree not to violate the rule again. Since court actions in which an agency is a party are often extended and costly and may be lost even if one is innocent, there is a pronounced tendency to submit to the consent decree. In this way the agency can avoid court battles and still create an image of success in doing its supervisory job.

Numerous other devices have been invented by agencies to ease their supervisory tasks. Of course, with so much coercive power available for supervisory use there is a possibility of abuse. If the agency itself is not effectively controlled, it may choose arbitrarily which of its supervised entities to investigate, coerce, and harrass and which to leave alone. An agency may well decide to overlook infractions by large companies with numerous government contracts and concentrate its supervision on others.

Advisory Opinions. Since it is possible that agency sanctions may be injurious to one, maybe it is better to ask the agency's advice when a question arises. Suppose Green Trucking Company, for example, has been engaged in a certain practice for an extended period. Then, after discussing the practice with others, Green is led to the conclusion that what he has been doing may have been a rule violation. Would it be better to clear the doubt by asking the advice of the appropriate agency or to let "sleeping dogs" lie? There are at least two risks to be run by asking for an *advisory opinion*. First, if Green's past practice is truly a transgression, he would attract attention to it and, likely, invite an investigation of his practice by asking about it. Second, even if Green's inquiry results in a stamp of approval by someone in the agency, the agency is not bound by that approval. Advisory opinions are not binding on the agency. Even if the agency were bound it could still make an interpretative rule holding the questionable practice to be a violation. So perhaps the less said about Green's customary behavior the better. Of course, this leaves Green in the unenviable position of suspicion about his practice and, perhaps, continuing a rule violation.

CONTROL OF AGENCIES

Courts exercise a limited degree of control over agency behavior, and legislative committees add a bit more. In the long run what agencies may or may not do is spelled out by legislation, and the legislation presumably responds to a public need. Most agencies are created by a legislative enactment; then, as a need becomes apparent, the behavior of agencies is modified by further legislation.

Standing. One who is injured usually has a right to take action to recover for the wrong done to him. Certainly a license applicant whose application has been denied has an "interest" to be protected and can show injury to that interest. But how about members of the public who might have benefited if the license had been issued? A few years ago this would not have been sufficient interest to give them standing to act. Recent cases have revealed a tendency of the courts to lower this barrier. Since actions by agencies affect large segments of the population at least remotely, the question of standing is frequently one of determining the degree of interest required to justify the action.

Ripeness. Ordinarily the harvesting of an agricultural product must wait until that product is ripe. Roughly the same meaning applies to administrative law actions to be taken before a court. The action must be *ripe* for review—there must be something for the court to settle before it will evaluate the agency's action (or inaction).

Ripeness reasoning is set forth in a Supreme Court decision. It "is to prevent the courts, through avoidance of premature adjudication, from entangling themselves in abstract disagreements over administrative policies, and also to protect the agencies from judicial interference until an administrative decision has been formalized and its effects felt in a concrete way by the challenging parties. The problem is best seen in a twofold aspect, requiring us to evaluate both the fitness of the issues for judicial decision and the hardship to the parties of withholding court consideration."[1]

Scope of Review.

The degree of reviewability of agency action depends upon the laws under which the agency operates. As a general rule, if a regulatory function has been entrusted to an agency by the legislature, a court has no right to replace the action taken by the agency. Usually judges are reluctant to decide such cases anyway, in recognition of agency expertise in an area in which the judge is likely not to be an expert.

Boundaries and limits are either established by statutes or practice, and when an agency exceeds these limits a call for review of the agency action may be successful. Challenges based on alleged procedural unfairness have an even greater chance for success.

One standard basis for review of agency action alleges that the agency action was taken with no reasonable or rational basis or the action was based on insufficient evidence. When a court examines this aspect of agency action, it is reviewing in its own area of expertise—the use of evidence and drawing inferences from it. The court is not substituting its judgment for the agency's in an area preserved by statute to the agency. Rather, the court is in a position to criticize the *manner* in which the agency did its job and require the agency to give a better performance.

Court control of agency action can only be a limited control. Reviews are limited to those features of agency action not delegated exclusively to the agency and to abuses of agency discretion. The only remaining control of unwise agency action is by the legislative body

1. Abbott Laboratories v. Gardner, 387 U.S. 136, 148–149, 87 S.Ct. 1507, 1515 (1967).

that created the agency—either by legislative "over-sight" committees or by legislative enactment. In creating agencies we have created controlling devices necessary in our society, but devices which, themselves, require control if we are to avoid abusive practices. The court system offers only a partial answer to agency control.

BOWLING GREEN-WARREN COUNTY AIRPORT BOARD v. C.A.B.

470 F. 2d 553 (1973)

Celebrezze, Circuit Judge.

This is a petition for review of the decision and final order No. 72-7-25, rendered by the Civil Aeronautics Board (hereinafter the Board) on July 7, 1972. By this order the Board granted the application of Eastern Air Lines, Inc., for amendment of its certificate of public convenience and necessity for Route 10 so as to delete the point Bowling Green, Kentucky, from that route.

The following facts, as adopted by the Board, appear in the initial decision of the examiner. Bowling Green is the county seat of Warren County, Kentucky, and the trade center for several counties in south-central Kentucky. In recent years Bowling Green and Warren County have experienced a trend of industrialization and relatively rapid growth. Thus Bowling Green's population has increased from about 18,000 in 1950 to about 38,000 in 1970, and the County's population increased from about 43,000 to about 55,000 during the same period.

Bowling Green is located approximately 60 miles north of Nashville, Tennessee, and approximately 100 miles south of Louisville, Kentucky, both of which cities are classified by the Federal Aviation Administration as medium air traffic hubs. From the Nashville airport, five trunklines and four local service air carriers provide single-plane service to over 65 cities throughout the United States. From the Louisville airport, four trunklines and three local service air carriers provide single-plane service to over 70 cities across the country. Louisville, Bowling Green, and Nashville are linked by Interstate Highway 65, a major north-south highway, as well as a major bus line providing frequent service between these points and beyond.

Since its certificate was amended in 1947 so as to add Bowling Green as a point on its Nashville-Louisville segments of Route 10, Eastern provided continued daily service to Bowling Green up to September 1969.[2] In fiscal year 1969, the number of origin and destination passengers for Eastern at Bowling Green had reached 11,852 per year or over 32 per day on its daily

schedules (southbound in the mid-morning and northbound in the late afternoon), and traffic had increased at a rate of about 2,000 passengers per year.

On May 1, 1969, Eastern filed an application requesting suspension of its service at Bowling Green and approval of an agreement between Eastern and Air South, Inc., whereunder Air South would be employed by Eastern as an independent contractor to perform replacement service to Bowling Green. Air South was to provide three daily round trips between Bowling Green and Louisville and two daily round trips between Bowling Green and Nashville, and bear its own expenses subject to Eastern's agreement to underwrite Air South in amounts of no more than $50,000 the first year, $10,000 the second year, and $5,000 the third year. In support of its application, Eastern cited its competition from numerous strong trunklines which are able to devote their full attention to dense and/or long-haul routes upon which Eastern is dependent for economic survival. Eastern noted that it would save $300,000 annually from suspension at Bowling Green and that Bowling Green would benefit from the more frequent service to Nashville and Louisville under the replacement service.

In August 1969, the Board approved Eastern's application for temporary suspension at Bowling Green and the agreement for replacement service by Air South. The Board's approval was made subject to the condition that the suspension granted to Eastern would immediately terminate if Air South should cease to satisfactorily provide the specified replacement service.

Air South provided reliable service from September 2, 1969, through March 31, 1970, when it terminated its replacement service due to a lack of financial resources and support. Notwithstanding Air South's morning, afternoon, and evening service from Bowling Green to Louisville and Nashville, the number of origin and destination passengers at Bowling Green dropped to an average of 21.9 per day during this seven-month period—a decline of about one-third from the traffic Eastern had carried just prior to its replacement by Air South.

Faced with the legal obligation of providing air service to Bowling Green when Air South terminated its replacement service, Eastern on March 30, 1970, applied to the Board for continuation of its temporary suspension at Bowling Green and for approval of a one-year agreement between Eastern and Northern Air-

2. Claiming an insufficient number of passengers at Bowling Green to support the two daily round-trip flights it was then providing to Nashville and Louisville, in 1961 Eastern applied for suspension and deletion of Bowling Green and replacement of its Nashville-Bowling Green-Louisville service by Ozark Air Lines, Inc. The Board denied this application in a decision rendered in 1964.

lines, Inc., which was then providing scheduled air service between Louisville, Bowling Green, and Nashville. Under the agreement Eastern would underwrite Northern in the amounts of $8,000 per month for the first three months of operation and no more than $4,000 per month thereafter for the latter's replacement service at Bowling Green.

Pending the Board's consideration of the above application, Northern's service was admittedly unreliable and unsatisfactory, and Northern in fact terminated service at Bowling Green on or about May 8, 1970. Bowling Green was thus without reliable and satisfactory air service from April 1, 1970, until May 25, 1970, and with no service at all during the last 17 days of this period.

On May 25, 1970, Eastern entered into a third contractual agreement for replacement service to Bowling Green, this time with Wright Air Lines, Inc. Whereas Air South and Northern in essence had been employed as independent contractors, retaining all revenues and bearing all expenses subject to underwriting payments by Eastern, Wright was essentially employed to provide substitute air service on a cost-plus-10 percent basis, subject to an initial ceiling of $28,000 per month. Under the agreement, Wright was to provide Bowling Green with at least three daily round trips to Louisville and at least two daily round trips to Nashville.

On September 24, 1970, the Board approved Eastern's application for continued temporary suspension at Bowling Green, subject to Wright's performance of the specified replacement service, and the agreement between Eastern and Wright for such replacement service. In so approving Eastern's application, the Board acknowledged that replacement service at Bowling Green had not been satisfactory. The Board was nonetheless of the belief that Wright's replacement service, sponsored and sustained by Eastern, would be superior to prior replacement service and superior to the service which would be provided directly by Eastern were the suspension denied.

On December 31, 1970, Eastern filed the present application for deletion of Bowling Green from its certificate for Route 10.

In his initial decision rendered after a public hearing, Examiner Sornson apparently recognized that there is no reasonable prospect that reinstitution of direct service at Bowling Green by Eastern would be economically feasible. The Examiner nonetheless concluded that Bowling Green should not be deleted from Eastern's certificate, but rather that Eastern should continue to be responsible for the community's air service needs through support of air taxi replacement service. The Examiner found Eastern's request for total relief

by way of deletion of Bowling Green to be unwarranted in that "Eastern (had) not shown that a substitute service arrangement at Bowling Green cannot be successful. . . ." In support of this conclusion, Examiner Sornson cited what he found to be inadequate subsidies paid by Eastern to Air South and Wright and Eastern's failure to effectively promote and advertise the replacement service.

Reviewing the decision of the Examiner, the Board rejected his finding that Eastern had failed to show that a substitute service arrangement cannot be successful at Bowling Green and his conclusion that Eastern should remain responsible for the community's air service needs through support of air taxi replacement service. Instead, the Board concluded from the evidence that:

> "Continued air taxi operations have only a limited chance of eventual success . . . there are no unusual or extenuating circumstances which would warrant support of the magnitude which would be required to continue such operations."

In support of its conclusion, the Board reviewed the decline in the number of passengers experienced by both Air South and Wright and the resulting operating losses suffered by these replacement carriers, notwithstanding the substantial subsidies paid by Eastern. Thus Air South, with its fully satisfactory schedules and performance, was able to generate only 22 daily origin and destination passengers, resulting in a loss of over $127,000 during its seven months of operation. And during its first year of operation, Wright experienced traffic of under 20 daily origin and destination passengers, resulting in a loss of $242,000 or $35 per passenger. The Board also relied on the evidence that after approval—without civic objection—of reduced service by Wright in May 1971 to stem continuing losses, traffic dropped to about 12 passengers per day.

The Board further rejected the Examiner's finding that the decline in passenger traffic is attributable to Eastern's failure to promote and assist the substitute service and Eastern's inadequate subsidies. In addition to providing support services for both Air South and Wright, Eastern spent about $3,500 in the year ended May 1971 advertising and promoting Wright's substitute service. Eastern paid Air South $50,000 in cash subsidy for the latter's seven months of operation and paid Wright almost $300,000 for the first year of its replacement service.

The Board therefore concluded that the public convenience and necessity require the amendment of Eastern's certificate for Route 10 so as to delete Eastern's authority to serve Bowling Green.

Under our narrow scope of review as set forth in 49 U.S.C. sect. 1486(e), the Board's findings of fact are conclusive if supported by substantial evidence. Beyond this scope of judicial review, we must defer to the Board's expertise and discretion in weighing the many factors and policy considerations which enter into Board decisions respecting public convenience and necessity. . . .

From the record before us we find that the Board's findings of fact are supported by substantial evidence. Relying upon the undisputed rates of traffic generation at Bowling Green between 1962 and 1969, the Board found that there is no reasonable prospect that a reinstitution of direct service by Eastern could be profitable in the future. This finding—which also appears to be a conclusion of the Examiner—is supported by evidence that during its peak year of 1969 with 11,853 origin and destination passengers at Bowling Green, Eastern achieved load factors of only about 30 percent and suffered an operating loss of almost $300,000 (about $25 per Bowling Green passenger) on its Bowling Green-Nashville and Bowling Green-Louisville flights.

We also find substantial evidence on the record to support the Board's findings that continued replacement air taxi operations supported by Eastern have an extremely limited chance of success and that traffic response to these operations does not warrant their continuation. As reviewed above, the declining traffic under Air South's and Wright's operations, and the substantial operating losses suffered by these replacement carriers despite Eastern's subsidies fully support these findings by the Board.

We find no merit in Petitioner's argument that the Board's order must be set aside because the Board failed to give sufficient weight to the several factors prescribed in 49 U.S.C. sect. 1302.[3] Petitioner asserts that the Board failed to adequately consider the future commercial needs of Bowling Green as well as the effects of its decision upon the Postal Service and the national defense.

With respect to Bowling Green's future commercial needs, its opinion discloses that the Board was fully aware of the factors favoring the maintenance of air service not only in Bowling Green but also in all smaller communities across the nation. On balance, however, the Board found that Bowling Green's future commercial needs and the community benefits from certified air service do not warrant continued requirements that Eastern—as a trunkline carrier—bear the responsibility and expense of the unsuccessful operations at the City. Finding no abuse of the Board's discretion, we are powerless to reweigh these factors which were before the Board. . . .

Moreover, we find in the record no evidence respecting the effects of the Board's decision on the present and future needs of the Postal Service and the national defense. Even if such evidence had been introduced, however, we do not believe that the Board is required in every case to make express findings on every factor set forth in Section 1302. . . .

The order of the Board is affirmed.

MARSHALL v. NORTHWEST ORIENT AIRLINES, INC.
574 F.2d 119 (1978)

Irving R. Kaufman, Chief Judge.

Northwest Airlines, Inc., ("Northwest") seeks to prevent representatives of the Occupational Safety and Health Administration ("OSHA") from inspecting one of its airport facilities, claiming that the safety aspects of the hangar in question are already regulated by the Federal Aviation Administration ("FAA"). It adopts this position notwithstanding the fact that an administrative record concerning the alleged overlap in jurisdiction has not been assembled and discovery is yet to commence. We agree with the determination of the district court that the challenge to OSHA's jurisdiction cannot be brought until Northwest has more adequately developed the record by exhausting its existing administrative remedies.

I.

On October 27, 1976, Efraim Zoldan, an OSHA compliance officer, attempted to inspect Northwest's Hangar No. 1 at John F. Kennedy International Airport. After being denied entrance by the agent in

---

3. 49 U.S.C. sect. 1302 provides as follows: "In the exercise and performance of its powers and duties under this chapter, the Board shall consider the following, among other things, as being in the public interest, and in accordance with the public convenience and necessity:

(a) The encouragement and development of an air-transportation system properly adapted to the present and future needs of the foreign and domestic commerce of the United States, of the Postal Service, and of the national defense;

(b) The regulation of air transportation in such manner as to recognize and preserve the inherent advantages of, assure the highest degree of safety in, and foster sound economic conditions in, such transportation, and to improve the relations between, and coordinate transportation by, air carriers;

(c) The promotion of adequate, economical, and efficient service by air carriers at reasonable charges, without unjust discriminations, undue preferences or advantages, or unfair or destructive competitive practices;

(d) Competition to the extent necessary to assure the sound development of an air-transportation system properly adapted to the needs of the foreign and domestic commerce of the United States, of the Postal Service, and of the national defense;

(e) The promotion of safety in air commerce; and

(f) The promotion, encouragement, and development of civil aeronautics. . . .

charge, he sought an inspection warrant from Magistrate Vincent Catoggio on November 4, 1976. Relying on affidavits establishing that Northwest's hangar had in the past been cited for 13 violations of OSHA standards, the magistrate issued a warrant.

The following day, Northwest again turned Zoldan away when he attempted to enter its facility, ostensibly because it would soon be moving to quash the warrant. It did so that very afternoon, arguing that section (4(b)910 of the Occupational Safety and Health Act ("Act") explicitly withdrew from OSHA any jurisdiction over safety matters already regulated by other federal agencies. Northwest contended that the FAA oversaw the occupational safety of hangar workers, and cited an opinion by Administrative Law Judge Jerome C. Ditore as support for this principle.

The opinion relied upon concerned the airline's challenge to a previous OSHA citation for failing to provide adequate protection to employees changing landing lights on aircraft. After a 24-day hearing, Judge Ditore determined that the FAA had preempted this area by promulgating regulations "affecting the occupational safety and health of ground maintenance personnel changing landing lights through the leading edge flap cavities of Boeing 747 aircraft." A member of the Occupational Safety and Health Review Commission subsequently granted the Secretary of Labor's petition for discretionary review of Judge Ditore's decision by the full Commission, but such plenary consideration has been delayed pending the appointment of a third commissioner.

Upon being apprised of Judge Ditore's decision, Magistrate Catoggio vacated the search warrant. He interpreted the earlier ruling to indicate that the FAA had preempted "at least part of the area (of airline safety)," and thus had, for section 4(b)(1) purposes, prevented OSHA from exercising jurisdiction over any safety hazards within the hangar. The Secretary of Labor then appealed to the district court, which reinstated the warrant, finding that the challenge to OSHA's jurisdiction was premature, and requiring the airline to first exhaust all administrative remedies.

II.

Section 4(b)(1) of the Occupational Safety and Health Act, 29 U.S.C. sect 653 (b)(1), provides that:

> Nothing in this chapter shall apply to working conditions of employees with respect to which other Federal agencies . . . exercise statutory authority to prescribe or enforce standards or regulations affecting occupational safety or health.

In essence, this provision is designed to eliminate any duplication of the efforts of federal agencies to secure the well-being of employees. At the same time, however, section 4(b)(1) was not intended by Congress to eliminate OSHA's jurisdiction merely on the basis of hypothetical conflicts. Employees should not lightly be denied the protection of OSHA for, as the Senate Report accompanying the Act noted, "(t)he problem of assuring safe and healthful workplaces for our working men and women ranks in importance with any that engages the national attention today." . . .Thus, as the section's wording makes clear, a sister agency must actually be *exercising* a power to regulate safety conditions in order to preempt OSHA. Were this not the case, many occupational health hazards might remain uncorrected merely because some agency whose prime concern is not safety has failed to take notice of that area.

In a similar vein, section 4(b)(1) is not designed to provide wholesale exceptions for entire industries. . . . The exact standard to be applied in determining the scope of preemption, however, is less than crystal-clear. The *Southern Pacific* court concluded that agency rule-making directed "at a working condition—defined either in terms of a 'surrounding' or 'hazard'—displaces OSHA coverage of that working condition." . . . The Fourth Circuit, on the other hand, has established a somewhat different test, concluding that "working conditions" encompass:

> an area broader in its contours than the "particular discrete hazards" advanced by the Secretary, but something less than the employment relationship in its entirety. . . . (They include) the environmental area in which an employee customarily goes about his daily tasks. . . .

As these vague standards demonstrate, a determination of preemption requires an inquiry into complex issues of law and fact. Accordingly, it is proper for a court to defer examination of such difficult questions of agency jurisdiction until a party has fully exhausted its administrative remedies. . . . The exhaustion requirement is particularly apt in cases such as this, where administrative review is forthcoming and the agency will be given a chance to apply its expertise. . . .

The airline asks this Court to conclude that an entire hangar, and the multitude of possible hazards within it, are excluded from OSHA protection. Given the breadth of the problem, our inquiry would of necessity be amorphous, unwieldy, and lacking in expertise. In contrast, following an OSHA inspection and its administrative review, the issues will have been greatly refined, and we will be made aware of the specific types of hazards that OSHA officials believe are regulated by the FAA. Certainly, given Congress's determination to create a "comprehensive, nation-wide" approach to improving occupational safety, the agency charged with that mandate should be accorded an initial opportunity to inspect potential safety hazards.

III.

In addition to disputing OSHA's jurisdiction, Northwest contests the constitutionality of the warrantless searches conducted by the agency's inspectors. The airline notes that in most instances, a warrantless search is inconsistent with the protections of the fourth amendment. . . . In fact, the greater number of courts to consider this issue have found unconstitutional the warrantless search procedure authorized by section 8(a) of the Act. . . . That question is now before the Supreme Court in *Marshall* v. *Barlow's, Inc.* . . .

We need not decide, however, whether Congress could constitutionally authorize warrantless searches of all business premises. Nor need we determine whether the "pervasive regulation" of the airline industry creates an exception to the warrant requirement. Assuming *arguendo* that warrantless searches are unconstitutional, it would then be proper for a court to imply a warrant requirement to preserve the statute's constitutionality. . . . The Supreme Court followed exactly this course of action in *Camara,* supra.

Adhering to these precedents, the district court issued a warrant, relying on Northwest's previous OSHA violations for a showing of probable cause. On this appeal, the airline does not dispute the existence of factual support for this finding. Accordingly, having determined that a warrant requirement can properly be implied if the statute, as written, were unconstitutional, we affirm the order of the district court reinstating the inspection warrant.

REVIEW QUESTIONS

1. Why must we have agencies? Why, for example, must we have an agency like the Civil Aeronautics Board to control air traffic? What could be a better way to accomplish this control?
2. What is the Federal Register?
3. What could an agency (say a local zoning board) do to a person or company whose actions it found undesirable?
4. How are agency hearings similar to and different from court trials?
5. How does rule-making differ from a legislative procedure?
6. What coercive tactics are available to agencies? Consider a local liquor control commission.
7. Who controls agency activities? Is the control adequate?
8. In *Bowling Green-Warren County Airport Board* v. *C.A.B.,* the C.A.B. was faced with the kind of problem it commonly handles. What other reasonable alternatives exist to the Eastern Air Lines problem posed by the case? Do any solutions other than no longer serving Bowling Green exist? What else could be done?
9. In *Marshall* v. *Northwest Orient* the problem seems to center on whether OSHA or FAA should inspect the Northwest Orient facility at JFK International Airport. In your opinion, which agency would do the better job of facility safety inspection? What problems would this agency likely encounter in carrying out this function?

24

Labor

A necessary component of all that we buy or sell is labor. According to one view of economic theory, all we really pay for when we buy something is labor in one form or another. Capital, it is said, merely represents stored compensation for past labor; management is just another form of labor. Other economists have argued that such thinking is illogical. However this may be, it is generally conceded that labor is a vital and, sometimes, volatile portion of all projects. For this reason we will consider here some of the problems posed when people's time and talent are bought and sold.

In this discussion such problems as cost, availability, and transportation of labor will be neglected to more thoroughly treat some of the legal problems involved in the settlement of labor conflicts. The discussion will center around unions. The reason for this is that without unions or the threat of them there is usually little conflict. Two powers must be fairly evenly matched for a conflict to occur—without any reasonable hope of winning a battle, it is pointless for one to become battle scarred. A single worker usually cannot successfully dispute a management edict, however wrong it may seem to him. He can be replaced. He can deprive his company of the service he renders, but in most cases others can be hired to do the job as well with a minimum of training or cost to the company. The laborer's answer to this rather unbalanced state of affairs is *organization*. A concerted refusal to work in which all employees participate can be a powerful weapon. To accomplish organized solidarity, unions were formed. Occasionally the balance of power shifts very heavily to the union side. When this occurs, management cannot afford the conflict that might be caused by its refusal of a union request. Refusal can lead to union economic action that would end the company's existence. The company must thus accede to the union demands.

Historical Background

Working people now have the right to form or join clubs or *unions*. Through these unions they may petition their common employer for improvements in wages or working conditions; under certain circumstances they may resort to economic warfare to enforce their demands. These things may be done lawfully now, but the legal right to do them was only recently acquired.

Criminal Conspiracy. Under the English common law existing at the time of the American Revolution the formation of an association of employees engaged in similar employment was unlawful. To a considerable extent law and the courts reflected the economic beliefs of the time—the *law of supply and demand* and the *wage fund theory,* for example. Reasoning from supply and demand, the courts claimed that it was unlawful to "artificially" regulate the price of labor or to alter working conditions; that the only fair, and thus lawful, price was that established by competition for a particular type of labor. The philosophy of the wage fund theory "proved" that for a worker to improve his wages or working conditions he must steal from another. Since the purpose of organizations of working people was known to be that of improving their lot in life, such organizations were unlawful "criminal conspiracies."

It was not until the 1840s that employees finally won court recognition of their right to organize. Meanwhile there were organizations of employees, and working conditions and wages were improved by them, but without court sanction. The demise of the criminal conspiracy doctrine in its application to labor unions intensified union activities during the next fifty years. New unions were formed and attempts were made to organize on a national scale. Gradually, the use of economic force to bring about improvements in working conditions began to win recognition in the courts.

Anti-Trust Laws. In 1890 the Sherman Anti-Trust Act was passed with the apparent primary purpose of preventing monopolistic practices of "big business." Whether or not labor unions were to be excluded from the act was not clear. A few years later, though, a case involving a union boycott was decided by the United States Supreme Court to be a violation of the anti-trust act, and triple damages were awarded against the union. Subsequent use of the act and threat of its further use were damaging to the union cause.

By this time two legal devices for preventing union-caused harm to employers had become popular. The "yellow-dog contract" prevented employees from joining a union or from forming a union among themselves. And the "labor injunction" could be used to prevent anticipated damage from threatened union activities.

Yellow-Dog Contract. The so-called yellow-dog contract was a clause in the employment contract stating, in effect, that the employee agreed, as a condition of his continued employment, not to engage in union activities. Under common law, a court had no choice but to uphold the agreement. If a union tried to persuade employees to become members, it was inducing breach of contract and was subject to either an injunction to prevent the activity or a damage action if it was successful.

Labor Injunction. Even if a union was formed, the employer had a means of controlling its activities. Anyone who is threatened with harm to his property has a right to request an injunction from a court having equity powers. Not only are the employer's physical assets, such as his plant and machines, his property—the concept extends to his good will in relations with his customers and the public. Delayed filling of customer's orders could be such an injury. Thus, an employer who was threatened with a strike or other economic action could show probable injury to his good will and could ask a court for an injunction to protect him. Courts soon came to respond to these requests quite freely with temporary injunctions or "labor injunctions" as they came to be known. Some courts even went so far as to direct the injunctions against "whomsoever" might harm the employer, thus setting up a small no-man's-land.

As a result of the use of these legal weapons in union-management warfare, there was considerable agitation for a law to end their existence or, at least, to curtail their use. The Clayton Anti-Trust Act appeared to be the answer; hailed as labor's *Magna Carta,* it seemed to eliminate most of the legal problems that had plagued the unions. The wording used to convey this meaning appeared to be clear. However, close examination revealed instances of garbled meanings in the text of the law. The result was that the Supreme Court interpreted the law to mean that Congress had merely intended to restate the rules as they existed before the Clayton Act was passed.

By 1932 court anti-union sentiment and popular sympathy had changed considerably. With the passage of the Norris-LaGuardia "anti-injunction" Act, most of what the Clayton Act had apparently attempted was accomplished. The anti-union contract clause was eliminated, nearly all labor injunctions were made unlawful, and a portion of the anti-trust legislation was made inoperative as to unions. Employee organizations could now undertake most of the familiar types of economic coercion without fear of successful court action against them. The courts were not rendered deaf to an employer's plea, but the balance of legal power had been shifted toward the unions.

National Labor Relations Act. Congress went even further in 1935 with the passage of the National Labor Relations Act (the Wagner Act), which pledged government support to unions. The only unfair labor practices (unlawful practices) spelled out in the act were acts of employers; labor could do no wrong. The Wagner Act set up the National Labor Relations Board (NLRB) to determine whether the federal law should be applied to a particular case, to hold elections to certify employee representatives, and to investigate and prevent or punish for unfair labor practices.

With the protection afforded by these two acts and the sympathetic attitude of government and the courts, it is not surprising that the labor movement thrived in the next few years. Old unions expanded and new ones were born. Collective bargaining and abiding by labor-management contracts became almost a way of industrial life.

Rapid growth and abusive conduct sometimes go hand in hand. Such seemed to be the case in the twelve years following the passage of the Wagner Act. Union action was aggressive and often managements gave up rights they considered "management prerogatives" as the price of temporary industrial peace. During World War II many managements voluntarily established precedents that proved unfortunate for peacetime operations. In an effort to more evenly balance the powers across the bargaining table, Congress passed the Taft-Hartley amendment to the National Labor Relations Act in 1947.

Taft-Hartley Act. The balancing of bargaining power in the Taft-Hartley Act required that certain union unfair labor practices be proscribed along with those of the employer. The law and NLRB rulings made unlawful the creation of a new *closed shop* arrangement with an employer (the arrangement in which a new employee had to be a union member before he could be employed). The secondary boycott (see p. 285) was made unlawful, and so were jurisdictional strikes (see p. 285) and featherbedding (see p. 288). A sixty-day notice of intent to strike was made a required precedent to a lawful strike. National emergency procedures were set up in an attempt to avoid national disasters and still preserve free collective bargaining. A federal mediation and conciliation service was created to aid in reaching collective bargaining settlements. The act also made unions responsible for their torts and allowed them to sue and be sued in court actions.

It is almost an understatement to note that unions objected to the new legislation; one of the more complimentary descriptive terms used for it was "slave labor act." Despite union objections to the act, the period following its passage was characterized by continued union expansion. Unions grew and combined, becoming nationwide and even international in their affiliations. The American Federation of Labor (an association of trade unions) and the Congress of Industrial Organizations (built along industry lines) merged to present a united front.

Unions, themselves, became big business. With the bigness came certain abusive practices. When people handle money belonging to others, there is always the temptation to divert some of it to personal gain, disguising the diversion or obscuring it by simply not keeping records. Accumulations of union dues, initiation fees, and assessments formed such a temptation. A senate investigating committee, headed by Senator McClellan, uncovered proof of such practices in some unions and strong suspicions in others. In at least one union many of the officers were found to have long prison records. The work of the McClellan committee was a main cause of passage of a second National Labor Relations Act amendment, the Labor-Management Reporting and Disclosure Act of 1959, the Landrum-Griffin Bill, by Congress.

Landrum-Griffen Act. While the main purpose of the Landrum-Griffen Act is to cause employers, labor organizations, and their officials to adhere to high standards of responsibility and ethical conduct, it also amends many sections of the Taft-Hartley Act. It differs from the Taft-Hartley Act in that it provides for a $10,000 fine or imprisonment up to one year, or both, for those who do not comply. Enforcement of the Taft-Hartley Act, on the other hand, is achieved mainly through cease and desist orders and contempt of court for non-compliance.

Labor and the Law

The main source of law governing the relationships between labor and management is the National Labor Relations Act. There are, of course, other federal acts such as the Fair Labor Standards Act, Walsh-Healey Public Contracts Act, the Work Hours Act, and the Equal Pay Act. There are also numerous state and local laws that have bearing on the relationship, but the central law of labor relations is the National Labor Relations Act.

As time has passed since the National Labor Relations Act became law, court cases and NLRB decisions have refined and interpreted the act. Many of today's controversies are decided upon the basis of the "settled law" of that particular area of labor relations conflict. But then with technological change and the seesaw bargaining of union-management contracts, new problems arise. The result is a legal field with a center core of hard and fast law and a continuously expanding outer edge in varying stages of refinement.

Policy. The avowed purpose and policy of the National Labor Relations Act is to minimize industrial strife and thereby promote the full flow of commerce. The means of accomplishing this is by defining certain rights of employees, rights of employers, and orderly procedures for settling disputes between them.

Employees are guaranteed the right to organize and to bargain collectively with their employers. They are also guaranteed the right to refrain from such activities unless they are subject to a union-management contract requiring membership in a union as a condition of their employment.

The entity charged with keeping this government promise to employees is the National Labor Relations Board (NLRB). It functions to prevent and remedy unfair labor practices and to conduct secret-ballot elections to determine employees' bargaining representatives.

NLRB Functions. Carrying out its two main functions requires the NLRB to engage in a wide variety of administrative procedures and practices. It must receive petitions and allegations, determine its own jurisdiction, investigate, hold hearings, issue orders, make rules, and become a party to controversies in federal courts. In short, it functions in much the same manner as do most federal administrative agencies.

Jurisdiction. The NLRB decides its own jurisdiction. It responds to petitions either claiming an unfair labor practice or requesting an election. Its first order of business in response to such a petition is to decide whether it has jurisdiction in the case. According to its rules the employer in the petition must be involved in interstate commerce for the NLRB to take the case; but involvement with interstate commerce does not necessarily mean that the NLRB must assert jurisdiction. If jurisdiction is refused the petitioner may turn to a state act under which to make his claim.

Employee Representation

In industries affecting interstate commerce, certification as the bargaining agent is largely a matter of winning an election. Section 9 of the Taft-Hartley Act (as amended by the Landrum-Griffin Act) describes the procedure.

Petition. Certification of a bargaining representative begins with a petition to the NLRB for an election to be held. The petition may come from employees, a labor organization, or the employer.

Investigation. Upon receipt of the petition, the NLRB must determine whether interstate commerce is substantially affected and determine the appropriate bargaining unit. One of several types of bargaining units could be considered as most appropriate to represent the employees involved. The unit might be an *employer unit*—that is, it would consist of all the employees of a particular employer, or a substantial portion of them; or it might consist of the employees of *one plant* or a *department* therein. The choice might be a *craft unit* if the employees involved in a particular trade or craft desire such representation. The bargaining unit determination is to be made in such a manner as to assure employees the fullest freedom in exercising their rights.

In determining bargaining units, special consideration is given two groups of employees: professional employees and guards. Professional employees (engineers, accountants, buyers, etc.) are not to be included in the bargaining unit representing other employees unless the majority of the professional group votes for inclusion. Guards employed for protection of company property and its employees may not be included in the same bargaining unit with other employees of the company; the guards' labor organization may not even be affiliated with unions representing other employees. Combining representation could partially defeat the guards' functions.

Elections

Elections to determine bargaining representatives are conducted by the NLRB. If the only choice is between a particular union and no union at all, a simple majority of the votes determines the outcome. If there are more than two choices and none receives more than half the votes cast, a runoff is held between the two choices receiving the most votes. Valid choice of a bargaining representative settles the issue for at least a year; after a year, certification can be removed by petition and another election.

Who May Vote. Each employee in the bargaining unit as determined by the NLRB is entitled to one vote to determine the representative. Shortly after passage of the Taft-Hartley Act, the question arose as to whether employees on strike could vote in a certification election or not. Rulings on this question proved difficult to follow in some situations and the law was clarified in the Landrum-Griffin Act. Employees on a

valid economic strike against their employer now retain their right to vote in an election for a year after the beginning of the strike. This right is lost, of course, if the strike is unlawful—a so-called wildcat strike.

Persuasion. Under the Wagner Act the employer could do very little to persuade his employees to join a particular union or to join none at all. He still is restricted in what he may say, but the limitations are much more lenient under the Taft-Hartley Act. Neither the employer nor a union may use coercion or threats of reprisal to attempt to influence an employee's vote. The employer cannot promise benefits to be given if the union is unsuccessful. He must be particularly careful, under NLRB rulings, during the twenty-four hours directly preceding the election. In short, he cannot do anything to create an atmosphere in which an election should not be conducted.

The limitations imposed on the employer are not intended to inhibit the normal conduct of his business. He can still hire new employees, discipline (even to firing an employee) for cause. He can speak to his employees on company time, or on their own time if attendance is voluntary. He can voice his opinion of unions or the result to be expected from joining a union as long as threats or promises of benefit could not be implied from his statements. He can state the company's legal position, the dangers and costs of union membership, and what the union can and cannot do for employees.

It may be well to consider who is an employer. The term *employer* includes the management of a company; not only the president and general manager, but generally, all salaried line or staff employees outside the bargaining units may be considered employers. Thus, what a foreman or an engineer or a production control clerk says or does prior to an election may be interpreted as the words or deeds of the employer.

The Contract

The contract between the management of a company and representatives of the company's employees is not an employment contract; no one holds his job by virtue of it. Rather, it is an agreement that sets forth the conditions under which those who are employed will work.

It has become almost standard practice to include certain provisions of importance to labor law in labor-management agreements. Usually there is a statement to the effect that the labor union agrees not to strike and the company agrees not to lock the union out during the life of the agreement. Nearly always the agreement sets up a step-wise grievance procedure—an orderly process for settling disputes without resort to coercive tactics or to the formal court system. An internal machinery of justice is provided. If the paint gang at Black Manufacturing believes a newly issued incentive rate to be unjust, their recourse is to petition for a change and take the route of the grievance procedure. A strike by the paint gang as a result of the rate issuance would be an unlawful *wildcat strike*. Such a strike would allow Black Manufacturing to permanently replace any or all of the paint gang members. Black Manufacturing could lawfully replace them, but if the paint gang members are allowed to return to work, they come back with the same rights they would have had if they had not engaged in the wildcat strike.

In a similar vein, Black Manufacturing must bargain with its employees—it cannot lock them out. If, for example, Black's bargaining sessions with its employees' representative reveals what Black considers to be unreasonable demands, Black must still bargain. Black may not even be able to go out of business to avoid bargaining. For example, if Black is a multiplant organization, it could not go out of business at, say, Dayton, where it has labor problems and move its Dayton operations to one of its other plants. To lawfully go out of business at Dayton to avoid the union, it would have to go completely out of business—at all its plants. Otherwise, it is an *unlawful lockout*—an unfair labor practice.

Unfair Labor Practices. It is an *unfair labor practice* for either a union or a company to restrain or coerce employees as the employees exercise rights guaranteed them by the NLRA. It is also an unfair labor practice for either party to refuse to bargain with the other. In this regard it is noteworthy that neither party is required to accept any proposal by the other or agree to any concession. *Bargaining* simply means meeting at reasonable times and conferring in good faith on employment-related subjects.

Since passage of the Taft-Hartley amendment to the NLRA in 1947 it has been unlawful to form any new *closed shop*. A closed shop is a contract provision according to which employees must be union members *before* they are hired. This results in the union rather than management selecting prospective employees. If an employee proves unsatisfactory the company has little or no right to replace him; generally, the company must keep whatever the union sends. Since 1947 the only lawful newly formed provisions of this kind provide for a *union shop*. In a union shop the employer hires new employees and has a period of at least 30 days (except for building construction industries) to examine the new employee and replace him if he does not perform satisfactorily. If Black Manufacturing existed and operated under a closed shop provision prior to 1947, it might be forced to retain that arrangement; but if the original contract provision were made after the Taft-Hartley amendment, Black might have a union shop or an *open shop* (where union membership is not required), but not a closed shop.

Boycotts. In this country, in fact nearly anywhere in the world, people may choose freely between dealing with one competitor or another. If the Black Company chooses to buy a die cast machine from Gray Enterprises rather than from Green, it is Black's choice to make. In fact, if Black wishes to deal exclusively with Gray rather than Green, that is still his option. The problem arises when someone forces Black to prefer one choice rather than another. The situation is shown graphically below. If A wishes to receive some benefit

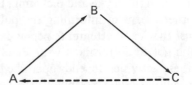

from C, he may bring added coercive force against C by forcing B to refuse to deal with C. This is known as a *secondary boycott* and it takes many forms. It is an unfair labor practice for a union to force or threaten to force a company to assign work to members of one trade union rather than another (involving a "jurisdictional dispute"). For example, a contractor might be required by the metal worker's union to assign the job of hanging metal doors to metal workers rather than carpenters, or the reverse.

Hot Cargo. It is an unfair labor practice to force or threaten to force an employer to refuse to handle the products of some other company. A union-employer agreement of this nature is known as a *hot cargo agreement* and is unlawful for both parties. The Black Company is threatened with a work stoppage and picketing if it continues to use chemicals produced by a nonunionized company. If Black agrees to cease using the chemicals under these circumstances, the agreement is an unlawful hot cargo agreement.

Lawful Union Coercion. There are, of course, situations in which a union has a right to take coercive action against an employer; and there are situations in which an apparent secondary boycott is really a lawful primary action. However, to be a lawful coercive action by a union it must meet three tests: (1) the objective sought by the union must be lawful (the objective of forming a new closed shop would not be lawful); (2) the means used must be lawful (use of the secondary boycott would not stand this test); and (3) the union must be the legitimate bargaining agent of the employees involved (picketing by a union that had lost a representation election at the plant picketed, would be unlawful).

As an example, consider the Black Company which has a labor-management contract with the representative of its employees, the UWW (call it the United Wood Workers). Sixty days before the contract is due to end Black receives a strike notice from the UWW. This does not necessarily mean that Black will have a strike on its hands two months hence. What it does indicate is that the union will enter negotiations for a new contract with a weapon it has a right to use when the current contract expires—the strike. It may also picket Black's place of business and attempt to persuade employees of other employers to refuse to cross the picket line. In addition to the strike and picketing, the UWW could use other means of informing the public of the strike against Black and attempt to persuade members of the public not to do business with Black. But the legality of these activities depends upon the UWW actually representing Black's employees and actually having a legitimate strike against Black.

Allies. An apparent secondary boycott may not really be a secondary boycott (sometimes one needs a roster of the players to identify their rolls). For example, a union may have a legitimate strike against Black but picket White, who is Black's main customer. Now this sounds like a secondary boycott against White. But suppose we manage to tie Black and White together in some manner. Maybe both are essentially owned and controlled by a common parent company; or perhaps they have formed a pact to the effect that they will assist each other in opposing union pressures. Their products may form an integrated link in a production network. In short, such situations as these or acts by the companies such that it is apparent that White is no longer a "neutral" give the union a right to act against him as Black's *ally*.

Common Site. Another problem of secondary pressures may arise when a company hires a contractor to do work on its premises. Suppose the contractor so hired has labor problems while the contracted work is being done. The union's primary and, presumably, legitimate target is the contractor, but the company for which the work is being done may well get splattered in the fray too. The *common site* situation occurs frequently enough so that special rules have had to be made for it. The rules are intended to minimize the injury to the second company without depriving the contractor's employees of their rights to act. If there is no conceivable way in which the contractor's employees' rights

can be exercised without injuring the second company, that company may well expect to be harmed without lawful recourse.

Subcontracting. Speaking of contracting work to be done, suppose the Black Company, being faced with a strike, subcontracted some of its work to Green. Certainly subcontracting is ordinarily lawful. But if Green takes the work involved, he may very well find Black's employees' union on his doorstep, lawfully picketing his plant and otherwise causing him problems. By taking the subcontracted work, under the circumstances causing Black to offer it, Green abandoned his neutral position.

Strikes. The NLRA specifically preserves a union's right to strike, but there are limitations on this right. In turn, the limitations depend on the objective sought, the means used, and the existence of a labor-management contract with a no-strike provision.

If there is a no-strike provision in a contract currently in force, the employees may still strike—but the right to do so is contingent upon the presence of a real hazard to the employees. If a real danger threatens—for example, the assigning of a welding job near a paint booth—there may not be time to resort to grievance procedure. Under such a circumstance it would be unreasonable to require employees to continue to work.

Economic Strikes and Unfair Labor Practice Strikes. If there is no contract provision for the union not to strike or if the contract time has run out, a union resort to strike may be quite lawful. If such is the case the strikers' rights depend to a considerable extent upon the objectives sought. A so-called *economic strike* is one in which the objective sought is an increase in wages, improvement of working conditions, a change in overtime policy, or some other such concessions from the employer. An *unfair labor practice strike* is a response to an unlawful labor practice by the employer. Economic strikers are still employees but they may be replaced by their employer. If the employer has hired permanent replacements by the time the economic strikers indicate a desire to return to work, the strikers are not entitled to reinstatement.

Strikers participating in an unfair labor practice strike are in a somewhat stronger position. If they are replaced by other employees, they retain their rights to reinstatement even though the replacement workers may have to be discharged.

Of course, there are acts by strikers that can bring their dismissal in any case. That is, if strike activities go well beyond those allowed, the employees involved lose their rights; and this is true whether they are economic strikers, unfair labor practice strikers, suffering from a mass "illness," refusing to work customary overtime, or simply engaged in a mass slowdown. Misconduct by the strikers—violence or threats of violence, for example—could be the cause of such a loss of rights.

The employer, just as anyone else, has the rights of dominion over and use of his property. The strike known as a *sitdown strike* deprives him of these rights and is, therefore, unlawful.

Picketing. We all have the right to picket. Whether we are employees, union members, or just ordinary consumers we may inform others of our grievances, and whether they are real or fancied makes little difference. Removal of this right would require a drastic change or complete upheaval of the first amendment to our Constitution. So pickets at an employer's place of business have the highest sort of legal sanction. Of course, when people exercise their rights they often run headlong into others' rights—this is what legal conflicts are made of.

Ordinarily the right of a union to picket an employer's place of business is a right reserved to the representative of the employer's employees. Particularly, organizational picketing by a noncertified union is barred as unlawful *blackmail picketing*. However, when picketing simply truthfully informs the public that the employer is nonunion, it has full legal sanction. It is lawful, that is, up to the point where it interferes with the employer's business—preventing pick up and delivery of goods, for example.

Speaking of people refusing to cross picket lines, consider an employee of the Black Company (with a sound no-strike, no-lockout contract) who must cross a picket line at the Brown Company to make a delivery. If the pickets are successful in keeping him from crossing the picket line, Black may lawfully discipline the employee for such refusal even to the point of discharging him.

Methods Changes, and Protected Work. The management of a company designs the methods by which the company's product is produced. When a company is formed it sets up whatever processes are needed to produce the goods and/or services it sells. It then arranges for labor to operate the processes. From the management point of view it seems right and reasonable that it should also be able to change the processes when economic analysis indicates the desirability of such change. But unions sometimes attempt to interfere with these changes. We will look at the law involved with this area of union-management conflict simply as one example of labor law.

What happens if two processes are merged into one by a methods change? Or suppose it becomes more economical to subcontract a process or a set of processes—even to the point of closing a plant. Perhaps a new plant is bought or built in a new location in another state to house some of the present processes. Maybe a merger with another company seems desirable. Each move is a management prerogative, isn't it? The short answer is that management generally has the right to make such changes (unless it has bargained the right away), but it must be willing to bargain over their effects on employees.

The merger of two companies into one is strictly management business. Black Company may merge with White Company to form Gray Enterprises without consulting any of the unions involved. Some mergers would have little or no effect on employees. Even if employee status is seriously affected by the merger, management is not obligated to bargain with the union *about the merger*—only about its aftereffects on the employees.

Similarly, if Black Company wishes to buy or build a plant somewhere else, this is strictly management business. It only becomes union business under the circumstance that employee jobs at the old plant are affected. For example, if so much work were to be moved away from the old plant to the new one that layoffs resulted, it could precipitate bargaining over employee rights.

The subcontracting of work is another management right as long as it can be shown that the inspiration for farming the work out was purely economic. There are some exceptions to this rather broad generality, and mention of them should help to clarify the rights involved. In one case[1] farming the work out to another precipitated a layoff, and the court supported the NLRB's contention that this was going too far. In another case[2] the subcontracted work (maintenance) previously done by union members on the company premises was to be done by nonunion people. Again the NLRB (with the backing of the U.S. Supreme Court) indicated that this was beyond reasonable limits of the management prerogative. In the construction industry, union-management contract provisions restricting subcontracting are permitted and upheld. One version of such provisions has come to be known as *work preservation agreements* and has the full sanction of both the NLRB and the U.S. Supreme Court. Subcontracting restrictions are also permitted in the clothing industry according to section 8(e) of the NLRA. The result of all this is that in most industrial activities, subcontracting of work is a management right as long as it is reasonably exercised. If the result is a plant closing or a layoff or nonunion people working in the midst

1. Weltronic Co. v. NLRB, 419 F. 2d 1120 (1969).
2. Fibreboard Paper Products Co. v. NLRB, 379 U.S. 203 (1964).

of union members on jobs that were formerly performed by union members, the subcontracting is not reasonable.

Another right management has traditionally had in a related area is the right to change production methods. It is management's right to overhaul processes, combine them, rearrange them, separate them, and add elements to or delete elements from them. In fact, many of our manufacturing advances and our high level of productivity have resulted from methods and process changes. Management has the right to change production methods, but the effects of such changes on employees may be subject to review.

Featherbedding. There is one form of union resistance to job deletion by management that is singled out for special treatment in the NLRA. This is the practice known as *featherbedding*. Suppose the Black Company completely automates a process involving ten people and because of the change, the ten jobs no longer exist. A reasonable move by management would be to retrain the people for other jobs and, perhaps, wait for normal attrition to take care of any excess personnel. The company might, of course, lay the people off or try to get them employment with another company. As long as Black Company treated the employees as fairly as it could under the circumstances, the union would have little to oppose. But the union could not by way of opposition require Black to retain and pay the employees as though they were still performing the eliminated jobs. Featherbedding, the requiring of payment for work not done or not to be done, is unlawful under the NLRA.

Employee rights is only one small segment of industrial law. It is used here as an example of areas of possible conflict between management and employees' representatives.

SO. PRAIRIE CONST. CO. v. LOC. 627 I.U. OP. ENG.

96 S.Ct. 1842 (1976)

Per Curiam

Respondent Union filed a complaint in 1972 with the National Labor Relations Board alleging that South Prairie Construction Co. (South Prairie) and Peter Kiewit Sons' Co. (Kiewit) had violated secs. 8(a)(5) and (1) of the National Labor Relations Act, as amended, 61 Stat. 140, 29 U.S.C. secs. 158(a)(5) and (1), by their continuing refusal to apply to South Prairie's employees the collective-bargaining agreement in effect between the Union and Kiewit. The Union first asserted that since South Prairie and Kiewit are wholly

owned subsidiaries of Peter Kiewit Sons', Inc. (PKS), and engage in highway construction in Oklahoma, they constituted a single "employer" within the Act for purposes of applying the Union-Kiewit agreement. That being the case, the Union contended, South Prairie was obligated to recognize the Union as the representative of a bargaining unit drawn to include Prairie's employees.[3] Disagreeing with the Administrative Law Judge on the first part of the Union's claim, the Board concluded that Prairie and Kiewit were in fact separate employers, and dismissed the complaint.

On the Union's petition for review, the Court of Appeals for the District of Columbia Circuit canvassed the facts of record. It discussed, *inter alia,* the manner in which Kiewit, South Prairie, and PKS functioned as entities; PKU's decision to activate South Prairie, its nonunion subsidiary, in a State where historically Kiewit had been the only union highway contractor among the latter's Oklahoma competitors; and the two firms' competitive bidding patterns on Oklahoma highway jobs after South Prairie was activated in 1972 to do business there.[4]

Stating that it was applying the criteria recognized by this Court in *Radio and Television Broadcast Technicians Local Union 1264* v. *Broadcast Service of Mobile, Inc., . . .*[5] the Court of Appeals disagreed with the Board and decided that on the facts presented, Kiewit and South Prairie were a "single employer." It reasoned that in addition to the "presence of a very substantial qualitative degree of centralized control of

---

3. The relevant portions of the Act, secs. 8 and 9, 29 U.S.C. secs. 158 and 159, provide in part: "Section 8(a) It shall be an unfair labor practice for an employer—

"(1) to interfere with, restrain, or coerce employees in the exercise of the rights guaranteed in section 7:

"(5) to refuse to bargain collectively with the representatives of his employees, subject to the provisions of section 9(a).

"Section 9(a) Representatives designated or selected for the purposes of collective bargaining by the majority of the employees in a unit appropriate for such purposes, shall be the exclusive representatives of all employees in such unit. . . .

"(b)The Board shall decide in each case whether, in order to assure to employees the fullest freedom in exercising the rights guaranteed by this Act, the unit appropriate for the purposes of collective bargaining shall be the employer unit, craft unit, plant unit, or subdivision thereof. . . ."

On the facts of this case, the Union first had to establish the Kiewit and South Prairie were a single "employer." If it succeeded, the existence of a violation under sec. 8(a)(5) would then turn on whether under sec. 9 the "employer unit" was the "appropriate" one for collective-bargaining purposes.

4. We need not for present purposes set out the facts as summarized at length in the Court of Appeals' opinion. . . .

5. "(I)n determining the relevant employer, the Board considers several nominally separate business entities to be a single employer where they comprise an integrated business enterprise, N.L.R.B. Twenty-first Ann. Rep. 14–15 (1956). The controlling criteria, set out and elaborated in the Board decisions, are interrelation of operations, common management, centralized control of labor relations, and common ownership.". . .

labor relations," the facts "evidence a substantial qualitative degree of interrelation of operations and common management—one that we are satisfied would not be found in the arm's length relationship existing among unintegrated companies". . . . The Board's finding to the contrary was, therefore, in the view of the Court of Appeals "not warranted by the record.". . .

Having set aside this portion of the Board's determination, however, the Court of Appeals went on to reach and decide the second question presented by the Union's complaint which had not been passed upon by the Board. The court decided that the employees of Kiewit and South Prairie constituted the appropriate unit under sec. 9 of the Act[6] for purposes of collective bargaining. On the basis of this conclusion, it decided that these firms had committed an unfair labor practice by refusing "to recognize Local 627 as the bargaining representative of South Prairie's employees or to extend the terms of the Union's arrgement with Kiewit to South Prairie's employees.". . . The case was remanded to the Board for "issuance and enforcement of an appropriate order against . . . Kiewit and South Prairie.". . .

Petitioners South Prairie and the Board in their petitions here contest the action of the Court of Appeals in setting aside the Board's determination on the "employer" question. But their principal contention is that the Court of Appeals invaded the statutory province of the Board when it proceeded to decide the sec. 9 "unit" question in the first instance, instead of remanding the case to the Board so that it could make the initial determination. While we refrain from disturbing the holding of the Court of Appeals that Kiewit and South Prairie are an "employer," . . .[7] we agree with petitioners' principal contention.

The Court of Appeals was evidently of the view that since the Board dismissed the complaint it had necessarily decided that the employees of Kiewit and South Prairie would not constitute an appropriate bargaining unit under sec. 9. But while the Board's opinion referred to its cases in this area and included a finding that "the employees of each constitute a separate bargaining unit,". . . its brief discussion was set in the context of what it obviously considered was the dispositive issue, namely, whether the two firms were separate employers. We think a fair reading of its decision discloses that it did not address the "unit" question on the basis of any assumption, *arguendo,* that it might have been wrong on the threshold "employer" issue.[8]

Section 9(b) of the Act, 29 U.S.C. sec. 159(b), directs the Board to: decide in each case whether, in order to assure to employees the fullest freedom in exercising the rights guaranteed by this

Act, the unit appropriate for the purposes of collective bargaining shall be the employer unit, craft unit, plant unit, or subdivision thereof. . . .

The Board's cases hold that especially in the construction industry a determination that two affiliated firms constitute a single employer "does not necessarily establish that an employer-wide unit is appropriate, as the factors which are relevant in identifying the breadth of an employer's operation are not conclusively determinative of the scope of an appropriate unit.". . .

The Court of Appeals reasoned that the Board's principal case on the "unit" question, . . . was distinguishable because there the two affiliated construction firms were engaged in different types of contracting. It thought that this fact was critical to the Board's conclusion in that case, that the employees did not have the same "community of interest" for purposes of identifying an appropriate bargaining unit. Whether or not the Court of Appeals was correct in this reasoning, we think that for it to take upon itself the initial determination of this issue was "incompatible with the orderly function of the process of judicial review.". . . Since the selection of an appropriate bargaining unit lies largely within the discretion of the Board, whose decision, "if not final, is rarely to be disturbed,". . . we think the function of the Court of Appeals ended when the Board's error on the "employer" issue was "laid bare.". . .

As this Court stated . . . ,

(i)t is a guiding principle of administrative law, long recognized by this Court, that "an administrative determination in which is imbedded a legal question open to judicial review does not impliedly foreclose the administrative agency, after its error has been corrected from enforcing the legislative policy committed to its charge.". . .

In foreclosing the Board from the opportunity to determine the appropriate bargaining unit under sec. 9, the Court of Appeals did not give "due observance (to)

6. See n. 1, *supra*

7. "Were we called upon to pass on the Board's conclusions in the first instance or to make an independent review of the review by the Court of Appeals, we might well support the Board's conclusion and reject that of the court below. But congress has charged the Courts of Appeals and not this Court with the normal and primary responsibility for granting or denying enforcement of Labor Board orders."

8. The ALJ's decision in favor of the Union included a conclusion that the pertinent employees of Kiewit and South Prairie constituted an appropriate unit under sec. 9(b). But that conclusion was of course preceded by the determination that the two firms were a single employer. In disagreeing on the "employer" issue, the Board was not compelled to reach the sec. 9(b) question in order to dismiss the complaint.

the distribution of authority made by Congress as between its power to regulate commerce and the reviewing power which it has conferred upon the courts under Article III of the Constitution.". . .

The petitions for certiorari are accordingly granted, and that part of the judgment of the Court of Appeals which set aside the determination of the Board on the question of whether Kiewit and South Prairie were a single employer is affirmed. That part of the judgment which held that the two firms' employees constituted the appropriate bargaining unit for purposes of the Act, and which directed the Board to issue an enforcement order, is vacated, and the case is remanded to the Court of Appeals for proceedings consistent with this opinion.

It is so ordered.

Affirmed in part, vacated in part, and remanded.

PEAVEY CO. v. N.L.R.B.

648 F.2d 460 (1981)

Bauer, Circuit Judge

Petitioner, Peavey Company, seeks review of an order of the National Labor Relations Board ("NLRB"). The NLRB cross-petitions for enforcement. We grant enforcement in part and deny it in part.

I

The Board found that Peavey violated section 8(a)(3) when it discharged Mellinda Snider. The Administrative Law Judge ("ALJ") found that Snider's discharge "was motivated at least in substantial part by her protected activities." While affirming the ALJ's conclusions of law, the Board labeled Peavey's reasons for the discharge a "pretext." The Board then found that "Snider was discharged solely because of her concerted and union activities." Peavey claims that legitimate business reasons justified Snider's discharge.

Since its decision in this case, the National Labor Relations Board issued its *Wright Line* decision. . . . Wright Line set forth definitive rules for resolving cases in which a "dual motive" discharge is alleged. The Board expressly rejected the "in part" test relied upon by the ALJ here. Instead, it applied the Supreme Court's test in *Mt. Healthy City School District Board of Education* v. *Doyle*, . . . to dual-motive discharge cases. Under the new test, the General Counsel must first make a *prima facie* showing that the employee's protected conduct was a motivating factor in the employer's decision to discharge the employee. Once this is established, the burden shifts to the employer to demonstrate that he would have discharged the employee even in the absence of the protected conduct.

. . . The Board ruled that the *Mt. Healthy* test aimed to determine the causal relationship between the employee's protected activities and the employer's action. Once found, a causal relationship justifies liability under section 8(a)(93), without any quantitative label such as "in part" or "dominant motive." *Id.*

This is the first "dual-motive" case to reach us for decision since *Wright Line.*[9] At least one other circuit has adopted the *Mt. Healthy* approach. . . . We have reviewed the decisions and have decided to follow the *Mt. Healthy/Wright Line* test in "dual motive" cases in this circuit.

Our review of the record as a whole convinces us that Peavey Company met its burden under the *Wright Line* decision. The evidence showed that, although a good typist, Snider was a sloppy worker and had a history of disputes with her supervisors. Peavey disciplined her in writing and advised her of possible discharge unless her work record and attitude improved. A few days before her discharge, she refused to insert notices of new pay scales into paycheck envelopes she was told to prepare. Snider's discharge was ultimately prompted by her refusal to retype some poorly typed letters.

The Board backed away from the ALJ determination that Snider's discharge was motivated "in part" by her union activity. In labeling Peavey's reasons as "pretextual," however, the Board relied on the same rationale as did the ALJ. It agreed that Peavey had "tolerated Snider's poor job performance for over eighteen months" until she began concerted activities. The Board also relied on Peavey's demonstrated "animus" towards the union and the timing of Snider's discharge.

Peavey's reasons here cannot be labeled pretextual. As *Wright Line* held, a pretext can be found to exist when "the purported rule or circumstances advanced by the employer did not exist, or was not, in fact, relied upon (sic).". . . Here, however, it is undisputed that Snider had been disciplined, for cause, prior to her contact with the union. Snider testified, in fact, that she went to the union as a result of her discipline. Her prior discipline also undermines the Board's claim that Peavey had tolerated Snider's poor performance without complaint for eighteen months. Unlike in *St. Luke's Memorial Hospital, Inc.* v. *N.L.R.B.,* . . . there were independent acts of misconduct at the time of Snider's discharge which justified Peavey's action. Moreover, an employer's silence does not extinguish its right to discipline an employee whose conduct continues to worsen. . . .

9. A recent decision, Sullair P.T.V., Inc. v. N.L.R.B., . . . cited but did not rely on Mt. Healthy and Wright Line, because there was no evidence of any illegal motive for the discharge.

Once Peavey's reasons for discharge are stripped of the label "pretext," it is apparent that Peavey met its burden under the *Wright Line* decision. Even though Snider engaged in some protected activity, Peavey showed that she would have been discharged even in the absence of the protected conduct. . . . The substantial evidence on the record as a whole does not support the Board's finding of an 8(a)(3) violation. We therefore deny enforcement of that portion of the Board's order calling for reinstatement of and back pay for Snider.

II

The Board also found five violations of section 8(a)(1) of the National Labor Relations Act. 29 U.S.C. Sec. 158(a)(1). The Board found that Peavey violated the Act when (1) its General Manager told Snider that she was a confidential employee and thus not entitled to participate in union activities; (2) Supervisor Sandy Noe followed employees and eavesdropped on their conversations; (3) it announced, after the union began organizing, that employees could see their personnel files; (4) its General Manager told an employee that persons who joined the union would be considered disloyal; (5) its General Manager promised the employees at a meeting that "he was going to see that things" got better.

After a review of the record as a whole, we conclude that substantial evidence supports the Board's finding of section 8(a)(1) violations. Peavey's contentions to the contrary are without merit. Accordingly, we enforce the rest of the Board's order.

Enforced in Part, Enforcement Denied in Part.

N.L.R.B. v. BROWN AND CONNOLLY, INC.

Cite as 593 F.2d 1373 (1979)

Aldrich, Senior Circuit Judge

This is an application for enforcement of an NLRB order arising out of an employer's alleged failure to abide by its oral recognition of a union in violation of sections 8(a)(1) and (5) of the Act. 29 U.S.C. Secs. 158(a)(1) and (5)(1976). Before addressing the facts we recite briefly the course of the Board's position on recognition short of an election. At one time the Board ruled that an employer faced with a demand *prima facie* supported, as with authorization cards apparently signed by a majority of its employees, was obligated to bargain, absent some good faith reason to doubt the union's showing. We accepted this principle. . . .

Thereafter the question arose in a modified form, where, after rejecting the union's demand supported by a showing of cards, the employer engaged in unfair labor practices. Although even here some circuits did not, we again agreed with the Board, and held that the employer's conduct making a fair election impossible destroyed any right it might otherwise have had to demand an election. . . . On certiorari to resolve the conflict, we were affirmed. . . .

After *Gissel*, perhaps recognizing the criticisms there expressed of the consequences of organization without the protection of secret elections and without permitting the employer to be heard, see . . ., the Board took the position that, absent other violations, the employer had a right to require an election regardless of the union's showing. In this it was supported by the Court. . . . On the other hand, if the employer once recognizes a majority union, no matter how informally, the Board holds that the right is lost. . . . This is the present case.

On September 14, 1976, 11 of the respondent's 17 employees,[10] together with two union organizers, called on respondent's president, Brown, at his office, unannounced, and followed what would appear to be a predetermined script to obtain an admission from Brown that he "recognized" the union. ("Do you recognize that we are a majority of your employees?" "Do you recognize that we all wear union buttons?" etc., etc.) Caught unprepared, with no prior knowledge of organizational activity, and quite possibly unaware of an employer's right to require an election, Brown ultimately, according to the credited testimony of the employees, said the magic word. Although it took a little longer, even on General Counsel's case the whole meeting might remind chess players of the fool's mate.

We could have some sympathy with respondent's attempt to require an election,[11] asserted promptly, and before any further steps had been taken, and when, at best, Brown had been the victim of an orchestrated encounter, 13 to 1, with considerable variation among

10. The company concedes that these employees constitute an appropriate unit.

11. No sympathy can be expected, however, in regard to respondent's conduct subsequent to its refusal to bargain which resulted in the Board's finding several unfair labor practices which respondent does not here contest. In light of our resolution, it is unnecessary to remand to the Board for a determination whether, given these violations, a fair election became impossible under NLRB v. Gissel Packing Co., . . .

those testifying against him.[12] However, even if we were the policy-maker, we would not quarrel with the Board's rule that once an employer had affirmatively agreed to recognize a union, it cannot change its mind. The facts in this case might suggest the desirability of a rule that recognition must be clearly and convincingly evidenced, and not dependent upon a staged performance and resolution of disputed, possibly perjured, testimony, which may have fostered here, at least in part, the very strife the Act is intended to prevent.[13] While voluntary recognition may be favored, *NLRB* v. *Broadmoor Lumber Co.,* . . . recognition versus election does not seem to us that important. The argument made to us, that if an employer could change its mind it would lead to unfair labor practices in an attempt to cause the union to lose the election, would also undercut the Board's policy recognized in *Linden Lumber Division,* ante, an inconsistency counsel for the Board avoided by not citing the case. We consider such policy matters, however, to be outside our province. . . . Equally, we reject respondent's request that we reverse the Board's evidentiary findings.

The order of the Board is to be enforced.

REVIEW QUESTIONS

1. Show graphically how Adam Smith's supply and demand theory might be used by a court to prove "unlawful" union action. Show by another graph how David Ricardo's wages fund theory might be used for the same purpose.
2. What do the following terms mean? What is their present legal status?
   a. Yellow-dog contract
   b. Labor injunction
   c. Closed shop
   d. Picketing
   e. Strike
   f. Wildcat strike
   g. Featherbedding
   h. Jurisdictional dispute
   i. Open shop
   j. Collective bargaining
3. What are the nature, purpose, function, and jurisdiction of the National Labor Relations Board?
4. Compare the effects on employers of the union shop and the closed shop.
5. What are the limits to which efforts may be taken to persuade employees either to join or not to join a union prior to a union election?
6. Describe how a secondary boycott works. Give an example of a secondary boycott involving a union. Give an example of one not involving a union.
7. Distinguish between an economic strike and an unfair labor practice strike. What are the rights of employees involved in each?
8. Reasoning from the Supreme Court opinion in *So. Prairie Constr. Co.* v. *Loc. 627 I.U. OP. ENG.,* what is the U.S. Court of Appeals function in such cases and what is the U.S. Supreme Court's function?
9. According to the decision in *Peavey Co.* v. *N.L.R.B.,* what employee activities justified discharge? What specific acts by the company were censured?
10. In the case of *N.L.R.B.* v. *Brown and Connolly, Inc.,* does it seem that the U.S. Court of Appeals has supported an activity that is at least unethical, if not illegal? What would be a better policy?

12. Particularly, we note that this gave the ALJ a variety of General Counsel's Witnesses to choose from for "principal reliance."

13. *Cf.* NLRB v. Gogin, ante, where the court accepted the Board's resolution of a telephone conversation, that the employer's attorney had perjured himself, without "intend(ing) adverse reflection upon counsel whatsoever.". . . A disputed telephone call seems an unhappy way of resolving the important question whether a union represents the employees.

25

Workers' Compensation

People who work for a living risk being injured. Some of the machines and equipment they must use are inherently dangerous. Sometimes the building or the work situation itself is hazardous. Occasionally it is dangerous to get to the job site or to return from it. There is some degree of danger associated with almost any human activity. Such being the case, who should run the risk of injury on the job—the employee or the employer? The answer a century or so ago was that the employee ran all these risks. The law heavily favored employers. The injured worker might take action against his employer for compensation for his injury, but his chances of winning were virtually nonexistent. The employer had three unbeatable defenses: assumption of risk, contributory negligence, and the fellow servant rule.

Assumption of Risk. In the law of torts if one voluntarily assumes a risk and is injured thereby, he has no cause to recover for that injury. Logically, then, one who accepts employment accepts the risks that are necessary components of that employment. If Green applies for work at the Brown Company and the Brown Company hires him as a machine operator, doesn't Green assume the risk of being injured? Isn't that part of his job? Until a century or so ago the answer to the questions was an unequivocal yes. Therefore, if Green were injured during his employment in the operation of a Brown Company machine, Brown might express sympathy or even offer Green a payment as a gratuity, but Green would have no available court action with any likelihood of success to *require* compensation from Brown.

Contributory Negligence. If the logic of assumption of risk should fail as a defense, the same or a similar set of facts could be used to establish contributory negligence by plaintiff. If Green lost a finger or a hand in one of Brown Company's machines, Brown could simply argue that working around machines was obviously dangerous and that Green was negligent in not keeping his hand out of the machine. Since Green was so negligent, he should have no proper cause of action against Brown. The logic is simply that Green's negligence caused his injury and Brown had no responsibility in it.

Fellow Servant Rule. Assumption of risk and contributory negligence usually covered the employer in all worker injury cases. But if they did not, there was a third line of reasoning that could be used as a defense. Let's assume that Green can establish that the machine that injured him was faulty, perhaps because of poor maintenance. Brown Company's answer could include as an added defense that a maintenance man or some other employee had been negligent and this caused the mechanical fault. Brown's next step, then, would be to allege that the real defendant should be the negligent fellow employee rather than the employer for whom both employees worked.

Employers' Liability Acts

The spectre of maimed and injured workers caused public concern. In various jurisdictions the law was changed by legislatures in the late 1800s to what were known as *employers' liability acts*. Under these acts the injured worker still had to take a legal action. This often meant he had to find an attorney willing to take his case on a contingency fee basis. This, in turn, would reduce plaintiff's recovery by 25% to 50% of the amount (if any) recovered from the employer.

Presuming the injured employee could find an attorney willing to take his case, he might have a chance to win under employers' liability acts. Changes from the common law of torts eliminated two of the employer's defenses and substantially changed the third one. Assumption of risk and the fellow servant rule were eliminated; contributory negligence was changed to *comparative* negligence. The legal battles frequently left it up to a jury to decide the question of "who was more negligent?" The rather natural result of this was that jury awards were tempered to reflect a sharing of the negligence. If a jury found both Brown and Green to be equally negligent and the damage award was established as $20,000, Green might be awarded $10,000. After paying his attorney, say 40% of the award, Green would be left with $6,000 to compensate him for a $20,000 injury. Other expenses, such as expert witness fees, could reduce Green's award even further.

Still, with employers' liability acts employers began to lose cases and pay awards to injured employees. So a means to avoid this was contrived—a practice that came to be a kind of "ambulance chasing." Green might be severely injured while working. As he recovered in a hospital he would receive a visit by a Brown Company representative urging him to accept an amount such as $500 from his employer to "help him in his time of need." Green would only be required to sign a "receipt" (which turned out to be a release from liability) to obtain the cash.

The employers' liability acts were a significant improvment over the common law of torts, but they still left something to be desired. The injured worker still had to find an attorney and initiate action; his award might be trimmed by comparative negligence and other expenses; and "ambulance chasing" practices were rather reprehensible. In addition, the injured worker often had difficulty finding fellow workers who would risk their jobs by testifying for him. The system known as workers' compensation had been adopted in most European countries by 1903. After a couple of false starts here, the federal government and a few of the states began to enact such laws. Between 1908 and 1948 all of our states adopted some version of the law.

WORKERS' COMPENSATION LAWS

It would certainly be surprising if the federal government version of workers' compensation and all state laws on the subject agreed on all details. The fact that the laws were enacted over a forty-year period doesn't do much to improve the probability that they will be identical. Even so, there is sufficient similarity in coverage among the various laws so that we may discuss a general concept of workers' compensation, pointing out prominent exceptions along the way. The laws attempt to reach the same general objective—to compensate a worker for injury arising "out of and in the course of his employment." Some reach this objective in one manner, while others differ in the details of coverage. In no sense, then, will our treatment here be correct in every detail for every (or any) workers' compensation law. Copies of individual state workers' compensation laws are generally available from each state's Industrial Commission (or Workers' Compensation Bureau).

Coverage

In almost all the laws industry coverage is either mandatory with penalties for noncoverage, or those industries choosing not to be covered are rendered virtually defenseless when sued. The law may require industry coverage of employees and state that each day of operation without coverage is a separate violation of the act with a fine or imprisonment to result from each violation. On the other hand, the law may merely state that coverage is optional but that if an injured employee sues his employer, the employer may not use assumption of risk, contributory or comparative negligence, or the fellow servant rule as a defense. In either case an industry is under legal pressure to adopt workers' compensation for its employees.

The worker never has to pay for workers' compensation coverage. The cost of the coverage is borne in some way by the employers. Generally, an employer may contract with an insurance company for workers' compensation coverage. In many of the states, though, he may elect to self-insure. In a few states he is required to buy his insurance from a state agency. In short, he must take the required steps as assurance that he is capable of paying an injured worker's medical expenses and a weekly compensation for lost wages.

In each of the workers' compensation acts there are certain exceptions to general coverage. Many of the laws exempt agricultural employees, domestic servants, independent contractors, casual workers, and/or workers in religious or charitable organizations. Some require that there be a minimum number of employees involved for coverage. Sometimes owners are counted as employees. As time passes there is a tendency to expand the coverage to more and more occupations.

Employer. The cost to an employer for workers' compensation may be judged from insurance companies' premium requirements. Generally, for the first three years an employer has workers' compensation coverage the premium he must pay for coverage on a given job is to be found in the insurance company's rate manual. Premiums are based on $100 of payroll cost. If Green operates a rather hazardous machine for the Brown Company, the premium Brown has to pay for workers' compensation coverage may be as high as $10 for every $100 Green earns. On the other hand, if Green works in the office where the only prominent hazard might be the possibility of tripping over a wastebasket, Brown's premium cost might be $.25 or $.50 per $100 of Green's earnings.

After the first three years of coverage the premium cost is raised or lowered according to the employer's experience rating. Few severe injuries over the period may result in reduced premiums. Numerous and very severe injuries may increase the premiums.

Second Injury Funds. Let us suppose Green is handicapped. He has lost the sight of an eye. Would the Brown Company hire him? Suppose he lost the sight of the other eye while working for Brown. He would then be permanently, totally disabled. The cost of such permanent total disability is far greater than the cost of losing the sight of one eye. In such a case Brown might well hesitate to risk such a heavy loss. "Hire the handicapped" would operate as "penalize the last employer." Under these circumstances few handicapped prospects would ever be hired. For this reason nearly all workers' compensation laws require the second employer to be responsible for only the extent of injury suffered while the employee was with him. If Green lost the sight of his other eye, Brown would be responsible only for the loss of sight in one eye. But Green, of course, would be totally blind, and this is where the *second* (or *subsequent*) *injury fund* comes in. That fund would make up the difference between what Brown would be required to pay and what Green would receive for being totally disabled. Second injury funds are created in a variety of ways, the most common being legislative appropriation.

Amount of Compensation

The amount of compensation an injured worker is to receive for a work-connected injury depends upon the nature of the injury and the specification in the workers' compensation law. Generally, workers' compensation laws require the payment of all medical expenses. The payment for lost wages, though, depends upon the nature of the injury. Four possibilities must be considered: (1) temporary total disability, (2) permanent partial disability, (3) permanent total disability, and (4) death.

A *temporary total disability* usually requires the employer to pay compensation that is some percentage of the employee's wage—say 2/3 of Green's customary weekly wage. But upper and lower limits nearly always accompany this provision. That is, while Green is waiting in the hospital for broken bones to heal he might receive 2/3 of his weekly wage providing this was no more than $300 per week and no less than $50 per week. Also, there is often a hold back feature in the law so that if Green is out only a few days he receives little or no wage compensation payment. If he is out two or three weeks the law may require Brown to go back and compensate Green for the first few days he was laid up as well as continuing payments until he is ready to return to work.

A *permanent partial disability* is usually the loss of function of some part of the worker's body. When Green lost the sight of one eye, that was a permanent partial disability. Loss of a hand, a finger, a foot, a leg, or the hearing in one ear would be a permanent partial disability. Workers' compensation laws generally have a schedule of times for which the worker will be paid a portion of his weekly wage for the disability. Green's loss of an eye might require his employer to pay Green 2/3 of his weekly wage (between the listed maximum and minimum) for perhaps 150 weeks. In addition to this, a majority of the workers' compensation laws provide for some form of vocational rehabilitation for both permanent partial and permanent total disabilities.

When Green lost the sight of both eyes he had a *permanent total disability*. Under about two-thirds of the workers' compensation laws, all his medical costs would be paid plus wage compensation for as long as he was disabled. If rehabilitation cannot be effective this means wage compensation for life. Under the remaining one-third of the laws, some limitations (usually as to maximum compensation total) is imposed, but the tendency in such laws is for them to become more liberal.

If Green lost his life while working for the Brown Company, Brown would have to pay all Green's medical expenses and then make wage compensation payments to Green's wife and children. This wage compensation would continue until a statutory limit had been reached or until Green's widow remarried. The amount of compensation might be modified when Green's children reached a certain age or married. Brown usually must also pay for Green's burial or, at least, is responsible for this up to a statutory maximum.

Determination of Compensability

Workers' compensation laws clear up the question of whether a worker injured while working will be compensated for his injury. They go on that to specify how much this compensation will be. Beyond that, the laws usually set up some kind of appeal procedure—which, perhaps, seems odd. After all, if all questions are answered by a statute, what is left to appeal? The reason for the appeal, of course, is that there are still unanswered questions. The main such question from which very large numbers of cases arise is whether an injury actually *was* work-connected. In other words, did the injury arise *out of and in the course of the worker's employment?* If the worker's injury occurred while he was mowing his lawn or painting his house or playing tennis on a weekend, it is difficult to conceive of workers' compensation coverage for him. If he is injured at work there is little question as to the application of the law. But what if he is injured while going to work or while he is on his lunch hour, for example? These are only two of numerous questions for which a case-by-case common law of workers' compensation has had to be built under each statute. We will turn next to answers that have been worked out for some of these questions.

Going and Coming. Generally, an employee is not covered by workers' compensation on his routine journeys to and from work. But there are enough exceptions to this generality so that a rather imposing body of case law has developed on this topic alone. The general statement is still true, but numerous special circumstances have caused decisions for coverage. Green, traveling in his car at his customary time of traveling over his customary route to or from work *probably* is not covered. Even this has an exception: if he is required to use his car in his work he would be covered by workers' compensation in many jurisdictions. Let us pass over that exception, though, and turn to some others that seem to be well established. If Green is responding to an early call-in or is returning home later than usual because of some unusual work requirement, he has a sound case for coverage. If he has taken an unusual route in response to a work requirement (even a mere suggestion by his boss), he is very likely to be covered. If his work has required him to be awake so long that he falls asleep at the wheel and is injured as a result, workers' compensation should cover him. In short, anything work-connected that causes him to alter his customary routine of travel to and from the job gives him a reasonable cause to claim workers' compensation. His travel (and injury) may be alleged to have arisen out of his employment and in the course of his employment.

Lunch Hour. A special set of cases is involved with the activities of persons during their lunch periods. If Green leaves Brown Company premises for lunch the generality runs that he is not covered. Again, enough exceptions exist to make the statement of the generality appear to be almost hazardous folly. If Green can show any connection between his job and his lunch hour activity he has a case for workers' compensation coverage. Even if the foreman only suggested that Green ride with him (Gray), and Green is injured in an accident involving Gray's car, Green has a case for coverage. And, for that matter, so has Gray. The coverage is more obvious where the lunch involves customers or vendors or co-workers on a business lunch, or where Green is asked to pick up materials or make a delivery in conjunction with his lunch period. In all of these Green has a reason to allege that injury arose out of and in the course of his employment.

Intoxication. If Green comes to work so inebriated that he cannot properly control his actions and, as a result, becomes injured at his job, should this injury be compensated? The question has been raised many times and compensation frequently has been denied. The logic for denial is that the injury was really caused by the employee's condition into which he voluntarily placed himself. Under many workers' compensation acts there are provisions that coverage does not extend to an employee who is intoxicated. So coverage may be denied to an injured worker who was intoxicated when the injury occurred.

Let us now change Green's situation a little. You might say that he is drunk, depending on your interpretation of the term. Perhaps it is better to note that he has imbibed numerous alcoholic beverages. But Green's job is now that of a traveling salesman. His job requires him to entertain customers. Brown Company actively abets Green's drinking habit or knows of it and tolerates it or ignores it completely. Green is involved in an auto accident after having entertained customers and is injured. Should he be covered by workers' compensation or not? The answer to this is almost universally in the affirmative.[1] The entertainment of customers was part of Green's job, so therefore, his injury arose out of and in the course of his employment.

Injury by Coemployee or Third Person. In many work-connected injuries it is possible to show that the cause was an error by some fellow employee or an outsider. If the injury arose out of and in the course of the employee's job, he has a right to workers' compensation. But this may not be the end of it. If strong evidence of a tort exists, there may be justification for the injured employee or the insurer (or both) to act against the one who caused the injury. Green is injured because a machine on which he was working malfunctioned. Green has a right to recover workers' compensation from Brown Company, his employer. He may also take a tort action, perhaps for product liability, against White Company, the producer of the machine. Brown Company's insurer, Gray Insurance, also has an interest in the tort action. Under subrogation they obtain the right to try to recover whatever they have paid to Green in workers' compensation payments.[2]

For workers' compensation coverage, injury by a coworker or outsider must have arisen from the injured employee's work. That is, if Green were injured in a strictly personal altercation with Black, coverage would not be appropriate. If the Black-Green altercation had nothing to do with Green's work, Green's only appro-

1. See, for example, Boyd v. Francis Ford, Inc., 504 P2d 1387 (Oregon, 1973).

2. A workers' compensation case in which a set of payments of this nature occurred is Moomey v. Massey Ferguson, Inc., 429 F. 2d 1184 (New Mexico, 1970).

priate recourse is a tort action against Black.[3] The injury did not arise out of and in the course of Green's employment.

Other Situations. It would be nearly impossible to describe all the injury-causing events that have occurred and their relation to workers' compensation. A few more general categories of cases might be mentioned simply as examples of problems that do arise. Suppose Green is injured by "an act of God" such as a tornado or other violent storm. Customarily, a person such as Green would be covered by workers' compensation, but only if his job exposed him to the hazard in greater degree than members of the general public were exposed.

Suppose Green disconnects a safety device on equipment with which he must work. Cases on this sort of situation go both ways. If the company (the foreman) knew of Green's added hazard and did nothing about it, the chances for coverage are good. Otherwise, under most of the workers' compensation laws, coverage is likely to be denied.

Green may intentionally injure himself (sounds unlikely, but it has occurred). If this can be shown, workers' compensation coverage is likely to be denied.

What if Green is called upon to live for short periods away from home? He may have to work on projects for his employer far enough away to require him to live in an apartment near the location of his work. Suppose further that Green suffers an injury in that apartment—the stove blows up or a wall or ceiling caves in or some other feature of the apartment causes him injury. Case law has not yet established a clear answer to the question of coverage in such circumstances. But, just as in the cases above, the answer depends upon the determination of whether the case arose "out of and in the course of" Green's employment.

TIETZ v. HASTINGS LUMBER MART, INC.
210 N.W. 2d 236 (1973)

Per Curiam

Relators seek review of a decision of the Workmen's Compensation Commission awarding benefits to respondent, widow of the deceased employee. The only issue is whether a drowning, resulting from a boating accident during a company picnic, was work-related and, therefore, compensable. We affirm.

The picnic was an annual outing sponsored and financed by the Hastings Lumber Mart, Inc., for the benefit of all of its full-time male employees. Full attendance was actively encouraged and actual attendance was usually close to 100 percent. The outing was

held on a workday afternoon chosen in advance to provide as little conflict as possible with other obligations of the employees. Those who attended received a full day's pay. Those who did not attend were not required to work, as the business premises were closed at noon on the day of the outing. However, some wage adjustment was made for those not attending, either by a reduction in the employee's sick leave or, in one case, by a direct docking of wages.

Although this occasion was not used to make speeches, present awards, or to otherwise enhance the vocational abilities of the employees, the commission found that the personal injury did arise out of and in the course of decedent's employment within the guideline of whether or not the employer derived a direct and substantial benefit from the employees' attendance at the outing "beyond the intangible value of improvement in the employee's health or morale that is common to all kinds of recreation and social life.". . .

We have weighed the factors which we regard governing,[4] and are convinced that the commission's findings are not manifestly contrary to the evidence and that they have followed the guidelines of *Ethen* v. *Franklin Manufacturing Co.,* . . . in reaching their decision, although this case is factually distinguishable and a different result is mandated.

Attorneys' fees in the amount of $400 are allowed respondent on this appeal.

Affirmed.

ATKINSON v. LITTLE AUDREY'S TRANSFER CO., INC.
212 N.W. 2d 350 (1973)

Spencer, Justice

Richard B. Atkinson, plaintiff-appellant, prosecutes this appeal from an order of the District Court for Douglas County, sustaining the order of dismissal of the Nebraska Workmen's Compensation Court. The cause was dismissed by a one-judge court, and on rehearing this finding was reaffirmed by the Nebraska Workmen's Compensation Court *en banc*. We affirm.

Plaintiff by vocation is an over-the-road truck driver. This action is predicated on his claim of a preinfarction angina on May 31, 1968, leading to a more severe myocardial infarction on June 3, 1968. He claims his heart condition arose out of and in the course of his employment with the defendant. Plaintiff's acute myocardial infarct occurred on June 3, 1968, while he was on a

3. One case of this nature is Highlands Underwriters Ins. Co. v. McGrath, 485 S.W. 2d 593 (Texas, 1972).
4. See, 1 Larson, Workmen's Compensation Law, Sect. 22.23.

cross-country journey from Fremont, Nebraska, to the west coast. The basis of the present action, however, is plaintiff's contention that he sustained a preinfarction angina on the previous trip, which originated at Fremont, May 25, 1968, and terminated on May 31, 1968, at Fargo, North Dakota.

On the trip in question plaintiff was working on a refrigerated unit with a cargo consisting of lettuce, carrots, oranges, and celery which had been picked up in California. The separate items of produce were segregated in the truck and were packed in cartons and crates which varied in weight between 35 and 70 pounds. At Bismarck, North Dakota, one-half of the load or 20,000 pounds, was unloaded onto skids furnished by the consignee. The unloading of the trailer was done by the plaintiff and the driver, individually picking up cartons of produce and placing them on the skids. The skids were then taken into the consignee's place of business by his own employees. Work commenced at the end of the trailer. As the trailer was unloaded the plaintiff and the driver worked their way into the interior. To unload this 20,000 pounds required 2 1/2 hours of work inside the refrigerated trailer. This same process was repeated with the balance of 20,000 pounds of produce at Fargo, North Dakota. Plaintiff worked another 2 1/2 hours in the trailer at that point.

Plaintiff testified that while unloading at Bismarck he had a shortness of breath and a feeling like he had drawn in too much cold air. He then experienced pain in his chest. These symptoms first appeared when he was inside the refrigerated trailer unloading produce. When plaintiff was unloading at Fargo, North Dakota, the pain increased. He didn't know what caused the pain and thought it was just cold air in his lungs. Two symptoms persisted, shortness of breath and the pain across his chest on both sides. This pain continued after he had unloaded the cargo at Fargo and when he arrived at Pipestone, Minnesota, where he left the truck. It continued during his return home to Valley, Nebraska, and was still present the next day, Saturday morning. It is plaintiff's contention that he was under unusual strain in temperature and work and that these conditions combined to produce the myocardial infarction.

On cross-examination the plaintiff admitted that he did not have any pain in his chest while he was in Bismarck. He did, however, have shortness of breath and thought he had sucked in too much air.

The testimony of the driver of the unit on which plaintiff was working does not support his position. He testified that the plaintiff made no complaints to him of chest pains. If he had made such complaints the driver would have remembered them because he liked the plaintiff.

The testimony of plaintiff's doctors tended to support his contention that there was a causal connection between his employment activities and his subsequent heart attack. Defendant's medical witness, however, testified that during the period in question the plaintiff had been engaged in ordinary work to which he was accustomed and there was no direct relationship between the work he had performed on May 31 and his subsequent heart attack on June 3.

It would serve no useful purpose to further detail the evidence herein. It is apparent that the evidence is irreconcilable and in direct conflict. A review of the record convinces us that we cannot say that the findings of fact are not supported by the evidence. This case therefore is controlled by *Gifford* v. *Ag Lime, Sand & Gravel Co.* . . . in which we said: "Upon appellate review of a workmen's compensation case in the Supreme Court, the cause will be considered *de novo* only where the findings of fact are not supported by the evidence as disclosed by the record."

Here, the triers of fact in each instance found against the plaintiff. The Workmen's Compensation Court *en banc* said in part: ". . . plaintiff failed to prove a causal connection between the work he did on May 31, 1968, and his subsequent heart attack which he suffered on June 3, 1968. . . . The burden was on the plaintiff to prove this causal connection."

We said in *McPhillips* v. *Knox Construction Co., Inc.* . . . "Where the claimant in a workmen's compensation case fails to show with reasonable certainty that the disability of which he complains arose out of and in the course of his employment, the proceeding will be dismissed."

We agree that the plaintiff has not maintained his burden herein. The judgment of the District Court sustaining the order of dismissal is affirmed.

Affirmed.

Smith, Justice, concurs in a separate opinion.

ANDERSON'S CASE

Mass., 370 N.E. 2nd 692 (1977)

Hennessey, Chief Justice

In this case we are called upon to construe the meaning of G.L. c. 152, sec. 7A, and to determine whether that statute was correctly applied by the reviewing board (board) of the Industrial Accident Board. We conclude that, since the findings and decision of the board leave it conjectural whether it correctly applied the statute, the case must be remanded to the board for further proceedings consistent with this opinion.

The plaintiff, widow of Albert S. Anderson (employee), filed a claim for compensation under G.L. c. 152, sec. 31. After hearing, a single member of the Industrial Accident Board ordered the insurer to pay the claimant-widow weekly dependency compensation in accordance with sec. 31 from March 28, 1972, to date and continuing at the rate of $45 a week. There were further orders for payments under other sections of c. 152.

The insurer claimed a review to the board. The matter was tried without witnesses, and the parties filed a statement of agreed facts. It was agreed that on March 28, 1972, the employee, then forty-nine, reported for work between 7 and 7:15 A.M. to perform his regular duties. As he was office manager, those duties were, in general, supervisory and clerical, and involved only occasional physical exertion, although his workweek almost always considerably exceeded forty hours. It is unknown what the employee did from the time of his arrival, but at 7:30 A.M. he was found by fellow employees at his desk, choking and semi-conscious. He kept breathing but never spoke. A police ambulance arrived and removed him to Worcester City Hospital where he was pronounced dead on arrival. A copy of the death certificate is attached to the record and was incorporated therein by reference.

By agreement, a report of John P. Rattigan, M.D., was submitted. He gave as his opinion, based upon the available medical data, that the employee's sudden collapse and subsequent death on March 28, 1972, occurred in the natural progression of coronary artery disease, and was not causally related to his employment. Dr. Rattigan regarded it as particularly significant that the employee died shortly after he arrived at work before he had engaged in any of his routine activities; and further, Dr. Rattigan gave as his opinion that the employee's general activities on the day of death were so completely void of suggestion of emotional stress that it was not possible to causally relate his collapse and death to work.

The board reversed the decision of the single member, and denied and dismissed the widow's claim. In its "Findings and Decision," after a statement of the agreed facts, the board stated: "Based upon the foregoing facts and the medical opinion of John P. Rattigan, M.D., whose opinion the Reviewing Board adopt, the Reviewing Board find that the deceased employee was found choking and semi-conscious at his place of employment; that his duties were supervisory and clerical; that there was no direct or inferential evidence of emotional or physical stress on the day of his death or involving his duties. Accordingly, the Reviewing Board find and rule that there is prima facie evidence that the employee was performing his regular duties on the day

of his death but that the claimant-widow has failed to establish by a fair preponderance of the affirmative evidence that the deceased employee sustained a personal injury arising out of and in the course of his employment. The Reviewing Board further find the claim does not come within the provisions of Chapter 152. The widow's claim for dependency compensation is hereby denied and dismissed." A judge of the Superior Court affirmed the decision.

General Laws c. 152, sec. 7A, as appearing in St.1971, c. 702, reads as follows, in its entirety: "In any claim for compensation where the employee has been killed, or found dead at his place of employment or is physically or mentally unable to testify, it shall be prima facie evidence that the employee was performing his regular duties on the day of injury or fatality or death or disability and that the claim comes within the provisions of this chapter, that sufficient notice of the injury has been given, and that the injury or death or disability was not occasioned by the willful intention of the employee to injure or kill himself or another."

The plaintiff argues that sec. 7A should be construed as establishing, inter alia, prima facie evidence that the employee's death was causally related to his duties as an employee. She also argues that, given that construction of the statute, the board's findings and decision do not demonstrate that the board correctly applied the statute to this case.

The plaintiff does not argue that the evidence did not support the board's denial of her claim. In this she is correct; the opinions expressed by Dr. Rattigan clearly warranted the board in concluding that the death was not causally related to the employment.

We look first to our standard of review in a case such as this. It has been well established that this court must sustain the findings of the reviewing board and they are final unless they are wholly lacking in evidential support or tainted by error of law. . . .

For a claim to be compensable it must arise out of and in the course of the employment. Clearly a causal relationship is required between the employment duties and the injury or death. In a case such as this one, where the employee was found dead at his place of employment, we construe the statute, sec. 7A, as establishing, inter alia, prima facie evidence of causal relationship between the employment and the injury or fatality. We believe that was the meaning intended by the legislature, particularly in its use of the words, "and that the claim comes within the provisions of this chapter."[5]

5. Cases construing the statute, sec. 7A, as it existed prior to its amendment in 1971, are not apposite, since the statute in its earlier wording was more limited in scope, and in its effective assistance to the claimant.

We turn next to the definition of "prima facie evidence," as we construe that term as used in the statute, sec. 7A. Prima facie evidence, in the absence of contradictory evidence, requires a finding that the evidence is true; the prima facie evidence may be met and overcome by evidence sufficient to warrant a contrary conclusion; even in the presence of contradictory evidence, however, the prima facie evidence is sufficient to sustain the proposition to which it is applicable.[6]. . .

In light of what we have said as to the meaning of the statute, we examine now whether the board has correctly applied the statute in this case. It is the duty of the board so to deal with cases before it that when a certified copy of the record is presented to the Superior Court, that court can determine with reasonable certainty whether or not correct rules of law have been applied to facts which could properly be found. . . .

It is possible that the board interpreted the statute, sec. 7A, as we have construed it, *supra,* and applied it correctly in this case. The result reached, denial of the claim, is consistent with a correct application of the law, since the board might have determined that the prima facie case which arose from the statute was controlled and overcome by other evidence, particularly the opinion of Dr. Rattigan. Nevertheless, the board's legal reasoning is far from clear in the record. Ambiguity is particularly shown in the board's conclusion that "the claimant-widow has failed to establish by a fair preponderance of the affirmative evidence that the deceased employee sustained a personal injury arising out of and in the course of his employment, and that his death was causally related to a personal injury arising out of and in the course of his employment."

There is no question in this case that the board was on clear notice that the legal effect of the statute, sec. 7A, was at issue before the board, because the statement of agreed facts by the parties posed, as an "issue presented," the question whether the statute warranted a finding for the plaintiff widow without actual medical evidence of causal relationship. As we have shown, that was a correct statement of the law as we have construed it, *supra.* It is at best conjectural whether the board applied the prima facie effect of the statute to the issue of causal relationship. The plaintiff is entitled to a clear and unambiguous statement of the board's reasoning.

The decree is reversed and a new decree is to be entered in the Superior Court remanding the case to the Industrial Accident Board for further proceedings consistent with this opinion.

So Ordered.

REVIEW QUESTIONS

1. What three defenses did early employers have when acted against by injured employees? How was this changed under the employers' liability acts? What further changes were made under workers' compensation?
2. Why should an employer be rendered virtually defenseless when an injured employee acts against him because of a work-connected injury, whereas he would have all the defenses normally available in a tort action by a nonemployee? Why should the employee be placed in such a preferred position?
3. Why were employers' liability acts unsatisfactory?
4. What basic proof is necessary for an injured employee to recover from his employer under workers' compensation?
5. What generally happens if an employer refuses workers' compensation?
6. What effect does experience rating have on an employer's workers' compensation coverage purchased from an insurer?
7. What is a second (or subsequent) injury fund? Why is it necessary, and how does it work?
8. Give two examples for each: (a) temporary total disability, (b) permanent partial disability, (c) permanent total disability.
9. Black, an engineer for the White Company, is injured while returning home from work. What circumstances might cause this injury to be covered by workers' compensation?
10. In the case of *Tietz* v. *Hastings Lumber Mart, Inc.,* list the reasons why workers' compensation coverage was allowed.

6. In Commonwealth v. Pauley, . . . see the following language: "According to the Massachusetts view, when by statute or common law, one fact probative of another is denominated prima facie evidence of that second fact, proof of the first or basic fact requires a finding that the second, the inferred or presumed fact, is also true. The finding is mandatory. To avert this result, the opponent must assume the burden of production (the burden of persuasion remains with the proponent). It is only when the opponent has introduced sufficient evidence, which, cast against the natural inferential value of the basic fact, creates an issue of the fact for the trier, that the opponent has satisfied his burden and the mandatory effect disappears. In a case tried by jury where the opponent does not assume his burden, the judge should charge that if the jury find the basic fact, they are required to find the inferred fact; if the basic fact is admitted or otherwise undisputed, the judge should charge that the jury must find the inferred fact, and if the inferred fact encompasses the substance of the case, the judge should direct a verdict.

11. Heart attack cases form an important and very difficult set of workers' compensation cases. Considering the *Atkinson* case, suppose Atkinson had returned home and suffered a heart attack (myocardial infarction) on the evening of May 31. Do you think he would have been covered by workers' compensation? If you think he would have been covered, suppose further that between finishing his workday and arriving home he had stopped at a local tavern for "a few beers." Would this alter his chances of recovery? What further proof do you think Atkinson would have needed in the actual case to turn the balance in his favor?

12. Based on your reading of Anderson's case, do you believe that an engineer found dead at his desk died out of and in the course of his employment? Suggest a scenario under which coverage might reasonably be denied.

It seems only reasonable and humane that the environments in which people work should not be hazardous to them. Furthermore, since each employee represents a significant investment in training (either formal or informal), an employer suffers a sizable economic loss when an employee is absent due to injury. The actual monetary costs of work-related injuries go beyond those of the employer, however. The wealth of a society is the goods and services produced by it. Each lost-time industrial injury diminishes that wealth. In addition, the public burden is increased by such injuries. Many of the people living on welfare and Aid to Families with Dependent Children and many of those living in state-run nursing homes can trace their plights to industrial accidents. Industrial injuries, then, are a source not only of personal misery, but also of social and economic problems.

In chapter 25 we discussed workers' compensation and its historical perspective. Workers' Compensation is a remedy, a device to partially compensate the primary victim for partial or total, temporary or permanent loss. It is not and was not intended to be a total replacement for the loss suffered. The fact that there *is* loss serves as a deterrent to industrial injuries for both employee and employer. Still, the strength of the deterrent (or the incentive for safety) does not seem to have been sufficient. In 1970 about 14,500 work-related deaths, 2,200,000 disabling injuries, and 390,000 new occupational disease cases were reported. To increase the incentive for industrial safety, the United States Congress in December of that year, passed the Williams-Steiger Occupational Safety and Health Act (OSHAct). It took effect April 28, 1971.

OSHAct's purpose is "to assure safe and healthful working conditions for working men and women. . . ." Of course, *complete* safety in a working environment is a virtual impossibility and probably would be undesirable even if it were achievable. That is, few of us would be likely to accomplish much in a "padded cell" atmosphere, and a total lack of movement might well lead to life-threatening tissue atrophy. So providing for "safe and healthful working conditions" necessitates compromises. The work environment should be safe and healthful, yet not so safe as to represent a stultifying atmosphere. The real, practical goal then is to provide

working conditions that are as safe and healthful as is technologically and economically feasible, with federal government representatives determining what that level of feasibility will be. The policy statement of the act is worded in such a way as to recognize the practical limits of providing a safe working environment.

OSHAct

The legal essence of the OSHAct is encapsulated in a statement of employer duties—"Section 5: a) Each employer—1) shall furnish to each of his employees employment and a place of employment which are free from recognized hazards that are causing or are likely to cause death or serious physical harm to his employees; 2) shall comply with occupational safety and health standards promulgated under this Act; b) Each employee shall comply with occupational safety and health standards and all rules, regulations, and orders issued pursuant to this Act which are applicable to his own actions and conduct."

Applicability.

As a federal law the OSHAct is limited in its jurisdiction to industries involved in interstate commerce. Of course, involvement with interstate commerce is often a matter of judgment. That is, White Company may operate only in, say, Oregon, but if it uses or handles goods produced in Kentucky, for example, it may be said to operate in interstate commerce. Or Green Company may be a road builder building roads only in the vicinity of Helena, Montana; still, the argument could be made that the roads are intended for interstate travelers as well as locals. So the restriction of interstate commerce may not be all that it at first seems to be.

Another restriction on OSHAct applicability is that it is not intended to replace coverage by other federal laws or the workers' compensation acts. The meaning of this restriction is not altogether clear, however, as may be noted from recent cases.[1] Black Trucking is involved in interstate commerce; this being the case, its

1. See, for example, Marshall v. Northwest Orient Airlines, Inc., at the end of chapter 23, "Administrative Law."

activities are supervised by several federal agencies including the Interstate Commerce Commission. Black might well be of the opinion that it has sufficient governmental supervision and, therefore, resist an attempt by OSHA to generate more paperwork and problems. A reviewing court, though, might conclude that the I.C.C. is insufficiently involved with safety and, therefore, require Black to also deal with OSHA. It seems that where a serious safety problem is found or suspected, some other device for exercising jurisdiction may also be found.

The OSHA Agency

OSHA (Occupational Safety and Health Administration) is an interdepartmental agency; it is mainly in the Department of Labor, but parts of it reach into the Department of Health and Human Services. Several new entities were created by Congress in the OSHAct.

The Secretary of Labor is the executive head of the agency. A company's main contact with the agency, though, is the Secretary of Labor's local representative, the OSHA inspector (or compliance officer). If the White Company has a problem with the local office, various appeals are possible. The OSHAct provides for a three-member Occupational Safety and Health Review Commission to review contested OSHA citations. Since this commission cannot handle all of the hearings requested, administrative law judges are appointed as commission representatives. White Company's complaint against the citation would take the form of an administrative law hearing. If White Company is unhappy with the outcome there (or if the Secretary of Labor is unwilling to accept the result), a request may be made for a hearing before the full commission. The commission may, at its discretion, review any hearing. When all commission review possibilities have been exhausted, the next step is review of the case by a United States Court of Appeals. The final step available in the process, of course, is a request for a writ of certiorari from the United States Supreme Court.

NIOSH

A third new entity created within the OSHA agency is the National Institute for Occupational Safety and Health (NIOSH). The director of NIOSH is immediately responsible to the Secretary of Health and Human Services (HHS), but is required to work closely with the Secretary of Labor. NIOSH is charged with safety research and education functions, particularly as these functions are concerned with toxic substances.

Of course, toxic substances also concern the Environmental Protection Agency (EPA) (which would make cooperation between the two desirable). The NIOSH findings as to safety requirements (e.g., maximum levels of toxic substances) are proposed to the Secretary of Labor as prospective industry standards. Approval and publication of the requirements in the Federal Register gives them the status of agency rules. One example of a toxic substance with which both the EPA and OSHA are concerned is lead in the atmosphere. The OSHA maximum (standard) has been established as $50\mu g/m^3$ (50 micrograms in a cubic meter of air). Three recent (1980) cases[2] read as a whole draw an interesting picture of the development of standards in the two agencies.

Section 20 of the OSHAct requires the HHS secretary to respond to employer or employee requests for workplace investigations. White Company or its employees may suspect a harmful concentration of lead in the air in the work environment, for example. In response to a request from either White Company or its employees, NIOSH would investigate the environment and report its results against the $50\mu g/m^3$ standard. The results of 41 such investigations are reported in "Health Hazard Evaluation Summaries."[3]

State Programs

Section 18 of OSHA provides for state occupational and health programs to replace those of the federal government. Of course, there are requirements to be met by a state program. There is a three-year developmental period during which the state must show it is capable of doing the OSHA job. If the state shows adequate legislative backing, standard-setting ability, the ability to enforce those standards, and competent personnel, OSHA may enter into an "operational status agreement" with the state. Final approval of the state plan may occur after an additional year or more of effective operation. One of the inducements for states to initiate their own programs is the provision that OSHA will pay up to half of the operating costs of state programs.

Provisions exist for decertification of state programs, and occasionally states voluntarily give up their programs. With such a flux it is difficult to indicate accurately how many states have occupational safety and health programs, but the latest count indicates that about half the states are so involved.

2. See Lead Industries Ass'n. v. Environmental Protection 647 F.2d 1130; Lead Industries Ass'n., Inc. v. E.P.A. 647 F.2d 1184; and United Steelworkers of America, Etc. v. Marshall 647 F.2d 1189.
3. U.S. Department of Health and Human Services, Public Health Service Centers for Disease Control, National Institute for Occupational Safety and Health, "Health Hazard Evaluation Summaries," Cincinnati, Ohio 45226, May 1981.

On-site Consultation

Much of OSHA's concern is in the area of work environment standards and questions of penalties for noncompliance, but this is not the complete story. Suppose White Company is sincerely concerned about the safety of its employees and turns to OSHA for advice. White's motivation could be economic as well as humanitarian—in the form of workers' compensation insurance premiums. White Company's request will result in a visit by a consultant to identify hazardous conditions and recommend corrections to be made. The consultation is free of charge to White Company—the consultant sent by a state agency is likely to be a state employee, but if the federal OSHA is called upon, the consultant will be a private firm or individual. The rules differ somewhat in the different states and in the federal agency, but using one state's[4] provisions as a pattern:

> On-site Consultants will . . . 1) Help you recognize hazards in your workplace; 2) Suggest general approaches or options for solving a safety or health problem; 3) Identify kinds of help available if you need further assistance; 4) Provide you with a written report summarizing findings.
>
> On-site Consultants will not . . . 1) Issue citations or propose penalties for violations of OHS regulations; 2) Report possible violations to EID (Environmental Improvement Division) enforcement staff; 3) Guarantee that any workplace will "pass" an EID inspection; 4) Prescribe specific engineering designs or identify specific firms to solve problems.

Thus, if White Company were a New Mexico firm it could benefit from free safety consultation without fear of penalty resulting from rule infractions found by the consultant.

Standards

The question of safety of a workplace environment is a relative one. Just as is true of many other engineering concepts, the absolute in safety is virtually impossible to achieve in any kind of practical circumstance. This implies that a decision must be made as to what is "safe enough." The OSHA attitude in making these workplace design decisions and publishing them as standards is to assure "to the extent feasible, . . . that no employee will suffer material impairment of health or functional capacity even if such employee has regular exposure to the hazard dealt with by such standard for the period of his working life."

According to the OSHAct the agency was given the first two years of its existence to examine and adopt (promulgate) so-called consensus standards. The result was wholesale adoption of existing industry standards, state standards, ANSI (American National Standards Institute) standards, and standards from various other sources. Most of these standards have proved to be highly useful, some have had to be modified, and others have been quite worthless.

As an example of OSHA standards, consider its *ground-fault protection standard*. This was one of the standards adopted from the 1971 National Electric Code at OSHA's inception. In addition to requiring proper grounding of all electrical tools, the 1971 NEC provided: "All 15- and 20-ampere receptacle outlets on single-phase circuits for construction sites shall have approved ground-fault circuit protection for personnel. This requirement shall become effective on January 1, 1974." This meant that the exclusive protection device was to be the ground-fault circuit interruptor. This device detects low levels of current leakage and trips the circuit breaker when this leakage exceeds some preset level, commonly 5 milliamperes. Since the time required for the device to react is quite short (as short as 1/40 sec.) electrocution of the worker is avoided, but the worker may still suffer a severe shock.

Shortly before the effective date of the ground-fault protection standard the OSHA advisory committee recommended a delay. The reason for this was a competing concept, known as an *assured equipment grounding program*. This program requires unusually stringent inspection and testing of each cord set, circuit, receptacle, and equipment for grounding before each day's use, plus other periodic tests. If this program is carried out, the risk of shocks of any sort is diminished to an insignificant level. As a result, the OSHA standard for protection against shocks, effective February 22, 1977, included the option of either method of protection.

Rule-Making. When the people at OSHA have formed an opinion that a particular toxic material or harmful physical agent must be handled in a certain way for the sake of safety, they create a standard. This is done by publishing in the Federal Register the proposed standard or rule along with a request for objections, data, or comments by interested parties. Those interested have a 30-day period in which to respond. If there is no response the rule may be finalized by a second publication in the Federal Register. If objections or adverse comments do appear, there is a hearing procedure specified in the OSHAct.

4. State of New Mexico Health and Environment Department, Environmental Improvement Division, Occupational Health and Safety Bureau, "On-site Consultation for the Employer", October 1980.

Variances. Sometimes an employer may legally avoid compliance with the OSHA standard. Exceptions can be made under both temporary and permanent variances. Suppose White Company a) has a better (or equivalent) means of protecting its employees than OSHA's standard provides, or b) cannot comply with the standard within the time allotted. As an example of the first variance reason, assume OSHA had passed the ground-fault electrical standard as first proposed and White Company already had an assured equipment grounding program. This would appear to be sound reason for White Company to request a permanent variance which, if granted, would permit it to avoid the standard.

As an example of the second kind of variance (temporary), White Company may find itself in the position of being required to comply with a standard in an impossibly short time. Reconstruction may be necessary, or personnel or materials to make the change may be hard to find. White Company's request for a time extension (temporary variance) may be honored by OSHA, but this is contingent upon White doing all it can to protect its employees from the hazard involved in the meantime.

There are, of course, many other reasons for granting variances. For example, suppose an OSHA standard conflicts with a religious requirement (remember, freedom of religion is part of the first amendment to the U.S. Constitution). To cite an actual instance, carpenters are required by OSHA to wear hard hats. The Old Order Amish are required by their religion to wear wide-brimmed black felt hats. A permanent variance was issued to allow Old Order Amish carpenters to comply with their religion rather than OSHA. Of course, if issuance of the variance might have endangered others, the problem would have been more difficult and the variance may very well have been withheld.

Standards Reforms. One of the major industrial complaints about OSHA involves citations about trivia. It is difficult for a company to understand why the design of a toilet seat or a two-inch variation in the location of a fire extinguisher or a one-inch variation in the distance between the rungs of a wooden ladder (12" for some ladders, 13" for others) might be important to someone's safety. The means by which such regulations came to be part of OSHA is the wholesale adoption of consensus standards at OSHA's inception. Not only were many trivial regulations picked up, but so were numerous rules having to do with dying processes, e.g., cooperage. To avoid the waste of resources on the enforcement of outmoded and trivial regulations, OSHA began a purge of rules in 1978. The editing efforts have now resulted in the deletion of over 1,000 unnecessary regulations, and OSHA's efforts to "clean up its act" are continuing.

Inspections

Probably the greatest single source of industrial complaint against OSHA is the unannounced inspection. White Company may have the least reprehensible safety practices in its industry and, therefore, should feel that any reasonable inspection would find no serious faults. But there are many disturbing aspects to OSHA inspections, many of which are discussed in the "investigation" section of the Administrative Law Chapter, p. 274. To make matters worse, OSHA suffers from an apparently well-deserved adverse image acquired in the early years of its operation. Many of the early investigators or compliance officers (Compliance Safety and Health Officers) apparently had little or no industrial experience. They committed horrible blunders of ineptness including investigations and complaints and arguments over trivia. One of their primary concerns was neatness—whether or not the floor was swept was a matter of great importance, for instance. The last thing White Company may desire is an unannounced interruption of its production system by a bungling faultfinder who has no knowledge of the effect of inept inspection upon the production facilities.

The OSHAct authorizes an OSHA compliance officer to: "enter without delay and at reasonable times any factory, plant, establishment, construction site, or other areas, workplace, or environment where work is performed by an employee of an employer"; and to "inspect and investigate during regular working hours, and at other reasonable times, and within reasonable limits and in a reasonable manner, any such place of employment and all pertinent conditions, structures, machines, apparatus, devices, equipment, and materials therein, and to question privately any such employer, owner, operator, agent, or employee." The reasoning behind the wording in the act, of course, is that surprise investigations are the only way to catch industries in their rule violations. If the investigator must first ask, be refused, and return with further authority, the employer has an opportunity to change the safety characteristics of the employment environment. On the other hand, the fourth amendment to the United States Constitution, modified by case law interpretations, indicates that such warrantless searches as described in the act are not to be condoned. Such controversies as this represent work for the U.S. Supreme Court. In the case of *Marshall* (Secretary of Labor) v. *Barlow's Inc.*[5] (an electrical and plumbing installation business in Pocatello, Idaho), 1978, the issue was decided. Barlow's, it seems, had twice refused the OSHA inspector access to its premises. Some of the court's statement in finding the act unconstitutional in regard to warrantless searches is interesting: ". . . the businessman, like the occupant of a residence, has a constitutional right to go about his business free from unreasonable official entries upon his private, commercial property. The businessman, too, has that right placed in jeopardy if the decision to enter and inspect for violation of regulatory laws can be made and enforced by an inspector in the field without official authority evidenced by a warrant." Thus, in *nonconsensual* instances (where consent for OSHA to enter is refused), the agency's authority to inspect is not removed, but some of the intimidation from the threat of a warrantless search is gone. OSHA can still get in to inspect, but it must go to court for a search warrant first if its original attempt to inspect is refused.

Citations. Just as an avid police officer could probably find something wrong with the way each of us lives, a zealous OSHA inspector can be expected to find rule violations present in almost any establishment. Just as traffic citations *could* result from your being observed speeding or failing to stop at a stop sign, OSHA citations *could* result from OSHA inspections. Whether or not such a citation will be issued is a matter within the discretion of the inspector and the inspector's boss, the area director.

Of course, the employer is not required to meekly submit to the citation, posting it for the employees to see and paying the penalties involved. OSHA allows fifteen working days to contest the citation, providing the employer has a disagreement with it and is willing to spend the necessary time and money to take the case to a hearing and subsequently, perhaps to trial.

There are numerous bases for appeal of an OSHA citation. One of the more common reasons is objection to the lack of specificity in the citation—occasionally it is difficult to tell from the citation just what the inspector's complaint was. Penalties required may be viewed as excessive, or the time period allowed for abatement of the hazard may be inadequate. Even when the citation is specific, it may be that the employer's safety practice is superior to the agency's rule.

Penalties. Citations may or may not include proposed penalties for the cited safety infraction. If the inspection reveals a *serious violation,* one involving a substantial probability of physical harm or death, there is a mandatory penalty assessment of between $300 and $1,000. A *willful violation* runs the risk of a considerably greater penalty. This is a violation in which the employer knew of the hazard and did nothing to correct it or to protect against it. The maximum penalty for such violations runs up to $10,000 and/or six months in jail. A second conviction doubles these maximum penalties.

Safety hazard citations usually state an *abatement period,* a time limit within which the employer is expected to remove the hazard. Failure to meet the time limit (or appeal the citation in this regard) may cause the assessment of up to $1,000 per day of abatement period violation.

Other penalties exist in the act for falsifying records, failing to post notices of citations, and assaulting OSHA inspectors.

Record Requirements

To the burden of keeping records to satisfy various federal, state, and local government agencies, the OSHAct adds one more. All but trivial work-related injuries or illnesses must be recorded, and the record must be available for inspection. The purpose, of course, is to assemble a body of knowledge of work-related human problems, an apparently worthy and desirable motive if record keeping were free or of trivial cost.

The OSHAct record requirement pertains to all employers having more than ten employees. There is an exception to the small-employer exception, however. The Bureau of Labor Statistics may ask for a sampling of the same information from small employers, so each such employer risks being required to keep those records.

The kinds of disabilities to be recorded include all occupational illnesses (assuming a determination can be made as to environmental cause). Also to be recorded are all occupational injuries resulting in a) death, b) lost workdays, c) restriction of motion, d) loss of consciousness, e) transfer to another job, or f) medical treatment other than first aid.

OSHA and the Political Environment

It may be observed that rarely, if ever, do government agencies such as OSHA go completely out of business—their tenacity is truly extraordinary. However, the vigor with which they pursue their tasks is influenced greatly by government attitudes. OSHA was born at a time when the business climate in the United States was healthy and the prevailing attitudes were concerns about the health of workers. With a much

5. Marshall v. Barlow's, Inc., 436 U.S. 307, 98 S. CT. 1816, 56 L.Ed. 2nd 305.

poorer business climate, concerns seem to turn to the health of companies, the height of the unemployment rate, and the avoidance of bankruptcies. This is not to suggest the complete inaction of the agency in such a climate—only a change of emphasis to an attitude more supportive of business. Agency attitude, then, is a product not only of the law under which it was created, but also of the currently prevailing economic and political environment in which it must operate.

WHIRLPOOL CORP.
v. O. S. & H. REVIEW COM'N
645 F. 2d 1096 (1981)

Bazelon, Senior Circuit Judge:

The Occupational Safety and Health Act of 1970[6] (OSHA) employs two devices to protect workers from the unconscionably high risk[7] of tragic death or injury: regulations, which define safety standards for specific industrial environments; and, a catch-all "general duty" clause[8] which requires employers to abate "recognized hazards" in the workplace.[9] As this court recognized in *National Realty & Constr. Co. v. OSHRC*[10], the laudable and sweeping mandate of the general duty clause must be focused through clear notice of any specific hazard, in order to ensure fairness to employers and open, reasoned decisionmaking by OSHRC (the "Commission").

As the commission acknowledges, the Secretary of Labor's (the "Secretary") citation here provided Whirlpool Corp. (the "petitioner") with inadequate written notice of the alleged general duty violation, and the evidence presented at the administrative hearing was not a "model of precision."[11] The predictable result of these haphazard procedures was a poorly developed record which fails to support OSHRC's findings. Because we cannot discern whether this lack of evidence reflects the confusion caused by the Secretary's procedures rather than an unmeritorious charge, we must remand this record for further development.

I. The General Duty Clause
A. *Substantive Elements*
    (1, 2) Section 654(a)(1) of OSHA, the general
        duty clause, provides that
    (a) Each employer—
        (1) Shall furnish to each of his employees employment and a place of employment which are free from recognized hazards that are causing or are likely to cause death or serious physical harm to his employees.[12]

As OSHA's legislative history makes clear,[13] this subsection does not impose strict liability on employers, but instead limits their liability to "preventable hazards."[14] The three elements of a general duty violation are: (1) a hazard likely to cause death or serious bodily harm; (2) recognition of the hazard either by the specific employer or generally within the industry; and (3) existence of a feasible method of abatement.[15]

The Secretary has the burden of coming forward with evidence on the feasibility issue.[16] This procedural burden is closely related to the broad sweep of the clause,[17] for proof of the specific method of abatement, perhaps more than the other substantive elements, helps provide the employer with notice of the precise hazard at issue.

B. *Notice requirement*
Section 658 of OSHA provides that an employer charged under the general duty clause must be given notice in the form of a citation which "shall be in writing and shall describe with particularity the nature of the violation . . . (and) shall fix a reasonable time for the abatement of the violation."[18]

Ideally, the citation should provide the employer with notice of the Secretary's contentions pertinent to each of the three elements underlying a general duty violation. Where detailed prehearing notice has been lacking, the reviewing court must carefully scrutinize the Secretary's presentation of evidence to ensure that the cited employer has been afforded a fair opportunity to address the specific violation charged.[19] As this

---

6. 29 U.S.C. sec. 651 et seq. (1976).

7. Prior to OSHA's passage, 14,500 persons were killed and 2.2 million were disabled annually as a result of industrial accidents. The staggering record of human suffering associated with just one occupational disease, byssinosis, is recounted in **AFL-CIO v. Marshall.** . . .

8. 29 U.S.C. sec. 654(a)(1) (1976).

9. *Id.* The text of the subsection is reprinted in text at Part 1(A) *infra.*

10. 489 F2d 1257. . . .

11. Joint Appendix ("J.A.") 43

12. 29 U.S.C. sec. 654(a)(1) (1976)

13. See 116 Cong. Rec.38377 (Nov. 23, 1970) (recognition requirement intended to mitigate employer liability); . . . (employer's duty "not absolute," but instead limited to protecting workers from "preventable dangers"). Although the employer's duty under OSHA extends beyond that imposed under common law . . . it must be "achievable and not a mere vehicle for strict liability."

14. H.R.Rep. No. 91–1291, *supra* note 8, at 21.

15. *See,* e.g., Titanium Metals Corp. v. Usery. . . .

16. *See,* e.g., Bristol Steel & Iron Works v. OSHRC. . . .

17. "Since the general duty clause is so broad, the evidence to support a charge of violation should be specific and detailed.". . .

18. 29 U.S.C. sec. 658(a)(1976).

19. As we noted . . . , administrative pleadings may be liberally construed, *"so long as fair notice is afforded. . . ."*

court found in *National Realty,* the virtues of adequate notice extend even beyond due process: "To assure the citations issue only upon careful deliberation, the Secretary must be constrained to specify the particular steps a cited employer should have taken to avoid citation, and to demonstrate the feasibility and likely utility of those measures."[20]

II. Procedural History of the Instant Violation

Petitioner manufactures appliances at its Marion, Ohio, plant. Overhead conveyors move parts through the manufacturing process. To protect employees working beneath the conveyors from falling parts, petitioner maintains a huge protective guard screen, which consists of multiple steel mesh panels secured by metal clips to angle iron frames, which are joined together by bolts. Maintenance personnel routinely traverse the guard screen to retrieve fallen parts.

In years prior to the instant violation, maintenance personnel fell partially through the guard screen. In 1974, an employee fell to his death when the bolts joining two frames failed.[21] After an OSHA compliance officer's inspection, petitioner was cited for: "failure to provide a safe walking and working surface on the screens under the conveyor."[22] The citation further required "immediate" abatement.[23] Petitioner contested the citation.

At the hearing, the Secretary offered the testimony of employees who described occasions on which workers had fallen partially through the screen. The Secretary's compliance officer refused to specify whether the source of the hazard was the bolts linking the panel frames or the tensile strength of the screen mesh.[24] A civil engineer testified for the Secretary, and suggested a third theory of the hazard: the absence of a heavy steel catwalk.[25] Petitioner's engineer testified on cross-examination that one-third of the screen's panels had been replaced by heavier-gauge mesh, but he added that complete replacement was architecturally infeasible.[26]

The Administrative Law Judge ("ALJ") vacated the citation without deciding whether the Secretary had proven a general duty clause violation.[27] OSHRC remanded the matter to the ALJ for findings under the general duty clause. One Commissioner dissented from the remand order, however, on the grounds that the Secretary had failed to specify or prove a feasible abatement method.[28]

On remand, the ALJ again dismissed the citation, this time on the grounds[29] that the record did not reveal a feasible abatement method.[30] The ALJ

assumed[31] that the hazard contemplated by the Secretary was the tensile strength of the screen panels. However, the ALJ accepted the unrefuted testimony of petitioner's expert, who stated that complete screen panel replacement was infeasible.

OSHRC again overruled the ALJ. The Commission was admirably candid in acknowledging the substantial deficiencies in the notice provided petitioner.

(T)he citation failed to specify (what condition rendered the screen unsafe) and accordingly facially lacked particularity. (In addition) a foundation had been laid in the citation for (the Secretary's) own confusion of focus and for (petitioner's) possible misconception of the case, not only by the absence of reference to the (tensile strength of the mesh) as the hazard, but by the requirement of immediate abatement, which most likely suggested abatement by replacing the bolts rather than by replacing a substantial part of the guard screen panels.[32]

The Commission concluded that, notwithstanding the confusion precipitated by its citation, the "purposes of the particularity requirement (were) fulfilled in subsequent stages of the proceeding." Although the "Secretary's evidence at the hearing was not a model of precision in identifying the hazard,"[33] the Commission found that repeated reference to the strength of the steel mesh gave

20. 489 F.2d at 1268.

21. J.A. 36. Because the instant citation was precipitated by this tragedy, petitioner had reason to believe, absent further clarification from the Secretary, that it was the bolts, not the tensile strength of the mesh, that was the hazardous condition. This ambiguity was compounded by the citation itself. See J.A. 43.

22. J.A. 2.

23. id

24. J.A. 72–78, 104–05.

25. J.A. 208–09.

26. The engineer's testimony is summarized first by Commissioner Moran. . . .

27. The ALJ found that a specific OSHA regulation, rather than the general duty clause, governed the instant citation. J.A. 19120.

28. J.A. 26–30.

29. J.A. 31

30. See National Realty & Constr. Co. v. OSHRC. . . . Only by requiring the Secretary, at the hearing, to formulate and defend *his own* theory of what a cited defendant should have done can the Commission and the courts assure even-handed enforcement of the general duty clause. (emphasis in original).

31. This assumption correctly anticipated the Commission's theory of the hazard. See J.A. 46.

32. J.A. 43

33. Id.

petitioner constructive notice of the hazard. Moreover, according to the Commission, petitioner apparently perceived that the tensile strength of the screens was the hazard, for it introduced rebuttal evidence on this point.

The Commission also rejected the ALJ's findings regarding the lack of evidence on the feasibility issue.[34] The Commission relied on the "record as a whole,"[35] and specifically: (1) the testimony of petitioner's engineer that heavier-gauge screens were safer;[36] and, the testimony of petitioner's employees, who acknowledged that heavier screen panels were typically deployed to replace screens that had torn. The Commission concluded

> Because Whirlpool systematically was replacing the mesh panels with heavy-duty wire throughout the plant, the feasibility of the heavy-duty wire to eliminate the hazard and its likely utility in Whirlpool's plant *is apparent*.[37]

The commission reversed the findings of the ALJ, and amended the citation to provide an abatement period of six months.[38] This appeal followed.

III. Notice and Evidence of a Feasible Abatement Method

A. Notice

OSHRC points to employees' references to the guard screen panels and to rebuttal testimony on the tensile strength of the screen as evidence that petitioner had adequate notice of the hazard. In so doing, the Commission ignores the importance of detailed notice to the fair administration of the general duty clause.

Assuming *arguendo* that petitioner's rebuttal suggests a general awareness of the hazardous condition,[39] it hardly follows that the Secretary ever gave petitioner a fair opportunity to address a necessary and independent issue: how the hazard could have been feasibly abated. The Commission acknowledges that there was no written notice. Nor was there constructive notice, for no witness outlined "the Secretary's own theory of what steps the (petitioner) should have taken to abate the hazard."[40] The Secretary's compliance officer addressed the subject of abatement only on cross-examination, and he pointedly refused to reveal the Secretary's abatement plan.[41] The Secretary's engineer did not even address abatement. Of course,

the Commission's post-hearing alteration of the citation clarified the hazard charged, but came far too late to provide petitioner with a fair opportunity to meet the Secretary's contentions.

B. Substantial Evidence

The substantial evidence requires a court reviewing an administrative adjudication to accept findings of fact supported by "such relevant evidence as a reasonable mind might accept as adequate to support a conclusion."[42] As tolerant as this standard is, the vague notice and unfocused evidence offered by the Secretary at the hearing has resulted in a record devoid of support of OSHRC's conclusion.

Although some witnesses called by the Secretary testified to the *efficacy* of the heavier-gauge screen, none addressed the *feasibility* of complete screen panel replacement.[43] On cross-examination, petitioner's engineer, after noting that one-third of the panels had been replaced before the fatality, stated that *complete* panel replacement was architecturally infeasible. In view of his unrefuted

---

34. In addition to the absence of evidence on the feasibility issue offered by the Secretary, the ALJ noted disparities in the credibility of the parties' witnesses. The compliance officer did not test the tensile strength of the various panels used in the guard screen, and the Secretary's engineer admitted that he had no experience with guard screen systems. On the other hand, petitioner's engineer was not only familiar with the special characteristics of petitioner's screen, but was also generally acquainted with guard screen structures. J.A. 28–29.

35. J.A. 47.

36. Id.

37. J.A. 48.

38. J.A. 49. Post-hearing alterations of the citation can signal deficiencies in the notice afforded respondents. . . . In this instance, alteration of the citation resolved an ambiguity in the precise hazard charged, see text accompanying note 27, supra. It would appear, however, that this ambiguity should have been resolved before or at least during the hearing to provide petitioner with a full and fair opportunity to meet the Secretary's charge.

39. Petitioner's rebuttal may represent an attempt to counter whatever unfocused allegations were made at the hearing, rather than evidence of fair notice. . . . Implied consent to the trial of an unpleaded issue is not established merely because evidence on that issue was introduced. . . . *It must appear that the parties understood the* evidence was aimed at the unpleaded issue.

40. National Realty & Constr. Co. v. OSHRC, supra, 489 F.2d at 1268. . . .

41. Q. Are you saying that the Secretary would agree that the wire, the heavy-duty wire type does comply. . . ?
A. No, Sir, I am not saying that.
Q. You're saying it does not comply?
A. I'm not saying it does, and I'm not saying it does not comply.
J.A. 73

42. *See,* e.g., Universal Camera Corp. v. NLRB. . . .

43. E.g., J.A. 104.

testimony, it is by no means "apparent" that complete replacement was a feasible means of abating the hazard.[44]

Accordingly, the order of the OSHRC is vacated and the record remanded for further development on the issue of a feasible abatement method.

So ordered.

IRWIN STEEL ERECTORS
v. OCC. SAF. & H. REV. COM'N

574 F.2d 222 (1978)

Per Curiam

The Occupational Safety and Health Act of 1970, 29 U.S.C. sect. 651, et seq., created the Occupational Safety and Health Review Commission (OSHRC), and authorized it to adopt standards, . . . make investigations, . . . and issue citations for violations. . . . It provides a procedure for enforcement of OSHRC orders. . . . Persons adversely affected or aggrieved by an order of the OSHRC may obtain judicial review. . . . In such review,

The findings of the Commission with respect to questions of fact, if supported by substantial evidence on the record considered as a whole, shall be conclusive. . . .

The employer who here seeks review was engaged in steel erection work. On the job in question, its welders were working on steel beams or joists in a single-story building about 23 feet above the ground. They were required to move along the beams in straddle position to do the necessary welding. The OSHRC ordered safety belts, lifelines, and lanyards to be used.[45] The employer contended that compliance with the standard would expose its welders to a greater safety hazard than non-compliance and, therefore, urged that the citation issued to it should be set aside and the proposed penalty of $600 be vacated.

While the evidence adduced before the administrative law judge was conflicting, there was substantial evidence to support the conclusion that the welders were subjected to the danger of falling, a serious violation of 29 CFR 1926.28(a), and that the use of the safety equipment ordered would not create a safety hazard.[46] The employer asserts that the preponderance of the evidence showed the requirement to be unwarranted and to create other hazards. We are prohibited by the statute and the authorities cited from reweighing the evidence. Accordingly, these findings must be affirmed.

The employer contends that the OSHRC increased the burden required for establishing the affirmative defense of "greater hazard" by requiring proof of (1) unavailability of alternative means of protecting employees, and (2) inappropriateness of a variance application, and cites *Secretary* v. *Industrial Steel Erectors, Inc.* 1974 . . . for the proposition that the only requirement of proof of the greater hazards defense is that the safety or health of employees would be endangered rather than protected by compliance. *Industrial Steel Erectors, supra,* and *American Bridge, supra,* involved fact situations, however, where employers used safety devices in compliance with statutory requirements except at specific points in their work. In both of these cases, a preponderance of the evidence showed that the employees were safer in not complying with the standard than if they had. In fact, the basis of the opinions was only that an employer would be permitted to assert an affirmative defense when the safety of employees would be endangered rather than protected by compliance with a standard.

Later, however, in *Secretary* v. *Russ Kaller, Inc.,* . . . the OSHRC spelled out specific requirements for the greater hazards defense:

The scope of the defense recognized in those cases is, however, narrow. It is not enough that compliance with literal terms of the standards would

44. J.A. 48.
At oral argument, counsel for petitioner noted that subsequent to the hearing *all* of the guard screen panels have been replaced.

OSHRC does not contend, however, that this disposes of the feasibility issue. As the Commission indicated in response to an initial remand from this court, eventual compliance with an abatement order does not moot the original citation, and our review of that citation is based on the record which purportedly supported it. The general duty clause's focus on preventable hazards, *see* note 9 *supra,* limits liability to dangers actually or constructively recognized at the time of the violation. . . . It would appear, then, that the feasibility of abatement must be judged as of the time of the violation as well. We cannot discern from this record whether petitioner's apparently recent success in abating the hazard contradicts the testimony on feasibility of abatement recorded at the 1975 hearing.

45. The citation alleged a violation of 29 CFR 1926.28(a), which states: Personal Protective Equipment.

(a) The employer is responsible for requiring the wearing of appropriate personal protective equipment in all operations where there is an exposure to hazardous conditions or where this part indicates the need for using such equipment to reduce hazards to the employees.

46. Under the Act, a serious violation shall be deemed to exist in a place of employment if there is a substantial probability that death or serious physical harm could result from a condition which exists, or from one or more practices, means, methods, operations, or processes which have been adopted or are in use, in such place of employment unless the employer did not, and could not with the exercise of reasonable diligence, know of the presence of the violation. 29 USC sec. 666(j). Under Section 666(c) a "nonserious" citation involves a determination that the violation in question was "specifically determined not to be of a serious nature."

create new hazards. . . . The record must show that the hazards of compliance are greater than the hazards of noncompliance . . . that alternative means of protecting employees are unavailable . . . and that a variance application under section 6(d) of the Act would be inappropriate. . . .

These are the standards that the Commission applied. It did not change the rules to the petitioner's prejudice in mid-course.

Moreover, we need not decide here, in any event, the propriety of applying the *Russ Kaller, supra,* standards, for the employer did not establish by a preponderance of the evidence the defense under the criteria it considers applicable. . . . The question for us is not whether the preponderance of the evidence test has been satisfied. That test is for the OSHRC, just as the preponderance of the evidence test in a civil jury case is for the jury. Once the OSHRC concludes that the evidence demonstrates a proposition by a preponderance, the only review available is whether there is substantial evidence on the record as a whole to support its conclusion.

The first criterion for a successful defense, admittedly valid, is for the employer to show that the hazards of compliance are greater than the hazards of noncompliance. There was substantial evidence to support the Commission's conclusion that the employer failed to show that the welders were in need of mobility and that the danger of dangling from a safety belt was greater than the danger of falling.

For these reasons, the petition for review is DENIED.

CHAMPLIN PETROLEUM CO. v. O.S. & H.R.C.
593 F.2d 637 (1979)

Roney, Circuit Judge:

An employer appeals an order of the Occupational Safety and Health Review Commission (Commission) finding a violation of the general duty clause of the Occupational Safety and Health Act (OSHA) which obligates the employer to

furnish to each of his employees employment and a place of employment which are free from recognized hazards that are causing or are likely to cause death or serious physical harm to his employees. . . .

The recognized hazard to which employees were exposed was the escape of hot oil. The Commission's order was based on the employer's failure to prevent such exposure by effectively communicating a rule against opening valves, through which the oil might escape, unless they are equipped with handles. Because we fail to find substantial evidence on the record considered as a whole, . . . that either the use of handles on valves or the effective communication of a rule against opening valves without them would have materially reduced the hazard of oil fire injuries, we reverse.

A pipeline control valve malfunctioned at the Corpus Christi, Texas, oil refinery of employer, Champlin Petroleum Company (Champlin). Isolation of the pipeline section and draining of its contents were necessary before the defective valve could be removed. A block valve was closed on each side of the control valve to permit the isolated crude oil, which flowed at a temperature hot enough to ignite on contact with air (auto-ignition temperature), to cool before draining through the bleeder valve. Several hours later, the unit operator, Cobb, and two maintenance employees, Benson and Bennett, prepared to bleed the control valve. Bennett stood up on the pipes a few feet to the side of the bleeder valve. Cobb stood to the right of and below the valve with the valve at waist or shoulder height. Benson stood up on the pipes on the same level as the valve. The valve had been newly installed with a handle four days before. On this occasion, however, the handle, a circle 2½ inches in diameter, was missing. Benson reached down and opened the valve by turning the valve stem with a crescent wrench. A thin stream of oil ran into the bucket which had been suspended from the valve. Shortly thereafter, smoke emerged from the valve indicating that auto-ignitable oil would follow. Benson was unable to close the valve, and in the ensuing flash fire the three employees were injured, Cobb fatally. Foreign matter had apparently been trapped in one of the block valves, preventing it from completely closing. The pressure created by opening the bleeder valve dislodged the sediment, permitting hot oil to flow into the isolated section.

Following inspection of the refinery by an OSHA compliance officer, a citation was issued charging a general duty clause violation in that:

(a) There was no fixed handle on the bleeder valve to control the flow of liquid hydrocarbons from the line. Employees were using a pair of pliers on the valve stem since the handle was missing.

(b) Liquid hydrocarbons were not piped away from the bleeder valve located approximately 3 feet from an in-service heater unit.

An $800 penalty was proposed.

The administrative law judge vacated the citation and proposed penalty, finding the hazard of exposure to auto-ignitable oil unpreventable because the employer could not have foreseen that its employee would open the valve without a handle in violation of the company's well-established safety policy. Reversing the administrative law judge, the Commission affirmed the citation and penalty, concluding that the company's safety policy was ineffectively communicated to employees.

We observe that in reversing the decision of the Commission we need not and do not assess the sufficiency of support for the administrative law judge's conclusions. The relationship between the ALJ and Commission differs from that of trial and appellate courts in that OSHA contemplates that the Commission be charged with fact-finding responsibility, 29 U.S.C.A. sec. 659(c), and the ALJ is merely an arm of the Commission for that purpose. . . . While the findings of the ALJ are to be considered on review and may weaken the contrary conclusion of the Commission, . . . we disturb the Commission's decision only because it lacks the support of substantial evidence. . . .

To establish a general duty clause violation, the Secretary must prove "(1) that the employer failed to render its workplace 'free' of a hazard which was (2) 'recognized' and (3) 'causing or likely to cause death or serious physical harm.' " . . . The general duty obligation, however, is not designed to impose absolute liability or respondent superior liability for employees' negligence. Rather it requires the employer to eliminate only "feasibly preventable" hazards. . . . It is the Secretary's burden to show that demonstrably feasible measures would materially reduce the likelihood that such injury as that which resulted from the cited hazard would have occurred. . . . The Secretary must specify the particular steps the employer should have taken to avoid citation, and he must demonstrate the feasibility and likely utility of those measures. . . .

At the hearing it was suggested by the OSHA compliance officer that such flash fires are preventable by attaching a drain pipe to the valve so hot oil would be piped away from the area of employee exposure and by maintaining handles on bleeder valves so they may be turned off quickly when smoke appears. Where handles are missing, the compliance officer suggested, an effective training and safety program discouraging opening of handleless valves could reduce injury. The administrative law judge found that use of a drain pipe would have been infeasible under these circumstances, and the Commission, assuming that an adequate safety rule regarding handles would have abated the hazard, restricted its discussion to the effectiveness of communication of the policy against opening handleless valves.

The conflicting evidence on effectiveness of company policy communication need not be confronted in this case. The decision properly turns on the lack of evidentiary support for the underlying assumptions of both the administrative law judge and Commission that either the use of handles or the strengthened communication of the company's policy against opening valves without handles would materially reduce the hazard of injuries from auto-ignitable oil fires.

We consider first the proposed improvement of the company's communication of its rule against opening handleless valves. The effectiveness of this communication is declared by the Commission to be the critical issue in the preventability of this violation. The emphasis of the Commission is misplaced, however, in its focus on what the company has taught rather than what the employees have learned. Improved education will effectively prevent repetition of a mishap only where ignorance was at least the partial cause of that mishap.

Close scrutiny of the record reveals no evidence that any Champlin employee has ever opened or is likely ever to open a handleless valve out of ignorance that it is contrary to company-approved procedures. Benson's opening of the valve on this occasion, the only known instance in which a handleless valve has ever been opened by a Champlin employee, was clearly done with knowledge that he was following an improper and unsafe procedure. Bennett, the other maintenance employee present, testified that he had never run into a handleless bleeder valve and suggested that he would know to get the handle replaced if he noticed its absence. He recalled being taught proper valve-opening procedure while coming up through training. Pascal, a unit operator, testified that standard company procedure was to open and close only valves with handles on them. It is incumbent upon the Secretary to demonstrate exactly how the company should and could improve communication of its policy so as better to reduce auto-ignitable oil fires. Because the record reveals no proof that any employee has ever opened a handleless valve before, in ignorance or otherwise, and because no witness testified that he was unaware of the correct procedure for opening valves, we conclude that the Secretary has failed to show that wider or louder broadcasting of the company's policy would have had any material effect on the likelihood of injuries of the type sustained here.

Even if the record revealed sufficient evidence from which to conclude that improved policy communication would reduce the opening of valves without handles, the record fails to demonstrate, as it must, that the use of handles themselves would effectively reduce the hazard that caused these injuries.

The administrative law judge stated

> It does not take a conscientious expert, familiar with the refinery industry, to recognize the factor of safety provided by the presence of a handle on a bleeder valve. Its utility enables the operator to crack this valve ever so gently, and if smoke is encountered from the flow the source of ignition can be halted abruptly.

The Commission too concluded that once smoke is observed, the valve "could be closed sufficiently quickly by means of the handle to prevent the hot oil from emerging." While common sense suggests that valves can be closed more quickly by use of handles, close examination of the record suggests that these conclusions are beyond the record evidence. . . .

The first witness, Champlin's chief supervisor, Cooper, testified that use of handles to open valves is standard company policy. He did not assert the efficacy of closing by handle in a case like this one. Rather Cooper commented that hanging the bucket from the valve instead of placing it on the deck below reduced the time available to close before flashing and speculated that the valve had been opened dangerously wide in this instance, perhaps because the valve itself was plugged. The OSHA compliance officer testified that increased maneuverability of a device with a handle is obvious, but he expressed doubt that use of a handle alone would have eliminated the hazard:

> Possibly if people were quick, without the hose there, if they were quick enough they might be able to control it. Who is to say, but at what point you are going to have a bleeder valve, assuming it is not plugged, in normal operations, who is to say at what point there might be a possible washout? And so therefore, a handle may or may not in itself solve a particular problem.

Bennett, when asked if the valve could have been shut in time with a handle, replied

> I would have to say that is an individual preference. I can't say that I would. I think from what I witnessed in this particular instance, the first thing I thought about was self-preservation. . . . I wouldn't have taken time to shut it, personally.

Bennett testified it would be standard procedure to try to close the valve "if you thought you could get it closed safely." Benson testified

> My first reaction was to try to close the valve and I reached for it and then there was so much smoke I realized I couldn't do it. . . .

Benson admitted that common sense directs the use of handles as the safest method to open valves, but explained

> In the case of this valve, there is no place to be that would be—how do I say this? The valve is so located that you can't get in a position that you can stay in, in order to close the valve and stay at the valve handle at all times.

Another maintenance employee testified that the standard procedure on seeing smoke would be to shut the valve off and speculated, "You wouldn't think to have enough oil to go out at one time to flash without you could shut it off immediately." In this particular accident there may have been no direct causal connection between the lack of handle and the flash fire. Evidence suggests, for example, the valve may have been opened so far that even a handle would not have closed it in time and that the employees may have been in unusually awkward positions. Because OSHA is designed to encourage abatement of hazardous conditions themselves, however, rather than to fix blame after the fact for a particular injury, a citation is supported by evidence which shows the preventability of the generic hazard, if not this particular instance. . . . We conclude, however, that the record fails to show substantial evidence that an employee, under any operating conditions, would be able to close this valve in response to the appearance of smoke signaling auto-ignitable oil if the valve were equipped with a handle. For example, there is no evidence of the time involved between appearance of smoke and ignition of the oil which followed. Similarly, the Secretary adduced no evidence that other Champlin employees had encountered smoke in bleeding valves and had been able to close valves handles in time to block the escape of hot oil.

Because the Secretary has failed to shoulder its burden of proof of the violation, the Commission's decision must be

REVERSED.

REVIEW QUESTIONS

1. Why was OSHA created?
2. In the business of OSHA, what are the functions of the inspector, administrative law judge, the Occupational Safety and Health Review Commission, and a U.S. Court of Appeals?
3. How is NIOSH related to OSHA?

4. In what ways could a state program for occupational safety and health be superior to the federal program? In what ways could the federal program be expected to be superior?

5. Consider the ground-fault protection standard. Which of the two standards discussed would be better under a particular set of factual conditions? Which should be better in general?

6. Consider a power press (punch press or brake press). List at least five ways to improve the safety of its human operator.

7. The U.S. Supreme Court decision in *Marshall* v. *Barlow's, Inc.*, indicates the necessity for OSHA to obtain a search warrant if an employer refuses to submit to inspection upon the inspector's first visit. What arguments can you propose for and against the warrant requirement?

8. In the *Whirlpool* case why did the U.S. Court of Appeals require that the OSHRC order be vacated and remanded? What would you expect OSHA to do next in regard to its citation against Whirlpool?

9. According to your observation and the reading of the *Irwin Steel Erectors* case, should structural steel welders be required to wear safety belts, lifelines, and lanyards? Compare the dangers of such a requirement with the danger if such equipment is not required.

10. In the *Champlin* case it seems obvious that the dangers of oil at an auto-ignitable temperature are life threatening. Why, then, did the U.S. Court of Appeals reverse the OSHRC finding and order regarding valves through which such oil flows?

Index